FROM THE LIBRARY OF
BERKELEY COLLEGE

New York:
NYC (Midtown and Lower Manhattan)
Brooklyn • White Plains

New Jersey:
Newark • Paramus • Woodbridge
Woodland Park

Berkeley College Online:
BerkeleyCollege.edu/Online

NETWORK LIKE YOU MEAN IT

NETWORK LIKE YOU MEAN IT

The Definitive Handbook for Business and Personal Networking

Andrea R. Nierenberg

Vice President, Publisher: Tim Moore
Associate Publisher and Director of Marketing: Amy Neidlinger
Development Editor: Russ Hall
Operations Specialist: Jodi Kemper
Cover Designer: Chuti Prasertsith
Managing Editor: Kristy Hart
Project Editor: Katie Matejka
Copy Editor: Krista Hansing
Proofreader: Chuck Hutchinson
Indexer: Lisa Stumpf
Compositor: Nonie Ratcliff
Manufacturing Buyer: Dan Uhrig

ISBN-10: 0-13-374290-3
ISBN-13: 978-0-13-374290-9

Pearson Education LTD.
Pearson Education Australia PTY, Limited.
Pearson Education Singapore, Pte. Ltd.
Pearson Education Asia, Ltd.
Pearson Education Canada, Ltd.
Pearson Educación de Mexico, S.A. de C.V.
Pearson Education—Japan
Pearson Education Malaysia, Pte. Ltd.

Library of Congress Control Number: 2013949116

To my wonderful parents, Molly and Paul,
who always taught me life's greatest lessons.

And to all of those who have made networking
a tool for their success in life.

Contents

Acknowledgments

Thank you to Tim Moore, Publisher of Pearson Education, for his hands-on ability to make things happen and for his superior skills that have made many books like this very successful.

A huge thank you to all of the terrific people at Pearson who contributed their amazing skills in pulling this book together.

Thank you to Russ Hall for his gift in writing and extraordinary editorial talents.

Thank you to Sean Stowers of Pearson Learning Solutions who thinks out of the box and was the one who "networked" me into the organization and opened the door.

Thank you to Linda Schuler for her excellent administrative and savvy skills.

And a warm and sincere thank you to all the wonderful people in my life who shared their stories and experiences that I incorporated into this book. The list goes on and on—and I thank every single one of you from the bottom of my heart.

Thanks so much to all of you.

About the Author

Andrea R. Nierenberg, author, speaker, networking strategist, and business coach and consultant is the force behind The Nierenberg Consulting Group. Called a "networking success story" by the *Wall Street Journal*, Andrea founded The Nierenberg Consulting Group in 1993.

Her firm provides training in networking, sales, customer service, and presentation skills—all skills that impact the bottom line.

With a stellar 30 years as a leader in sales and marketing, Andrea is an in-demand business expert both at home and abroad. Her firm partners with an array of the world's leading financial and media industry businesses.

Introduction

May I have your card?" I asked Melinda, a woman I met at an event. She had told me she was in real estate, a business, like most, in which everyone is constantly "networking" for new clients. I offered to send her a copy of my first book on networking.

She didn't have her card with her, yet she did tell me her name and where she worked. At the end of the evening, we said goodbye, and I'm sure she thought I'd forget to send the book (follow-up sometimes falls through the cracks). I wrote down her name and company info on my electronic notepad (an important networking tool). The next morning, I called her company, found out she worked in the main office (the company has 10 branch offices), and sent her a copy.

A week later, she emailed me and wrote, "Thank you. I'm pleasantly surprised for three reasons." What were they?

1. I'd remembered her name and her company (I'd immediately recorded it on my phone.)

2. I'd found her company address and her specific location. (I was resourceful, and technology makes it so easy.)

3. I'd sent her the book (I'd followed through).

She was so impressed that she told me she'd give the book to Bill, the vice president of sales, with the hope that he might invite me to speak with the other agents in her firm. A week later, Bill left me a voicemail and invited me to meet with him to discuss the possibility of speaking about networking to 200 agents. Before my next step, I sent an email to

Melinda (her preferred method of communication) to thank her, as my original contact.

I then looked up Bill on both LinkedIn and the firm website, to do my homework before we connected. I learned about his background, and I prepared some conversation starters for our meeting.

Fast-forward to the day of the workshop. My meeting with Bill had gone well. I looked around the large room and saw three people I recognized. One was a neighbor of mine, Diane. We had always smiled and said hello, but we'd never formally met. Now Diane and I are both friends and working colleagues, and since I'm a referral broker, I always send connections her way to anyone looking for a real estate agent. I recognized another woman from my yoga class. Now when we see each other in class, we always greet each other warmly. The third person was someone I'd previously seen in a store speaking rudely to a salesperson. Needless to say, I'd be hesitant to refer her to any of my clients. We all have bad days, yet in the world of business networking and in life, the golden rule always applies.

So because of that chance meeting at the industry event, and because I had taken the opportunity to follow up, was resourceful, and had thanked my networking contacts in the firm, I landed the opportunity and ended up working with several of its branches.

It all began when I went to the event prepared with these tools:

- Networking toolkits
- Primed "networking awareness"
- A system for follow-up and follow-through

I've also continued to thank Melinda and Bill every time I'm referred to another office. Why? Because they were the first to recommend my service, and it keeps me on their radar. (By the way, in case you're wondering, I immediately went back and thanked my friend, Bruce, who had invited me to the event, and have kept him posted about my success with the firm.)

In fact, I make it a practice before any engagement to say "thank you" to *all* the people who've referred me, which is part of my "thank you chain" (more about that later). And I always thank them by their preferred method—email, voicemail, text, or social media.

I've seen over and over how personal contacts can turn into professional ones. In fact, the art of effective networking is absolutely vital to building solid business relationships; finding, growing, and keeping your business; and enhancing your life.

To make sure this book covers everything people need to know about networking, I asked people in my network to share their questions about networking. Here's what they asked and what you will learn in this book:

- How do I start a conversation with someone I find intimidating?

- How do I ask tough questions tactfully?

- How do I start and exit a conversation at internal and external business events?

- How do I "network" with someone I might not like but who is key in the department or industry?

- What are some topics to avoid?

- What are examples of great opening lines, icebreakers, and small talk when I'm networking?

- How do I follow up?

- How do I establish and create advocates and referral opportunities?

- How do I know when I'm networking?

- Where can I find a systematic approach to networking?

- How can I keep all my contacts organized and easy to reach?

- How can I continue to find, keep, and grow my business all the time?

- How do I develop my own "self-brand"?

These kinds of questions always come up, along with remarks about how networking can be scary or cringe-worthy. That might be the reason you shy away from the very skills that can help you both personally and professionally.

Before you go further, take a minute to answer these questions yourself:

- How did you find out about your current (or any previous) job?
- How did you meet your spouse?
- How did you choose your neighborhood?
- How do you decide on a vacation spot and accommodations?
- How did you get your last promotion?
- How do you find clients for your business?
- How did you find your doctor, dentist, accountant, day care provider, health club, or favorite restaurant?

When you sought advice from people you knew, when someone introduced you to a person who could help you, or when someone championed your cause, you were networking. Have you done the same for others? If so, you were networking. You might not have realized it, but that is the essence of networking.

What you might lack is a systematic approach to networking, a way of life that can help you draw upon the vast number of people with whom you come in contact, by choice or by chance.

If you are already a seasoned professional and consider yourself a good networker, some of what you'll find in this book will be a refresher course, a checklist for following up, and a guide to new techniques for building your network and keeping it growing. If you're new to the strategies of reaching out to your personal and professional contacts and making them part of your business plan, you'll find concrete tools for tapping your social skills, becoming a resource for others, and building a network that can help your business and profession—and your personal life.

Many of us already know why we need to network continually. Unfortunately, the word *networking* has been misunderstood and often has a negative impression because so many people are interested only in "What's in it for me?" and want quick results.

Instead, look at networking as a process of developing and maintaining quality relationships that enrich your life and empower you to achieve your goals. It's about giving first and realizing that we can learn from everyone we meet.

What you need is a step-by-step approach to networking effectively and methodically, to work it into your everyday life, no matter who you are or what you do. You also need to practice consistent networking and make it work in your life and lifestyle. One size does not fit all. Someone in a class once told me that networking is similar to flossing your teeth: If you fail to do it every day, you won't reap the benefits.

Network Like You Mean It: The Definitive Handbook for Business and Personal Networking focuses on how to increase your business and achieve your goals—by reaching out to people. It also explores how to network in your personal life and expand and enrich your circles. You'll soon see how both personal and business networking have many similarities.

You'll discover a system that's simple to remember and incorporate into your life, based on five practices:

1. Meet new people and nurture your current networks.
2. Listen and learn from everyone with whom you connect.
3. Make quality connections for others.
4. Follow up consistently.
5. Stay in touch creatively.

You'll see in these pages that networking is a lifelong process and a state of mind. The opposite of *networking* is *not working*. Ross, a client who's become a friend, told me that many business professionals understand how to provide their clients with excellent customer service during the "state of the transaction." The challenge is learning how to maintain and cultivate that same relationship—and more—in between transactions. This is building a relationship.

How do you distinguish yourself from others, move your business relationships to the next level, and also be time sensitive and efficient? One goal, as Ross told me, is to find a way to leverage relationships into "dynamic partnerships." Each part of finding, growing, and keeping business relationships weaves into another, and you need to have all three components to create really strong business and personal relationships that will help your business. Ask yourself these questions:

- Who am I? Am I an entrepreneur, part of a small or large company, a manager, or a salesperson?
- What are my goals, and how do I want to achieve them?
- What do I have to offer others?
- What can I give, and how can I be a resource?
- How do I market myself with my experience and expertise?
- Where and when will I do it?

This book is divided into three parts. In Part 1, "Find (Meeting People)," you'll discover how and where to find new connections, and you'll build your checklist for maximizing every event you attend. Part 2, "Grow (Building on Your Strengths)," shows you how to grow your relationships to their fullest potential. Part 3, "Keep (Maintaining Your Hard-Earned Relationships)," helps you keep your contacts, friends, clients, and all relationships coming back. Each chapter includes stories from my personal experience and from people like you who have shared their experiences. Each chapter also concludes with exercises you can do as you build on the skills you've learned, and you'll find an appendix of reference materials to consult for more.

You might be thinking, "Easy for her! She makes this all sound so simple—but I think this is hard!" I understand entirely—I'm an introvert. I've spent my life researching, learning, and developing the skills that now make me someone others many times perceive as an extrovert. At public events or when I'm connecting with someone individually, I often say that I'm a "learned extrovert." You, too, can use the strategies I offer in this book to personalize a plan that works to make you an effective networker.

You already have all the tools inside you—it's just a matter of developing a system and sticking to it.

PART 1

Find (Meeting People)

1

Who Do You Know?

"Everyone has a story to tell. Bring new people into your life. Everyone you meet is an opportunity to learn from, give to, and be a resource."
—Anonymous

On a trip to Kenya, you can imagine my surprise when Massai warrior Chief William asked for my card and then emailed me! Remember, the tribe lives without electricity. The chief walks 10 miles to the village daily and uses the computer at the store where he buys beads for his tribe to make jewelry. We've stayed in touch over the years, and he has created and developed a nonprofit foundation that reaches across East Africa.

In whatever you do, be sure to *get and retain* business *and/or a fulfilling position* and also find relationships that will continue throughout your life. In order to "find," you must have a strategy, plan, and tactics that you can implement for daily help. Some people might consider themselves the "hunters," or the ones who find new opportunities, but you also need to fine-tune your skills as you create new relationships and build and nurture the ones you have.

In the first section of this book, you tackle only those aspects involved in finding relationships and business opportunities—everything from meeting new people to identifying where and how you can do it easily and efficiently. You learn what to do at an event to make your time more efficient and productive as you're networking. I have also put together a model that you can modify according to your own needs and a strategic guide to help you in any business—or, for that matter, any life situation.

The opposite of networking is *not* working. Every day, I start out by thinking, "Who will I meet today?"

Sitting on an airplane one day awaiting takeoff, I looked around the cabin and realized that each person had his or her own story and many different networks. Any conversation could teach me something new or let me help the person I talked with.

I decided to experiment and noticed that the woman sitting across the aisle was reading a book on sales and marketing. When we were served our sodas and nuts, I asked her whether the book was interesting and mentioned that I hadn't read that one yet. We began our conversation, and I learned that she was a new sales manager for a software company and was on her way to a sales meeting in Los Angeles. Through some open-ended, conversational questions I asked, I learned the following:

- She lived in New York City, in the same building as a friend of mine, and they knew each other from their condo board.

- She formerly worked for a company where I had presented a workshop.

- She was an active alumni member of a university that a friend's daughter was interested in and said she would write a letter of recommendation to the admissions office after speaking with the young woman.

Through this exchange, I realized that, in business and in life, networking happens anywhere, anytime. You never know how starting a conversation with someone can open doors and opportunities for both parties involved. In a Woody Allen movie, I once heard the comment, "Life is networking"—and I agree.

The art of networking, which I define as the combination of people skills, interaction, and opportunity, is an absolutely vital tool for building business and keeping it. Networking is about creating and developing opportunities by meeting and connecting the dots among the people you know. Over time, as you build rapport and trust, these relationships lead to other contacts, relationships, and opportunities—and friendships develop. As you read this, I hope you are saying, "Of course! This is life and what I do daily—I just don't call it *networking*."

The power created by this amazing link of trusted advisers, friends, and advocates is stunning. Think of those you know who are truly masterful at networking, and ask yourself, "How do they do it? What do they do?" You'll find that their "best practices" vary greatly, but regardless of their communication and personality style, these people all have confidence and respect for each other.

Now think of all the networks you already have:

- Jobs (clients and colleagues)
- Social activities
- Religious affiliations
- Neighbors, friends, and relatives
- Clubs (social and business)
- Business and professional associations
- Social media
- Hobbies and interests
- School alumni

The list goes on and on.

I read years ago that we all know at least 250 people. Look at the group of people you know who fit in this list. You can multiply your network by helping many of these people, who can then connect you with some of the 250 people each of them knows. In my own life, this number has multiplied many times over!

By the way, I've stayed in touch with that woman from the plane. She was able to help my friend's daughter get into the university she wanted (of course, the young lady did have good grades and was both an athlete and an all-around terrific young lady, yet my new friend's influence helped), and I ended up doing an executive coaching project for her company. I also reconnected with her former company, which I had previously worked with. Just by taking some action steps, I was able to make more connections that led to other business opportunities that I'm nurturing today.

Here's one reason I hope you're reading this book: to learn to look at life with a networking eye and ear and realize that opportunities can unfold anywhere, anytime. You just have to be ready, willing, able, and open to starting some conversations. Be open to serendipity and the path to synchronicity. There are no accidents—everyone we connect with can be a resource or lead us to the next opportunity.

Write down the names of up to three people you know in each of the following categories:

Job/workplace:

_____

_____

_____

Social activities:

_____

_____

_____

Religious affiliations:

_____

_____

_____

Neighbors/friends

_____

_____

_____

Clubs:

_____

_____

_____

Professional associations:

_____

_____

School/alumni associations:

_____

_____

Now look over these names and recall how you met some of these people. How were you introduced? Did you introduce them to others? Perhaps you have to jog your memory a bit. The end result is that you'll realize that networking has been part of your life, even if you've never consciously thought about it.

Part of growing and strengthening your business networks is remembering who else was involved when you met and realizing that each of you probably does know more than 250 people. Let me share a few of my examples.

While sipping espresso at a coffee shop, I was talking with a friend about his advertising agency. Noticing that the man at the next table was listening, I introduced myself and asked if he was in advertising as well. He said he was, but he was currently looking for a job. I introduced the two men and later heard that the man at the next table got an interview at my friend's firm.

In another case, I was in an art class and complimented a woman on her bracelet. We began talking, and I ended up ordering the bracelet from her firm and attended an event held by the designer. Now she and I are working on a consulting project. All that came from admiring a piece of jewelry and following up.

As a third example, one afternoon, Bill, a successful realtor, received a call from a woman who left this message: "I am in Los Angeles at a hotel with my two kids, and I'm unemployed and need to find a house." He called her back and agreed to meet to see how he could help. This woman turned out to be the wife of the new coach of a major sports team, and they were relocating. Bill sold the family a great house and has gotten several more referrals from other team members. Following up made the difference: The woman had left the same message for five other brokers, none of which returned her call. When Bill told the initial part of the story to the other 90 agents in his office, they all remarked, "Waste of time." But who's laughing now?

These examples, and countless others, show that almost any person you come in contact with is a potential networking contact. Be aware, and develop new business opportunities when you're on an airplane, at the dentist's office, in line for movie tickets, and even at the dry cleaner.

People You Need in Your Network

The first step in building a network is to identify the people with whom you want to build relationships. You will be pleasantly surprised by how many of them you already know. The types of people you need in your network most likely include the following categories:

- Customers and clients
- Suppliers
- Coworkers and colleagues
- People in your profession
- People you went to school with or met at a seminar or workshop
- Like-minded people
- Neighbors
- Friends
- Family
- People you meet "in everyday life"

Customers or Clients

These people are the lifeblood of your business, and it is important to build positive relationships with them. The more you know about them, and the more they know about and trust you, the more both of you will prosper.

You might be thinking, "This category doesn't apply to me. I don't have customers or clients."

In my workshops, I often ask, "By a show of hands, how many of you are in sales? How many in customer service? How many in public relations? How many own and run a business? How many manage a team of employees?" Some hands go up.

Then I ask, "How many of you have to convince another person to use an idea of yours? How many of you are looking for a new job, a promotion, or a raise?" By the end of my questions, almost everyone has raised his or her hand. The fact is, we are all in sales, customer service, or public relations, regardless of our formal job description.

When you think about it, you are constantly communicating messages and selling your ideas to others. We are all public relations specialists when we act as representatives of our companies or ourselves. Your "clients" include coworkers, staff, other department heads, and, certainly, your boss. In fact, anyone you "sell" your thoughts or ideas to is a client.

If you are in sales, keeping customers happy and profitable members of your network is essential. Besides being the lifeblood of your current business, they can be your advocate by referring you to prospects, thereby helping your business to grow and prosper. And you can do the same for them. Many of us don't like the word *sales* and almost cringe at the thought of it. Let's look at it from the perspective of hotels such as the Ritz-Carlton or the Hilton, where everyone in the organization is part of the customer experience—let's think of it that we all work to create the best experience.

CREATING A POSITIVE EXPERIENCE

Use these networking tactics to keep those you connect with satisfied and happy.

- **Know them.** Find out their hobbies, names of family members, likes and dislikes, birthdays and anniversaries, and even their favorite foods. Keep good records of this information, and use it to build on your relationships.

- **Keep in touch.** Share information and ideas with customers when you think it will help them. Even if nothing develops, it will provide an opportunity to be on their radar screen. Remember, your goal is to make lasting impressions.

- **Handle complaints and concerns promptly.** Take responsibility for problems, no matter who caused them. Your customers will see you as their lifesaver and will want to help you in return.

- **Prove that you are dependable.** When you make promises, keep them! This builds trust, an important factor in any relationship.

We expand on this later as we move into keeping your relationships.

Suppliers

Whether you own a business or work in a company, you buy goods and services from suppliers or vendors. Think of all the products and services you buy in your business and in your personal life.

Your suppliers can be anyone. Other than your business contacts, they could include your dry cleaner, your hairdresser, and even your doctor. My IT tech, John Mazzaraco, once overheard me on the phone with someone as he was installing some software and said, "Andrea, I know the head of purchasing of the company you're calling." Turns out they were friends growing up. As you can imagine, having the referral from John was a huge help and got me through right away. I also returned a favor to him by introducing him to one of my strategic partner clients, and now he is doing that person's computer work. Remember, this is a two-way street. Over the years, we have exchanged many referrals and opportunities because of the trust we have in each other and feel comfortable referring each other.

Just as I was writing this book, my hairdresser, who knows the real color of my hair, was planning a surprise birthday cruise for his significant other. He asked me who I knew, and I was able to connect him with my new part-time neighbor in Florida, who lives in the same condo building and is a cruise specialist! Bingo—a true win/win on all fronts.

Again, 24/7 networking awareness helps everyone.

FUNNY THING IN THE DOCTOR'S OFFICE

As I walked into the office, my doctor came out front to meet me. I'm always impressed by how he greets each patient by name, no matter how full the waiting room is. As I walked back to the exam room, I passed his office. On his desk was the first book I had written.

I said to him a few minutes later, "Dr. S., you are good!" He looked at me curiously, and I explained. "Well, here I was visiting your office today, and you pulled out my book to put right on your desk. That's great, and it makes me feel important." He smiled and said, "Andrea, I've got to tell

> you, it's been there since you gave it to me! It's a great paperweight, and other people always pick it up and ask about it!"
>
> Whether you've written a book or not, you can always give others something that will help keep your name in their mind. (He will now get a copy of this book!)

Coworkers and Colleagues

Look around your office and throughout your organization. Some people you know fairly well—they might even be your friends. For the others, you could set a goal to get to know them better. Start your action plan by asking them out for lunch or coffee, or volunteer on a task force so that you'll have more interaction with them. The fact is, the people who work with us and know us are a powerful source for networking.

Janice works in the legal department of a large organization. Through her relationships, she found a new apartment, got in touch with a new carpenter, and was able to help one of her friends at another company get a job at her organization. How? It all happened through the power of internal networking. She has also gotten into the habit of learning more about her colleagues and coworkers. Janice takes the time to learn about their interests. One day at lunch with a colleague, she discovered that her best friend's husband was the sales director of a company where her sister was interviewing. Her sister was very qualified, yet many other people were, too, and the interviewing process was tough. Thanks to the personal introduction, her sister got the "job of her dreams." That's just more evidence of how the concept "You just never know" applies here. We'll look into how to develop your internal business relationships across departments more later.

Yet too often I hear this: "In my company, we work in 'silos.' How can I strengthen my relationships with other departments?" This is a critical question because we're all working for the same bottom line, and each person with whom we interact is someone we can learn from and possibly cooperate with at work. Larger companies often find out too late that one department is working with a prospective client, and other departments could have added their expertise to help close the sale or move the business along. Sadly, no "crossover" discussion occurs, and business is lost because of it.

You and your coworkers form a "chain of value" that can reach more potential clients than your efforts working in isolation from each other. You are all internal invaluable resources for one other. You might ask yourself:

- What links do I have with other coworkers and departments?

- Do people know what I can do to help them? And do I know what they do?

- What are our common goals?

- Are we committed to learning from each other's ideas and creating new possibilities together?

One law firm that I consulted with realized that it could develop more business if the partners and associates learned more about each other's practice areas. In putting together a workshop for the firm, I asked the members what questions they had about their firm's other departments. Each attorney came to the program with a mission statement of what his or her department did and suggestions on how all of them could work more productively with other areas.

At the end of the program, each person was charged with staying in touch with someone from another practice area, to see what new opportunities could develop. The challenge after these events is always whether people will get out of their comfort zone and change. Most lawyers, like all professionals, are already overworked, yet this internal networking focused on the bottom line. Partners saw how they could gain new business. I'm happy to report that, after six months, this law firm developed two new pieces of business from the internal relationships they established.

A NETWORKING OPPORTUNITY FOR YOU

We can all do this. Think about your own internal teams. See where you can uncover new business opportunities right in your own backyard while also making everyone better team players.

Effective networking is often woven throughout the mission statements, core values, and career growth models of corporations:

- Provides access to key contacts to help you grow in your career

- Permits informational exchanges

- Leverages the knowledge and experience of others to understand what drives the firm's business

- Connects you to a wider array of people who can help educate you, and vice versa

STARTING A NEW JOB

Pete, a young man I have worked with, really goes out of his way to learn about people and their interests. When Pete took a new job, one of the first things he did was draw a map of his new office area, noting each cubicle and office. As he met people, he wrote down their names on the corresponding space on his map, along with interesting things he learned about them in conversation: the names of their children, their favorite vacation spots, any sports they play and other outside interests, and favorite restaurants, as well as work information. Pete created a foundation for strong business relationships with these people right from the start. From my last report with him, he has steadily moved up the ranks of his firm—and he credits much of it for his internal networking and alliance-building practices.

People in Your Business or Profession

I enjoy developing relationships with other people in my different businesses. Some people view this category of people as competitors, and in some ways we are—yet we can also refer, help, and leverage our relationships with each other. I know, for example, that often when I am called for a large project, I must bring in a team of consultants. Because I continually develop strong relationships with other subject matter experts, I always have a "team" of people waiting. They feel the same way, and sometimes I work with them as part of their virtual group. By removing our egos, we both make room for more new business.

I have developed contacts in companies that were not initially interested in my services. Yet because I was working with others in my business who already had relationships with those businesses, they came to see what I can do to help them. Carol is a perfect example. She also has a communications consulting firm and has hired me on several occasions to team up with her to conduct a part of a program in which I have expertise. Another time, I called on another executive coach friend to do a project for one of my clients. It all boils down to the fact that I trust these people, and I know their work. We have formed great strategic alliances. No person is an island, and we work better knowing that we have formed great networks.

You can do the same. Start to observe the people you know in your business and profession. They can become your network of advisers, and their connections will be helpful after you build a relationship with them.

Obvious places to meet people in your profession are on LinkedIn and in physical business meetings, conferences, association meetings, trade shows, meet-ups, and wherever people gather formally or informally to share ideas and news about your industry. As you become more successful in your profession, be sure to join professional associations and special-interest groups; attend seminars, workshops, and conventions; and become an active participant in these programs and groups.

Be willing to share your experience and expertise with those you are getting to know. Think of it this way: A fist tightly clenching what it has is unable to grab new opportunities. Be open to others, and you can receive from them. Such was the case with Margaret, a successful trainer and someone I have shared with generously. Because of our business relationship, she referred me to one of her clients to speak at a conference. Margaret knows my work, and she knew that I would honor her client relationship and be sure to keep her in the loop. We also have a business relationship and alliance. Want this technique to work for you? Find one professional contact whose business you'll offer to help grow. You'll see other opportunities emerge over time.

People You Went to School with or Met at a Workshop or Seminar

I'm involved with my college alumni organization and was asked to speak at one of its meetings. The contacts I reopened there led me to opportunities in two new industries, and I was asked to return to my former college campus to speak with the students. This came about because a former classmate of mine, now one of the managing directors of a large securities company, heard me speak at a conference and referred me to my college's business school. Take a closer look at your alumni e-zine or magazine, with an eye toward people who can help you or whom you can help in your profession. On LinkedIn, connect with those people and then follow your university or grad school. Make sure you also keep that college magazine abreast of your achievements for inclusion in the publication—you never know whom you might reconnect with. Again, the opportunities are limitless.

A colleague's niece, a recent graduate of a leading technical college, launched a successful career as a photographer's stylist in New York City based almost solely on contacts with alumni of her school. She actually knew very few of them before moving to New York City, yet she sought them out and found them willing to help her because they were fellow alumni. At a recent workshop, a young woman named Sarah mentioned, "Everything that has happened to me since college is a result of the people I met in classes and my sorority."

In another instance, a good friend had just landed a large project with the U.S. Air Force. I asked her how she'd been able to get connected, and she said, "Andrea, this goes back to a friend in my college sorority. Of course, it didn't happen overnight. We've been friends and always found ways to stay connected." Just for the record, my friend has been out of school for at least 25 years. It pays to stay in touch.

At one of my yoga classes, I always talk with Norma, who is in the public relations business, in between poses. Over time, she invited me to speak at an association lunch when the featured speaker canceled at the last minute. At that meeting, I connected with two people I have started to build professional relationships with—all because Norma and I shared conversations over time in yoga. Of course, I always keep her in the loop whenever an opportunity comes up as a result of her help. This is *key:* Always keep your initial introduction sources in the loop on any referral or introduction, whether they come together or not.

Meeting Ross is an example of giving and getting much in return. He sat in the front row of a seminar where I donate my time for a nonprofit professional association. After the program, he sent me a note, and we stayed in touch. (Talk about a wonderful note writer! Ross wins the award: He regularly sends me cards and articles of interest.) After about a year, I was invited in to work with Ross's team at one of his company's sales meetings. I got to help Ross, too—as I was getting my real estate license, I ran into someone he used to work with and reconnected them.

YOU ALREADY HAVE A MUCH LARGER NETWORK THAN YOU THINK

Curious about how big your current network might be? Find out by answering these questions:

- How many people do you work with now?

- How many people have you worked with in the past?

- How many clients or customers do you have, both past and present?

- How many people do you know from professional organizations?

- How many people do you know from other organizations, such as health clubs, your homeowners' association, or your children's school groups?

- How many people do you know from your religious affiliations or organizations?

- How many professionals (doctors, lawyers, accountants, and so on) do you come in contact with?

- How many former schoolmates do you stay in touch with?

- How many people do you know in your neighborhood?

- How many friends and relatives do you have?

Add them up. Chances are, you already have a large network of contacts.

Like-Minded People

Often the easiest people to talk with are those who have common interests and ambitions, or who share similar life experiences. And not just professionally—after all, you have a personal life, and that's a huge part of our networking! Think language classes, charity groups, kids' soccer games and recitals, vacations, and religious groups. The people you find at these events and places like the same things you do, and that leads to a perfect networking opportunity. You form your own niches when you start hanging out and meeting with people who share a passion or interest.

I like to collect jewelry. It's something I inherited from my wonderful mother, and I know she's smiling down at me from heaven. You might wonder what this has to do with my business. Well, one day, one of my former clients asked me to have breakfast with him and his friend, Dan, who had been the publisher of a jewelry magazine and was now looking for another position. We had an interesting meeting, and because I was engrossed in the subject matter of the jewelry industry, I was able to give him some leads. He eventually landed the top position at one of the leading jewelry publications through one of the connections I'd introduced him to. I was thrilled. It feels good to connect and help great people when the opportunities arise—and they often do. Just live life with that 24/7 networking awareness.

It just so happened Dan's editorial offices were in Bangkok, and I was going to be visiting there. Dan put me in touch with the chief editor, Robert, and I was able to become a contributor and write articles for the publication on developing new business. As I wrote for them on the very topics we are discussing here—how to find, grow, and keep your business—I had a great deal of fun: After all, I was doing it for an industry that I'm personally interested in. And you never know who will read the articles. How can you do the same with an industry that you are interested in expanding into more?

What do you really enjoy, and how can you start to create new connections for business in that area? Find ways to be visible. For example, you could write an article or make a presentation on your area of expertise at a business function where potential clients will be.

Neighbors

Neighbors can serendipitously become valuable members of your network. One small independent publisher of children's books has found several of her best authors in the small town where she lives. Most of us could get to know our neighbors better. Too often we just wave as they drive by, or we chat about our gardens, traffic, or the weather. Living in New York City, sometimes I see people only in the mailroom or elevator. I decided to change that and, over the years, have gotten to know quite a few people—not only in my building, but also in a two-block radius.

Start an experiment to take relationships with your neighbors to a new level. Go beyond the back-fence or mailroom conversations, and really get to know them by using some of the techniques you'd use at a business networking event. You might be surprised to find a neighbor in the same business, or a related one, or one who knows someone you want to meet. Of course, good neighbors are always an invaluable source for such things as cleaning services, contractors, organizations, decorators, or, when the time comes to move or expand, real estate agents. If you're reading this and thinking, "I need some down time," I understand—take the best and leave the rest! I'm just reinforcing that the potential of meeting new people has no limit. Operate within your pace and style—this is not a race.

NETWORKING IN YOUR ELEVATOR

John always said hello to a certain man in the elevator of his building. The man always nodded and asked how John's dad was doing. One day they started talking. John learned that the man, Tom, was the publisher of one of his favorite publications. John confided that he worked in the advertising business but was not in a position he particularly enjoyed. The two men stayed in touch, always saying hello when they met. Then one day Tom mentioned that he had an opening on his staff and asked John to send his resume. "I ended up working for 14 of the best years of my life for the man in the elevator," says John. The two became close friends, and when Tom passed away, his wife asked John to give the eulogy at his memorial—and specifically requested that he tell the elevator story as part of his "Tales with Tom."

Along the same lines, I know someone in Chicago who routinely strikes up conversations in the elevator. When he meets someone new in his office building, he looks at the button the person pushed and says, "Hi, my name is Bill. May I ask what kind of business you are in on the seventh floor?" He makes great new connections in less than 30 seconds.

Friends

Friends make the world a happier place. We need to welcome and nurture these people in our lives, as well as consider them important members of our network. What better advocate can we have, or can we be, than a friend? Take time to nurture and cultivate your friends. Network with them in a positive way, never with expectations. Give without the thought of receiving or keeping score, and you will receive the greatest gift of all: a good friend. When something more comes of it, consider that a gift.

My friend Bill, who works in the financial services industries, is one of those people who always looks for ways to help his friends. He gives freely of himself and receives introductions all the time. Why? Because he stays on all his friends' radar screens; when someone needs a financial adviser or is looking for help, he immediately comes to mind. I know that I look for ways to introduce him to others and keep an eye out for opportunities that would be good for his business. I also trust him and admire Bill's knowledge of his field and the pride he takes in his work. I know that he would do a great job in any project he undertakes.

How do you find the time to see your friends? Make plans to meet for breakfast, lunch, or dinner. Even better, look for unusual activities to share. I have met friends for walks (the new "in" for meetings and health benefits at the same time), afternoon tea, shopping excursions, workouts at the gym (chatting on the treadmill or bike is also good for your heart), and art lectures. Go to a sports event; play golf, tennis, or any other sport; or have a drink together after work. Take the time to do these things for your friends and for your own enrichment.

Family

Network with your family? When you know them well and believe in them and their work and ambitions, creating connections is easy. A friend of mine recently told me she recommended her nephew, a graphic artist, for a project for her company. She was familiar with his work and was confident he could do a quality job, quote a reasonable price, and meet the deadlines. Remember, her reputation was at stake, as it would have been with any recommendation she made. She also wisely distanced herself from the financial negotiations. Both she and her nephew were very clear with one another that this was a business arrangement and that, no matter the outcome, it would remain so. In this case, it worked out just fine. He did a good job, as she knew he would, and has received several subsequent assignments.

Networking with your family can work. Just be sure to maintain your integrity and be mindful of the reputations involved.

I'm always looking for opportunities to refer my dentist, Dr. Allan Miller, who is also my cousin. He has been my dentist my whole adult life. At a cocktail party last year, a couple mentioned that they lived in the same community as Dr. Miller, and I asked if they'd heard of him. The wife already is a patient, and the husband was impressed because Dr. Miller had referred him to an excellent specialist for work my cousin doesn't do. Again, this is networking and building connections at its finest.

People You Meet by Chance or in the Serendipity of Life

This is where the fun starts. These people seem to come into your life by chance and from almost anyplace: on planes and trains, at the grocery store, at Starbucks or Dunkin' Donuts, or wherever you happen to be. To make these chance encounters work for you, treat those you meet as important people to have in your network. Keep your ears and eyes open for these opportunities through chance encounters.

While visiting a friend in the hospital in Florida, I was sitting in the waiting room and started talking with the woman next to me. I was fascinated by her time management and organizational skills, even in the hospital waiting room.

As we talked, I learned about her business and the types of clients she worked with. By the time I was allowed into my friend's room, I had made a new contact and had already referred her to two new business projects. And from her, I learned many new tips and tricks on being better organized than I already was. We can always learn something new from someone when we are open to it.

One time in a New York taxi on my way to a dinner party, I started chatting with the driver, who told me that he loved the people of New York because they were so helpful. I learned during our 10-block ride (you might know about New York City traffic) that he was a lawyer from another country. When he'd moved to the United States, he'd had to start over in law school, all while he was working as a paralegal and driving a cab to support his family. Talk about determination! I gave him my card and asked him to email me his resume to see if I could do anything to help. I first wanted to see if he would follow up and whether he was for real. Well, he did—and he does have the credentials. I have already sent his information to two people. You never know what will happen, yet I'm sure my driver, Sangiv, will find some wonderful opportunities. I'm so glad that I was in his cab and, as always, had on my networking eyes and ears. You just never know!

Keep your eyes and ears open—serendipitous opportunities happen all the time, anywhere. This can happen when you log in to Twitter, Facebook, or LinkedIn and answer a message in a group question; when you comment on a picture; or when you reply to a tweet. Be open to the opportunities that develop.

Virtually everywhere is open ground. Those who might still think that networking is *getting* may think this seems like too much. Separate yourself from that mindset by remembering the most important aspect of networking: that it's about being open and willing to help and *give* first. Just make a connection. You might have heard that people come into our lives for a reason, a season, or a lifetime, and often we don't know which they fall into. Over time, we realize it.

Resist being cynical—concentrate only on the good things that happen when you surround yourself with positive thoughts and vibes.

Reconnect with People You Already Know

Make a game plan for reconnecting with the people who are already in your network. Start with a list of people in each of the categories we've just discussed, and add a few others that come to your mind who will accept your phone call, email, text, or social media invitation. Now reach out to them to touch base, say hello, or catch up on what has been happening in your lives. With all our technology tools and engines, we all know this is a daily "to do" and a common way people connect—and, more importantly, reconnect.

This happened to me recently. I received two emails from people from my "history." Both had read an article in which I was quoted, along with several others, and they'd gone to my website and reached out. One person had been the president of the company where I'd worked in my first sales job. Although I knew him somewhat, all these many years later, it was so nice to hear from him. I might even do a consulting project for his firm. (If not, it's still a great reconnection.) The other person was a woman who had worked for me when I was the publisher of a magazine. She called to say how excited she was to reconnect. We caught up, and I found out that she has her own business. I've already sent some people to her store in Minnesota.

I also recently reconnected with someone from my past as I was doing research on LinkedIn. I found a fantastic subject matter expert who is one of the top gurus in listening, Dr. Manny Steil. He'd spoken at my first sales meeting when I was starting out in advertising sales. I'd been so impressed with Dr. Steil and always remembered how he left an indelible print in my mind on the power of superior listening skills (something we work on daily). We reconnected and are now talking, and I've referred him and his book to many others. What a wonderful reconnection for me!

When you make that first reconnect, instead of feeling awkward, keep in mind the positive impact. The person might have been thinking of you and meaning to reach out, yet life got in the way. This has happened to me countless times. These reach-outs are easy to make because you're not going to be asking for anything. Be prepared. If you've been out of touch for a while, the person might respond cordially, yet you know he or she is thinking, "What do you want?" Imagine the person's surprise and pleasure when this turns out to be purely a friendly catch-up. Perhaps you are reaching out to congratulate him or her on something. LinkedIn gives us this opportunity daily.

FOUR-MULA FOR SUCCESS

Connect with four people per week from your universal database, including people from these categories:

1. A client or prospect with whom you have not been in touch for a while

2. A former business colleague

3. A friend you haven't been in touch with recently

4. A current friend

The final connect, to a current friend, will be the easiest and most fun— think of it as a reward for making the other three. This is a great way to keep nurturing our friendships—they're part of our network, and they also want us to be happy, just as we want the same for them. It's a win/win always. And no matter how well we know someone, we don't know everyone he or she knows. So many times, I've found mutual connections that we never initially realized. As you work through your list, you will find that many past relationships have become current ones. Keep it going. It's easy to fit four connects a week into your busy schedule. It breaks down the formidable task of reconnecting with your contacts into manageable, bite-size tasks—baby steps, as I like to call it. Make it a practice you continue as your network grows. Most important will be the results. Imagine, once you've solidified your relationship, how simple it will be to ask later if you ever need a favor.

Identify Key Business Contacts You Would Like to Meet

Make a list of key people in your industry or profession that you'd like to meet. Make them specific individuals (or specific titles of individuals, if you don't know the name of the current person in that position) within an organization or industry group who would be beneficial to your career or business goals. Aim high! Include high-level executives and high-profile people in your field. Again, LinkedIn makes this simple to navigate.

With LinkedIn or any search engine, do your research and determine organizations, interest groups, or places you could meet these people. Think about people they know, people you know, and the possible connections that might lead to a meeting. No connection is impossible.

One new woman in my network, Karen, owns a graphic arts company. She and I met on the chance that we might have opportunities to work with one another or people each of us knew.

I liked Karen's style, and I sent four letters of introduction to some of my clients for her. She, in turn, wrote a great letter of introduction to a company that I have always wanted to work with and that she already has as a client. When I sent my initial email, I connected right away, and the process of working with the organization is steadily underway. I knew this company and the person I wanted to talk with, yet I didn't have a connection until Karen referred me to someone who could start the process.

You can see how we have all sorts of people in our network without even realizing it. We have also looked at whom you need to get to know to strengthen your universal network. In the next chapter, you'll be getting ready to step out to the places where you'll get to network with current and new contacts. Before you attend your next meeting, take some time to look into your current network with the following exercise—it will lay a foundation for many opportunities in the future.

Exercise: Who's in Your Current Network?

This exercise is designed to help you bring to mind the people in your current network. When you think long enough about the people you've connected with throughout your life, you'll realize that you're in a much better position than you might have originally thought.

Your Immediate Network

This network includes people who would quickly answer or return a call, email, or text from you. For each type of person listed, name up to three people you would consider as part of your immediate network.

Customers of clients

1.

2.

3.

People from whom you buy products or services

1.

2.

3.

Coworkers

1.

2.

3.

Professional colleagues

    1.

    2.

    3.

Friends and neighbors

    1.

    2.

    3.

People in Your Secondary Network

Your secondary network includes people you connect with periodically. They might include people you went to school with, people you worked with at a previous job, friends from an old neighborhood, or people you met by chance and have found interests in common with. List up to five people in this category; beside each name, note how you met the person.

    1.

    2.

    3.

    4.

    5.

People in Your Universal Network

If you had to create an Excel spreadsheet of everyone you know, how many people would be on it? Chances are it would be a much longer list than the names you just listed in your immediate and secondary networks. This long list of your universal network is something to go back to every few months, to see what has changed in your business life that warrants getting in touch. Say you have several medical industry contacts you haven't worked with for years. Right now they could be part of your universal network. If you change jobs, however, and start working with medical products, these people would move to your secondary or immediate network. Your network is a living database that you need to nurture and maintain.

Networking Ladder

- **Top rung:** Your immediate network—people who connect via any form of communication from you right away

- **Middle rung:** Your secondary network—people who know who you are when you contact them

- **Lower rung:** Entire list of everyone you have ever known

Take-Away Reminders

Key exercise point: Check this list every three months to make sure you keep your network current. That way, you'll always have a list of people to reach out to when you're looking for a new opportunity or have something to help someone in your network.

Accountability: After each chapter, review and highlight the specific action steps you will take and how you will personally measure and monitor them.

In the Part 1 Appendix, you'll find a strategic networking guide that will help you with your action plans.

> *"Networking is the tool to open up doors. If you don't network, then get used to looking at a closed door."*
>
> —Jeri Sedlar, writer and coach

2

Where to Meet People

O n my way to an adventure travelers' lecture, I stopped off to get a cup of tea. I started talking with a man in line who had a bag with the logo "World Traveler." I asked him his favorite country, and as we talked, I found out that he was the lecturer that evening for my travel class. I got to know John and have taken several of his tours around the world.

Today you have so many opportunities to meet new people both on- and offline. In this chapter, we focus on meeting and connecting face to face. Later we will look into the vast opportunities of meeting people online.

Where do people you want to know gather? Identify the different kinds of places, events, associations, trade organizations, and conferences where people in your profession, or the professions you are interested in, meet. Think about your potential and current clients and advocates—where do they go to connect? These are the types of locations where people get together to exchange and share information, contacts, and knowledge, as well as to purely enjoy each other's company.

Start building your list. What do you already know about these organizations? Do you belong to them and attend meetings? If so, how can you get more out of the organization and become more involved? Would you like to know more about these organizations and their members to find others who can help you build your network?

When you need to start a list from scratch, think first about your own professional and personal interests and passions. Do you go to your kids' parent–teacher meetings, watch their swim meets, or lead their scout troop? Do you belong to your neighborhood association or local historic group, sing in the choir at your church or synagogue, or work out at a local health club? Do you like to travel? Do you volunteer or contribute to charities? Do you belong to a book or financial club? Do you take dance, art, or language classes, or do you have any other hobby that you have a strong interest in? Thinking that conferences, meet-ups, and business meetings are the only places to go is too limiting. Most of us can think of how we started up a lifelong friendship or a business partnership from a chance meeting far outside a business environment. That's why I always say life is networking and serendipitous opportunities are everywhere. We just need to have what I call a 24/7 networking awareness.

Events and Organizations

You can meet potential business contacts at all different types of events. The first that comes to mind is the structured event whose stated purpose is to actively network and learn from each other. These can take place at associations and industry-specific group events, as well as at meetings of networking organizations. People who attend these events expect to introduce themselves and briefly discuss their business, in hopes of making a helpful business connection. In some ways, it's easier to go through the process of "active" networking at these events because that's their stated purpose. As you know, it takes time to make connections that stick and turn them into opportunities for both sides. Sadly, some people think that they simply need to show up a few times. But these types of events are the perfect place to start learning a little about the people you'd like to connect and start the process with. These exchanges can start the process of building trust, and people do business with those they trust and like. This accomplishes two goals: You find out whether you want to join the organization, and you expand your network by two.

Another opportunity to meet and make connections is at association and professional industry events. Here the stated purpose is either to conduct business or to address a specific topic of interest to the group. This is also a perfect opportunity to network and connect with other like-minded people. These events are great venues for creating the opportunities to make solid connections.

Industry organizations also hold social and cultural events either specifically to raise funds for a charity or to recognize industry leaders. As we all know, when you get involved in any group, there are often several opportunities to pursue. The key is to find the right group (or groups) where you can make a difference during the time you spend there and with those you connect with. The process is to get involved, attend meetings, and build relationships. The next sections describe some types of groups you might want to consider.

Associations and Industry-Specific Organizations

I grew up in the advertising and direct marketing industry. Like any industry, it has many different forums, councils, and meetings. Plenty of contacts, relationships, and business opportunities are developed at these events, all the result of active networking. You simply need to keep your eyes and ears open and have a process to follow (more on this when we discuss your networking checklist for every event you attend).

Often the stated mission of these organizations is educational, informational, or, for some trade associations, to review industry trends to identify any future opportunities. Most organizations are open to those who work in, or aspire to work in, the industry or profession they represent. I think of how many organizations I've found online and how much I've learned about social media by getting involved and attending different educational forums. I've met people who have helped me, and vice versa, and those who have become friends, vendors, and clients. All of these organizations provide a wide variety of services to members, including the opportunity to meet and connect with like-minded people. Becoming involved gives you the opportunity to meet people with whom you will feel a rapport and possibly build a relationship.

I have been involved and active in several organizations over the years that have helped me in my business. Two that have worked for me are the Financial Women's Association and Advertising Women of New York. Through the years, I have found clients, suppliers, friends, and mentors through these groups. I did not join them specifically because they are women's organizations; I joined them because they represented two industries I work in and wanted to learn more about. After I did my research and attended some meetings, both of these organizations kept coming to the top of my list.

Although I have reaped many rewards from these associations, I believe joining an organization is foremost about *giving*. Getting involved in committees, participating in webinars and workshops, and helping others along the way opened many doors for me. I always know that what gets remembered gets rewarded. The "it's a small world" effect holds true here. Countless people I've met at these associations have connected me to businesspeople I never would have met on my own. My secret? I do what you should do:

Take the time to get involved instead of just being a spectator.

You can find these groups and industry associations by asking others in your business or profession, or by reading online trade magazines and going to LinkedIn and joining different groups. Do an Internet search for organizations you know about, and also search with keywords to find others. When you find a group you think you'll like, be sure to check out its links and resources page. You'll likely be overwhelmed with the content and links to other organizations in the industries you have an interest in. Most organizations have a local chapter in your community, and you'll find everything on their home page. You can also visit the home page of the Center for Association Leadership (ASAE), www.asaecenter.org.

Joining and becoming active in one or several of these groups will provide you with many profitable networking opportunities and give your career a boost.

Networking Organizations

These are groups whose primary stated purpose is to network, build relationships, and exchange leads, contacts, and tips. Instead of being industry specific, they have members in different fields, yet with collaborative and partnership opportunities to grow your business opportunities. Search for any type of group you are interested in—business, hobby, special interest, cause that you support—and you will find organizations to choose from; simply decide what is the best use of your time, energy, and money.

Many groups are national in scope, with local chapters, so visit a couple meetings and employ the 2-2-2 strategy (see the "My 2-2-2 Strategy" sidebar in this chapter). Meeting schedules vary greatly, and with the mobile way we work today, you can find the right venue for you. Many organizations allow some or all attendees to give a brief elevator introduction (we talk more about preparing yours for this situation in Chapter 3, "Techniques for a Successful Networking Event"). With your networking checklist (discussed later and found in the appendix), you will be armed and totally ready to go.

Some networking organizations keep their members accountable. They keep track of who is actively receiving and giving leads to other members—and your membership often depends on being a giver first. Again, I look at many of these types of organizations as creating your own advisory board for business: You learn about others, and they learn about you. The end result is that you want to refer opportunities to them. What results can you expect? It depends on how much you and other members of your group are willing to contribute. If I had to offer a formula, it would be this:

Networking organization you like

+

Frequent attendance

+

Giving more than you receive

+

Following up with new contacts

+

Reporting back to the person who gave you the referral

=

Networking success

The best thing about these groups is that they are structured, have a facilitator, and keep the meeting on point with an agenda. This format seems to work well for many people, especially those of us who are introverted or uncomfortable with the activity of networking or asking for referrals. You can be great at your particular profession yet not be comfortable with this way of building your business. Let me show you how one of these groups works.

Several years ago, I was asked to be a luncheon speaker for the Executives' Association of New York (www.eanyc.com). I walked into a room of 85 people, all owners or principals of midsize businesses who come together weekly to share information, offer leads, and help with each other's businesses. They were excellent networkers and relationship builders, and here I was speaking to this group! Reading the audience, I quickly adapted my remarks to show how they could help coach their staffs to network and find new opportunities. As a result, they invited me to become their official "networking guru." This group operates like a business and has a clear business model for its members. Some of the members have been together more than 20 years, and the organization is international. I have made great connections and gotten some terrific and trustworthy vendors from the group, including my caterer, my travel agent, and even a business coach that I have also referred to many.

The system truly works. It's built on hardworking professionals, all experts in their fields, who come together to learn from and do business with their colleagues. Many wonderful friendships have also formed over the years.

Other types of networking groups you find might focus on job hunting. These are invaluable resources for networking and offer helpful tips and opportunities. The groups host meetings for networking, publish e-zines, and provide workshops and webinars to aid in job searches. In many cases, the group's website alone is an invaluable resource. A quick search on the Internet will yield similar sites, many of which are specific to your industry and interests.

Internal (Company) Meetings and Events

An important yet often overlooked opportunity for meeting and developing contacts is the internal business meeting or social event within your company. Recognizing the value of employees' internal networking, one company I know invited me to present at its annual meeting. We started off with an exercise that has since become a tradition for the group. The firm's employees start the first evening of their sales conference with this assignment. Each person is to find someone at the opening cocktail party event that he or she doesn't know well and learn something new about the person. Often the participants have already done an internal online search and visited each other's LinkedIn profiles. This builds a foundation for forming new alliances and contacts. The company has found that this simple exercise helps its associates work well together throughout the conference, as well as later when they return to their home offices. It also improves interactions with senior staff members. Our technology makes so much of this easy, possible, and fabulous!

All organizations have internal meetings, which are necessary for conducting business and continuing the lines of global communication. Companies also recognize the importance of making these opportunities internal networking environments: They seek to create and build internal alliances and develop more opportunities. One corporate program I delivered for 500 employees, from different departments and at all job levels, was titled *Building Your Internal Alliances and Advocates*. I approached the assignment with the strategy that, for the most part, this was a diversified group with a shared interest in the company's goals and mission. I was able to discuss the opportunities and advantages of meeting and developing associations with people across the firm, regardless of their position or title. To facilitate this, I incorporated tips and techniques for a successful event, such as creating a networking checklist (discussed in Chapter 3).

Many of us do this type of training on- or offline with professional services firms and corporations where people tend to work in what are sometimes referred to as "silos." We may rarely think of the resources available to us in other parts of their firm. The great reward is the feedback I get from people who mention that, as a result of some of the tools we discussed, they were able to connect and get to know someone in another department who has subsequently helped them in their work—and enabled them to help others as well.

An exercise that often works well for a regional or national company meeting is to have everyone drop his or her business card into a bowl. When people leave the meeting, they take out a card. Their assignment is to communicate with that person electronically. They need to introduce themselves, ask about the other person's goal from the meeting or session, set a follow-up date, and then actually speak for a few minutes to show some accountability. When the system works correctly, two connections are made: You make one, and someone else connects with you. This is a great way to start some internal team building, learn from each other, and make each meeting count. Try this in your own organization or department, and see what types of new connections and collaborations are made. In Chapter 3, we talk about finding out people's preferred method of communication. In this initial case, I find that people often email or text first and then follow up with a "live" conversation.

WAYS THAT I CAN HELP OTHERS

- Introduce and make connections for others

- Recommend products and services that have benefited me

- Share information I have learned

- Learn about other people's business so I can refer them

- Send them items of interest through multiple channels of communications

Everywhere Else...

Finally, there is everywhere else. Industry-related classes, seminars, and workshops where you go to further your skills are prime networking opportunities. Doing volunteer work or joining a neighborhood association or the board of your church or synagogue also provides opportunities to meet people you need in your universal network. However, avoid at all costs joining any group just to seek quick results. It won't happen. Follow your interests first. Enjoy yourself, learn a new skill, make a contribution, and meet and develop new contacts while you're at it.

I've included some ideas for you here, depending on your interests. You'll find a full guide in this book, with strategies and tips that will help you network and connect for any type of group you find yourself in. (Refer to the Part 1 Appendix.)

Service Groups

The mission of most nonprofit service organizations is to serve humanity. Members come from various walks of life and a variety of professions, so consider this another opportunity to build your network. Some organizations include these:

- Rotary clubs (I have had the great fortune to speak and attend chapters all over the world.)
- Chambers of commerce
- Political clubs
- League of Women Voters
- Charitable and fund-raising groups
- Museum and art leagues
- Religious groups
- Parent–teacher associations
- Homeowners' associations

The following are some of the largest organizations that provide service to those in need:

- Lutheran Services in America
- YMCA
- Salvation Army
- United Jewish Communities
- American Red Cross
- Catholic Charities USA
- Goodwill Industries International
- Boys & Girls Clubs of America

Whether you belong to any of these and leverage them as a networking resource depends on your interests and your inclination to volunteer your time and expertise to your community. These groups exist to serve the community; meeting and connecting with people is the bonus. As I have said, like-minded people are the people you want in your network; you will find these people at these organizations. In addition, at many charitable and fund-raising events, you will find executives and other business leaders who volunteer their time. What better way to get to know them, and for them to get to know your abilities, than to work together on such an event? Join, volunteer, and profit from these organizations.

MAKING AN INTEREST PAY OFF

For a great example of making an interest pay off, consider the case of a real estate agent I worked with on an article for the Women's Council of Realtors. She's also actively involved on the March of Dimes board in her community and in her church. Being part of these local groups has helped her build credibility in her community—and has also helped her real estate business. When people see that you're part of the community and a contributor to its welfare, they begin to trust you. You will become known to them as "the go-to expert" in your area of work, and people will start coming to you for your advice when the need arises. This can lead to business opportunities with them or recommendations to their friends and colleagues. Remember, you join these groups because you are sincerely interested and believe in them. However, you're always willing to give friendly advice or offer your services to those you know you can help.

Special-Interest Groups and Activities

Networking opportunities are everywhere—at your gym or yoga class, book club, chess club, salsa dance class, round-robin racquetball game, Wednesday evening church fellowship group, and exotic vacation destination of your choice. All of these groups are personally rewarding, but they can also help you make connections with like-minded people who could become valuable members of your network. I recall a friend worrying about an organized tour of Europe she was about to embark on: "What if I don't like any of the people I meet?"

"You will like them," I replied. "They enjoy the same things you do, or they would have chosen another tour."

I was right. She had a great time and came back with not only new friends, but also a number of professional contacts that subsequently benefited her business.

It's Not Just About the Event—Get Involved

By now, you have perceived that, to grow your network, you have to do more than join and attend. You have to get involved to meet new people and make a name for yourself. Here's my three-step process for involving yourself in any organization where you've identified people you'd like to know:

1. Go to meetings, meet people, and then *join* the organizations that best suit you.

2. Volunteer, join a committee, and *become active.*

3. Write an article, give a speech, and *become known.*

Go to Meetings, Meet People, and Join the Organizations That Best Suit You

As I've said before, if you're going to invest time and energy in an organization, make sure it's the best one for you. Most organizations encourage a prospective member to attend a couple meetings before joining. I highly recommend this, no matter what you think you already know about the organization. Use your networking techniques, and set a goal to meet at least two new people at each meeting you attend. Then set up a follow-up meeting with each person you met, to get to know him or her and find out more about the organization.

You'll discover from their answers whether future meetings will help you achieve your reasons for joining the organization. Yes, it's true that you always need to be open to connecting with people. However, you also have to make the most of your resources, your time, and money.

Research online the organization's past and upcoming meetings and events. Are these of interest and benefit to you? Are the speakers people you want to hear and meet? Are other programs and workshops offered that would help you in your profession? Read the group's newsletter and online materials. Read and rate its website. Is it useful and informative? Would you have something to contribute to a newsletter or a program? Start making your notes.

For each group or activity you consider, ask yourself:

- Who attends meetings and actively participates?
- Are these the people I want in my network?
- Is the group network friendly, willing to give and share information with others?
- Are the meetings, speakers, and activities of interest and benefit to me?
- What can I contribute that will be of interest and helpful to the group and its members?

When you feel satisfied with the answers to these questions, sign up. Join and become an active member.

MY 2-2-2 STRATEGY

Before you decide to join a group, apply this strategy:

- Attend two meetings.
- Meet two people and exchange business cards.
- Arrange two follow-up meetings for breakfast, lunch, or coffee.

This achieves two goals: You find out whether you want to join the organization, and you expand your network by two.

Volunteer, Join a Committee, and Become Active

Connecting with like-minded people is one of the reasons you join an organization. Becoming actively involved in what the organization does helps make you visible and get known.

Join the program committee, for instance, one of the most interesting and profitable committees in any organization. As an active member of this committee, you'll meet and interact with all the speakers and presenters—the experts in their field. Who in your industry would you like to meet yet have no logical way to do so? Perhaps you will be able to invite him or her to give a speech for your organization, and you will start to be on that person's radar screen.

If the program committee doesn't seem right for you, join another one that interests you. You will meet and get to know more people in a shorter time, and they will get to know you. When you only attend meetings, you limit your ability to really connect with other members. After all, the majority of the time spent at a meeting is devoted to the program, which usually involves listening to a speaker. And remember to take great notes and always find a reason to send a thank you note (either electronically or handwritten), to thank the speaker for his or her remarks and tell what you learned. You'll differentiate yourself and, over time, add new people to your network.

Or maybe you want to volunteer for the greeting and welcoming committee. The greeter meets everyone who attends the meeting, so you're guaranteed a chance to introduce yourself to everyone. Then you'll have an opening line to connect with them again later in the meeting. I love to do this, and it's a sure way to meet people. Also, for someone like me who can be introverted, it's a great icebreaker.

Become active in the organizations you join. Doing so will expand your network quickly and efficiently.

Write an Article, Give a Speech, and Become Known

One of the best ways to get your name in front of the members of an organization is to get your name in print. Remember how you checked out the organization's newsletter and website before you joined to see whether you could make a contribution? Now you know about the types of articles published in the newsletter or on the website, and it's time to make that contribution. Write an article and submit it to the editor or webmaster. Even if your article is just a recap of the last meeting, do it, get a byline, and get it published. You will start to gain name recognition—and, as I say, "Repetition causes recognition." Meeting people will be much easier when they remember your article and your professional credentials, which that article mentioned. In addition, you will be making a valued contribution to the organization and its members.

Giving a speech or presentation to your organization is another way to become known and meet more people. Organizations are always looking for program ideas or breakout sessions for larger meetings or conventions. Show them your expertise, and seize the opportunity to become a presenter on a topic you think could be beneficial to the group. If you fear public speaking (we all work at this throughout our lives), take a course in presentation skills and practice what you've learned whenever you have an opportunity. The ability to speak in front of a group is a necessary skill in the business world, even if it's a tough one for many of us. I've been teaching presentation skills for more than 20 years to hundreds of clients and thousands of participants, and I can assure you that learning and practicing these skills greatly boosts confidence and ensures success. I practice every single day. Offer to do a webinar or online video—let people see your expertise and passion.

Now that you know most of the places to find people (some tips and suggestions for online networking are found in Chapter 8, "The Introvert's Networking Advantage: The Quiet Way to Success"), you're ready to network in the traditional sense: at a structured event. The next chapter gives you a detailed checklist of what to do when it's time to network.

TEACH A CLASS

Giving a speech or presentation can be as simple as teaching a class on a topic you know. In addition to speaking and teaching in corporations, I keep myself fresh with the courses I teach at universities around the country. My participants have come from many different professions and industries. For example, last year my classes included a store owner, an attorney from a major firm, the owner of a midsize advertising agency, an intern at a large public relations firm, a seasoned orthodontist, an international banker, and a digital marketer, to name a few. It was wonderful to see these people making connections among themselves. In this class, as in so many others I've taught, I've made friends and business connections; my network continues to expand.

Developing a Niche as You Network

When you create a niche, you separate and differentiate yourself from others. You become the go-to person in your business for your specialty or expertise. As you network within a particular niche, you gain three main benefits: credibility, visibility, and differentiation.

Ask yourself some questions as you develop this area:

- What are my strongest interests?
- What makes me excited about a specific hobby, charity, or special interest?
- How do I like to spend my time when I'm not at work or with my family?
- What are my talents?
- How do I differentiate myself from others who also share my interest or passion?

Consider some ways to get started:

- Look at your existing list of connections and contacts, and identify the ones you enjoy spending the most time with and those who leave you feeling energized and valued.
- Determine common characteristics, and look at demographics, personality traits, and interests. Look at what solutions you provide for your clients and how your experience makes you a specialist or expert.
- Start to paint a mental picture of what your ideal niche or passion connection looks like, and craft an outline and script to describe them. Create a template and information profile where you develop talking points as you continue the discussion. This can include demographics, business and occupation, passion and hobbies enjoyed as a common link, and what events they might be facing in their personal and professional life. You will start to see how your talking points and discussion start to resonate with the people you meet, and you will be developing your own specific best practices.

- As you are enjoying your specific passion, hobby, or charity, start to customize your introduction statement for this particular audience when you find yourself in their company. For example, if you're a financial adviser looking to create a niche, you might say, "I help triathletes plan their retirement," or "I work with art enthusiasts to eliminate their financial anxiety so they can buy more art."

- Start attending events and speaking within the community of your interest. There's a group for everyone, as we discovered in earlier sections.

- Focus and be consistent as you add a niche component to your networking process. Another example is, "I have practiced yoga for over 10 years. I really enjoy it."

Over the years, I have met many people, strengthened my networks, and been introduced to new clients—all with a lot of time and patience.

Exercise: Where Can I Meet People?

Make a list of at least three industry-specific organizations you would like to research for joining. Use their websites to conduct your research.

1.

2.

3.

List your personal interests. How can you combine these with your professional interests?

1.

2.

3.

List at least three organizations or activities related to your interests that you would like to participate in and that you can make a contribution to.

1.

2.

3.

Make a list of five unusual places where you can talk to new people. (Have fun with this!)

1.

2.

3.

4.

5.

What is your action plan for the next three months?

Where will you go, who will you meet, and how will you follow up? (See the strategic guide in the Part 1 Appendix.)

_____

_____

_____

_____

Your own accountability questions:

Month 1

1. What did you put into action?

_____

2. Your successes and opportunities:

_____

3. Challenges, roadblocks, and how to improve:

_____

Month 2

1. What did you put into action?

   _____

2. Your successes and opportunities:

   _____

3. Challenges, roadblocks, and how to improve:

   _____

Month 3

1. What did you put into action?

   _____

2. Your successes and opportunities:

   _____

3. Challenges, roadblocks, and how to improve:

   _____

Do your research. Join. Contribute. Meet new contacts!

> *"The world is a great mirror. It reflects back to you what you are. If you smile into it, it smiles back; and if you frown, it returns that greeting. The world is what you make it."*
>
> —Anonymous

3

Techniques for a Successful Networking Event

S arah easily registered, put on her name tag, and moved down the hallway to where she could look through the doorway and see people milling about and chatting. She suddenly got cold feet and butterflies in her stomach. This wasn't comfortable for her at all. The meeting coordinator smiled at Sarah and waved her to come inside.

"Welcome," the coordinator said. "Let me introduce you to some people."

The crowd looked harmless, and most people were smiling, but Sarah still felt uncomfortable.

You begin by taking a small step, she thought. Before she knew it, she was talking to someone and exchanging business cards. She moved through the crowd, briefly joined a small group, and then talked with three different people one on one. She even got into a conversation while moving along the refreshment table that introduced her to three more people and turned out to be one of the most productive moments of the evening.

Taking that plunge had been the hardest part, yet once she got started, she was connecting and making new contacts throughout the evening. Being prepared made all the difference.

Maybe you would feel the same at first and, in a similar situation, wonder, "How do I begin?"

Why does the thought of going to any type of business or industry event, or even a regional meeting for your firm, sometimes seem so daunting? Often it is because you feel you have to put yourself in an uncomfortable position with pressure to *network*. You might not know how to engage in this activity correctly, and you might still think of the word *networking* as being negative. I've even seen people break out in a sweat just thinking of what they have to do. Every gathering of people coming together is, in fact, the basis of a "networking event." You can develop a process of what to do before, during, and after an event to make it a great use of your time—and to walk away renewed, refreshed, and armed with opportunities to give and receive help.

My goal is to help people first discover what makes them feel uncomfortable and then plan the steps they will take to shift their mindset and see how networking in an event setting can be an excellent experience.

Few of us are ever taught the process of networking, or perhaps we didn't have a mentor to encourage us and show us the way. We internalize the concept that networking is just a way to learn and help others. Does it seem too simple? The issue is that many of us feel we need permission to walk up to someone at an event or in another department of our company, introduce ourselves, and begin a conversation. Many people have confided in me that they just don't know how to do it or what to do. Almost everyone asks, "How should I begin?" and "What if I look foolish before senior management?" and "What are they thinking of me?" These are some of the thoughts that bombard them.

How would you feel if your CEO announced at a meeting, "Let's all get to know each other better. I want everyone to network!" What goes through your mind when you attend a networking event at a convention, business meeting, or seminar? What is your attitude when you join an association, trade group, or interest group? Is the answer, "I think I'll just stand off to the side and see what happens," or "I'm going to meet new people today, and it's going to be a great experience." (Don't worry if you're not at the point of jumping in to meet new people, because I trust your attitude will change by the time you finish this book.)

To assess your networking comfort level at events, think about how you would answer these questions:

- Where would I start in a room full of strangers?

- How would I approach another person and introduce myself?

- How would I keep the conversation going?

- How would I even remember the other person's name?

- Would the person think I was rude if I handed him or her my card and asked for his or hers?

- What if I was the only new person and everyone else knew each other? Would they think I was intruding? Would they let me into their group?

- How would I break away from someone so I could keep on mingling?

- If I connected with someone, how would I follow up?

If you've ever asked yourself any of these questions, you're in good company. Many people who attend my seminars and workshops express these feelings about traditional networking events. Breaking old habits can be hard. When you're unfamiliar with the simple techniques of effective networking, you tend to stay within your comfort zone at these events—it's easier to hang out with friends or stand in the corner and wait for lunch to begin. Yet as we all truly know deep down inside, unless we're developing new contacts and deepening the relationships we have, great success in the future will evade us.

The next sections offer some helpful techniques for a successful networking event.

Give Yourself Permission

"You must give yourself *permission* to network and enjoy the process," I advise my clients. Many of us lack the self-assurance to walk into a new group. We create all types of self-talk and worry that we'll fail somehow or that people won't like us. We can forget that a business event is often where people expect to meet and connect with other people. That's why they are there, and adjusting your mindset to a positive one is the first step to success. Allow yourself to use your confidence to adopt a positive attitude. You will also have more confidence when you're prepared with effective techniques to use when you walk into that room full of people who *do* want to connect with you.

Preparation—Before the Event

Technology prepares us for everything! With LinkedIn, Google, or any search engine, your research gives you the competitive edge. Do the tasks discussed here. You'll feel better and be ready to meet, greet, and connect. In fact, preparation is the ultimate key, because it's one way to make sure that you feel better about yourself and have greater confidence. Just like anything important in life, preparation is 80% of success.

Do Your Research

Type the name of any topic, person, or organization into a search engine, and in seconds you have access to unlimited information. Look first for the most current material. I check the "press room" or "news center" to find the latest information, or look for the latest press release about the company, person, or industry I am researching. I often also set up a Google alert for my subject.

Read either print or electronic versions of industry, association, and trade magazines and newsletters. I find lots of articles and news items about promotions, job changes, and other news events that present opportunities for me to start a conversation with someone. The time you spend researching will be "net-worth it," and this is so easy to do on your phone or tablet.

See who will be speaking, and learn as much as you can about the speakers and their topics. If awards are to be presented, do some quick research on the recipients. Just by doing this simple research, you'll be able to develop some opening lines that will make approaching new people much easier and more enjoyable.

Think about the presentations you've had to make at college, at work, or for an organization. Networking at a structured event takes similar preparation. When you are well prepared and know your subject matter, you'll find yourself much more relaxed when meeting new people who could turn out to be great contacts.

Identify Whom You Want to Meet

Before any event, I strategically think of some of the people I want to meet and how to make that happen. As you know, if you go to a two-hour event with, say, 300 people, it would be physically and mentally impossible even to just say hello to each person. (And if you did do that, you would be what I call a "negative networker.") So identify a couple specific people or types of people to focus on (such as marketing personnel or human resource directors). Of course, it's great to identify people you already know that you can reconnect and catch up with, and possibly connect with people they know. The great realization is that you can begin to network the moment you walk in the door by connecting with the person at the registration desk who helped plan the event.

When I'm attending a meeting with a group for the first time, I often email or call the person who is organizing the event in advance to introduce myself and say that I look forward to the event and meeting him or her. I also often send a note after our conversation or exchange: I thank him or her again and ask if he or she would be comfortable introducing me to some of the members when I arrive. I did this recently, and my advance contact, who happened to be the president of the organization, was delighted that I recognized her as I walked in. She was graciously enthusiastic about introducing me to several new contacts. By the way, I knew exactly who she was because I recognized her from her picture on the group's website and also from a Google images search.

At the end of the evening, I thanked her and let her know that I'd enjoyed meeting the people in her organization. The following day, I sent her a note, and she responded with an email inviting me to the next meeting. By doing simple research in advance, which we all do, and learning something about the people I wanted to meet, I could be more self-assured and relaxed in my conversations with my new contacts. Taking the step to connect with the organizer or board member is the added bonus. Try this with your next event.

Take Your Toolkits, Intangible and Tangible

For any event, you need to be properly equipped. For networking events, I've created a couple toolkits that are easy to carry with you. They ensure that all your interactions and follow-ups will appear seamless and natural. As I say about these or any of my suggestions, remember to use what works for you and come up with a few new ideas to show your "networking personality." And if you're more of a natural networker or you feel very confident networking, these will only be a reminder for what you already carry with you.

Your Intangible Toolkit

The first toolkit, which weighs the least yet has the greatest value, includes the intangibles, or items that reflect the state of mind you bring with you to every event. Here's what to include in the intangible toolkit:

- **A positive attitude:** Come with a positive outlook. Table what happened at the office, and walk in relaxed and open to opportunity.

- **Self-confidence:** Keep in mind how much you have to offer to those you meet at this event. You're an expert in your field, and you want to share your knowledge with your new contacts. I often give myself a mini pep talk before I walk in, something like, "There's someone in this room I can help today" or "Today I will learn something new from someone."

- **An open mind:** Forget your preconceived notions—just go to give and learn, without any grand expectations. That will certainly alleviate any pressure. Think of your mind as a sponge: What great new information will you absorb?

- **Your presence:** Before you enter the event, silence your phone. Be present in the here and now, and avoid distractions. This shows respect for the people you are speaking with and for the event. When we focus on people, they focus on us.

- **Ears:** Make sure that your ears are open and you're ready to listen and learn. Talk less and listen more. We were given two ears and one mouth; remember to use them in that proportion.

- **Eyes:** Be ready to observe. Make eye contact to assure people that they have your full attention and interest. Eyes truly are the windows of the soul.

- **A smile:** This is the universal greeting and the key approachability factor. Plus, we all look more attractive when we're smiling. Research also tells us that when we smile, we become more confident and immediately approachable.

- **A firm handshake:** Show that your greeting is sincere with a firm, confident handshake. Make sure it's not a bone crusher or a jellyfish!

- **A goal for the event:** Make it specific and strategic to your business situation and needs.

- **An opening line:** Also prepare idea generators and "get to know you" questions.

- **A 30-second introduction about yourself:** Be ready to easily and confidently answer the inevitable question of "What do you do?"

Now that you have these "tools" in your kit, remember that true life networking takes place anywhere and anytime. Be prepared with your easy-to-carry intangible toolkit.

Your Tangible Toolkit

The items in your tangible toolkit prepare you to meet, connect, and follow up with ease. These are small items, but using them can dramatically improve your image with the people you meet. Your tangible toolkit should contain items such as these:

- **Breath mints:** It's only polite to be concerned about your breath. I've found that when you're talking a lot, your mouth becomes dry, and the quality of your breath deteriorates over the course of the event.

- **Hand sanitizer:** You will shake a lot of hands during any event and, unfortunately, collect a lot of germs you don't want to pass along. No need to be compulsive—just use it occasionally and subtly.

- **Business cards:** Make sure you have an adequate supply of cards in good condition and within easy reach.

- **Business card cases:** Take one for your cards and one for the cards you collect. Keep them in separate pockets. You never want to give away someone else's card accidentally as your own!

- **A nice pen:** Consider this as an accessory and part of your image. I'm always on the lookout for fun, interesting pens, since I collect them. They need not be expensive—just make sure they look good. Take two, in case someone wants to borrow yours to write a note.

- **A small notepad:** Use this to jot down what you learn about a new contact. I like to write something about each person to remember and follow up on. Don't write on the back of the person's business card, as some cultures consider this rude. Some people just type the information into their phone, but I prefer to write on a small, attractive pad. Use your discretion here. If I'm in a conversation with someone and I'm learning some new information, I often ask permission to take a few notes. No one has ever said no. Or wait until you walk away, and either write your notes for follow up or send to yourself on your phone.

- **Notecards and stamps:** I carry these so that I can write my personal follow-up notes immediately. Definitely send within 48 hours.

- **Highlighter:** I use this to highlight my name on my name tag, if possible. People always ask me, "How did you get your name highlighted so that it stands out?" It's a conversation starter.

- **Name tag:** Wear this on your right side so that people will see your name as they shake your right hand.

- **Mirror:** Take a quick look before you walk into the event, to make sure that you have a big smile and nothing between your teeth, that your hair is tidy, and that no tags are sticking out of your collar.

Have an Opening Line

Think about what you will say before you meet someone new. Prepare several opening lines, and practice them in front of the mirror at home. Then when you use them at an event, they'll easily flow off your tongue. And the more you do it, the more confident you'll become.

Here are some "opening lines" to consider:

- "I'm thinking of joining this group. Are you a member? What do you think of its programs (meetings, get-togethers, resources, and so on)?"

- "What brought you to this meeting?"

- "This is my first time at this meeting. What can you tell me about this group?"

- "How does this first meeting at this convention (seminar, conference) compare to others you've attended?"

- "How have you found these meetings to be helpful to your business?"

- "Have you heard the speaker before? What do you know about her?"

- "What are some of the benefits of this association?"

- "That's a great suit (tie, pin, bracelet, and so on). Where did you get it?" or "What is the story behind it?"

- "Hello, I don't think we've met yet. I'm (name), and you are...?"

Notice that most of these are open-ended questions, which require more than a one-word answer. The tip is to start the other person talking and to begin a conversation. When you've done your homework, you might even know something about the person you are meeting and be able to ask a pertinent question about his or her work or interests. This breaks the ice, and the conversation starts to flow.

AN UNUSUAL ICEBREAKER

My friend Barbara uses this unusual yet effective icebreaker to kill two birds with one stone. When she meets someone and learns the person's name (Tom, in this case), she immediately says, "So nice to meet you, Tom." Then she uses his name again a few minutes later, as she talks about how hard it can be to remember names and how she has been working on this for some time. She reveals that one of the things she has learned is to repeat the name. She and Tom get into a conversation about remembering names, and guess what? Not only has she broken the ice, but she's also sure to remember Tom's name! I also ask how to spell the person's name. I have clients who spell their names differently, as in Scot, Jon, and Ric. This helps me remember their name and spell it correctly when I do follow up.

Have a List of "Get to Know You" Questions

Opening lines help you enter a conversation; "get to know you" questions are different. They focus on the person you're speaking with instead of the event or organization, and they help you develop a more personal relationship that grows your network.

Two years ago, I was in Europe to give a workshop and speech at a conference. As I entered the auditorium, there was a room full of people all staring at either their notes or at me. They were early, so as I was setting up, I said, "Take this opportunity to get to know the people around you." I was pleased, of course, to see that many people were already becoming engaged in conversation.

Yet for some, you would have thought I had asked them to give a State of the Union address! Some sat in silence. One woman finally said, "It can be uncomfortable." I said, "I understand—so what if you just turn to someone you haven't met, introduce yourself, and ask why he or she came to this session? Have some fun, and remember that this room is almost like a laboratory class."

By the way, the workshop was titled *Networking to Build New Relationships*. Knowing that people love to follow specific instructions, I asked them to turn to their neighbors and ask one or more of the following questions:

- Why did you come to this session?

- Where do you live?

- Where do you work, and what do you do?

- How can someone know when a company might need the services you or your company provides?

- What do you do when you're not working? Do you have any hobbies or special interests?

- What do you most enjoy about your work?

- What types of projects do you get involved in, and what have you done recently?

- What are some of the trends going on in your field?

At first, many people just sat there. Then about 30 seconds later, they all started talking at once and kept at it. It was hard to get them to stop so I could start the session. When I finally got their attention again, I asked one of my favorite questions: "Who just met someone interesting?" Of course, every hand went up. Then I asked them to share a few things they had learned about each other. People discovered they had friends in common, grew up in the same neighborhoods, and had shared interests and hobbies. More important to their business lives, they met colleagues who could help with projects, learned about parts of the company they had never known, and discovered how they could become a resource for others.

Develop your own set of "get to know you" questions using these as a guide. Add questions relating to family, travel, hobbies, favorite books and movies, and the like. Add business-related questions appropriate to the situation. Use them at your next event, and I guarantee you'll meet someone interesting.

Develop a List of Idea-Generator Topics (Small Talk)

Some people are great at small talk. They seem to know something about many subjects and start a conversation on any of them. You can conquer small talk, too. Write down ideas as you think of them or when you read or hear something of interest to others. Become conversant about current affairs, best-selling books, movies, business news, the stock market, and certainly the latest news and trends in your own industry. Keep a journal of such topic ideas, organized by subject, right on your phone. Develop opening lines around topics that are current and in the news.

We are bombarded by interesting news 24/7. Just be careful that a topic you start to discuss isn't too controversial—you don't really want to find yourself in disagreement with your new acquaintance. If this happens, gracefully move on to another topic that is a little less provocative.

The bonus for doing your small talk research is that you become knowledgeable and more well-rounded. People enjoy talking with people who are both interesting and knowledgeable. Small talk is also part of the exploration process in conversation that leads to discovering opportunities and common interests. As you feel more at ease with the art of small talk and learn how it helps you get to know another person, you'll see how effectively it opens the door to trust and rapport. Most of us walk with a mobile news source, so you can gather something new to talk about as you're walking in the door.

A TIP ON WHERE TO FIND IDEA GENERATORS

Read a special-interest e-zine, look at a search engine cover page for the daily news, or read one of the many blogs or tip sheets that arrive daily in your inbox.

I read the front page of the *Wall Street Journal* and Google News for a quick update of what's happening in the world. Read the industry paper or magazine related to the events you attend so that you have current information about that industry. I like to prepare by reading as many of these as I can find online.

Prepare a 30-Second Introduction About Yourself

How many times have you been asked, "What do you do?" Thousands, I'm sure. It's the most common question at a networking event and, for that matter, at many meetings and gatherings. And it's one you must be prepared to answer in a clear, concise, enthusiastic, and memorable way—all in 30 seconds or less! Think of this as your personal mini infomercial. Remember, first impressions count, and you have limited time to make a good impression. Work at making this a brief and punchy sound bite—you don't want to see people's eyes glaze over when you're going on about yourself.

When preparing your introduction, start by answering the following questions:

- How do I want to be remembered?

- What headline and benefit statement do you want to stand out in someone's mind?

- How do you differentiate yourself?

- How can you best tell people who you are and whom you work with (your target market)? What benefit do you offer?

Create several introductions that have a core consistency yet can be customized for the group or particular meeting.

If you merely state your job title and assume that other people will light up with excitement, it won't happen. Stating only your title, position, or profession might be easy, but it's far from memorable. Don't say, "I'm an investment adviser," or "I'm vice president of sales," or "I'm a computer consultant," or "I'm a real estate agent," or "I own a consulting firm." These statements tell the other person nothing about you—and usually bring the conversation to a quick end.

When you want to make a more appealing introduction, consider these instead:

- "I help people retire early [or send their kids to college, or build their dream house]."

- "I coach salespeople on how to exceed their goals."

- "I develop winning marketing campaigns."
- "I find people their dream home."
- "I assist people in developing their financial goals."

As you build your introduction statement, try this exercise to cut the words to seven or fewer, and leave out the word *I* or the name of your firm (no one cares yet anyway). Think of this as your headline:

- Help people retire comfortably and with dignity
- Remove the anxiety from networking and public speaking
- Develop and grow small businesses
- Make training entertaining
- Help companies find executives effectively and efficiently

The key to your response to the question "What do you do?" is a memorable statement that will lead to further questions about you and your business (your 30-second infomercial). Or, in the case of my doctor, "I keep people breathing."

How to Test Your Personal Infomercial

Advertisers often test their commercials long before they go into production to see how effectively they communicate. You can do the same with your personal introduction; here's how to do just that:

- Ask yourself whether your opening statement makes the other person say, "Tell me more!" Regardless of your response to "What do you do?" or the opening of your 30-second infomercial, make your statement leave the other person wanting to know more. Sometimes I open with, "I remove stage fright," and the response is, "How do you do that?" I then respond, "Workshops, consulting, and speaking engagements." Now I can develop and build the conversation based on the interests of the other person. Often I am asked who attends or books these workshops, seminars, and speaking engagements. This gives me an opportunity to describe my target audience. Yet before I do that, I usually switch gears and ask the person about him- or herself—I find out what the person does and in what industry. Listening intently and for key-words, I can then, when given back the opportunity, describe one of my target audiences; it might be in the same industry, or the other person might know someone in that industry.

- Determine whether you are specific enough. Paint a word picture in the other person's mind. We all meet many people—take the time to differentiate yourself. You don't want to be just one in a sea of names that all end up underwater. Here are two examples—one bad and one good—of putting a picture in the mind of the other person:

  Hard to see: "I'm a nutritionist, and I create diet plans with supplements to help people lose weight."

  Easy to visualize: "I help people get and stay in control of their eating patterns. I helped one woman go from 250 pounds to 140 pounds. One man had a 42-inch waist, and now size 34 pants are loose on him."

Staying enthusiastic and upbeat is key. Do you enjoy what you do, and does it show? When you're excited about your work or professional interests, you'll naturally come across as a passionate and energetic person. I've seen it so many times. Regardless of your personality type and whether you're introverted or extroverted, you'll come across as someone worth learning more about.

POSITIONING YOURSELF

Positioning revolves around your core marketing message, which should clearly state these elements:

- Who you are
- Whom you work with
- What solutions you provide
- What benefits you offer
- What results you produce
- What is special and unique about you

What benefits and solutions to problems do you provide? Always think of how you convey what you do as a benefit to the other person or a solution to a problem. I heard one person put it very well in communicating the problems she solves: "I work with organizations that are facing the many challenges of a slow economy." Here's another one that works: "You know how many businesses struggle to find new customers? I have a service that guarantees them new business."

Reflect on what makes you and your services unique. We all should know enough about our markets to have distinguished ourselves from the competition. Part of your 30-second infomercial should convey this information. It might be a process you use in your business, or a special type of client you service, or a brand-new product you offer. Be sure to communicate your uniqueness. Look at these examples:

- **Lawyer:** "My firm works with zoning cases for churches, synagogues, and mosques. We've helped houses of worship buy property when it seemed impossible."

- **Image consultant:** "I help people make 'million-dollar' first impressions by showing how just one good hairstyle and three attractive outfits will make them more appealing to new clients."

- **CEO of a computer software company:** "When small businesses think they can't afford powerful client-management software, they call us. We help businesses, even with just a dozen employees, run like a Fortune 500 company."

- **Book publisher:** "We publish business books for the busy executive. When someone wants best practices for customer service, she can read our books in the least amount of time to get the best information."

- **Real estate agent:** "First-time home buyers are anxious about their upcoming purchase. I take all the pressure of finding properties within their budget that they can move into as soon as they want."

Video is the game of today. Visit YouTube to watch different examples of introductions. Then practice your own and continue to refine and record. Keep updating it, and over time, it will be perfect.

Remember to be brief, be brilliant, and be ready to listen to other people as they tell you what they do; you will then be able to weave in more about your work.

DEVELOP A SOUND S.T.R.A.T.E.G.Y. FOR YOUR 30-SECOND INTRODUCTION

S	Make your introduction *short and succinct.*
T	*Think* of it in advance, and practice.
R	Remember the *results* you want to achieve.
A	Be *articulate* in your message.
T	*Time* is of the essence—20 to 30 seconds is optimal.
E	Speak with *enthusiasm* and *energy.*
G	Set a *goal* to attain.
Y	Focus on the *"you,"* meaning the other person you are speaking to.

Set a Goal for Every Event or Meeting You Attend

Most managers know how to define realistic goals for their departments and plan strategies for meeting them. Before you attend any meeting, set a realistic goal for that event, even if it is to establish contact or reconnect with two people.

A former colleague, Jerry, used to stand in a corner at company meetings and other gatherings while people around him were greeting each other and getting into conversations. Although Jerry was a highly respected executive, he suffered from severe shyness (familiar to many of us) that made him very uncomfortable in structured networking situations. Often he attended these meetings with his associate, Nick, who was extremely gregarious and social. Jerry knew he had to make business contacts, and he also desperately wanted to have more interactions. Attending these events with Nick put added pressure on Jerry because he thought he couldn't keep up with him.

"Begin slowly," I told him. "Set a goal before you leave the office to meet at least two new people. Plan on meeting just two new people with whom you will engage in conversation, ask some open-ended questions, and exchange pleasantries." I told Jerry that he could meet more people, if he wanted, but his goal was at least two. And if he felt there was a reason to meet again, I suggested that he send a note or email or place a call to set up a follow-up meeting over breakfast or lunch. In any event, he should send a short thank you to the two people for their time and conversation. (If he had his tangible networking kit handy with its note cards, he'd be set.)

The key for Jerry—and for you—is to set a goal to make a specific number of quality connections (Jerry's goal was two) at every meeting, gathering, or event you attend. Two is a realistic goal for everyone. Think quality rather than quantity.

In the discovery conversation, I told Jerry to concentrate on four things as he connected with people:

1. Learn something new—names, what they do, why they are there, and whatever they share with you.

2. Give back a comment based on something they said, perhaps a suggestion or just a thought.

3. Take something away. If the conversation is progressing, you might take away the opportunity to talk further and get permission to follow up in the other person's preferred method of communication.

4. Think of your follow-up action plan, and implement it within 24 to 48 hours. Make this a note, an email, a text, or a similar communication.

Even if you're shy (and 20% of us are), take a risk and make it your goal to approach two people. In one of my workshop exercises to help people meet each other, I say, "Take two minutes and meet someone new. Ask the people who they are and where they work; if they're in your organization, ask what department they work in and ask what comes to mind when they hear the word *networking*." I then ask everyone, "Who approached whom first?" Usually the people who were approached felt happy and complimented that someone had chosen them. I then say, "Use this technique and, at every event, you'll start to enjoy this part of networking." By being the approacher, you'll be a better networker and you'll make others feel better and more comfortable. Take the initiative.

Arrival: Take a Deep Breath

You made it to the event. You did your research; you have opening lines, you've identified small talk topics, and you've polished your 30-second infomercial. You're now ready to connect.

Introduce Yourself to the Host

Usually, one of the jobs of the host is to introduce people to each other, especially when new members or visitors are thinking of joining the group. You did your research and know who to find in the crowd. So find the host or designated greeter and ask for help. A major bonus here comes from dropping this person a note in advance saying that you're attending the meeting and that you hope he or she can help you meet several people. This shows your appreciation for the person's time and your enthusiasm for the event in advance. The host or greeter just might be ready for you when you arrive.

One night at an association event cocktail party, I lingered after checking in and, after reading the name tag on a woman at the registration desk, said, "Barbara, it's nice to meet you. I've read your organization's e-zine, and it sounds like you have a lot of active members. May I ask your help in introducing me to a couple people here to break the ice?" She gladly took me around to several people I was able to talk with for the remainder of the evening, and I made some solid new connections. When I arrived at the next meeting, I was more comfortable and walked right over to reconnect with those I had met earlier. Of course, we'd followed up in between, and I also followed up with a short note to thank Barbara for introducing me.

Get in Line

A great strategy for meeting people at the beginning of any event is to walk to where people congregate—the bar, refreshment table, registration desk, or wherever there's a line. Most people aren't fond of lines, but at events where you want to meet new people, lines provide a natural opportunity to start a conversation with the person in front or behind you. I actually like lines. Here's an example of how networking while standing in a line worked for me.

It was 11:45, right before lunch, and there was a line in front of the ladies' room (where else?) at the restaurant where I was attending a meeting. I noticed the name tag on the woman in front of me and realized we were attending the same meeting.

"Have you come to these meetings before?" I asked her. I also complimented her on the interesting necklace she was wearing. As we chatted, I learned she was the vice president of marketing for a large New York media firm. By the time we reached the beginning of the line, we had exchanged contact information and I'd promised to send her some information about my workshops and consulting business the following week. Three months later, when she was planning a sales meeting, she contacted me and hired me to do a presentation at her event. In the time between, I continually stayed in touch with a card, a note, and a text, and I certainly had her and her organization on my Google alerts and in LinkedIn.

Now she has become a valued client—all because we started talking in the line for the ladies' room. Just be open and aware, and realize that an opportunity could be right in front of you. Be aware of what I call my 24/7 networking mindset.

Dive into a Group

Approaching a group of people engaged in active discussion is hard to do. Look for a group that looks friendly. They might be laughing, smiling, or enjoying each other's companionship. Wait for an opening, and say, "I don't mean to interrupt, but you seem like a friendly group. I'm new here. Would you mind if I joined you?" Or simply walk up and just say in a gentle, approachable voice, "May I join your conversation?" Who could say no to that? Often when I use this approach, people smile and say to me, "You have courage. I admire the fact that you can do this. It's nice to meet you." This is something I do a lot because I walk into many places where I'm new and have to jump in. I'm also more introverted than extroverted, so I've learned to do this over time. Actually, I recently discovered that, like many of us, I'm more of an ambivert—I have the qualities of both an introvert and an extrovert. It's a continual practice in motion.

I had just arrived in Los Angeles and was going to be speaking the next day to a group of anesthesiologists on presentation skills. That's right, I was going to be talking about presentation and speaking skills to a group that normally puts people to sleep. There was a cocktail party that evening, and as I walked into the room, everyone was engaged in conversation. I looked around and saw that most of the people were talking in pairs. I usually don't dive into conversation with two people who are talking together because they're both engaged, and it's generally rude to walk up and disrupt a conversation.

Then I spotted a group of three people smiling and chatting informally. I walked over and said, "May I join your conversation? You seem like you're enjoying yourselves." They were great, and I ended up talking with the chairman of the meeting for the next day. By the time I spoke the next day, we were pals and had made a great connection. Take a risk, and you'll meet some very interesting people along the way.

Admittedly, approaching others who are already in a group isn't easy. Even with all your preparation, it can still be uncomfortable. I often give myself a pep talk before approaching people I don't know. Think of positive and interesting things about yourself, such as these:

- "I'm glad to be here because it's going to help me grow professionally."

- "I'm an expert in my field and eager to be a resource to others."

- "I'm a great listener."

- "I'm a friendly person and eager to learn and meet new people."

It's all in your attitude. Positive self-talk really works. I remember watching the Olympics and observing top athletes giving themselves a pep talk before their performance. If it works for them, it can work for you.

However, be sure to give your pep talk silently. Once, on a plane to Chicago, I was going over my notes for a speech. Part of my preparation is, of course, always a mental pep talk. After I did my pep talk, I took off my iPhone and disconnected. As the plane descended, several people around me started to applaud. I had forgotten where I was, and everyone heard me talking to myself!

NETWORKING GOES TO THE DOGS

I practice smiling and saying hello to people who are walking their dogs. People are generally friendly—and even if they aren't, their dogs usually are. Try this exercise if you're uncomfortable about approaching new people; it's good practice. Also, as you continue to see some of the same people, it's a way of getting to know them over time and perhaps making a new contact.

Start a Conversation with Your Dinner Partner

Look to your left. Look to your right. Your dinner partners could become important members of your network. At a seated meal, use your icebreaker opening lines and your idea generators, and start the conversation rolling. As my dear friend Jon would always say, business meals are certainly not about the food; they're about connecting with and learning from others.

At many events, you'll have opportunities to speak with more than just the people beside you at a meal. Here are a few suggestions to meet others besides those seated directly next to you:

- When there's a lull in the conversation, clink on a glass and suggest that the group introduce themselves to one another.

- Get up and walk around between courses to chat with other people at the table or around the room.

- When everyone has finished eating, trade seats with the person next to you or with someone seated across from you so that you can get to know others at the table.

Of course, ask your dinner colleagues for permission to do this as a way for all of you to connect and meet several others; you don't want to insult anyone by moving around. People will probably be glad you were the one to take charge and create more interaction. You'll be the hero.

During the Event, Make a Connection and a Plan to Follow Up

When you first meet someone at an event, your goal should be to make a connection and learn something about the person that will create reasons to follow up and allow you to begin to build a relationship. I discuss communicating and connecting with others and then following up in Chapter 10, "Stay in Touch." Until then, here are a few essential tips to use during a networking event.

Listen and Learn

My goal is to first learn about the other person before I talk about myself. I want to learn something about the person so that I can be a resource to him or her. Networking is about giving first—you might get something back later over time, or you might not.

Think giving and learning first and foremost. As you are speaking and connecting with someone, pay specific attention to what the person is saying, as well as what he or she doesn't say. Watch the person's body language, and listen with both your ears and your eyes. We were given two ears and one mouth to use in proportion. (Take a look at the Appendix to take a simple listening quiz and get some everyday tips on being a better listener.)

Find Out Preferred Ways to Stay in Touch

Busy people know how they want to hear from others. When you meet someone you want to stay in contact with, be sure to ask, "What's the best way for us to keep in touch?" Everyone has a preferred method of communication. I know that we use them all and that, with different generations, the communication forms and devices continually change. With email, phone, text, social media, and more as viable venues, I always like to find out the absolute preferred way for me to reconnect with someone. Again, we use all forms—I like to ask once and then file that away in my database.

I have one client who does not like email. Of course, she knows she needs it (it's still our number one form of business communication), yet she's not prompt in returning all the correspondence she receives, if at all. On the other hand, as soon as she receives a phone call, she responds immediately. Therefore, I know exactly how to communicate with her. In my contact information template, I have a *V* for *voicemail* next to her name. You'll find a full contact information template in the Appendix that you can customize and use in any way.

Another man I know rarely returns a call. He even told me, "I don't use my phone to speak." Clearly, I know how to communicate with him. He does return his emails and text messages, so I put an *E* for *email* next to his name in my contact list, with *T* listed as secondary. You might be thinking, "This is weird." Maybe—yet we all have our preferred method of staying in touch and conducting business. With any networking contact, whether a client or a prospect who wants to connect, we need to learn to follow suit. Of course, we use all methods of communication as business professionals; I just believe we're a step ahead when we ask someone, "What is your preferred method for me to use to follow up with you?"

Donna, a financial adviser, told this story about communicating with various people in her network:

She and a colleague at her firm, Michelle, were both engaged in supplying information to a client. The client clearly preferred email for communicating and wanted information quickly—he checked his email 24/7. Michelle's colleague, Joe, thought he was being a good time manager by checking his email only three times a day and was not responding quickly enough with the information Michelle needed. This was a problem for Michelle because the client needed speedy communication. The problem was solved when Joe offered to give Michelle his assistant's name and email. Joe's assistant replied quickly to Michele's emails, and the client was happy. This time Joe found a solution, but I would advise him in the future to realize that, as a service provider, he needs to alter his preferred method when he is in this role.

We often meet people who prefer a different form of communication from the one we use. If we want to build a relationship with them, we need to learn to be flexible. I'm almost always the service provider, so I always ask what the client wants and accommodate him or her.

> I heard a great line once about being flexible: "Praised be those that are flexible—you will never be bent out of shape."

It's important to ask your contact about his or her preference and make a note of it, either mentally (I don't trust my memory), on a small notepad, or in your notes section on your phone (then enter it into your database so that you'll always remember to use it when following up and keeping in touch).

Have an Exit Strategy

When you have a room full of people to meet, or even your designated two, it's a good idea to make sure that you don't monopolize people's time. (They most likely also have goals for people they want to meet.) Even when you're engrossed in a great conversation, it's perfectly polite to leave something for next time and close your conversation with a follow-up suggestion.

The other scenario that calls for an exit strategy is when you're talking with someone and you find yourself mentally counting the minutes until you can get away. We've all been there. Whatever the situation, you need some conversation enders and ways to wrap it up with grace and style. Here are a few that work well:

- "It was great meeting you, and I hope we can continue our conversation sometime over lunch or coffee."

- "Thank you for sharing the information about your new project. It sounds exciting. Best of continued success."

- "My time has already been well spent with the pleasure of meeting you. Enjoy the rest of the program."

- "I enjoyed hearing about your company and look forward to seeing you again."

- "Let me introduce you to_____. He may be a good person to discuss some of the opportunities you're working with.

- "I'm so glad we met. Lots of good luck, and if I hear of anything that might be a fit for you, I'll definitely be in touch."

Before I start my exit, I always ask for a card or see if we can exchange contact information right into our phones. I know that I will follow up with at least a short note according to the person's preferred method of communication if I've been able to get it. I usually wait until people ask me for my card instead of just giving them one of mine. Remember, I asked for their card first because I was interested and knew I would follow up. Over time, when we continue to build rapport, they will learn all about me.

In my conversation, I always aim to do the following:

- Learn something about the contact, such as the person's area of business.

- Give something—for example, a suggestion, a piece of advice, or a business idea.

- Take something away, if only a piece of knowledge and a way to stay in touch.

- Follow up—but only if you plan to act on it. Otherwise, it could have been a brief conversation in which you met an interesting person, learned something, shared, and moved on.

When you follow up with a personal connection, you differentiate yourself and start to solidify a relationship.

Also, before I disconnect, and if this is someone I feel I would like to get to know better, I always ask, "How do I know if I'm speaking to someone you might like to meet for your business?" At least now, I can keep the conversation going for another time, and I have created more interest. Who knows who I might be able to connect that person with over time?

"SORRY, I CAN'T TALK TO YOU—I'M HERE TO NETWORK!"

I had just walked into an evening event with my friend Robert at an Ivy League college event when we ran into a woman Robert knew. She looked at us both and, without saying hello, announced, "Sorry, I can't talk to you—I'm here to network!"

How sad for her. She was clearly out for her own gain and was trying much too hard to get something, certainly without giving first—and that's not to mention the fact that she made her friend Robert feel like he wasn't that important.

Had she been a smart networker or business communicator, she would have spent a few minutes chatting and catching up before disengaging to meet new people. It was such a negative incident that it left an indelible mark on my brain. Networking is not only about making new connections, but it is also about nurturing and digging deep into your current contacts that you are continuing to build. In fact, reconnecting with some of your contacts and clients can and should be a real goal for an event. Besides, it's nice to visit with old friends, get back on their radar, and create a stronger relationship. Remember, networking is about building strong relationships, and this takes time.

You've walked through the entire networking event, from research and goal setting, to your exit strategy. Make sure you arrive ready, and when you're there, start the process and accomplish your goals. We've also touched on the importance of listening. In the following chapter, you take that skill to the next level: discovering a process that transforms ordinary conversations into extraordinary discoveries to benefit your business life.

What's the point of using techniques for networking success? Success at networking functions doesn't always come naturally for many of us; it requires some planning and preparation. Without it, your network is unlikely to grow. With it, you'll succeed far beyond your expectations, regardless of your previous perceptions and experiences of networking.

Exercise 1: Setting Goals

List five goals that will help you be more successful when attending an event with a group of people you have never met.

1.

2.

3.

4.

5.

Write down what event(s) you will attend in the next month and up to two goals you have for each event. What type of research will you do, and who will you identify to meet?

Name of event: _____

Goal(s):

_____

_____

Research:

People I have identified to meet:

_____

_____

Exercise 2: Meeting People in Line

List five places where you can meet people standing in line—or anywhere in life.

1.

2.

3.

4.

5.

Exercise 3: Use Your 30-Second Introduction in Different Situations

Throughout the year, you might experience one or more of the following situations in which you want to use your introduction sound bite. Although your core information is the same, you want to position yourself a bit differently in each situation. Take a look at these situations and tailor your infomercial to address your audience.

- Industry-structured networking event
- Firm or company party
- Business-related volunteer group
- Chamber of commerce, Rotary, or any civic organization meeting, or a meet-up
- Business seminar
- Charity event
- Neighborhood association meeting

Exercise 4: Opening Lines

Opening lines are important for connecting with people. Write an opening line for each of the following situations:

1. At a holiday party, you are meeting someone from your company whom you do not know.

_____

_____

_____

_____

_____

_____

_____

2. While on a plane, you want to start a conversation with the person sitting next to you.

_____

_____

_____

_____

_____

_____

_____

3. While getting coffee, you realize that a key business contact you want to know, and with whom you have never spoken, is standing right next to you.

_____

_____

_____

_____

_____

_____

_____

4. You are standing in a buffet line, and you overhear some people talking about something you're interested in. How do you politely jump in?

_____

_____

_____

_____

_____

_____

5. You meet some people on vacation while on a tour.

_____

_____

_____

_____

_____

_____

_____

Appendix

The following checklist will help you get the most out of any business event where you are expected to meet and connect with prospects and other people to add to your networking universe. Your objective is to reach out, take the initiative, and make a positive impression. Your ability to capitalize on contacts and connections will be a key part of your continued career success.

Before You Go

☑ **Set a goal for the event.** Make it specific and strategic to your business situation and needs. Be realistic and know that, for your goal to be a reality, you have to follow up and take the action steps after the event.

☑ **Do your research.** Find out all you can about the event, including any interesting facts about the location, its purpose, the organization sponsoring it, and people likely to attend. Identify your reason for attending this event and determine your networking potential. Check the website to find out who the organizer is, who is on the advisory board, and what the mission and agenda are. If you are hosting, you have the opportunity to research all those invited.

☑ **Identify whom you'd like to meet.** Think strategically about the people attending. Set a goal to research three to five people you'd like to meet. Also consider calling or emailing ahead to introduce yourself to those hosting or planning the event—differentiate yourself.

- ☑ **Prepare your "opening line."** Think in advance what you will say as you meet people for the first time. Frame some open-ended questions to start a conversation:

  - "What brought you here today?"

  - "Hello, I don't believe we've met yet. I'm _____, from (company name)—and you are?"

- ☑ **Have a list of "get to know you" questions.** Prepare some questions that help you build rapport as you're connecting and keep the conversation going. From your advance research on the group, you'll already have some material to frame your questions.

  - "What brought you to the meeting?"

  - "I'm thinking of joining the group. Are you a member? Tell me a bit about what you like."

  - "What are some trends you're seeing in your business?"

  - "How would I know if I'm speaking to someone you would like to meet or someone who could possibly become a client for you or your business?"

  - "How long have you lived in the community?"

- ☑ **Develop a list of idea-generator topics (small talk).** Become conversant in current affairs, best-selling books, movies, business news, the stock market, and certainly the latest news and trends in the financial industry and your special niche. Keep a running journal of such topic ideas, organized by subject, so that you're always prepared. Every day, read your preferred news medium for general news, industry news, and firm news so that you have topics ready to discuss.

- ☑ **Prepare a 30-second infomercial about yourself.** Be ready to easily and confidently answer the inevitable question, "What do you do?" Plan positive and interesting sound bites and a provocative value proposition about you and your company that will get people interested enough in you to get to know you better. Practice your sound bite so that it flows. It should vary according to the event, audience, and person you are talking with. The core message should be consistent, yet practice how you can change accordingly. Say enough to garner interest, and then move the conversation to what the other person does. As you prepare, remember to address these questions:

- Who are you?

- Whom do you work with (target market)?

- What solutions do you provide?

- What benefit do you offer?

- What differentiates you?

☑ **Decide on your signature prop.** Make it a conversation starter.

☑ **Prepare your tangible toolkit.** Keep these items handy to help you meet and follow up with ease:

- Grooming essentials. These simple items are often overlooked.

- Business cards. Have an adequate supply, in good condition.

- Two card cases. Use one for your cards and one for those you collect (keep them in separate pockets).

- A nice pen, an accessory for your image.

- A small notepad to jot down things you learn immediately after speaking with someone you will follow up with.

- Note cards and stamps. Have the note cards already stamped so that you can easily follow up immediately with a quick thank you note to those you've connected with.

At the Event

☑ **Employ your discovery process.** Think about these goals before every encounter: Learn something new, give something (such as a piece of advice or a suggestion), take away a piece of information you can use later, and find a way to follow up with those you've made a solid connection with.

☑ **Take a deep breath.** You've arrived, you've done your homework, and you're ready!

- ☑ **Be present.** Turn off or silence all electronic devices, to avoid distractions.

- ☑ **Have a positive attitude.** Be ready to engage and enjoy the prospect of meeting new people and reconnecting with those you know.

- ☑ **Have self-confidence.** Remember what you have to offer as an expert in your field and the company that stands behind you. Have your 20- to 30-second introduction prepared for this event. Think about how you want to be remembered—what is your headline and benefit statement, and why should others care?

- ☑ **Have an open mind.** Go to give and learn, without any immediate expectations—except to learn, connect, and give away something. Think, "There's someone here today I can learn from and give something away to" (such as a piece of advice or information).

- ☑ **Smile.** Have a genuine smile ready to show your interest and approachability (a smile is also a great confidence booster).

- ☑ **Offer a firm handshake and connect.** Make a positive, human connection. Keep your ears and eyes open and ready to connect.

- ☑ **Wear a name tag.** Highlight your name—it's a conversation starter. Wear the tag on your right side, to be seen as people shake your right hand, the way our eyes naturally look.

- ☑ **Listen and learn.** Ask about the other person first. Remember that true networking is about giving, without concern that you will get something back. Make a point to actively listen, and you will learn something new and useful. Listen with your eyes and ears, don't interrupt, and jot down later what you learned. (I'm amazed at the information I pick up when I least expect it.) Be sure to ask people what they do—people love to talk about themselves and their interests, and you will be remembered as a good conversationalist because you listened.

☑ **Be ready to take the initiative.** Approach others with positive expectations and genuine interest. Besides the people you identified in advance that you hope to meet, remember to say hello to these folks also, to maximize your attendance:

- The greeter and/or organizer

- People you meet in line as you are checking in

- People in line to get a drink or food

- Someone standing alone

Remember, you only have to say hello, smile, and be pleasant. You won't have a full conversation with everyone you meet—yet you never know unless you reach out.

☑ **Dive in!** Look for a group of three or more that's smiling and engaged; say hello and engage them yourself. (If it's just two people, they're already deep in conversation.)

☑ **Sit next to someone new.** Set a goal to sit next to someone new and get to know him or her. Also plan to follow up.

☑ **Start a conversation with your dinner partner.** If there's a meal, talk to the people on either side of you—and even those across the table, when feasible. Make a point to sit with new people.

☑ **Make connections and create a plan to follow up.** Have a goal to learn something about the people you meet, and create reasons to follow up and start building a rapport—and, hopefully, a relationship.

☑ **Find preferred methods of communication.** Every busy person has a preferred method of communication. Ask, "What is your preferred method of communication for us to connect?" Email, telephone, text, or even social media? Make it easy for the person to reply to you when you reach out.

☑ **Have an exit strategy.** At events, everyone wants to talk and mingle. If you've made a concrete connection, you will have your agenda to follow up (when and how). To diplomatically disengage at the event, use these suggestions:

- "It was great to meet you, and I look forward to continuing our conversation. As we discussed, I will follow up with you [when they told you to follow up] via [their communication preference]."

- "It was great chatting with you—I look forward to seeing you at another event. Thank you, and enjoy the rest of the meeting."

- "I'm very glad we met. Continued success, and when I have an opportunity or suggestion for you, I will definitely be in touch."

After the Event: Your Follow-up Action Plan

☑ **Within 24 hours, send an email to those you connected with.** Also consider sending a simple and sincere handwritten note, stating your pleasure at meeting them, your appreciation of their time, and any information you promised to send. You will differentiate yourself.

☑ **Send materials immediately.** People who follow up promptly always stand out. Send only what you promised (less is more)— you will have time to bring more as you deepen the connection.

☑ **Call or email within two weeks of the event to suggest a meeting with contacts who said they would enjoy the next step.** Be strategic in your follow-up. If someone expressed interest in further contact after the event, be the one to follow up with something specific, suggesting an activity, time, and place.

☑ **If a contact of yours provided you with a referral, be ready to tell that person of your follow-up and the results.** Let people know what happened, keep them in the loop about next steps, and offer a sincere thank you for the connection and introduction. Referrals are the key to many new and successful opportunities. Always thank the referrer and keep him or her in the know.

Remember, the event is only the starting point. To build strong connections into your universal network, you have to take the next steps to build the relationship—and to do so consistently.

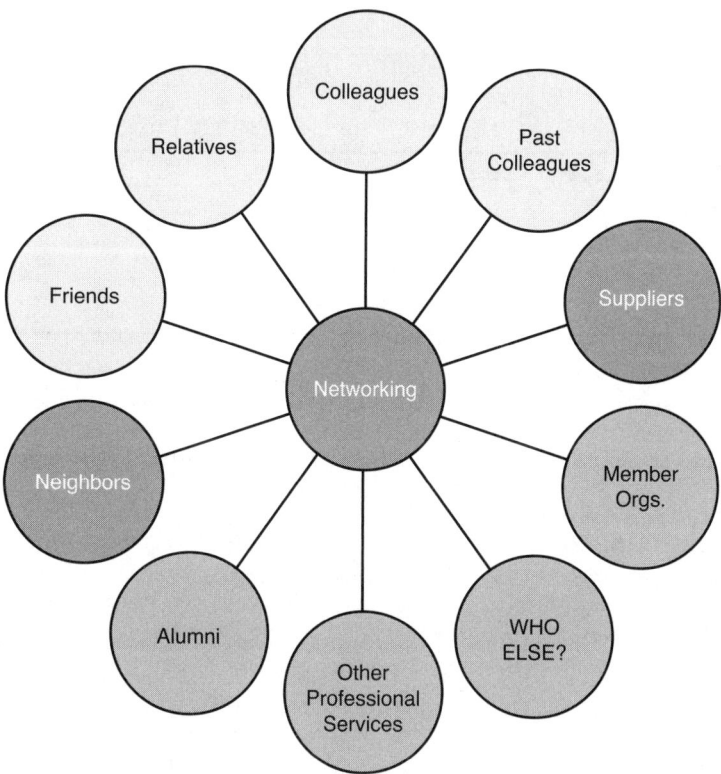

Figure A1-1 Who Is in Your Network?

Networking Goal	Who?	Action Steps	Follow-up	Results

Figure A1-2 Networking Action Plan

"The Opposite of Networking is Not Working"

How do you define networking?

7 Rules of Networking

- Smile
- Look the person in the eye
- Listen—I.R.A. formula
- Be aware of body language
- Reach out—be proactive
- Come across positive
- Look for common interests

Where are your strengths and areas of improvement?

5 Types of People Who Can Help Your Network

- Satisfied client
- Friend
- Someone who is a joiner and active participant
- Supplier or vendor
- Circles of Influence

Networking Strategies

- Become aware of everything—24/7 awareness.
- Have a plan and goal.
- Do your homework consistently.
- Be proactive. Get involved.
- Go global in your thinking.
- Be clear about your expertise.

Figure A1-3 Guidelines for the Event

PART 2

Grow (Building on Your Strengths)

4

Listening and Learning

"Listening is the single most important ingredient and skill to effective communication and networking. Driven by the simple reality that when you listen, you learn more about others and thus create deeper rapport and relationships. Become an active and aware listener. Listening is the trump card to meaningful networking."
—Dr. Lyman K. (Manny) Steil, Chairman and CEO, International Listening Leadership Institute

As you continually find and build the key relationships in your business and personal life, you must *grow* both your business and your relationships to keep them prospering. In this section, we address the skills and tactics to do just that.

You will start to enhance your listening skills and other key communication skills to use every day of your life so that you can become the ultimate professional. You will discover the mysteries to communicating and working with all the personality types easily and with minimal effort. You will also embark on opportunities to develop and create your own "self-brand" so that you can market yourself in a seamless way anywhere and everywhere. We look at the advantage of the quiet or introverted networking style in depth, and we finally move into the key components for effective follow-up.

This section is chock full of information and materials that you can put to use immediately.

"If I listen, I have the advantage; if I speak, others have it."
—Arabic proverb

The Golden Rule of Listening

Two men were walking down a busy New York City street one day when, above the noise of the cars, trucks, and honking horns, one said to the other, "Listen to that cricket." His companion replied, "How can you hear a cricket in the middle of all this noise?" Without saying a word, the first man took a coin from his pocket, flipped it in the air, and let it bounce on the sidewalk with its familiar metallic sound. A dozen heads turned and feverishly looked for the bouncing coin. "We hear what we listen for," the first man said.

I often use this story to illustrate the importance of good communication skills—especially listening—in making contacts and building relationships. The first step in building trust and respect with your new contacts and your current network is to listen and learn. We have the opportunity to do this daily. This requires good communication skills, effective listening, and the ability to recognize and honor different communication styles and personality types.

Communication Skills for the Effective Networker

As you continue to master the techniques for meeting people and gaining more confidence, you are ready to enhance the communication skills that will help you connect and develop a relationship with those you want in your network. It's all about building rapport and learning how to interact with ease. Many of you know these skills and already use them to the utmost. Consider this a reminder as you put them into action in all your interactions.

Start with a Smile

Everyone responds well to a smile. When you meet someone, it's the most important thing you can wear. It's also the first step in building rapport. Remember to smile when you enter a room, begin a business meeting, answer the phone, and even start typing electronically. When you smile, the other person or persons become the mirror that reflects your expression. A smile can raise your spirits and even affect the way you sound.

Research confirms that there's "magic in a smile." When you have a genuine smile on your face as you walk into a room of strangers—or anywhere, as a matter of fact—you appear more confident and approachable, and a smile becomes contagious. A smile is also good for your brain: The act of smiling releases the neuropeptides that work toward fighting off stress. (Neuropeptides are tiny molecules that allow neurons to communicate. They facilitate messages to the body when we have a whole range of emotions.) We're also perceived as being more attractive when we smile, and people treat us differently. If you don't believe me, see how many looks you receive when you walk outside with the smile you're wearing right now. Be open to the power and control you have with the universal greeting of a smile.

When you speak on the telephone, I suggest that you use mirrors with the phrase printed on the case, "Can your smile be heard?" Put the mirror on your desk so that when you're sitting there talking on the phone, you can see your facial expressions. You can use the mirror app on your iPhone to do the same when you're speaking. You might be very surprised—yes, a smile can be heard. I always remember what my dear friend Florence used to say before picking up the telephone: "Have a smile on your face, and visualize the words *opportunity* and *decorum*." It's amazing how doing this changes your inner perception.

You might be rolling your eyes thinking, "How can I keep a mirror on my desk? My colleagues will think I'm vain." Don't worry. I've seen mirrors on the desks of many very successful people who are merely checking out their presentation image when they're on the phone.

Remember that a smile can disarm another person. Your face speaks volumes and encourages people either to open up to you or to walk away. It is a powerful tool to use when meeting new people in any situation, so use it to your advantage. I make it a habit to walk into every meeting, event, or encounter with a smile on my face. I've also gotten into the habit of smiling at three new people every day. It's warm and refreshing and totally diffuses any tension. Remember to be discreet, however. I live in New York City, so I advise people not to walk down the street grinning. I'm talking about sincere, feel-good hello smiles—and nothing else.

Look the Other Person in the Eye

Have you ever been talking with a person who was looking over your shoulder instead of at you? Did you think to yourself, "He doesn't think I'm important" or "She's not even listening to me"? Making good eye contact shows respect and interest, and it's good manners.

At a casual networking event, Carol, a vice president of human resources for a large financial services company, and her assistant, Barbara, talked to an external partner. During the entire conversation, Bill, the external, never looked at Barbara. He focused totally on her supervisor, Carol, whom he thought was the sole decision maker. As it turned out, Barbara actually made the purchasing decisions for Bill's services. He paid no attention to her and, when it came time to order, she gave her business to another supplier with comparable services.

Eye contact is one of the strongest communication skills we can develop. It's been said, and I believe it's true, that the eyes are the windows to the soul.

Another time I was at an event where a man started talking with me because I had just been on a panel. During our conversation, he kept looking past my left shoulder. At first I thought I had something hanging from it or a stain. Then in midsentence, he left me standing and seemed to fly over to talk with someone else. I thought it was rude, yet these things happen. It was ironic that, as I was walking to get a cup of tea, I heard my name called out, and a friend motioned me for me to join him. As I walked over, I saw my former acquaintance (the one who had left me to talk with someone he thought he could sell something to). Little did he know that the "someone" happened to be my friend. I can still see him squirming when my friend said, "Have you two met?" I smiled, and somehow Mr. Rude decided to take a more proper exit strategy with no immediate sales.

MAKING EYE CONTACT

Fifty-five percent of communication is visual. When you neglect to make eye contact, you might be communicating that you're uninterested, bored, or, worse yet, sneaky and untrustworthy. In reality, you might be shy or nervous about attending the event. If you find eye contact challenging, practice making eye contact with yourself in the mirror while you're on the phone. When you're in front of someone and can't look into his or her eyes, try to focus somewhere around the eyes between the nose and forehead. I call this area the "third eye." Soon it will become easier for you.

Remember Names

Dale Carnegie, author of *How to Win Friends and Influence People*, a lifetime classic, wrote, "[A] person's name is to him or her the sweetest and most important sound in any language." It really pays to remember names because people then know you've heard what they've said. Here are four ways to sharpen your name-recall skills.

1. Form an impression of the person's appearance, and embed it into your mind. Note height, stature, color of hair and eyes, facial expression, and any distinguishing physical features. I always remember my late friend Fred White, who had the whitest hair you ever saw. His name was easy to remember! Don't concentrate so much on dress or even hairstyle, though—these might be different the next time you meet. (I'm a perfect example of that!) Concentrate on remembering the person's face.

2. Repeat the person's name after you meet and a couple times during the conversation. When you repeat the name, two things happen: First, you make your contact feel good. Second, the name goes into your memory bank. Often when I teach, I meet many people with very unusual and wonderful names. I always ask them to repeat their names so I can pronounce them correctly.

Then I use the name several times. However, be sure not to turn it into a distraction and use the name too often in a short conversation. The best policy is to repeat it at the beginning when the person first says it, in the middle, and again at the end when you are exiting. I also ask people how to spell their name. John can be Jon, Rick can be Ric, and one of my clients is Scot. It's great to remember this, and people appreciate it.

3. Make up a visual story about the person's name. Associate the person's name with something that will remind you of it. Use your imagination and paint a story in your mind. Put the person into your visual story. The sillier the story, the easier it will be to remember. For example, I met someone in one of my workshops named George Whitehouse. I remembered his name by picturing him standing in front of the presidential White House, and he was shaking hands with none other than our first president, George Washington. Hence my new contact, George Whitehouse (an attorney, at that!). At your next meeting, take time to practice this with several new people you meet. It might seem challenging at first, yet it becomes fun and is truly a great way to remember people's names.

4. Write down the names of people as they walk into a meeting, and write a word or two describing them to jog your memory. I always do this when I'm speaking or training and want to remember the names of people in my audience so that I can address them personally. With effort and practice, you can remember anyone's name.

You Are a Star (Whatever Your Name Is...)

Once I was working for a company and had the opportunity to speak with the president of that company at a luncheon meeting. He was in the business of personalized stationery and prided himself on remembering names. You can imagine my surprise when I received a beautiful card from him a few weeks later. On the front it said, "You are a Star." The inside note started with, "Dear Angela" (oops).

Introduce and Reintroduce Yourself

"Oh, my gosh! I hope he doesn't see me!" It's that awful feeling that comes over you when you see someone whose name you should remember, but your brain has just turned off. There's no need to panic. Chances are, if you draw a blank on the name of someone you've met before, that person might not remember your name, either. Simply put out your hand as I do and say, "Hi, I'm Andrea Nierenberg. We met at the last meeting." Most people reciprocate happily and reintroduce themselves. If not, just ask, "Please tell me your name again" or "Refresh my memory. What is your name again?" or "Forgive me, please tell me your name again." No one will ever say: "Guess!" I then repeat the name aloud, then repeat it silently several times again, and make a mental note to remember it. I write it down, too.

It's also a good practice to reintroduce yourself to those you have just met. Although you might remember their names and use them, they might have forgotten yours and will appreciate your gesture.

Be Aware of Your Body Language

A friend of mine always scratches her head when faced with something unpleasant. We might not realize we have these habits, so it pays to become aware of them. They could convey a less than positive body image. Avoid nervous habits such as blinking your eyes, licking your lips, fidgeting, twirling a strand of hair, stroking your mustache, or drumming your fingers. Remember Ralph Waldo Emerson's wise words: "What you do speaks so loudly that I cannot hear what you say."

You can say a lot without opening your mouth. Research tells us that we form perceptions in three ways: Verbal makes up 7%, nonverbal is 38%, and visual is 55% of our perception of others. Notice that body language makes up the biggest percentage. Make sure your body language communicates what you truly want to say. This is why the phrase "Actions speak louder than words" is so true.

Practice good posture. Standing tall and straight reflects confidence. Be aware of your facial expression. Your expression says a lot before you even open your mouth. Remember to look relaxed and happy to meet the person. Use good eye contact, smile, and react to the conversation with appropriate nonverbal actions, such as nodding and showing encouragement and interest. You might want to ask a trusted adviser or friend whether you do anything that could take away from creating a stellar impression. My sister, Meredith, has helped me a lot here. I remember her asking me, "Do you realize that you say *really* a lot? In fact, I counted 27 times once during a conversation!" At first, I was taken aback. Then I realized, "Wow, she's right!" I've become very aware of this and other pet phrases that can take away from my presentation. Meredith is a great help, and she certainly tells it like it is!

Your handshake is also part of your body language. A soft and floppy grip can imply that you lack confidence or are unenthusiastic, whereas a vicelike grip can imply that you are overly forceful and aggressive.

Robert E. Brown and Dorothea Johnson offer this sage advice in their book, *The Power of Handshaking*: "Handshakes reveal inner traits, personality, and motivations. The hands can't conceal messages as the spoken word can. Your hands are messengers of your subconscious mind, and whether you like it or not, your handshake will often betray your emotional state."[1]

They are very right. You want to appear self-confident, friendly, and open to your new contact. Here are some tips for a proper handshake:

- Grip the other person's hand firmly at the point where the webs of your thumbs meet.

- Shake from the elbow, not the shoulder, and just a couple times.

[1] Robert E. Brown and Dorothea Johnson, *The Power of Handshaking* (Herndon, VA: Capital Books, 2004).

- Hold for only a few seconds and end cleanly.

- Use only one hand. Don't use your other hand to cover the other person's hand.

Brown and Johnson call this the all-American handshake: "This is the handshake delivered by corporate executives and champions of both genders. This person makes eye contact, smiles, offers a firm grip, and two or three firm strokes. The handshake delivers a feeling of relaxed self-confidence. This is a warm and genuine greeting acceptable worldwide."

Other gestures are just as important as a firm, friendly handshake and reveal your readiness to meet and connect with new people.

B	**Breathe** deeply and consistently. This steadies your nerves and gives you a pleasant facial expression that says, "I'm glad to be speaking with you."
O	**Overtures** can speak volumes. Nod to show encouragement and confirm that you're listening. Keep an open posture to show you're receptive.
D	**Demeanor** is the part of your personality demonstrated by body language. A blank stare, crossed arms, and nervous gestures all convey the opposite of what you want to communicate. Instead, be open and receptive in your presence.
Y	*You* means, "I am focused on you." Observe how others interact, and find a way to match it. For example, if you're sitting across the table from a person who's leaning in to create a closer connection, follow suit. Don't lean back; this could say to him or her, "I'm not interested." Remember that actions often speak louder than words.

Consider a few more pointers on body language, which is truly an art and science all to itself:

- Notice the signals people might be giving out when you meet them.

- Pay attention to how close someone is standing or sitting next to you. It's also important to note that personal space is culturally fluid; what's considered close in one country is too far away in another. To be safe, always observe how closely people stand in lines when you're in another country and even when attending events that include people from all parts of the world.

- Watch the head position. Keep it in a straight position looking right at the other person. Someone who tilts his or her head to the side could be confused or even challenging you.

- Eye contact speaks volumes. People who look to the sides a lot are nervous or distracted. Look directly at your colleague. Someone who looks down at the floor could be shy, timid, or possibly upset. Some cultures believe that looking someone in the eyes is a sign of disrespect, so be cognizant of the person you're speaking with, so as not to make him or her uncomfortable.

- Use mirroring. When we try to replicate the body language of the person we're talking with, it's a sign of trying to establish rapport. Use this wisely.

- Monitor gestures and arms. If you stand with closed arms, others might perceive that you're closing yourself off—or that you're cold! Some people just have a habit of standing this way, and it can indicate that they're reserved or uncomfortable. People standing with their hands on their hips often convey impatience, so this can signal that it's time for you to wrap up the interaction, especially at an event. If someone's hands are closed or clenched, it could be a sign of nervousness.

- Watch for nervous gestures when connecting. Raised eyebrows could mean disagreement; someone who's constantly pushing up glasses onto his or her nose and slightly frowning could be in disagreement.

- Clue into the feet. A fast tapping or shifting of weight shows impatience and nervousness. If people shuffle their feet, they could be bored.

To play it safe, be sure to mentally observe your own body language to see what messages you might be giving out. You can lean in to show interest to the person you're speaking with. When observing others, be subtle. If someone doesn't look you in the eye during a discussion, he or she could be shy. Never take it personally.

To continually get better at this skill and become more aware, watch television with the voice off every night for three weeks in a row. Just by guessing what's going on from body language, you will improve your ability to read it. You can also go to your cellphone and check online for a quick description about something. I use this constantly and am always learning.

Keep in mind that each person has a unique body language, called baseline behavior. It's easy to spot a confident person—these people make prolonged eye contact and have a strong posture. They might also sit or stand very erect. Their faces often have an open and direct gaze.

Be Respectful of Others' Boundaries

The invisible boundaries around us that define our personal space vary from culture to culture. Most Americans become uncomfortable when someone is closer than 18 inches. In some countries, standing as close as we do in the United States is considered too far apart. In other places, it's too close. People's boundaries are not only an issue for travelers: America is a melting pot, so we need to be aware of the diversity within our own country.

Brown and Johnson advise: "Watch how far an individual extends the arm to shake your hand. As a general rule, the straighter the arm, the more protective he or she is of personal space."[2]

Look for Common Interests

Ask open-ended questions and listen to what others say in response. Practice your list of "get to know you" questions so that they come automatically. Phrase them so they can't be answered with a single word. And be sure to have a follow-up question ready.

Some people you meet will take your questions quite literally. "Did you enjoy the speaker?" you ask, hoping to start a conversation. "Yes," is the answer you get, followed by silence. So change your question to, "How did you find the speaker's presentation?" You might still get, "Fine."

---

[2] *Ibid.*

Then you can follow with, "What did you particularly like about it?" or "What did you think of his message?"

After you establish your common interests, the conversation will begin to flow. You can learn something from the other person, possibly give a suggestion or thought, take away contact information, and find a reason to follow up and stay in touch. For example, you might be able to say, "I have an article you might enjoy based on what the presenter talked about. May I send you a copy?"

Give Genuine Compliments

When you listen to people carefully, often they mention something they're proud of. Think for a moment and find a way to acknowledge their achievement. Make a goal of finding at least one positive trait or characteristic in each person you meet that you can compliment. It might seem awkward at first, but it will soon become second nature. I guarantee you can do this when you truly listen to the other person.

For example, I think one great accessory is a good pen. In fact, I often give nice pens to my clients and friends. I was at a meeting once and saw a woman with a beautiful pen in her hand. I commented how much I liked it. This simple compliment on her taste in writing utensils started the conversation rolling. Eventually, as we got to know each other, we found we had other, very similar preferences. I practice this continually; it's both fun and empowering, and it makes the other person feel good. Again, it must be authentic—you must truly take an interest.

I think back to a woman I used to work with early in my career. She was never one to mince words, and sometimes they came sounding less than encouraging. I remember saying to her over lunch, "You've taught me a lot with your direct, no-nonsense approach to things. I know that sometimes people don't understand you; however, I do, and I thank you for who you are." She was silent for a minute and then said, "Thank you. That means a lot to me."

As a general rule, most of us don't give out compliments as often as they're deserved. We worry that we'll come across as insincere or as if we're doing it because we want something. This is why it's so important to be genuine and to give a compliment only when you mean it. Only then will it be truly meaningful to the recipient. Otherwise, the less said, the better.

Sometimes you may give someone a compliment, and the recipient doesn't know how to receive it. This is a common reaction, but it shouldn't stop you. Most everyone likes to receive a sincere compliment, even if some of us have a hard time showing our appreciation. I have also found that some people crave public praise, whereas others prefer private praise. When I ask in my workshops about people's preferences in this regard, much discussion results. When I ask for a show of hands, it seems most people don't mind public praise. However, some people just don't want to be the center of attention, even if it's really good attention; they're most comfortable in a support role. Most likely, they won't tell you that they'd rather not be praised publicly, so if you sense that this might be the case, don't be afraid to ask. Then simply tell the person at an opportune time what he or she did well or how it impressed you. Also, a thank you card can mean the world to someone who prefers private praise. Take the time to observe and find out how people like to receive compliments and honor their preferences.

Right now, think of something you admire about a coworker, colleague, client, friend, and family member. Take a few minutes to jot down your thoughts, and share them either verbally or in a note. Make a practice of doing this frequently, sincerely, and consistently. It's a wonderful exercise.

FIVE A DAY

Look for positive attributes in the people you come in contact with during the course of your day, and compliment them. Make a goal to give "five a day." Put five pennies in your left pocket in the morning. Each time you give a sincere compliment, take out a penny and put it into your right pocket. By the end of the day, you should have transferred all five pennies—and you will have made at least five people feel good!

Talk Less, Listen More

One of the greatest compliments you can give another person is to let him or her know that you are listening to everything said. As Emerson said, "It is a luxury to be understood." Find the hidden word in *listen* using all the letters. The word is *silent*. That's what our internal voice must be to get the full impact of what others are saying. Remember that when you're networking with a new contact, it's like reading the paper. Let the person tell you his or her story so you can discover the news within that he or she would like to share.

More people have literally talked themselves out of a job or a sale by speaking instead of sitting back and actively listening. It takes real concentration to listen. I read once that we hear only half of what is said to us, understand only half of that, believe only half of that, and remember only half of that.

Great salespeople have learned to listen first and then tailor their sales presentation to their potential clients' needs as presented in the first few minutes of conversation. The same holds true for meeting new people and deepening our relationships with others. People know that you're genuinely interested in them as a person if you can tailor your comments to what they've just told you about themselves. Relate your experiences to theirs. For instance, often I say, "That reminds me of...," based on what I just heard. When one participant in a workshop told me how she often got nervous before speaking in front of a group because she felt her heart beating so fast, I said, "I totally understand. That reminds me of when I was a young girl and would have to speak in front of my class for a report. I would remember my heart beating so fast, I thought everyone could hear it." I also told her what my wonderful father, Paul, would say to me, and I still hear him from heaven: "No one can hear it beating, and just be glad it is!"

Are You an Effective Listener?

I recall a friend telling me this story about a dinner party she had attended. She'd been seated next to the guest of honor, a very distinguished older gentleman. After the meal, the host relayed a compliment to her from her dinner partner: "He thought you were the most fascinating person he'd met!" She told me she'd hardly said a word all evening to this man. "He was so interesting, I just listened." Well, I know this woman very well. She's a fascinating woman, successful in her profession, and a very effective networker. She knows that if you sit back and listen, people will tell you a lot about themselves, how they like to communicate, and what's important to them. It's a great communication strategy and tool. The bonus is that you learn a lot also. I'm curious by nature, so I take in every encounter as an opportunity to learn and observe—and, of course, listen.

Good networkers, like my friend, take what they've learned to the next step, making a real connection with people they can help and who can help them. As we build on our networking and realize the skills we need to find, grow, and keep our business, one of the most critical skills we must develop is the ability to listen and find ways to make a connection.

How Do You Rate as a Good Listener?

Consciously using active listening skills is a must. Rate yourself on a scale of 1 to 5 on these essential listening skills. Give yourself a 5 if you can answer, "I always do this with ease and confidence." Rate yourself a 1 if you say, "I rarely do this and feel awkward when I do."

1. I make eye contact. I always look the other person in the eye during our conversation and focus my full attention on him or her.

2. I ask questions for clarification. If I don't understand or need further clarification, I ask the other person to explain so that I can understand better. I restate what I think I understand, and then I ask to make sure that's the intended meaning. For example, I say, "What I'm hearing you say is..." or "Am I correct in understanding what you said is...?"

3. I show concern by acknowledging feelings. I also listen with my eyes. I use positive body language by nodding and smiling when appropriate. I am empathetic.

4. I try to understand the speaker's point of view before giving mine. I recognize that the other person is far more interested in stating his or her point of view than in hearing mine. I also realize that my understanding of the other person's point of view leads to building a better relationship and a better response on my part.

5. I am poised and emotionally controlled. I hold back from jumping to conclusions or interrupting with what I want to say when the other person is speaking.

6. I react nonverbally with a smile or a nod. I know this shows my interest and allows the person to continue without interruption.

7. I pay close attention and do not let my mind wander. I am careful not to allow my mind to take a mental excursion. I concentrate on what the other party is saying instead of formulating what I'm going to say next.

8. I avoid interrupting. Someone once gave me a great sign: "The most successful people have teeth marks on their tongue. "Don't interrupt—let the other person finish. (This one can be tough—count how many times you interrupt someone or, easier, how many times someone interrupts you, and think about how it makes you feel.)

9. I avoid changing the subject without warning. I make sure the conversation on one subject is closed before jumping to the next subject. Changing the subject abruptly relays that you are not listening and want to talk about only whatever is on your mind.

How did you do?

> If you scored 35–45, you're an exceptional listener.
>
> If you scored 25–34, you're a very good listener.
>
> If you scored 20–24, you're an average listener.
>
> If you scored 15–19, keep working; you'll improve!

Take a good look at the areas where your rating could improve. Start to work on these, while continuing to practice the skills you've already mastered consistently. Take the quiz again in two weeks. Watch how your ratings improve when you commit to improving your listening skills.

Listening Skills Pay Off

Effective listening skills are not only critical to understanding and building relationships, they also pay off in business and life. I once asked the president of a company if he ever measured how much business his firm lost because someone didn't listen. He told me that the company once lost a million-dollar sale that he thought would be a sure thing. Two salespeople were involved in a conference call with the customer to close the deal. One didn't hear an important piece of information from the customer, and although the other one heard it, he misinterpreted its significance. The result was a lost sale.

The incidents and situations differ, yet the impact is the same: In most cases, when someone fails to listen and learn, the costs associated—in time, relationships, productivity, and money—are extraordinary.

ARE YOU ALL EARS?

Rate each on a scale of 1 to 5, with 5 being the best. Add the scores; then imagine your score on a continuum. On the very left, representing the lowest number, is a brick wall; on the right, representing the highest score, is a field of corn. Are you stuck up against the brick wall, or are you "all ears" in a field of corn?

How would the following people in your life rate you as a listener?

- Your best friend

- Your boss

- Your spouse or partner

- Your client(s)

- Your employee(s)

- Your dinner partner at the last party you attended

- Someone who is challenging to listen to (this is a tough one)

Keep this LISTEN-ing reminder handy:

L **Look** at the person (body language, eye contact)—be aware.

I **Involve** yourself in the conversation. Be present and ask specific questions.

S **Steady** your nerves and emotions. Refrain from interruption.

T **Translate** the meaning of the person's remarks. Put yourself in his or her place.

E Avoid mental **excursions**. Concentrate and be silent.

N **Needs** and **nurture** are both key in all relationships.

Interact with Ease

Think of someone you know who can walk into a room full of strangers and immediately make friends. Can you recall someone who instantly made you feel at ease when you first met him or her? How about someone who makes you feel as though you're the only person in the world when speaking with you?

If you know such a person, take a moment to think about what personal traits he or she possesses. Confident, empathetic, enthusiastic and energetic, tenacious, caring, appreciative—the list can go on.

I often ask this of participants at my seminars and workshops. Based on the answers from hundreds of them through the years, here are 10 common characteristics of people who interact with others with ease and grace:

1. They are able to make others feel comfortable.

2. They appear confident and at ease.

3. They are able to laugh at themselves, not at others.

4. They show interest in others by maintaining eye contact, self-disclosing, asking questions, and actively listening.

5. They extend themselves to others, leaning into a greeting with a firm handshake and a smile.

6. They convey a sense of enthusiasm and energy.

7. They are well rounded, well informed, well intentioned, and well mannered.

8. They know vignettes or stories of actual events that are interesting, humorous, and appropriate.

9. They introduce people to each other with an infectious enthusiasm that inspires conversation.

10. They convey respect and genuinely like people.

People at my seminars and workshops who know or observe others with these characteristics and who possess some themselves tell me they are successful at their business; have a wide and effective network of friends, associates, and contacts; and tend to achieve their goals. Let's look at these characteristics in more detail.

Confident

Bill is the president of a runner's club that meets for runs on Saturday mornings. He exudes confidence. It shows in the simplest of matters, like how he's able to silence 50 eager runners to make announcements before a run, and in far more important matters, such as how he's able to muster an army of volunteers to raise thousands of dollars at a run to benefit cancer research. His confidence is a magnet. People gravitate to him and eagerly offer their time and expertise. Where did his confidence come from? You can't buy it. If a store sold it, we'd all be in line. Confidence comes with experience and grows over time. What kind of experience helps us develop it? Not sitting still or doing the same thing repeatedly and expecting different results. To build confidence, you have to step out of your comfort zone and take some risks. It helps if you start with small steps and then keep going as your confidence grows.

You have to step out of your comfort zone to meet and follow up with the people you want to connect with at every event. Take small steps, develop a plan, and think about conversation starters and your follow-up. The more you set your intentions, the easier this becomes—and you will soon be more confident.

Compare this process to any new thing you have mastered—learning to play tennis, learning a new application, speaking in front of a group, and so on. You started with small steps and progressed as your competence and confidence grew. Most important, you had to step out of your comfort zone, take a risk, and do something different; as you continued to practice and got better at the skill, you gained confidence. Did you also notice that people were more interested in what you had to say than before? Expanding your contacts in your new field of expertise was suddenly easier.

REACH HIGHER

In my seminars, I ask everyone to stand and raise their hands as high as they can. Then I say, "Now, go an inch higher!" Everyone does it. The point is, we can always do better than our best. So keep reaching even higher as you develop your confidence.

To develop confidence, practice the skills you want to attain. Over time, the confidence you have developed in your abilities will show.

TO GROW YOUR CONFIDENCE, START WITH "BABY STEPS"

Taking a ride one lovely Thanksgiving holiday in Cape Cod, I never imagined I would wake up hours later in a hospital emergency room in Boston with 46 broken bones. During my recovery, I had a lot of time to reflect. This terrible automobile accident had shattered more than my bones. I thought I was a confident person, but it all seemed to disappear as I embarked on my journey to recovery.

For starters, I had to learn to walk again. I literally started with "baby steps." With each small step I took, my confidence grew. One day in the hospital, I was able to walk across the room using only a walker to push me along. Granted, it took 45 minutes, but it was a major accomplishment for me. The doctors and nurses were so proud of me, and I had gained back a bit of my lost confidence. Confidence grows in small increments: Inch by inch, it's a cinch; yard by yard, it can be hard!

Empathetic

An empathetic person puts him- or herself in someone else's shoes. Being empathetic doesn't necessarily mean you share another person's point of view; it does mean you are concerned about others and interested in their point of view.

Empathetic people pay attention to the details. They take the time to look at and listen to others. They observe and interpret body language. They listen as carefully to what people leave unsaid as to what they say. They have the ability to read between the lines. They can tell when a friend is preoccupied, and they respect these boundaries. They have the ability to make the other person truly feel heard and valued.

One afternoon, as I was working on a speech, I received a call from a business colleague, Susan. Although she tried to sound upbeat, I could tell something wasn't quite right. Her voice sounded vague and disconnected. I respected her nonverbal but obvious wish not to discuss what was bothering her over the phone, so I suggested we meet for coffee the next morning. It turned out she had just lost her job and was in a state of shock. Her dismissal had clearly come out of left field. Only the week before, her work had been highly commended.

I listened, observed her body language, made a few comments, and encouraged her as she began to develop a plan. Even though I didn't directly offer advice, she told me later that I had helped her a great deal. A week later, I received a call from a contact at a company who was looking for someone with Susan's skills. I made some calls, meetings were set up, and soon Susan had a new job. I like to think that being empathetic to Susan helped this process. I understood how she felt and what she wanted to do. Then, because both of us are good connectors, she was able to take advantage of an opportunity when it presented itself.

Appreciative

The quality that makes people charismatic networkers is their natural instinct to give sincere appreciation. I believe you can never tell someone thank you too many times when it is done sincerely.

You can say thank you in many ways. There's the handwritten note sent via the U.S. Postal Service. There's email, which is quick, easy, and immediate. In addition, there's the face-to-face thank you, delivered sincerely with special emphasis on the communication style of the person you're appreciating. You can also show appreciation by sending a gift. I'm a big believer in giving gifts and will share some of my techniques and resources when we get further into the book. Saying "thank you" might seem like simple etiquette, yet it's amazing what it can do for your professional and personal growth as a networker.

An email message I once received confirmed the value of saying thank you. The message was from the CEO of a company for whom I'd done some programs. His message was, "I want to thank you and compliment you on the work you've been doing for us. I also would like to share some of the flattering remarks that several of our senior people have for you...." It took the CEO just 30 seconds during his busy day to write this message, but it had such an impact on me that I kept it in my inbox for a very, very long time.

We all strive to be remembered positively by others. Showing sincere appreciation always makes a lasting impression. People want to do business with people they enjoy being with, and they seek out these people. In addition, an affirming communication has a way of leading to other opportunities.

Here's how a personal expression of gratitude led to a referral and a new client. After I thanked one of my suppliers for helping me meet a nearly impossible deadline, he said he wanted to do something for me in return. He told me about another client of his whom he thought might use my services and gave me the referral. I followed up and now have a new client—all for a simple thank you.

Tenacious

About 10% of my business has come from people who turned me down the first time. When I realized this, it was a lesson to me in how being tenacious can pay off for networking and for business.

I remember how one current client was particularly tough to win over. For three years, I called, emailed, texted, and tried to stay on the radar screen of this client, but I got nowhere. What organizations and events,

I thought, would she be likely to attend? I belong to several business networking groups I thought could be a possibility. At least if the person I was trying to reach might not attend a meeting, perhaps I could connect with someone from her company who knew her. My break came when I was giving a presentation at a meeting of one of these groups. After my presentation, a woman from my potential client's company approached and suggested I meet with someone in her company who could use my services. She offered to set up the meeting. Guess who this someone turned out to be? None other than Ms. "Never Returns My Calls."

The story does not have a happy ending quite yet. We did meet, and at first, I could tell the woman was doing it out of courtesy for her coworker and really did not want to meet with me. However, things got better as the meeting progressed, and it ultimately went from the 20 minutes she'd allotted to an hour and a half. At the end, she said, "I like your proposal, but frankly, we're working with plenty of consultants and it takes about five years for outside consultants to land work in our firm. However, you can call me [her preferred method of communication] every quarter just to stay in touch." At first I was discouraged, but then I thought, "At least I got in the door! And now, with five years to go, I'd better hang in there [as my father would say]." I sent my thank you note, and a month later, when I heard she'd been promoted, I sent her a note of congratulations. When the first quarter was up, I called her and left her a message that said, "I'm just touching base." I continued to keep in touch for another quarter or two, when, to my surprise, she called me. She awarded me not one, but two projects with her firm. I have since done more than 30 projects with the company; it's one of my largest clients. My tenacity paid off. Instead of getting discouraged, I just put on my schedule to call her every quarter and stayed in touch. I also added her to my "stay in touch" campaign (more on this later).

There's a fine line between being tenacious and being a pest. Be careful not to cross this line. Much of it has to do with getting permission to keep in touch. She'd invited me to keep in touch, so it was appropriate to follow up with the phone calls and notes. We linked in, and over time, I learned more about her. Being tenacious in a positive way means taking advantage of opportunities, as well as looking at the setbacks that come along as opportunities in disguise—and keeping at it.

Enthusiastic and Energetic

Enthusiasm and energy are contagious. When you're enthusiastic, you bring out the enthusiasm in others. If you're full of energy, the energy in the space around you rises. If you don't believe me, watch what happens at a gathering when folks are waiting for a speaker to take the floor. If the speaker arrives with energy, watch how the expressions on the audience's faces change and the room becomes "charged." Energy and enthusiasm make communication easier. It puts people at ease. It makes people relaxed and receptive to your message.

Realize, though, that enthusiasm and energy come in many forms. You do not have to be loud and excited to be energetic or enthusiastic. Enthusiasm can be a quiet passion that shines and makes people want to be a part of it.

I.A.S.M.

Look at the last four letters in the word *enthusIASM*: I Am Self-Motivated.

You have to believe in yourself and your ideas first before others will join you.

Caring

I believe that when you truly care about others and you don't expect a payback for your efforts, you will indeed get the ultimate reward. You will make others feel good about themselves and about you.

Often the act of caring produces unexpected, positive networking results. Recently, I received one of those "voice from your past" phone calls. It was from Gloria, who had been the receptionist at a company I had called on years before. I had last seen her 14 years before. She was now the vice president of marketing for another company. She'd recently read an article of mine and decided to call me about doing a project for her new company. I was quite flattered by her call and her invitation to do a project. When I asked her what had made her call me, she said, "You always made me feel important whenever you called. Moreover, you even told Jim, our president, that I had a great voice and a smile that truly came across the phone." She was right—I remember when I told him. (Remember what we discussed about sincere compliments?) She told me how she'd always remembered my kindness, and now she wanted to return the favor. As far as I was concerned, there was no "favor to be returned," for she did have a great voice, and I still remember how nice she was to me when I was calling on her company. When I complimented her, it was sincere and without a thought of any payback. Yet here it was, 14 years later, and she still obviously treasured my remark.

Effective networkers are always networking not because they "need" to, but because they want to create lifelong connections with people. They embrace networking as a way of life. They network without the thought of getting an immediate or specific payback. Effective networkers know they're making positive connections in which all parties ultimately benefit. How very different this is from the image many hold of networkers, which is what I call the "pathological networker" who engages in "negative networking." These folks never think of picking up the phone, writing a note, sending an email or a text, offering a heartfelt recommendation on LinkedIn, or extending a helping hand until they need something. They are not networking.

IT'S NOT ABOUT A QUICK HIT

You know the pathological networker. This is the individual you see at events passing out cards in a frenzy, obviously there for no other reason than to get a job or make a quick sale. A woman once walked up to me at an event, tapped me on the shoulder, and thrust her card into my hand. "I'm a photographer," she announced, oblivious to the conversation I was having with others. "Call and email me for work." Needless to say, that brusque introduction did not inspire me to communicate with her. Sadly, her approach is all too common at many functions today.

Each communication style has its own language.

Visual	Auditory	Kinesthetic
See	Hear	Feel
Look	Listen	Touch
Picture	Sound	Feeling
Appear	Discuss	Aware

Being a good listener and an effective communicator is key to showing empathy. When you hear someone say, "This doesn't sound right to me," an empathetic response is, "What exactly are you hearing to make you say that?"

An empathetic person is an excellent listener who understands and adapts to the needs of others. Being empathetic doesn't mean changing your personality. Nor does it mean being solicitous or manipulative. It is a positive, sincere, and proactive approach to understanding another person's feelings and interests. The dictionary definition of *empathy* is "the action or understanding, being aware of...the feelings, thoughts, and experience of another...without having the feelings, thoughts, and experience fully communicated in an objective, explicit manner." Therefore, to become empathetic, you need to be aware of communication styles and personality types.

Exercise 1: How Do You Communicate?

The following list contains eight essential communication skills for effective networking and life skills. Rate yourself on a scale of 1 to 5, with 5 being the highest and 1 needing improvement. Mark the skill(s) that you didn't rate highly (1–3). What's holding you back? What can you do to improve these skills?

_____ Smiling

_____ Looking the person in the eye

_____ Listening

_____ Remembering names

_____ Being aware of body language

_____ Respecting other people's boundaries

_____ Looking for common interests

_____ Giving genuine compliments

Exercise 2: Complimenting Others

Make a list of five coworkers or people with whom you associate, and write down at least two compliments you can give each person. Pick a day when you will see them all, and use the five-a-day penny exercise in this chapter. Your goal is to transfer all five pennies.

1. Name_____

_____

_____

2. Name_____

_____

_____

3. Name_____

_____

_____

4. Name_____

_____

_____

5. Name_____

_____

_____

Exercise 3: How Well Are You Listening?

I often say that listening skills are the most effective skill in being a successful business networker. Now it's time for you to see if you can retain what other people tell you.

Talk with other people in the room, at your office, or at a meeting about any of the topics we've covered so far. After you speak with them, tell them three things that stood out from what was said. Now consider the following questions:

Were you able to remember what they said?

_____

_____

_____

What did they remember about you?

_____

_____

_____

Is that what you wanted them to remember?

_____

_____

_____

How can you improve your communication so that people remember what you want them to?

_____

_____

_____

_____

_____

_____

Exercise 4: Characteristics of Best Practices of Great Networkers

Who is good? Write down the names of at least two people you consider to be good networkers. Then write down what characteristics they have that you think help them succeed.

1. _____

_____

2. _____

_____

3. _____

_____

Exercise 5: Are You Effective?

Look at the traits of effective networkers. Rate yourself on a 1–5 scale, where 5 is the highest and 1 is the lowest. Mark which ones you need to improve on (1–3). What strategies can help you make those areas stronger?

_____ Friendly and approachable

_____ Confident

_____ Empathetic

_____ Appreciative of others' help

_____ Tenacious in overcoming obstacles

_____ Enthusiastic and energetic

_____ Caring

_____ Good listener

_____ Able to rebound quickly from rejection

_____ Nurturing in relationships

_____ Appearing poised and polished

5

What Is Your Communication Style?

Communication Styles and Personality Types

Effective networkers are aware of communication styles and personality types. They know their own style, with its strengths and weaknesses, and have learned to recognize and honor other people's styles of communication and personality types. They also adapt their style to accommodate others, when appropriate.

How Are You Wired to Communicate?

Sometimes trying to communicate with someone who communicates differently from the way we do is like two ships passing in the night. We don't understand them, and they don't understand us.

To communicate effectively, be ready to alter the way you communicate. Once I was in France and was trying to communicate with a shopkeeper. I thought that if I spoke louder and more slowly in English, she would understand me. Of course, there was no way she could. The louder and more slowly I talked, the more frustrating it was for both of us. I needed to alter my style (talking at a regular volume in English) and try something else she could understand, such as pointing and gesturing, smiling, or finding someone who could translate for us (which I eventually did).

The frustration I felt before I altered my style is exactly the same feeling we have when we don't connect with someone else. We might even be in our own country speaking the same language, yet our communication styles are so different that we have a hard time making a connection. We need to understand and adapt our style to communicate effectively.

I'm a bottom-line person. Often I see the big picture first and then find a way to go for it, sometimes without thinking it through completely.

My friend Steve, on the other hand, is a process person. He looks at every detail, weighs both the positive and negative, and really thinks it through. Another fellow who works with Steve is even more of a process person! I have learned to communicate with them so much better now. I take the time to listen and hear every word and suggestion they give me, and I learn along the way. In the past, though, I know we all got frustrated sometimes because we wanted to communicate only "our" way. However, when we adapt, we do see things from the other person's point of view, and we can work together much more clearly and effectively. At your next meeting or networking event, practice altering your style with each person you meet or connect with. In the course of a day or event, you will most likely find yourself changing your communication style with everyone you encounter.

Everyone uses a style of communication when giving and receiving information. Harry is auditory—he learns by hearing information. He rarely takes notes at a meeting and prefers a verbal briefing to a written report. He has told me that he listens to the news every morning and night instead of reading a newspaper or online material. When I speak with Harry, the auditory type, I am sure to incorporate phrases such as, "Are we in harmony?" or "How does this sound to you?" I recognize that he will remember things he hears rather than sees, so I leave him voicemail messages instead of email or text reminders.

Ann is visual—she needs to "see in it writing." She takes many notes in a meeting and treasures handouts and written reports. She loves Power-Point presentations and videos. YouTube is one of her favorite channels. When she communicates, she often draws what she's talking about on a pad. When I talk with her, I say things like, "How does this look to you?" or "Picture this...." I know I need to paint a picture for Ann.

Bill is kinesthetic—he needs to act things out, be involved, or have things demonstrated to him. He talks with his hands and explains how to do something with a demonstration. He learns things best by actually doing them. With Bill, I say, "Are you comfortable with this idea?" or "How does this feel to you?"

Think about how you like to give and get information. What is your preferred communication style? What is that of your boss, various coworkers, your subordinates, and even your spouse? Have you ever been frustrated trying to communicate something when the other person just didn't get it? Maybe your communication styles were too disparate. Think about how you can adapt your style to accommodate the other person's. Keep in mind that people won't tell you their style. You'll learn their preferred methods only by observation and careful listening. Hear the words they use, and watch their behavior. Then you can match your words to theirs to communicate with them effectively.

Recognizing Personality Types

In addition to being aware of communication styles, a good communicator adjusts to other people's orientation or personality type. Some people are more oriented, or sensitive, to the concerns and feelings of others; others are more bottom line or results oriented. Still others are interested in and concerned with details and the way things work.

Certain ways to identify personality and temperamental categories help predict how people react and relate to each other. One popular personality style indicator many companies use is the Myers-Briggs Type Indicator. I also use the DISC profile, which explores behavioral issues. It has been around for more than 40 years and is an effective tool for understanding personality traits and styles. I definitely recommend researching these and other personality indicators. However, for you to be effective, all you really need to do is listen carefully, observe behaviors, and then respect others' personality orientation. I have found that this works time and time again. Still, it takes practice.

For example, I once walked into a corporate conference room and found myself giving three different presentations at the same time! I was there to present a training proposal to three top decision makers in the company. Having met them all, and through careful observation and listening, I knew that each had a very different personality style. My main goal (besides selling my program) was to speak to their needs and convey the benefits to each one. Therefore, I needed to adjust my presentation to each one individually. As I spoke with each person, I switched the way I conveyed the information I was giving to match his or her personality.

The head of human resources and training was amiable in her approach. What I remembered most about her was her comment to me about being sure to "get everyone involved" and her obvious caring and concern for all the employees. Clearly, I had to focus my presentation to her on the personal benefits for her employees and make sure she felt that the time her employees spent in training would be worthwhile for their growth and development.

The chief financial officer, however, was interested in the return on investment he expected from my program. In addition, he wanted details and numbers. I decided to give him the same proposal that I had given to the head of human resources, but to include a specific outline for each module, with costs clearly defined. The more data I presented to him, the better!

The CEO told me he had only six minutes to hear me out. (I actually clocked how long he was in the room, and it was exactly six minutes!) All he wanted to know was, "What are my people going to learn?" and "How much will it cost?" I was prepared with the same presentation (in case he had questions), but I gave him only the executive summary: a brief, succinct paragraph followed by bullet points and the bottom line.

These were three very different people, all wanting the same thing yet needing it delivered in three very different ways. To succeed, I had to read each person carefully and provide exactly what he or she wanted to hear.

Later, after I had done several programs with this firm, each person told me separately how much he or she enjoyed our working relationship because, "We communicate in exactly the same way." I smiled to myself, knowing that my extra work and effort to understand each personality type had been well worth it!

TRAITS OF COMMON PERSONALITY TYPES

Dominant:	Bottom line oriented, competitive, direct
	Makes decisions quickly
	Best approach to use:
	Focus on the "what"
	Be efficient

Expressive:	Persuasive, animated, expressive, emotional
	Enjoys helping others
	Best approach to use:
	Focus on the "who"
	Be empathetic
Amiable:	Patient, agreeable, amiable, quiet
	Is very dependable
	Best approach to use:
	Focus on the "how"
	Be supportive
Analytical:	Compliant, cautious, accurate, analytical
	Likes a lot of details
	Best approach to use:
	Focus on the "why"
	Be logical

Not a Chameleon

An effective networker is an excellent listener who understands and adapts to the needs of others. Be aware, however, that this does not mean constantly changing your personality. Nor does it mean being solicitous or manipulative. It is a positive, sincere, and proactive approach to understanding another person's feelings and interests. You want to appear empathetic, not opportunistic. The dictionary definition of *empathy* is "the action or understanding, being aware of...the feelings, thoughts, and experience of another...without having the feelings, thoughts, and experience fully communicated in an objective, explicit manner." Therefore, to become empathetic, just be aware of communication styles and personality types.

Men and Women: Do We Network Differently?

If personality types were the only thing that made us different, that would make communication challenging enough! Take all these different types and mix in the fact that men and women perceive the world much differently—now you have a real challenge! That's right—in our diverse world, we need to take a good look at how being male or female affects how we listen to, learn from, and network with one another.

Female vs. Male Bonding

First, let's look at how the sexes relate to members of the same sex. When we see what requirements men have to feel good about their communication with each other, and when we look at how women bond with each other, we can understand what we might do to communicate better with the opposite sex. These are generalities and are useful only in providing a framework of understanding. As helpful as these can be, there's no substitute for really getting to know other people and their communication preferences. The biggest difference to remember about understanding how women communicate with each other is that women often bond more easily than men do, and in a different way.

In one accounting firm I work with, the women partners often try to give business to other women. We bond. Often by the time coffee is served, we know another woman's life story...and then we turn to business. We like to help each other once we have developed some trust.

Men tend to have some brief small talk and then dive right into doing business. They tend to think, "Why spend all that time getting to know each other, unless I know this will be a good business proposition? After the deal is done, then we can get to know each other. That will help us, since we'll be working together. If all goes well on the business end of things, and there is some mutual respect, then we might recommend each other to our associates for further business opportunities." This is what I hear from my male counterparts. We all help each other, and we do it in different ways that seem natural to us.

As you interact with the opposite sex, keeping these ideas in the back of your mind will help when you deal with any "speed bumps" in your communication. When communication is hard or breaks down between men and women, more often than not, it's because we forget there are primary differences in how we relate to each other. Remember, in most cases, both parties are trying to communicate in good faith, and it helps to consider gender differences before assuming anything different.

Men Are Thinkers, Women Are Feelers—Generally

Why do there seem to be clear and fundamental differences between men and women? Why do men tend to want to talk about external issues and women want to talk about internal ones? This has much to do with how they make decisions and determine what is important.

For example, the Myers-Briggs Type Indicator, perhaps the most widely used tool for measuring individual style and preferences, distinguishes between how "thinkers" and "feelers" make decisions and communicate them to others. Thinkers believe that the best decisions are rational, logical, and dispassionate and that everything is governed by objective, consistent rules. There are absolute rights and wrongs, and the rules can't be changed to fit a situation. They think that emotions can distort and negatively affect the quality of decisions.

Feelers, on the other hand, highly value emotion when making and acting on decisions. Their frame of reference is subjective. Making a sound decision means that everyone involved should feel as good as possible. To feelers, there are no absolute rights and wrongs. The most effective way to behave is to accommodate all styles. Their approach is sensitive to emotion and unconcerned about whether everything makes perfect sense.

Not surprisingly, two-thirds of all men who take the Myers-Briggs score highly as thinkers, and two-thirds of all women score highly as feelers. Again, these are general ideas; the important point to remember is that everyone, regardless of gender, is unique. This means that we must relate to people first and foremost as individuals.

Communication Tips Between Men and Women

If we understand ourselves and the opposite sex better, and make some slight adjustments, we'll be able to bridge communication gaps.

Listening and Body Language

The first thing that's different between us is the way we listen. Men and women do listen to each other, yet they do it differently. Women generally listen actively and often nod and smile. Men rarely do this. Men think of the nodding and smiling as agreement, seeing it as a sign encouraging them to speak. One woman I know was turned down for some business because of her continual nodding—the client thought she agreed with everything and made no decision on her own! He thought she was weak; she thought she was being polite! The client exhibited common male listening traits: wandering gaze and neutral facial expression. Many women think this is rude and inattentive. As a result, women might act defensively when men don't even realize that their listening can trigger this behavior.

A tip to women when networking with men: Cut down on the nodding and smiling, and lessen the intensity of your gaze.

A tip to men: Keep steadier eye contact and assume nothing if you see a smile or nod.

Changing Topics

Men often feel that interrupting someone is the logical way of changing speakers, while women often wait for their turn out of politeness. Women need to jump in, or they might wait a long time to speak at an event or meeting.

Advice to women: Learn to jump in—this is a skill. Speak a bit louder and faster, with more enthusiasm. Give a comment about what is being said, such as, "John, you're right, that seems relevant, and here's another point to consider." Keep the rapport going without pausing, and know that you'll be interrupted.

Advice to men: Interrupt less and wait for pauses in the conversation. Ask a woman what she thinks, and then you'll get feedback.

On the Lighter Side

Men and women look at humor and joking differently. While men may think everyone will laugh, it is not always appropriate and women may sometimes hesitate. Know your audiences and err on the side of being more conservative.

Women: Know that men exchange a lot of one-liners, and learn to follow. Just know that if the ball is tossed your way, you can throw it back. Keep it positive.

Men: Know that women prefer direct communication, such as, "Good morning. How was your weekend?" instead of: "You look exhausted. Didn't you sleep last night?"

Making Small Talk

For small talk, find gender-neutral topics, such as trends in the industry and current events rather than too much family conversation. Also, women tend to talk about themselves and their feelings more than men do. Men need to realize that this is just women's way of making small talk at times.

TIPS FOR MEN AND WOMEN TO "MEET IN THE MIDDLE" WITH COMMUNICATION SKILLS

Communication Skill	How Women Can Improve	How Men Can Improve
Listening	Keep a blank face	Maintain eye contact and listen without interrupting
Speaking	Jump in, increase volume, begin on a positive note	Wait for pauses in the conversation and avoid interrupting
Small talk	Minimize talk about yourself	Talk about something other than sports and politics
Humor	Go with the flow and learn to respond to joking politely	Avoid trying to be too witty and telling jokes that not everyone will appreciate

Tying It All Together

Building the right communication skills is a key to effective networking. These can be as simple as making eye contact and remembering people's names. Understanding the variety of personality types out there, coupled with the knowledge of men's and women's basic "wiring" when it comes to communication styles, can greatly enhance your networking opportunities. It will be a more satisfying experience for you and those with whom you network. Now that you have the basics of understanding others and making contact, we look at personal marketing—how to best present yourself in the "grocery store of life."

Exercise 1: Networking with Someone Whose Natural Communication Style Differs from Yours

Look at three emails and texts this week. Assign each a *V* (for "visual word"), *A* (for "auditory"), or *K* (for "kinesthetic"), and pay attention to the responses or reactions you receive in replies. Also pay clear attention to the sensory receivers in the messages you receive, and force yourself to reply in kind. Do this three times, and then continue being aware so that you consistently put this element into your correspondence and conversation.

Exercise 2: Networking with Each Communication Style

Fill in the following according to your style, and then look at the descriptions that follow the exercise. Think of how you will network and interact with people you meet, knowing that you have to flex your style to their way of communicating.

Communication Styles

Find your natural or primary communication style here. Even though you have one dominant style, you use all styles, some more than others. On a scale of 1 to 4, with 1 being your primary style and 4 being the style you use the least, rate the following:

The Expressive Rating: _____

You are animated, energetic, and spontaneous. You easily communicate your ideas, sometimes throwing out half-formed ideas to gather more input. You enjoy involving people. You like variety and are curious and sometimes impulsive. You could overlook details. People say you are expressive, innovative, persuasive, and outgoing.

The Amiable Rating: _____

You are empathetic, sympathetic, and friendly. You have a warm tone of voice and frequently show concern for the people with whom you work. You are very steady and caring. You are good at anticipating people's needs. You are often described as being patient, controlled, concerned, and cooperative.

The Analytical Rating: _____

You live in the world of the mind and like to keep your ideas private. You are quite deliberate. When solving a problem, you like to weigh each alternative and consider all the facts. You are organized and systematic. You tend toward perfectionism. You are detail oriented, thorough, and orderly.

The Dominant Rating: _____

You are a possibilities thinker. You value action, get impatient, and are easily bored. You are results oriented. It is relatively easy for you to make decisions and take calculated risks. You do not like to spend time considering a lot of alternatives. People say you have a lot of drive, make a good leader, and are assertive and outspoken.

The Four Major Communication Styles

Expressive:

- Be social, be able, and stay on track.

- Give special attention; plan interaction that supports others' feelings and intuitions.

- Enjoy talking about themselves, work, and style of life.

- Put what you want them to remember in writing.

- Be prepared—you will be interrupted.

- Use visuals.

- Best way to deal with these types: Get excited with them, show emotion.

Amiable:

- First win them over as a friend.
- Show sincere interest in them as people—find common interests and agreement.
- Patiently draw out their expectations and work with them.
- Present your case softly and without threat.
- Let them move at their own pace.
- Assure them that all promises will be kept.
- Make sure the closing of your visit is a logical, natural conclusion of the conversation.
- Best way to deal with these types: Be supportive, show you care.

Analytical:

- Plan your work and work your plan. Use time to be accurate.
- Approach in a straightforward, direct, yet low-key way.
- Support the logical, methodical approach. Build your credibility by listing pros and cons to the subject.
- Use comparative data and expectations to be derived.
- Be sure to answer all questions, both those that are asked and those that you think they want to ask.
- Handle all objections completely.
- Appeal to their sense of logic.
- Know that they are interested in research and statistics, and need time to think and consult before making a decision.
- Best way to deal with these types: Provide a lot of data and information

Dominant:

- Be brief, get to the point quickly, and be clear and specific.
- Stick to business. Come prepared, be well organized, and have support material that you might never open.

- Start with WIIFM (what's in it for me)—for them professionally.
- Be sure of yourself; be firm.
- Present the facts logically, and plan to be concise and efficient.
- Hit quick and hard—they make decisions on impulse.
- Bottom-line the facts.
- If you disagree, take issue with the facts, never the person.
- Close by asking for action on their part.
- Be ready to deliver on short notice.
- After talking business, depart graciously.
- Best way to deal with these types: Let them be in charge.

6

Your Best Foot Forward

recently connected two friends. Bill is in the disability insurance business, and Joel is a Certified Public Accountant. I thought there might be some synergy between the two, and I was right: They had a good first meeting—they sincerely enjoyed meeting each other, yet what business connection might be made was not apparent.

Then we all happened to be at a business cocktail party, and as we were casually talking, Bill mentioned his supervisor. Joel's eyes lit up and said, "You work with Dan? That's great to hear! He's terrific and someone I respect a lot. Can we talk again next week and set up a time when the three of us could meet? I've read what Dan has said about developments in your company, and I'd like to share some helpful ideas that fit into your plans."

Later, as Bill and I were talking, he said, "Isn't that amazing what happened as soon as I mentioned Dan?" I said, "Yes, and it's truly remarkable when people get connected and then find something in common, and the conversation seems to flow better as your interest in each other increases." In this case, it was a true win/win situation. The connection was made.

I love sharing this phrase: *The opposite of networking is not working.* When used positively and correctly, networking can be the most important business skill you can use anywhere you go. Every time you meet someone, you have an opportunity to learn from that person and to be a resource as well. Remember, you can even learn from someone you don't like or respect, in that you can learn what *not* to do or how *not* to act. Often I say that in my workshops, and everyone agrees. We see in other people what we either want to emulate or avoid. And truly and most important, networking starts with giving—being able to find a way to help the other person.

Networking is at its best when our interpersonal skills create an atmosphere of respect and trust. We all want to do business with people who make us feel comfortable, and if we like them, that is a true home run. This chapter focuses on what it takes to present yourself as someone with character and integrity. Read the news to learn about how business leaders conduct themselves. CEOs with integrity are respected (those without it go to jail). It's about putting your best foot forward and knowing how to market yourself and build your brand.

CHARACTER CHECKUP

When you want to evaluate the character of someone with whom you'd like to connect, here are some questions to consider:

- Does the person look you in the eye when speaking, or do his or her eyes roam around the room?

- When you help someone with a referral or contact, does the person acknowledge what you did?

- Does the person answer questions honestly?

- Do you get a sense that the person is sincere, or does he or she simply see you as a business target?

Nobody is perfect; however, character does matter. Make sure the people you connect with appear to have integrity. We know that if you are reading this book and are constantly improving yourself, you certainly do. We go to school throughout our life.

Marketing Yourself

Many years ago, when I was a magazine publisher, I received a call mid-morning from one of the senior vice presidents who asked if I was free for lunch with him and the president of the division. Of course, I went. However, when I look back on all the mistakes I made, I shudder. For some crazy reason that particular day, I was going to be in the office all day, so I wasn't dressed in my normal business meeting style. I know that today we live in the world of business casual, but I realized then and there that if you want to make a great impression—you're always "on" in our world today—you have to look the part that will make you feel at your best. If that weren't enough, I was also too immature at the time to use the sage advice I have since learned: "Talk less and listen more." I came across nervous and not sure of myself instead of as someone who could have been groomed for a new job opportunity. Granted, I had the business credentials and had built a great name at my magazine, yet I didn't do a good job of really marketing myself in front of my senior management team. What a lesson I learned on the spot—and never forgot.

Fast-forward many years later. I'm still in touch with that vice president, who has since retired after serving as chairman of a major corporation. It's great to remember how I have learned over the years that you *always* have to be ready to present your "self-brand."

Think of some well-known brands that you use. Why do you always go back to them? What makes them stand out in your mind? Usually the reason you remember them is twofold: marketing and consistent quality.

We are surrounded with marketing for new ideas and products. In this book, the focus is on the opportunity to market the most important product each one of us has: ourselves. Knowing how to market and sell ourselves is the way to get noticed. Being noticed in a good way depends on *how* we do it. I find that one of the best ways is to have others believe in our brand so much that they talk about us.

The way we appear, communicate, interact, and are perceived by those in our workplace and by our clients is a direct result of the tools we develop as self-marketers. The Carnegie Institute of Technology conducted research (which other studies confirmed) showing that technical skills account for 15% of financial and career success, while interpersonal skills account for 85%. I believe that much of our success comes from our efforts to build a network of people who fully appreciate our talents, recognize our potential, and support us in getting where we want to go as we help others get what they want.

Your Personal Brand

So what is your own personal brand? It's how you express who you are and what you have to offer. Think of the vision you want to create. The brand you develop for yourself is what people will think of when they hear or see you. A brand is a reputation of credentials, and personal branding is how we market ourselves to others. Our brand ultimately serves to create an image.

Your brand will create buzz, and that informs more people about you. When you've created a recognized brand for yourself, then your clients, friends, and contacts will be your biggest advocates, and they will want to refer prospects to you. You have credibility in their eyes, and that comes from trust and believability.

Think of what distinguishes you from others in the same business. Think about what you are best known for, and write it down. Why are you known for that? Back it up with some examples.

YOU ARE THE PRODUCT

Answer these questions as you "package" your brand:

- Why did you choose to go into the business you're in? Or why are you choosing the business you want to be in?

- What types of people do you most enjoy serving and working with?

- How do you uniquely help those people solve their problems?

- With whom do you compete, and what do they do well that you should work to do as well?

- What makes you different from the competition that your current clients like?

A brand is simply what people think when they hear a name or see a logo.

As you refine and redefine your brand, always keep in mind, what do people think of when they hear your name? What immediately comes to their mind in an authentic and understood way?

Keep in mind the 10 C's of a strong personal brand:

1. Correct

2. Concise

3. Clear (less is more in your sound bite)

4. Consistent

5. Compelling

6. Clever

7. Connected

8. Committed

9. Constant

10. Current

Everything you do should be reflected in your brand, including your communications, appearance, social media presence, daily interactions, and any instances when you are speaking and writing about your brand.

You also need to incorporate your Unique Promise of Value—the feelings, words, and associations that people attribute to your personal brand. Here are some factors that will enhance your self-brand:

1. Know that your reputation is valuable. We are what we continually do and how we treat others.

2. Do what you say you are going to do. Follow up and follow through.

3. Return all forms of communication that ask for a reply, and always say thank you.

4. Treat everyone with respect and courtesy. Everyone is part of the universal network.

5. Listen. I can't say it enough.

6. Keep improving and adding to what makes *you* who you are.

THE GROCERY STORE OF LIFE

If you were sitting on the shelf, like a box of cereal, why would someone decide to buy you?

- Do you grab people's attention?

- What "ingredients" do you list that are better for the consumer?

- Are you new and improved?

Frosted Flakes has been around for many years, yet today's version is healthier and has an updated image for modern consumers. (It's okay for you to be sweet—just not sugary.)

Create Alliances

When you read newspapers, you often see stories about political and social causes that include such words as *coalition, pact,* and *associations.* These are people and organizations that join together for a common good. Joining forces brings strength and many benefits. The same is true when building your network of people.

I met Audrey, who has her own consulting business, more than three years ago at an industry networking event. After the event, I followed up with a suggestion to meet for lunch, and we have kept in touch ever since. I stay on her radar through my e-zines, tweets, LinkedIn, and marketing campaigns. Over time, we decided to create an alliance and market one another's services. Recently, Audrey called to tell me that several of her clients were interested in my services. She had made calls and sent notes to people, and some opportunities were starting to develop. I am doing the same for her. I believe that the essence of personal marketing is convincing others to believe in you and to become your advocate. This is very different from self-promotion, which often comes across as aggressive and negative.

I spoke with Audrey recently to thank her for all the connections she has started to make for me. Her answer has stuck with me: "You make me look good in front of my clients." Again, that's all the more reason to develop your alliances and connections through trust and respect. Ask yourself as Audrey did about me, "Would I want that person representing me or reflecting on my hard-earned and developed contacts and universal network?"

THE PERSONAL MARKETING ALLIANCE THREE-POINT SYSTEM

Look at how world leaders build alliances between their countries. It takes planning and patience. Look at the European Union. Years ago, it was just a dream; today it's a powerful collaboration. Here's how you can do the same:

- **Be known.** Go out and speak and write. Be a presence in your community. Be sure to keep a high profile among the people you are aligned with.

- **Be liked.** Take good care of people, and they'll take care of you. Your allies will want to hear from others how much you respect people.

- **Be trusted.** Be a true professional and always stay true to your word. Your reputation will precede you, whatever anyone says about you.

Your allies want to know from others that their association with you is an asset.

Become a Resource for Others

We all have skills and knowledge that can be helpful to others. When you become a resource for others, people will recognize your expertise, refer you, and help your network to grow.

One day I received a call from Jim, who was referred to me as someone who might help him find a job. I was happy to help him, and in turn, he offered many resources that helped me. Through our several phone meetings, I met more than 10 people and received two new projects. Jim also got his dream job through one of the connections I made for him. Both of us work our networks and believe first in giving and helping others. The result was a benefit to both of us. How do you also incorporate that into your life?

Making yourself an "expert" in an area is important. People remember what you are best known for and what expertise you have. Just think of some of the various products and services you use and why. Which product comes to mind when you think of a dependable family car? Fast pizza delivery? Delicious dinner for two? Your favorite search engine? Just as is the case with these products, your goal needs to be that your contacts see you as the *only* person who can help them in certain areas.

What skills, expertise, and resources do you have that you can give to others? How can you best communicate this? Here's a way to begin.

List your skills that you think could help others, such as persuasive writing skills, excellent computer knowledge, and social marketing expertise. I think of my IT guru, John. He's a whiz on all aspects of computers and stays up-to-date on everything, which makes my life easier. He also speaks in human terms, which is important for all of us—he makes it easy for the other person to understand him.

List areas in which you are knowledgeable. This includes specific comprehension of your industry or any new developments and trends in your field. Dr. Allan, for example, is a dentist extraordinaire. He is continually reading, taking courses, and learning new advances in the protection and care of teeth; he's always full of advice and tips on how to best care for my teeth. He never stops learning, and I'm always happy to be updated, knowing that I'm working with a pro.

Think of people, places, and things you know about that would be helpful to others—office equipment, websites, restaurants, stores, workshops and seminars, books, newsletters and recent articles, trade organizations, and the like. I continually learn new information and trends from everyone and every source in my network, and I share it with the people in my alliance to show that I am a team player. Engage in all sorts of social media, tweet, and post on Facebook and LinkedIn. Share your information with others. You will also become known over time as a thought leader.

My late friend Bruce was a master at being a resource to others. He researched 20 to 30 magazines and papers every week, both on- and offline, and sent out email memos to his database according to their interests. I was on several of his lists and always found the information interesting and helpful. What was Bruce doing besides giving out great information that he'd researched? He'd stayed on many people's radar screens, and the "buzz" about him continued. He was almost like a personal Google Alert that kept on the radar of people.

Bruce's mastery of networking went even further. He routinely sent a letter to two different people to make an email introduction and let each person know something about the other and why they would want to connect. This is an excellent exercise—it is all about creating advocates and helping each other. Again, it's so easy to implement into your weekly schedule; just keep a 24/7 networking awareness with everyone you meet and connect with. Ask how you can help them and whom you can introduce them to. Never worry about it coming back—it always does.

THE NETWORK IS ALWAYS OPEN

"The network is always open," said my friend Bruce Dorskind. He passed away shortly after he sent me this note.

Every time I venture into a store, board a train or plane, or attend a meeting, I view it as a networking opportunity. I always carry cards and a plethora of vertical trade publications. I'm not hesitant to say "Good morning" in the elevator or speak with the receptionist or security guard; I always observe what's on the desks of people with whom I am visiting. I attempt to take rigorous mental notes of important subjects. In this way, I can send relevant material, which can serve as a foundation for adding someone to my network.

I recall flying first class to Los Angeles, and I was reading 20 trade publications, ranging from a banking publication, to an engineering journal, to a magazine on Hollywood celebrities. As fate would have it, the person sitting next to me was a world-famous talent agent who was curious about my eclectic reading habits. After we established a connection, he referred me to an opportunity in the United Kingdom, which resulted in a very large fee.

> Networking, like breathing, must be a natural and everyday occurrence. Everything you see on the screen, every shop you visit, and every item you read presents a potential networking opportunity. Look for those opportunities—capture them and leverage them.

Help others fine-tune their 30-second infomercials. We all need a good sounding board to test how well we communicate our image. Ask the people in your alliance to tell you what they do in a clear, concise, compelling statement. Then critique their infomercials and offer suggestions to make them better. A friend once told me in astonishment about how she overheard someone say people were describing her to others as a "specialist in landscape photography." Actually, my friend had just started a studio for children's portraits, yet in conversation she had mentioned something about her landscape photos, not her new children's studio. Although she was flattered to be mentioned to other people, she realized she had not communicated her current focus on children's portraits.

As it turns out, my photographer friend was speaking with someone who not only had children of her own (a potential client), but also was on the board of directors of a riding school that taught children with handicaps. Another photographer learned this, volunteered to take publicity photos for the school, and ended up with several paying clients. I just asked a friend who is in the final round for a position at the White House to send me his 30-second introduction on his iPhone so that I can go over it with him and prepare for the different audiences he will be interviewing with. He's a geriatric physician who also heals his patients through dance. I look forward to helping him craft his sound bite to help him win this life-changing opportunity.

Supply people in your alliance with support materials. Be sure members of your alliance have easy access to all your electronic marketing communication.

Share speaking opportunities: When you're invited to speak on a panel, in a webinar, or in any online and offline opportunity, find out whether the presenting organization needs more presenters. If so, contact appropriate people in your alliance to join you. This can even work for writing articles or creating a noncommercial, information-based website where you and several of the people in your alliance make information available.

The most important attitude with those in your close circle is to be a giver and to share every resource that helps to develop the partnership and builds greater trust.

Personal Power

Communicating a sense of inner strength comes from a belief that you are determined to reach your goals. Powerful people empower others and encourage them to express themselves openly. You communicate a sense of personal power by developing these traits:

- **Authority:** Authority is inner confidence, a trust in your skills and abilities. It comes from an attitude of "I can do that." This attitude radiates outward as you politely assert your knowledge to establish who you are while, at the same time, helping others.

- **Assertiveness:** Assertive behavior is active, direct, and honest. By being firm, we view our wants, needs, and rights as equal with those of others. An assertive person wins by influencing, listening, and negotiating so that other people choose to cooperate willingly. There's a thin line between being assertive and aggressive. When it comes across as attacking and arrogant, it's aggressive. When you're firm and getting your point across, it's assertive.

- **Accessibility:** The powerful person is a master networker. Good networking increases your visibility and provides you with a valuable circle of people to whom you can give and from whom you can receive support and information. Imagine yourself as the hub of a wheel surrounded by spokes (your contacts).

- **Image:** You communicate power through your image. How do you continually project an image consistent with strong leadership? Stand tall and walk proudly, yet with humility. Always remember that you have value as a person, regardless of anything negative people might say about you. When you meet others, make direct eye contact and keep your handshake firm and friendly. Clearly state who you are and what you do.

Confidence is a key ingredient in projecting personal power. Often I ask my classes, "Who here, besides me, would like to buy some confidence?" Almost every hand goes up. Unfortunately, confidence isn't something you can buy. You have to work at it. Confidence comes from experience—making mistakes, doing something over and over again until you get it right, and being proactive.

Think how much more confident you are today in your position than you were the first week, month, or year. How much more comfortable are you speaking in public than you were when you first took the podium? Building confidence takes time and patience.

First Impressions Count: Appearance

It takes only three seconds to make an impression. While we all believe we should be judged on our character and innate worth, unless that first impression is a positive one, we often do not get the chance to reveal who we truly are. That's why it's worth the time to look our best whenever we come in contact with those we need in our network—and that's all the time, everywhere. This doesn't mean you have to wear the latest trends and fashions. My style is to dress on the conservative side, always looking professional—and when in doubt, leave it out! (for example, avoid wearing pins for religious or political organizations). If you simply follow a few commonsense guidelines for looking your best, you can turn that first impression into a gateway to making profitable connections.

A colleague, Sarah, told me an unfortunate story that might have happened to someone you know. Sarah left New York late on a Sunday afternoon to fly to Los Angeles to present a training program the next morning. She decided to fly in comfort in a warm-up suit and tennis shoes, with no carry-on except her handbag and iPad and laptop. She checked her bag at the curbside check-in.

At nine o'clock that night, when her bag didn't come off the plane in Los Angeles, panic set in. How could she show up to teach a class on communications at nine the next morning in her unprofessional attire! Luckily for her, an all-night discount store was open, and somehow she was able to piece together an outfit. It was a miracle that she was able to look presentable when she greeted her class the next morning. However, she did confide to me that her improvised wardrobe affected her confidence. It always does. Strive to be at your best daily, no matter what.

After I heard her story, I told her my two travel rules: First, always dress professionally when traveling. You never know whom you may meet and, if something happens to your luggage, you have an outfit. Second, always carry on a bag with enough essentials to make it through a day.

Exercise: Did You Make the Connection?

After you have had a conversation with someone you want to connect with, ask yourself the following:

- Were you able to remember what the person said?

- What topics did you talk about that could lead to further connections or networking opportunities?

- What do you think the person remembers about you?

- How did the person respond to your 30-second infomercial and the other information you wanted to communicate?

- Were you able to establish a reason to make a further connection? How did it go?

- Do you know how to get in touch with the person and whether he or she prefers email, text, social media, or phone (office, home, or cellphone)?

7

Networking Etiquette

Hello, my name is Linda," she said, walking over and introducing herself to Sharon, whom she met in line at an event. Without knowing how the other would react to a complete stranger, both began an eclectic discussion, ranging from Linda's childhood career dreams to Sharon's current endeavor as a personal shopper for clients interested in shopping in Paris.

After about 20 minutes, someone rudely interrupted them by standing right in front of Linda and completely taking over the conversation. The man introduced himself to Sharon as the publisher of an online magazine yet failed to acknowledge Linda. Taken aback, Linda stayed there only in an attempt to join the conversation he began about the different trends in their operating system and advertising. He never even looked at her. When the time was right (Linda's goal was to maintain her composure and redirect any negative feelings away from the situation), she injected herself back into the conversation by explaining *her* position as a media buyer. To the man's total surprise, she turned out to be a buyer for one of his top accounts.

He started to realize that perhaps he was selling the wrong person and decided that Linda was now worth speaking to. She was turned off, however, and never gave him her card or expressed any interest in talking further. She did get Sharon's card, though, and the two have stayed in touch and laughed at the circumstances under which they met.

It was truly poor networking etiquette—or negative networking, as I call it. Networking is all about establishing relationships and building trust instead of trying to make a quick sale. That never works—and it's truly self-serving and not what true networking is all about.

TUNING INTO THE PODCAST IN YOUR HEAD

Two on-air stations are constantly playing in our heads. Which one you tune into more often determines how successful you are at networking. Take a listen:

- **WII-FM—What's in It for Me:** Unfortunately, this one often spells trouble because it tells the other person that you are interested only in getting something—and usually *now*.

- **MMFI-AM—Make Me (the other person) Feel Important about Me:** I work at always tuning into this station. I ask myself, "What can I do to make the other person feel good and build rapport?"

A survey we conducted asked our participants what is the worst thing someone did to you when "networking" at a traditional event. Table 7-1 shows what we learned.

Table 7-1   Survey: The Worst Things People Do While Networking

Option	Response
Seemed interested only in selling me something	44%
Left as soon as they realized I wasn't someone who could help them	26%
Talked only about himself/herself	14%
Gave advice I didn't ask for	9%
Asked too many personal questions	7%

Courtesy of Nierenberg Consulting Group

As you can see from the survey, when you tune into only yourself, others want to turn you off!

Once at a seminar, a quiet man, George, raised his hand to share his worst experience. At a cocktail party, he'd been talking with a certain woman. Later in the evening, the woman came back to him and said, "Please give me back my card. I realize that you can't help me." I know your jaws might have just dropped because, although it's true, it's difficult to believe. You'd be surprised at some of the negative networking that goes on daily. I have often wanted to record some of the incidents I've seen on my iPhone, yet I think everyone reading this book has some interesting stories!

Etiquette is good manners and common courtesy. Growing up, most of us learned our manners from our parents, school, peers, and mentors. A friend told me about a young investment banker who attended a dinner with his boss and a potential client at an upscale restaurant. Uncertain of the proper dining etiquette, he learned to survive by closely observing the manners of others. Although it worked in this situation, he knew that, to really survive in the corporate world, he would have to learn the rules of business etiquette.

I share here some etiquette tips and techniques to help you in many networking and business situations. Check your business etiquette skills with these common questions and answers.

1. At a business meal, when should I start the business discussion?

   Your answer:

   _____

   _____

   It's a good idea to let your guest have an appetizer and a beverage before starting to discuss business (or, at breakfast, let the other person have some coffee and a bite of a muffin). Use that time to get to know the person through casual conversation. Build the rapport.

2. After an initial meeting, what is the best way to follow up?

   Your answer:

   _____

   _____

   It's best to send a handwritten note over email, which most people use to communicate. Email is immediate, yet a handwritten note shows that you took the time. I often send a quick email first, and I always follow that with a handwritten note, which is my "trademark." You will differentiate yourself.

3. I'm expecting an important call. Do I leave my cellphone on during a networking meeting?

Your answer: ☐ Yes ☐ No

A: *No!*

Never leave the ringer on; turn it off and put the phone on vibrate only. Then when you feel it go off, you can excuse yourself at the right time and check for messages in private. This rule also applies to any other personal electronics that could start buzzing or ringing at a bad time.

4. I'm going to a networking event and have been advised to hand out at least 25 business cards. Is this a good goal?

Your answer: ☐ Yes ☐ No

A: *No!*

A better goal is to make a certain number of quality contacts and to follow up after the meeting. Just handing out your card is not making a quality connection. I once watched a man enter a networking event, walk around, and hand his card to the first 20 people he met. He just said, "Hi, I'm [name] with [his company name]. Here's my card. We can help you save money on [his product]." I'll bet he told everyone the next day how many "contacts" he made and how hard he "networked." I don't think so. He's an example of what not to do.

5. I'm looking for new clients. Should I send a mass email to my contact list asking for referrals?

Your answer: ☐ Yes ☐ No

A: *No!*

Thoughtfully go through your list and your LinkedIn connections, and send a personalized message or call each person you feel might be of some help or might give you advice on finding new business. Take the time to personalize this—it's a clear picture of your image and how the world receives you.

6. I would like to develop business for my firm. I know that a friend of a contact of mine knows the director of marketing. Should I use that person's name when calling for an appointment?

Your answer: ☐ Yes ☐ No ☐ Maybe

A: *Maybe!*

Do this only when you have permission from both parties, your contact and his friend. Also take the time to learn something about each of them. Be sure to send a thank you note to each and let them know what happened. This is critical and why true networking is also about the reflections back to the first source of referral. Make it positive.

Common Networking Situations and Rules of Etiquette

I was at an event and noticed Jill, an association manager, rushing into the program, which was already in progress. The registration desk had closed, so she had no name tag, was frazzled, had missed the short networking time before the seminar began, and had a hard time calming down to listen to the program. During the lunch break, she started talking to a woman in the line for drinks. When Jill wanted to give her a business card, she couldn't find them! She'd changed purses at the last minute and had forgotten to transfer her card case.

Jill was so anxious that she spent the 10-minute break searching for a stray card instead of listening to her new colleague, who eventually moved on to someone who would listen to what she was saying.

Jill hurried to another group, pushing in aggressively in her haste not to waste any more time. She blurted out her name and thrust her hand at one person in the group. Everyone politely backed away from her as they hurried to their lunch tables. During the meal, Jill just couldn't relax. She spoke too much, talked with her mouth full of food, and managed to offend everyone around her.

Poor Jill became a networking disaster at this event. What I also learned about Jill is that she doesn't do well under pressure or when everything doesn't go according to plan. What can we learn from Jill?

Following are some common networking situations and rules of etiquette that address the negative approach Jill took.

At a Networking Event or Meeting

Come prepared to your next meeting or event. Here are some reminders to make the next one seamless for you to meet, connect, and follow up.

- It's better to arrive early than late. Arriving late signals that you think your time is more valuable than the time of those at the meeting. An early arrival shows enthusiasm for the event and respect for other people's time. An added benefit is that an early arrival gives you the opportunity to meet more people. Someone once told me when you're on time, you are already late.

- Place your name tag on your right-side lapel. This places it in direct eye contact of the person you meet and allows others to see who you are and to remember your name when they are shaking your hand.

- Exchange business cards with ease. Place your cards in your right-side jacket pocket, where you can easily access them. Make sure you have enough to last through the event. Be sure they're fresh and don't look like they've been collecting lint in your pocket. Place the cards you receive from the people you meet in your left pocket. This way, you won't inadvertently give out someone else's card thinking it's your own. Or remember your toolkits and have two attractive business card cases, one for your cards and one for those you receive.

- Make eye contact—and keep it. Looking someone in the eye shows respect and interest. People can always tell when your eyes are wandering over the room looking for your next contact. Then you're are silently saying, "You are not that important to me." This isn't the message you want to communicate.

- Shake hands firmly. Nothing is worse than a fishlike or death-grip handshake. Make your handshake firm and professional.

- Be aware of personal space. Moving in too close makes people uncomfortable. Most people consider anything less than 18 inches to be too close and will back away from you.

- Join conversations in progress with grace. Be sure to ask for "permission" to join a conversation. Say something like, "This looks like a fun group—may I listen in?" People enjoy having you join them when you are courteous.

- Exit a conversation politely. Express pleasure at having met the individual and the hope that you will meet again.

- On eating and carrying on a conversation: Simple. Don't do it.

- On drinking and carrying on a conversation: A nonalcoholic drink without ice is the easiest to handle. Why no ice? Frigid handshakes aren't pleasant. Why nonalcoholic? You'll pay better attention.

Meals at Large Events or Private Functions

People were walking into the meeting room at the hotel to an industry cocktail party and dinner. Jim was very visible and audible, in that he was trying to manage his beeping digital handheld device while balancing a drink and a plate. As he walked around talking to people, he kept peering into his mobile device and kept his other cellphone in his hand, just in case it rang. By the time everyone sat down for the meal, Jim was hungry, so he started eating before it was appropriate. He tried to talk over everyone and started a conversation with one of the guests at the far end of his table, which made for an uncomfortable situation.

Unfortunately, he also picked up his neighbor's glass of water and used the wrong fork for the salad. Poor Jim—on top of all of this, he jumped right into a sales pitch at dinner, letting everyone at the table know who he was and what his company does.

Sad for Jim. (His picture should be in the dictionary next to the entry for *negative networking*.) Look over these tips to see how he might have done much better.

- Turn off your mobile device or switch to vibrate mode. Talking, texting, emailing, or, worse, making a call during a meal shows disrespect. It says, "The person I'm talking to is more important to me than you are." One woman I know thinks she is being sly by having her handheld email device in her hand and casually peering into it. Everyone knows what she's doing, and it's rude. I do also know that "everyone does it"—it's still not showing good networking etiquette.

- Introduce yourself first to the person seated to your right and your left. Then introduce yourself to the rest of the table. As others join your table, introduce yourself and others to them. You might even arrange with another colleague at the table to switch seats with you during a second course or dessert so that you both get to know more people.

- Wait for the head table to begin eating or, if it's a private meal, wait for the host or hostess to begin. When you are the host or hostess, you must begin first.

- When ordering, allow your guest(s) to order first. Direct the server first to your guest(s); then select your entrée. It's safest to pick something in the midprice range and something easy to eat. Remember, it's not about the food—it's about making connections.

- Choose your fork wisely. If you're unsure about which utensil to use, working from the outside in is the safest bet. Alternatively, watch the host, hostess, or other guests, and do as they do.

- Keep your napkin in your lap until you leave the event or restaurant. If you leave the table temporarily, leave the napkin on your chair.

- Not sure which water glass or salad plate is yours? Remember, liquids on the right, solids on the left. If your neighbor forgets and takes yours, just ignore it.

- When you're finished, place your knife and fork in a parallel position across the center of your plate. This signals the waiter to clear your setting.

- Even if you're still hungry, stop eating when everyone else is done. Slow eaters, you can always get a snack later. Conversely, if you're a fast eater, slow your pace to match that of others.

- Never talk with your mouth full. Yes, I know, you learned this when you were 6. At your next event, just watch how many adults still do this, and make sure you're not one of them.

- Refrain from talking about business until people have settled in and had their appetizers. This allows ample time for making small talk and getting acquainted.

- Ask before you take notes. It is perfectly acceptable to take notes at a business or networking meal—just ask first, out of courtesy. Then use a small, attractive notepad and pen. Always keep these in your toolkit, ready to go.

REMEMBER, YOU'RE ALWAYS "ON"

Recently, I was invited in to make a sales presentation to a company. When I met the executive vice president, I thought she looked vaguely familiar, although I couldn't place her. During my presentation, it hit me. The week before, I had been at a restaurant having dinner with a friend and had noticed her at the next table because she was yelling at the server in a disgraceful fashion. Obviously I kept this revelation to myself. However, based on the scene at the restaurant, I decided that she might be a very tough client to work with. I declined the project. The incident reminded me that we should always be on our best behavior, because, in truth, we are always "on."

We never know who's watching, and that's why 24/7 networking awareness is good to keep top of mind.

Making Introductions

At an important meeting, Bill got nervous when he ran into Mr. Davis, the president of a large manufacturing firm he wanted as his client. He was walking with an intern, Josh, who had started recently right out of college. As they approached Mr. Davis, Bill said, "Mr. Davis, I'd like you to meet Josh, who has just started with our company." Mr. Davis was professional and gracious; he spoke for a few minutes with Bill and the intern, asked a couple questions, and then made his exit. What did Bill do wrong? Here are a few clues:

1. In the business world, defer to position and age. Gender is not a factor. An introduction is normally made in a logical order:

   Introduce younger to older.

   Introduce your company peer to a peer in another company.

   Introduce a junior to a senior executive.

   Introduce a fellow executive to a client.

   Introduce a personal contact to a business contact. For example, my friend Linda accompanied me to an industry luncheon, and we found that we were seated with one of my clients. I then said to my client, "May I introduce my friend Linda? Linda, this is my client, Bob Smith."

2. When making introductions, give a brief statement about each person's interest or profession. In the best case, mention something the two might have in common. This is polite and gets the conversation going. My client Al is a master at this. As he introduces different people to me, he always tells me something about the other person and, in many cases, mentions a common interest. We then have a perfect place to start our conversation, and Al can exit gracefully.

Email Etiquette

Our work and life can get controlled by the amount of email we receive. We are constantly wired, and it's part of the new normal of today.

Although email is an essential business communication, it can be misunderstood if you don't follow certain conventions. Email lacks the vocal inflections of a phone call, the body language of a face-to-face communication, and the impact of a handwritten note on fine stationery. Yet we also know that you can tell when an email has some "attitude"—and, one hopes, a positive attitude.

Here are some email etiquette tips to make sure your recipients read and respond to your messages promptly:

1. Keep your emails brief and focused. Think of how many you get, and do the math on how long it takes to read each one. Brevity is

the winner here. Consider the fact that the Lord's Prayer is only 56 words, and the Gettysburg Address was 226.

2. Use meaningful subject lines. These are your "grabbers" and convince the recipient to open and read your message. Examples are "Thank you for your help," "Attached is an article you expressed interest in," and "Referred by...."

3. State your point as soon as possible and tell what action you want the other person to take. (Think of your email message as a mini presentation.) Be cautious, clear, and concrete.

4. When you need to send a long document, send it as an attachment.

5. Utilize the Three B's: Be brief, be brilliant, and be gone. Time is of the essence.

6. Always reread your message before you hit Send. Make sure your tone is what you want it to be. Avoid anything that could be construed as sarcasm or innuendo. Many a sad tale is told of how someone hit the button before rereading what he or she just wrote in a moment of anger, passion, or stress.

7. Answer all emails within 24 to 48 hours. A quicker response is always better. Even if you don't have an answer, at least acknowledge that you received the message and will be in touch soon. Keep people in the loop and give a status update.

8. Let people know when you'll be away. When you know you won't be able to check your email regularly, engage the automatic "away from my desk" message for your emails. Better yet, send out messages to key contacts that you will be leaving in a few days and ask if they need anything urgent before you go. As we all know, true professionals are checking even when away. Business and life go on. Stay in touch.

9. Email is never personal. Be professional at all times. Leave out emotion.

10. Have a proper introduction, body, and close with a call to action (again, mini presentation).

11. Politeness always pays—"please," "thank you," and "sorry" go a long way.

Telephone Etiquette

Although some will say that the telephone is soon joining faxes and other so-called "endangered species," we still need the phone, and it's a critical tool for interpersonal communication and human relations. In fact, I believe the popularity of the telephone and its power are coming back in vogue.

For telephone success, keep these pointers in mind:

1. Return all phone calls within 24 hours.

2. When making a call, ask if it's a good time to talk and follow the lead of the person you're calling.

3. State the purpose of your call and indicate how much time it might take to complete the conversation. If you think the call will take a half-hour, and the other person only has a few minutes, schedule another time to speak.

4. When leaving a message, state your name, purpose, and action needed clearly and succinctly. Most important, when you leave your phone number, speak s-l-o-w-l-y and repeat it. I usually write my number in the air as I say it, which makes me slow down.

5. When calling a contact referral, state your name and who referred you. For example: "Hello, Steve. My name is Andrea Nierenberg. John Baker suggested I call you about customer service training. Is this a good time to talk for a few minutes?"

6. Never do other tasks while you're on the phone. People can hear you typing on your computer or shuffling papers. This shows you're not focused on them. Even if you're just reading your email, you can't concentrate on the person on the phone. One of my clients, Roger, tells a funny story. He was on the phone one day with a client and was reading his emails at the same time. He was reading one from his wife, and when he was ready to say goodbye to his client, he said, "Bye, Honey. I love you!" Remember, doing two things at once is doing neither one well.

Avoid these voicemail mistakes:

1. Don't leave a message unless you have done your research.

2. Don't leave a long message—less is more.

3. Don't be a pest. There's a thin line between being a pest and being persistent.

4. Don't hang up without giving your connection a reason to call you back. Think about the benefit to him or her, and make your message impactful.

5. Don't speak too quickly. Don't be the Roadrunner.

6. Don't give an unrehearsed presentation. Don't mumble or be disorganized.

7. Don't be a bad listener. Pay attention to how the recipient wants information.

Non-networking Events Etiquette

Some people think that nonstop networking means making new contacts anywhere you go. Yes, you want to keep your radar up as you are meeting and connecting with people everywhere in life. Life is networking, and serendipitous opportunities pop up all the time. You have distinct advantages to forming connections at personal events, the main one being that these are people whom you've known most of your life (or their friends and relatives are), so you have a common bond. You can share a built-in sense of trust and understanding that takes much longer to develop with total strangers. However, like everything else you've learned about proper networking, there are right and wrong ways to conduct yourself.

When I want to talk business at these personal events, I keep a few ideas in mind to prevent any embarrassment:

1. Ask permission to follow up at a more appropriate time and opportunity. If I'm speaking to my friend's cousin from St. Louis and I find out she's the head of human resources training, I ask for her contact information and inquire if it's okay to get in touch at a future date and in her preferred method of communication.

2. Remember where you are. If you're at a funeral and happen to find out the person next to you is part of a chamber of commerce organization in your community, think about how to approach being invited to a meeting. Before you disengage, ask the person how best to follow up. Doing anything else would be considered very bad taste.

3. What do you do when someone else wants to talk business? If the other person is pushing to discuss business, graciously suggest, "Who would have thought we'd meet at this event? However, this is probably not the right place to discuss business, so may we connect tomorrow and see when we can discuss this further?"

4. Exchange contact information and get back to the event at hand.

5. Play by the rules. Recognize that there are establishments, such as some private clubs, where conducting business simply is not allowed. Be sure to follow the prescribed behavior.

This has changed a lot, yet always pay attention to the rules so you will be invited back.

Never Keep a Scorecard

It's always better to give than to receive, and things have a way of coming back to the giver. When you look at business leaders, from Andrew Carnegie to Bill Gates, you see how their generosity in giving to others gets them a lot of good press. The same can be true with you. When you give to others, you build up your own personal public image, which goes a long way in developing business contacts now and well into the future.

Here's my advice on keeping track of exchanging favors when it comes to networking:

1. Give more than you get. Even when someone does a favor for you first, think about how you can return it and add something extra. If someone gives you a client lead, think about how you can offer a referral and possibly a gift of some sort to say thanks for the referral and belief.

2. Continually asking for a favor in return is a big mistake. People work hard to refer people they know, like, and trust, and that takes time and relationship building.

3. Have a giving attitude. Mother Teresa is much more famous than most people in the world. She was a giver who looked at life from an eternal perspective. Be a giver, and it will come back to you in better ways than you ever imagined.

4. One of my favorite phrases is, "Give without remembering and receive without forgetting." It was one of my wonderful dad's favorite lines. He lived by it.

Social Media Netiquette

Social media networking is here to stay—and is also changing at lightning speed. The world of social media blends professional and personal communication. Keep these tips in mind to better navigate this terrain:

1. Offer something of value. Is it useful and valuable?

2. Observe people's habits before engaging with them. You may tweet a lot; another person might not. Again, find out preferred methods. The same goes with IM, LinkedIn, and Facebook.

3. Stop and think before you say something you might regret. If in doubt, leave it out.

4. Make your style clear and obvious. Many of us are glued to the Internet; others are not. Be sure to let others know your communication styles also.

5. Resist the temptation to multitask.

6. Be respectful of everyone's content and blogs.

7. Be sure your LinkedIn profile is up-to-date and 100% complete. When connecting or inviting, always add a personal message stating what you have in common and why you would like to connect. LinkedIn is your online professional resume, bio, and brand builder all wrapped into one.

8. On LinkedIn, as with Twitter and other forms of social media, think quality versus quantity.

9. Become known as a thought leader and a true professional networker on LinkedIn. Share, introduce, and stay connected.

10. Remember, all forms of social media and online networking are tools and technology that make the ultimate goal of connecting offline easier. Our primary goal of networking is to build real relationships, face to face and eyeball to eyeball. Social media helps facilitate some of our initial approaches, offers ways to stay in touch and connected, and helps us expand our networks through people we are connected with.

People build trusting relationships with others by looking them in the eye, shaking their hand, and getting that intuitive feeling about them. You can do a lot with social media, yet real chemistry is built offline. The technology is a tool to support what we primarily do in person.

THE "GOLDEN RULES" OF EFFECTIVE NETWORKING

- Respect other people's time; it's a precious commodity for everyone.

- Offer to help others sincerely. People can tell the difference between an opportunist and someone doing a good deed for people.

- Always show and convey appreciation. Gratitude can be in the form of a gift or a simple note of thanks. Either way, do it consistently.

- Share information. If you know something that can help someone, pass it on. Imagine—if previous generations hadn't shared with us their knowledge, the world could not have progressed. I learn something new daily from my universal network. It is a true gift.

- Follow up, follow through, and keep others in the loop: Avoid being a "missing in action" networker. Find a good reason to stay connected, even when there's no "breaking news." Staying in touch and connected is key.

Networking "Are We There Yet?"

Like children traveling in the backseat of a car, we often get impatient having to wait to arrive at our destination. When people network, they often think, "I made contact, I received the person's contact information, and we had lunch. So why is it taking so long to get their business?"

Generating genuine trust with someone takes time and patience. The items at the top of your priority list might not even get an honorable mention on someone else's. Many of my best networking connections that led to new business took years—yes, two to five years. There's no set time, and each situation is different.

Networking works much like bamboo grows. It takes between 4 and 15 years to grow, yet once it starts, it can shoot up to 90 feet in six weeks. What was it doing during that time? It was building a root system, much as we do as we build and expand our networks.

Remember, your personal image has to last over the long term. Think about major brands of consumer products such as Coke, Apple, and Starbucks. They took years to develop into respected names in the minds of consumers. The same is true with you. When you plant your networking "seeds" with business cards or meetings, give them time to grow. Pull an apple off the tree too soon, and it's bitter.

Put your best foot forward as you continue on your networking journey. We looked at establishing your personal brand through making alliances, becoming a resource, and showing respect for others. You know the basic rules of etiquette—although they're constantly changing, you got the basics here. In the next chapter, we tackle one of the most interesting and popular aspects of networking: how introverts can network effectively. If you or someone you know is shy when it comes to meeting new people, get ready. You'll be surprised to discover that introverts have more going for them in networking than one might think.

Exercise: Self-Evaluation for Your Best Networking Traits

Take a look in the networking mirror to see what about you shines and what you should focus on when you network more frequently. Here's one exercise to help you:

1. Make a list of three things you're comfortable doing in your business and personal life. You might say, "I'm a good listener," "I enjoy setting up meetings," or "I always send people information to help them do their jobs better."

2. Now take those behaviors and look at the strengths you bring to your work and your networking opportunities. For example, as a good listener, I'm able to hear the most important information on a call and then direct the person to other resources that can help the most. How do the things you wrote down distinguish you from others? You might find that you're more skillful than anyone else in your department in building relationships with people from other cultures.

"For lack of training, they lacked knowledge; for lack of knowledge, they lacked confidence; for lack of confidence, they lacked victory."
—Julius Caesar

8

The Introvert's Networking Advantage: The Quiet Way to Success

My friend Jorge goes to the gym early every morning and sees the same three people almost every day. He exchanges a brief hi with two of them, but never the third, and the chatting has never gone beyond the weather. He doesn't know the names of any of them, or why they come early to the gym, whether they have jobs they go to later, or anything about them.

He figures that they, like himself, would feel crowded or intruded upon if the conversation got more than superficially casual. And the woman might even think he was hitting on her. So he keeps a space or distance between them. He says it's because he's shy, an introvert. Plus—and, mind you, this is important—he has no incentive to know them better because he can envision no future moment when knowing them better might benefit him or them.

He is probably wrong. What if he's missing a connection that could someday lead to a significant business or personal breakthrough? What if just knowing them might make his life a little richer and build his networking skills for general usage?

If you relate to Jorge and know yourself to be more introverted than extroverted, you might benefit from considering Cyndi's story, which I share next.

A Quiet Networker's Success Story

When the door opened and I walked in to start a business development meeting with several executives at a firm, Cyndi clearly struck me with her approach to communication. I had heard beforehand that she was a rising star in the corporation, yet her challenge lay in the fact that she was unable to look me—or her colleagues, for that matter—in the eye. Her shoulders were slumped, she made no small talk, and as she started to talk about some of her projects, she gave just the facts in a monotone voice. Then like a lightning rod, she spoke about her newest project, which was an initiative she was starting. It was as if a different person emerged from the Cyndi we first met. Her voice changed, she came "alive," and she spoke in such a way as to paint a real word picture of what she was looking to accomplish.

What happened that transformed her from seemingly shy and withdrawn to a passionate communicator about her work? Bottom line, Cyndi is an introvert. As I got to know her, she explained some of the challenges she faced in the business world. She felt she had to be "on" continually to sell herself, which she didn't like at all. As we began to talk and work together, she saw that she could keep her own style and personality and still "market herself"—she could communicate her ideas and strengths in a positive way. As her perceptions changed, her actions did, too, along with the way her colleagues and management perceived her.

I've known Cyndi for 10 years now, and she is currently a senior vice president of another large corporation, where she runs a whole business unit and frequently speaks around the country. When I visit with her, she always goes back to the time when we first met, when she never thought she would be able to come out of her shell.

One way that I always spot the Cyndis, Jorges, or other quiet networkers and communicators when I do a workshop is by the response I get from my first question on my prework questionnaire: "When you hear the word *networking*, what immediately comes to mind? How do you feel about networking for your career advancement?"

This icebreaker is very telling. People pour out their feelings, and what I usually hear is: "I hate it. I'm not good at it," or "I don't like having to sell myself" or "It's not me."

If you're like Cyndi, Jorge, or any of those people who feel uncomfortable extending yourself into what you view as other people's space, then the first step is to realize that networking is a state of mind. You continually network in the way you interact, connect, and build on your relationships, regardless of your style. What you might view as just the way you are or as a personal weakness might actually be a strength you can use to your advantage, to get started on the road to positive personal marketing. There's a way even you, as an introvert, can work in the most passionate and organized way, follow up with efficiency, and develop alliances with others in the organization who will market you.

The Introvert's Business Advantage

Did you know that Albert Einstein, Socrates, Mahatma Gandhi, Angelina Jolie, and Colin Powell are all introverts? It might surprise you to find out that some very famous introverts out there have achieved great success and left their mark on the world. The success they achieved came from being able to take what's inside and bring it to the outside, to share it with the world. Extroverts are naturally good at this—they're wired to live outside themselves. Introverts, however, need more internal time. They also need a little understanding of themselves and need to adopt some techniques to move what's inside to the outside.

Studies have shown that introverts account for 25% of the population (you guessed it, extroverts comprise the other 75%). Table 8-1 shows the main characteristics of introverts and extroverts. To be able to interact with the majority, if you're an introvert, you have to learn what your strengths are so you can be heard and fully appreciated. Here are some of the most important strengths introverts have in business.

Table 8-1 Characteristics of Introverts and Extroverts—Which Are You?

Introverts	Extroverts
Recharge by being alone	Energize by contact with others
Prefer to listen	Are talkative
Are thoughtful and reflective	Are action oriented
Focus well	Multitask
Can be mistaken for being aloof	Seen as friendly and outgoing
Need time and space for themselves	Like to surround themselves with others
Keep their thoughts to themselves	Can "think out loud" through talking

Introverts	Extroverts
React internally	React externally
Are quiet	Are expressive
Don't enjoy small talk	Love small talk
Listen first, speak later	Speak first, listen later

Strategy and Organization Come Naturally

Let's say your company wants to be the number one provider of widgets in the country. First, it needs to make production plans; then it needs to establish and send out a sales team, build out its social media channels, and create marketing and public relations plans. When many ideas have to be considered, assimilated, and organized, give this work to an introvert. Introverts like to put puzzles together and make them work in a synergistic way.

An extrovert is often the first person out there shaking hands and making initial connections, but an introvert might need to busily work away at a "master plan" to systematically achieve his or her networking goals. Days might pass before an introvert actually starts making calls. Each approach has its benefits, and neither is wrong. Extroverts can generally build multiple relationships more quickly, which energizes them more and more. Introverts, on the other hand, intuitively know that they have only so much "people energy" available, so they usually create a systematic plan to get the job done.

Problem Solving

Because of their temperament, some introverts can be very intense problem solvers. This intensity is a definite advantage. For instance, introverts process all the pros and cons of a situation, and they intuitively know where the snags will be. This can be a great asset when networking. Whereas an extrovert might be able to offer a variety of possible solutions in a sales call, the introvert is often able to pinpoint the obvious solution on the spot because of his or her ability to solve problems.

I recently benefited from the problem-solving skills of one of my introverted associates. I was telling three clients at lunch about my great fortune in possibly having CNN interview me for an international event. I said that it might be in front of the United Nations building, and while I was talking about it, two of the three people were right there with me, full of energy and enthusiasm.

Then Karen, the head of the department, whom I had noticed was sitting there pensively, quietly asked me, "Have you checked it out with the UN? Do you have all the details from them? Have you considered the insurance issues?" She continued her mental checklist of questions in a very organized manner.

I realized immediately that, no, I hadn't done or even thought about any of these things. I was too excited about the actual happening!

Thank goodness for her detailed, organized, quiet approach. At first I felt as if my bubble had burst. Then I realized that she was right, and her approach and information were going to save me from a lot of headaches and panic. I learned not to get too excited and was saying a silent "thank goodness" that I work with a very organized and processed team whose members made sure that all details were taken care of beforehand.

Good Readers, Good Writers, Good Listeners

Let's say you run a company and want to tap the strength that introverts bring to your staff.

If I want to find out what's going on with one of my introverted business associates, I often ask the person whether he or she is reading any good books. The person usually answers yes. A passionate discussion often follows. Books are the introvert's best friends. Many introverts are very well read and have a broad understanding about a variety of topics. This is due to their natural need for more alone time, and that's exactly what it takes to get through a number of books a year.

If your company is going to a networking event and several large potential clients are going to be there, assign researching these companies to an introvert. The thrill of getting paid to go online to find the latest news on these prospects will almost be too much for the introvert to handle! Have the person put together a mini summary of each potential client for you and the other salespeople, and it will be a great resource for your entire team.

Introverts often feel much more at ease using the written word to communicate their ideas. If they're presented with the option of making a pitch in person or writing a 20-page proposal, the proposal almost always wins. For personal communication, email is often an introvert's best friend. Here introverts can lay out all their ideas clearly and in the exact order they prefer. Writing also allows introverts to nuance their communication, using exact word choices to precisely spell out their thoughts and feelings. Extroverts can also effectively communicate through the written word, but introverts should use this to their advantage in networking. If they can use email communication to get their networking process going, this will give them a great advantage when it comes to making the actual in-person connections.

Your introverted employees' ability to listen could be their greatest asset. Extroverts often find it amazing that introverts can sit and listen to another person for a long time. Extroverts' exuberance naturally makes them want to jump in and make a contribution. However, they often miss or do not share points because there isn't enough time for anyone else to communicate. For introverts, listening comes a little easier. In fact, they might just want to listen and then go back, process the information, and schedule another meeting to talk about solutions. Especially with sensitive clients, introverts can make a great impression with their listening ability. Introverts should know how rare a good listener is, and they should know the difference this makes to the customer. Customers often emotionally embrace their introverted vendors because they feel so cared for when others listen to them.

Dale Carnegie, the grand master of communications skills, always said in his classes that one of the top human relations principles is to let the other person do a great deal of talking—that is, listen to the person! This is music to introverts' ears, for they would rather listen than talk.

Think back to a time when you were at a meeting or event, and as you were introduced to someone, you asked some open-ended questions. What happened? Most likely, the other person started talking and sharing, and you most likely jumped in with other prompter questions. Before you knew it, you were getting ready to leave, and after your exit strategy, the other person probably commented to the host, or at least thought, "I enjoyed talking with you so much. What an interesting person!"

Although you didn't say much, you did do the following:

- Asked open-ended questions
- Paid attention to what the person said
- Showed your interest with your eyes and ears

This is the power of good communication and rapport-building skills. For any cynics reading this and thinking, "That seems manipulative," it is *only* if it's done insincerely. As I always say about anything we discuss in this book, it must be done with the utmost of sincerity, credibility, and character.

EMBRACED OR THE EMBRACER?

Think back to a time when you connected with someone at a business meeting or function.

- Did you approach the other person, or did that person approach you?
- If you were approached, how did it feel?
- What did you think of the embracer?
- How did the conversation go, and who seemed to control it? Or was anyone controlling it?
- If you were the embracer, how did you feel, and what was the reaction of the person you approached?
- How did the conversation go?

In a survey I've conducted at several workshops, I've asked this question after the initial ice breaker exercise in which two people meet and begin a conversation: Who approached whom, and how did it feel?

We've gotten into a lot of discussion about it, and people have overwhelmingly said, "It's a nice feeling to have someone approach or embrace me."

It *is* a nice feeling. Reach out of your comfort zone and make a note to start being the "embracer," or initiator, at the next few meetings, functions, and events you attend. Do this for the next month, and keep track of the results. It could be going into a staff meeting and walking over to greet a colleague from another department, or it could be at your next industry cocktail party where you approach some of the strategic people we talked about previously.

At the end of the month, look at the new contacts and reconnections you made by taking that first step!

Passionate Conversationalists

Now, if you're an introvert, verbal communication might be a challenge. You tend to process your ideas and feelings internally. Extroverts often *need* to verbalize ideas and feelings to get them sorted out. This can be a great advantage for the extrovert, especially in fast-paced environments where answers are needed *now*. However, you, as an introvert, should be encouraged that you can make sure your ideas are heard and considered in a number of ways. When you are passionate and knowledgeable about a given topic and have found a comfortable venue for sharing your views, you can be a quite brilliant communicator and highly effective networker.

Caring

It's hard to say that one temperament style is more caring than another. It's usually a matter of personal choice. The point is that even though introverts might hesitate to share as many of their feelings as their extroverted counterparts, they certainly can care about a situation or business decision just as intensely. When introverts say a few caring words, they have been chosen carefully, and each word has great emotional value attached to it. An introvert might use 10 words to get his or her feelings across to someone, whereas an extrovert might use a hundred words to share the same emotion. Both are valid ways to show emotion and need to be appreciated for their different styles.

If you're an introverted networker, you might want to go the extra mile and send a card or quick email later to reinforce that you truly care about the situation.

Introverts Are Great Networkers

Introverts are quieter by nature, yet they can be great networkers. They just do it differently from the other 75% of the world. The important thing for introverts is to have a networking plan, to provide structure for verbalizing their feelings and ideas most effectively. Introverts' ideas and input are needed; the idea is to work within their own nature. This means being comfortable with the fact that they network differently and have their own style, which might be different from the majority's. Personal marketing and networking are also just as critical for introverts, of course. The key is to grow in the areas you find challenging and to have a toolkit of skills that will help you get your valuable ideas out to the world around you.

Growing Your Introverted Networking Skills

I usually can spot the people who dread coming to my session on networking. How? From the survey I send out in advance. Here are some of the responses I get to the question "What comes to mind when you hear the word *networking*?": "It's selling, and I don't sell." "I'm not good at it—I don't like asking people for things." "It's sleazy." The list goes on, and I can usually pick out these people as soon as I enter the room.

People in the session come to realize that all of us have our own best practices when it comes to networking and personal marketing. However we connect these dots, positive alliances and advocates can help us with what we want to create.

Determine the Areas That Are Most Uncomfortable

What area of networking are you most uncomfortable with? Is it starting conversations? Making small talk? Giving presentations? Cold calling? Think about as many different networking opportunities as you can remember from the past. These can be in business settings, at social events, or at your place of worship. List the top three "I strongly dislike doing" areas of networking. Post them on your computer screen or phone. These are the areas that we're simply going to take some time to learn more about.

Develop a Learning Plan

Now that you have your top three "fear factor" topics of networking, it's time to start turning these into positives in your mind. I'm not saying that you'll ever love doing these things. But you can get to the point that you will no longer avoid these areas, and you'll have these skills in your networking toolkit to use when the time is right.

Make a commitment to do some reading, go to a seminar, or get personal coaching in these areas. Work this into your yearly plan. I suggest giving yourself at least 3 months, and not more than 12, to gradually get some training in these areas. Of course, this depends on how critically you need to get these skills in place. If you're developing a new sales territory and need to increase the business by 400% by next year, then an abbreviated period will have to do. The next step is to start to be purposeful in implementing this learning in your daily work life.

Set Goals for Personal Meetings, Business Parties, and Events

You've become familiar with the three areas of networking you'd like to conquer. I hope the books, articles, webinars, and personal coaching have been helpful and encouraging. You've seen that this is something you can do with a little focused work and effort. Now the challenge is to set some attainable goals that will help you get started using these newfound networking techniques. You want to set goals for personal meetings, business parties, and events.

Often the hardest part is knowing how and where to start. For example, a client of mine, Doug, was overwhelmed. He knew he had to get out in the field and attend new functions and associations. Yet there were so many functions that he could literally go to something every day. I always stress quality versus quantity, and it certainly applies here.

Doug made a list of the top priorities he wanted to get out of the associations he joined. He knew that unless he got involved and went to meetings, it would be a waste of time and money. He started by listing the top 10 organizations from his local chamber of commerce and an industry organization to which his clients belonged.

He used the 2-2-2 strategy (attend two meetings; meet two people and exchange business cards; and arrange two follow-up meetings for breakfast, lunch, or coffee) that we discussed previously. He set a goal of going to at least two meetings of the group, meeting two people, exchanging cards, and arranging two follow-up meetings. Therefore, whether he joined the group or not, he had learned something and had expanded his network by two.

He then narrowed his list to three organizations in which he knew he had a strong interest and whose mission he respected. He carefully cultivated people he knew would like him and got involved in committees to become known in the organization. Over one year, Doug was able to incorporate these three organizations into his life with consistency, ease, and a positive impact.

Write down the associations in which you'd like to invest your time and money to help your career and continued business development. What will be your time commitment each month? What will you do to become known in the group? (*Hint:* Serve on a committee, offer to speak, or write an article for the newsletter.)

With practice, these skills will start to become second nature. The key is to stay focused and committed. Again, we're not talking about changing an introverted nature. We want to gently push ourselves out of our comfort zones, honoring who we are while at the same time stretching beyond ourselves to reach out to others with all that is inside us.

Start in Your Comfort Zone and Work Your Way Out

Who are the people you're most comfortable with? Make a list of family members, friends, and business associates with whom you can establish a networking home base. These people are your comfort zone, so this is where you want to start using your newly developed skills. These people will be the most forgiving when you take some risks and make mistakes. Remember, mistakes are natural. Be easy on yourself. Imagine learning to walk—and soon you'll be running! These people will also give you honest feedback. If the situation is appropriate, you might even tell them about your quest to build up these skills. They will be impressed that you are taking proactive steps to help yourself and still be yourself.

The challenge here is to get out of your comfort zone quickly. When you've had some success networking with those you're comfortable with, it's time to take some bigger risks. The best time to take a risk is when you've had a success. You're at the top of your game, and your confidence is high. Is there a client you've been wanting to call, yet haven't been able to? Now is your time. Go for it! You might not strike gold on the first hit; the goal is to build habits that will make you successful in the long run.

Body Language

As we discussed previously, body language and visual image are 55% of our communication. Introverts need to be especially aware of posture. It's been said that posture is the foundation of your presence. Make sure you look up and stand tall. If you're not in the habit of doing this, it might seem awkward at first. Soon it will become second nature, and you'll see that others find you much more approachable. Then they'll reflect the positive feeling you radiate back to you in their conversation.

Eye Contact

Introverted men should especially be sure to make eye contact. Women, both introverted and extroverted, tend to have less trouble with this. For most men, the tendency is not to relate face to face; side to side is much more comfortable for some. Most of your interpersonal networking will be face to face, though, so make sure you stay focused on the person talking to you. This might not feel completely natural at first, so try to avoid "locking onto" the other person with your eyes. This is where it feels as if someone is trying to drill holes in your head. It's completely normal to look around a bit, yet your attention should always bounce back to the other person's eyes. And remember to look at the "third eye," the space on the forehead right between the eyes.

Creating an Introvert-Friendly Networking Plan

Introverts' networking success can greatly increase with a plan. As I mentioned earlier, this will come easily for most introverts, with their organizing and strategizing temperament. Everyone's plan is different.

Here I have attempted to give you some ideas that you can incorporate into your own personal plan, if you're an introvert. The important part of the plan is to maximize your strengths, yet stretch yourself in areas that tend to not come as naturally. Consistency will be your best friend in following your plan. I recommend that you ask the following questions in making your networking plan:

- "What is my ultimate goal for networking? Is it finding new business? Developing current accounts? Becoming known in my industry or in one that I serve? Building a stronger internal team and developing new alliances? What are my personal strengths as an introvert, and how can I maximize these in networking toward my goal? Are they organizational skills, writing skills, or problem-solving skills?"

- "What is my strategy for blending my strengths in areas in which I need to stretch? How much time will I spend networking using social media and electronic communication? How much time will I spend networking on the phone? Do I have goals for myself in this? How much time will I spend networking in person? Again, what are my goals for these types of events? How can I stretch myself in this and also honor who I am as an introvert?"

- "How can I integrate all forms of networking into a system that will work for what I do? Will I use an opener letter before I call my contact? When appropriate, will I always try to get an in-person appointment when I am networking over the telephone? How can I integrate my organizational strengths to be more prepared for when I am in a person-to-person situation? How might I use my writing strengths to add to what I present in person?"

- "What books and educational or coaching resources might I tap to continue to sharpen the areas in which I am strong while not neglecting the areas that challenge me? Do I have a yearly schedule for this? Have I set some goals on reading articles or books that will help me improve this year?"

- "Do I need to include in my plan regular reminders about areas of personal development, such as making eye contact, having good posture, using proper etiquette, and/or developing character?"

Let's walk through some of the ways you can maximize your introverted temperament to develop new business and build your networking skills.

Maximizing Your Writing Strengths

If you're in a fast-paced or highly interactive environment, you'll want to conserve your social energy, to avoid being tapped out when you really need it. One technique that can work well for introverted networkers is maximizing the amount of written communication in their networking approach. A caution up front: The idea is to maximize this strength, yet not totally rely on the computer and social media, because it might be more comfortable than being face to face or talking on the phone with people. You'll still need to be personally out there as much as possible. Nothing takes the place of an in-person meeting.

Writing for Publications and the Web

Introverts can maximize their networking effectiveness by raising their profiles by writing articles for magazines, newsletters, and newspapers; guest posting on blogs; and posting on social media sites.

When I'm looking through industry e-zines, I often see if they take contributed articles. If it looks like they do, I email or call the editors to see if they're interested in an article. As they tell you about the topics they might be covering in upcoming issues, you might say that you'd like to send a one-paragraph proposal for an article you could write. Or if you have an idea right there on the phone that you can really write about with proficiency, pitch it and see what they have to say.

If they don't need an article at that time, let them know that you'd like to send them a letter with your information, in case they ever need to interview someone in your field. I usually include a short, casual letter thanking them for their time and offering my time as a resource in case they need someone to talk about something in their industry. I might also include an article I've written or other articles for which I have been interviewed. If I think there's some potential with the publication, I add it to my follow-up plan and find ways to keep in contact periodically.

It's often easier to get published on the web than it is in print. My articles usually run on a magazine or trade organization's e-zine, and I track them with Google Alerts. And remember to thank all for the connections you make. This is part of the thank you chain I introduce in the next part of the book; it works well and should be a consistent part of the plan.

Put your articles on your own website, tweet them, and, in some cases, post them on Facebook. You might have to make them less industry specific to reach a more general audience, and this is easy to do. In fact, it's possible to change the same article to fit a wide variety of industries. Remember, the material is fresh to the accountants, even if you already used it in the cosmetic industry. Just make sure you take the time to research each industry and customize your article using industry-specific language and phrases.

Another up-and-coming way to get your name out using the written word is to capitalize on the current fascination with blogs. What is a blog? A blog, short for *weblog*, is basically a diary or log of your thoughts about a particular topic that's posted on the Web for the whole world to see. Blogs are especially useful if you deal with cutting-edge news. For instance, if you're a political consultant, people can go to your blog and see if you have anything in there on the President's new initiative to reform Social Security. If you're an expert in your industry, or even if you're not, you can start a blog to get your thoughts out to see what people think. From there, you can set up a chat room for them to respond to your thoughts, or they can simply email you if they would like to talk further. This can be a great way to make contacts on the Web. If your blog is particularly good, people will start to add it to the Links page of their websites. Soon you can become the "expert" in your particular area of interest as the momentum of your blog grows on the Web. Today everyone is an author and has a blog—find a way to make yours stand out.

Online Networking Communities

Online communities are where *you* have to be. The enormous opportunities made available by all online communities could take a book to explain. Be sure you have a LinkedIn presence, set up a Twitter account, and know about Facebook; when appropriate, set up a business fan page. Be sure to post on LinkedIn groups, and ask and answer questions to gain visibility and get known for your expertise and knowledge.

Please go ahead and post it. This can often open up a conversation online and then lead to face-to-face discussions. I am always an advocate of real live people getting together face to face—there's no greater form of communication. Try what's comfortable for you—it will be a great way to meet people.

Social Media Networking

Introverted people tend to agree that online they become "online extroverts." The same people who say it's challenging to introduce themselves in a room full of people feel at ease striking up a conversation on LinkedIn, Twitter, or Facebook. The whole awkward feeling seems to be removed.

This is the best foot in the door; however, as with anything, use these vehicles wisely. They're tools for our interpersonal communication. Make every interaction personal. My biggest pet peeve is getting LinkedIn invitations that just have the default message to link in. Take the time to say something to introduce yourself for either connecting or reconnecting. I do this with each invitation I send out and then do the same when I reply. Make the message personal—for example, I might use, "Great to link in from Andrea Nierenberg" in the subject line and then add a line or two on something that I read from the person's profile. Your response rate will rise dramatically.

I do send out a monthly tip-of-the-month e-zine that often gets forwarded throughout a company. And to a variety of people, this has been a great way for an introvert like me to also start to connect with people I might not have otherwise met.

With every reply you get, send a personal note of thanks, no matter what. The idea is to get the conversation started, not close the deal. You might just follow up with someone you'd like to get to know because you saw the person mentioned in the newspaper or trade journal, heard about his or her recent success, or thought the person could benefit from a product or service you offer. You might have seen it on LinkedIn, Google Alerts, or any material that arrives in your inbox. You might not always get a response, but that's okay.

The next step is to get on the phone and talk with the person. Then at least you have an opener: "I'm following up on the email I sent you about such and such." Usually the response is positive, such as, "Oh, I was meaning to get back to you...." You might even put in your email that you'll follow up via phone, if that's appropriate—better yet, ask for the person's preferred method of communication for next steps. Again, the goal is to find common ground and eventually have a chance to talk with others face to face if you can really help them with a need, be a resource, or learn something from each other.

Opener Letters

Another technique to get things started is to use the opener letter. After I've determined whom I want to contact, I try to figure out how to customize an email that might open some doors when I call the person to follow up. Usually I try to work one type of business or industry at a time. For example, one month I concentrate on my prospects in the legal profession. During the following months, I might focus on real estate, cosmetics, and fashion and ad agencies, in that order. As I work on each industry, I do my best to follow its current trends by reading online blogs, journals, association newsletters, and, of course, Google Alerts that are specific to that industry. I do this between appointments or while traveling. When I know I'll be writing my opener letter for a particular industry, I make sure to take written and mental notes as I do my reading.

Does a current trend make it possible for me to help people in an industry improve their communication skills in some way? Even new legislation that might affect a particular industry could provide a lead on where my services are needed. The most effective way to write the opener letter is to know what's going on in the particular companies you're writing to. When I'm writing to an industry for the first time, I research only the top 10 companies I want to reach out to. This usually gives me a good idea of what might be happening in all the companies I'm writing to. The key is not to pretend you are *the* expert in your letter—just show them that you're informed and ready to let them know how you can be of genuine service to them. We have so much online research at our fingertips—we all expect people who connect with us to be totally informed. As introverts, we know this is key in our communication.

No formula dictates how to write an opener letter, although you might find some samples or examples on the Internet. The basic letter has an introduction, a body, and a conclusion or point of action you'd like the recipient to take. Take some time to introduce yourself, point to your product or service, and identify how you think you might be able to work together. In the body, you might include some industry-specific details that grab the reader's attention, along with possible solutions that you could provide. In the closing, let the recipient know that you will follow up on the phone, and give a specific time frame for when you will be doing this. Then make sure you follow up within that time. This formula works also when you're reaching out for an exploratory interview or even when you're connecting with someone within your global firm. The template and basic formula are the same—what you put in will be unique and yours alone.

By the way, you can also add a postscript to the letter. People often skip down to the P.S. to see what the email or letter is about, without reading the whole thing. The idea is to capture your main idea and reiterate it in one or two sentences. For example: "P.S. Please remember, I'm offering a free consultation this month on how the art and science of networking can help you find, grow, and keep the best business relationships."

Using a Script

When you do get someone on the phone, ask whether the person received your letter. If not, or if the person hasn't gotten to it yet, have a script ready to keep you from stumbling. Go through in your head all the different answers you anticipate, from "Yes" to "I'm too busy right now," and have some idea of what you will say to each response.

You might have a few questions ready about the firm or some interesting ways others in the industry have benefited from your product or service. If the person can't talk at the moment, which is usually the case, ask when you can follow up. Be prepared that, 99% of the time, you will go right into voicemail, so think in advance with your script what you will say that will give the recipient a reason to listen and take your next call and correspondence. Remember to be as gracious as possible; we all have gotten calls from people at the wrong time. Put yourself in the other person's shoes. Above all, be friendly, courteous, and respectful. The person might be busy now, and later when you call, when the person needs something you have, he or she will probably show a much warmer side.

POST IT AND PRACTICE

Be prepared, write a script, and practice. I call it P.O.S.T.

P   Prepare your script in advance.

O   Organize your thoughts and what you want to say. Less is more.

S   Succeed with your own system.

T   Take your time.

Follow-Up

Follow-up is key. As I like to say, after all is said and done, much more is said than done. Email your follow-up immediately. Make sure you email a week before your meet-up, to make contact, and then contact the person again the day before the meeting, to confirm. Email articles from LinkedIn and all the different sites and information you receive. Always send a follow-up email thanking the person for the time he or she did give you. Then, while your call is still fresh in the person's mind, elaborate briefly—only one paragraph, at most—on why you were calling and what action you would like to take with the person. You might ask for more information about how the person selects vendors or internal partners, or what the person does when he or she needs a custom solution in the area in which you specialize.

Person to Person

Person-to-person connecting can often be the hardest area for the introvert. However, whether you are an accountant, dentist, author, or artist, personal marketing is the key to giving what you have to give to a world that needs it. Personal marketing is about putting your best foot forward in front of other people.

I've already mentioned many of the challenges and strengths you possess as an introvert. You're known in your field for your expertise through your written articles and personal publicity. You've maximized your introvert traits by using social media to make good contacts. You've done your phone work, and now here you are, face to face with your contact. Perhaps this is a sales presentation, a "meet and greet" where your company comes in and does a presentation on your products or services, or a networking event where, by "chance," you've run into your contact. Regardless, now is the time to really connect with others in the most personal of ways, face to face.

The important point is to be yourself. That's right—you can only be one person, and that's yourself! Just put your best foot forward and let those ideas and goals come out; you'll be surprised at how positive a response you get from others when they see your passion for what you are doing. Remember, you do have good ideas and want to help people where you can. You're a giver, and you want the opportunity to learn and to serve. You are naturally the internalizer. Your gift is to process situations and challenges from within and create new paradigms for the outside world to use. Even though introverts make up 25% to 35% of the population, the other 75% of the population needs what you can contribute. Let them know who you are and what you can offer, and I believe you'll eventually see all your thoughts and dreams come to life.

Even if the people you meet aren't an exact match for what you do in business, focus on them and learn something from them. You might have to politely break conversation and move on in your networking, yet you'll have connected with the person and feel good about it. This respectful treatment of others will come back to you in many ways. Believe me, as I've told the story before, when I, an introvert, first came to New York City after graduating from college years ago, I knew no one. Now I have many colleagues, clients, connections, and friends in every realm of life and business. Your network takes time to build and is continually growing, and I am richer in my experiences for it.

Small Talk for Introverts

The biggest challenge for most introverts in face-to-face communication is small talk. Small talk is simply the social lubricant that gets conversations started.

You've probably been in group discussions where the speaker comes up with an icebreaker to get people talking. This is all small talk; only it's in the context of two individuals instead of a group. Some introverts think there's something wrong or less than honest in making small talk. This need not be the case. You can make small talk with people while holding on to your integrity. Just be honest when you speak and respectfully withhold your opinion if you disagree. Most people won't press you too hard to agree with them when you're first getting to know them. If they do and you're uncomfortable, simply excuse yourself politely and find someone else to talk with. This will apply to maybe 1% of the people you run into; the other 99% will be just as eager as you are to make good connections and learn something along the way.

Of course, some practical tips are especially helpful for the introverted networker. Earlier, I mentioned using a script. This can be a huge help for the quieter networker and will give you something to get the conversation started. For the introvert, I also suggest having a few questions or comments ready as conversation starters. Extroverts tend to have an easier time finding things to talk about. Introverts will want to map these out in their head beforehand. Consider this example of a mental list:

- Ask what others thought of the speaker tonight.

- Ask why they came to this particular event.

- Ask how this event compares to other, similar events they've been to.

Remember that 75% of the people you talk to love to talk. All you have to do is ask a few questions, and the conversation will flow on and on—and they'll walk away thinking you're a brilliant conversationalist. And the fact is, because you're such a good listener, you are! And you will have learned some new things along the way. Listening is the key ingredient to great networking, and introverts, as a whole, do this with almost perfection.

Of course, be ready with your 30-second introduction when other people ask you about yourself. If you sense they're truly interested in what you're saying, be bold and let them see your passion, whatever it might be. This can be a great way to go from the small talk stage to really forming a personal relationship with someone. And remember the four must-do's: Learn something, give something, take something, and find a way to follow up.

Partnering with Extroverts

One way to capitalize on the natural skills of quieter networkers is to encourage them to work with extroverts who will naturally be good at making introductions and getting the conversation going. While this is happening, your introvert has picked up on the mood of each person, has analyzed the potential for doing business, and is thinking about how he or she can solve the potential customer's problem. The introverted executive has probably also figured out the personality style of the prospect or new connection. When the conversation naturally reaches the point where a solution is needed, it's time for the introvert to take the stage. The extrovert will need to defer to the introvert as the "expert" and move out of the way. This is especially effective at business events when engaging companies that you'd like to do business with yet have never interacted with.

Tag-Team Sales Call

Back from a sales call, Steve and Bill had totally different takes on what happened. Steve, the extrovert, walked into the manager's office saying, "What a great call! We aced it! They're definitely going to go forward with the proposal." Bill, on the other hand, looked puzzled as he expressed the opposite point of view and scratched his head in bewilderment. He was thinking, "Did I actually just participate in the same meeting Steve did?" Of course he did—what happened was that these two people looked at the meeting in completely different ways.

When Steve was telling the client, Rochelle, all about their suggested proposal, he was talking without listening as much and wasn't paying attention to details or body language. He was focused only on what he was saying, not on the nonverbal gaze he was getting from Rochelle. Bill, on the other hand, paid close attention to Rochelle and saw how she stiffened every time Steve blurted out another claim about why their product was the best and why they had to move forward. Bill watched her get interrupted if she tried to speak until she finally sat in total silence waiting for the meeting to end. Because her style was also that of the introvert, she smiled and said "Thank you." As she ushered them to the door, she said she'd think about it and that she had to dash off to another meeting.

Steve interpreted the meeting as a definite sale, where Bill saw it as a definite no-go. What could each of them have done differently to help the other and create a winning situation? Steve needed to carry his intangible toolkit—he needed to bring his ears and eyes. If he had observed Rochelle's body language, stopped talking, and started listening, he could have asked open-ended, high-gain questions.

Bill, on the other hand, with his strong intuitive and detail skills, saw what was happening. If he could have jumped in at the appropriate time to save his colleague by asking a question or giving a fact based on the research he had done before the meeting, he could have turned the meeting around. He was totally organized before he left the office and had a script in place, complete with potential objections and answers.

Steve and Bill needed to prepare before the meeting, go over the possible scenarios to decide what to do, and look at the situation from both vantage points. "Tag-team" meetings with opposite personalities can produce amazing results. Each person sees the situation differently; with some preparation and time management, together they can work wonders.

Look at your own situation; then go to your next meeting with one of your extroverted colleagues and plan in advance. Write down and discuss your strengths and areas in which each of you is challenged. After the meeting, debrief what did or didn't happen and how you can move forward and learn from each other.

Recharging for Introverts

You might be thinking that all this talk about personal marketing is starting to wear you out. That's okay! It's just the way introverts are wired. Introverts need to take time to recharge and not feel guilty. Remember, you're processing things at a much deeper level than most people do. This is your strength, but it's also a great challenge because you need the time to disengage from your external environment to give your internal self time to think, resolve, and rest.

The lunch meeting can be a great time to get business done. I recommend using mealtimes as often as possible to get to know people. This is one way we humans really connect with each other—by eating together. "Let's get a coffee" is also a very effective way to take things from the purely business to a more personal level. However, if you're an introvert, you need to plan some time for yourself throughout the day, if possible. If you can do this over lunch with a good book or when watching a webinar or catching up on emails, great! If you need to use your lunches to conduct business, then I strongly suggest taking a couple 10-minute breaks in the morning and afternoon to recharge. This can be spent simply by reading an e-zine, going for a quick walk, or even taking a short power nap (5 minutes—I don't want you getting fired for napping at work)! Many firms, like Google and Facebook, have created relaxation rooms for their employees to decompress and regain energy and creativity. You might not think you have the time to do these things, yet in the end, you'll get more done every day by keeping yourself recharged.

Quiet, Yet Quite Successful

As I have tried to stress, in many ways, introverts rule. They make excellent networkers and engage in their own powerful and strategic way. Their natural ability to process things internally and their great listening skills make them valuable assets to any team or business, especially when teamed with extroverts who know and value their abilities.

Introverts' intrinsic desire to have things organized and to formulate a plan often sets them apart from the crowd. In time, it makes them very successful at whatever they set out to do. For many introverts, writing is a hidden talent they need to take advantage of. Writing lists for assignments, writing names of various contacts, and devising a networking plan are all safe and comfortable activities for introverts. Then they can sit down by themselves, review the lists, and evaluate their next steps in connecting with people face to face. Remember to use your internal passion to your advantage in person-to-person conversations. People love to talk with someone who's passionate about something they're also passionate about. Always stretch yourself, while honoring who you are, and take a break now and again to recharge. That way, you'll be your best for yourself and for your client.

TWO GREAT NETWORKERS, TWO DIFFERENT STYLES

When I visited my lifelong friends Trudy and Bill, who are also my godparents, I was reminded again of the networking strengths of both extroverts and introverts. Trudy meets and greets, talks, and acts friendly to everyone. She's also the first to stand up and give a short speech. Bill, conversely, would be content to hold a conversation with just a few people. He sometimes looked as if he was holding court when people gathered around him waiting to hear what he would say, because anything he said was important. He was intelligent and articulate. Together they were a powerful couple and both superb networkers, yet each would say, "I'm not a networker; I'm just being who I am." Of course, this is the key. They both have superb interpersonal skills that have brought them a lifetime of friends and contacts. At this writing, Trudy and Bill were married 68 years, and she's still going strong at 93!

Consider these six ways introverts can get networking results:

1. Take quiet time. It's your time to restore and recharge, and often creativity emerges.

2. Prepare. Work ahead of time to lay out the steps for the results you want to achieve.

3. Listen closely. Utilize your strengths as an engaged listener, and be totally focused.

4. Have a focused conversation. This combines listening and purposeful talking.

5. Write. Think, process, compose, and create.

6. Use social media thoughtfully and purposefully through the channels of LinkedIn, Facebook, Twitter, YouTube, and everything else emerging daily. Start by taking 10 to 15 minutes a day to network through social media and see what develops over time. Focus on a few sites only—don't spread yourself too thin.

These need to be your networking "I am" statements—and keep adding to this list.

- I am prepared and focused.
- I am a good listener.
- I am approachable.
- I am interested in others and what they have to say.
- I am someone whom others trust.
- I AM....

In the next chapter, we focus on how to use follow-up to make your network really thrive.

Exercise: Networking Self-Test for Introverts

1. When is the best time to think of networking?

_____

_____

2. What is the mistake people most often make in the way they define or describe networking or personal marketing?

_____

_____

3. What are the three top things you want to learn about every person you meet?

_____

_____

4. When you meet someone, what two things can you do to build rapport and trust?

_____

_____

5. What is one thing you can do to inject some small talk into your conversations?

_____

_____

6. What can you do to be totally prepared for every networking encounter, to make each one totally comfortable?

_____

_____

7. How do you continually work on your introduction and get to know your questions and exit strategies according to your own organized plan?

_____

_____

8. How many people would you consider to be true advocates who could explain what you do and who you are to someone else in less than 30 seconds?

_____

_____

9. How do you want to be remembered when you meet someone, and what's your approach?

_____

_____

10. What are you going to do starting today and every day to keep your network alive, growing, and building for you?

_____

_____

9

Follow-up: A Road Map for Growth

"Avoid shortcuts. They always take too much time in the long run."
–Anonymous

After any event, as I'm walking out, I have my exit strategy in place for building my network. I'm ready to input information about new people I've met into my contact database, write follow-up notes, email any articles I've promised, and get the contact information of at least two people to set up meetings with. I might be masterful at working the room and making contacts (though introverts and extroverts do it differently), but without follow-up, one thing is certain: Nothing will ever happen.

I repeatedly hear people say, "I was going to follow up, but I got so busy!" or "I wasn't sure if the contact I made really meant for me to contact him." Whatever the excuse, if I've learned anything about finding, growing, and keeping contacts, it's that follow-up is the key to growing your network and your business. What I remember has a way of being rewarded over time.

"Must-Do's" After a Meeting

After any event or meeting, you have a number of opportunities to follow up quickly and efficiently, based on conversations you had and contacts you made. Timing is of the essence. Tomorrow you will only have more things to do and more excuses for not doing it, so do it now.

At least 24 hours after a meeting, send a note or email, or call to say any of the following, depending on the circumstances of your meeting:

- **"It was nice to meet you."** I attended an association dinner where one of the guests, Nick, was sharing some information about his company. Even though we met and chatted only as we were walking out the door, I sent him a note the following day telling him how much I had enjoyed meeting him and hearing his presentation. He responded, and we met several times over the years. I now work with his company as a client. He refers me all the time, and we've had many collaborations. We've also formed a great friendship. It never would have happened without follow-up.

- **"Thank you for your time and consideration."** Anyone who knows me or has heard my advice knows that I strongly believe in the power of the handwritten note. Here's how the power of a note can work: After a long day of meetings and interviews with the partners of a company where I was presenting a proposal for management coaching, I left armed with my note cards. Two days later, everyone received a personal note from me, thanking him or her for taking the time to meet with me. As it turned out, I didn't get the project and was told I was a "close second." So I sent each of them another note, this time email or text, depending on their preferred method of communication. I wrote "Thank you for your time and consideration" and expressed my hope that our paths might cross again. Some people might think that was a lot of work because I didn't get to close the deal. Yet it paid off, because a couple months later, I was called back in to do a more extensive project with some of the organization's internal people and created a strategic alliance to work with some of its clients. You never know how your thank you notes will work. The personal note tells the client or prospect that you took the time to write, which will make you stand out. If you say that your handwriting isn't good, I have two options for you: Either print or utilize a great system that I also use (see my website, www.appreciationpower.com).

- **"Perhaps we can meet again."** When I speak with people, I always ask how it might be best to follow up. Remember, at various networking events, your goal is to establish rapport and ask for permission to meet again. This was the case when I attended a huge industry event not long ago. I started chatting with the woman sitting to my left at lunch. Shortly into our conversation, it was time for the program to begin, and she had to dash out. She didn't have her card, so I wrote down her name and her company; then I went to the company website and emailed her the next day, suggesting we meet for breakfast the following week. We did. I was able to hook her up with a new supplier, and she is now a new contact for me. Find opportunities to pay it forward.

- **"Thank you for the useful information."** I always practice this suggestion—and it's also nice to be on the receiving end! Recently, I received several nice notes and emails after giving a short presentation at an event. I remember one, in particular, that came to my email box the next day, with the subject line, "Thank you for sharing some helpful thoughts." I always remember the people who follow up with me to say thanks or tell me that my information was helpful. We all like to hear this. Take the time today to think about someone who has recently given you some useful information—whether the person is an existing contact or someone you met recently—and drop him or her a note or email to say so. Doing these follow-ups is more than courteous; it distinguishes you from the other people your contact has met. You will differentiate yourself.

If you've promised to send materials, call to set up a meeting, or pass on a referral, keep your word and do it within the time promised—or sooner. It's easy to make these promises at a meeting or event, but a person who follows up in a timely manner is remembered and trusted.

Call within two weeks after suggesting a get-together, whether over a meal or at a more formal meeting. "Let's do lunch" is just an old cliché, unless you make it happen. And we have many times in the day to meet for a meal or snack or drink. Suggest it only if you mean it, and then follow up to set a specific date and place. And remember to call or send an email to confirm the day before. Things happen in life, and people appreciate it when you take the time to do this added courtesy. If they must cancel, you'll have an opportunity to make other plans. Either way, you come across as being sincere and professional.

When a contact provides you with a referral or offers to pass on your information to help you, be sure to say thank you and keep your contact in the loop by letting him or her know the results, whatever happens. The same holds true for any tangible advice you get from a contact. People who offer to help you, and then go out of their way to do it, deserve to know the results of their advice. And they certainly deserve a thank you! Again, these people are some of your advocates—they are helping to market you, and I consider them my "clients," too.

Several months ago, when I spoke to a group about this subject, Jane, who had invited me, said, "Andrea, I must share a story, because as you are explaining the importance of this simple courtesy, I am seething with anger regarding a recent situation." She told me that her husband had referred their friend, Bill, for a project at her husband's client's company. They heard nothing from Bill until several months later at a party, when a mutual acquaintance told them that Bill had gotten the project. Never once had Bill thanked them for the referral, let them know how the project was going, or even had the courtesy to let them know he'd been successful. Jane was angry about Bill's rudeness after her husband had gone out of his way to help him. Some weeks later, she called me to say that Bill had recently left a message on her husband's machine asking if he could help out a "friend"—yet there was still no thank you! Needless to say, no further help was offered.

You've probably been in situations like this when people forget their most important client, advocate, or referral source. Be sure to avoid those kinds of mistakes, and take the time right now to repair any inadvertent damage you might have done. Usually it's an innocent mistake— we simply forget. Dig deep and go back through your entire database. This is a useful and helpful exercise.

Doing these follow-ups is good manners, helps build solid relationships for the future, and shows respect for others. *Respect* is the key word here. Remember, people do business with those whom they know and respect. They will want to help you again when the opportunity arises.

AFTER YOUR FIRST MEETING

A gentle touch is often required as a follow-up with people we have just met. First and foremost, take the time to build rapport. If you've met someone new and then the next day you ask to set up a sales call or ask for a referral, you risk coming across as aggressive and self-centered, and you could damage a developing relationship. Remember to ask for permission to stay in touch. Send a note first, saying how much you enjoyed meeting the person and suggesting another meeting.

As I was waiting for my dinner guest one night at a restaurant, the woman in the next booth and I struck up a conversation. It turned out she had been a speaker at an event I had attended. The world is small. I'd thought she was very interesting and insightful. I began discussing a few of the things I remembered from her talk, and we were still talking when our respective dinner partners arrived. I sent her a note the following day, along with a copy of my first book. She called me soon afterward and invited me to give a speech for her organization. Follow up! These serendipitous opportunities happen all the time when we are open and aware.

Thank You Notes

As I have said, one of the best follow-up techniques is a simple thank you note. It seems so obvious to thank someone, yet many people fail to do so. A handwritten note clearly makes you stand out and separates you from the others. At the very least, send off an email or pick up the phone after your meeting just to say thanks, or send a text—you'll begin to build a relationship. I remember this from several years ago when I sent a new contact a handwritten note. He responded to me by saying, "I know I shouldn't have been surprised, yet in this day and age of everything electronic, your note certainly made an impact." I still remember this—and it was five years ago. Now a handwritten note makes even more of an impact in our electronic world.

Eight reasons to send a thank you note follow:

1. **For time and consideration:** This is one of the four "must do's" after a meeting. It also applies to many other situations, such as interviews, one-on-one meetings, and social encounters.

2. **For a compliment you received:** I met a woman at an event who had one of the most amazing pens I've ever seen. It was a great conversation starter. She told me it was her "signature piece," and she loved it. I later sent her an article that I saw on pens, and she sent me a note written with her special pen thanking me for the compliment!

3. **For a piece of advice given:** A client called me to offer her advice on how to design an upcoming presentation for some decision makers in her company. She spent quite a bit of time with me, so I immediately sat down and wrote her a thank you note for her time and help.

4. **For business:** This is a "must do"! Every time someone does business with you or gives you an order, drop the person a thank you note. Remember, someone else could have gotten that business instead of you. Remember also to send a thank you note to all those who were responsible for making the decision. Too often people thank only the top person; however, most decisions are made with input from many people. Be sure to send a note to everyone who was part of the decision. This will show your appreciation and reinforce your name with others in your client's business. It also strengthens what I call "surrounding the account," where you expose your potential client to your name and business on as many fronts as possible.

5. **For a referral:** After I spoke at a real estate company, one of the agents in the audience referred me to one of his clients. I sent him a note immediately. He continually tells me how much he appreciated that simple note. When you thank in writing the people who go out of their way for you, it guarantees you will stay on their radar screen. It shows you took the time.

6. **For a gift:** I read a wonderful story about a little girl who learned the power of thank you notes when she was only 7. She thanked her mom and grandmother for every gift she received, often with a little drawing or card. Once she was so excited about the unique toothbrush her grandma had given her that she wrote up a little

note saying she would think of her grandma every night when she brushed her teeth with her new toothbrush! You might be smiling—this kid is bright. Who do you think is remembered and rewarded all the time?

7. **For help on a project:** I think of all the great people on my virtual team who continually help me with my projects. My assistant, Linda, is always there to proof, and I always know my work will look great. Margie, Scott, and John are always helping me by adding their wonderful expertise. Even though we've worked together for years, I always send notes and delicious brownies to show my appreciation.

8. **Even when you're "rejected":** The door is never shut. My mantra is, always thank people for their time and consideration, even if nothing comes of it—because sometimes it does! And you can always learn something. One of my clients told me how her rejection of a consultant turned into an offer. When the first candidate she chose for the project didn't work out, she looked again at the other possibilities. She recalled one consultant who had sent a note thanking her for her consideration, despite the rejection letter he got. She called him in for another meeting and subsequently hired him for the project.

THANK YOU NOTES PAY OFF

Recently, I found out that Dave, a former client of mine, had left his company to pursue another passion. I sent him a note, thanking him for all his help in coordinating our projects and making my work so easy at his company. I also sent thank you notes to the senior people with whom Dave used to work, in addition to his former assistant. Over the next two months, there was a flurry of activity at the company. I came up on the radar screens of all the people I'd contacted, which came from my note to each of them. As you can see, it's important to take the time to write these notes—they'll pay off over time.

My Thank You Chain

I've mentioned my thank you chain before and said that I often use it to thank everyone who has helped me along the way. It's a simple, efficient, and powerful way to follow up and be remembered. I have thank you chains throughout many companies where I work. For instance, I was giving a speech at an association meeting and met three new people who hired me for projects. The first thank you went to the organizer of the association meeting, and the others went to all the people I knew from the group. I also sent over a basket of goodies because, without them, I never would have met these people. I have done several projects at one of the companies and continue to thank my original and secondary contacts so the thank you chain can grow.

I even have a system for my thank you chain. I track every single opportunity back to the first introduction. I put this information into my database so that I can easily go back and see how the connection began. I thank all the people in my chain by phone, email, text, social media, or note, depending on their preferred method of communication. People are often surprised by my thank you because they might not have realized the part they played in the chain. It's fun to tell them how it evolved and that, if it hadn't been for them, I wouldn't have had this success. And I thank them! This suggestion is both simple and powerful.

YOUR PERSONAL THANK YOU CHAIN

Working from present to past, think about the chain of events and people who led you to your current job (business, profession, or a major client). Make a list of the people who helped you through referrals or in other ways. Write, call, or send each of them an email to thank them. Start by asking yourself:

- How did I get my current job?

- How did I get into this industry?

- How did I meet my last two major clients?

Every day, I go through my database and do the following:

1. Send three handwritten notes.

2. Send three additional emails or texts.

3. Make three additional phone calls.

4. Bonus: I link in with someone daily.

My database includes people's names and their preferred means of communication (*E* for email, *V* for voicemail, *T* for text, and *L* for LinkedIn) so that I can say thank you or just touch base in the way and system they prefer. When combined with my personal notes, this becomes a powerful and effective way to maintain meaningful business relationships. It takes only about 16 minutes of your day, and it's very "net worth it"!

Building Trust

People do business with those they trust and respect. *Trust* is the key word, and building trust takes time and patience. When we network, we need to learn to respect others' timetables. Often new contacts don't respond in a timely fashion—at least, it seems that way. They may be busy with their own deadlines and have many responsibilities that keep them from responding to you immediately. So how can we move the process forward without "pushing" other people too hard, which will only make them more reluctant? If someone you've met doesn't call back after being given a great introduction or offer, avoid being seen as a pest. Life is busy and challenging, and we never know what is going on in someone else's life. Stay the course, touch base periodically, and see if something develops over time. Take the high road—there's always less traffic there.

When you do connect, ask a few productive questions for your follow-up. "How do you and your organization prefer to learn about new suppliers or external partners?" or "What is the best way to present product information to you?" This way, you make it easy to do business with you, and you ultimately receive the response you're looking for.

Rushing a communication—hurrying off the phone or sending an email that's not carefully written—can be another networking stumbling block. It tells the new contact that you're trying to move through the process in a cold and mechanical way. Even when we have long lists of people to contact, it takes very little effort to develop a personalized approach. Here are three ways to do it:

1. Ask your contacts how they want the issue to be handled and how they prefer to communicate. Some people prefer that everything be done in writing; others would rather receive a quick follow-up phone call or email letting them know about new opportunities that can benefit them. This is so simple. For example, many of your calls might elicit no response. However, when you email, text, or send something through LinkedIn, the response is immediate. You have just learned to communicate with people the way they like.

2. Check on new contacts regularly. Have your follow-up plan in place. Mark your calendar for the next significant date on your contact's calendar. Connect by phone or electronically before sending new information and say that you hope to connect with him or her at an upcoming conference or meeting.

3. Develop a networking game plan. New contacts will never develop into anything important unless you have a long-term plan in place for keeping in touch with them. Keep a readily available list of all contacts. Using that list, develop a plan that is appropriate for all the contacts, and choose which ones should receive special treatment. For instance, you might see that an effective follow-up strategy with a key contact could be looking for him or her at an upcoming business function. Another contact might appreciate a note with helpful information. When you find out which method is most effective with each of your contacts, build on what works and develop the skills you need, such as writing and speaking, to make meaningful connections with those people. Look at the client/contact profile and see how much you learn about people as you get to know them over time.

Remember that the true key to growing your network is follow-up. Now that you have an expanding network, you need to figure out how to keep it alive. In the next chapters, we check out some great strategies for staying in touch with your contacts. Before you move on, try these quick exercises to help you follow up and grow your network.

Exercise 1: Eight Ways to Say "Thank You"

Look at the following eight reasons for sending a thank you note. Next to each reason, write down at least one name of someone to whom you can write a thank you note this week.

1. For time and consideration _____

2. For a compliment you received _____

3. For a piece of advice given _____

4. For business _____

5. For a referral _____

6. For a gift _____

7. For help on a project _____

8. Even when you're "rejected" _____

Exercise 2: Other Notes

Other types of notes you can send anytime to stay in touch and be helpful. Write down at least one name of someone to whom you can write a note this week. Consider the following reasons:

1. FYI (for your information) _____

2. Congratulations _____

3. Nice talking to (or meeting) you _____

4. Thinking of you _____

5. Other _____

Exercise 3: Who Will You Help?

Think of people in your network whom you can help or provide with a connection, information, or a referral. Write down their names and take action.

1. _____

2. _____

3. _____

T   Take the time to say thank you to someone.

H   Have a plan of action to incorporate this strategy every day.

A   Articulate your note or compliment with powerful language.

N   Notice something special about each person.

K   Keep in touch sincerely and in your own style.

Y   *You* is the most important word when thanking someone; tell others what is special about them.

O   Organize yourself so that this process becomes seamless.

U   Understand the power of a sincere and considerate thank you.

"Life is like a soap opera. God is the head writer, your story line keeps changing, it's a daily event, and there are Friday cliffhangers."
—Anonymous

Appendix

Characteristics of a Good Listener

On a scale of 1–5, with 5 being the highest, fill in the blank to indicate the degree to which you already practice these positive listening behaviors. Go through the list twice, first rating yourself with the person you listen to the best and then rating yourself with the person to whom you find it most difficult to listen.

Best	Worst	
_____	_____	I make regular eye contact with the speaker.
_____	_____	I ask questions for clarification.
_____	_____	I show concern by acknowledging feelings.
_____	_____	I restate or paraphrase some of the speaker's words to show that I understand.
_____	_____	I seek first to understand, then to be understood.
_____	_____	I am poised and emotionally controlled.
_____	_____	I react nonverbally, with a smile, a nod, a frown, or a touch, if appropriate.
_____	_____	I pay close attention and do not let my mind wander.
_____	_____	I act responsibly with what I hear.
_____	_____	I don't change the subject without warning.

Bad Habits of Listening

On a scale of 1–5, with 5 being the worst, indicate the degree to which you are guilty of these poor listening habits. Rate yourself twice, first with the person you listen to the best and then with the person to whom you find it most difficult to listen.

Best	Worst	
_____	_____	I interrupt often.
_____	_____	I jump to conclusions.
_____	_____	I finish other people's sentences.
_____	_____	I am parental and answer with advice.
_____	_____	I make up my mind before I have all the information.
_____	_____	I am a compulsive note taker.
_____	_____	I don't give any response.
_____	_____	I am impatient.
_____	_____	I lose my temper.
_____	_____	I think about my reply when the other person is speaking.

Some Helpful Listening Tips

- Be an active listener. Use good eye contact; nod your head; give some verbal cues that you are listening to the person.

- Show an interest in what the person is saying. Imagine yourself being faced with the same predicament.

- Listen to understand instead of listening to argue and judge.

- Don't let the other person's emotional display or choice of words throw you off course. Keep the purpose of the conversation clearly in the forefront of your mind. When necessary, keep the other person focused.

- Check out what you *think* you heard by restating what the other person said.

- Listen more intensely for *what* the person is saying instead of *how* he or she is saying it (for example, poorly enunciating, mispronouncing, or misusing words).

- When you need to gather more information, ask open-ended questions. (What? How? When? Why? Who?)

- When someone is angry, a good rule of thumb is to remain silent and listen to what he or she is saying—and, more important, what he or she is trying to say.

- Keep your emotions in check by taking an ongoing inventory of how you're reacting. Pay attention to signs like these:

  - Jaw muscles tighten

  - Stomach turns into knots

  - Breathing gets shorter and choppier

  - Hands get sweaty

  - Heart begins to pound

- At some point, your physical responses might be a clue that you are no longer actively listening to the person.

- When emotions get out of control, the purpose of the conversation typically gets lost. It might be best to end the discussion at that point and resume it at another time.

- Keep in mind that good listening is a skill and requires ongoing practice. So when someone comes into your office for a casual chat, make a point of giving this person your undivided attention—that means avoiding the tendency to want to continue typing, writing, reading, or filing papers while he or she is talking.

- When you give someone your attention, not only are you giving that person your time (a valuable premium), but you are also sending a complimentary message that you respect that person.

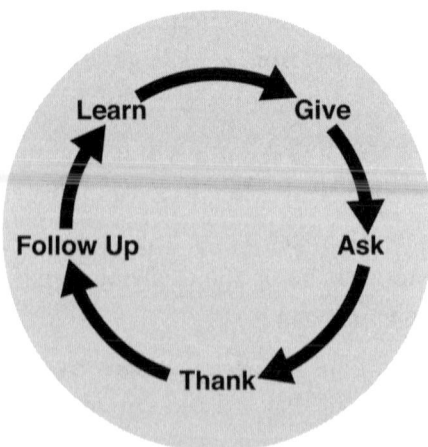

Figure A2-1 The Golden Circle of Strategic Networking

PART 3

Keep (Maintaining Your Hard-Earned Relationships)

10

Stay in Touch

*"The opposite of networking is **not** working—it takes time and effort that will pay off."*
—Andrea Nierenberg

This section is probably the most compelling because you can spend a lot of time finding and growing your business through the relationships developed using the powerful art of networking. However, to see that everything is running productively, you must make sure that you keep your business and retain those amazing relationships and the business they've helped you develop.

It's time to explore creative ways to cultivate advocates in your networking relationships and be aware of continually identifying potential opportunities to do so. You'll find out how to earn referrals for your business and make sure everyone on your team realizes that they both help bring in business, as "rainmakers," and help to keep the business you have. You need to explore how to be proactive and stay in touch by remaining on your advocates', ambassadors', and clients' radar screens. You'll also learn how to manage all of this with your own contact management system—wherever you are conducting business.

Finally, you'll tie it all together and consider how to make networking part of your DNA (Dedicated Networking Always). You will learn my 10 easy-to-remember networking suggestions based on my acronym out of (what else?) the word *networking*.

Following up in a timely manner with materials promised, an immediate thank you note, or a "nice seeing you" note is a must for effective and strategic networking. The sure way to lose a contact is to fail to follow up and follow through. However, the next step is an equally important, yet often neglected action in today's busy world. This is the process of keeping in touch on a continual basis. Imagine how awkward it would be to contact someone you once met out of the blue and ask for a favor if you hadn't stayed in touch. This is an example of the kind of action that gives networking a bad name and makes people dislike these "What's in it for me?" types. Our surveys indicate that people are turned off by contacts who call or email them only when they need something. If you stay in touch with your networking contacts and nurture your network regularly, you'll receive a much more positive response to future requests.

Ways to Stay on Your Contacts' Radar Screen

To keep a relationship going, you need to stay connected. Recently a friend mentioned to me that although it's easy for her to send an email or a note after she meets someone, it's much harder for her to stay in touch after that. Follow-up, she told me, is reacting to a situation that calls for a response or action on her part. However, when she heard my comment about staying on your contacts' radar screen, she asked me, "After the follow-up, what 'opportunity' do I have to contact this person?"

"Sometimes," I told her, "you have to invent the opportunity, and you have to vary the contact methods."

If follow-up is reactive, think of staying in touch as proactive. It involves looking for ways to stay in touch and building on the relationship so that when an opportunity arises to ask for some advice, you can do it easily because you have a solid relationship. Here are some methods I use to stay connected.

Notes

Besides the thank you note, which is a follow-up must, you can send several other types of notes at any time to stay in touch, be helpful, and be remembered. Because handwritten notes are so rare, yours will really make an impression.

- **"FYI" (For your information).** Send articles to people in your network with a note saying, "I thought you might be interested in this." The articles can be related to the person's business or personal interests. I have a contact who is a huge Yankees fan, so I've sent him pictures from the Sunday newspaper and several articles on his favorite team. He's been appreciative of those, especially because I took the time to find out what he cares about. How did I remember what he likes? I wrote it all down, and now it's on my database under his name and information (look at the Client Profile Template in the Part 3 Appendix).

Other ways you can give your contacts helpful information is by sending them information from a seminar you've attended or forwarding information about an upcoming conference or class. Any information that helps them understand the latest trends in their business is good, too, and remember to send any helpful leads.

- **"Congratulations!"** Send a note of congratulations for a promotion, an award or honor, or an anniversary. I sent a former colleague a note of congratulations when I saw an article that a mutual contact, an editor we both knew, had written about him. I wrote to them both, congratulating my colleague on his promotion and complimenting my editor friend on his great article. It was a good opportunity to reconnect with both contacts and helped us keep in touch. My former colleague ended up hiring me for a project. He's a busy person, and although he might have considered me among others for his project, I clearly believe it was because we stayed in touch with each other. It made him think of me instead of my competition. He's also totally bottom line oriented—his emails are never more than about 10 words. I respond and write to him in exactly "his" way.

- **"Nice talking to (or meeting) you."** You can send these notes any time you speak with someone on the phone or at a meeting. I even send them after a chance encounter and conversation. I have some great note cards with a picture of a phone and "Nice talking to you" on the front. Use any technique you can think of to make you stand out from the crowd. I call this the power of "remember-ability." People are always amazed, and it reinforces our discussion and makes me stand out.

- **"Thinking of you."** I've found that when I send this type of note to people with whom I've not been in touch for a while, it often reopens the relationship. Laney had been a student in a presentation skills class years ago when she was in advertising. We stayed in touch at her next job, and then she started her own business—in, of all things, greeting cards. Now I'm one of her best clients.

- **"Wish you were here."** I send postcards wherever I go. I travel quite a bit and have found that this is a great way to stay in touch with contacts when I'm away from my office. My good friend and client Bob always sends me postcards from his world travels. He has a great system. He prints labels from his mailing list and takes them with him. Then he just writes the card and sticks a label on it. Easy!

You might be wondering how I have the time to send handwritten notes. I always carry notes and stamps with me. I use the time in airports, on trains, while waiting at the doctor's office, or while watching television to dash off a note, address it, and drop it in the mail. All it takes is carrying note cards in your networking toolkit, keeping a supply of stamps on hand, and, of course, being organized.

Holiday Cards and Special Occasions

Sending season's greetings cards to everyone in my network is a practice I have done for many years. I also send greeting cards on special occasions and other holidays. Many people throughout the world, for instance, celebrate Chinese New Year or the Jewish New Year (Rosh Hashanah), St. Patrick's Day, Mother's Day, or Veterans Day. I even send e-cards on Chocolate Day, if I know my clients like chocolate. (Yes, there is such a thing as Chocolate Day!) In fact, to be really creative, consult with Google or your favorite search engine—and type in "holidays" and see what comes up. There's usually a holiday daily.

Birthdays, anniversaries, and other important events are also opportunities to keep in touch with a note or small gift. Pay attention to what people mention about these dates. Some people are proud of work anniversaries, so you can send a note of congratulations on these occasions. Others mention an upcoming award, honor, or promotion. If you haven't heard about these important days from your contacts, you can find out about them from their coworkers, in articles, through Google Alerts, or from whatever the latest and greatest "search engine news aggregators" are. I've been collecting these days of importance for a while, and some months I send out as many as 80 personal greeting cards! My recipients continue to be surprised and happy to hear from me.

The key is to consider the profile and interests of your contact when sending a card. The card industry has millions of choices for you to give your contacts a little loving care—and to remind them of you.

BENEFITS OF SENDING GREETING CARDS

The Greeting Card Association tells us that sending a greeting card is a simple yet powerful gesture that reminds people someone is thinking of them. When you make someone else feel good, it also makes you feel good!

People often ask me how I find out my contacts' birthdays. I just casually ask them what month they were born after I've known them for a while. Then I record it in my client profile. My contacts usually forget they've told me their birthday.

Stay Connected

Set aside 10 minutes every day to reach out to a client, a prospect, and a new connection in their preferred method of communication to say hello and share an idea, thought, or suggestion. This is in addition to your regular calls and meetings for the day.

- Keep it brief and concise. You want to show they're on your mind.

- You can send an article, email, or quick message.

- Once a week, go through your universal list and call three people to say hello.

- Once every two weeks, have breakfast or lunch with a business friend, client, center of influence, or prospect.

Listen and Learn

We work on active listening skills, yet we sometimes forget to be totally involved in the process and exchange.

Track how well you're really listening with at least one call and interaction daily. Stop anything else other than writing notes as you listen. Focus on the message. If you're on the phone, note tone and inflection. If you're together in person, focus on the eyes to show you are connecting. (Hopefully you will do this with all interactions. Give yourself a daily goal, to be sure to monitor at least one—you'll see that it gets easier as you practice and focus.)

Learn at least one new piece of information daily as you connect. Write it down as you keep a running log of information learned. It can be a tip, an idea, a business strategy—the list is limitless. It's all in the focus and concentration.

Create Advocacy and Centers of Influence

Create advocacy and centers of influence as you build your brand and business. Think, "Who can I connect with each week?" Perhaps it's a center of influence with a client, a vendor or internal resource, or someone else. As you learn more about the people involved in your business, you will find opportunities to create other synergies and build your brand. Your advocates offer you valuable third-party endorsements and are part of your business marketing. Be their best ambassadors also— reach out to someone daily.

Do this monthly: List 10 contacts (clients, centers of influence, colleagues, friends). These are also your advocates. Ask these questions:

- How often are you two in contact?
- What is the biggest challenge the other person faces in business?
- When did you last visit the contact's website?
- What is one action item you can do for your contact in the near future:
  - Write an article.
  - Give him or her a referral.

- Help him or her solve a challenge.

- Have a face-to-face meeting.

Follow-Up

Follow up on something specific. Every day you follow up in your regular work, yet something on your desk right now needs a follow-up action. It could be from someone you met at an event, and this is your time to call or email. Maybe you have a connection that you promised to send an article or information. You might need to return a call or email, or link in. Whatever it is, besides everything you're doing in your action steps, you need to take five minutes to do one additional follow-up.

You have many creative ways to stay on your contacts' radar screen as you continually build and grow your relationships (you learn many things about your contacts) that will surprise and delight them when you pop up just to stay in touch and be on their radar.

- Set up a Google alert, to get an alert any time your contact appears in the media or anywhere on the Web. This gives you an opportunity to touch base—to say hello, offer congratulations, and so on.

- Adapt a list of topics to know about your connections over time. Create the ones that will be most important for you and an opportunity to be on the radar screen.

- Take time to reflect on what is important and of value in your life. I started my own "gratitude and nice card file," where I put a note each time I think of something for which I am grateful. Doing this is also a way to remember the strong personal connections I've created.

Reflect your own personality when reaching out to people.

Interesting Emails

Even though a handwritten note is a unique and thoughtful way to stay in touch, emails can also make you stand out. They can be used for the same reasons as notes, and you can use your own unique style to create them. Send links to interesting online articles and websites, inspirational quotes, pictures, and videos. You can also include articles, video clips, or pictures in the body of your email, with a personalized, friendly note on top.

Another way to use email to stay in touch is to let your clients know about any charity or community work you're doing. For instance, if your company is involved in a tutoring program, you can send an email to your clients about it, along with your note and pictures.

Many discussion forums and weblogs online cover a wide range of topics; find some that would interest your client. Start the email with something like, "I saw a discussion on this website about the distribution issues we were talking about. Thought you might be interested." Then include the link to the website.

I also use email to send monthly tips to people who have signed up for them on my website. Or you can include a signature at the bottom of your email that says, "Click here to get monthly tips." Some people send emails to their contacts every time their websites are updated with new information, products, or articles. Tweet and blog often to your network universe. Keep adding to your wealth of knowledge and expertise.

Whatever you do, make sure you have a valid reason for sending emails, and tailor your message to the recipient. Also remember to reply to emails within 24 hours of receiving them—even if only to acknowledge that you've received them—and promise to reply in detail later.

Your Own Article or Newsletter

If you've published an article in a trade publication or e-zine, email a copy of it to your contacts with a personal note. If you haven't yet gotten an article published, create your own. You can print it on nice stationery, email a copy to your contacts, or post it on your website and email your contacts the link. You can also post it on LinkedIn, Facebook, Twitter, and whatever the latest online vehicle is.

Gifts

Everyone enjoys a nice gift to celebrate a special occasion, such as the completion of a project, a promotion, a birthday or holiday, or someone doing a special favor for me. Sending a gift sets you apart, but you need to be careful about the nature of the gift. Keep in mind that this is a gesture of appreciation, and avoid placing the recipient in the awkward position of having to turn down your gift because of company policy. In general, food and flowers are good choices because the whole company can share them. I like to send a fruit basket, a tin of popcorn, a box of candy, or other goodies. I am also a big sender of the most delicious brownies. Of course, when your food gift is shared with others in the company, your name gets in front of others—an added bonus.

Make sure you consider the recipient's preferences and habits in deciding what gifts to send, and respect people's diets. These days, I'm careful to avoid giving candy or popcorn to clients who are watching their carbohydrate counts. I'm always on the lookout for items that people will like and can accept. One workshop participant told me about sending a bouquet of flowers to a client to thank him for some business. It turned out that his client was allergic to flowers. After the client's assistant assured him that a different plant was fine, he immediately sent one, along with an apologetic note. He then recorded his client's allergy in his client profile so he wouldn't make this mistake again.

I met one of my favorite vendors over the Internet when he emailed me to ask permission to use one of my articles in his newsletter. I was happy to do so and was in the market for a gift basket, so I tried it. (Pretty clever networking on his part!) Be creative with your food gifts. I've sent everything from chocolate telephones to fruit-flavored flowers.

Give the gift of a book that you like or one that has a special message. Send it with a note about why you thought your contact would also like it. People rarely throw away books; at the very least, they pass them along to someone else. I've actually incorporated what I call "give away a book a day to keep your networking growing day by day": Every week, I give or send a book as a gift to someone. I'm always reading and like to share with others.

I've given gift certificates so that people can choose what they want—all they have to do is order it. The fact that you ordered it at a store or website they like will show them that you went the extra mile. The important point is to do what works for you and makes your clients happy, and to keep it professional.

People in your network enjoy receiving gifts. Think of how the following words in this acronym can be a reminder when you are building your network.

GIVE A GIFT

G **Giving gifts** that make you memorable

I **Invite** and **involve** people in special events

F **Friendly** people are giving people

T **Time together** with somebody

Premiums

Invest in premiums with your company's name: pens, notepad holders, magnets, paperweights—anything useful and memorable. I give premiums to everyone who attends my seminars and to people I meet at events. Each premium has my name, company, and contact information, including my website. Most important, all my premiums are useful. My signature piece is a pocket mirror that says, "Can your smile be heard?" Every year I look for a new premium that will put my name in front of my contacts as they go about their working day. I love giving gifts that stay on people's desks. When they're functional, they're a constant reminder of your services.

Personalize each premium with a brief note and individualized message, just as you would for any gift.

Face Time

Despite the immediacy and efficiency of our online communication today, spending personal time with a client is memorable and more powerful. Finding the time to get together might seem difficult because we're all busy and live far apart. However, if you're persistent and creative, you can schedule these all-important personal meetings. Besides the traditional breakfast, lunch, and dinner meetings, suggest meeting for coffee or afternoon tea. Coffee shops are always in vogue for networking meetings. Or try playing a game of tennis or golf; going for a walk; meeting at a museum; getting a manicure; shopping; attending an industry event; or attending a play, concert, or sporting event. Share a cab to a meeting, or meet at the sky club at the airport when you're between flights in your colleague's city. Before going on a business trip or vacation, look up everyone you know in the places you'll be visiting; then call or email before going, to arrange meetings.

I had dinner recently in Atlanta with several business friends, found out they had common interests, and made a wonderful connection with each of them. Our telephones can now do all of this with ease through Facebook and LinkedIn. We can always be connected to our connections.

Everyone is busy, yet many still manage to spend time with people in their network. I meet with some people at least once a quarter and others a couple times a year. I see closer associates and friends more frequently.

Because of my travel schedule, I like to become familiar with, and then recognized at, the better restaurants and hotels for entertaining clients. I often find these through recommendations from people in my network. After eating or staying there, I send the hotel or restaurant manager a thank you note saying that I'll be visiting again in the near future. I have been happily surprised to receive very nice treatment when I return. Again, just showing appreciation and saying "Thank you" have set me apart and made these people remember me. It takes only a few minutes to do—and add their information to your Client Profile Template.

Here is a reminder of what to remember on every in-person connection. Enjoy it, be adaptable, connect and find community, and know when to go.

F.A.C.E. TIME

F   Make it <u>F</u>un. Find unique things to do and places to meet.

A   <u>A</u>dapt to the other person's timetable and surroundings.

C   <u>C</u>onnect and find common interests.

E   Know when to <u>E</u>xit—be respectful of the other person's time.

Share Your Expertise

I have a friend who is a consultant and a magician. He's often asked to perform his magic show at charity events, and he gives his time willingly. He contributes to the cause through his magic, stays in touch with people in his network, and even meets some new contacts at these events. He always walks away from these events with new business. People see him in action and remember him. What better way to build name recognition?

Think of your own expertise. When you offer your writing, proofreading, publicity, computer, or organizational skills, or any of your business or personal skills, you'll experience the satisfaction of knowing that you're helping others. When you take some time out of your hectic schedule to help someone else, you never know when the favor will be returned. Others appreciate and seek out knowledgeable people who want to give generously of their expertise. And when you've been a resource to people, they're more than willing to help you when you ask. Just avoid keeping score; do it because you want to help instead of keeping track of what is owed to you. Again, that says "negative networking" to me.

Technology

Videoconferencing, text messaging, and instant messaging are cost-effective and convenient. Whether you're using email, using the phone, or meeting face-to-face, decide what works best for you—and your contact—and what will make you stand out while maintaining meaningful personal contacts.

A DAILY, WEEKLY, AND MONTHLY PLAN TO STAY IN TOUCH

1. Every day, send an email to three people you haven't been in touch with for a while (or create variety with one note, one email, and one phone call).

2. Once a week, go through your contact list and reach out to three people just to say hello.

---

3. Once a month, have lunch with a friend, colleague, or client you haven't seen for a while.

4. Add or send a message to 10 people in LinkedIn or Facebook every month.

5. Write a quick how-to blog post or article for your own blog, e-zine, or fan page weekly.

6. Record a video tip about your own expertise, along with a call to action, and post it on YouTube, linking it to your social sites and blog.

Setting Up and Managing Your Contact Database

So many tools for managing your database effectively are right at your fingertips. I still keep my system simple, flexible, and usable for me. It's a part of my KISS theory (Keep It Simple, Sweetheart). My system for organizing and keeping track of a network database works on any system you have. I have a friend who says, "My life is in three different CRM programs in my office." It works for him, and he's very successful.

You can use any contact management application that works best for you. So many are available that I encourage you to consult with an expert or someone you trust to find out what might work best for you. The key for any type of contact management system is to find one method that's easy to use and that you can use consistently. The best networkers use a system that's organized and accessible.

I live with my iPhone for all mobile communication, and it has been my favorite tool. It took a long time for me to also give up my Blackberry, and now I can't imagine how or why I kept it for so long. More than 50% of our electronic communication is now done with a mobile device. That percentage is quickly growing, and so are the different versions and tools available.

Setting Up a Contact Database

Whatever formal system you decide to use, go back to the Client Profile Template and modify and insert it into your system to have all pertinent follow-up and "deepening the relationship" information that you need. I fill in as much information as I continually gather, and I also note whether they're introverts or extroverts so that I remember how to best communicate with them.

I continue adding information and meeting notes with the dates they occurred to the notes section. This gives me a complete record of interactions I've had with each person in my database. I also track how I came to know each person—who introduced us and how, when and where we met. This is critical information for my thank you chain contacts.

Prioritizing Your Network

My current database continues to grow, as I know yours will also. I'm frequently asked how I manage to keep in touch with all the people on my networking list. First, the majority of the people in my database comprise my mailing list, and I reach them regularly with my Tip of the Month.

I divide the rest of my list into three categories (A, B, and C), and I have a contact plan for each category. I organize all my contacts, professional and personal, in the same database because business opportunities can happen through different kinds of connections, and there's so much interchange and flow among various areas of my life.

My C list has people with whom I touch base. These are casual acquaintances with whom I am not currently doing business. They might also be former clients or people who are part of my thank you chain. I email each of them my Tip of the Month, and I send them a card or note once or twice a year, plus a holiday card. Currently, about 350 people are on this list.

My B list has "associates" with whom I am actively involved. I find a way to meet everyone on this list in person at least twice a year for a meal or coffee. I also send them at least six personal notes a year. If we're unable to get together, I call them every other month. I also send them holiday and premium gifts, my Tip of the Month, and a holiday card. This list includes about a hundred people.

My A list is made up of close friends and associates. I see each of them at least four times a year for a meal—or longer, if possible. I send them special gifts, holiday cards, and premiums, and I also frequently send them personal notes and articles. I look for opportunities to send flowers, theater tickets, or dinner certificates. I constantly think of ways to stay in touch with the 40 people on this list. They are my top ambassadors and advocates.

As you can see, because my contacts are categorized, I'm very realistic about how I can stay in touch with them in a quality way. I'm thrilled to have a huge contact base, yet the majority of these people are my electronic buddies—and the growing popularity of social media will only make this grow further. I'm often asked how many contacts I have on LinkedIn. I always say that, as with any network you build, it's quality versus just quantity. People have moved from this list to become closer associates when we've been in touch, they've followed up with me, or I've reconnected with them at an event or function.

These categories change continually because my network grows every day. I add new people to the appropriate category and move people between the lists, depending on what happens in life and how different connections occur.

My D list includes people who are no longer in my life, either for a period of time or forever. It's not personal. On the other hand, last year I reconnected with three people I knew from different venues 8, 10, and 12 years ago. They all reappeared at different times, and we just picked up where we left off. One of them has become a client, and I've been able to help another with a training plan for her company. I'm glad that all three are back in my life! That's one of the greatest parts of continual networking.

Birthdays

I keep track of birthdays by adding the contact's birthday month into the database. Then I create a birthday file in a simple MS Word file folder and make each month a separate document. Once a month, I print the list and mail each person a birthday card. Recently, I've started to add anniversaries and other special dates in the appropriate months, so I have all the important dates in front of me and can send my greetings. This makes it easy to remember. Plenty of software programs will do this for you, but my low-tech system still works for me.

Business Cards

The more you network, the more business cards you will collect, so you'll need a system to record all that information. Here's what I do when I get a card: I immediately add it to my database. Often I get a large stack of cards from people who simply want to be on the newsletter list. I go through these quickly, separate out the ones I made a connection with, and find an additional reason to follow up and say thank you. I send my follow-up notes and enter the information into my database, and I set the rest aside for my assistant to enter into the mailing database. With my iPhone, I also can add people immediately, and then it syncs with my Outlook system. Again, there are so many systems out today and another one tomorrow—find the one that works for you and develop it.

If the contact is going to become a client or prospect, I staple the card to a file folder in which I keep materials and other information. I put other cards into the "circular file" next to my desk because I've already captured the information in my database—and I like things to be clutter free!

Conversations and Meetings

I take notes on all the conversations I have, including business matters and important follow-up tasks and dates. I also enter any personal information, such as a favorite team, hobbies, or upcoming family celebrations. Again, refer back to the Client Profile Template that includes all these topics. These notes serve as conversation starters for the next time we meet, as well as reminders to send a note. I record all the notes in the Activities section of the contact's record in my computer database, including the date, purpose of the meeting, highlights of our discussions, and follow-up tasks and dates. I make sure I have a running log of every contact and conversation, and I always date them. Very often I also save our email correspondence in a folder, on my computer, with the person's name and company so that I have a complete information trail at my fingertips that's simple and organized.

STAYING IN TOUCH WITH A NEW CONTACT

When you meet someone at an event, do the following:

- Record the information from the business card in your contact database, or use one of the apps from your phone and sync to your database.

- Enter the date, where you met, and how (if it was through someone else), as well as notes about the person's profession, family, and interests.

- Record notes about your conversation.

- Send a "Nice to meet you" note.

- Mark down in your calendar that you will follow up in two weeks or when you both decide for a follow-up meeting.

On the Road

You live in a mobile world, and staying in touch with your universal network is easy, no matter where you are and in what time zone. Whether you take your laptop, your iPad, or just your phone, everywhere you go, there's an Internet connection. And that's all you need.

Between Go to My PC, Dropbox, and every other cloud connection, you can always be connected. This makes networking online so much easier and efficient.

Decide on the system that works for you and your organization. Being— and staying—connected is simple and also great for time management. Think when you're waiting in an airport or in your hotel room. Use all the different technologies and apps. Stay in touch, reconnect, start a conversation, go back to the Customer Profile template, and say hello to someone whose city you are visiting—and maybe set up a meeting.

The list is limitless—just start.

A Game Plan to Stay in Touch

Decide how often you want to contact the people in your universal network. I review my contact list every month. It usually takes a few hours, and I manage to do it by breaking it up into small blocks of time. First, I review every contact record to see if it's up-to-date, and I make any necessary category changes. Then I print or highlight the records for each of my A and B contacts. From this, I make a contact plan for the month. I determine whom I need to contact, why, and when, and I record on my calendar. My goal is to list at least nine people to contact every day during that month. It's what I call the Power of Nine.

As I add new people to my database, within 24 hours, I send them a "Nice to meet you" note or email to start the process. My calendar has follow-up dates and tasks that become a part of my daily "to do" list, the names of the nine people I should contact, and any cards I should send.

A TYPICAL DAY

Here's how I stay in touch on a typical day when I'm not in my office and at a client meeting:

- I check phone messages and prioritize them to determine who has to be called immediately.

- I return the priority calls right away and return the others within 24 hours.

- I check and respond to emails. For those that take more time, I send an email referring them back to later in the day.

- I call a prospect that has been referred to me. We speak briefly and set up a future phone appointment. This gives me a chance to check the prospect's website so I will be prepared when we speak. I also email the referral contact (his preferred method) to say thank you and ask if there is anything I need to know about the prospect. All this I record into my phone.

Then, when I return to my office, I make sure to do the following:

- Send the prospect a handwritten note.

- Send my referral source a handwritten note to thank him for the referral. I also utilize my automated software system, appreciationpower.com.

- Enter all the information into my database.

- Visit the prospect's website and prepare for our phone meeting the next day.

- Return the rest of my phone and email messages.

Staying in touch with everyone in your network is an art and a science. People like to be remembered and contacted in thoughtful ways. However, as your network grows, you need to create a system for staying connected with so many people. The successful networker knows how to combine these two tasks to create a seamless networking fabric in his or her life.

In the next chapter, you'll look at how to create your own "fan club," which involves building and maintaining a group of advocates who take it upon themselves to help you succeed in your business life. You also learn how to build your referral pipeline, develop a niche as you develop your network, and explore networking across the different generations.

Exercise 1: The Power of Three (or Nine)

The best way to stay in touch with people is to make a habit of contacting at least three of them a day by note, email, phone, or text. This enables you to make staying in touch a part of your busy schedule. Beside each category, write the name of at least one person to whom you will write a note, make a phone call, or send an email or text. You can extend this exercise by writing up to three people's names for each day of the week. Make a copy of this form, and do this exercise every day for a month, to make it a habit.

Coworker: _____

Prospect: _____

Client: _____

Friend: _____

Service Provider: _____

LinkedIn Connection _____

Contact from an Event _____

Family Member: _____

Note: I keep raising the bar for myself, and I have increased the Power of Three to the Power of Nine. Many of my colleagues and workshop participants have done the same. Take small steps—start with three a day, and make it a part of your life.

Inch by inch, it is a cinch—yard by yard, it is hard.

Exercise 2: Strengthening Your Network

The longer a working relationship has been in existence, the stronger it gets. However, it takes effort to make that happen. The following questions help you think about ways to build better and stronger connections with others.

What do you think are the three most effective ways to show appreciation after someone has given you business referrals?

_____

_____

_____

What are three important dates most people celebrate that you can recognize by sending a card, making a call, or sending a text?

_____

_____

_____

What could someone do for you that would justify sending a thank you gift? (List up to three.)

_____

_____

_____

11

Creating Advocates

ne afternoon, I received a phone call from the division of a large financial services firm asking me to come in for a meeting regarding an extensive consulting project.

During our conversation, I asked the representative how she had received my name and contact information. I knew that I could have cold-called and sent information and proposals for months and probably had no success. So why was I called?

I had an advocate at the firm: Erinn, a young woman I had helped several years ago after she attended a college class I was teaching on networking in business. Erinn was now a rising star at this firm, and she'd recommended me to her colleagues and to the selection committee.

I emailed Erinn immediately to thank her for the referral and said I would let her know what developed. As she later wrote back, "I never forgot how you helped me when I was starting out, meeting for a soda at the diner, listening, and offering your suggestions. You don't know how much I appreciated it."

Well, I do, and I'm thankful that Erinn is my advocate!

You know that networking is a necessary skill for finding and developing new clients and keeping those you have. It's also an opportunity to create advocates for your business. These advocates will be your best sales and marketing champions because they know and respect you.

They will talk about you and your business in a positive way. This is a credibility factor that no one can buy—it comes from working hard and smart to create powerful and strategic connections.

A colleague recently received an email with the subject line, "You come highly recommended." It was from the executive vice president of human resources for a large holding company, asking for a meeting to discuss her firm's products. As she read the email, she saw that a former client had referred her. As she said to me, "Even with both of our crazy schedules, we manage to keep in touch with each other in person or by email and notes." That client and I had met for breakfast not long before. After our breakfast meeting, he told a colleague about me, and I then received the email requesting a meeting.

Of course, even when you do have your advocates, you still need to market yourself directly to your prospects and clients. When your advocates open the door for you, you must stay in there and close the deal. It pays to create these advocates who believe in you and who can leverage your marketing efforts.

Identifying Potential Advocates

Creating advocates and ambassadors is key to expanding your networks. People who know you, trust you, and believe in you are all possible alliances and resources for you and your business. Look at the various people that are in your life.

The Satisfied Client

Who can be better advocates than satisfied clients or employers? They can give testimonials and refer you to others. Sometimes you might feel awkward about asking for referrals; however, there are ways to make asking easier. I had just finished a project at a new company where I had gotten to know several people quite well. While we were talking during our celebration lunch, I said, "As we debrief, tell me what you liked best about our program and what could have been changed or different." It was a positive discussion, and I thanked them all. Then I said, "I would be happy to work with anyone you feel comfortable referring me to within the firm." Two weeks later, I received a call from a colleague of one of the people at the luncheon asking me for an appointment to learn about my services.

Another time, I was referred to the former supervisor of a person I had worked with on a project. When Natalie called me, she said that Allison, who used to work for her, had recommended me to do the same project for her organization. Of course, I thanked both Natalie and Allison, and I kept Allison in the loop as the project progressed. Your advocates stay with you when you stay in touch. This is part of the thank you chain we talked about in Chapter 9, "Follow-up: A Road Map for Growth." Be sure to always keep everyone in the loop and in their preferred communication method.

Good times to ask satisfied clients for referrals are after a success, when you're meeting during a social gathering, and when you've solved any challenges that might have occurred.

People You Work With: Your Team

Whatever someone's job description might be, it's ultimately a sales job. You might be thinking, "Wait—my assistant doesn't sell" or even "I don't sell." What does sales have to do with that type of job? Anyone who has a client contact, whether direct, as in sales and customer service, or indirect, as in production or accounting, is ultimately responsible for selling and marketing the company. In fact, as you build your internal networks and alliances, you are always selling ideas to others, so you are in sales. You need to help everyone around you think like this. Your assistant might speak all day to your clients, internal support teams, and management. The way he or she communicates is a direct reflection of you. Empower your team members to think of ways to create and develop more business opportunities, regardless of their job function.

Conrad Hilton built his hotel empire on the principle that every employee is responsible for sales, from the groundskeepers, housekeepers, and bellhops, to the front-desk staff. Every interaction with a customer is a sales opportunity, even if that is well-kept ground, spotless rooms, or a smile and greeting at each contact.

If everyone on your team could think, "How is what I'm doing helping the client, whether internal or external?" then everyone would be an advocate for your firm. Helping an internal client—coworkers who depend on you to help them get their jobs done—is as important as helping an external client. First and foremost, you must build and maintain a strong foundation.

Creating advocates in your company takes the same networking skills we've been discussing. Find out who you need in your network, and get to know them—listen and learn. Then make the connection and stay in touch. Go through the same processes we've been discussing. Think of every meeting as an opportunity to further build your internal network.

EVERYONE IS IMPORTANT

Too often people network only up the corporate ladder. My theory is that every single person is important and is part of your internal team. Smart people know to build relationships and alliances with those up, down, sideways, and across. Create and build relationships throughout the company.

Contacts and Colleagues in Your Business or Industry

In today's world, many of the contacts you make in your industry will refer business to you because you specialize in an area that is needed. Here's where your self-marketing skills are necessary. Fine-tune your 30-second infomercial, become known in your field by giving presentations and writing articles, join and participate in professional organizations, and follow up and stay in touch with your network contacts.

Judy, a woman I met in a yoga class, had launched a photography business. Several years later, she now has a successful portrait studio. Much of her business comes from referrals from other photographers who specialize in commercial work. They refer their clients to her for portraits and executive head shots, and she refers clients to them for websites and corporate photography. She's a specialist in her area and has a reputation as one of the best. The key here is to identify what you do best and to make sure that becomes your "brand"—when people need what you do, you will pop up on their radar screen.

Others at Your Client's Place of Business

It's important to reach beyond your comfort zones and meet more people, develop more relationships, and learn that, even with your strongest business accounts, it's critical to "surround the account" and know several people at the firm or organization. Think of the different people at a firm you meet during a job interview, or those you're working with on a specific account, or the different people on the internal team. Get to know the different people as you build your networks.

At one firm I work with, Linda used to be my main contact, Claudette was her assistant, Alice worked next to her, and David and Michael were assistants. By creating and developing relationships with all these people and staying on their radar screens, I have expanded my network and set the scene for more business. Recently, Linda left the company and went to another one. I kept in touch with her and will soon be presenting a proposal to her new company. Claudette, her assistant, was promoted, and because of my relationship with her and others, I have kept my business at that company. This is a story that has been around for ages. Every person who takes on a leadership role brings in his or her own teams. Make sure you've done your homework to know them.

Several years ago, I helped Carol find a new job. Then she introduced me to the head of marketing in her company, who hired me to do a program on presentation skills. In the last few years, I have done many projects with this company. Carol left the firm after a year, yet because I created many internal connections in the company, I have worked in all its branches throughout the country. I continued to work with Carol in her next job, which was more suited for her. Now she's thinking of starting her own business in the next year, and she knows that I will be one of her biggest advocates, as she has been for me.

START YOUR THANK YOU CHAIN

1. Think right now of all the connections you have within a firm.

2. Go back and put into action the thank you chain to touch base with some of these people. Connect to say thank you—call, write, text, email, or use social media. Just do it!

3. Then before you do anything else, go back to your contact management system and enter the names of these people, your relationship to them, how you know them, and what business you might have gotten from or given them. (Use the Client Profile Template in the Part 3 Appendix.)

4. Watch the relationships in each of your accounts begin to multiply, and see your network grow.

How many times have you lost business when your main contact left the company? You have to start all over again to win back the account. Better to have advocates throughout the organization who will champion your services.

Think of the companies you work for now and possible advocates you have developed. Remember to use your thank you chain, and be sure to show your appreciation for referrals others give you. Keep this information in your contact management system, and stay in touch. Business can come from anyone on the other side of your door.

Your Friends and Neighbors

You work hard at building friendships that include mutual trust and respect. As you find out more about your friends' work, you'll want to help them, and over time, they will most likely want to help you with referrals.

Recently, my friend Norma experienced some challenging times in her business. She lost several key clients through circumstances that had nothing to do with her ability. I introduced Norma to another friend of mine who was looking for a top person in his company. Now Norma is working there happily, and she has also become my advocate. I spoke at a meeting of one of her industry organizations, which resulted in three new contacts for me. We both make sure we stay on each other's radar at all times.

Turning neighbors into advocates might take more time, yet it will be worth the effort. Take the time to strike up conversations with people in your building or neighborhood. Often you find that you have common interests.

My friend Jan struck up a conversation with a young man in her elevator and found out that he was a coin collector. She knew someone else whose hobby was coin collecting and arranged to have the young man attend a showing. His parents were so impressed with Jan's gesture that they invited her and her husband for cocktails at their home. During the evening, they discovered they shared a lot of common interests. The young man's father is the managing partner at a large law firm, and Jan is a publicist who works with law firms. Several months later, Jan has this firm as a client, along with another firm the father referred to her. Like Jan, when you look at life with a networking awareness, your contacts will develop into something more.

You never know what can happen when you get to know your neighbors. It all starts with a smile, genuine interest and curiosity about others, and self-marketing skills to create advocates. We meet people in a variety of ways, develop relationships, and then see opportunities present themselves—often when we least expect it.

People many times ask me the underlying question, "How do I convert a friendship into business without jeopardizing the friendship?" We never want our friends to think we are exploiting our relationship, and we also may worry that a poor result will sour the friendship. The remedy for this dilemma is twofold. Half is mindset, and half involves tactics.

Think about the following:

- Your friend might have a need for what you or your firm specializes in. You already have a vested interest in your friends, and you can say that you would like to refer them to a trusted source that you work with.

- Your friend might also wonder why you haven't brought up the subject in the past.

- You are successful at what you do and consider that working together might actually deepen your friendship because your friend will see you in a role in which you shine.

When you develop a different mindset, you are ready to plan a strategy for suggesting that you work together. Preplan the conversation in your mind, to make you more comfortable in something that you might perceive to be an awkward discussion.

Here's one approach:

> Elizabeth, I'd like to talk about the possibility of our doing business together, and I don't want it to impinge on our friendship. Would it be okay to come to your office on Tuesday and discuss your financial/estate planning needs to see if there's an area in which my firm or I might be able to help you?

This approach has several advantages:

1. It clearly acknowledges that you value the friendship and don't want to jeopardize it.

2. It lets your friend know that you recognize the boundaries between friendship and business, and it makes clear that you do not intend to convert your "friend time" into an endless barrage of sales pitches.

3. It puts you on a businessperson-to-businessperson footing when talking business.

If even that approach seems too direct, here are some other ways to get friends to start thinking of you as the solution to their business concerns instead of seeing you as just a great tennis partner or another mom on the soccer sidelines:

1. Ask them about their businesses. This typically leads to questions from them about your business.

2. The next time you're scheduled to have lunch, ask them to meet you at your office. When they see you in your business environment, they might see you in a new light.

3. Showcase your business acumen by inviting them to a seminar put on by your firm at which you are a featured speaker.

4. Forward an article of professional interest to them that relates your expertise. Include a personal note highlighting why it might be of interest to them and how it relates to your practice.

5. Invite them to be your guests at a business-related program on a topic of mutual interest. Picking up the tab sends the subtle message that you consider this a business opportunity.

Which friend have you overlooked as a great prospect for your services? What could you do this week to broach the possibility of doing business together? With the right mindset and approach, doing business with friends can be comfortable, fun, and profitable!

Building Your Referral Pipeline

Positive networking is your way of marketing yourself. You build business when you receive referrals from your clients, contacts, and friends. They believe in you so much that they want to send opportunities your way.

Sometimes they need a reminder—and that's why it's so important to stay on people's radar screens: You want to come to mind when they want someone with your expertise. When others take the time to refer you, it means they trust you because you have earned that trust.

Here are some ways to earn trust and stay on your contacts' radar screens every day:

1. Get to know your clients as friends. Have a meal with them, take them to an event, and develop a relationship with them as you would with a friend.

2. Provide service that dazzles your clients. Credibility is everything. Make it easy for them to brag about you because you provide top service and always go the extra mile.

3. Always think of them and what they need. Be proactive. Think of how you can make their life and work easier and more productive. Be the go-to person to fix things for them.

4. Continually give added value. Whatever you currently do for them, do some more and spice it up. Send them a note or a tip of the month (or week) to keep them informed about things they want to know and information that could help their business.

5. Make connections for them. Help them find new business, a valuable connection, or anything that enhances their life or solves a problem.

6. Never keep score. Do it because you like and respect them. If you show that they're always on your radar screen, you will find yourself on theirs as well.

Over time, you will earn their trust and respect and will see the results in a solid network of contacts that you can rely on and go to when you need help. From time to time, however, you might want to ask your clients and contacts for a "report card." Find an appropriate time to ask the following questions:

- What makes you do business with me?

- What could I be doing better?

- When you refer me to someone, what qualities about me come to mind?

Always remember that a referral is earned and is never given without thought and consideration. Here's a checklist of more suggestions on how you can grow your referral pipeline without asking for them:

- Make a daily thought of "Who will I meet today?" or "Who will I be introduced to today?" At the day's end, have a friend or family member ask you, "Who were you introduced to today?" This just helps keep your awareness and focus more in tune.

- Fall in love with the word *curiosity*. It's a great probing word, and people are more likely to open up when we're curious. It also works well with any objection. "I see. Tell me more—I'm just curious."

- Make sure your advocates and ambassadors know how to refer you and know that you are a reflection of their trust when they do refer you.

- Keep them in the loop. I know I say this a lot, but it is important.

- Receive every referral graciously. How you receive the referrals you get will either encourage or discourage your contact, client, or networking resource for future referrals.

- When the referral turns out favorably, offer to take both your source and the new contact to lunch. This makes it more collaborative.

- Become proactive at giving first. Always ask others, 'How do I know when I'm speaking with someone you would like to meet?" and "How do I know your ideal client or someone who can use your services?" Give first and build on the relationships, and the referrals will come. Even if you can't always give other people a concrete referral, you're letting them know that they're on your radar and that you want to know how to introduce them when the opportunity arises. One of my dad's greatest lines has served so well in receiving referrals: "Give without remembering, receive without forgetting."

- Strive for introductions with your strongest clients and advocates. In conversations, you might ask, "What made Bill come to mind? How do you know him, and what will make him take my call?"

Networking Across Generations

You currently interact with four generations, especially at work: Millennials, Generation X'ers, Baby Boomers, and Traditionalists. Whatever generation you are in, you look to the others as different and have to adjust.

Phyllis Weiss Haserot, Practice Development Counsel Consulting/ Coach to the Next Generation, says that networking and dealing with people of different generations is similar to the recipe for any kind of successful networking—with a few twists. Have a sincere interest in the other person. If you really want to learn about their interests, how you can help them, what makes them tick, it will show. (If you're bored and uncomfortable, that will show, too.) Ask questions about them with enthusiasm.

Here's what Generations X and Y and Millennials want:

- To feel important
- To be heard
- To have their ideas sought out
- To feel respected and valued

- To feel that you enjoyed the conversation

- To sense your authenticity

When you're networking, if you know people in the room, introduce the young people to them. Make those people feel comfortable by telling a snippet about them, to lay a foundation for common ground or a conversation starter.

Also offer to introduce your new young acquaintances to people outside the event. They're hungry to build their networks and learn from experienced people, and your offer shows that you respect them and the value they might bring to an older person. Don't worry about having to be an expert in their music, sports, or other interests if you don't really care to be. That's inauthentic, and they will pick up on it.

One of the keys is to get outside yourself and feel excited by what you can learn about and from each new person you meet. It's a state of mind that you can adopt if it doesn't come naturally. I'm lucky that it does come naturally to me. I feel fortunate to have many good friends who are much younger than I am, and I love their company and hanging out with their friends. We energize each other, and it's a great feeling.

Creating Rainmakers in Your Business

A rainmaker is someone who thinks about growing the business and finds ways to bring it in continually—someone who generates opportunities for new and current clients and thinks of ways to solve their problems. If everyone on your team did this, business would improve. To help everyone think like a business developer, you need to create awareness and communicate the idea to your team.

An accounting department manager at one company I know trains her team to speak in "user-friendly" terms to customers. Instead of calling only to ask about payment, her team listens to the clients to understand their problems and finds ways to solve them. The team members have come to see how everything they do, from the way they speak to clients, to the way they handle complaints, has a direct connection to the bottom line. While listening to a client's questions about a transaction, one staff member discovered both a concern and an opportunity for new business. She handled the concern and relayed the conversation to staff members who were able to correct a problem that could have lost the business. They were then able to take advantage of an opportunity that created new business. This staff member in accounting now truly believes and understands that she is part of the rainmaking team and understands the value of internal networking.

> The dictionary definition of *rainmaker* is "a person (as in a law firm) who brings in new business; also: a person whose influence can initiate progress or ensure success."

Salespeople work hard to sell and create relationships with clients, yet everyone in the company also needs to build and maintain good relationships with clients. Everyone is in sales. The operations manager, the marketing associate, and the IT technician represent the company every time they contact a client or a potential client. I like to say that we are all in sales, public relations, and customer service for the companies with which we work. In fact, customer service isn't a department—it's part of everyone's job, from the CEO down to the receptionist.

A dentist I know embraced the concept of rainmaking when she was losing patients because of the way her office staff treated them. In one case, a patient who left also took five family members, three people from her office, and two friends from her health club! My friend was fortunate to find out about this, since most people who receive poor treatment don't complain; they simply go away and then tell everyone about their experience. The dentist took immediate steps with her staff to correct the way they were handling patients and to stress the importance of their role in the practice. She was able to turn them into rainmakers.

People on your team need to know and understand a couple ideas to think like business developers and strategic networkers. And if your "team" is only you, then you'll have to work even harder and smarter because you are your business and you are the product. First, ask what business you're in, whom you serve, what your clients' needs are, who your competitors are, what makes you different, and what unique benefits clients derive from your services. Second, ask what your mission statement is and how that applies to your clients.

At one company I recently worked with, I asked the group to tell me its mission statement; only 2 out of 40 people knew it, and most had no idea how it applied to them. It's your job to explain your mission and turn your employees into advocates. Look at your employee roster. How well do you know the employees who are in a position to relay your message? What can you do to incorporate some networking techniques into your day by going to a different area and spending a little time with each employee or department? I read that Sam Walton, the late founder and CEO of Walmart, not only knew the name of each of his employees, but also empowered them with a sense of ownership of their company. To this day, when I walk into a Walmart, I always feel welcome, as if each person contributes to all the great customer service and sales there. I'm glad I also own stock in the company!

Find ways to listen to your team and hear their concerns and problems. It's important that you know how they interact with customers and that they understand how their relationship with customers affects the company. When people feel their work is important, they become advocates for the company, which is the ultimate in building relationships.

Give members of your team some appreciation; find ways to say thank you and to compliment them. Be sure to compliment them when they handle clients well or when they're advocates for your business. Studies show that people often work harder when they feel appreciated and that behavior that is rewarded is repeated. Instill in your people the power of networking and that it is everyone's job. Reward them when they succeed at it. Lead by example.

SEVEN STEPS TO CLIENT RETENTION

1. Spend 20 minutes daily talking with two existing clients or networking connections. Ask them what they want, what they need, what they like, and what they dislike. Ask them how they feel about the service they're currently receiving. Listen, implement changes, and suggest new ideas.

2. Invite your "champion clients" to serve on an advisory board.

3. Partner with your client in a workshop or special event. The more time you spend together, the more you bond.

4. Provide value every day. Offer something unique to show that you are creative, resourceful, and open to new ideas.

5. Find ways to connect on common ground, such as through hobbies, sports, special interests, religious affiliations, or school alumni groups.

6. Spend some time with your competitors and learn what they're doing. Find out from your clients what they hear in the outside world.

7. Conduct regular client satisfaction surveys or interviews, both formal and informal. These also provide valuable feedback.

Grow and Keep the Business You Have

Getting new business is much tougher than growing, managing, and building the business you already have. What can your team do to grow existing business?

1. Make your relationship with your customer's job number one. Find ways to stay focused on the client. I know one firm that only calls or emails clients at billing time. Needless to say, several clients have found other firms—ones that they feel are there for them in between the billing periods.

2. What do your clients need? What worries them? When you provide solutions, or at least show them that you care, you become a valuable addition to their team.

3. Who are your best customers, and why do they buy from you?

The principal objective of developing customers is to focus on the customers' needs. Happy customers are then cultivated as tremendous referral sources. When you have a customer on your side, generating high-profit word-of-mouth referrals is always easier. At the same time, your employees can be thinking beyond current ideas about what to do and how to help when they hear clients' concerns, problems, or situations (positive or negative). This affects everyone's job by contributing to the bottom line.

We all want personal attention, and we are all someone's customer. See how you feel the next time someone you work with treats you well or not so well. You might consider assigning every customer someone whom they can call at any time, so at least there's always a "real person" to help. If that person is unable to handle the situation, he or she can direct the call to someone who can.

Your personal advocates can offer you the most valuable third-party endorsements. Think of them as part of your personal "buzz marketing" campaign. Be sure to take good care of the connections you have with them.

It's hard to believe that it's time to wrap up everything we've discussed so that you can build on what you've discovered to create a terrific networking future.

Exercise: Who Are Your Advocates?

1. List 10 contacts (clients, coworkers, employees, friends) who are advocates for you and your business. What quality made you think of them?

2. How often are you in contact with each of them?

3. What is the biggest challenge each of them faces?

4. What associations or organizations do they belong to, and have you been to a meeting? Recently?

5. When did you last visit their website or respond to something you saw on Google Alerts?

6. List at least one thing you could offer to do for them in the near future:

   a. Write an article for a publication.

   b. Offer to do a workshop pro bono.

   c. Send an article of interest.

   d. Give them a referral.

   e. Make a useful introduction.

   f. Help them solve a problem.

   g. Send a card or note for a special occasion.

"When all is said and done, much more is said than done."
—Anonymous

12

Today, Tomorrow, and Your Future

Each day holds amazing networking opportunities for you. It truly is a small world, and you never know what will come from the connections or contacts you make. This is part of the fun of life, and I always hold on to that wonderful phrase, "If you want to make God laugh, tell him your plans." We just never know what's in store for us and how our lives can change or be enhanced, or how something entirely new can suddenly unfold. This can happen just because someone we've met makes a connection for us, we've reconnected with an old friend, or we've met someone through a chance encounter. Of course, much of this has to do with our following up. Things happen when we take that action step after life has presented us with a variety of opportunities.

In business, which is such an integral part of our lives, the power of connection is the key. It's all about whom you know, and who knows you, and how you enhance and learn from those relationships. Often in my workshops, I ask, "Is it always the smartest person who rises to the top of an organization?" Unanimously, people say, "No!" The truth is that being smart and capable is your ticket in the door and staying there. However, to succeed and keep building your business, you also need to have great alliance and people skills—just what we've talked about throughout this book. The philosophy is simple; it's the consistent implementation that takes discipline.

In today's crazy, time-starved world, people want information quickly and succinctly so they can act on it. Did you know that Abraham Lincoln's Gettysburg Address was a total of 226 words, and the Ten Commandments only 297 words? These are documents that get their points across succinctly.

EVERYONE HAS A MOTHER...

Having just reconnected with a friend about a year ago, I established a business relationship with the association she heads. I met her second-in-command, Marshall, who, when not working for the association, runs his own marketing company. Just recently, Marshall hired me to conduct a media training program for one of his clients, a doctor.

As it turns out, I told the doctor during our session that his last name was uncommon and that I also knew a very nice woman with the same last name in the direct marketing industry, where I started my career. I asked him if he knew her. "Yes," he said, "she's my mother!" Life is funny. You never know when one connection may lead you to another.

Another time, sitting in a client's office, I was looking at his family picture and saw his sister. This was another great experience. I knew her from an industry association where I had been active. However, she has a different last name, lives in another city, and works in a different industry. I just was being observant and commented on the picture. What are the odds that I would have been in her brother's office?

Again, you just never know. The world is truly connected.

WHEN YOU NEED A RELATIONSHIP, IT'S TOO LATE TO BUILD IT

Live life with the state of mind that networking is everything—it is life. Greet each day with a "networking eye and ear." Learn and be aware. To do this, incorporate these practices daily—or at least be aware of them:

1. Meet people and nurture your current network.
2. Listen to and learn from all the people you connect with.
3. Make connections for others.
4. Follow up.
5. Stay in touch.

New stories and "aha" moments happen every day. People like you connect with me all the time to tell me of their success. Often they realize that they have been networking all along and never realized it, or they tell me how they have become more aware of this interesting phenomenon and state of mind. I especially enjoy when they tell me about their best practices and success stories, and how they've passed them down to their staffs, colleagues, and teams at work.

You've been on quite a journey in this book. Very simply stated, you have gone through tips, strategies, and techniques for finding, growing, and keeping your business through the art and science of networking. The magic formula for all this is in the doing of it. Start today with your awareness of it all, and just remember these final few facts.

Networking is truly a misunderstood word. Yes, some work is involved, and when you implement what we've discussed in this book, you will see results over time and without keeping score. Just try to be aware of everything and live life with your networking eyes and ears open. Continually do your homework—always be prepared and organized, and consistently apply the techniques we've discussed in your daily life.

Whenever I give a speech or a workshop, I always finish my program with what I call my Networking Acronym. It really condenses everything we've discussed in this book to its simplest form, and I hope you can take one thought, one idea, or one "aha" moment from it and put it into action starting today. And if you come up with some thoughts that I've left out, please connect with me and let me know, and I will add them into my next speech, workshop, or seminar.

N   Remember people's **names**. To each person, his or her name is golden. On that same thought, continually **nurture** the relationships of your current networks and find out what they need.

E   **Enthusiasm** and **energy** are key; have the **empathy** to understand that everyone has his or her own agenda; remember that **eye** contact speaks volumes; and know when to **exit** gracefully. **Execute** the skills, **engage** in the process, and realize that it **evolves** over time.

T **Talk** less and listen more. Networking is about listening and learning from everyone you meet. Developing **trust** takes **time**, and you always need to be in the mode of **thinking**, "How can I help this person?"

W **Write.** In this electronic age, a handwritten note or message stands out and will be remembered. **Work** is involved that you will incorporate into your daily life.

O **Organization** is key. Keeping your contacts, records, and information is essential to your success. Remember, whenever you meet others, it is an **opportunity** to learn from them and be a resource to help them. To do this, get into the habit of asking **open-ended**, high-gain questions to develop rapport.

R **Research** everything. Know that the goal is to develop a **rapport** that will lead to a **relationship** encompassing both trust and **respect**. Your **reputation** is crucial because you have built on it your whole life, so be careful when you **refer** anyone—that person is a **reflection** on you. Be **resilient** and **respectful** of all. Everyone has a lesson to teach us.

K **Knowledge** is power...only with execution. Much of our discussion has been common sense—it's just not always common practice. Take the action steps to make things happen. Keep in touch, and be creative about it. Also, I think every day about what my wonderful father said to me and continues to say as he smiles down from heaven: Be kind to people; give everyone you meet a smile and a handshake. My dad was the master of this and lives in my heart daily.

I **Integrity** is everything we have discussed. Your character and reputation are so important—remember that, with integrity, nothing else matters. To make your networking work, be sure to always take the **initiative**. Waiting for someone else to make the first move is not the style of a proactive networker. Also, become **interested** in other people and what you can learn from them.

N Sometimes you have to say **no**—when you say yes to everyone, you say no to yourself; know your limits. On the other hand, when I hear "No," I often reverse the letters to *on* so that I am resourceful and creative in making and keeping my connections.

G Set **goals** for your networking achievements, and remember to show **gratitude** to those who help you. Also **give** of your time and expertise to others. In the end, it's all about **going** for it and being **gracious.**

One Final Story: How Networking Has Changed My Life

I remember March 1993 very well. I had been working as a magazine publisher and was enjoying my work very much. Then one day that March, I received a phone call. It caused me to remember a promise I'd made to myself a few years earlier after I was in a bad car accident and had to be hospitalized.

I'd promised myself that I'd start my own business. I didn't know how, but I did know that this was what I really wanted to do in life. In fact, I had been preparing myself all along as a student of psychology and business. I had already been speaking publicly through my work at a variety of associations and at any opportunities that popped up. I had also started teaching other workshops, yet I had not taken that leap of faith.

When that call came, it was from one of my publishing clients, Max, who was asking me to come and speak to his sales staff at their annual meeting. That morning, as I was reviewing my notes for my presentation, I had a funny feeling that this experience might change my life. Fast-forward to the next day. The presentation went very well, I thought.

Apparently, Max did as well. Afterward, he invited me in as a consultant and said, "We will be your first client." And for three years, two days, and a week, his company helped me lay the groundwork for my business. This gave me the opportunity to interact with a whole company of people—from the junior people who were just starting out and learning some of the rules of business etiquette, to the senior people who needed to brush up on their presentation and pitching skills and wanted to learn how to work more effectively with their growing staffs.

As I met and worked with each person, I learned so much about each of them and practiced all the techniques and strategies outlined in this book. The 200 or so people with whom I worked there started another huge network in my life and business. People I had connected with left and went to other companies and brought me in to work with them and their teams (hence the beginning of my thank you chain).

During the three years I worked at that company, I also worked diligently on figuring out what other industries I most wanted to work in. I practiced my 2-2-2 strategies, went to a lot of meetings and associations, met a lot of people, and then decided to join several organizations and become involved. More doors opened, and the very steps we talked about in Part I, "Find (Meeting People)," became, and still are, a devout daily practice of mine. I realized there was, and is, so much opportunity everywhere when you just take the time to live life with a networking eye and ear as I have learned to do—by offering to give first and be a resource to others.

After my accident, while I was lying in the emergency room of a local hospital, in Massachusetts, waiting to be airlifted to one of Boston's top hospitals, I asked the doctors to call my parents so they would know what was happening. I still remember what my father, who had been recuperating from open-heart surgery, said to me as they held the phone to my ear: "Keep fighting—you are my whole life."

Through the years, I have thought about what my dad said and how I promised myself that when I got well, I would go out, find a way to make a real difference, and give back to all the people who have helped me along the way. For me, being able to give back like this has been one of the most fulfilling parts of being alive. I now realize how this attitude and my dad's loving words really are what changed my life and made me want to be a giver as much as I possibly can. To me, that is what networking is really all about. The human relations principles we discussed in this book are all practices we can use in our lives every day. You will see, or you have already seen, how everything we do is linked to others in our life—the way we touch them or the way they touch us—and how we influence them and they influence us.

As I look at my business and how it continues to grow, I see that every single aspect of my life relates to finding, growing, and keeping lasting, powerful relationships. These have opened doors for me and created amazing opportunities. My hope is that you will close this book now and promise to act on some of the tips, ideas, and strategies we have discussed and then contact me and let me know about all the wonderful successes that continue to come into your life.

Thank you for the opportunity to come into your life through this book, to share and discuss some of the interesting business strategies and lessons I have learned along the way from the many masters who have touched my life.

Exercise 1: What Do You Think Now?

Now that you've finished reading this book and doing the exercises, think about how your thoughts on networking might have changed. Please answer the following questions:

How has your definition of networking changed? How can you now create more business opportunities and stronger personal relationships through your own power of networking? What are you going to do consistently?

_____

_____

_____

List three new ideas about networking that you've learned.

1. _____

2. _____

3. _____

Exercise 2: Know Yourself

When you know effective networking techniques, you can use them in any situation. Wherever you network in business and in life, remember the following:

1. **Know who you are.** Write down, in one or a few lines, how you want people to remember you. What would people say were your positive personality attributes?

_____

_____

_____

2. **Focus on others.** Write down your best conversation starters.

_____

_____

_____

3. **Have a goal.** Which goals are you most concerned with now in your life?

   a. Promotion

   b. New job

   c. Political aspirations

   d. Career change

   e. Lifestyle change

   f. New business venture

   g. Move to a new location for work and/or life

   h. Clients for your business

   What can you do today to start achieving those goals?

_____

_____

_____

Exercise 3: Do It Today

Which person will you contact today whom you haven't thought of before you did these exercises? Write down that person's name, how you will contact him or her, and what you want to accomplish.

_____

_____

_____

_____

The Networking Acronym: Fill in any other traits or techniques that come to mind. Take the next step, and write next to each letter an experience that corresponds to that letter, to make it real for you.

For example...*E:* Remember a time when you had a successful *exit* strategy. Or *W:* Think where you started the process of *writing* handwritten notes. Keep this going for yourself to maintain a networking tip log.

N _____

E _____

T _____

W _____

O _____

R _____

K _____

I _____

N _____

G _____

Exercise 4: Networking Action Plan

As a result of reading and working through this book, what are you going to do in the *first week*?

More of:

_____

_____

Less of:

_____

_____

Change:

_____

_____

By the *end of the month*, I will:

Do more of:

_____

_____

Do less of:

_____

_____

Change:

_____

_____

In the *next three months*, I will:

Do more of:

_____

_____

Do less of:

_____

_____

Change:

_____

_____

Remember, positive networking is all about giving more to others than you receive and always being a resource for them. Until we meet again, all the best in your networking!

Appendix

Client Profile Template

As you build your network connections and turn them into relationships, the more you know about someone the better. Collect data through conversations over time, and then you can use it to reach out, show that you remember important information, and continue to build the relationship.

Business Information

- Company/firm
- Business background and previous work experience
- Address and phone number
- Assistant's name
- Promotions and business opportunities
- Key relationships
- Corporate culture, levels, and politics
- "Why do you work with us?"
- How you met
- Business issues they are working on now
- Who you refer them to and why
- Immediate business and career objectives
- Personality type: Driver, Expressive, Analytical, Amiable

- Did you ask for their advice? Information given?
- How you've handled challenges in the past
- Which competitor they're most concerned about
- How they receive information: online, print, TV/radio
- What contributions are they most proud of?
- Preferred method of communication: email/phone/text/other
- Anniversary of doing business together
- What motivates them
- What achievement makes them proud
- Professional associations

Personal Information

- Birthday
- Birth state or country
- Activities in the community and charities
- Education: high school, college, fraternity or sorority, degrees
- Military service
- Hobbies and personal interests
- Favorite foods and restaurants
- Vacation interests
- Spouse: name, occupation, and interests
- Children: ages, names, schools, and interests
- Pets
- Personal objectives
- Key extended family members
- Special holidays
- Any specific likes and dislikes

- Book genre that they enjoy reading
- Collections they have
- How often they want to be communicated to
- Idiosyncrasies
- What else?

52 Nonstop Networking Tips (Practice over Time)

1. Give yourself permission to network. Maintaining a positive attitude is the first step to networking success.

2. Make a list of "opening lines" to use when meeting someone new. Use open-ended questions to create dialogue.

3. Develop a 20-second introduction about yourself. Practice it until it becomes spontaneous and natural. Create several for different audiences.

4. Do your research before attending an event or meeting. Learn the basics about the organization and the people likely to be there.

5. Have a list of "get to know you" questions." These go deeper than opening line questions; they help you to get know the interests of the person you just met.

6. Keep a journal of "small talk" topics, such as current events, industry topics, books, movies, community topics, and the like.

7. Set a goal for every event or meeting you attend. A good goal is to meet two new people; make a connection; and send a follow-up note, call, or email.

8. Smile when meeting people, entering a room, or talking on the phone. A smile is the first step in building rapport. Smile for 10 seconds when you enter a room. (Research says that this makes you more approachable.)

9. Look the other person in the eye. It shows that you are focused on the conversation and interested in what the other person is saying. The eyes are the windows of the soul.

10. Listen with care. Be aware of what the other person is saying instead of thinking about what you will say next. *Listen* has the word *silent* in it—silence your mind to focus and listen.

11. Learn to remember names. This skill will set you apart. Listen carefully when the name is said, repeat it in the conversation, and create a mind picture that will help you associate the person with the name.

12. Give compliments. Make a goal to look for positive attributes and give five compliments a day. Make sure they are sincere.

13. Make a list of the key people in your industry or profession that you would like to meet. Determine what organizations, places, and people you know that might help you connect.

14. Reconnect with four people a week. Call a client, prospect, colleague, and friend you haven't spoken with for several months.

15. Join a networking group and attend the meetings. Practice techniques such as your 20-second introduction, and keep expanding your circle.

16. Research and join industry and professional groups. Go to two meetings, meet two people, and set up two follow-up meetings before you make your decision to join. (2-2-2 Theory)

17. Join service groups such as your chamber of commerce, local Rotary chapter, or fund-raising organizations. Follow your interests in this matter. Join for the sake of giving, not getting.

18. Follow your interests. Remember, you need like-minded people in your network.

19. Volunteer, write an article, or join a committee in your organization. Becoming known helps you meet people and develop relationships faster and more profitably than just attending meetings. Be involved.

20. Send three handwritten notes a day. Send these to people in your network to say thank you or congratulations, send an article of interest, extend an invitation, or just keep in touch. Use found time during the day, and make these short and simple. Carry note cards and Forever stamps with you.

21. Write an article or newsletter to send to your contacts. This promotes your business and also helps you keep in touch with your contacts and stay on their radar.

22. Send gifts. Remember those who help you, or remember a special occasion for those in your network. Develop a list of reliable vendors of unique gift items for these occasions. Think of the person, and send a gift that you picked especially for him or her.

23. Use premiums that remind people of you and your business. Look for something that will be appreciated and that will keep your name in front of others.

24. Follow up within 24 hours of a meeting to say, "Nice to meet you" and "Thanks for your time and consideration," and to set another meeting.

25. Call within two weeks of suggesting another meeting. "Let's do lunch" is not an effective networking technique. Make it happen and set the date.

26. Send materials or information promised—on time or sooner than promised.

27. Thank your contact for a referral and let him or her know what happened. Keep your contacts in the loop.

28. Become a resource for others. Give generously of your time and expertise.

29. Look for unique and creative ways to have face time. Be creative and think outside the box.

30. Remember birthdays and special occasions, and send a card.

31. Review your list of contacts on a regular basis, and make sure it is revised and updated.

32. Develop a system to keep in touch with everyone in your network on a regular basis. As your list grows, divide it into categories and have a contact plan.

33. Maintain the system. It should work for you; you should not have to work for your system.

34. Collect information about each contact besides the basic information. This includes interests, family, awards and promotions, special dates, how you met, and other pertinent facts.

35. Determine the contact's preferred method of communication: phone, email, text, social media, in person. Note this on the person's database record.

36. Make and keep notes about each meeting with each contact. Refer to these when following up or before the next connection with him or her.

37. Have a system for keeping track of your contacts.

38. Enter information about a new contact within 24 hours of your meeting.

39. Answer all communications within 24 hours, even when you are on the road.

40. When you're out of the office, let people know with a message on your phone and an automatic email message.

41. Every day, send an email to someone in your database whom you have not been in touch with recently.

42. Once a week, go through your contact list and connect with three people to say hello.

43. Once a month, have lunch with a friend, colleague, or client.

44. At a company function, set a goal to sit next to someone new and get to know him or her. Also plan a method to follow up with them.

45. When making a phone call feels uncomfortable, use a script and practice until it becomes natural.

46. Begin with a compliment. This is a wonderful way to start a conversation when you might not know what to say to break the ice. Be sincere.

47. When a conversation gets off the topic you want to talk about, use a "bridge," such as "That reminds me of..." to get back on track.

48. Attend meetings with a purpose. Have a specific goal in mind when attending an industry event or other traditional networking meeting. It could be to meet the speaker or reconnect with a new client or prospect.

49. Set a time limit. When spending an entire meeting with an unknown group seems daunting, give yourself permission to leave after a specific time—at least one hour.

50. Send articles and interesting research electronically to keep in touch.

51. Give yourself a reward for your continual networking practice, whether for attending an event or reconnecting with someone from your past.

52. Network on the Internet with professional search engines.

ABC's of Life Networking

A Take **action**, monitor your **attitude**, be an **ambassador** of the firm, create **advocacy**

B **Belong** to groups (industry, professional, special interest, client focused)

C Call your **clients** and **contacts—connect**

D **Deliver** what you say immediately and consistently

E **Empathy**, **execute**, **evolution**, **eyes**, and **ears** (opened), **Engage** in the process

F **Friendly** approach, **find** opportunities to be in touch

G **Goals, give, grow**

H **Humor** and **help**—they go hand in hand

I **Initiate** and show **interest**

J **Join** and be involved

K **Keep** in touch with your contacts' preferred method of communication

L **Listen** and **learn**

M **Motivate** yourself to keep the process going, think like a **marketer**

N **Nurture** your relationships

O Be **open**, ask **open-ended** questions, take the **opportunity** to learn from all

P **Process, plan, practice**

Q Set your **quota—quality** versus **quantity**

R **Research**, be a **resource, refer** others

S **Strategy, system, success**

T **Trust** takes **time**

U **Understand** first, everyone is **unique**

V **Versatility** counts

W **Write** to stay in touch

X **XO**—really like the people in your continual networks

Y Focus on the other **you**—what are your contacts' interests?

Z **Zero** in on all opportunities and possibilities with new and nurtured connections

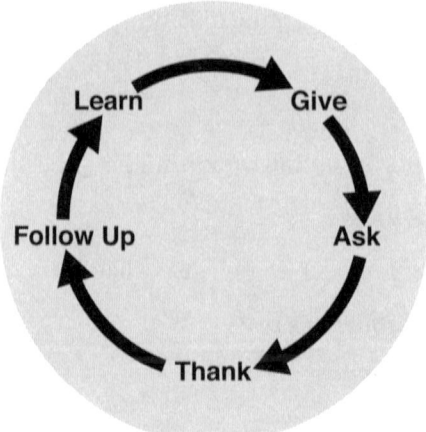

Figure A3-1 The Golden Circle of Strategic Networking

Index

E

thank you chains, 206, 244

thinkers versus feelers, 131

thinking of you notes, 220

third eye, 98

toolkits, 87

   intangible, 58-59

   tangible, 59-60

traits of common personality types, 129

travel tips, 151

trust, 145, 169

   building, 207-209

U

Unique Promise of Value, 143-144

uniqueness, communicating, 68

universal networks, 32-33

V

visual, communication styles, 126

visual stories, remembering names, 100

voicemails, etiquette, 165

volunteering, 46-47

W

Walmart, 252

Walton, Sam, 252

web, writing for, 184-185

WII-FM (What's in It for Me), 154

wish you were here notes, 220

women versus men

   bonding, 130-131

   communication, 132-133

   thinkers versus feelers, 131

worst things people do while networking, 154-155

writing

   articles, 47-48

   introverts, 176

   for publications and the web, introverts, 184-185

writing utensils, 60

Y-Z

You (focusing on), 103

Long Ago and Far Away

Hollywood and
the Second World War

Robert Fyne

THE SCARECROW PRESS, INC.
Lanham, Maryland • Toronto • Plymouth, UK
2008

ROWMAN & LITTLEFIELD PUBLISHERS, INC.

Published in the United States of America
by Scarecrow Press, Inc.
A wholly owned subsidiary of
The Rowman & Littlefield Publishing Group, Inc.
4501 Forbes Boulevard, Suite 200, Lanham, Maryland 20706
www.scarecrowpress.com

Estover Road
Plymouth PL6 7PY
United Kingdom

British Library Cataloguing in Publication Information Available

Library of Congress Cataloging-in-Publication Data

Fyne, Robert.
  Long ago and far away : Hollywood and the Second World War / Robert Fyne.
     p. cm.
  Includes bibliographical references and index.
  ISBN-13: 978-0-8108-6124-4 (hardcover : alk. paper)
  ISBN-10: 0-8108-6124-0 (hardcover : alk. paper)
  1. World War, 1939–1945—Motion pictures and the war. 2. Motion pictures in
propaganda—United States—History. I. Title.
D743.23.F96 2008
940.53'1—dc22   2007050198

∞™ The paper used in this publication meets the minimum requirements of American
National Standard for Information Sciences—Permanence of Paper for Printed Library
Materials, ANSI/NISO Z39.48-1992.
Manufactured in the United States of America.

All photos in the book supplied by Photofest

This book is for Jo-Ann,
who deserves much more.
Mon bijou précieux,
mon étoile brillante.

Contents

Chapter One

We've Never Been Licked

1941–1945

"It was the best of times, it was the worst of times."—Charles Dickens's antistrophic appraisal of everyday life prior to the unsettling events that eventually propelled eighteenth-century France into a long period of conflict, turmoil, and mayhem in *A Tale of Two Cities*

"Ever read *Guadalcanal Diary* by Richard Tregaskis? That was a best-seller and I read it!"—Amherst undergraduate Jonathan Fuerst (Jack Nicholson) arguing with his roommate, Sandy (Art Garfunkel), about belles-lettres in Mike Nichols's scathing 1971 depiction of sexual mores, *Carnal Knowledge*

On Thanksgiving Day 1941, many American families—clustered around a holiday table—still felt unclear about their nation's future. Why wouldn't they? Now in the ninth year of President Roosevelt's revolutionary New Deal—a complex organization of alphabet agencies designed for social and economic reform—the country witnessed a dramatic drop in the unemployment rate as eager recruits swelled the ranks of the Civil Works Administration (CWA), Civilian Conservation Corps (CCC), and the Work Projects Administration (WPA). Certainly this innovative surge created a better lifestyle, but off in the distance—in faraway Asia and Europe—another world war raged. Nazi Germany occupied many European nations, Imperial Japan swallowed up huge regions of China, and Stalin's Russia verged on collapse as *Wehrmacht* (German armed forces) troops approached Moscow. How long, many Americans pondered, before this conflict involved the United States? When would the homeland's youth—like their fathers before them—leave their families, enter the military, and fight on foreign soil?

Certainly, this global situation seemed bleak as each day's newspaper headlines bemoaned the British Empire's precarious state, Vichy France's fascist directives, and prime minister Hideki Tojo's Far East saber-rattling policies — while back in the States the right-wing isolationists, spearheaded by their hero Charles Lindbergh, argued neutrality with the interventionists. At the same time, magazine articles, radio commentators, and motion-picture newsreels added more information about Axis expansionist goals. And, of course, Hollywood feature films — the most popular form of entertainment — depicted one scene after another in an array of preparedness titles, warning audiences that war was lurking around the corner. No wonder many holiday guests, munching sweet potatoes, turkey breast, and pumpkin pie, seemed apprehensive about the future. While much of the Great Depression's misery had dissipated and a bouncy song proclaimed "We're in the Money," the looming overseas conflict worried everyone. On most people's minds a simple question gnawed: were they living in the best or worst of times?

A few days later all speculation ended when Japanese air squadrons attacked the Pacific fleet moored at Pearl Harbor. Within hours, Americans heard the news. Casualties were high at the Hawaiian outpost, and the threat of invasion alarmed the nation. Spurious sightings of Japanese vessels rattled West Coast residents, unsubstantiated rumors of fifth-column activities frightened everybody, and railroad stations, jammed with thousands of servicemen hurrying back to their bases, bulged at their seams. The following morning President Roosevelt, with Congress applauding his Day of Infamy proclamation, declared war on the Japanese Empire and warned about the uncertain days ahead. In the meantime, the Axis Pact — spearheaded by Germany and Italy — issued their formal declaration, and by week's end dozens of nations officially joined one side or the other. Clearly, these events removed any ambiguity. Without question, the worst of times had arrived.

Almost overnight, the nation prepared. Young men flocked to recruiting stations, civil-defense leaders implemented precautionary policies, manufacturers retooled for military armament, mayors of large coastline cities decreed blackouts, consumer rationing appeared, Boy Scouts organized scrap drives, public schools doubled as air-raid shelters, and in California studio executives stepped forward. With FDR's imprimatur, the motion-picture industry, now on a wartime footing, produced feature films that fostered morale, reassuring every American that the nation — with God's blessing — would emerge victorious from the global conflict. For the next four years, Hollywood created numerous photodramas that heralded the Allied cause, extolled democratic institutions, and applauded America's fighting men — while at the same time vilifying Axis leaders, denouncing expansionist policies, and disparaging the enemies' combat forces. Collectively, these war-related, black-and-white titles, with their two-dimensional characterizations, stereotypical plotlines, and clichéd dialogue, reminded audiences of their nation's commitment to victory. All of these pictures, of course, with their subliminal storylines, were propaganda films.

For Hollywood, this call to colors was old hat because many of the studios, especially Warner Bros., had already released feature films that in one way or another contained anti-German or anti-Japanese sentiments. In 1938 MGM's *Test Pilot*, with Clark Gable in the aviator's seat, argued for a strong bomber fleet; in Paramount's *Men with Wings*, an American airman, Fred MacMurray, died fighting for China against Japan; in RKO's *Hawaii Calls*, a young crooner, Bobby Breen, helped U.S. officials wreck a German and Asian undercover operation, stealing plans for the island's fortification; and in Columbia's *Smashing the Spy Ring*, Ralph Bellamy broke up an espionage gang nabbing U.S. military secrets. But in 1939, Warner Bros. declared war on Germany with its blatant *Confessions of a Nazi Spy*, an elaborate denunciation of Third Reich agents working on American soil. Likewise, Producers Distributing Corporation's *Beast of Berlin* warned about Hitler's persecution of Jews, Catholics, and non-Aryans in graphic concentration-camp scenes.

One year later, in 1940, the furnace reached full blast. MGM's *Escape*, *They Met in Bombay*, and *The Mortal Storm*; United Artists' *Foreign Correspondent* and *The Great Dictator*; Fox's *The Man I Married* and *Four Sons*; and Paramount's *Mystery Sea Raider* denounced Nazi Germany in unequivocal language. By 1941 Warner Bros.' *Dive Bomber*, *Underground*, *Sergeant York*, and *International Squadron*; Paramount's *I Wanted Wings*; Fox's *Man Hunt*; and United Artists' *Sundown* warned audiences that war with Germany and Japan was just around the corner. After all, Joel McCrea, in the concluding minutes of *Foreign Correspondent*, pleaded with his countrymen to "keep those lights burning—cover them with steel, ring them with guns, build a canopy of battleships and bombing planes around them. Hello, America, hang on to your lights; they're the only lights left in the world!"

So in the broadest of terms, December 7 did not surprise most Hollywood producers. In a matter of hours numerous department heads huddled in smoke-filled rooms, plotting their next move. For these experienced moviemakers, this Sunday-morning Hawaiian attack ended all sugarcoating. Now cameramen received blunt instructions. Remove the kid gloves, load up your equipment, and go after the Axis Pact with both barrels. By war's end, this high-powered industry—even with unprecedented shortages and ambiguous U.S. Office of War Information (OWI) directives—delivered approximately four hundred motion pictures that in one form or another were outright propaganda films. Both entertaining and persuasive, these feature stories and optimistic storylines—as President Roosevelt often bragged—became an important component of morale.

Sizing up the situation, a New York City journalist (Joel McCrea) and his girlfriend (Laraine Day) keep a sharp eye on some fifth columnists operating near the Dutch coastline in Alfred Hitchcock's 1940 Foreign Correspondent. *Courtesy of United Artists.*

Like all moving pictures, propaganda films were easily categorized. Some screenplays concentrated on the Japanese offensive—depicting American troops assaulting heavily fortified South Pacific islands. Others focused on the European theater—showing the GIs' eastward advance toward Berlin. Still others extolled the Russian and Chinese armies—newfound allies—as these nations, often using rudimentary equipment, fought their invaders. Many described home-front life, reminding audiences about fifth columnists, black marketeering, food points, blackouts, housing shortages, and meatless Tuesdays. Musicals and comedies entered the fray, with popular songsters taunting the Japanese with "You're a Sap, Mr. Jap, to Make a Yankee Cranky" or rallying against the Nazis with "Let's Knock the Hit out of Hitler," offering some levity to a war-weary nation. At the same time, the American cowboy saddled up against the Axis, often in anachronistic plots, where galloping horses raced across the plains and caught up with foreign saboteurs. And, finally, Saturday-afternoon serials, those once-a-week cliffhangers, and Technicolor cartoons, featuring such staples as Popeye, Donald Duck, and Mighty Mouse, took potshots at their nemeses, Hitler, Tojo, and Mussolini.

For Hollywood directors, the Oriental enemies, with their distinctive facial features, became easy to caricature, ridicule, and malign. Soon, dozens of anti-Japanese pictures appeared, depicting the soldiers as diminutive, banzai-spouting automatons, wearing Coke-bottle eyeglasses, ready to commit hara-kiri at the drop of their funny-looking hats. Hastily produced B-potboilers— *A Yank on the Burma Road*, *Secret Agent of Japan*, and *Remember Pearl Harbor*—indicted the nation for treachery, while *Two-Man Submarine*, *Corregidor*, and *Manila Calling* reminded edgy audiences that the United States, now gearing for offensive war, would emerge triumphant. Why not? As another B-title reaffirmed, *We've Never Been Licked*.

Certainly, these "B for budget" screenplays, with their seven-day shooting schedules, unknown actor rosters, and painted backdrops, promised victory in every frame. But these sixty-minute motion pictures lacked the complexity of their big brothers, the feature films.

Full-length titles such as *Guadalcanal Diary*, *Gung Ho*, *Thirty Seconds Over Tokyo*, and *Flying Tigers* glamorized America's fighting men, led by tough, wiry officers, routing the Japanese on remote islands or blasting their aircraft over Chinese skies. Other photodramas—*Wing and a Prayer*, *Destination Tokyo*, and *God Is My Co-Pilot*—destroyed the Oriental foe on land, sea, and air. Occasionally a few movies, *The Purple Heart*, *Wake Island*, *Bataan*, and *Cry Havoc!* among them, detailed unavoidable setbacks, but even in defeat these titles demonstrated U.S. determination. Major Brian Donlevy, the Wake Island marine commandant, rejected the Japanese surrender offer, radioing to the superior force, "Come and get us," while another leatherneck in *Air Force* defiantly bragged, "Send us more Japs!" Even Robert Taylor, trapped behind enemy lines on the Bataan Peninsula, blasted some encroaching Japanese soldiers moments before his death, screaming, "We're still here; we'll always be here!"

Without question, Hollywood portrayed the Japanese foes as sadistic, inhuman, bestial animals, a nation of fanatics lacking compassion, dignity, or decency, happy to kill American prisoners of war, torture civilian workers, or rape captured nurses. Frequently called monkeys, rodents, rats, or snakes, these Orientals—like the epithets used to describe them—required immediate extermination. For the German enemy, however, different criteria prevailed. Caucasian by birth and admirers of Beethoven, Bach, and Mozart, this ethnic group spoke a language similar to English and enjoyed food found on most U.S. tables. Haughty, well dressed, and punctual, this European foe, for the most part, resembled a clown, buffoon, or simpleton. Feature films such as *To Be or Not to Be*, *Once upon a Honeymoon*, *Hotel Berlin*, and *Five Graves to Cairo* depicted *Wehrmacht* officers as silly, inept, and boastful men who constantly tugged at their suede gloves, polished their monocles, clicked their heels, uttered Heil Hitler salutes, and goose-stepped on the parade ground— while behind their backs Allied soldiers blew up bridges, rescued their friends, and captured strategic strongholds.

Why joke about a military force that committed unremitting atrocities, deported millions of civilians to death camps, and indiscriminately bombed major cities? Why depict the Nazis in such superficial terms? Was it to downgrade their power and minimize the threat? Or was Hollywood following a propaganda tenet: make your enemy look foolish and useless and downplay his strengths and accomplishments? In *Casablanca*, a supercilious Nazi major (Conrad Veidt) locked horns with an American expatriate, Rick Blaine (Humphrey Bogart) about civilian control in the Vichy-occupied city. Proud as the proverbial peacock, the German—fingering a small black book— bragged about his research, "We have a complete dossier on you." Without missing a beat, Rick's deadpan retort, "Are my eyes really brown?" derided the *Wehrmacht* officer, rendering his meticulous record keeping ineffective. Or how about a Nazi major's (Raymond Massey) serious comportment when an Allied officer (Ronald Reagan) mockingly explained a secret bombsight's design, detailing the "thermotrockle's" interaction with the "dermodyne" in *Desperate Journey*?

Not every motion picture contained laughs. Some titles portrayed Nazism's darker side. Somber screenplays—such as *The Moon Is Down*, *Edge of Darkness*, *Hitler's Children*, and *This Land Is Mine*—lacked humor but, instead, detailed the New Order's draconian occupation policies, portraying civilian deaths in Norway, a public flogging of a young German girl, and an execution of a simple French schoolteacher. Similar storylines, *Hangmen Also Die*, *Hitler's Madman*, *Hostages*, *The Seventh Cross*, and *Action in the North Atlantic* reiterated Nazi brutality with their depictions of village reprisals, concentration-camp crucifixions, and strafing unarmed mariners. In all, these anti-Germany propaganda films seemed evenly divided. On the one hand, the Third Reich was ridiculed in zany comedies such as *Hitler—Dead or Alive*,

That Nazty Nuisance, and *The Devil with Hitler*; on the other hand, this Teutonic enemy was vilified as harsh, unrelenting, and cruel in such unsmiling productions as *The Cross of Lorraine*, *Joan of Paris*, and *Above Suspicion.*

While Japanese and German belligerents received most of Hollywood's propaganda efforts, a few shows took swipes at their Axis partner, Italy, but in muted format. Historically, Benito Mussolini aligned his nation with Hitler, hoping to capitalize on the führer's lebensraum conquests, only to witness, a few years later, the Allied invasion and subsequent homeland surrender. For America's filmmakers, this abrupt change of sides involved finessing a delicate situation. Initially, a few pictures—*Casablanca*, *Sahara*, and *Five Graves to Cairo*—depicted Italian combatants as passive conscripts, men oblivious to *Il Duce*'s the-grandeur-that-was-Rome mentality. Basically friendly, almost comical, these nationals seemed interested in enjoying robust meals, sipping hearty vino, and chasing pretty women instead of obeying military directives. After Italy's capitulation, two additional screenplays—*The Story of GI Joe* and *A Bell for Adano*—focused on the positive side of America's defaulted ally. In both pictures Italian villagers befriended advancing GIs, aided in their comfort, and swore allegiance to Jeffersonian democracy.

While most of the propaganda films hammered away at the Axis Pact, other screenplays reminded moviegoers that both China and Russia, two important allies, were in the fight, routing America's foes in different parts of the world. On the Chinese mainland—where a large army thwarted Japanese advances— the nationalists slowly began their offensive. Topical motion pictures, such as *Flying Tigers*, *God Is My Co-Pilot*, *China Girl*, and *China Sky*, praised this faraway land and acclaimed its leader, Chiang Kai-shek, a soft-spoken hero. Likewise, two other titles, *Thirty Seconds Over Tokyo* and *The Purple Heart*, acknowledged this country's role in rescuing some Doolittle Raiders, those airmen who crash-landed after their April 1942 Tokyo bombing run. Still other photodramas—*Night Plane from Chungking*, *China's Little Devils*, and *Dragon Seed*—bonded the strong loyalty between America and China, a friendship that would soon drive the Japanese army into the ocean. After all, a wounded Army Corps pilot (Van Johnson) thanked his Chinese physician for skillful, makeshift surgery, saying, "You saved my life, Doc."

As for the Russians, other problems abounded. For over twenty years, ever since the Bolshevik Revolution, Hollywood motion pictures depicted this Communist nation in unflattering, almost pejorative terms, labeling the population as godless, Leninist, and, of course, anticapitalist. But Pearl Harbor changed everything, and now the Soviet Union—with its large Eastern Front army battling the advancing Germans—stood firmly in the Allied camp. Almost overnight, the American film industry changed its tune, producing one title after another extolling its Slavic friends, those gallant defenders of life, liberty, and happiness. Skewed screenplays, such as *Miss V. from Moscow*, *The Boy from Leningrad*, and *The North Star*, glamorized Russian victories while *Days of Glory*, *Song of Russia*, and *Counter-Attack* documented the similarities between Russian and American people. One title stood out. Warner Bros.' *Mission to Moscow* raised propaganda one step up the ladder with its distorted view of Kremlin politics, anti-Trotsky rhetoric, Purge Trials whitewashing, and unabashed Stalin-worshipping. In one scene the American ambassador (Walter Huston), standing proudly next to the Soviet ruler, prophesied, "History will record you as a great builder for the benefit of mankind."

The Chinese and Russian people were not the only groups receiving high praise from America's filmmakers. Back on the home front, millions of civilians kept the factories, steel mills, and shipyards rolling, producing equipment for the overseas fighting man. This workforce—now augmented with women, employees jocularly called Rosie the Riveter—frequently labored long hours, as manufacturers often ran their plants around the clock. Faced with food and gasoline rationing, an unprecedented housing shortage, and wartime separation, everyone adapted to a different way of life. Hollywood, of course, understood these changes and quickly produced films lauding Uncle Sam's matériel force. Strong photodramas, such as *Joe Smith, American*, *Pittsburgh*, and *Gangway for Tomorrow*, praised the assembly worker, exhorting this group to even higher levels of production, while similar stories— *Saboteur*, *Swing Shift Maisie*, *They Got Me Covered*, and *Keeper of the Flame* warned about Axis subversives plotting to undermine factories or social institutions.

Other home-front problems emerged. Wartime family separation appeared in such multilayered dramas as *Since You Went Away*, *Tender Comrade*, and *I'll Be Seeing You*, while the frustrating housing shortage—especially for transplanted workers—provided some levity in lighthearted romps such as *The More the Merrier*, *In the Meantime, Darling*, and *Johnny Doesn't Live Here Any More*. For sheer pathos no wartime title ever attained the heartbreaking poignancy of *The Fighting Sullivans*, the true story of the five apple-pie, Iowan-bred brothers who perished on the USS *Juneau* during the 1942 Guadalcanal offensive. Certain unsavory practices such as black marketeering and stockpiling were decried in *Rubber Racketeers*, *Rationing*, and *The Racket Man*, three titles that explained how daily hoarding and unscrupulous purchasing aided the Axis. Warnings about Nazi agents inside America's borders highlighted *Watch on the Rhine*, *Secret Enemies*, and *Busses Roar*, while Japanese spy rings operated in *Little Tokyo, U.S.A.*, *Betrayal from the East*, and *Texas to Bataan*.

Out on the high plains, fast-galloping cowboys lassoed Axis saboteurs in *Riders of the Northland*, *Wild Horse Rustlers*, and *Cowboy Commandos*, insuring that America's beef and mineral supplies would reach their armed

With his hands gripping the newly crowned Miss America (Amelita Ward), a smooth-talking publicity agent (Wally Brown) explains to her boyfriend (William Terry) that the beauty queen must give up her social life for the next twelve months in John Auer's Gangway for Tomorrow. *Courtesy of RKO Radio Pictures.*

forces. On city streets, quick-thinking detectives uncovered fifth columnists in *Secrets of the Underground, Eyes in the Night,* and *Quiet Please, Murder* while a few independent sleuths—Sherlock Holmes, Bulldog Drummond, Ellery Queen, and Charlie Chan—found time to ferret out Third Reich operatives before these spies could blow up defense plants or poison city water supplies. And, finally, popular songsters, comedians, and dancers provided rousing entertainment in such rip-roaring wartime musicals as *Yankee Doodle Dandy, Reveille with Beverly, This Is the Army, Stage Door Canteen,* and *Here Come the Waves,* foot-stomping screenplays that reminded audiences to keep an upbeat attitude, put their faith in President Roosevelt, and always "Ac-Cen-Tchu-Ate the Positive."

In all, approximately four hundred Hollywood motion pictures bore the propaganda imprint, and these screenplays, in one form or another, provided viewers with a biased interpretation of the global war. When Randolph Scott and his Marine Raiders charged up Makin Island's beach in *Gung Ho,* audiences knew these tough leathernecks would overrun their enemy. After Humphrey Bogart dug those trenches around an abandoned water well in *Sahara,* moviegoers understood an approaching German squad would never breach these makeshift fortifications. How could they? With Bogart barking orders, checking and double-checking the ammunition supply, and, finally, drawing a line in the sand, what hope did the *Wehrmacht* have? And how about Errol Flynn? He parachuted into the uncharted jungle, trekked his squad miles inland, and—after some minor setbacks—routed the Japanese in *Objective Burma*.

Other Hollywood stars fought gallantly. Two tough Marines, William Bendix and Lloyd Nolan, leaped out of their assault boats, dashed across the beach, and eventually pushed the Japanese into the ocean in *Guadalcanal Diary*, while on another South Pacific island, Pat O'Brien moved inland and fought hand to hand against Nipponese defenders in *Marine Raiders*. Over on Norwegian soil, Paul Muni led his attack team through a precarious fjord, climbed a hill, and rescued his countrymen in *Commandos Strike at Dawn*, while in another village, a local fisherman, Errol Flynn, organized the townspeople in an armed rebellion against their German captors in *Edge of Darkness*. For airborne adventure, two photodramas highlighted the Doolittle Tokyo bombing raid. In *Thirty Seconds Over Tokyo*, Spencer Tracy portrayed the flamboyant leader who took his men from a dusty Florida training field to the enemy's major city, while in *The Purple Heart*, another pilot, Dana Andrews, dropped his bombs right on target. But some bad weather forced his crew to crash-land in China, where—after some hit-and-miss adventures—they were captured by the Japanese, dragged before a kangaroo court, and subsequently executed. Even though this mission ended tragically, American audiences took pride in their martyrdom. After all, these airmen refused to divulge military information and accepted death rather then betray their cause.

With their many victories, strong homilies, and patriotic exhortations, these propaganda films defined the war for most Americans even though many of the storylines were distorted or even untrue. So what? Doesn't a little prevarication offer more reassurance? While U.S. Marines and civilian workers fought to the last man in *Wake Island*, historically this closing scene was a fabrication since the Japanese captured many survivors. But what a perfect Alamo ending! Refusing to surrender, the nation's famous leathernecks—machine guns blazing—killed hundreds of their Oriental enemies before capitulation. Have no doubt, the storyline blared, just wait until we return.

And look at the famous Doolittle Raid. While, factually, a few bombs fell on Tokyo, only miniscule damage occurred, but Hollywood went one step further. In *Behind the Rising Sun*, a Japanese national, J. Carroll Naish, walked ruefully through a city reduced to rubble, lamenting that the Greater East Asia Co-Prosperity Sphere brought this destruction upon itself. But what destruction? Not this April 1942 air raid. Maybe it was that nighttime B-17 raid in *Bombardier*, a motion picture glamorizing the men who dropped explosives on enemy targets. This fiction-as-fact mission, likewise, left the capital city in ruins.

Colonel Jimmy Doolittle (Spencer Tracy) ponders the upcoming April 14, 1942, bombing raid in MGM's Thirty Seconds Over Tokyo. *Courtesy of* TV Guide. *If the Doolittle Raiders had actually flown B-52s on that spring morning, the results would have been much different.*

Similar problems existed in these V-for-Victory titles. During the closing scenes of *Air Force*—a screenplay glamorizing a B-17 crew—U.S. aircraft wrecked a large Japanese flotilla in the South Pacific a few days after Pearl Harbor, glossing over the reality that the Army Air Corps lacked a bomber fleet in December 1941 so, of course, no battle took place. What difference did it make? Audiences understood one thing: American airmen destroyed Japanese ships. Why wouldn't they? According to Hollywood, U.S. servicemen possessed remarkable skills. In *Flying Fortress*, a pilot walked on his starboard wing at 10,000 feet; in *Call Out the Marines*, two impecunious leathernecks spent their off-duty hours in expensive nightclubs, wooing pretty women; and in *The Fighting Seabees*, a construction worker clobbered Japanese soldiers with his bulldozer. Even the supernatural helped out. A dead pilot's ghost roamed around an air base, helping an inexperienced flyer hone his volant skills in *A Guy Named Joe*.

As a motion-picture genre, the Hollywood World War II propaganda film—with its red-white-and-blue storyline—reassured the nation that victory was right around the corner. After all, Humphrey Bogart broke up an

Axis plot to demolish the Panama Canal. And Van Johnson positioned his B-25 right over Tokyo and bombed that city. Bow your heads for Vladimir Sokoloff, who defied his Japanese captors, refusing to lower the American flag. Do not overlook Wallace Beery. This overage sergeant snagged some saboteurs outside his base. Do not forget Randolph Scott. He guided his corvette safely to the Irish coast. And tip your hat to Tyrone Power. He and his submarine crew blew up a strategic Nazi oil depot. Clap your hands for the Andrews Sisters and their wonderful songs about Old Glory. Show appreciation to George Montgomery and his flying skills. How many Japanese Zeroes were destroyed over China? Wave a flag for Errol Flynn, who trekked many Canadian miles to capture a stealthy fifth columnist. Say a prayer for Comrade Dana Andrews. He crashed his Russian aircraft into a row of Nazi tanks to halt their offensive. Give Captain Don Ameche some credit for his fancy aircraft carrier maneuvering. And what about Robert Taylor, who sank a Japanese vessel? And stand up and cheer for Blondie, Dagwood, Mr. Dithers, and Daisy. Collectively, their home-front work brought their nation one step closer to victory.

By early 1945—as the Allies pushed eastward toward Berlin, and Japanese cities smoldered in ruins from U.S. bombing raids—the motion-picture industry toned down its propaganda-film production and, instead, returned to traditional entertainment. Why not? the moguls asserted. The war was basically over, and audiences no longer needed reassurances their side would win. Besides, a good comedy or musical feature brought in greater revenue. Months later, the announcement finally came. A beaming President Truman proclaimed that after four years of sacrifice, the Second World War had ended. As the country celebrated, Hollywood also took its bow. During the conflict, their photodramas—an important component of the victory effort—galvanized the nation. These propaganda films, for better or worse, offered hope during the darkest hours and jubilation in days of triumph. And now these motion pictures were no longer needed. Their work was completed.

For Hollywood, the Second World War was far from over, because moviegoers—still interested in a subject that for the most part contained death, destruction, and brutality—wanted more frontal assaults, European bombing raids, and hand-to-hand combat. Why was this? Why did audiences enjoy World War II films? Did they create a chauvinistic, self-congratulatory mood? Or was it something more basic? A primordial function? An atavistic need? Does anybody know? For the motion-picture entrepreneurs, this subject, the pivotal event in twentieth-century history, became money in the bank. Hollywood returned to this war on a monthly basis, churning out one show after another catering to current public tastes and changing ideologies.

Some of these pictures waved Old Glory, others denounced U.S. officers, goldbrickers, 4-Fs, and opportunists. A few dramas poked fun—either in burlesque or black comedy format—at historical events, citing the conflict's absurd nature, while a handful of revisionist screenwriters penned the Axis foes as kindhearted and gentle people. Some blockbuster titles won cinematic awards, while lesser B-stories vanished into oblivion. Many pictures offered explanations for battles, campaigns, and mistakes, while a handful focused on larger-than-life commanders, generals, and presidents. For budgetary reasons, screenplays were made in overseas locations, utilizing unknown foreign actors, anachronistic equipment, and unsynchronized dubbing. Some photodramas were blatantly antiwar, even accusatory, depicting American servicemen in pejorative terms.

What prompted such an abrupt change? For Hollywood, one event explained everything: the World War II propaganda film ended—not with a bang, but with a whimper—on a large battleship, moored in Tokyo Bay, on a historical September 1945 morning. In that fateful hour, America no longer needed its motion-picture heroes. Now these remarkable men could leave quietly, echoing Walt Whitman's sentiments, "The ship has weather'd every rack, the prize we sought is won."

Chapter Two

Victory and Memory

1946–1949

"You've been watching too many war movies."—Colonel Vince Johnson (Powers Boothe) badmouthing his oversexed wife, Jessica Lange, in Tony Richardson's 1994 exposé of army nuclear testing shenanigans, *Blue Sky*

"I hate war movies."—Mrs. Johnson's surly reply

On September 2, 1945, a group of diffident, high-ranking Japanese officials—many of them incongruously decked out in formal attire, including top hats and walking sticks—stood demurely in the hot morning sun on the U.S. battleship *Missouri*'s starboard side anchored in Tokyo Bay. Here, these worried delegates listened nervously as the American war hero and newly appointed occupation director, five-star general Douglas MacArthur, still puffing on his worn-out corncob pipe, dictated the surrender terms and peace conditions. A few minutes later, these Japanese dignitaries affixed their signatures on the surrender document. At that moment, witnessed by hundreds of stern-faced American GIs jammed into the backdrop, the Second World War was finally over.

Back on the home front, the elaborate celebration that started on August 15 was winding down. For two weeks, merriment became the chief order of the day. Strangers danced together in the streets, motorists honked their horns, church bells rang out, and in Times Square a jubilant sailor, wearing winter blues with his hat tilted at a rakish angle, smooched an unsuspecting nurse while a few feet away, Alfred Eisenstaedt snapped their picture.

For Hollywood, the surrender meant a quick return to normalcy. Now the studios could shelve those propaganda films and concentrate on new material. How about more romance with fancy clothing and stylish prancing or some musical comedies with plenty of laughs? As entrepreneurs, the production heads knew that American audiences were tired of war movies. Entertainment, not combat, was the ticket for financial success. Give the public some fun and happiness.

True, a few war pictures were still in production, but their release in late 1945 or early 1946 merely brought closure to the global conflict. MGM's *They Were Expendable* placed Robert Montgomery in the thick of the South Pacific fighting, while over in the Italian theater, RKO's *Step by Step* paired Lawrence Tierney and Anne Jeffreys as two innocents who grabbed some California fifth columnists. Fox's *A Walk in the Sun* downplayed an army squad's routing of a Nazi stronghold a few miles from the Salerno invasion. Back in New York, the FBI, always vigilant and led by Lloyd Nolan, broke up an Axis spy ring working out of the Yorkville section in Fox's *The House on Ninety-Second Street*. MGM's *The Courage of Lassie* pitted America's favorite collie against Japanese soldiers, while RKO's B-meller, *The Bamboo Blonde*, showed off a B-29 crew's fighting skills, and Columbia's *Out of the Depths* extolled the fast-moving naval officers who prevented a Japanese suicide attack against the USS *Missouri*, moored in Tokyo Bay, minutes before the surrender document was signed. Similarly, three titles heaped praise on the Allied espionage network—Warner Bros.' *Cloak and Dagger*, Paramount's *O.S.S.*, and Fox's *13 Rue Madeleine*. Finally, one screenplay put the matter to rest: United Artists' *A Night in Casablanca*, the Marx Brothers' zany war-picture spoof. Clearly, the laudatory days of World War II filmmaking, as personified in more than four hundred propaganda movies that glorified Allied intransigence, were over. Now, after fighting in Uncle Sam's armed forces these four years, Marion Morrison could put his khakis in mothballs and, without missing a step, mount his horse—with guns blazing and eyes hell-bent for leather—and gallop back to the range.

Why not? By now, American audiences wanted enjoyment on their night out, and a good shoot-'em-from-the-hip Western always provided vicarious thrills when the man in white rescued some comely widow from the clutches of a greedy, mustachioed cattle baron. How about some music and romance? Bring out Jack Carson and Dennis Morgan for *A Song, a Dance, and a Girl*. Rather watch some bill-and-cooing? How about Cary Grant and Alexis Smith in *Night and Day*?

But not everyone seemed satisfied with escapist movies. After all, the events of World War II—the greatest political, social, and economic upheaval of the twentieth century—simply would not go away. Thousands of returning veterans, wearing their Ruptured Duck decorations, flooded the workforce, causing unemployment in certain sectors. Racial violence, especially in the South, flared up as Jim Crow laws forced black GIs into direct confrontation with local officials bent on keeping their segregated lifestyle. Other problems included marital infidelity, war profiteering, and short memories. And, of course, there were the wounded veterans who returned to their hometowns with permanent injuries. These disabled servicemen frequently were unable to walk, see, or hold someone's hand.

Soon a few titles emerged that took a hard look at the readjustment many veterans suffered as they entered mainstream U.S. life. Warner Bros. led the way with *Pride of the Marines*, a combat story that featured John Garfield in the real-life role of Al Schmid, a marine sergeant who lost his eyesight at Guadalcanal. Laden with examples of social consciousness, the film—directed by Edward Dmytryk—forged a few swipes at America's three-tier system, pointing out the war was fought both at home and abroad, and it was generally the men from working-class origins, such as Al Schmid, who bore the casualty brunt.

Another photoplay—RKO's *Till the End of Time*—focused on three marines as they reentered California's mainstream middle-class life. Starring Robert Mitchum, Guy Madison, and Bill Williams as close friends, who, like Al Schmid, fought at Guadalcanal, the threesome confronted their own postwar dilemmas. Mitchum, recovering from a head trauma, suffered nightmares, while Bill Williams, unable to walk because of spinal injuries, could not adjust to wheelchair life. Only good-looking Guy Madison, with a modicum of stability, offered some comfort to his pals while romancing a pretty widow. Eventually, the three ex-jarheads confronted some war profiteers and, in an elaborate barroom-fight scene, showed off their Marine Corps stuff. As social commentary, the film fired some lukewarm salvos at stateside opportunism, but its tepid treatment of this ongoing situation seemed mute. That would soon change. Just five weeks after *Till the End of Time* premiered, RKO released a motion picture that defined the World War II experience better than any other movie ever made, either before or after. Finally, an elaborate three-hour film epic detailed—in the simplest of human terms—the high cost, both tangible and intangible, of the Second World War.

Strictly speaking, *The Best Years of Our Lives* was not a combat picture but, instead, an elaborate human document pointing out the frustrations that most returning veterans experienced firsthand as they slowly uncovered the many unsavory practices that abounded on the home front while they were overseas. With an all-star, Academy Award cast that included Dana Andrews, Fredric March, Myrna Loy, and Hoagy Carmichael, the photodrama, like *Till the End of Time*, followed three veterans—now back in their hometown—and their gradual perception about the war itself and its aftermath on family and friends.

Directed by William Wyler, it was no coincidence that *Best Years'* opening scene took place in a large stateside airport terminal where an anxious Air Corps captain, Fred Derry (Dana Andrews)—a recently discharged, decorated B-17 bombardier—pleaded with a ticket clerk about a flight for Boone City, his hometown. No chance at all, she answered sympathetically. It was summer 1946, the fledgling airline industry catered to a civilian clientele, and business was booming. Because the war had ended almost a year ago, servicemen no longer received priority and, like any cash-paying customer, must wait their turn. Why should they have first choice, the scene implied? What do we owe the armed forces? Haven't we said thank you enough times?

Now what? As a well-heeled businessman curtly stepped in front of him to check his golf clubs, Derry's frustration level moved up another notch. Why all those European bombing runs over enemy territory with his life and limb in peril? And what about the numerous deaths of friends and squadron members? What was that all about? To ensure this overage civilian—who stayed behind reaping huge profits from the matériel industry—an airline seat, always at his beck and call, clean and comfortable.

In this opening sequence—less then one minute of script time—William Wyler's taut direction established the confrontational theme that continued for three more hours. Simply put, the war, now over, no longer prevented most Americans from pursuing the good life. Normalcy prevailed: no more rationing, blackout shades, food points, and gasoline stickers. And what about returning veterans? Give them a hearty pat on the pack, a few governmental handouts, and a victory parade. No more special privileges. Here, in this municipal airport—surrounded by well-dressed, well-fed civilians—came the moment of truth for Derry. Stranded, pushed aside by some golf clubs, what was next? How would he get home?

If the civilian world would not help, how about the military? "You might try the ATC, Captain," the ticket agent proffered, "off the terminal, to the right, across the field." Minutes later Derry—his name on a makeshift boarding list, his B-4 bag nearby—was standing in the modest operational room of the Air Transport Command, surrounded by dozens of GIs, sailors, and marines milling around, grabbing seats on space-available military aircraft. While Derry waited for the call, a quiet seaman, Homer Wermels (Harold Russell), stared pensively at the wall, mulling over the future. Already, the tar had balked when some GIs, lifting a skid, called for help. "What's the matter sailor, tired or something?" an Air Corps private sneered.

What was wrong? Why didn't the sailor pitch in and help the GIs move the skid? Was he a goldbricker? A slouch? Derry, eyeing this small interservice rivalry, couldn't care less. Chair tilted, head back on the wall, feet up, he was through with that. Let the army and navy bicker all they want. Finally—after dozens of bombing runs, dodging hundreds of ack-ack blasts, and witnessing untold carnage—he was going home.

Hours later came the good news: "Got a call from Base Ops. There's a B-17 taking off in a few minutes for Boone City." Quickly, Derry—followed by an enthusiastic Wermels—stood at the counter. "Probably have a long ride cause she's making a lot of stops," the NCO explained. "OK, sign here!" At last, the words every serviceman waited to hear. "Boy, it sure is great to be going home," the bombardier retorted. After signing the manifest, Derry handed the pen to the bluejacket. Here, in a quiet, unassuming, and polite manner, Wermels—the navy man, who demurely sat off to the side, lost in his own thoughts—grasped the pen between the two hooks on his right prosthetic arm and wrote his name. Stunned, both officer and NCO quietly sized up the situation. "What's the matter," the sailor voiced, "think I can't spell my own name?"

Using the hooks on his left prosthetic arm, the double-amputee sailor hoisted his duffel bag, and the two Boone City residents scooted toward the aircraft, a modified B-17. Here, they picked up a third GI, Sergeant Al Stephenson (Fredric March), a tired combat infantryman, who, like any veteran, just wanted to go home. Soon, the threesome—now airborne, sequestered in the snug quarters of this converted bomber plane—recounted their wartime stories. Derry, a former soda jerk in the town's simple drugstore, saw plenty of action in the German skies, while Stephenson, a respected

Smiling from ear to ear, two discharged servicemen (Harold Russell and Dana Andrews) head toward a military aircraft boarding area for their long flight home in William Wyler's story of lost time and short memories, The Best Years of Our Lives. *Courtesy of MGM.*

banker turned ground-pounder, fought on Pacific islands, finally reaching Hiroshima. But Wermels, a shy, ordinary flattop seaman, worked belowdeck. "When we were sunk, all I know there was a lot of fire," he recalled. "When I came to, I was on a cruiser. My hands were off."

What about their families back home, who waited these four long years? Derry, married only ten days before shipping overseas, hardly knew his bride, a Texas beauty he met while in flight training. Stephenson, a husband for twenty years, felt confident about his wife and two children. Only Wermels seemed apprehensive. "Well, you see, I got a girl," he started. "Wilma's only a kid, she's never seen anything like these hooks." Eventually, the all-night talk shut down, and soon all three men, secure in the womb of this B-17, fell asleep.

Using less than twenty minutes of exposition time, William Wyler, a former World War II military cameraman, reaffirmed the uncertainty every veteran knew when the fighting ended and peace was restored. Many, of course, remembered vividly their friends who died during this global conflict. Others, like Wermel, suffered horrendous injuries that impeded any type of normalcy. For the rest, everything was unclear, ambiguous. What awaited them? Could they ever pick up where they left off? Would these veterans—the men who gave their country the best years of their lives—reap the benefits of the postwar society?

Finally, after interminable hours in the air, the new friends reached their hometown airport, and now, sitting in their taxi, each man felt uneasy. As the car pulled into Wermel's street—a pretty, lawned neighborhood dotted with clean single-family houses—the nervous sailor balked. "Say, how 'bout the three of us going back to Butch's place? We'll have a couple of drinks and then we can go home," he suggested. No dice, the sergeant gestured, "You're home now, Kid." After the taxi stopped, the young seaman, shaky and insecure, lumbered out. Wermels, a double amputee, the clean-cut boy next door, the youth who joined the navy to fight for his country, was home.

Probably no motion-picture scene has ever captured the pathos, warmth, nuance, and happiness associated with a veteran's return as these brief cinematic moments when Wermels emerged from the taxi and stared at his boyhood house, recalling the joyous, idyllic moments of growing up on this block. Immediately, his eleven-year-old sister, followed by their parents, dashed out and greeted him. Then Wilma—his fiancée, the sweet girl-of-his-dreams—rushed over. Now what? How could she not see those prosthetics? Looking past the two sets of hooks, she hugged and kissed him. "I'm so glad you're back."

Watching from the taxi window, Derry and Stephenson eyed this wholesome scene with quiet approval, hoping for a similar happy homecoming. A few minutes later, Stephenson, the battle-weary, middle-aged former GI who once dodged Japanese bullets on a South Pacific island, stepped into a swank apartment building only to confront a surly doorman, who obviously was not a veteran: "Just a minute," the man brayed, "I'll have to announce you first." Here was another moment of truth. All those months in the combat zone—for what? Some ill-tempered lip from a mealy-mouth draft dodger? "Put that phone down," Stephenson interjected, "I'm her husband."

Ignoring the man's confusion, Stephenson rode the elevator to his floor and rang his doorbell. What a reception! A teenage son could not believe his eyes while a twenty-year-old daughter beamed. From the kitchen emerged his comely, dignified, and faithful wife (Myrna Loy) who stared ecstatically at her returning husband. Finally, after months of uncertainty, Stephenson—like his newfound navy friend on the other side of town—was home. But unlike the young sailor, Stephenson could wrap his arms around his smiling Milly.

As for Derry, his welcome-home party proved less satisfying. Standing in his father's run-down kitchen, while a few feet from the building, a steam-engine-locomotive train chugged by, the former Air Corps bombardier, the man from the wrong side of the railroad tracks, received his dad's gratitude for a job well done. Only, where was his wife? What happened to the pretty girl he married after a ten-day, whirlwind Texas courtship? "She took an apartment downtown," his stepmother hesitated, while his father added it was near her job. "Some nightclub," he whispered, "I don't know which one."

Nightclub? What nightclub? What did her absence mean? Was she another Allotment Annie, a gold digger? Was he a chump? Had he, like so many other GIs who hastily married before going overseas, been screwed, blued, and tattooed? For Derry, here was another realization. Now that the war was over, what did the future hold? Could he ever pick up where he left off with his sexy wife? Was there a place in this booming economy for an ex-bombardier? Now for a few answers. Leaving his father's tenement district, Derry pondered his fate. This much he knew: nothing would ever be the same.

Here, in less than one hour of screen time, William Wyler's storyline emerged as a caustic social criticism of America's shaky values during the postwar period. Using these three men as his fulcrum, Wyler's cameras followed their ups and downs as each man tried to find a niche in the Boone City prosperity. Wermels, after much soul-searching, eventually married his high school sweetheart while Stephenson, now a bank loan officer, fidgeted uncomfortably with applicants as he pondered their financial woes. As for Derry, his readjustment was more complex. Eventually he located his wife, and, as her unsavory, adulterous past spilled out, he had no choice but to leave. Later, a new romantic interest—with Stephenson's grown-up daughter—would blossom, but first another indignity pushed him against the wall.

Derry's first order of business was finding a job. Before enlisting in the Army Air Corps, while working as a soda jerk at a busy drugstore, scooping ice cream sundaes and malts for local teenagers, Derry seemed content in small-town America. But like thousands of other uprooted fellows—who joined the service and traveled overseas—that provincial way of life, with all its innocence and charm, was inextricably lost forever. No more banana splits or cherry cokes, Derry vowed. After flying all those combat missions, he was ready for something better. But what?

One afternoon, Derry strolled into the old drugstore but was dumbfounded by its upscale appearance. A big chain had bought the owner out and remodeled its interior, transforming this quaint turn-of-the-century shop into a slick departmental emporium. Everything was changed, including the personnel. At first the manager appeared pleasant, but soon his haughty, patronizing mood took over. "We're under no legal obligation to give you your old job back," he cautioned. "Old job," Derry retorted, "I'm looking for a better one." Soon this informal interview soured as Derry's military experiences unfolded. "But, unfortunately," the manager sneered, "we've no opportunities for that [Air Corps bombardier] in Midway Drugs." For Derry, those bitter comments said it all: the young men who fought in the war and were lucky enough to come home, were now at the mercy of the overage 4-Fs and draft-dodgers who stayed behind. Here, in their safe, capitalist, civilian world, opportunism flourished. While he spent three years behind the Norton bombsite—the best years of his life—these stateside civilians gobbled up everything. "I think I'll look around," Derry concluded, "thank you."

A few weeks later, Derry, wearing the familiar white jacket and apron of a soda jerk, stood behind the counter serving customers. What choice did he have? Where could an ex-bombardier find work in postwar America? With his mustering-out pay almost gone and his marriage in shambles, he swallowed his pride and grabbed his old job. As a combat officer, he reflected, the pay was over $400.00 a month. Now he earned $32.50 a week. To exacerbate matters, his boss was a former teenage assistant. At least he knew the ropes: no one needed to show him how to dish out a hot fudge sundae or a bacon, lettuce, and tomato sandwich. What difference did it make? Everybody parroted the same bromide: the war was over.

However, this employment was short-lived. One morning at the counter, Derry listened idly as his friend Wermels and a customer bantered about the war. At first, the stranger seemed sympathetic to Homer's plight—even appreciative—but soon the talk turned nasty. "We let ourselves get sold down the river," the man jeered, "by a bunch of radicals in Washington." One word led to another, and soon a loud argument developed. A shoving match ensued, and Wermels teetered. That was enough for the former bombardier turned soda jerk. Leaping over the counter, eyes riveted, Derry sucker-punched the agitator, sending him crashing into a perfume display. As scented bottles rolled around the floor, Derry knew his time was up. "I'll meet you outside in a minute, Kid." Turning to the manager, he discharged both barrels. "Don't say it chum, I know, the customer is always right, so I'm fired—but this customer wasn't right."

Now what? For Derry, the answer was obvious: leave town and start fresh somewhere else. Next stop: the Air Traffic Command. Here, the former officer stood in the local airport bumming another military ride. No problem with that. A plane, leaving in a few hours, would take him eastward. Killing time, Derry strolled over to the runway's edge where hundreds of obsolete, discarded Air Corps bombers—the cream of America's offensive attacks—were parked ignominiously in the afternoon sun, awaiting demolition. Armament and engine parts, strewed all over the place, transformed this airplane graveyard into an eerie memory of their formidable power, a ghostly recollection of past victories. Pausing in front of a dusty B-17, the *Round Trip?*, Derry could feel those volant days when he was jammed into a turret, carefully aligning a target, and then yelling "bombs away."

Without hesitating, he quickly slid into the *Round Trip?*'s escape hatch and wiggled into the bombardier's pit. Finally, after all these months of readjustment, he was back in the saddle. No more unfaithful wife, loudmouth store manager, or draft-dodging opportunists giving him grief. No more lost dreams or right-wing pamphleteers. Absorbed in his memories, recalling the dangerous European flying missions, Derry seemed stupefied as recessed events slowly emerged. Enclosed in this earth-mother womb, with his eyes shut, throat parched, and body taut, Derry's thoughts meandered back to the ethereal world of air combat. Oblivious to any stimuli, the young man—who left rural America to fight for his country—had, perhaps unknowingly, drifted off to another dimension.

"Hey, bud, what are you doing up there?" Hearing these words, Derry quickly snapped back to reality. Standing in front of the fuselage, a burly man yelled, "Hey, you, what are doing in that plane?" Flustered, he left the plane and backpedaled his daydreaming. "I used to work in one of those," he told this construction boss. "Getting some of them [memory demons] out of my system." The men sized each other up, then, after some introductory banter, compared war stories. Out of the blue, Derry saw an opportunity: "You don't need any help, do you?" The former tank sergeant, who battled his way across Europe, squeezed his brow. "Hey, Gus," he barked down the line, "see if you think this guy can be of any use to us."

What a perfect Hollywood ending: one veteran helping another. Both men eyed each other, and their facial expressions said it all: military bonding— that was the ticket—always help your buddy. Now Derry could stay in town, his readjustment completed. True, many problems loomed ahead, but with both feet on the ground he was ready. Like his two pals, Wermels and Stephenson, he was back in mainstream America. As for the war, forget it, that counted for nothing. Whether he liked it or not, 1946 began a new era. Don't ponder the past, move on.

As a social document, *Best Years* combed through the myriad of problems veterans faced, indicting the different modes of home-front opportunism. While many of the young men went into the service, those who stayed behind reaped countless benefits. Derry's teenage assistant (known as "Sticky") worked in the drugstore and, by war's end, became a manager in the new conglomerate. When Derry capitulated and returned to soda jerking, he endured added humiliation because this floor supervisor—an obvious 4-F—crowed with new authority. Likewise, during the three-year marriage, Derry's wife squandered her monthly allotment check, lavishly entertaining various boyfriends. While her husband constantly endured harm's way, she spent her evening hours as a nightclub hostess, making eyes at anyone wearing pants.

What did America owe its veterans? Everything, according to *Best Years*, and Wyler's storyline, sometimes subtle, occasionally blatant, reiterated that point. Certainly, there was not a dry eye in any theater when homespun Wilma removed the prosthetics from Wermels and was confronted by the reality of his wartime injury. Over in a fancy banquet hall, a few capitalists did not appreciate Stephenson's diatribe blasting the U.S. economic system. While back in shantytown, Derry's simple father, a quiet man from the lower class, glowed with amazement while reading his son's Distinguished Flying Cross citation: "Despite intense pain, shock, and loss of blood, with complete disregard of his personal safety" he told his wife, "signed by Lt. General Doolittle."

After *Best Years*, where could Hollywood go? This Academy Award picture said it all and closed the book on the Second World War. Why not? It was time for the moguls to churn out traditional entertainment or escapist titles. No more war pictures; instead of watching American GIs mounting barbed steeds, postwar audiences applauded when hoofers like Donald O'Connor clicked his heels or when crooner Bing Crosby wowed some pretty lass with his mellifluous melodies. How about Tommy Dorsey's throbbing trombone or Benny Goodman's wailing clarinet? Bring on the dancing, singing, or music. Who needed to be reminded of the war?

So for a brief period—1947 and 1948—only a handful of photodramas used the war as backdrop. MGM's *The Beginning or the End* declassified some of the secrets associated with the Manhattan Project, while Paramount's *Golden Earrings* allowed British officer Ray Milland, now disguised as a *Mitteleuropa* gypsy—with Marlene Dietrich's help—to elude Gestapo agents. On a lighter side, jokester Danny Kaye fantasized heroics in RKO's screen adaptation of James Thurber's classic short story *The Secret Life of Walter*

Mitty. A few titles—MGM's *Homecoming*, Universal's *All My Sons*, Warner Bros.' *To the Victor*, MGM's *Gallant Bess*, United Artists' *Arch of Triumph*, and MGM's *High Barbaree*—reminded moviegoers that infidelity, opportunism, equine loyalty, collaboration, and lost love were universal themes, found both in peace and war, while two B-potboilers—Fox's *Jungle Patrol* and Southern California Pictures' *Women in the Night*—retold the Australian and China fighting in their simple, budget formats.

But the motion picture industry—never known for consistency—soon realized that while most moviegoers enjoyed song-and-dance entertainment, they also needed tangible reminders of their nation's prowess. After all, didn't the United States just win a war? Why keep World War II films on the back burner? Why not celebrate America's victories? After this brief two-year hiatus, Hollywood reloaded its cameras, and soon moviegoers watched Edmund O'Brien climb into his pursuit aircraft's cockpit and, with his fellow pilots, blast the *Messerschmitts* out of the crowded European skies in Warner Bros.' *Fighter Squadron*. Once more, the floodgates opened, and now the World War II photodrama—with all its glories and tragedies, its triumphs and mistakes—became a prominent fixture in theaters everywhere.

Every aspect of the war flickered on the screen. In MGM's B-meller *Act of Violence*, an embittered army veteran (Robert Ryan), now stateside, tracked down his former officer (Van Heflin), seeking revenge for some misdeeds in a German prisoner-of-war camp. Told in flashback, the storyline ignored heroism and, instead, emphasized that under duress, any soldier became vulnerable. After a suspenseful cat-and-mouse chase back in Southern California, the two men confronted each other, and in an ironic twist, Van Heflin's accidental death atoned for his POW actions. As a dark melodrama, *Act of Violence* proved that self-interest, a basic human instinct, overshadowed everything else in wartime. A similar MGM title, *Desire Me*, paired Robert Mitchum and Greer Garson as a Brittany married couple separated by the June 1940 call-up. When the pretty wife learned her POW husband died in an escape attempt, a quiet despondency eventually turned into a reclusive lifestyle. Later, a smooth-talking stranger appeared at her oceanside cottage, detailed her spouse's death, offered comfort and solace, and finally suggested marriage. Unaware of this man's duplicity, the lonely woman reluctantly acquiesced but—in a typical sudsy ending—her husband returned home, assaulted the opportunist, and reclaimed his bride—proving once more the Shakespearean maxim that "love is not love that alters when alteration finds." As a World War II moving picture sharing the problems of a French couple, it defied imagination to insinuate that Robert Mitchum, a well-known, rough-around-the-edges, Hollywood tough guy and the London-born Greer Garson, an actress with a distinct British accent, could convince moviegoers they were two simple Brittany villagers. Likewise, Paramount's *Beyond Glory* told the difficult story of a West Point cadet (Alan Ladd), whose tormented memories of his enlisted-man's North African combat experiences interfered with the academy's rigid discipline system. With the help of pretty Donna Reed, these problems dissolved, and as an added bonus, General Eisenhower delivered the graduation address. Paramount's *Sealed Verdict* recounted the complexities of assigning guilt, as a U.S. major (Ray Milland), examining a Nazi general's role in some wartime atrocities, found ambiguous evidence that suggested exoneration.

In the Air Corps, other problems abounded. MGM's elaborate *Command Decision* took a hard look at the high casualty rate caused by the daylight bombing raids over Germany. While the British tacticians ordered nighttime attacks—a calculated operation with fewer losses—U.S. strategists demanded accuracy. In this highly charged, all-male photodrama, an American general fought not only the Nazis but also fellow officers and a buttinsky congressman.

Loosely structured on *The Dawn Patrol*, Warner Bros.' 1938 World War I drama *Command Decision* updated a standard Hollywood theme: the difficulty of sending men into risky aerial-combat situations. Each day—from his British countryside air base—General Casey Dennis (Clark Gable) ordered another maximum effort against the German factories that were assembling a jet fighter—an aircraft that, if mass-produced, would blow any Allied plane out of the sky. For General Dennis, these raids represented the difference between victory and defeat. Unless these war matériel sites were obliterated, the European theater, at best, would bog down into an agonizing stalemate. At worst, the Nazis could emerge victorious.

In human terms, the cost was astronomical: forty-eight crews lost the first day, fifty-two on the second, on a target, a staff officer bemoaned, the American people couldn't find on a map. Now what? Should the bombing continue? After a heated discussion, everyone balked. An up-for-election congressman—fearing public outcry and a possible November defeat—appeared penitent, while a senior general—his eye on another star—also demurred. However, off to the side, General Dennis understood the military necessity for the next day's mission. "It's on," he instructed his operational chief, "There's a mission tomorrow, maximum effort."

As a major Hollywood production, *Command Decision* took numerous potshots at World War II politics, blasting the many opportunists who placed their self-interests above the important task of maintaining low casualties. While American airmen routinely risked their lives, their senior officers—basking comfortably in field headquarters—seemed oblivious to the moral question of death in warfare. Instead, they pondered the efficacies of each day's mission,

Two grim-looking Air Corps officers (Clark Gable and John Hodiak) mull over a recent strategic offensive against a German munitions factory in Sam Wood's airborne saga Command Decision. *Courtesy of MGM.*

examining such personal dilemmas as career advancement, interservice rivalry, military appropriations, adverse public reaction to high fatalities, inaccurate bombing runs, and the oft-repeated frustration that—unlike the military troops—the weather could not be controlled. True, this motion picture sanitized aerial combat—no scenes depicted airmen being blown apart from a direct ack-ack blast—but it still pointed the *j'accuse* finger at numerous noncombatants, especially high-ranking personnel, who for one reason or another reaped lavish benefits from their authoritative positions.

Another screenplay that continued Hollywood's examination of the controversial Allied precision daytime-bombing program, Fox's *Twelve O'Clock High* reaffirmed the daily dangers each Eighth Air Force airman experienced when his B-17 left the comfort of the English landscape and headed east toward Axis targets during the fall 1942 offensive. In this screenplay, Gregory Peck portrayed General Frank Savage, a hard-nosed disciplinarian assigned to a jinxed bomber group that no longer functioned efficiently. Here, he observed that military protocol and regulations were lax, pilots were drinking heavily, and morale seemed nonexistent. Soon, Savage implemented changes that gradually transformed this hard-luck company into a well-honed fighting unit. Along the way, he encountered rejection, animosity, antagonism, and, finally, appreciation from the crewmembers, who, stereotypically, learned the difficulties of command. However, Savage's hard work vanished one early morning on the runway, prior to an important bombing mission. In full view of his officer staff, he suffered a complete mental collapse, requiring restraint and observation. His overpowering sense of mission had, in fact, destroyed him.

Released only twelve months after *Command Decision* and directed by aviation expert Henry King, *Twelve O'Clock High* confirmed that the daily daylight attacks—waged by human blood—extracted a high cost from American airmen. At his first briefing, General Savage's draconian instructions, "Write yourself off, tell yourself you're already dead; once you accept that fact, it will be easier to fly," set the tone for the many casualties that followed. Almost devoid of flag-waving antics, this film weighed those myriad personal relationships and psychological profiles found in combat, including self-aggrandizement, elaborate glorification, and overblown egos. Clearly, this motion picture, along with *Command Decision*, exposed a darker side of the European air war.

On a more positive note, Warner Bros.' *Task Force* heaped dollops of praise on the U.S. Navy's airpower, asserting that aircraft carriers won the Pacific war and now, in 1949, would protect the nation against any foreign (specifically, Russian) aggression. Starring Gary Cooper in the role of the indefatigable Admiral Jonathan Scott, the part-fictional, part-documentary storyline traced this officer's twenty-seven-year career beginning with his first carrier takeoff in the early 1920s, then into the congressional appropriations battle where isolationists opposed military funding, and finally, World War II, where the navy warships proved a major component of the armed service. Unlike *Command Decision* or *Twelve O'Clock High*, this motion picture downplayed the heavy combat losses. Instead, it glamorized all facets of seagoing victories, as America's powerful Pacific fleet, spearheaded by its flattop warships, pulverized the Japanese into ignominious defeat.

Still other titles appeared in 1949 that recounted different aspects of the War. Fox's *I Was a Male War Bride* poked fun at the marriages between American GIs and their foreign spouses, spoofing the bureaucratic difficulty of arranging stateside passage. Here, Cary Grant, a French army captain, married an American officer, and the twosome faced a red-tape dilemma: how to enter the United States as man and wife. Actually a male war "bride," Grant donned women's clothing, hoping this distaff disguise would bring him to America's shores because military regulations did not cover his unusual conjugal situation. In Columbia's *Jolson Sings Again*, Larry Parks portrayed the popular songster Al Jolson as he entertained the troops in various combat zones. Now, a new generation of fans applauded the singer who—back in the thirties—made "Sewanee" a household word. Warner Bros.' *My Foolish Heart* recounted the anguish a young woman endured after her GI sweetheart died in a training accident. Starring Susan Hayward and Dana Andrews, this soap opera ignored combat heroics and, instead, concentrated on the heartache associated with lost love. RKO's sixty-three-minute meller *The Clay Pigeon* put an American seaman into first gear after he spotted a former Japanese prison guard hiding out in a California town. Once again, the Hawaiian-born actor Richard Loo—famous for his fanatical roles—portrayed another Japanese villain brought to justice by a fast-moving bluejacket.

A few more photodramas returned the war to American audiences, but in different formats. MGM's *Malaya* heated up the Southeast Asian peninsula, where two American mercenaries, Jimmy Stewart and Spencer Tracy—in a series of make-believe adventures—hoodwinked their Japanese occupiers by smuggling huge quantities of unprocessed rubber to a nearby U.S. Navy ship. Basically devoid of any realism, *Malaya* contained many flimsy situations, suggesting that the Japanese military commanders were nothing more than overblown bags of wind. However, United Artists' *Home of the Brave* was a different matter. Here a black GI (James Edwards), fighting on a South Pacific island, experienced racial gibes from his fellow soldiers, causing hospitalization for paralysis hysteria. With the help of a psychiatrist, the root of his physical breakdown—he could not move his legs—was traced to an inferiority complex about being a black man in a white world. For a 1949 movie, *Home of the Brave* opened new doors by attacking America's two-tier racial-segregation system and blatantly criticized the military for maintaining this policy. Who were the real enemies in the South Pacific, the film asked, the Japanese hiding in the jungle or the southern GIs loathing most black people?

Still the European fighting continued. MGM's *Battleground* replayed the 1944 Christmas defensive at Bastogne, where thousands of American troops dug in as the German war machine, now with its back to the wall, launched its last hurrah. Hampered by the coldest Belgian winter in recent memory, the U.S. front lines, caught completely off guard, resembled a fragile protuberance on the military map as the *Wehrmacht* pushed forward, hoping to press the Allies back into the sea. Eventually, the GIs reassembled and—with a lucky break in the weather—repelled the German attack. In retelling this famous Battle of the Bulge saga, director William Wyler followed the adventures of one airborne platoon, highlighting each man's fears, aspirations, and anguish in this forest battleground.

Starring Van Johnson, John Hodiak, and James Whitmore as hardened members of the 101st Screaming Eagles, an outfit known for its esprit de corps, *Battleground* bared the frustrations every combat GI knew as supplies dwindled, rumors replaced information, casualties mounted, and cold weather prevented uninterrupted sleep or cooked meals. For over two cinematic hours, this squad—a microcosm of faraway American life—shared its laughter, joys, and sorrows as each man mused the same question: would he live through this battle, this war? As Private Van Johnson bantered, "I'm just a PFC—praying-for-civilian."

With the platoon as motif, *Battleground* downplayed heroics and empha-sized each man's introspection as they pondered their fate. One GI fiddled with dentures, wondering if their loss would constitute reassignment out of the combat zone, another trooper waited anxiously for an official letter approving a hardship discharge, while happy-go-lucky Johnson just needed a few min-utes to scramble some peculated eggs. Another dogface pooh-poohed the *Stars and Stripes*, mocking this newspaper's sanitized reporting, while a young re-placement, the Kid, searched for an old buddy. Amid the occasional death and misery, *Battleground* eschewed any blame or incompetence but, instead, fo-cused on quiet virtues and American values. In one scene, Johnson casually re-minded an officer—who stumbled over some Texas-leaguer password infor-mation—of the national pastime's importance: "May I suggest, Sir, that you study up on baseball." Later, this same levity appeared in command head-quarters when a German major, confused by General McAuliffe's laconic, one-word no-surrender dictum, inquired, "Das ist negativ or positiv?" With a wry smile, an American colonel sneered, "'Nuts'—is strictly negative."

While *Battleground* low-keyed its characterization of heroes by portraying most GIs as nonbelligerent, Republic's *Sands of Iwo Jima* showed viewers the other side of the coin by glorifying the U.S. Marine Corps' many Pacific is-land victories. Starring the indomitable John Wayne as Sergeant John Stryker, *Sands* followed a rifle squad from their early fighting at Guadalcanal, then on to Tarawa, and, finally, to the lava beachheads of Iwo Jima, where they watched in awe as six marines raised the American flag on Mount Suribachi in a scene that can only be described as breast-pounding. Probably no Holly-wood picture made since V-J Day inspired such patriotism, pride, and loyalty as this 1949 production. Has any movie ever equaled it? Probably not. Was this film—released during the Cold War—a strong warning to the Soviets? Without question.

Directed by Allan Dwan, *Iwo Jima* began in elaborate Hollywood fanfare. First, Republic Pictures' logo—the outstretched eagle—stood defiantly as the Marine Corps hymn blared, followed by the semper fidelis emblem, super-imposed by the screen credits that included a dedication for valor that "left a lasting impression on the world and in the hearts of their countrymen." Also listed were the three surviving flag raisers—Rene Gagnon, Ira Hayes, and John Bradley—captured in the photo taken by Joe Rosenthal, who played cameo roles. Then, the omniscient voice-over introduced the photoplay. "This is the story of marines," the narrator intoned, "a rifle squad." What a rip-roaring opening. Where was this picture heading? Only one place—victory.

Why not? With America's best fighting man, John Wayne, riding roughshod over his charges, his familiar cry, "Saddle up," echoed the Marine Corps' credo for tough training. "You joined the Marines because you wanted to fight," he bellowed, "well, you're going to get your chance and I'm here to see that you know how." In the end, of course, his martinet policies paid off. Each man, now ready for combat, owed part of his survival to the sergeant's persistence. But for Wayne/Stryker, it was a different matter. Basically a fatalist, he understood his father-figure/tragic-hero role and seemed ready for the inevitable. Charging up a volcanic hill, at the exact moment the Mount Suribachi flag was raised, a sniper's bullet pierced his heart. Stunned, his squad balked in disbelief. After a few reflective moments—while an unfinished letter, written by Stryker to his son, was read—the marines stood tall. "Saddle up," a private mimicked, "let's get back into the war."

As a 1949 Hollywood Film, *Sands of Iwo Jima* glorified every facet of World War II, recalling such previous propaganda titles as *The Purple Heart*, *Gung Ho*, *Wake Island*, and *Thirty Seconds Over Tokyo*. Standing alone, John Wayne, the leader of a finely tuned Marine squad, personified the best of America's military. Here was a film character that refused to take no for an answer, a rough-and-ready fighter willing to stand up for his beliefs. Without question, John Wayne, this former B-actor and stunt cowboy—who, after many trials and errors on Poverty Row, metamorphosed into an indelible, blast-'em-from-the skies, hard-drinking, fist-flying, anti-Communist image—articulated a mythic adventure that kneaded a nation's psyche during this foreign war. Unknowingly, *Sands of Iwo Jima* became Wayne, and Wayne became America. Then what happened? Did America become Wayne?

Probably. How far does an icon's mystique travel? In 1976 Vietnam veteran Ron Kovic wrote in his best-selling indictment, *Born on the Fourth of July*, that watching John Wayne in *Sands of Iwo Jima* inspired him to join the Marine Corps and volunteer for combat. For Kovic, the ineffaceable John Wayne image in Iwo Jima—the unrelenting sergeant who charged a Japanese pillbox, pulled the safety from his explosives, tossed the pack into the enemy's lair, and then somersaulted away—said it all. Why hold your manhood cheap? Next stop: the dotted line.

As the prototype recruitment film, *Iwo Jima* rammed heavy doses of patriotism down American moviegoers' throats with its many red-white-and-blue scenes proving, once again, the Marine Corps would fight their battles in the air, on land, and sea. True, it took John Wayne four years to kick off his cowboy spurs, change into khakis, grab a rifle, and blast away at enemy snipers, but his return brought new meaning to Old Glory. As the decade came to an end, America's World War II memories really boiled down to one man and one movie. What was World War II all about, a youngster might have asked back in 1949? How did we win the war? Who were our heroes? Easy answer. Go watch John Wayne—the marine with steely eyes, taut muscles, and poised fingers—charge up the ashen hill in *Sands of Iwo Jima*. On that hot February day, America won the Second World War.

Chapter Three

The Cold War Turns Hot

1950–1953

"I didn't see you at our movie tonight. I thought Errol Flynn was your kind of guy."—Navy doctor Scott (Richard Thomas) poking fun at a fellow officer in Robert Iscove's 1990 harrowing tale of shipwreck survival, *Mission of the Shark*

"Actually, I don't find motion pictures about the war all that informative."—Marine captain Wilkes (David Caruso) explaining his absence.

"No, well, they're meant for the civilian population, I imagine."—Dr. Scott's rationalization.

During the final week of January 1950, president Harry S. Truman, at a dramatic news conference, promised the nation that—unlike many Eastern European countries now trapped behind what Winston Churchill had recently labeled the Iron Curtain—the United States would never capitulate to Communist expansion. To ensure our safety, the chief executive stressed, a new retaliatory weapon, the hydrogen bomb, was basically operational. For many Americans, the White House's strong words evoked a ten-year-old rhetoric, reminiscent of President Roosevelt's fireside chats. What did this announcement mean? Was war with the Soviet Union inevitable? Would young servicemen fight another global conflict? Could atomic weapons fall on American cities? Certainly, it wasn't easy—as the popular songster, Evelyn Knight, warbled—to powder your face with sunshine.

While the question of a future war loomed ominously, many Americans— looking for the elusive better life—turned their attention to a novel entertainment format, the television set that by 1950 was quickly becoming a permanent home fixture. Each night millions of viewers plopped down in front of their twelve-inch black-and-white screens to catch the Paul Whiteman, Fred Waring, or Aldrich Family shows. In the afternoon only test patterns were available. As most demographers prophesied, this electronic medium, now in mass production, would transform the nation's social, economic, and political life.

Hollywood, of course, could read the handwriting on the wall. As more people purchased these sets—a Philco cost $199, a TeleKing was $159, and for the well-heeled, a DuMont Rumson was $329—motion-picture attendance edged downward. Now people could watch their favorite movies from the convenience of their home. No more nightly walks to the neighborhood shows and, for the practical-minded, no admission charges. However, one drawback offered the moguls some optimism. Television networks could not air current films. Instead, they reached back to the many photodramas from the thirties and early forties. So the movie industry had this one advantage. If audiences wanted to see a recent title, they still needed theaters.

As for the Second World War, many viewpoints prevailed. For ex-servicemen—especially combat veterans—that four-year event evoked painful recollections that, realistically, would never go away. In many households, Gold Star mothers still agonized on Memorial Day as elaborate civic parades and religious services remembered the many deaths required for victory. Still others saw the war in distant terms, stating it was time to move on and forget the past. One large group, however—the young men called into military duty by the selective service system—heard about the war on a daily basis as their drill sergeants reminded the draftees about the lessons learned from the recent conflict and their possible application against a new enemy, the Soviet Union.

As expected, Hollywood continued to churn out World War II feature films that—in one way or another—still glorified America's dominance. In early February, Fox released *When Willie Comes Marching Home*, an offbeat tale that starred song-and-dance-man Dan Dailey as a West Virginia GI who, despite his best persuasive efforts, remained stationed near his home. After some wheeling and dealing, this happy-go-lucky lug convinced his superiors to send him behind enemy lines, where he procured strategic information. His homecoming, however, downplayed this secret mission, much to the townspeople's chagrin. Modeled after the Preston Sturges 1944 madcap comedy, *Hail the Conquering Hero*, this updated version likewise lampooned unbridled patriotism. On a more somber note, Fox's *Three Came Home* dramatized the harrowing events in a Japanese prisoner-of-war camp. Here Claudette Colbert and her four-year-old son suffered many indignities in a Borneo compound, under their captors' draconian rule. Based on the novel by Agnes Newton Keith, *Three Came Home* indicted the Japanese for their hatred of all Caucasians.

Over in the European theater, Paramount's *Captain Carey, U.S.A.* placed a former army officer (Alan Ladd) in Italy months after the war to hunt down a renegade foe. After a few setbacks involving some stolen art treasures, he found the traitor and, as a bonus, an old girlfriend. Up in northern Germany, Fox's *The Big Lift* highlighted every aspect of the 1949 Berlin Blockade, depicting the air force's herculean effort to supply the old capital after the Russians imposed their cordon. One afternoon a former POW (Paul Douglas) bumped into the *Wehrmacht* soldier who had abused him six years earlier, and now with the tables turned, the confrontation offered retribution. As with *Three Came Home*, this screenplay reiterated the cruelty inflicted upon American captives.

However, on June 25, 1950, stateside television viewers stared incredulously as news commentators interrupted their Sunday-night programs to announce the North Korean army had crossed the demarcation line—formed by the thirty-eighth parallel—pushing toward Seoul. Vowing to stop this Communist aggression, Truman ordered combat troops into this faraway peninsula. Within hours, U.S. soldiers stationed in Japan were hastily dispatched into the fighting zone and told by their commander, World War II conqueror General MacArthur, to halt the advancement. Euphemistically dubbed a police action, the Korean struggle would seesaw for three years, resulting in approximately fifty-four thousand American deaths until a July 1953 armistice agreement was signed.

Within the first weeks of this unexpected conflict, the Hollywood machine reloaded its cameras and after a shaky start released its first Korean conflict screenplays. Titles such as Eagle Lion's *Korea Patrol*, Lippert's *The Steel Helmet*, RKO's *Tokyo File 212*, and Fox's *Fixed Bayonets* glorified fast-moving GIs blowing up a bridge, surviving a POW massacre, knocking off a Communist spy ring, and attacking from a cave hideout. While these motion pictures exalted American prowess and promised victory, the newspaper accounts of the hostilities told a different story. After winning an important battle at Inchon in September 1950, U.S. forces ran into stiff opposition as thousands of Chinese "volunteers"—now part of the North Korean military—curtailed further advancement. To exacerbate matters, Truman, in a sudden volte-face, relieved America's popular hero Douglas MacArthur of his command when the general, hoping for a quick triumph, threatened to bomb China.

What happened? How could the nation's greatest champion—the larger-than-life officer who kept his I-Shall-Return promise to the Philippines—fall from grace? Did this mean that the United States, the indisputable victor of the Second World War, would suffer its first defeat? Against an Oriental foe? At least in the movie houses, Americans found comfort with past glories as

their popular male stars continued to blast their Axis foes at every turn, reminding audiences that no matter who the adversaries were, the republic
would prevail.

While Hollywood slowly fine-tuned its Korean battle stories, the stable
World War II photoplay—also in full production—offered tangible proof of
the nation's military strength. Early in the police action, titles such as Co-
lumbia's *Okinawa*, Fox's *An American Guerrilla in the Philippines*, RKO's
Flying Leathernecks, Warner Bros.' *The Tanks Are Coming*, MGM's *Go for
Broke*, and Universal's *Target Unknown* were released. These recapped
Japan's kamikaze defeats, navy steadfastness behind enemy jungle lines, ma-
rine airpower, a tank sergeant's heroism, the nisei's role in routing Hitlerism,
and fast-moving GIs battling in Nazi-occupied France. Other screenplays—
Warner Bros.' *Operation Secret*, Columbia's *Eight Iron Men*, Universal's *Red
Ball Express*, Allied Artists' *I Was an American Spy*, and Republic's *Fighting
Coast Guard*—re-created a traitor's perfidy in an Allied division, a squad's
perseverance to thrash the Germans, the pertinacity of an integrated outfit that
drove trucks supplying the Normandy breakout, a Manila chanteuse's bravery
against the Japanese, and the Coast Guard's skill in pounding the Axis.

Still other motion pictures idolized past victories: Universal's *Mystery Sub-
marine* heralded a U.S. officer's role in destroying a German *Unterseeboot*
operating furtively off the South American coast; Republic's *The Wild Blue
Yonder* saluted the B-29 crews' many Pacific triumphs and allowed two fliers,
in their spare time, to woo the same nurse. Another Republic B-formula,
Thunderbirds, also venerated Air Corps pilots and their wartime role in Italy.
Again, two airmen, during their idle moments, chased the same girl. Allied
Artists' *Flat Top* exalted the training and combat record of aircraft carrier avi-
ators while Paramount's *Submarine Command* traced a naval officer's role in
both World War II and Korea and the heavy burden involved with life-and-
death decisions. Warner Bros.' *Breakthrough* told the rousing story of an
American infantry unit from its basic training to the Normandy invasion,
where an eager platoon fought diehard Nazis. As one GI bragged, "Nobody
breaks through those stinking hedgerows—you got to fight for each one,
sixty, seventy yards at a time."

Occasionally a few titles departed from the God-is-on-our-side storylines
established years earlier by the propaganda films. Two Fox releases, *The
Desert Fox* and *The Desert Rats*, heaped praise on the military skill of Field
Marshal Rommel, downplaying his role as an adversary, while Columbia's *El
Alamein* applauded the English troops for North African victories. Fox's *Decision before Dawn* glorified a German POW (Oskar Werner), who returned
to the Fatherland as an agent, hoping to glean information that would end hostilities and spare his birth land further destruction. For the young idealist, his

mission seemed noble: "I did it because I wanted to help my country and, now, more then ever, I am sure what I did was right." Another Fox production, *Five Fingers*, conversely, glamorized the exploits of a Nazi spy, who surreptitiously photographed strategic British operational orders in wartime Turkey. RKO's *Sealed Cargo* heralded a Newfoundland fishing-boat captain who exposed an intricate Nazi plot to supply their submarines—hidden off the Canadian coast—with fuel and torpedoes. Here, Dana Andrews realized that a derelict sailing vessel was really "a mother ship for the U-boats." With a nod to science fiction, Briskin-Smith's *The Magic Face*, a B-meller, depicted the unlikely story of a German actor who became Hitler's valet, quietly murdered the führer, assumed his identity, and then, without missing a beat, canceled a scheduled British invasion by asserting, "We should deal with the Bolsheviks first."

American casualties were not forgotten. United Artists' *The Men* told the sobering story of some paralyzed veterans and their arduous road to recovery. With Jack Webb and Marlon Brando portraying disabled servicemen, the screenplay emphasized the high cost of the recent victory. Likewise, Universal's *Bright Victory* explained a blind soldier's gradual adaptation to his postwar life. Here, the soldier (Arthur Kennedy), with the help of a sympathetic caretaker, slowly adapted to his sightless world. A similar storyline, Columbia's *Purple Heart Diary*, allowed a mutilated GI to find comfort with a caring nurse. Another Columbia entry, *The Juggler*, offered a somber look at a concentration-camp survivor (Kirk Douglas) and his difficult adjustment, without his wife and family, in the new nation of Israel.

In a different mood, some high jinks lightened up military drudgery. Fox's *You're in the Navy Now* starred Gary Cooper as a ninety-day wonder, working hard to make a decrepit destroyer seaworthy. Inadvertently, he rammed this vessel into a flagship carrier, much to the chagrin of some top-heavy brass. Warner Bros.' *South Sea Woman* highlighted the unauthorized comings and goings of a marine sergeant (Burt Lancaster), who broke up a friend's marriage, fled to a South Sea island, posed as a deserter, joined the French Resistance, seized a Nazi supply ship, and sank a Japanese destroyer, even though he was technically AWOL. Universal's *Up Front*, based on Bill Mauldin's cartoon book, turned the European war into a series of laid-back, breezy moments for two ground pounders, Willie and his sidekick Joe, a streetwise dogface, who crawled through mud and rain exclaiming, "I can't get no lower, my buttons is in the way." On the soap opera circuit, MGM's *Teresa* confronted the problems a returning GI (John Ericson) endured when he brought home an Italian bride, a situation that angered his domineering mother.

Other photodramas, however, explained the war more realistically. The Marine Corps, with its reputation as the first to fight, charged the beaches in Fox's CinemaScope production, *Halls of Montezuma*. Directed by Lewis Milestone and released in 1950, this combat picture followed Republic's *Sands of Iwo Jima* by a few months, and the two titles seemed cast from the same mold. Naturally, no Corps film would ever outdo John Wayne's performance as Sergeant John Stryker, the hard-boiled NCO who blasted Japanese pillboxes, but *Halls of Montezuma*, featuring Richard Widmark as a push-pull squad lieutenant, proved, as always, that the quick-moving jarheads, standing behind their semper fidelis credo, would keep their honor clean.

With the stirring martial refrains of the Marine Corps' hymn blaring in the background and the distinctive anchor, eagle, and globe emblem superimposed over the opening credits, this motion picture glamorized the all-volunteer outfit's go-get-'em daring. Here, in 1944, America's seafaring fighters stood ready to disembark from the safety of their transport ship into a vulnerable, flat-bottomed landing craft that would bring them to the hostile shores of another Japanese-held Pacific island. But this time, a senior officer adjured, the strategy was different. "We used to say," the colonel barked, "that the only good Jap was a dead Jap. That's changed! From here on in, the only good Jap is a Jap prisoner who tells us things."

Now what? How do you capture a crazed enemy that prefers death to surrender? For one company the rules were simple, "Keep your eyes on your squad leaders and platoon leaders." Soon the men applied these principles as they slowly moved away from the beachhead into jungle warfare's terra incognita. Using many of the classical propaganda film tenets, *Halls of Montezuma* focused on the marines' diversity: The lieutenant was a high school chemistry teacher, his medic a South Dakota farmer. Other riflemen—including a boxer, a stutterer, a petty hoodlum, a writer manqué, a brewer, and a Japanese-speaking aesthete—were Guadalcanal and Tarawa veterans. As always, this 1950 motion picture restated that the leathernecks represented all facets of American society, and this eclectic background, a reiteration of national pride, honored the Corps.

Since John Wayne had already seized Iwo Jima, director Lewis Milestone (whose World War II film credits included *The Purple Heart*) realized that a similar victory was needed to establish *Montezuma* as a significant screenplay rather than another humdrum. Instead of assaulting Mount Suribachi, the marines—now embarked on a risky search-and-destroy mission to wipe out a hidden Japanese rocket-launching pad before H-Hour—cautiously moved forward. After a circuitous trek, this tightly knit squad reached the Japanese stronghold and—in an obvious nod to Lewis Seiler's 1943 red-white-and-blue extravaganza *Guadalcanal Diary*—wrecked their Oriental foes, diehard fanatics burrowed in-

A Marine translator (Reginald Gardiner) explains the contents of a Japanese message to his squad lieutenant (Richard Widmark) while another gyrene (Jack Webb) listens in Lewis Milestone's Pacific victory adventure Halls of Montezuma. *Courtesy of Twentieth Century–Fox*

side hilltop caves. With this threat eliminated, hundreds of leathernecks, waiting patiently behind their front lines, moved ahead and quickly secured the island.

Certainly, this hard-driving Marine victory, coming months after John Wayne's flag-waving triumph, reassured moviegoers that the same fate awaited those North Korean invaders now fighting on that faraway peninsula. Why not? If John Wayne and Richard Widmark, the best of America's prowess, could push the Japanese off an island, the new enemy was next. After all, in the closing moments of *Montezuma*, didn't Richard Widmark stand up, hand-signal his squad, and order them frontward, barking, "Give 'em hell!'"?

Other themes mirrored the war's consequences. Warner Bros.' *Operation Pacific* allowed submarine commander John Wayne many trial-and-error opportunities to unravel a defective torpedo problem and then blow up some Japanese ships while, on the Italian front lines, another Warner Bros.' story, *Force of Arms*, showcased William Holden routing the *Wehrmacht*. During his spare time the good-looking army officer courted pretty Nancy Olson, proving once again Virgil's maxim that true love conquers all, while an army

Romeo (Kirk Douglas) learned, in United Artists' *Act of Love*, that military life was not a bed of roses. Here, the decorated soldier, fresh from combat, found that his Paris command assignment offered unexpected problems when a loudmouthed officer, unsympathetic to any enlisted-man's situation, quashed a romance with a fragile French woman. In another area, tough-talking Richard Widmark—basking in *Halls of Montezuma* triumph—led his underwater demolition team into hostile South Pacific waters in Fox's *The Frogmen*, destroying enemy targets whenever they found them. In Allied Artists' *Torpedo Alley* a former World War II pilot (Mark Stevens), unable to adjust to civilian life, joined the submarine service as a tribute to the men who rescued him years earlier after a failed aerial mission.

Probably the best Hollywood screenplay to explain the Korean conflict era was MGM's *Above and Beyond*, a docudrama depicting the top-secret training of the men assigned to fly the *Enola Gay*, a high-powered, modified B-29 that on August 6, 1945, dropped the first atomic bomb on Hiroshima. With matinee idol Robert Taylor portraying the fly-by-the-book flight commander, Colonel Paul Tibbets, this 122-minute part-history, part-soap-opera drama detailed the intricate crew selection process, the daily, repetitive stateside training flights, the surreptitious trek to the Mariana Islands, and, finally, the early morning westward deployment to the Japanese mainland. Directed by Melvin Frank, this glorification-of-airpower adventure tale reassured anxious moviegoers that the military machine responsible for a swift and decisive end to the Pacific War—by using two nuclear bombs—would defend the nation again, if necessary, by the same means.

With its January 1953 opening date—a time when many Americans feared the Korean War could escalate into a deadly conflagration with the Soviet Union—*Above and Beyond* reaffirmed the popular 1941 propaganda song's slogan, "We Did It Before and We Can Do It Again." Why not? With Robert Taylor in the cockpit bellowing orders to specific crew members, checking and double-checking various control settings, and then pulling back the throttle and screaming off into the wild blue yonder, audiences knew their nation's defense was inviolable. After all, Taylor rode roughshod over his staff, demanding impeccable performance, firing or demoting anyone who sullied their training's secretive mission, constantly reminding his men, "Each of you has a job that could shorten the war." Even his wife— unaware of the reasons for his late night hours, unexplained absences, and vague dinner conversations—patiently endured one frustration after another until that fateful August afternoon when radio commentators interrupted all scheduled programs and told the nation about this historical mission, explaining that for all practical purposes, the atomic-bomb attack meant the end of World War II.

Still other low-budget screenplays showed the diversity of global fighting. Deep in the African desert, a GI mechanic (Rod Cameron) tinkered with an abandoned, run-down Panzer tank and turned it against the Axis in *The Steel Lady*, while over in the Asian theater, Edmond O'Brien's marine patrol captured an important Japanese naval commander needed for interrogation in Columbia's *China Venture*. In Allied Artists' *Fighter Attack*, Sterling Hayden recalled his last combat flying mission over Italy, and Dan Duryea dealt with leadership responsibility in Columbia's *Sky Commando*. Helmut Dantine frustrated the Nazis on his native Greek soil in Lippert's *Guerrilla Girl*, while Alan Ladd, a former U.S. officer turned British enlisted man, fought the Germans in Columbia's *Paratrooper*. Another Fox title, *Destination Gobi*, placed naval meteorologist Richard Widmark deep in the isolated Central Asian desert sending weather reports to various command posts. In United's part-comedy, part-melodrama *Stalag 17*, William Holden, an American POW wheeler and dealer, shuffled in and out of lighthearted situations with his captors in a manner that sugarcoated Nazi cruelty in these prison compounds. As with any motion picture that portrayed the war as one laugh after another, many scenes lacked any reality about the ongoing conflict.

But one photodrama took a hard look at military life and pointed the finger at the U.S. Army, denouncing this organization for its officer-caste elitism, unfettered brutality in the ranks, and harsh regulations. Based on James Jones's acclaimed novel, Columbia's Academy Award–winner *From Here to Eternity* opened the floodgates with its unforgiving, microcosmic portrayal of barracks life on a sunny Hawaiian base, weeks before the December 7 attack. With an all-star cast that included Burt Lancaster, Frank Sinatra, Montgomery Clift, Deborah Kerr, and Ernest Borgnine, this 118-minute moving picture downplayed those John Wayne mock heroics found in most World War II screenplays. Instead, it excoriated the armed forces for a variety of unpleasant practices. Clearly, screenwriter Daniel Taradash crossed the Rubicon with *Eternity*, indicting the military as an undemocratic institution precariously sinking from the weight of its quasi-fascist policies.

In telling the story of the rise and fall of army private Robert E. Lee Prewitt (Montgomery Clift), stationed at the Schofield Barracks Field near Honolulu, director Fred Zinnemann slowly limned every nuance of 1941 military life as most enlisted men—often victims of loneliness, alienation, and insecurity—sought camaraderie through hard soldiering, payday drinking, and weekend catting. But Private Prewitt, with his slow-talking, quiet behavior and tattered postbellum mannerisms, kept away from this crowd and, instead, derived satisfaction from his intrinsic claims about honor and integrity. For this simple Kentucky-born soldier, orphaned at seventeen, the army meant everything. "I'm a thirty-year man," he once reflected, "I'm in for the full ride."

On a bright November morning Private Prewitt, wearing a freshly starched, gig line-perfect, Class-A khaki uniform, explained to his new top sergeant (Burt Lancaster) and commanding officer (Philip Ober) why, as a corporal, he left an easy-living bugle assignment to join a no-nonsense rifle company, a voluntary transfer that, along with other disadvantages, mandated a reduction in rank. Shifting his weight from one foot to another, the spit-and-polish private's explanation seemed hollow. "I was first bugler for two years," Prewitt asserted, "the topkick had a friend who transferred in from another outfit. The next day, he was made first bugler over me. I was a better bugle player." Unimpressed by this answer the captain offered a remedy. "I'm the regimental boxing coach, you know," he boasted, alluding to the numerous photographs on his office wall, "all I need is a top middleweight."

But Prewitt, a one-time contender, quickly demurred, "I'm sorry, sir, I quit boxing." He apologized, detailing an unfortunate event months earlier that resulted in blinding a friend in a military sparring match. "That's why I decided I would quit, sir." Aloof to his subordinate's predicament, Captain Holmes pushed his authoritative button. "Looks to me like you're trying to establish a reputation as a lone wolf, Prewitt," he barked. "You should know that in the army, it's not the individual that counts." Minutes later, the slick-sleeved private, walking across the quadrant with the first sergeant, explained his refusal: "A man [that] don't go his own way, he's nothing." Smiling sardonically, Sergeant Warden retorted, "You'll fight because Captain Holmes wants to be Major Holmes."

Clearly, in less than ten minutes of screen time, the plot of *From Here to Eternity*, unlike any previous World War II photodrama, ignored patriotic themes but instead became a vehicle for social criticism with its inflammatory messages. As an impersonal institution, the U.S. Army, with its low pay, meager facilities, and dubious enlisted-man recruitment standards sharply contrasted the well-paid, pleasant accommodations and elitist selection found in the commissioned ranks. Here, in balmy Hawaii, a lone infantry private, unwilling to join a boxing squad, soon felt the brunt of sadistic field sergeants and unpleasant work details, while his commanding officer, standing in the background, encouraged this treatment.

Other problems emerged. In an unusual turn of events, Captain Holmes's love-starved wife (Deborah Kerr) seduced her husband's first sergeant, and soon the twosome sneaked around the island looking for seclusion. Likewise, Private Prewitt fell for a club hostess, a friendly Oregon girl (Donna Reed), while his new barracks friend Private Angelo Maggio (Frank Sinatra), waving his whisky bottle, smiled approvingly. For Prewitt, this unexpected romance, coupled with Maggio's congeniality, offered brief solace from the miserable treatment on the training field. Finally, after weeks of harsh military discipline, the former bugler, lacking any family ties, became warm and affectionate now that he found both a girlfriend and an army buddy.

Checking out the Hickman Field parade ground, Private Angelo Maggio (Frank Sinatra) envisions a respite from soldiering with a Saturday-night foray into the Honolulu bar scene in Fred Zinnemann's indictment of military authority, From Here to Eternity. *Courtesy of Columbia Pictures.*

But *Eternity* was not a soap opera. Mrs. Holmes, angry that her lover would not apply for a commission and marry her, broke off the affair. For the ramrod sergeant, the whole idea seemed implausible. "I'm no officer, I'm an enlisted man," he bragged. "If I try to be an officer, I'll be putting on an act." As for Private Maggio, another difficulty arose. Caught on a drinking binge that involved guard-post dereliction, he received a six-month stockade sentence, placing him under the heel of a sadistic guard, Fatso Judson (Ernest Borgnine). Finally, following weeks of physical torture, Maggio escaped only to die hours later from blunt trauma. Enraged, Prewitt swore revenge and, in few days, lured Fatso into an alley and after a short scuffle, killed this tormentor. Knifed in this fight, Prewitt squirreled away in his girlfriend's Honolulu apartment to recuperate. For Private Prewitt, the southern idealist who only wanted to soldier, the future seemed ominous.

What future? On Sunday morning, December 7, Japanese planes strafed Schofield Barracks, and immediately the soldiers ran to their posts, firing at the low-flying aircraft. Spearheaded by Sergeant Warden, the troops shot down a few Zeroes and then regrouped at water's edge, ready to repel an amphibious invasion. That evening, everyone's nerves were taut. When a guard spotted a lone figure zigzagging furtively on the beach, he first warned the intruder and then fired. Immediately other sentries pulled their triggers, and moments later they stood over the lifeless Private Robert E. Lee Prewitt, the loner returning to his squad. Sergeant Warden, summoned to identify the body, looked pensively at Prewitt's anguished face and uttered a makeshift eulogy, "He loved the army more than any soldier I've ever known."

As a naturalistic tract, *From Here to Eternity* offered moviegoers their first glimpse of the unsavory elements found in military life. Unlike any previous World War II story, this photodrama raised serious questions about basic rights and rigid authority. Really, how many young men would rush out to enlist in the armed services after eyeing Fatso Judson bludgeon a helpless GI? What mother, with a son in the army, would feel comfortable after watching Private Prewitt spend hours digging an elaborate five-foot hole so a smart-aleck noncom could bury a newspaper? But in 1953, with the selective service pulling men into the army, recruitment was not an issue. The real problem was the Korean conflict. On a monthly quota, thousands of draftees routinely shipped out to stateside basic-training bases and each man pondered the same thoughts: How long would this war last? When would they go home? Or, would they suffer the same fate as Private Robert E. Lee Prewitt, an unknown cipher looking for a modicum of comfort, a fallen victim to a harsh, impersonal system?

Chapter Four

Public Attitudes and Revisionism
1954–1967

"We can tell lies about the good old days in the war."—Detective James Doyle (Wendell Corey) reminiscing with his World War II pal, photographer-turned-voyeur L. B. Jefferies (James Stewart), in Alfred Hitchcock's 1954 thriller, *Rear Window*

"Hollywood just never caught on. In their casting they looked in the wrong places. Well, that's how old Georgie Patton wanted it. He wanted a very couth looking soldier. Sanitized killers."—Former World War II infantryman, Bill Mauldin, creator of the popular cartoon series *Up Front*, featuring Willie and Joe, two dogfaces hoping to make it home, bemoaning that combat offered the GIs little chance for clean clothes, hot showers, and regular meals, unlike the handsome, tidy, and well-fed soldiers portrayed on Hollywood screens

By early 1954 Americans seemed divided about the recent Korean police action. For some, the high death toll—over fifty-four thousand servicemen—was excessive, especially for a seesaw war that, basically, ended the same way it began, at the thirty-eighth parallel. For others, serious questions remained unanswered. What happened? Why didn't Uncle Sam roll up his sleeves and push these Orientals into the ocean? Why did the strongest military force in the world, the nation that eight years earlier brought the Axis scourge to its knees, agree to a stalemate with its Communist enemy? And what about General MacArthur? Why was America's World War II hero removed from command?

The most challenging question involved nuclear weapons. While numerous voices advocated dropping the atomic bomb on Red China, saner minds realized that such a dramatic act would only bring a retaliatory attack from their puppeteer, the Soviet Union. Clearly, this three-year conflict altered the rules of warfare. No longer would a frontal assault guarantee success. As for airpower, what good are destructive weapons if they cannot be used? What choices did the United States have? According to the wags, only one: Hobson's choice.

As public interest in this faraway war waned, the Hollywood moguls—realizing this conflict lacked the visceral qualities of the rousing World War II titles—quietly phased out this genre, and in 1954 only a handful of Korean conflict photodramas opened in American theaters. For the producers, the bottom line prevailed. Audiences were not interested in lost causes, they averred, because ticket buyers wanted clear-cut victories and red-blooded heroes to cheer when the Stars and Stripes, a tangible symbol of the republic's strength, flew defiantly over the enemy's stronghold.

So in 1954, Hollywood—staring at the handwriting on the wall—quickly returned to previous glories, heaping more adulation on World War II victories. United Artists' *Beachhead* praised the U.S. Marines for their tough stance in the Philippines, a feat that allowed MacArthur's invasion fleet untroubled access. Starring Frank Lovejoy and Tony Curtis, this eighty-nine-minute testimony glamorized many aspects of the dangerous, behind-enemy-lines strife. Similarly, MGM's *Betrayed* placed Clark Gable and Lana Turner in the Dutch underground movement, thwarting the Nazis at every turn and allowing the King to utter sweet nothings to the sweater girl: "You're beautiful when you're angry." On a lighter note, Universal's *The Glenn Miller Story* told the quiet narrative of the musician whose snappy rendition of "Little Brown Jug" became a household song, and his combat-related death reiterated the high cost associated with V-E Day. With the venerable Jimmy Stewart in the leading role, this heartwarming movie received accolades from everyone. Another musical, Fox's *Carmen Jones*, offered a GI version of the famous Bizet opera. As predicted, an army corporal, Harry Belafonte—stationed in an all-black unit training for overseas duty—fell victim to the sensuous wiles of an off-base Circe, Dorothy Dandridge.

Another title, Columbia's *The Caine Mutiny*, projected a moral dilemma encountered during wartime service. Based on Herman Wouk's best-selling novel, this screenplay depicted the not-so-glamorous adventures of a minesweeper's captain, Philip Queeg (Humphrey Bogart). Queeg's many shipboard failures, coupled with ongoing irrational behavior, resulted in an unprecedented mutiny as junior officers—fearful of capsizing—seized control of the vessel during a raging storm. Eventually, a court-martial exonerated the accused when a persuasive navy lawyer (José Ferrer) pushed the commander over his edge with rapid, no-nonsense questions, causing an obvious nervous breakdown in the witness chair. But for the victors, their joy fizzled out after their slightly bibulous defense counsel, now on the high ground, berated his charges, "Queeg was sick, he couldn't help himself. But you—you're real healthy. Only you didn't have one-tenth the guts that he had."

As a major World War II feature film, *The Caine Mutiny* posed several ambiguous questions: how many neurotic officers still commanded naval vessels, and at what point can military directives—those regulations responsible for maintaining authority—be overridden? Certainly, Wouk's novel sided with Queeg, with his discernible shortcomings, and, for the most part, the movie echoed those sentiments. Even with Queeg's emotional entropy, the defense lawyer rationalized, this officer deserved respect. "When I was studying law and Mr. Keefer here was writing his stories," he blurted out, "and you, Willie were tearing up the playing fields of dear old Princeton, who was standing guard over this fat, dumb, happy country of ours? Not us!" he screamed. "Oh, no, we knew you couldn't make any money in the service. So, who did the dirty work for us? Queeg did! And a lot of other guys. Tough, sharp guys who didn't crack up like Queeg."

Another screenplay offering similar equivocation was Warner Bros.' *The Sea Chase*, an oversimplified revisionist tract expostulating that not all Germans were rabid, goose-stepping Hitlerites but instead intelligent, sympathetic nationals snared in a vicious system that, by 1939, was out of control. In his most atypical role, John Wayne portrayed a German hero, a sea captain, whose freighter—moored in an Australian port—awaited shipping orders. Then, news of the Poland invasion changed everything. Considered an outcast, Wayne quickly took to the high seas, setting his compass toward the other side of the world hoping to reach his birth land. After much travail and months of perilous adventures—including an elaborate pursuit by the British navy—he abandoned this course and, in a misty, surreal ending, disappeared into a Norwegian fjord.

Was this the John Wayne who dashed between Japanese bullets to blast his foes from their pillboxes? The man who constantly barked, "Saddle up!" to his marine squad? Would audiences accept their red-blooded, anti-Axis fighter in a new role as a good German, a type of spiritual exile, an ironic hero, a citizen who can love his nation but not its politics? Who knows? For all its symbolism, *The Sea Chase* wasn't really a World War II motion picture but, instead, a Cold War metaphor. Here in 1955, as the USSR menaced NATO forces with their saber-rattling choreography, it was time to reinstate Germany—not the Nazis—into the Allied fold against a contemporary threat. Who was the best man for this job? Who could convince American moviegoers that most Germans were oblivious to Hitler's lebensraum? Who could wear a German naval uniform with the same authenticity as any rough-and-tumble leatherneck? Only one person, the plain-talking, in-your-face, flag-waving, Iowa-bred Marion Morrison.

For the next thirteen years, Hollywood continued to turn out an array of photodramas that in one shape or another recalled the World War II glory days when American forces rammed their enemies at every turn. Warner Bros.' *Battle Cry* heaped dollops of praise on the Marine Corps and their many South Pacific victories, as the young men in this all-volunteer unit—led by competent, father-figure officers—leaped out of LSDs, slammed the beaches, pushed inland, and obliterated the Japanese menace. Likewise, Universal's *To Hell and Back* offered quiet admiration for an average soldier, Audie Murphy, a bashful, gee-whiz, Texas GI whose exploits in the European theater culminated with the coveted Medal of Honor. Similarly, in Warner Bros.' *The McConnell Story*, Alan Ladd portrayed the American air ace, Joseph McConnell, expounding his World War II career, his Korean conflict experiences, and his accidental death testing an experimental jet aircraft.

Other titles continued the fight against the Axis in different formats. Columbia's *The Cockleshell Heroes* extolled the surreptitious adventures of some British kayakers as they paddled up a Bordeaux inlet to destroy Nazi warships moored in this strategic waterway. Starring José Ferrer, this photodrama embellished the daring exploits of an exclusive commando unit. Likewise, Fox's *The Man Who Never Was* unraveled a complex espionage tale involving a British cadaver—set afloat in the Iberian Peninsula—which lulled the German high command into false security. With Clifton Webb in the starring role, this unusual story offered some insight about the English intelligence operations. Universal's *Away All Boats* was another Pacific naval tale about an attack transport commander (Jeff Chandler), who, after much trial and error, fine-tuned an inexperienced crew into a precision team that repelled the kamikazes. One anachronistic scene—depicting a black sailor firing at incoming enemy Zeroes—offered a special nod to Dorie Miller, the real-life mess gob who received the Navy Cross for manning a machine gun at Pearl Harbor, probably destroying a Japanese aircraft. Another navy tale, Columbia's *Battle Stations*, highlighted the hard work involved in saving a carrier after a Japanese bomber blow. Here, Richard Boone bellowed many orders to keep his ship from sinking and, finally, after some Yankee intransigence, brought this damaged flat-top back to its Brooklyn port. In Lippert Pictures' B-potboiler *Silent Raiders*, two U.S. commandos (Earle Lyon and Richard Bartlett) knocked out a Nazi communications center hours before D-Day.

In RKO's *The Bold and the Brave*, Wendell Corey and Mickey Rooney routed the *Wehrmacht* in the 1944 Italian hills, while over in England, Tom Tryon, in Columbia's seventy-nine-minute B-meller *Screaming Eagles*, dropped behind enemy lines hours before the D-Day invasion, disrupting enemy fortifications. Paramount's *The Proud and the Profane* placed William Holden in the South Pacific jungle, fighting the Japanese. As in most of his photodramas, the good-looking colonel found a love interest. Another Paramount title, *When Hell Broke Loose*, a low-cost B-quickie, showed off the efforts of a smooth-talking GI sharpie (Charles Bronson) as he broke up an assassination attempt on General Eisenhower, days before the Normandy invasion. Fox's B-picture *Under Fire* put Henry Morgan and three lost GIs in a tight spot when Nazi soldiers donned American uniforms. Eventually, these Axis infiltrators were dispelled. Warwick's *Tank Force* placed an American sergeant (Victor Mature), a GI who tried to assassinate Josef Goebbels, in North Africa leading an escape from a Nazi prison compound. After some desert adventures that included a spy in their group and a flight from a German-sympathizer sheikh, the men seized a Tiger tank and reached Allied lines.

A few soap operas offered personal insights into everyday life. Fox's *D-Day—The Sixth of June* revealed the complexities of wartime separation when a married American intelligence captain (Robert Taylor) could not keep his romantic hands off a pretty English social worker (Dana Wynter), whose husband was fighting in the North African campaign. Eventually, wounded during the Omaha Beach assault, the captain, now older and wiser, proffered a sudsy farewell to his British girlfriend and headed back to his wife. Similar unhappiness abounded in MGM's *Gaby* (a remake of MGM's World War I tearjerker, *Waterloo Bridge*) in which a French ballerina (Leslie Caron), unable to cope with the battle death of her American fiancé (John Kerr), reverted to promiscuity, believing that such unbridled behavior would purge all tormenting memories. When the "dead" sweetheart returned to London, their reconciliation proved that true love never faltered. A similar situation existed in Columbia's *The Key*. Here, a disillusioned woman (Sophia Loren) gave numerous naval men her room key, hoping such romantic trysts would alleviate seagoing dangers, even though one officer (William Holden) exclaimed he didn't want to become "another jacket on the hanger." In Fox's *The Man in the Gray Flannel Suit*, a former airborne captain (Gregory Peck)—ensconced in the New York City corporate world—belatedly learned that his cozy liaison with a lovely signorina during the 1945 Italian Campaign had produced a son. Now married to his American dream girl, some difficult decisions were made to rectify this problem. Down in New Zealand, a marine major (Paul Newman) wooed a steadfast woman (Jean Simmons) in MGM's *Until They Sail*, despite the many frustrations found in wartime separation when American servicemen, away from home for the first time, courted local females.

Similar issues moved forward. For many years Hollywood's portrayal of U.S. armed services officers—those men selected to lead others into combat—was exemplary. No one questioned the skill of Colonel Van Heflin in *Battle Cry*, Commander Jeff Chandler in *Away All Boats*, General Clark Gable in *Twelve O'Clock High*, or Admiral Gary Cooper in *Task Force*. Who could fault them? Fair-minded, down-to-earth, and perspicacious, these officers, according to filmdom's interpretation, fostered victories through wisdom, inspiration, and fortitude even though a frontline captain (Brian Fox in *Breakthrough*) could use a grammar lesson after bellowing, "I ain't gonna let no second guesser foul them up." True, occasional problems surfaced: Captain Humphrey Bogart in *The Caine Mutiny* or Captain Philip Ober, the ineffectual company commander in *From Here to Eternity* who allowed his boxing squad to ride roughshod over Montgomery Clift. By their malfeasance, both men violated their leadership roles and, subsequently, were drummed out of the service, allowing the officer corps' system to remain intact.

Other officers likewise did not fare well. In Warner Bros.' *Mister Roberts*, a Napoleonic supply-vessel captain, James Cagney, stood on his bridge bellowing one inconsistent directive after another, in a manner that was both comical and irrational. Clearly, the crew—infused with loneliness, uncertainty, and boredom—realized that their commander had lost his marbles. In turn, they looked to a junior lieutenant, Mister Roberts (Henry Fonda), and a kindly naval doctor (William Powell) for advice and assistance. After many shipboard mishaps, including the obsessive cultivation of a palm tree, the captain begrudgingly approved a transfer for his lieutenant, much to the chagrin of the enlisted sailors. But worse news followed. Months later, Mister Roberts, now on a combat destroyer, perished in action.

As a comedy turned tragedy, *Mister Roberts* depicted a naval captain who was both loony and paranoid—an officer who had slipped through the cracks and was given command of a supply vessel—while his foil, the always smiling Henry Fonda, worked unsuccessfully to restore civility in a hostile workplace. Frequently kibitzing with the crew, the easygoing ensign represented the best of the commissioned corps while his nemesis spouted one contradiction after another. In many ways, audiences could laugh at James Cagney's foolery because he posed no danger—his ship was on a logistical mission, safely ensconced from harm. More of a clown than a villain, his behavior elicited belly laughs rather then anger or protest. Here was an officer who was a fool, not an opportunist.

This was the exception to the out-of-control command leaders. Putting aside the portrayal of high-strung, easily duped commissioned bumpkins in such lighthearted comic-book stories as *Francis* (a lieutenant and a talking mule held discourse) or *Don't Go Near the Water* (junior naval officers ran amok in a public relations section), the irresponsible, incompetent combat officer presented a deadly threat. In Fox's *Between Heaven and Hell*, a psychopathic army captain (Broderick Crawford) ran his frontline Pacific island stronghold in a manner reminiscent of a medieval fiefdom. Surrounded by obsequious but degenerate goons who addressed him as "Waco," he arbitrarily punished any soldier who did not kowtow while he heaped rewards on his many sycophants. Almost frothing at the mouth, this officer encouraged brutality and sadism on a regular basis. When challenged by a liberal-minded National Guard private (Robert Wagner), "Waco" exploded with rage, sending the soldier on a dangerous scouting mission.

Would this film play in Peoria? Probably. Released eleven years after V-J Day, *Between Heaven and Hell* provided a replay for many veterans who knew firsthand about those unstable combat officers whose judgments were mired by their numerous mental problems. Clearly, these ex-GIs remembered screwballs like Waco and the misery associated with their command. For these viewers, this motion picture downplayed heroics and, instead, told a realistic story about military life's seamy side. Finally, Hollywood—after years of tap dancing around this sacred cow—broke new ground with this unconventional screenplay. Now, the die was cast; the days of the sanitized officer corps were over. No longer would this privileged caste system's misdeeds go unnoticed.

Why should they? Why should the officers eat fresh meat while the ground pounders gulped down K-rations? Why should the commissioned ranks enjoy showers while the enlisted men remained unwashed? How do you effectively control a rigid separatist system—allowing pleasing accommodations to one segment while denying basic comforts to another—during wartime? These annoying questions formed the backdrop of Warner Bros.' scathing antiofficer, antiauthority photodrama *The Naked and the Dead*, another screenplay that purported the armed services contained a good percentage of unstable individuals. Based on Norman Mailer's naturalist novel, this 131-minute indictment portrayed military regulations and contemporary fascism as two elements cut from the same cloth.

In some ways *The Naked and the Dead* followed a conventional plotline. U.S. Army troops, controlled by a megalomaniac commander, invaded a fictional Japanese-held island, moved inland, attacked their enemy, and, finally, secured every objective. Along the way, one squad, headed by a misogynistic, rabid sergeant, killed Japanese prisoners and—with an eye toward his financial future—extracted their gold-plated teeth, while other GIs either smiled approvingly or displayed disinterest. For the foot soldiers, only one concern mattered—survival.

For the high command, stronger issues prevailed. Standing in his commodious tent and reaching into his well-stocked refrigerator for a cold beer, General Cummings (Raymond Massey), a steely-eyed patrician, offered his young aide (Cliff Robertson) a beverage, explaining that such niceties were inherent with rank. "Every time an enlisted man sees an officer getting an extra privilege," he bragged, "it makes him fight harder." For the Ivy-league-schooled lieutenant, his superior's callous viewpoints jarred his liberal upbringing, and soon a polite, but formal, downward-thrust discussion ensued. "I don't care what kind of man you give me," the commander pontificated, "if I have him long enough, I'll make him afraid." As a concluding taunt he accused his charge, "Under that mask of humanism," he sneered, "you're a reactionary, just as I am."

Clearly, General Cummings's crypto-fascist ideas rattled his aide, but every lieutenant knew the imprudence of contradicting a commander. A few days later, a conversation proved more difficult. In a show of absolutism, General Cummings, his face livid with rage, ordered his subordinate to pick up a crushed cigarette butt or face many years in a military prison. After an unhealthy pause, Lieutenant Hearn, the idealist who espoused humanism, bent over, picked up the butt, and tossed it into an ashtray.

As a reformist film with strong leftist ideals, *The Naked and the Dead*'s weak ending did not spawn much optimism. Lieutenant Hearn, wounded behind enemy lines, recovered and in a syrupy homily, argued that love, not fear, motivated the fighting man (even though in the novel, a Japanese sniper killed him). The misfit sergeant's death seemed ample punishment for his unsociable behavior, and General Cummings, with his autocratic ideas still in tow, remained in power, while off to the side, the foot soldiers grubbed along,

In a rage, a one-star general (Raymond Massey) rebukes his orderly (Edward McNally) for bringing flowers into the command tent in Raoul Walsh's scalding condemnation of autocratic rule, The Naked and the Dead. *Courtesy of Warner Bros.*

realizing another island invasion loomed. Clearly, at the next battle site, General Cummings would enjoy more alcoholic beverages while the enlisted men—those GIs who bore the brunt of combat—sipped their powdered milk.

Another title that hammered away at the self-serving officer was United Artists' *Attack*, a strongly worded indictment that blasted command figures for a variety of opportunistic offenses. Here, Eddie Albert portrayed a sniveling National Guard captain, Erskine Cooney, leading an infantry company during the 1944 French offensive. Completely unfit for a combat assignment and displaying blatant psychotic tendencies, his bad judgments, flagrant blunders, and high casualties frustrated his battalion superior, a fellow southern-hometown politician manqué, Colonel Clyde Bartlett (Lee Marvin). The colonel needed the support of this subordinate's father—an influential county judge—to tout him for public office when the war was over; "Tippecanoe and Bartlett too," he envisioned. At the same time, the platoon's popular lieutenant, Joe Costa (Jack Palance), vowed to protect his men from the irrational behavior of their misfit captain: "If I ever lose another man on account of you, just one, you'll never see the States again," he threatened.

As a 1956 photodrama, *Attack* took American audiences into the officer caste system's terra incognita with all its quid pro quo shortcomings, double-dealings, elitism, cover-ups, privileges, and watch-my-back protection, while off to the side the enlisted men endured poor food, hard work, and constant danger as they wondered what dopey plan their captain would concoct. Even Colonel Bartlett, the man who fantasized about postwar political glories, knew the judge's son was unfit for command but did not want to relinquish that old-boy network so important in determining a stateside election. Rather, he admonished his subordinate, "You're commanding this company for one reason, as a favor to the judge. He always wanted a son, now I'm trying to give him one." But that suggestion was wishful thinking. Within hours, Cooney ordered an attack on a small village. Minutes later a handful of GIs lay dead, the squad lieutenant badly wounded, while huddled in a cramped cellar, an out-of-control Captain Cooney, yelling incoherently, opted for capitulation to the rampaging Nazi forces: "The way I see it, we're trapped! There's only one thing to do—surrender."

Now what? Would this out-of-it officer hand over his squad to an enemy that would probably shoot the GIs on the spot? Could anyone stop him? As the enlisted men watched in disbelief, Lieutenant Costa, bleeding profusely, aimed a pistol at his captain but collapsed and expired before he could pull the trigger. Moments later, Captain Cooney, shaking his rifle toward the GIs, sneered, "I'm still in command here! And the first wisecracker that gets out of line is going to get it right in the head. How about it? Any takers?" Seconds later, a lone shot resounded in the cellar. Captain Cooney—the man responsible for numerous casualties—dropped to the ground, killed by a junior officer, Lieutenant Harold Woodruff (William Smithers). Stunned, the GIs eyed him cautiously. "Good shot," a private uttered, "from the hip." Minutes later, the enlisted men, anxious to protect their lieutenant, took their weapons and, in a solidarity gesture, fired into the corpse. "The Krauts got the captain," a private scoffed, "they got him coming through the door," while another soldier argued, "Look Lieutenant, if ever a man needed killing it's that no-good putrid piece of trash laying there."

Certainly this motion picture pulled no punches with its depiction of those deranged individuals assigned to the U.S. Army's command positions, and this soldier's words clearly emphasized the anger every GI knew when their superiors simply lost it. While Colonel Bartlett and Captain Cooney—two men cut from the same cloth—oozed opportunism in every frame, the junior officer, Lieutenant Woodruff, represented their antithesis. Clear-minded, agile, and resourceful, he understood the dangers the squad faced following Cooney's orders. But was his killing justified? Would two wrongs make a right? Apparently not. In typical Hollywood fade-out, Lieutenant Woodruff—the young officer who witnessed so much military corruption—began the redemptive process by notifying the general staff.

In this Pollyanna ending, director Robert Aldrich abruptly shifted the storyline from hard-boiled realism to Hollywood mush by insinuating that Lieutenant Woodruff would get a fair shake from his superiors. What happened? After blasting the officer caste system for over a hundred minutes, could Aldrich suggest that—according to basic American ideals—the truth would set Lieutenant Woodruff free? Perhaps he forgot the admonition of the PFC down in the cellar, scoffing at Captain Cooney's bullet-ridden body, "Some sharp operator, bucking for his majority, will make you look like a blood-thirsting maniac." Apparently, Aldrich wanted to end *Attack* on a positive note, so he downplayed the private's warning and, instead, waved the flag during the final sixty seconds.

Without question, no other World War II moving picture depicted the officer corps in such derogatory terms as *Attack*. Years later, of course, titles such as *M*A*S*H*, *Apocalypse Now*, *Dr. Strangelove*, and *Seven Days in May* ran these men into the ground with their nasty depictions of command life, while similar screenplays—*Catch-22*, *What Did You Do in the War, Daddy?*, *Fail-Safe*, and *In Harm's Way*—also took potshots. Another picture, the Academy Award–winner *The Bridge on the River Kwai*, portrayed Colonel Nicholson (Alec Guinness) in a slightly ambiguous role. Released at the same time as *Attack*, David Lean's *Kwai* re-created the ordeal of British and American prisoners of war who were forced to build a railroad bridge in Japanese-occupied French Indo-China. Here a senior officer became obsessed with this project, and cooperating with his captors was either an act of treason or the ultimate

Unable to contain his anger toward an unfit company commander, an infantry lieutenant (Jack Palance) swears retribution for any future mishaps in Robert Aldrich's denunciation of frontline incompetency, Attack. *Courtesy of United Artists*

insanity. Finally, the structure was completed, but the following day, British commandos wired the bridge. In a controversial ending, Nicholson fell on a detonator, destroying his creation. But a bigger question remained unanswered: did Nicholson blow up the bridge as an expiatory gesture, or was his fall merely an accident, caused by his stupefaction and imbalance?

In the late fifties, most Hollywood producers—eager to reap large returns on World War II photodramas—kept the old red, white, and blue at high mast. United Artists' *The Sharkfighters* placed a navy officer (Victor Mature) in the warm Cuban waters until his research team perfected a repellent that would protect downed flyers from the marauding sharks found in both oceans. Determined to protect U.S. servicemen, the no-nonsense commander argued, "There's only one way to prove what we're doing, we must try it with a man in the water." Another seagoing man, submarine commander Ronald Reagan, attacked many Japanese warships in Columbia's *Hellcats of the Navy*, as his girlfriend, Nancy Davis, smiled enthusiastically.

Tough-talking Robert Mitchum kept the enemy at bay in two combat zones: first, as a naval officer chasing a lone Nazi U-boat in Fox's *The Enemy Below*; then, as a stranded marine corporal, protecting a Roman Catholic nun from the Japanese in Fox's *Heaven Knows Mr. Allison*. Another hard-drinking, chain-smoking hero, John Wayne, portrayed the real-life aviation pioneer Frank "Spig" Wead in MGM's *The Wings of Eagles*. Here, Commander Wayne explained his "jeep carrier" idea, an innovative plan to supply depleted flattops: "That's it—jeep carriers, that's what we've been needing."

Other films that glamorized America's past victories included Warner Bros.' *Darby's Rangers*, a salute to the unorthodox volunteer battalion that advanced in North Africa and Italy. Starring James Garner, this spit-and-polish homage cheered every aspect of his maverick fighting unit. Fox's go-get-'em title, *In Love and War*, verified the Marine Corps' prowess as the leathernecks seized another Japanese island. Conversely, Warner Bros.' *The Deep Six* downplayed the quiet conversion of a Quaker naval officer (Alan Ladd), who modified his pacifist views while fighting Nazi forces. A similar moral issue occurred in MGM's *Torpedo Run*. Here, a submarine commander (Glenn Ford) unknowingly sank a Japanese transporter carrying fourteen hundred civilians, including his wife and son. Over in the Philippines, AIP's *Suicide Battalion* highlighted the exploits of two GIs who sneaked into a Japanese-occupied building and destroyed coded documents. Mike Connors starred in this seventy-nine-minute B-potboiler. In southern France, a lieutenant (Frank Sinatra) halted German forces in United Artists' *Kings Go Forth*, unaware that an enlisted man (Tony Curtis), annoyed by the junior officer's authority, sneered sardonically. In another AIP contribution, *Warrior's Five*, an American soldier (Jack Palance), along with five Italians, destroyed a strategic bridge, aided by a pretty national (Giovanna Ralli).

Action pictures always waved the flag. In MGM's *Underwater Warrior*, song-and-dance man Dan Dailey, now wearing khakis, developed the principles of below-the-waves demolition proving, "A man underwater could sink a battleship, foul up an enemy landing, or neutralize a minefield," while Columbia's B-tale, *Tarawa Beachhead*, showed Kerwin Matthews spearheading his squad during this important Pacific island invasion. Back in London, an American agent (Jeffrey Hunter) duped the Axis intelligence service about the upcoming Normandy invasion in Fox's *Count Five and Die*, while a surreptitious second-story man (Ray Milland) was recruited to steal German documents in MGM's *The Safecracker*. A similar storyline appeared in Allied Artists' seventy-two-minute caper, *The Secret Door*. Here, two likable yeggs (Robert Hutton and Peter Illing), expediently released from prison, traveled to neutral Lisbon, where after some cloak-and-dagger episodes they stole a Japanese codebook. Columbia's *The Two-Headed Spy* fictionalized the exploits of Alexander P. Scotland, a Berlin sleeper spy who worked with Hitler. With Jack Hawkins in the leading role, the British Empire remained intact even though the führer (Kenneth Griffith) claimed, "The defeatists! They are the enemy." Another Columbia drama, *Ghost of the China Sea*, placed a seaman (David Brian) in the midst of another Philippine skirmish aboard a dilapidated ship, facetiously dubbed the USS *Frankenstein*. Moving fast, the quick-thinking bluejacket lured an enemy cruiser into an ironclad trap. On another issue, Fox's *The Inn of the Sixth Happiness* told the simple story of an English missionary (Ingrid Bergman) and her many experiences in China under the Greater East Asia Co-Prosperity Sphere.

Not every movie was about combat. Eventually, a few titles surfaced that accented the frivolous side of the World War II experience, motion pictures that downplayed the horror and mayhem and, instead, looked at human nature's droll side. For starters, Danny Kaye and Curt Jurgens romped together in Columbia's *Me and the Colonel*, a screenplay based on Franz Werfel's *Jacobowsky and the Colonel*. Here an anti-Semitic Polish officer and a Jewish refugee, scheming an escape to England, frolicked in a foolish, lighthearted manner. Over in France, Glenn Ford and Red Buttons pushed the comedy button in MGM's *Imitation General*, an easygoing farce about a master sergeant who inadvertently impersonated a one-star general in the countryside during the 1944 fall offensive. Under the waves, Commander Cary Grant enjoyed many laughs harassing the Japanese in Universal's *Operation Petticoat* even though he worked from a pink submarine. On the other side of the ocean, Jack Lemmon and Mickey Rooney schemed to host a madcap, off-base party in a small Normandy town in Columbia's *Operation Mad Ball* while Rossano Brazzi and Mitzi Gaynor rhapsodized about an upcoming enchanted Solomon Island evening in Fox's elaborate musical, *South Pacific*. Universal's *The Secret War of Harry Frigg* offered many laughs as a recalcitrant army private (Paul Newman), sent to rescue five Allied officers from an Italian fortress, outwitted Nazi officials.

Naval lieutenant Jack Lemmon took to the Bismarck Sea aboard a broken-down scow used as a decoy in Columbia's *The Wackiest Ship in the Army*, while over in the Far East, Don Knotts and Ernie Kovacs used their ingenuity to build a fancy hotel from army supplies in Fox's *Wake Me When It's Over*. Later, ABC capitalized on this whimsical theme in a made-for-television yarn, *Wake Me When the War Is Over*. In this comedy a German baroness (Eva Gabor) convinced a bumbling American officer hiding in her chateau—five years after V-E Day—that the conflict was still raging. A similar idea appeared in Paramount's *Situation Hopeless—but Not Serious*, in which Alec Guinness creaked along as a lonesome German national who kept an American airman (Robert Redford) prisoner in his cellar long after the war ended. United Artists' *The Last Time I Saw Archie* starred Robert Mitchum and Jack Webb as two leftovers from a stateside training program for overage pilots, while an army intelligence officer (Jim Hutton) slid from one escapade to another in MGM's *The Horizontal Lieutenant* as he searched for a Japanese soldier still hiding on a South Sea Island. Over in sunny Italy, two smoothies (Charlton Heston and Harry Guardino) spoofed army regulations with their numerous shenanigans in Paramount's *The Pigeon That Took Rome*, while in the North African desert two romps offered more laughs: in Columbia's *The Best of Enemies* a British officer (David Niven) crisscrossed paths with an Italian adversary (Alberto Sordo) as the two armies tried to outwit each other, and AIG's *War Italian Style* paired two American GIs sparring with a high-ranking Nazi general (Buster Keaton) about some phony invasion plans.

Other lighthearted screenplays included Universal's *Captain Newman, M.D.*, in which a stateside army psychiatrist (Gregory Peck) encountered daily bureaucratic mishaps, exclaiming that his office was "short of beds, doctors, orderlies, nurses—everything except patients," while over in the Pacific, Warner Bros.' *Ensign Pulver* continued the *Mr. Roberts* saga as Robert Walker pulled numerous pranks on his dour-faced captain (Burl Ives). Another South Pacific romp, Universal's *Father Goose*, placed an easygoing beachcomber (Cary Grant) in unusual circumstances when he hid a gaggle of schoolgirls from the Japanese forces. Universal's *McHale's Navy* and *McHale's Navy Joins the Air Force* highlighted the oddball antics of a PT crew stranded on an unmarked Pacific island, while United Artists' *What Did You Do in the War, Daddy?* was a madcap spoof of military regulations. In this screwball story, James Coburn and Dick Shawn lampooned the 1943 Sicilian campaign, deriding every aspect of the armed services and prompting an exasperated company officer to exclaim, "The village is in an uproar and I'm queen of the May." Likewise, Paramount's *On the Double* contained laughs aplenty when mild-mannered Danny Kaye impersonated an English general, a ruse that fooled the gullible Germans, while Warner Bros.' harmless frolic,

Onionhead, placed Andy Griffith as a likeable Coast Guard cook aboard a combat vessel that attacked an Axis submarine. Another hide-and-seek romp, Fox's *Kiss Them for Me* gave three navy aces a few days' shore leave in happy San Francisco before returning to Pacific combat duty. Here, Cary Grant chased pretty girls, spoofed military regulations, and enjoyed—as the title suggested—many osculations in the City by the Bay.

Most of these breezy shows seem mute when compared to MGM's dead serious, antiwar, black comedy, 1964 masterpiece *The Americanization of Emily*. Directed by Arthur Hiller and adapted from the novel by William Bradford Huie, *Emily* vacillated between slapstick, satire, exposé, and serious drama in telling the high-jinks story of an admiral's aide, Charlie Madison (James Garner)—stationed in London during the volatile, pre-D-Day invasion—whose main assignment was to provide high-ranking officers with plush hotel accommodations, unlimited alcoholic beverages, succulent food, and friendly women. A natural at this job, the good-looking lieutenant commander weaved in and out of pleasant situations, enjoying the many advantages available to a smooth-talking officer well connected to the general staff. Soon, he courted a comely English war widow, Emily (Julie Andrews), a woman who originally resented his privileged status but, subsequently, capitulated to his boyish charms with one request: "Don't show me how profitable it will be fall to love with you Charlie—don't Americanize me." Frequently at odds with her glib lover, she listened to Charlie's many rationalizations about the goldbricking life. "I'm yellow, honey, clear through," he bragged, "I'm a practicing coward."

His lackadaisical life fell apart when an eccentric senior admiral, William Jessup (Melvyn Douglas)—anxious to create a public relations coup—concocted the perfect plan: "A lot of brave men are going to die on D-Day," he gloated. "The first brave man to die on those beaches must be a sailor." Unavoidably caught up in this cockamamie, steamrolling scheme, Charlie was drawn into the logistical planning and ordered ashore on D-Day with an advance photography team to record this auspicious event. Now, in the early hours of June 6, Charlie Madison, the self-avowed dodger, after weeks of unsuccessful finagling, crouched on a French beachhead, movie camera in hand, as hundreds of bullets whizzed by. "What's the matter with you?" he yelled at another officer, "They're shooting at us." Suddenly, he fell. Minutes later, the news reached London: D-Day's first fatality was a sailor.

Elated by this news, Admiral Jessup ordered an elaborate testimony, complete with medals and a statue, for his fallen aide, while Emily quietly withdrew into her private world of pain. "What was admirable about Charlie was his sensation of life, his cowardly, selfish, greedy appreciation of life," she recalled. Finally, after days of preparation, the tribute was in place. Only one thing went wrong.

Living high on the navy's hog, two smooth-talking officers (James Coburn and James Garner) contemplate their next move as they scheme to fulfill their superiors' every whim in Arthur Hiller's runaway spoof of military shenanigans, The Americanization of Emily. *Courtesy of MGM.*

The first casualties from Normandy were returning to England. In this group, one man limped unobtrusively: Charlie Madison—a well-known opportunist famous for milking the system—had returned. Now what? The first man to die on Omaha Beach was, in fact, very much alive. Without missing a beat Admiral Jessup beamed, "We're going to make a brass-band hero out of Charlie."

As an unruly satire, *The Americanization of Emily* fired off both barrels deriding military authority, unbridled opportunism, male lasciviousness, and mock heroics while giving the thumbs-up signal to men like Charlie Madison. Certainly, in 1958, no U.S. service base would allow *Emily*, a wide-eyed picture that mocked every echelon, in their PX movie houses. Who could blame them? In scene after scene, director Arthur Hiller reduced World War II from a global conflagration to the youthful silliness found at most university fraternity parties: drinking, sex, jealousy, bragging, affectation, role-playing, and gibberish. No wonder this screenplay was taboo. What commander in his right mind wanted his servicemen to watch a film that lampooned regulations, caricatured senior officers, praised goldbricking, and championed unlicensed behavior?

Certainly, most Hollywood productions from 1958 to 1966 contained enough fast action and visceral thrills to fulfill those vicarious experiences enjoyed by many moviegoers. MGM's *Up Periscope* praised the Silent Service for its good work by having a navy commando (James Garner, fresh from his successful *Americanization* role) stealthily infiltrate a Japanese headquarters and remove vital secrets. Nearby, Admiral William "Bull" Halsey routed the Japanese seagoing forces in United Artists' *The Gallant Hours*. With James Cagney in the starring role, this 115-minute hagiography detailed the minute planning necessary for his Pacific Ocean victories and his wartime philosophy, "There are no great men, only great challenges that ordinary men are forced by circumstances to meet." A few miles away, a submarine captain (John Bentley) torpedoed many Japanese vessels in AIG's B-quickie, *Submarine Seahawk*, while another underwater-vessel captain (Cliff Robertson), stranded on an enemy island, relayed important messages to American commanders in Columbia's *Battle of the Coral Sea*. Later, the good-looking Robertson portrayed Lieutenant John F. Kennedy's South Pacific combat experiences in Warner Bros.' *PT 109*. Here the future president used skill and ingenuity to save his crew from encroaching enemy troops. On the Japanese-occupied island of Guam, a young bluejacket (Jeffrey Hunter) avoided capture for three years in Universal's *No Man Is an Island*, while another Universal title, *The Outsider*, replayed the life story of a Pima Indian, Ira Hayes—one of the leathernecks who raised the Mount Suribachi flag—his unaccustomed fame, and subsequent postwar death. With Tony Curtis in the leading role, this motion picture glamorized every facet of the Marine Corps Pacific island victories. In AIP's B-story *Operation Bikini*, a trio of U.S. soldiers destroyed a submarine containing secret information, even though one of the GIs (teen idol Frankie Avalon) paused to sing a few anachronistic rock-and-roll songs. Over in China, the Allies routed their Oriental nemesis in Columbia's B-potboiler, *The Mountain Road*. Here, Major James Stewart, an army engineer, braved both Japanese soldiers and rebel bandits before destroying a strategic roadway.

For Tinseltown producers, the war in the Philippines—against the Japanese invaders—provided plenty of excitement in thirteen motion pictures. Associated Producers' *Blood and Steel* was another B-quickie in which some rough-and-tumble Seabees, led by John Lupton, rescued island villagers, while down on the beach, Michael Parsons battled encroaching enemy soldiers in Hemisphere's *Raiders of Leyte Gulf*. Over in a nearby valley, Keith Andes rallied native soldiers from their hideouts in Allied Artists' *Surrender—Hell*, while Van Heflin deployed ground forces in Allied Artists' *Cry of Battle*, determined, for mercenary reasons, to protect his young charge (James MacArthur), boasting, "No Jap is going to get their hands on this kid."

Myriad's *W.I.A. Wounded in Action* dwelled on developing love interests between wounded soldiers and their nurses in a Philippine infirmary. With Steve Marlo and Maura McGiveney in leading roles, this wartime B–soap opera offered few resolutions. John Saxon eluded the encroaching Japanese army in Hemisphere's *The Ravagers*, while in Warner Bros.' *The Steel Claw*, a Marine captain turned guerrilla and minus his right hand (George Montgomery) routed the Japanese forces during a rescue attempt of a one-star general. In AIG's *Lost Battalion* Diane Jenkins and Leopoldo Salcedo kept one step ahead of enemy troops. Likewise, Hugh O'Brien trekked through this archipelago, disrupting enemy forces in United Artists' *Ambush Bay* even though his private (James Mitchum) wore a bright red hat, visible for many miles. Jack Mahoney attacked Japanese troops holed up in Manila's Intramuros (the Walled city) in Hemisphere Pictures' *The Walls of Hell* while Jimmy Rodgers and Jack Nicholson, two Intelrecon rangers, undertook a dangerous reconnaissance mission in Fox's *Back Door to Hell*. There, another GI (John Hackett) took a fatalistic approach: "Yeah, we're all gonna die anyway tomorrow, next week, thirty years from now. Did that little thought ever penetrate your thick skull?" Another Fox production, *Battle of Bloody Beach*, saw Audie Murphy, a civilian working for the navy, help the insurgents defeat their invaders, while in F-8 Productions' *Once Before I Die*, Major John Derek encountered many close calls in the dense, mountainous terrain.

Four more films took American forces into the Burmese hinterland: General Jeff Chandler led his machete-wielding fighters in Warner Bros.' *Merrill's Marauders* to attack a Japanese stronghold at Myitkyina but privately admitted, "Sneaking 3,000 men through this damn jungle is gonna drive me nuts." Likewise, Ron Foster eluded Japanese forces, saved some Oriental girls, and blew up a strategic supply line in United Artists' B-quickie, *Operation Bottleneck*. Squadron leader Gregory Peck, haunted by memories of his deceased wife, endured both emotional and flying problems in United Artists' *The Purple Plain*, and Captain Frank Sinatra chased the Japanese in MGM's *Never So Few* while his girlfriend (Gina Lollobrigida) waited patiently for his return. Later, Sinatra—now demoted to a chief navy corpsman—aided the wounded during the Solomon Islands fighting in Warner Bros.' *None But the Brave*. Back on Guadalcanal, two leathernecks (Keir Dullea and Jack Warden) fought their Oriental enemies in Allied Artists' adaptation of James Jones's novel *The Thin Red Line*, while George Segal, James Fox, and other Allied POWs struggled in Columbia's *King Rat*. In Filmgroup's sixty-four-minute B-travesty, *Battle of Blood Island*, two GIs (Richard Devon and Ron Kennedy) stranded on a Pacific island put aside their religious differences to avoid capture. Another B-meller, Fox's *Seven*

Women from Hell, depicted the horrors of Japanese prison camp. Here, Patricia Owens spearheaded an escape from a sadistic guard (Richard Loo) in their New Guinea compound. Rank's *A Town Like Alice* likewise depicted the misery of internment on the Malaysian Peninsula, where a spirited English woman (Virginia McKenna) fell for an Australian outbacker (Peter Finch), a man who helped her during this ordeal. In a different tempo, an American C-47 pilot (Victor Mature), making daily runs across the Hump, married a local beauty in United Artists' *China Doll*. One year later both perished in a Japanese attack while their infant daughter, only a few months old, survived. Rescued by friends, the baby drifted from orphanage to orphanage until, fourteen years later, the airman's pals located the teenager and brought her to America.

On the European front, the battle continued. In MGM's *The Angry Hills*, an agile war correspondent (Robert Mitchum) escaped from Athens with important data for the Allied command, while on a nearby Greek island, Gregory Peck trekked many kilometers and experienced numerous close calls before his undercover team destroyed two monster cannons in Columbia's *The Guns of Navarone*—even though his British explosive expert complained, "I prefer to leave the killing to someone like you, an officer and a gentleman, a leader of men."

Nearby, on the island of Crete, a British national (Shirley Eaton) joined a band of female guerrillas disrupting Third Reich advances in Universal's B-drama *The Naked Brigade*, while miles away in neutral Stockholm, William Holden personified the quiet heroism of an American-born businessman, Eric Erickson, who infiltrated the Nazi war machine, gleaned intricate secrets, and sent this information to British agents in Paramount's *The Counterfeit Traitor*. Another spy meller, Fox's *I Deal in Danger*, highlighted Robert Goulet in the tricky role of an Allied operative posing as a fervent Hitlerite, gleaning needed logistical information while gloating to his Berlin superiors that he would, "Convince the American people they can't possibly win the War." Likewise, Glenn Ford, a Parisian bon vivant, obtained critical war news from high-ranking *Wehrmacht* officers in MGM's remake of the 1921 Rudolf Valentino silent classic, *The Four Horsemen of the Apocalypse*, a grim story of brothers who fought on opposite sides. Also in France, an SNCF (national railway) Resistance fighter (Burt Lancaster) derailed a locomotive loaded with priceless stolen art treasures in United Artists' fast-moving cat-and-mouse cliffhanger, *The Train*, even though an effete Nazi colonel (Paul Scofield) claimed, "A painting means as much to you as a string of pearls to an ape." A similar screenplay involving an Italian high-speed rail chase was Fox's *Von Ryan's Express*. Here, an American colonel (Frank Sinatra) seized a POW freight train, and after many close calls the escapees reached Switzerland. But in an atypical Hollywood ending, Frank Sinatra perished, another victim of Axis brutality.

Other themes continued the fight against Hitler's forces. United Artists' *The Secret Invasion* paired Stewart Granger and Mickey Rooney as two criminals recruited to liberate an Italian general imprisoned by the Axis, while an OSS officer (Van Johnson) and a French Resistance fighter (Jean Pierre Aumont) rescued a high-ranking German officer who wanted to defect in Columbia's *The Enemy General*. Over in Ireland, Robert Mitchum, an IRA member, battled a comrade who worked for the Third Reich in United Artists' *The Night Fighters*. Not to be outdone, Marlon Brando, now an anti-Nazi, helped the Allies capture a German cargo ship in Fox's spy thriller *Morituri*, while Cliff Robertson, flying for the British, attacked a strategic Norwegian fuel factory in United Artists' *633 Squadron*. Still in Scandinavia, Kirk Douglas and Richard Harris traversed many miles to destroy an enemy heavy-water plant in Columbia's *The Heroes of Telemark*, while deep inside the Fatherland George Peppard obliterated an underground V-2 factory in MGM's double-agent thriller, *Operation Crossbow*. Alexandra Film's *Then There Were Three* told the B-story of six GIs (including Frank Latimore and Barry Cahill) searching for lost soldiers, unaware that a friendly stranger offering aid was a Nazi spy gathering logistical information. Similarly, in Filmgroup's wintry B-for-budget *Ski Troop Attack*, five GIs became stranded behind German lines, and in Universal's *Tobruk* some Jewish commandos fighting for the British destroyed critical oil reserves stored at this heavily guarded North African port. With a Canadian major (Rock Hudson) overseeing this unorthodox squad, everyone understood Captain George Peppard's warning, "If those tanks reach El Alamein, the Germans have Egypt."

Fox's *Up from the Beach* matched Cliff Robertson and Red Buttons as two GIs moving inland after the D-Day invasion. Along the way they encountered retreating Germans and pretty French women. Allied Artists' *Armored Command* assigned Howard Keel and Burt Reynolds as two U.S. Army men who thwarted the efforts of a charming Axis spy (Tina Louise). In another venue, equestrian master Lilli Palmer worked hard to protect her prized Lipizzans from German and American troops in Disney's *The Miracle of the White Stallion*. In Paramount's *Five Branded Women*, a group of unwanted Yugoslavian peasants (Jeanne Moreau, Carla Gravina, Barbara Bel Geddes, Silvana Mangano, and Vera Miles) fled their small village and joined the Resistance, where they fought their tormentors. Another B-production, Warner Bros.' *Hitler*, starred Richard Basehart as the führer in a role that portrayed the National Socialist leader as a demented, lovesick schoolboy bemoaning, "Compulsion turns me away from every woman."

A few blockbusters examined the European conflict with more detail. Fox's *The Longest Day* documented the planning and implementation of Operation Overlord, the multifaceted Normandy invasion. Here, the storyline weaved in and out of various command posts, asserting each side's strengths, weaknesses, joys, and failures even though the German defense commander Erwin Rommel (Werner Hinz) prophesized, "Not a single Allied soldier shall reach the shore." Another elaborate production, Paramount's *Is Paris Burning?* traced the numerous quid pro quo arrangements responsible for countermanding Hitler's draconian order and saving the French capital from destruction after the military commandant declared, "We're soldiers, not tourists." Using many famous movie stars, this screenplay spotlighted Gaullist determination to preserve its City of Lights. Warner Bros.' *Battle of the Bulge* fictionalized the details of this 1944 Belgian confrontation. With Henry Fonda, Robert Ryan, and Dana Andrews in leading roles, this 165-minute screenplay offered new problems associated with the Allied victory. One accurate scene, however, the German massacre at Malmedy, reiterated the *Wehrmacht*'s unbridled cruelty toward captured Americans.

Sometimes a motion picture looked philosophically at the European war. Columbia's *The Victors* contained poignant vignettes as U.S. servicemen moved cautiously from Sicily toward the Fatherland, experiencing pleasures, hardships, defeats, even romance. One episode, a thinly disguised version of Private Eddie Slovak's death, spooked moviegoers because an incongruous holiday song—Frank Sinatra's warmhearted version of "I'll Be Home for Christmas"—accompanied this controversial execution by a firing squad. United Artists' *Judgment at Nuremberg* explained the international court trials that brought Nazis to justice, even though a German lawyer (Maximilian Schell) waggishly suggested to a senior American judge (Spencer Tracy), "In five years, the men you sentenced to life imprisonment will be free." Another title concerned with punishment for Nazi leaders was Allied Artists' *Operation Eichmann*. Here, Israeli agents traced this prized fugitive to a South American hideaway and returned him to trial.

But Hollywood never strayed far from the real foes. Columbia's *The Last Blitzkrieg* highlighted the *Wehrmacht*'s destructive efforts during the Battle of the Bulge, where German soldiers, dressed in American uniforms and speaking excellent English, infiltrated Allied lines, disrupting their communication network. This time, Van Johnson—in an atypical role—played the leader of this Axis spy force. Another Columbia title, *Night of the Generals*, depicted the perverse killings of some French prostitutes during the Nazi occupation and the subsequent capture, some twenty years later, of the murderer. Starring Peter O'Toole, this revisionist screenplay suggested that the German judicial system was fair, honest, and unrelenting. Universal's *In Enemy Country* placed a French Resistance colonel (Anthony Franciosa) in a cat-and-mouse espionage plan near the Normandy coastline. After many close calls, he destroyed a German torpedo plant.

A few screenplays focused on the prolonged Italian campaign. AIG's *Tank Commandos* found two demolition specialists (Wally Campo and Robert Barron) thwarting some advancing Germans before they could fortify an Italian city, while Parade Releasing Organizations' eighty-four-minute B-clunker *Shell Shock* emphasized the comings and goings of a frontline army squad whose sergeant (Beach Dickerson), fearful that one of his men was faking battle fatigue, set out to expose him. Another B-quickie, AIG's *Paratroop Command*, placed U.S. airborne troops in the thick of battle during the 1943 offensive. Here a corporal (Richard Bakalyan) performed heroically in the grape-growing countryside. Beckman's low-budget filler *The Quick and the Dead* placed B-actor Larry Mann as a stealthy GI working with Italian partisans to rout the Nazis during the northern offensive, while in Fox's B-yarn *The Cavern*, five Allied soldiers and a German sergeant were trapped in a cave with a pretty woman (Rosanna Schiaffino). As expected, everyone survived. Nearby, an American spy (Rory Calhoun) moved quickly to avoid capture by the Gestapo in Embassy's eighty-one-minute thriller, *A Face in the Rain*. In Columbia's *Verboten*, an American sergeant (James Best) fought his way across the Rhine and after VE-Day took a fast discharge, married a German national, worked as a civilian adviser, and, using his army training, broke up a neo-Nazi group.

Near the Siegfried line a recalcitrant private (Steve McQueen), harboring a death wish, clashed with army regulations and Nazi soldiers in Paramount's *Hell Is for Heroes*, a blatant photodrama acknowledging that American forces contained a good percentage of sadistic and mentally unbalanced foot soldiers. A similar storyline about the unstable fighting man, Columbia's *The War Lover*, again showcased Steve McQueen as a monomaniacal B-17 pilot obsessed with dropping bombs on German targets regardless of the danger. In United Artists' *The Great Escape*, McQueen's portrayal became more mainstream. As a captured American pilot—rotting away in a POW camp—he joined other officers in an elaborate tunnel escape from their stalag. After a long countryside motorcycle chase, the hard-driving McQueen, just meters from the Swiss border, could not clear the fence. Nabbed by the *Wehrmacht*, the never-say-die Captain McQueen, undaunted by this setback, planned his next breakout attempt. In another vein, MGM's *36 Hours* offered a *Twilight Zone* D-Day scenario. Here, an American intelligence officer (James Garner)—after being drugged and taken to a German base disguised as an U.S. hospital—slowly emerged from a deep sleep. For the next day and a half, German officers posing as American doctors explained away his amnesia, concocting a wild, hocus-pocus story, hoping the disorientated major would fall for their ruse and reveal Operation Overlord information. Using bogus newspapers, magazines, and radio programs, an elaborate tale purported that World War II ended five years earlier. Ever vigilant, the quick-thinking major picked up on their scheme, and in one deft moment, turned the tables on his captors.

Even though many World War II titles depicted combat adventures, a few screenplays put aside flag-waving heroics and, instead, examined the emotional vicissitudes and psychological disorders the global conflict produced. AIP's *The Pawnbroker* told the poignant story of a concentration-camp survivor (Rod Steiger) living in suburban Long Island, tormented by horrific memories of the Nazi prison camp where his family perished. As one flashback after another emerged, the film accentuated the hopelessness this moneylender faced each morning—anger, poverty, and deprivation—as locals, cast-offs looking for a few dollars, stumbled into his Spanish Harlem shop. For the pawnbroker, the Holocaust reduced his worldview to simple nihilism: "I do not believe in God, or art, or science, or newspapers, or politics, or philosophy." Another motion picture about a concentration-camp survivor, Paramount's *Judith*, added to the despondency theme. Here, Sophia Loren—after many hardships—reached Israel, looking for her husband, the opportunist who betrayed her to the Gestapo. Likewise, Fox's *The Diary of Anne Frank* recounted the tragic story of a Dutch household, hiding from the Nazis in a makeshift Amsterdam attic. With Millie Perkins in the leading role, the photodrama recalled the daily frustrations an unassuming Jewish family endured in such cramped quarters. Two similar storylines, told in low-budget format, Hammer Film's *The Camp On Blood Island* and its sequel, *The Secret of Blood Island*, offered gruesome scenes of Japanese atrocities against British and American prisoners of war, portraying their Oriental captors as uncompromisingly vicious and arrogant.

MGM's *A Bridge to the Sun* examined the unusual circumstances of Gwen Terasaki (Carroll Baker), a Tennessee belle who married a Japanese diplomat stationed in Washington, D.C., but was reassigned to Tokyo just before the war started. After Pearl Harbor, her world turned upside down, resulting in one problem after another for a blue-eyed American blonde living in Japan. Paramount's *Another Time, Another Place* told the age-old story of lost love. Here, a woman (Lana Turner) working in London enjoyed an extramarital affair with a BBC correspondent (Sean Connery) until his combat death. In a strange, remorseful mood, she befriended her dead lover's wife, offering the widow many consolations. Another screenplay depicting problems of the heart, Warner Bros.' *Miracle in the Rain*, recounted the poignant story of two lovers (Van Johnson and Jane Wyman) brought together in New York City only to experience sorrow by a combat death. In a different format, Warner Bros.' *The Incredible Mr. Limpet* provided some levity, as a mild-mannered Brooklyn bookkeeper (Don Knotts) held discourse with a porpoise and, using his special skills, trained this mammal to destroy Nazi submarines operating in the North Atlantic. Fox's *The Rookie* added a few more chuckles after two GIs (Peter Marshall and Tommy Noonan)—stranded on a deserted island with a gorgeous model—bump into two inept Japanese soldiers. On a harmonious level, Fox's *The Sound of Music* offered wonderful melodies as the von Trapp family moved quickly to elude encroaching Nazis in their native Austria.

Columbia's *Bitter Victory* paired Richard Burton and Curt Jurgens as two British officers—with antithetical viewpoints—fighting both the Axis and each other during the difficult North African campaign. Schooled in the romantic tradition, the Welsh captain often berated his superior, pontificating, "War is inhuman." In nearby Tunisia a wounded GI (Wally Campo), separated from his unit, employed old-fashioned American know-how to escape from a German officer in AIP's sixty-four-minute *Hell Squad*, while over in the Pacific, a hard-minded fighter pilot (Sterling Hayden) who lost a leg in a combat crash, inspired his men to defeat the enemy in Republic's *The Eternal Sea*. Many miles away in an Indian courtroom, Fox's *Man in the Middle* focused on a controversial court-martial of an American officer (Kenneth Wynn) charged with murdering a British soldier. The defendant argued that the dead man's personal life provoked his shooting, while off to the side, his lawyer (Robert Mitchum) offered a more realistic defense, purporting that his client—suffering from numerous mental problems—could only be classified as insane, an argument that infuriated the English prosecutors, tight-lipped men demanding the death penalty. Another Fox melodrama, *The Revolt of Mamie Stover*, downplayed heroics when a mismatched couple (Richard Egan and Jane Russell)—stumbling to resolve their romantic differences—watched Japanese aircraft attack Pearl Harbor, prompting the buxom nightclub hostess to exclaim, "They're all running scared." As predicted, this incompatible twosome never found happiness.

Sometimes the motion-picture industry drifted off into another dimension. Science fiction titles, always a popular genre, offered weird interpretations of postwar activities. Paragon Films' *They Saved Hitler's Brain* told the creepy story of escaping Nazis, fleeing toward the South American country of Mandoras, carrying the führer's brain sealed in a vacuum-packed jar. Hoping to regroup and use a deadly G-Gas weapon, these officers planned to resume the war against the Allies and promised this preserved head, "You will see a great victory, mein führer." With Walter Stocker as a federal agent searching for the cerebral organ, this screenplay—often paired with *Attack of the Killer Toma-*

toes as one of the worst pictures ever made—appealed to many cult-film followers. Three other titles followed this screwball formula. Gold Star's *The Frozen Dead* permitted a demented scientist to keep the heads of Nazi war criminals alive until appropriate bodies were located for reattachment. Screencraft Enterprises' *She Demons* showed a German scientist mutilating pretty girls, removing their faces, and attempting a reconfiguration with zombielike women. Majestic's *He Lives* chronicled Hitler's bunker escape to an Argentine castle where in 1967 he roamed around large rooms extrapolating about the Fourth Reich, while Martin Bormann—his devoted follower—proclaimed, "Yes, the Führer is old but he is still our guiding force." Both died when Israeli troops attacked their mansion.

Not all motion pictures took potshots at former foes. As the events of the global conflict slowly receded, old villains and past misdeeds were sugarcoated as revisionist titles appeared. Columbia's *I Aim at the Stars* backpedaled the career of Werner von Braun, a leading German V-2 rocket scientist, and his role in creating weapons that attacked London and, instead, highlighted his work in developing America's postwar missile program. Here Curt Jurgens played another stellar role as a "good" German who did not accept Hitlerism. A similar persona appeared in Paramount's *Under Ten Flags*, in which a benevolent Nazi captain (Van Heflin) behaved humanely toward the survivors of ships he destroyed. To continue this positive image, United Artists' *Ten Seconds to Hell* portrayed Jeff Chandler and Jack Palance as two German weapons defusers in postwar Berlin, disabling thousand-pound, unexploded British bombs.

Universal's *A Time to Love and a Time to Die* depicted an ordinary *Wehrmacht* private (John Gavin) as a kind and sentimental individual who eschewed Nazism and was himself a victim of an out-of-control system. Based on the book by Erich Marie Remarque (of *All Quiet on the Western Front* fame), the screenplay dismissed most of the German brutality and in a closing scene, with an obvious nod toward Cold War politics, indicted the Russians for their cruelty. Another title that portrayed kindly German nationals, Fox's *Fräulein* told the romantic story of an American officer (Mel Ferrer) who escaped from a POW camp, received help from a university professor, and, at war's end, discovered happiness with his daughter (Dana Wynter). As another Cold War tract, this motion picture accused the Nazis, not the German people, for the recent conflagration.

Now what? Was the tide turning? Why were old enemies becoming new friends? For American filmgoers the answer seemed simple. The nation's current enemy was the Soviet Union, and the postwar German Federal Republic, headed by members of the pro-Western Christian Democratic Union—Konrad Adenauer, Ludwig Erhard, and Kurt Kiesinger—stood firmly as a partner against this Communist threat. After all, was every German bad? Didn't some of them resist Hitlerism? What about Marlon Brando? As a German national, didn't he abhor Nazism and help the British destroy a ship in *Morituri?* And how about *The Young Lions?* Didn't Brando, that handsome, blond-haired Nazi officer, behave charitably?

As an elaborate 167-minute, black-and-white CinemaScope production, Fox's *The Young Lions* traced the joys and sorrows of two American draftees, Michael Whiteacre (Dean Martin) and Noah Ackerman (Montgomery Clift), and a *Wehrmacht* officer, Christian Diestl (Marlon Brando) from their prewar civilian lives, induction into military service, their combat experiences, and finally, a serendipitous April 1945 meeting on an isolated German hilltop. Directed by Edward Dmytryk, this screen adaptation of Irwin Shaw's leftist novel—with its synchronistic storyline—juxtaposed the comings and goings of these three individuals as each man searched for his own niche in the global conflict.

On New Year's Eve 1938, a high-spirited Diestl, working as a ski instructor in a cozy Bavarian resort, flirted openly with an American tourist, Margaret Freemantle (Barbara Rush). For the German lothario, this pretty foreigner, easily charmed by his Teutonic smile, represented another possible sexual conquest. However, at midnight—as the happy Germans raised their glasses, sang patriotic songs, and praised their führer—Margaret, upset by this annoying chauvinism, ran from the restaurant. Moments later, Diestl, standing on the porch, explained his country's lebensraum policies. "Hitler will bring us a better life," he bragged, referring to the nation's lopsided caste system. "He has promised to change all of this." Unimpressed, the young American abruptly walked away, leaving Diestl alone to ponder his *Nationalsozialist* slogans.

Two years later, at a fancy New York City cocktail party, Margaret and her boyfriend, Michael Whiteacre, chat amiably with Noah Ackerman about social and political inequities. Both men, recently classified as 1-A, realized their carefree civilian days were numbered. But Ackerman, a department store salesclerk, seemed more philosophical about the impending induction and later told his future father-in-law, "I make $35 a week and am 1-A in the draft." But Whiteacre, a successful Broadway showman, expressed disdainfully, "I've read all the books. I know that in ten years we'll be bosom friends with the Germans and the Japanese." For both men, however, their personal views meant nothing. A few months later, on a southern basic training base, they listened to sergeants bellow orders, regularly cleaned their weapons, scrubbed the barracks floor, and marched on the parade grounds.

After an arduous training period—that included some AWOL punishment for Ackerman—the two friends parted. Whiteacre's connections landed him a cushy Washington, D.C., assignment and then, after Pearl Harbor, another soft London public relations job. Ackerman remained with his rifle squad and eventually landed at Normandy in June 1944. Weeks after this D-Day invasion, Private Whiteacre, reassigned to his old outfit, joined his New York pal, and for the next ten months, their unit advanced eastward. Finally, in April 1945, as part of a forward operation, this group liberated a German concentration camp. For a few days, the two friends remained here, helping the Nazi victims. One afternoon, these GIs, hoping to clear their minds, took a few hours off and strolled around the countryside.

Back in France, Diestl, now a dashing *Wehrmacht* lieutenant, found many of his 1940 Paris occupation duties distasteful. Assigned to a martinet captain, he routinely arrested Frenchmen for minor violations and complained, "I am not a soldier, I'm a policeman." Later, he was transferred to a North Afrika Korps fighting unit and watched in disbelief when his attack team routed a British patrol, killing everyone including the wounded. A few months later, when the tide changed, he escaped from the advancing Allied offensive and, after some good luck, returned to Berlin. Here in the Third Reich's bombed-out showcase city, he confronted the utter futility of war: children were orphans, wonderful homes destroyed, churches burned to the ground, and food nonexistent. For Diestl—the idealist German who envisioned Adolf Hitler as the New Order's messianic savior—Nazi horrors loomed everywhere.

For the German army, everything was in disarray, and Captain Diestl became part of a retreating horde. After U.S. fighter planes strafed his ragtag unit, everyone dispersed into the forest. Alone and without resources, Diestl traveled for days until he finally reached a concentration camp. Standing in a dilapidated office, he watched the commandant destroy military documents until another sight caught his eyes: the remnants of Hitler's Final Solution. For the one-time believer in National Socialism, here was the moment of truth. Quickly, he left this killing site and, after scrutinizing the timberline, chose a hilltop hiding place. A few days later, secretly watching American troops liberating the camp, Christian spotted two GIs walking nearby. Slowly, he began a cautious descent toward these two soldiers, struggling to maintain his balance on the steep terrain.

When Private Whiteacre spotted a German soldier noisily stumbling down the hilltop, he impulsively aimed his rifle and fired off some rounds. Seconds later the two GIs stared at the lifeless body of a *Wehrmacht* officer, Christian Diestl, the former Bavarian ski instructor who, six years earlier, attempted to seduce Whiteacre's fiancée. Here in a rain-filled ditch lay a one-time Hitler devotee who blindly accepted the Master Race's doctrine of purity, loyalty, and strength but, after witnessing his nation's collapse, renounced all these ideas. Standing over another dead German, the two Americans shrugged their

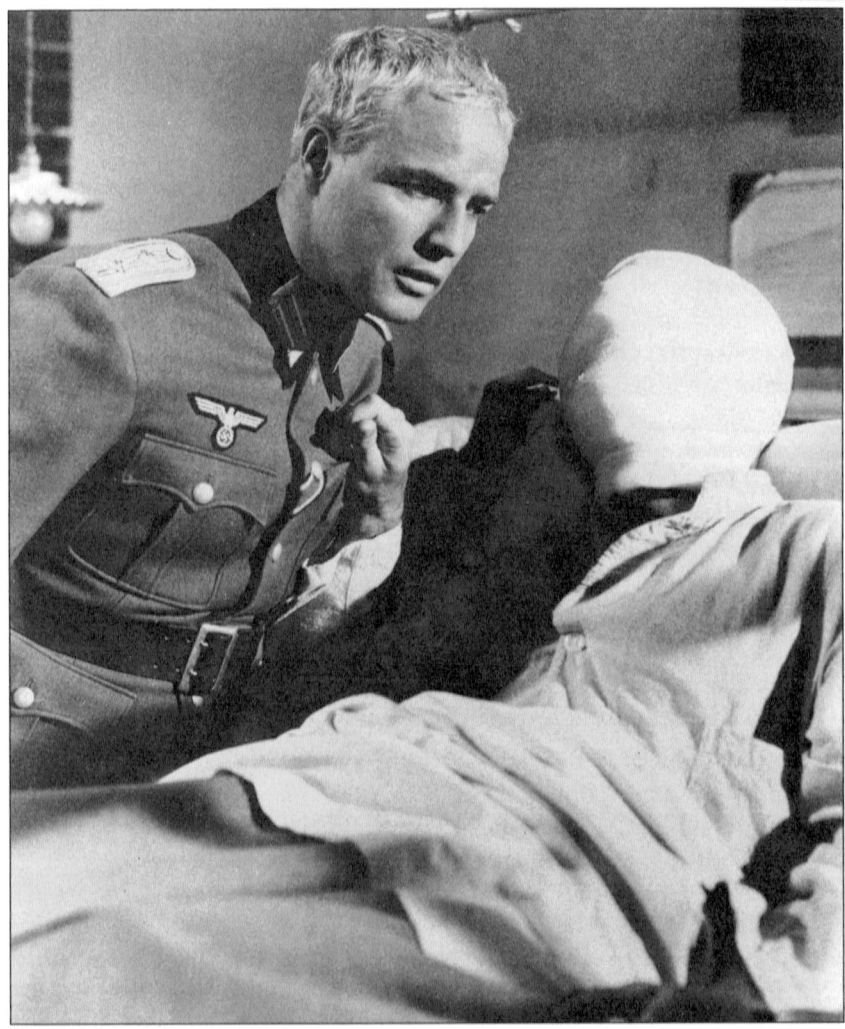

Demoralized by his commanding officer's horrific injuries, a Wehrmacht *lieutenant (Marlon Brando) realizes that total capitulation is close at hand in Edward Dmytryk's three-tier saga of love and war,* The Young Lions. *Courtesy of Twentieth Century–Fox.*

shoulders and continued down the road. For these victors, men who had witnessed hundreds of combat deaths, this Axis soldier was just another fallen cipher of the European carnage.

Certainly this Hollywood ending exulted the fighting prowess of the common GI, but on a spiritual level Captain Diestl's accidental (or sacrificial) death symbolically atoned for Germany's misdeeds. Was it coincidental that this *Wehrmacht* officer's first name was Christian? What about his untimely end? Was it an act of redemption? A modern-day crucifixion? An expiation? Clearly, his sinuous path—from a rabid Hitlerite to pious humanist—offered some consolation for a former enemy, especially a nation aligned with the Western bloc.

By 1967, while many Americans watched (and enjoyed) World War II motion pictures, these moviegoers realized that larger issues—emanating nightly from the television news—seemed ominous. Every evening the popular commentator Walter Cronkite reminded the nation that a civil war was raging in a former French colony, Vietnam, pitting the Communist forces from the north against the Western-aligned government of the south. Routinely, President Johnson shipped thousands of servicemen into this red-hot combat zone. For the second time since V-J Day, American casualties from a foreign battlefield appeared in daily newspapers. Once more, the United States, the perennial arsenal of democracy, ordered its young men into harm's way. Now what? How would Hollywood handle this new crisis? Was it time to load up the cameras, call up the special effects department, and send John Wayne, complete with rifle, ammunition clips, and hand grenades, back into combat?

Chapter Five

Vietnam Boils Over

1968–1976

"The Japanese were right to do it. From their point of view, we were their mortal enemy. As long as we existed, we were a deadly threat to them. Their only mistake was that they failed to finish us at the start." — Finger-snapping, Brylcreem-laden, right-wing political science professor and U.S. presidential adviser Dr. Walter Groeteschele (Walter Matthau) justifying the Japanese Pearl Harbor attack in Sidney Lumet's 1964 Cold War tract *Fail-Safe*

By January 1968, the red-hot Southeast Asian cauldron — fueled by repeated American B-52 high-altitude bombing strikes around Hanoi — finally boiled over after Communist leader Ho Chi Minh, hoping for a decisive win, launched his Tet Offensive. Soon, Vietcong forces, confident of a quick victory, attacked more than thirty South Vietnamese cities, including Hue and Saigon. For many stateside undergraduates watching this elaborate winter assault on nightly television, the news painted a grim picture. This ongoing war — a conflict that by now had polarized the nation — was far from over. Where does this leave us, the male students, who were always nervous-for-the-service, pondered, who will the draft board grab next? What time does the next bus leave for Canada?

For Hollywood, it was business as usual. The motion-picture industry, keeping its eye on the bottom line, wanted profitable screenplays, not liabilities. The facts of capitalist life were clear. Any movie glamorizing the Vietnam fighting would collapse at the box office. No producer in his right mind would touch this political hot potato with the proverbial ten-foot pole. But World War II films — with their uplifting, red-white-and-blue endings — were a different story. After all, didn't last year's audiences flock to watch MGM's *The Dirty Dozen*, an action drama that showed hard-boiled GIs annihilating a

Nazi command center? Who could forget former football star Jim Brown's dash across an Axis courtyard, zapping hand grenades into air vents as bullets and explosives went off everywhere after Major Lee Marvin barked, "Blow it!"?

As the fighting escalated in Vietnam with no end in sight, new World War II photoplays recalling past glories and achievements kept popping up in stateside theaters. Controversy was everywhere. The protest movement viewed these pictures askance, claiming they were nothing more than right-wing propaganda, while the let's-go-in-and-win-the-war crowd argued that here was America at its rough-and-tumble best. Just look at United Artists' *The Devil's Brigade* (a *Dirty Dozen* copycat), they argued. Watch tough-talking William Holden hone those recruits into a deft commando unit that eventually routed the *Wehrmacht*. How about Richard Burton and Clint Eastwood, two behind-the-lines experts, who rescued a U.S. general from an Alpine Gestapo fortress in MGM's *Where Eagles Dare*? Don't forget Major Lloyd Bridges's assault team fighting on the Normandy shoreline. These Allied soldiers destroyed an enemy naval base in United Artists' *Attack on the Iron Coast*. Why wouldn't they? Didn't Major Bridges, urging his men forward and (with a nod to the Vietnam conflict), exclaim, "This is a war we have to win!"?

Certainly, the American people needed a Vietnam victory, but by 1969 that goal seemed far away as casualties climbed to fifty thousand, threatening to eclipse the Korean conflict's grand total. For many stateside viewers, the same questions dominated every discussion: when will this war end? Who will lead us out of this quagmire? While President Nixon and his supporters proposed numerous offensive policies, his opponents argued, conversely, for a quick withdrawal. Back and forth the debates resounded off the congressional walls with no resolution in sight. Then, in 1970 a Hollywood motion picture appeared that suggested the United States could win the war. An elaborate 171-minute, Academy Award screenplay recalled the let's-go-get-'em demeanor of a modern-day warrior, detailing his numerous World War II exploits that resulted in solid European victories and earned him the sobriquet, "Blood-and-Guts."

As a monumental cinematic production, Fox's *Patton* told a straightforward story of the controversial general, beginning with his North African and Sicilian campaigns, then the French eastward advances, until, finally, his triumphant Berlin entry. Patton was noted for his salty language and frequent expletives—he told the foot soldiers, "We are advancing constantly," and reminded them when encountering a German "to kick the hell out of him all the time." As a flag-waving photodrama, *Patton* emphasized the many World War II triumphs and (with George C. Scott in the leading role) articulated that victory comes from strong leadership and a determined will to win. "No bastard ever won a war by dying for his country," he exhorted. "He won it by making the other poor dumb bastard die for his country!"

Without question, American moviegoers understood Patton's bellicose words and their obvious analogy to the Vietnam problem, "We're gonna keep fighting. Is that clear? We're gonna attack all night, we're gonna attack the next morning." Certainly this motion picture pleased the chief executive. Why wouldn't it? George C. Patton was a no-nonsense soldier, the three-star general who bragged, "Americans have never lost and never will lose a war, because the very thought of losing is hateful to Americans." He personified the best of U.S. military determinism. When he prophesized, "We're going to have to fight the Russians eventually anyway. It might as well be now while we've already got the army here to do it," it was no wonder that Nixon gave private White House screenings to numerous subordinates, hoping this film, or at least George C. Scott's persuasive oratory, would inspire them.

Patton was not the only World War II photodrama to remind audiences that U.S. military forces were invincible. Over in the Pacific theater, Paramount exalted the navy's determination to turn the tide by starring the quintessential icon, John Wayne, in a role that gave stronger meaning to Old Glory. Directed by Otto Preminger, *In Harm's Way*—a 180-minute extravaganza glorifying the intricate planning and logistical support needed for victory—glamorized every facet of America's seafaring, fighting manpower. Without question, when Admiral John Wayne stood on his flagship bridge,

A tough-talking navy commander (Kirk Douglas) blasts a spoiled-brat ensign (Brandon De Wilde) for his double-dealing, backstabbing behavior in Otto Preminger's three-hour epic about seafaring prowess, In Harm's Way. *Courtesy of Paramount Pictures.*

peered at maps, discussed underwater currents, and, finally, gave the go-ahead order, moviegoers knew that the Japanese vessels, navigating through a narrow strait, would end up at the bottom of the ocean.

As a major Hollywood production, *In Harm's Way* gathered many established stars, including Dana Andrews, Henry Fonda, Kirk Douglas, Patricia Neal, and Burgess Meredith. It wove one subplot after another, detailing the uncertainties associated with the Pearl Harbor bombing, the U.S. Navy's slow recovery, some opportunistic backstabbing, a father-and-son reconciliation, the perils of alcoholic consumption, the joys of new love, a suicidal redemption, the importance of fast-moving PT boats, the impeccable high-command planning, and, finally, the routing of Japanese forces. Certainly, this film echoed America's unremitting prowess, and only Admiral John Wayne could raise his glass, turn to his fellow sailors, and express these sentiments: "To our country, our Navy, and all the best things they stand for."

While *In Harm's Way* depicted a fictional South Pacific naval battle, another major screenplay, Universal's *Midway*, told the high-powered story of the June 1942 clash in which the Japanese lost four aircraft carriers and over two hundred aircraft—destruction so great that it ended any future threat of a Hawaiian invasion. *Midway* was saturated with famous movie personalities, including Henry Fonda, Charlton Heston, Glenn Ford, Robert Mitchum, and James Coburn. Replete with juxtaposed subplots involving high-risk planning, code breaking, Japanese pride, an admiral's bout with shingles, intricate air battles, and uneasy miscegenation, this 132-minute screenplay highlighted this important American victory even though U.S. casualties included one aircraft carrier and approximately 150 planes.

In embellishing this decisive win, director Jack Smight re-created both sides of the story by interweaving American and Japanese commands as stony-faced officers, unsure of the other side's strategy, peered ominously at oceanic maps, hoping to find a vulnerable spot. For the U.S. Navy, under the control of Admiral Bull Halsey, his succinct words said it all: "Don't worry about what I would do. Your only job is to go to sea, find Yamamoto, and chew his ass." A Japanese officer, Tamon Yamaguchi (John Fuioka), realizing his precarious situation, seemed more realistic: "Once, we filled the sky with our aircraft, we win or lose with six fighters and ten torpedo planes."

While both *In Harm's Way* and *Midway* provided moviegoers with overwhelming U.S. military victories, everyone seated in the audience already knew the dire outcome of Fox's Pearl Harbor saga, *Tora! Tora! Tora!* This 144-minute production detailed the December 7 attack, an event whose impact was prophesized in the cinematic (and no doubt, apocryphal) words of Admiral Isoroku Yamamoto (Sô Yamamura), "I fear all we have done is to awaken a sleeping giant and fill him with a terrible resolve." In retelling this often-discussed, frequently argued day of infamy, three directors pooled their talents for a standard historical interpretation. They elaborated on America's lackadaisical, "we-are-protected-by-two-oceans" philosophy while the Japanese nationalists, intent on continuing their expansionist policy, felt threatened by the Roosevelt embargo—even though Yamamoto advocated, "There is no last word in diplomacy."

As a major Hollywood screenplay, *Tora! Tora! Tora!* unfolded in sequential order between the American military command in Hawaii, the Japanese officers aboard their aircraft carriers streaming eastward, and various Washington, D.C., departments, where high-ranking officials examined incomplete logistical information, argued about Tojo's Greater East Asian policies, and scheduled meetings with Japanese diplomats. For the U.S. forces stationed on this mid-Pacific island, everything seemed to work against military logic. The Hawaiian Park Service, concerned with maintaining a mountaintop's natural beauty, prohibited a radar screen installation, while a junior officer, staring at the fighter aircraft tightly aligned on the runway, warned, "We got 183 combat planes on this base. The way they're parked right now, a one-eyed monkey, hanging from a ten-cent balloon, could scatter them all to hell with just one hand grenade."

Other problems highlighted these ambiguous days. A senior intelligence colonel (E. G. Marshall) spent hours deciphering intercepted communiqués and concluded from his Washington office, "Japan is going to attack us. We're going to be attacked on Sunday, the 30th of November," while back at Pearl Harbor, General Walter Short (Jason Robards) listened attentively as his aide read a standing order, "If hostilities cannot be avoided, the United States desires that the Japanese commit the first overt act." With such equivocal information, the Hawaiian command, unaware of the enemy task force heading toward them on December 6, acted indecisively. Back in Washington, in the early hours of December 7, the U.S. cryptologist finally pieced together the last segment of an intercepted message, prompting General Marshall (Keith Andes) to announce, "I am convinced the Japanese intend to attack at or shortly after one o'clock today." However, his warning—stamped highest priority—would not arrive in time. Meanwhile, dozens of Japanese aircraft, using a Honolulu radio station as their beacon, reached their target, dropped bombs and torpedoes on the unsuspecting ships, blew up parked aircraft, machine-gunned scores of servicemen, and triumphantly returned to their carriers.

In its own investigatory way, *Tora! Tora! Tora!* sustained cinematic interest by projecting a few hypotheses. What if, the photodrama suggested, the radar sighting, issued minutes before the Japanese planes arrived, was sounded instead of frivolously dismissed by a young officer, whose smart-aleck remark, "Don't worry about it," reflected the slapdash nature of prewar life? And how about General Marshall's directive? Would a four-hour warning have made a difference? And, do not forget the Japanese ambassador! If he was a better typist, would the ultimatum have reached the White House, as planned, before H-Hour? And what about the numerous American officers and diplomats who foresaw the handwriting on the wall? Why were they ignored? In all, the screenplay asked, was this attack preventable?

While *Tora! Tora! Tora!* allowed moviegoers to speculate about history, other Hollywood titles continued to pulverize the Nazi war machine. In United Artists' low-budget production, *Submarine X-1*, a Canadian naval officer (James Caan), after losing his first battle to a Nazi predator, utilized a midget submarine to foil his enemy. Back on land, Allied soldiers, led by Tony Franciosa, infiltrated the Fatherland, wrecking a secret torpedo factory in Universal's *In Enemy Country*. Down in Italy, army troops, after many setbacks, finally advanced inland in Columbia's *Anzio*. Here, an American war journalist (Robert Mitchum) chronicled the intricacies of this hard-fought campaign.

In United Artists' *Hornet's Nest*, an American GI (Rock Hudson) received help from some spirited children when he blew up a heavily guarded Nazi dam in southern Italy, reminding the youngsters, "If we do it right the Germans will never know we were here." Closer to Berlin, George Segal and Ben Gazzara spearheaded their army troops across the Rhine in United Artists' *The Bridge at Remagen*, a screenplay that exalted the fighting man while taking numerous potshots at an opportunist general (E. G. Marshall) who, oblivious to the human cost, ordered, "We're not going to blow that bridge—we're going to take it!" Down in North Africa, a motley crew of British Tommies became pawns in an upper-echelon debate about military deployment tactics in United Artists' *Play Dirty*. With Michael Caine in the starring role, this 117-minute desert tale blasted the British command structure for blatantly sending troops on a suicide mission. Also in North Africa, a U.S. Army sergeant (Lee Van Cleef) and his attack team decimated a fascist oasis, disrupting *Wehrmacht* advances in Heritage Enterprises' *Commandos*. A third North African tale, United Artists' *Massacre Harbor*, recounted the exploits of a four-man team, dubbed the Rat Patrol, who concocted a mass prisoner escape from a German compound using local fishing boats.

A few screenplays examined the Balkan Peninsula hostilities. Continental's *Operation Cross Eagles* paired Lieutenant Richard Conte and Sergeant Rory Calhoun with some Yugoslavian guerillas to free an American general. Another drama in the mountainous region, Bosna Film's *The Fifth Offensive*, depicted the Nazi effort to destroy Marshal Tito and his followers. With Richard Burton portraying the Communist leader, these craggy fighters easily outflanked their Axis foes. Republic's version of the Yugoslavian campaign, *Battle of Neretva*, placed glabrous Yul Brynner as a spirited partisan at odds with Curt Jurgens, a Nazi commandant, in the rugged terrain. Avala Film's *Hell River* pitted two adversaries, a Serbian loyalist (Rod Taylor) and a reluctant Nazi (Adam West) in the hostile countryside. Dubraya Film's *The Ravine* cast David McCallum as a German special agent who chased down a pretty Tito partisan (Nicoletta Machiavelli) in an isolated mountainous region. Stranded by an elaborate snowstorm, the twosome, after a shaky start, put aside their differences, fell in love, and, in an unexpected volte-face, left together.

Other photodramas glamorized the heroics found in combat. United Artists' *The 1,000 Plane Raid* detailed the planning, implementation, and bombing of numerous German factories. With Christopher George and Gary Marshall cramped in the cockpit, this aviation story highlighted the Air Corps' role in halting all Axis matériel production, while another airborne saga, United Artists' *The Battle of Britain*, chronicled the 1940 defense that repelled the *Luftwaffe*, compelling Winston Churchill's words of praise, "Never in the course of human endeavors have so many owed so much to so few." On the espionage front, in Warner Brothers' *Triple Cross*, a light-fingered safecracker (Christopher Plummer), released from a London jail, feigned Axis loyalty but, in reality, served as a British double agent. This screenplay was loosely based on the real-life story of Eddie Chapman, the man who claimed, "I'm a realist. I'm in prison and I want to get out!" In Sagittarius's B-yarn *The Last Day of the War*, a U.S. sergeant (George Maharis) rescued an important scientist secluded in an Austrian hideaway, while an American agent (Stuart Whitman) likewise freed a German rocket maker from a Nazi stronghold in United Artists' *The Last Escape*. Hispamer Films' *When Heroes Die* told the weird story of some commandos assigned to kidnap General Rommel. The plan backfired after the Germans caught these GIs, took their uniforms, and, in a reversal of ideas, planned to kill General Eisenhower. Fast-moving Craig Hill saved the day in this ninety-minute clunker.

Another off-the-wall idea, Silverton Production's ninety-minute *Death Race* clashed a disabled American fighter plane—that could not take off—against a Nazi tank in an African desert duel to the death. Sitting in the cockpit, the lieutenant (Doug McClure) employed Yankee know-how to outmaneuver his Nazi nemesis (Lloyd Bridges) and, eventually, gain the upper hand and obliterate his enemy. A similar high-jinks tale, AIG's sixty-four-minute romp *Hell Squad*, depicted a small American patrol, led by Wally Campo, that spent many days eluding a German intelligence officer (Brandon Carroll) in the uncharted Tunisian desert. In Clover Films' *The Cut-Throats*, an infantry officer (Jay Scott), along with five unsavory volunteers, attacked a secret stronghold, killed

every German, retrieved some top-secret Axis battle plans, and—seizing an opportunity—helped themselves to Nazi gold. As an unexpected bonus, a few
sexy women living in this enemy compound provided a little prurient diversion.
Another behind-enemy-lines drama, American Allied Picture's *Operation Day-
break*, re-created the assassination of Reinhard Heydrich, the infamous Nazi
controlling Czechoslovakia. Here, a group of expatriates, led by Timothy Bot-
toms, parachuted into their native land and, after a series of close calls, assassinated the führer's handpicked man. Based on historical facts, this made-for-television reenactment detailed much of the intricate planning necessary for
success. In ABC's *Carter's Army*, a racist army captain (Stephen Boyd), commanding an all-black rearguard outfit, defended a strategic dam from the Nazi
army even though his many solecisms—"I've never seen no one stand guard
like that"—seemed contradictory. Later, this B-potboiler, with its eye on the
African American audience, was renamed *Black Brigade*.

Occasionally, other nations, hoping to capitalize on the American motion-
picture market, produced World War II screenplays utilizing one or two Hollywood stars (or former box office draws), in leading roles. Mostly Italian directors—in concert with stateside distributors and financiers—created a novel
type of photodrama as European and American actors mingled in rehashed,
cost-efficient storylines, usually with unsynchronized dubbing, a process that
permitted lips to move in one direction while words went somewhere else.
These wartime movies, produced in Italy, borrowed unabashedly from their
motion-picture cousin, the spaghetti Western genre. Fast-moving dramas such
as *The Battle of El Alamein*, *The Battle of the Last Panzer*, *A Bullet for Rommel*, *Code Name—Red Roses*, *Churchill's Leopards*, *Desert Commandos*,
Desert Battle, *Dirty Heroes*, *The Dirty Two*, *Eagles Over London*, *The Fifth
Day of Peace*, *Hell Commandos*, *Hell in Normandy*, *Heroes in Hell*, *Kill
Rommel*, *Probability Zero*, *Suicide Commandos*, and *War Devils* showcased
American GIs fighting the Nazis in various locales. One title, *Attack and Retreat*, employed a different approach, sugarcoating the Axis's ill-fated Rus-
sian campaign, an invasion where many Italian troops perished.

Occasionally, a few pictures took a prurient look at the European conflict.
Another made-in-Italy drama, *The Damned*, chronicled the uneasy relationship between German nobility and the emerging Third Reich. With numerous
scenes depicting homosexuality, pedophilia, and incest, this production—a
condemnation of Hitler's industrialists—left little to the imagination with its
sadomasochistic presentations. Going one step further, an American clunker
defied all conventions with male castrations, vicious floggings, onanistic or-
gasms, and toenail extractions. WIP's *Ilsa: She-Wolf of the SS* pushed the limits of World War II drama with its voyeuristic, perverted, and pornographic
images. With Dianne Thorne in the starring role—as a *Schutzstaffel* (SS)
dominatrix who tortured, mutilated, or raped anyone in sight—this cult fa-

vorite, frequently referred to as disgusting, filthy, and degrading, offered, in its own exploitative fashion, another interpretation of Nazi cruelty. Three mirror copies, Olympic International's *Love Camp 7*, Coralto's *Salon Kitty*, and Italian Stallion's *SS Special Section Women* also titillated viewers with nude prisoners, bootlicking females, suspension bondage, forced lesbianism, brothel madams, and kinky foaming at the mouth.

Frequently, the World War II film examined complexities beyond the rigors of combat. Universal's *Counterpoint* depicted the adventures of a European symphony orchestra, under the baton of Charlton Heston, forced to perform for the Nazis, while MGM's *The 25th Hour* told the existential tale of a Rumanian peasant (Anthony Quinn) and an eight-year separation from his family. Columbia's *Castle Keep* treaded openly into the ontological nature of battle as eight soldiers sought refuge in a baroque castle while the Battle of the Bulge raged nearby. With Burt Lancaster in the starring role, the screenplay deftly pronounced the absurdity of war. United Artists' *The Secret of Santa Vittoria* portrayed Italian nationals as fun loving and antifascist. Here, Anthony Quinn presided as the mayor of a small, hilltop town. When the Germans arrived to confiscate their prized wine collection, the townspeople quickly revolted, preventing the *Wehrmacht* from taking their harvest. Over in Scotland, a tough-talking intelligence officer (Brian Keith) played a cat-and-mouse game with Axis prisoners of war in MGM's *The McKenzie Break*. After some sub rosa planning, the Germans launched a well-coordinated escape with a nearby U-boat, while the British, asleep at the switch, recaptured only one man. Another taut drama, Universal's *The Birdmen*, detailed the planning of an airborne escape from an alpine castle by an American officer (Doug McClure) in a secretly constructed homemade glider. Hemisphere's *The Only Way* heralded the efforts of a few Danish folks, led by Jane Seymour, who saved their Jewish countrymen from the Nazi roundup.

Sometimes productions looked askance at the war, depicting the global conflict in amusing terms. In Universal's *Slaughterhouse-Five*, Michael Sacks portrayed the stumbling Billy Pilgrim, an inept GI who eventually became a prisoner in Dresden. Basically, an antiwar tract (with black comedy overtones), the screenplay—based on Kurt Vonnegut's acclaimed novel—took a science fiction approach to the February 1945 firebombing of this baroque city. Scimitar Films' *Hannibal Brooks* told the peripatetic saga of a British POW (Oliver Reed) working in the Munich zoo, who—after an Allied bombing attack and numerous adventures—walked the town's elephant many kilometers to neutral Switzerland. In an offbeat fashion, ABC's fast-moving *The New, Original Wonder Woman* highlighted this comic-strip heroine's fight against Nazi soldiers and spies. With Lynda Carter twirling her magic lasso, the Axis foes quickly capitulated.

MGM's *The Extraordinary Seaman* told the easygoing story of three American sailors who teamed up with an eccentric Englishman aboard a dilapidated ship on a Pacific island, only to learn the British officer was really a ghost, doomed to roam the high seas until a heroic deed redeemed him. With David Niven as the wraith, this seventy-nine-minute fairy tale, with its supernatural motif, offered many chuckles, especially when the staid Englishman confessed, "I died approximately at 1430 hours, the tenth of October 1914, and that is the real reason why I have no need of food or sleep." Allied Artists' winter tale *Snow Treasure* explained how Norwegian children, living in an occupied village, smuggled gold bullion across the border right under the nose of a Nazi commandant (James Franciscus). Another MGM title, *Kelly's Heroes*, spoofed the war, as four enlisted men with itchy fingers (Clint Eastwood, Telly Savalas, Don Rickles, and Donald Sutherland) planned a bank robbery behind German lines, while perennial jokester Bob Hope entered the fray in United Artists' *The Private Navy of Sgt. O'Farrell*. Here, on a South Pacific island safely ensconced from any combat, the ski-nosed comedian—along with Phyllis Diller—poked fun at military life, including a parody of the famous Deborah Kerr, Burt Lancaster, *From Here to Eternity* beach scene. Warner Bros.' zany *Which Way to the Front* portrayed Jerry Lewis in the unenviable position of the world's richest man. Classified as unfit for military service, this tycoon, determined to help Uncle Sam, recruited other 4-Fs into a private army, traveled to Italy, impersonated a Nazi commander, was introduced by a general to "Von Pabst, Von Heineken, Von Busch, and Von Schlitz," and, after a few mad, comic routines, attempted to assassinate Hitler.

One zany title took the cake with its brooding dark humor and trenchant satire of military life. Based on Joseph Heller's madcap first novel, Paramount's *Catch-22* lampooned every aspect of a B-25 squadron operating from a small Mediterranean island and assigned to bomb strategic Axis targets. With Alan Arkin, Orson Welles, Richard Benjamin, and Buck Henry in starring roles, and directed by Mike Nichols, this screenplay blasted all aspects of military directives and command protocol. Here, in balmy weather, American pilots heard one absurd comment after another about daily mainland bombing runs. "To those of you who won't be coming back, I like to say we're going to do our best to take care of your wives and/or sweethearts," an operations major gibed, "and don't forget, a nice tight bombing pattern on those aerial photographs."

However, one experienced bombardier, Captain John Yossarian (Alan Arkin) reached his limit after thirty-five combat missions and naively asked, "Why are they shooting at me?" A medical deferment went nowhere because regulations clearly stated that any pilot who avoided danger was perfectly sane. As the flight surgeon pronounced, "It's Catch-22." Overall, the base resembled a loony bin. One officer traded parachute silk for cotton, bragging, "We're going to come out of this war rich," while another commissioned man became a squadron commander without earning his wings. A chaplain prepared "a nice snappy prayer that will send the officers out feeling good." A bigwig general flaunted his mistress and barked inconsistent orders while his son-in-law smiled docilely. A medical officer bribed an errant pilot to list his name on the manifest, enabling the doctor to "get my flight pay without doing anything stupid like going up in a plane," while other flyers received decorations for bombing an inlet, killing many fish. A smooth, wheeler-dealer lieutenant arranged a nighttime attack over the base and, finally, the magical go-home number reached eighty missions.

An Air Corps colonel (Martin Balsam) gleefully ups the ante, telling his bomber squadron that the magic go-home number requires eighty combat missions, while his commander (Orson Welles), accompanied by his son-in-law (Austin Pendleton), couldn't care less in Mike Nichols's zany satire, Catch-22. *Courtesy of Paramount Pictures.*

As a runaway 1970 satire, *Catch-22*—with its obvious analogy to the current Vietnam conflict—contained much of the caustic rhythm of Arthur Hiller's 1964 *The Americanization of Emily* with its ongoing put-down of military command. One funny scene depicted a bird colonel (Martin Balsam) bellowing directives while seated on a toilet bowl during a morning self-purification ritual. Later, this commander listened to a smooth-talking lieutenant (Jon Voight) outline a circuitous get-rich scheme involving bartering some base supplies for needed durable goods, while a few yards away, a B-25 crashed and burst into flames. Oblivious to the exploding aircraft, both officers agreed, "There are tremendous profits to be made." As for the one-star general (Orson Welles), his corpulent body oozed opportunism, avarice, gluttony, and sensuality in every frame. Clearly, this motion picture raked every aspect of military life over the coals with its clever depiction of a world gone mad.

Not every storyline was frivolous. In Universal's North African tale *Raid on Rommel*, a captain (Richard Burton), with the unlikely help of a conscientious objector, led a dogged attack team—composed of Jewish refugees fighting for the British—against the strategic fuel depot in Tobruk, halting Field Marshal Rommel's offensive. But in National General Pictures' *Massacre in Rome*, the Welsh-born actor switched sides, portraying a cynical SS colonel who ordered the mass execution of some Italian nationals after a partisan strike in the Nazi-occupied city of Rome. As an antireligious officer, the nasty-talking Burton, a fervent believer in Hitlerism, ridiculed a cleric's plea for mercy, telling the man, "I would prefer a religion that didn't need priests." In Eguiluz Films' *Battle of the Commandos*, a Scottish Colonel (Jack Palance) recruited some British ex-convicts, nudged them with esprit de corps, and then crossed the English Channel, where after hard fighting, they destroyed a huge Axis railroad gun on the Normandy coast hours before the June 6 go-signal. Down in the warm Caribbean, a lone Irish merchant seaman (Peter O'Toole) destroyed a Nazi submarine hiding in an estuary in Paramount's *Murphy's War*. And, in Paramount's *Hitler: The Last Ten Days*, Alec Guinness portrayed an out-of-control führer, hidden deep in his Berlin bunker, screaming one inconsistency after another—including unwarrantable criticism of Wagnerian divas: "Some of our most talented singers have allowed themselves to become absurdly fat"—while aboveground, Soviet troops blasted the German capital. In Fox's D-Day espionage tale, *Fireball Forward*, a general (Ben Gazzara), after some fancy intelligence work, dislodged an Axis spy working in a nearby French town. This discovery provided Allied forces a clear road to Paris. In Universal's *The Young Warriors*, a tough sergeant (James Drury) guided his outnumbered, untried recruits into battle against oncoming Germans. Also, in Brighton Pictures' *Underground*, a maverick U.S. major (Robert Goulet) left his English hospital, parachuted into France, and, after some perilous adventures, thwarted a Nazi general's coastal defense plans, while in Filmstar's *Five for Hell*, a few untoward GIs infiltrated *Wehrmacht* headquarters and walked off with the führer's Italian offensive orders.

What about the home front with its joys and sorrows when American soldiers were fighting their enemies in those faraway places with strange-sounding names? Warner Bros.' beautiful *Summer of '42* told the coming-of-age story of a Nantucket Island teenager (Gary Grimes), infatuated with a lonely woman (Jennifer Jones) whose husband was in an overseas combat zone. When the dreaded telegram arrived—explaining her spouse's death—everything she knew fell apart. In a moment of cathartic weakness she found solace with the boy. A similar photodrama (without the death scene), Columbia's *The Way We Were* spotlighted the wartime courtship of a conservative naval ensign (Robert Redford) and his left-wing girlfriend (Barbra Streisand). In this outspoken screenplay, much of the capitalist system's shortcomings were decried, while, concomitantly, President Roosevelt received ongoing praise as the wartime leader. On the eastern seacoast, Raisen Company's *Remember When* re-created the heartwarming saga of a Connecticut family's four sons in combat zones. In this Norman Rockwell world, every aspect of American life—Mom, apple pie, baseball, and church—confirmed the need for victory.

In sharp contrast, Universal's *Farewell to Manzanar* told the poignant chronicle of West Coast Japanese Americans, rounded up after Pearl Harbor under Executive Order 9066, and their difficult times in relocation camps. Here many good-hearted and patriotic families—victims of wartime hysteria—endured numerous indignities and deprivations during this dark side of national history. A similar title, Aaron Spelling Productions' *If Tomorrow Comes*, told the Romeo and Juliet story of a California girl (Patty Duke) who married a Japanese American (Frank Liu) on Sunday morning, December 7, and the husband's subsequent internment. Another photodrama, Lorimar Productions' *Returning Home* (a remake of the 1946 classic *The Best Years of Our Lives*) depicted the slow integration of three veterans back into their unfamiliar civilian world. With Tom Selleck, Dabney Coleman, and James R. Miller in the starring roles, this lackluster, made-for-television, color version toned down most of the social criticism found in its Academy Award–winner predecessor. Columbia's *Baby Blue Marine* finessed the apple-pie story of an inept recruit (Jan-Michael Vincent) who failed marine boot camp training and was sent home wearing faded baby-blue fatigues, an outfit that symbolized washout. After being knocked unconscious by a battle-fatigued marine deserter, he woke up, discovered his clothes gone, and replaced them with the man's bemedaled uniform. Wearing this spiffy outfit, he soon became involved with local townspeople and was acclaimed a combat veteran. Eventually, the truth came to light and all was forgiven, reaffirming the epistemological maxim that honesty becomes its own virtue. On a super-natural level, Cinema Center's made-for-television clunker, *Sole Survivor*, told the eerie mystery of a B-25 that crashed in the Libyan desert in 1945, killing everyone except the navigator who bailed out to safety. But twenty-five years later, in 1960, this surviving officer (Richard Basehart), now an air force general, learned the plane was unearthed, contradicting his story that the aircraft crashed into the Mediterranean Sea. To complicate matters, the ghosts of the doomed crew, headed by the pilot (Vince Edwards), waited these long years, hoping their bodies would be properly interred. As a supernatural tale capitalizing on the World War II theme, this drama, with its wraithlike twists and turns, resembled any number of episodes from the popular television se-ries *The Twilight Zone*.

In a similar science fiction mood, Viking International's *Flesh Feast* de-tailed some Nazis in Florida guarding Hitler's corpse and waiting for the right moment to revive him for further conquests, even though a concentration-camp-victim's daughter (Veronica Lake) placed grubs on the restored body, badgering the führer, "What's the matter, don't you like my little maggots?"

Still other motion pictures depicted the human suffering associated with the war. World Wide Pictures' *The Hiding Place* examined the misfortunes of two middle-aged Dutch sisters (Julie Harris and Jeannette Clift), arrested by the Nazis for harboring Jews, and their subsequent ordeal in a concentration camp where their Christian beliefs kept them from total despair. While the older woman died, her sibling lived through the nightmare and, later, in a nod to her religious convictions, learned to forgive her tormentors. In a jurispru-dence mode, ABC's 390-minute epic *QB VII* paired an American author (Ben Gazzara) against a German doctor (Anthony Hopkins) in a heated courtroom drama, as British jurors debated the innocence and guilt of wartime crimes. Cinévision's thinly disguised interpretation of the Adolf Eichmann trial, *The Man in the Glass Booth*, retold the story of a New York City Jewish entre-preneur (Maximilian Schell), who was kidnapped by Israeli agents, taken to Jerusalem, and after an emotional courtroom drama, revealed as a concentra-tion-camp commandant. Associated General Films' peripatetic tale of callous indifference, *Voyage of the Damned*, examined the seafaring saga of 937 Jew-ish refugees, who in 1939 left Hamburg looking forward to a new life in Cuba. However, under Nazi pressure, this island government denied these ex-iles entrance permits and sent them westward to Florida, where for a second time, national officials refused docking rights. Without hope or recourse, the ship returned to the Fatherland, where a concentration camp awaited them. With Faye Dunaway and Oskar Werner in starring roles, the entire screenplay, from the book by Gordon Thomas, denounced rigid U.S. immigration laws that allowed a democratic country to look the other way.

Another photoplay depicted a nation's shame. Universal's *The Execution of Private Slovik* re-created the heart-wrenching tale of a borderline Michigan draftee and his inability to comprehend military regulations that, eventually, led to his January 1945 execution by firing squad. In his portrayal of the inept Eddie Slovik, Martin Sheen captured every nuance of this unfortunate GI, who, after arriving in France, drifted away from his unit, wandered aimlessly, and, finally, was convicted of desertion, a decision approved by General Eisenhower. Adapted from the scathing book by William Bradford Huie, this made-for-television drama—an indictment of autocratic military power—attacked the high command for its draconian rules.

From a different slant, United Artists' *Beach Red* combined an odd mixture of antiwar sentiments with marine bravado. Here, a captain (Cornel Wilde), leading an attack team on a Japanese-held island, harbored many misgivings about the daily mayhem. Finally, his doubts dissolved in a horrific skirmish, where both American and Japanese forces clawed at each other. A similar screenplay involving a leatherneck's qualms about killing, Warner Bros.' *First to Fight*, re-created a Medal of Honor recipient's gradual metamorphosis from warrior to peacemaker when a rough marine (Chad Everett), after returning stateside and marrying a local girl, reevaluated his outlook about war and its consequences.

Another title that examined a serviceman's change of heart—Cinerama's *Too Late the Hero*—told the repentant tale of a navy officer (Cliff Robertson), whose boyish charms provided a soft life away from hostilities. Eventually ordered to join a reconnaissance patrol, he fell victim to enemy forces in a gory, symbolic ending. In Cinerama's *Hell in the Pacific*, a naval pilot (Lee Marvin), marooned on an uncharted Pacific atoll with a non-English-speaking Japanese officer, forged an uneasy truce for basic survival. Universal's *Flying Misfits* glorified the exploits of the legendary Flying Tiger commander, Pappy Boyington, whose unorthodox methods destroyed the Japanese at every turn over the China skies. After Pearl Harbor, he rejoined the Marine Corps and—following many top-level confrontations—created another fighter squadron, composed of recalcitrants, whose daily sorties harassed the enemy.

The Philippines' jungle fighting contained many perils. In Universal's 100-minute B-yarn *Warkill*, a Marine colonel (George Montgomery) and his Filipino guerrillas fought the Japanese in thick underbrush. Another Universal title, *The Longest Hundred Miles*, explained how a hard-punching American corporal (Doug McClure), an army nurse (Katharine Ross), and a cleric (Ricardo Montalban) saved a busload of children from the advancing Japanese forces, while just a few miles away, in a third Universal screenplay, *Escape to Mindano*, two Bataan Death March survivors (Nehemiah Persoff and

Ronald Remy) fled their jungle compound with a top-secret enemy decoding device. In Manson's B-tale *Mission Batangas*, a mercenary pilot (Dennis Weaver) crash-landed on a small island, and, after a quick transformation, aided the army by caching some gold from the encroaching Japanese forces. In Box Office International's B-yarn *A Taste of Hell*, two American GIs (John Garwood and William Smith) teamed up to rescue a pretty woman (Liza Lorena) from a prison camp. Another reference to the netherworld, Tigielle's *A Place in Hell* positioned a war correspondent (Guy Madison), with the honorary title of major, in the thick of battle destroying an enemy radar station.

By January 1973, after incessant chessboard maneuvering, the United States and North Vietnam reached a cease-fire agreement that ended hostilities, and just two months later, the last ground troops left this faraway battlefield. For most Americans there was a strong feeling of relief—by now the death toll was fifty-eight thousand—even though it meant a strong ally, the South Vietnamese, were on their own. Almost immediately, the fighting resumed, but in April 1975, as expected, Ho Chi Minh's nonstop forces roared into Saigon and took control of the country. Back on U.S. soil, many voices expressed concern about this capitulation. The hawks claimed the nation's honor was impugned, while the doves reiterated the shortcomings that sent GIs to war in the first place. But one thing seemed certain. Hollywood, always ready to capitalize on current themes, lacked material for a rip-roaring Vietnam conflict movie. How could it? If audiences wanted reassurances of the past glories and unbridled triumphs, there was always old faithful—the World War II photodramas, with their uphill pillbox charges and hard-fighting tank breakthroughs—still waving the flag, reminding moviegoers about America's determination, under adverse conditions, to achieve victory.

Chapter Six

The Last Hurrah

1977–1989

"Rock, in the morning, what's it like, a surface battle?"—Commander Egan Powell (Burgess Meredith) feeling apprehensive about an upcoming ship-to-ship battle in Paramount's 1965 tribute to naval prowess, *In Harm's Way*

"Like any other battle, I guess. Maybe a little noisier."—Admiral Rockwell Torrey (John Wayne) trying to downplay the situation

"I'm so scared that my bones are clicking like dice on a Reno crap table. I should be back in Hollywood, sitting in front of a typewriter, making all this up for a movie, not living it."—Commander Powell's wishful thinking

Somewhere in the mid-seventies, many American households could not shake their love/hate relationship with a fledgling technology that promised more enjoyment for a lifestyle already imbrued with instant gratification. In exchange for a monthly fee (that always spiraled upward), local cable television companies provided additional programming that included major sporting events, unbridled pornography, sweet-talking you-must-own-this shop-at-home outlets, and commercial-free, first-run feature films. For many television watchers, this innovative format basically altered leisure time when a small electronic box entered the home. Why bother with the time and expense of driving to a local show when forty, fifty, even sixty channels were available in your living room? And, what about the future? Some companies touted that by the 1980s, every subscriber could access a hundred channels. Clearly, the days of the downtown movie houses—like the small neighborhood theater featured in Columbia's *The Last Picture Show*—were over.

This was not the first time Hollywood found itself on the ropes. During the 1950s, when audience attendance dipped, production companies introduced wide-screen formats—Cinerama, Todd-AO, CinemaScope, VistaVision, plus the three-dimensional photodrama that required cumbersome cardboard glasses—to bolster sales. Now in the 1970s a similar question unfolded. How do you lure audiences away from their cable networks, that once in a while offered a made-for-television movie, and return them to their roots? For the moguls, a simple answer prevailed: build multicomplexes with fifteen, twenty, even twenty-five large-sized screens, install elaborate sound systems, provide unlimited parking, mount coin-operated video games, and offer glamorous concession stands overflowing with food, drink, and cinema paraphernalia. After all, everyone enjoyed a night on the town.

Soon, the megatheater appeared, anchored inside high-powered malls, with acres of parking spots, eclectic fast-food chains, credit-card ticketing, and, of course, numerous motion-picture selections. Clearly, a new era emerged. Moviegoers were no longer restricted to a single title found on the marquee of those old-fashioned neighborhood shows. Now they could pick and choose a photodrama to their liking. Combined with shopping and eating, these user-friendly emporiums quickly found their niche in the American landscape.

As for the World War II action film, these storylines, glamorizing American GIs routing their Axis enemies, still drew excited crowds. In 1977 United Artists released an elaborate 176-minute title that highlighted the planning, implementation, and eventual failure of the September 1944 Market Garden offensive, an unprecedented British, American, and Polish foray into the Dutch countryside where thirty-five thousand paratroopers struggled to secure four strategic Rhine overpasses. Directed by Richard Attenborough and using numerous established actors—Sean Connery, Anthony Hopkins, Lawrence Olivier, Michael Caine, James Caan, and Robert Redford—*A Bridge Too Far* re-created the strengths and weaknesses, the achievements and failures, and the unpredictable serendipity coupled with bad weather conditions affecting both sides during this nine-day invasion.

Even though this photoplay depicted one of the worst Allied defeats of the war, Richard Attenborough fashioned an upbeat, multilayer drama that examined every aspect of this brief campaign, pausing to blame various command personages for their logistical myopia. First, a leading British officer, General Frederick Browning (Dirk Bogarde), eager for a high-profile victory, downplayed reconnaissance reports and, instead, envisioned a quick sweep, reminding various subordinates that this plan "would end the war by Christmas, in less than 100 days." He bragged the airborne invasion—a concept that had "never been attempted before"—would overwhelm the few German defenders, men who "were second-class, not frontline caliber." Adding to this whimsical idea, an operations officer saw nothing wrong with a drop zone approximately ten miles from their target while another colleague, fearful of reporting unpleasant news to General Browning, remained quiet about some malfunctioning field radios, claiming, "If anyone's going to rock the boat, it won't be me." But an intelligence officer, who confronted his general with Panzer tank photographs in the landing area, was quickly scolded: "Are you seriously thinking to ask us to cancel the biggest operation since D-Day? Because of three photographs? Sixteen consecutive drops have been canceled in the last few months—for one reason or another—but this time the party's on! And no one is going to call it off."

Call it off? Who would want to call it off? Certainly not the British high command. Richard Attenborough—in these first thirty minutes—unequivocally placed culpability for this impending disaster on high-ranking English officers, citing their haughty, aristocratic demeanor coupled with a supercilious desire to show up both American and Polish troops. While General "Boy" Browning received the brunt of the blame, Field Marshal Montgomery (Edward Fox) also took it on the chin. Here, the First Viscount, wearing his trademark turtleneck sweater, resembled a cruise-ship recreation director, offering lighthearted pep talks to various staff officers, fast-driving a jeep throughout his convoy, and bantering sophomoric we-will-win shibboleths to the enlisted men, suggesting that when all was said and done, war, like a Caribbean seafaring voyage, was really fun.

Let the party begin. On September 17, 1944, the Market Garden airborne offensive, after weeks of intensive planning, began as hundreds of planes and gliders blackening the skies, lumbering toward the German border. Within minutes, the go-signal flashed, and thousands of paratroopers, many hardened from the Normandy invasion, landed safely over a wide swath of land, quickly assembled, and trekked toward assigned targets. But hopeful success soon turned sour as German troops began an aggressive assault, scattering Allied troops, creating confusion, and blocking roadways. Within hours and then days, the situation seemed marginal as desultory reports reached unit commanders. One logistical officer reported, "We're more or less surrounded. So far we're holding our own but we're desperately short of food, medicine, and above all, ammunition. The Germans have overrun the dropping zones." Another communiqué revealed more bad news: "The Germans have trapped these men in a pocket and they're squeezing it smaller and smaller."

What happened? Why did this carefully plotted assault turn sour? As predicted, the British radios that did not work hampered communications while airborne supply drops, crucial to this offensive, fell into German hands. The Polish troops, held in England by fog, arrived days late, suffered heavy losses, and became inoperative. Soon, a grim reality permeated the Allied camp: the two Panzer divisions, pounding away at their perimeters, were unstoppable. As one British officer lamented, "We just didn't make it this time, did we?" Finally, a disgruntled General James Gavin (Ryan O'Neal) issued the retreat order, "Well that's it, then. We're pulling them out!"

Field Marshal Bernard Montgomery (Edward Fox) slowly digests the news that his highly touted Market Garden offensive has turned into a major Allied debacle in Richard Attenborough's A Bridge Too Far. *Courtesy of United Artists.*

Certainly this fast-moving motion picture, with its rousing military musical score, offered moviegoers many vicarious thrills as American paratroopers, members of the famed 82nd and 101st Airborne, routed their German foes in one skirmish after another as they headed toward their objective until, eventually, the sheer numbers of the *Wehrmacht* proved unbeatable. As for the British, their leadership left much to be desired. One commander ordered his batman to pack both his golf clubs and dinner jacket with his combat gear, while another top-ranking officer pranced around with an umbrella, pointing it in different directions to punctuate an order. Overall, the film implied, the failure of this operation rested with the British. Why not? If this had been an American operation under General Eisenhower's authority, U.S. troops would have seized the bridges in record time. What did the English accomplish? According to an area commander, General Roy Urquhart (Sean Connery), the results demoralized everyone. "I took 10,000 men into Arnhem, and I've come out with less than 2,000." Even General Browning rationalized the failure. Comfortably seated in his leather chair, he proffered a neat throwaway line for the debacle: "Well, as you know I always thought we tried to go a bridge too far."

While the British extended themselves by one bridge, on the eastern front the Russians fared much better with their westward advance. In a typical revisionist storyline, EMI's *Cross of Iron* exonerated most German soldiers from their nation's lebensraum policies and, instead, accused their Prussian-bred officers, those rabid men wearing the coveted Iron Cross, who insisted on death before dishonor as the maddening Russian forces breached their flanks. Here, a resourceful *Wehrmacht* noncom, Sergeant Steiner (James Coburn), fought both Red Army attackers and his superiors' draconian orders, arguing, "God is a sadist, but probably doesn't even know it," as the Third Reich's war machine, once the strongest force in Europe, deteriorated into a mere shell of its former power. Directed by Sam Peckinpah—whose trademark style incorporated slow-motion bullets piercing human organs as an antiwar statement—much of the screenplay insinuated that the Soviet Union, not Nazi Germany, was the Allies' real enemy.

Capitalizing on Sergeant Steiner's heroics, Maverick International's *Breakthrough* transferred this unconventional *Wehrmacht* soldier to the June 1944 Normandy coastline where Third Reich forces, now in a humiliating retreat, suffered many casualties. Once more, Sergeant Steiner disregarded his officer's instructions and, following some close calls, reached Allied headquarters, revealed information about Hitler's planned assassination, persuaded an American colonel (Robert Mitchum) to call a truce, and eventually entered a French town. As with *Cross of Iron*, this 1979 screenplay contained many antiwar, anti-Hitler, and anti-Gestapo remarks and reiterated the prevailing Cold War, backpedaling philosophy that the Nazis, not the German people, were responsible for the horror of World War II.

Another screenplay that humanized the German people, Wardway's *From Hell to Victory*, told the universal story of camaraderie, love, separation, and heartache when six friends gathered at a happy August 1939 Paris party, oblivious that a global conflict loomed weeks away. Soon each person—two Americans, two French, one English, and one German—went off to the war, fighting unseen enemies for unknown reasons. Finally, in a serendipitous nighttime skirmish, the Frenchman killed a *Wehrmacht* officer, unaware that this fallen soldier was the German friend who years earlier sat next to him in that Parisian café. A similar motion picture that used a happy gathering as the jumping-off point, Film Ventures International's *Battle Force* traced the comings and goings of some American, British, and German officers from their affable 1936 Berlin dinner through many battles until they met again in the North African desert, where the Afrika Korps capitulated to Allied forces. With seventy-one-year-old John Huston and seventy-two-year-old Henry Fonda in leading roles, much of the screenplay suggested that wars were fought and won by the geriatric generation. As a low-budget 1977 production, *Battle Force* did not fare well at the box office. Hoping to generate sales, it was released numerous times under different titles: *The Battle of the Mareth Line*, *The Biggest Battle*, *The Great Battle*, and *The Greatest Battle*.

Frequently, a big-scale production, depicting major Allied advances against the German forces, fared much better. United Artists' *The Big Red One* glamorized the army's First Infantry Division beginning with their initial assault-landing in Morocco, through Sicily, Normandy, the Battle of the Bulge, and lastly, a concentration-camp liberation. With Lee Marvin starring as a combat-hardened, World War I veteran, this aged noncom guided his squad through hazardous skirmishes, frequent patrols, ongoing tragedies, castle-in-the-sky dreams, and lost aspirations during their three-year eastward advance, always reminding his charges, "You don't murder animals; you kill 'em." Directed by Sam Fuller, this autobiographical screenplay downplayed heroics and, instead, restated the enlisted man's doctrine that wars were created by politicians and behind-the-lines officers but fought by average soldiers: "You know how you smoke out a sniper? You send a guy out in the open and you see if he gets shot. They thought that one up at West Point."

Sometimes historical events veered off into the galaxy. Associated General Films' *The Eagle Has Landed* told the fictional story of Winston Churchill's planned assassination by some Nazi commandoes led by Michael Caine. United Artists' fast-paced espionage yarn, *Eye of the Needle*, re-created the arduous narrative of a surreptitious Third Reich devotee (Donald Sutherland), working quietly in London, obtaining D-Day information. Eventually, on a remote Scottish island he confronted a determined British woman and realized, "The war has come down to the two of us." In a gruesome finale, she stopped his espionage activities. Fox's *Julia* traced the strained relationship between the noted playwright Lillian Hellman (Jane Fonda) and her mentor and occasional lover Dashiell Hammett (Jason Robards). These two American writers clashed on numerous social, political, and literary issues, including her rapport with a lifelong friend, Julia (Vanessa Redgrave), an outspoken liberal involved in many antifascist causes. After some soul-searching, Miss Hellman threw caution to the wind and smuggled money into Nazi Germany. However, this episode ended badly. Arrested by the Gestapo, Julia died in prison.

In similar chronicles, Paramount's *The Sea Wolves* re-created the unlikely tale of some retired British cavalrymen living in Calcutta who formed an attack team and, after elaborate planning, blew up three Nazi warships moored in a nearby harbor. With Gregory Peck, David Niven, and Roger Moore leading this unorthodox group, success was, of course, guaranteed. Trading International's *Bridge to Hell* allowed three prisoners, including B-actor Andy Forest, to escape from a Nazi camp, team up with Resistance fighters, and locate hidden war booty. In American-International's *Force 10 from Navarone*, good-looking Harrison Ford joined a demolition team that parachuted into Yugoslavia, fought with local guerrillas, infiltrated a Nazi base, and, with the help of a British sergeant (Edward Fox), who claimed, "I'm an expert at blowing them up," destroyed a strategic bridge, bringing the *Wehrmacht* to a grinding halt.

More photodramas depicted breakouts behind enemy lines. MGM's *Victory* told the pie-in-the-sky story of some Allied POWs who agreed to a Paris soccer match with their captors but secretly planned a mass escape, even though an American officer (Sylvester Stallone) complained, "This frigging game is ruining my life." Another meller using Operation Overlord as its backdrop, MGM's *Code Name: Emerald*, elaborated the close calls of a double agent (Ed Harris), who parachuted into France just before D-Day to rescue an American airman familiar with the invasion plans. Satori's *Brady's Escape* detailed the adventures of an American bomber pilot (John Savage) who was shot down over a Hungarian plateau, hidden by some antifascist locals, and— with the aid of Tito's partisans—reached safety in Yugoslavia.

Titles made exclusively for television audiences spotlighted Allied espionage achievements against the Fatherland. Universal's *The Rhineman Exchange*—a five-hour extravaganza—explained the comings and goings of an undercover American plant (Stephen Collins) operating in Argentina, where in a drawn-out storyline, diamonds were exchanged for a needed gyroscope. In Columbia's *Keefer*, beefy William Conrad headed a small group of secret agents working behind enemy lines, while Lorimer's six-hour potboiler, *A Man Called Intrepid*, told the unlikely story of an Allied team privately funded by a wealthy Canadian (David Niven). Over in North Africa, Nazi spies vied against British interests in Lawrence Productions' four-hour tale of intrigue, *The Key to Rebecca*. With Cliff Robertson in the leading role, this cat-and-mouse tale featured David Soul as an elusive German spy, while, in bizarre casting, Robert Culp played General Erwin Rommel, the famed Desert Fox.

Another farfetched idea, HBO's *To Catch a King* low-keyed the convoluted propaganda scheme employed by some Axis agents hiding in Lisbon, hoping to kidnap the Duke of Windsor. However, a well-known man-about-town and nightclub owner (Robert Wagner) sidetracked their plan. With a slight nod toward *Casablanca*, this made-for-television dud proved, once again, that no German undercover agent could outwit a fast-moving American. A similar oddball story, Warner Bros.' *Lassiter*, placed a handsome, smooth-talking London jewel thief (Tom Selleck) in an awkward situation. After an embarrassing arrest, the second-story man must choose between imprisonment or a government-approved burglary of the heavily guarded German embassy, a feat that would help his country. "Why not?" the experienced burglar groused, "I'm standing in a frame and you're gonna wrap me in the flag, too."

In Phoenix Entertainment's made-for-television dark thriller, *Monte Carlo*, sexy Joan Collins, working as chanteuse, spied for the Allies on the eve of World War II. In a flippant mood, Universal's burlesque *The Gypsy Warriors* paired Tom Selleck and James Whitmore Jr. as two American intelligence officers who, after some silly cloak-and-dagger escapades, destroyed a German chemical-weapons factory. In MTM Enterprises' espionage suspense film, *Behind Enemy Lines*, a professor-turned-spy (Hal Holbrook) planned a rescue mission to Nazi-occupied Norway, where a prominent scientist with doubtful loyalties was holed up. Another action screenplay depicting capture and escape, TNT's *Breaking Point* (a remake of MGM's 1964 intrigue, *36 Hours*), retold the roundabout tale of an American intelligence officer (Corbin Bernsen), who, after being drugged and tortured by Nazi operatives, escaped with important information.

Two other made-for-television programs examined familiar stories. Columbia's *The Caine Mutiny Court Martial* detailed the vitriolic courtroom battle between an aggressive navy defense attorney (Eric Bogosian) and a neurotic senior officer, the vulnerable Captain Queeg (Brad Davis), resulting in an acquittal for his clients. Directed by Robert Altman, this updated version, laden with the director's trademark—background scenes juxtaposed against the main frontal action—complemented the earlier Humphrey Bogart and José Ferrer version, even though much of the action took place in a gymnasium (with anachronistic basketball floor markings) instead of a staid military chamber. NBC's *Mister Roberts* used Charles Durning and Robert Hays in the James Cagney and Henry Fonda roles about seafaring shenanigans aboard a supply vessel hovering in the noncombatant South Pacific, where an irrational captain sparred with his ensign about decorum. Basically a comedy with a few somber overtones, this 100-minute version reminded audiences that laughter was still the best way to handle an out-of-control officer.

Sometimes World War II made-for-television photodramas emphasized distaff members and their role in the global conflict. Penthouse Productions' *The Secret War of Jackie's Girls* re-created the spirited adventures of five female pilots—stationed in England and using experimental helicopters—flying covert missions behind enemy lines. With Mariette Hartley in the title role, this exaggerated storyline stretched aviation history with its anachronistic scenes depicting helicopters in aerial combat. Another potboiler, Harlech's *Jenny's War*, told the unusual saga of an American mother (Dyan Cannon) who learned that her RAF son (Hugh Grant) was shot down over Germany. Soon she traveled to Berlin where her ex-husband—now a Nazi major—rejected her pleas for help in finding the airman. After a series of arduous exploits—including working as a maid in a fancy brothel, killing an SS officer, struggling in a Russian POW camp, and escaping in an onion sack—she went into hiding after a Gestapo agent (Robert Hardy) ordered, "If you find her, shoot her on sight."

Hitler's world-domination plans were a popular theme. Circle Films' *Inside the Third Reich* heralded the career of the führer's architect, Albert Speer, the man who once rebuked a field marshal by asking, "Do you realize who you are talking to?" With Rutger Hauer in the title role, every aspect of Germany's grandiose project for a New Order was examined in this five-hour epic. Time-Life Productions' 180-minute re-creation of Hitler's final days, *The Bunker*, starred Anthony Hopkins as an obsessive megalomaniac führer, switching between hot and cold moods, speaking incoherently—"I've never acquired anything of value in my life"—as fast-moving Soviet troops entered the capital city. Metromedia's *Hitler's SS: Portrait in Evil* dissected the Gestapo's fourteen-year history, so enveloped in brutality that it prompted an imprisoned professor (José Ferrer) to contemplate, "I wonder what Goethe would have to say now."

Other motion pictures presented similar problems. Cannon Group's *The Assisi Underground* showcased the cat-and-mouse efforts of some Italian priests hiding Jewish nationals in their village church, while outside the cloister walls Third Reich officers nonchalantly strolled by, harassing the townspeople and examining resident permits. With James Mason as a levelheaded bishop orchestrating many ruses necessary to avoid detection, and Ben Cross as his youthful cleric, these hapless victims remained hidden until war's end. A similar storyline, ITC's *The Scarlet and the Black*, honored a Vatican official (Gregory Peck) who hid many downed pilots, escaped prisoners, and Resistance members inside the Holy City. Anthea's *Forbidden* examined the clandestine love affair between a German countess (Jacqueline Bisset) and her Jewish lover (Jürgen Prochnow) as the Berlin Gestapo hovered nearby, unaware that their fugitive was ensconced in a windowless apartment. In Castle Hill Productions' *Reunion*, two secondary-school friends, one Jewish, the other Christian, enjoyed many carefree days, oblivious to emerging ideologies in 1933 Stuttgart. After Hitler seized power, the Jewish boy, Hans, left for America while his Christian pal, Conradin, remained behind. Years later, an older Hans (Jason Robards) returned to his birthplace and searched for his lost chum, only to learn about his execution in the failed 1944 Hitler assassination plot.

Over in France, HBO's *The Blood of Others* depicted the ordeals associated with the New Order's occupation of this Gallic country, while another melodrama, Newland-Raynor's *Arch of Triumph* (a remake of the 1948 Charles Boyer and Ingrid Bergman classic) paired Anthony Hopkins and Lesley-Ann Down as star-crossed lovers being harassed by their Nazi nemesis, Donald Pleasence. Another Sunday-night photodrama, NBC's *The Great Escape II: The Untold Story*, served as a sequel to United Artists' popular 1963 screenplay about Allied soldiers who tunneled out of their stalag, fled into the countryside, and were captured and hastily executed by German soldiers. In this awkward, non-sequential account, two American officers (Judd Hirsch and Christopher Reeve) pestered their captors for straight answers about missing men.

Other titles continued the fight against heel-clicking Nazis in more flamboyant terms. Capitalizing on the success of its 1967 blockbuster *The Dirty Dozen*, MGM produced three made-for-television sequels heralding the misadventures of these ill-disciplined soldiers, who for survival, formed a tough fighting unit. *The Dirty Dozen: The Next Mission* brought members of the original cast on another high-risk Fatherland operation. Once more, Lee Marvin—now eighteen years older—led a motley team of murderers, degenerates, and rapists behind German lines to disrupt a Hitler assassination plot, because an army general (Ernest Borgnine) claimed, "Hitler is our best ally, we need him alive." Two years later, with Telly Savalas in charge of this unsavory group, they destroyed a nerve-gas plant in *The Dirty Dozen: The Deadly Mission*. The following year, in the third installment, *The Dirty Dozen: The Fatal Mission*, Major Savalas took these mavericks into the hot Middle East to obliterate an elite Nazi team, twelve handpicked Hitler devotees planning an insurgent Fourth Reich movement, capable of continuing the war.

Copycat versions of *The Dirty Dozen* saga soon followed. Film Concorde's *Deadly Mission* involved the misadventures of five imprisoned GIs, who, after a strafing attack, escaped from their guards and headed toward Switzerland. Following an array of comic-strip events—where they strangled, speared, shot, and stabbed many Germans—they inadvertently joined a

French Resistance team, entered a V-2 plant, and, following a wild railroad ride, grabbed a gyroscope. An American colonel, holding this crucial part, bragged, "That's what we came for." As a ninety-nine-minute B-travesty, this film, like the phoenix, had numerous rebirths. Reissued four times, the producers deftly created spiffy titles with different twists: *Counterfeit Commandos*, *GI Bro*, *Hell's Heroes*, *The Dirty Bastard*, and *Inglorious Bastards*.

American cast-offs were not the only group in hot water with their superiors. Another spin-off of the renegade-soldier motif, Panorama's *The Misfit Brigade* bellowed the same shenanigans except this time, the heroes were slovenly *Wehrmacht* prison battalion recalcitrants. Sent on a suicide mission, they fought not the Americans but, instead, the encroaching Red Army. After some Looney Tune adventures, this dysfunctional unit killed many Russians, lost some of their own men, and finally reached a village, where—to their surprise—they found both German and Soviet soldiers romping harmoniously in a nude swim fest with pretty girls. Basically an antiwar tract, this B-spoof contained one caricature after another, including the pompous SS colonel fingering his monocle and the pudgy general threatening to execute everyone within hearing range. One scene in particular, the screening of some Soviet propaganda call-to-surrender motion pictures in a no-man's-zone, pushed the misfits over the edge. This Red Army ploy promised a beautiful woman, wearing a gossamer nightgown, in exchange for capitulation. Besides their sexual frustration, these men realized the futility of Hitler's expansionism and, coupled with the SS's fight-to-the-death dictum, understood everything was lost, prompting one man's facetious observation, "If we lose the war, we win."

Frequently, a screenplay emphasized the difficulties of the heart when American soldiers found new love interests. In a mushy tale, Columbia's *Hanover Street* re-created familiar problems when a carefree B-25 pilot (Harrison Ford) fell for a lonely, married British woman in war-torn London. To complicate matters, the husband and lover were paired on an intricate French intelligence mission. After some close calls dodging Nazi troops, both men returned to England, where the conscience-bound aviator, sadder but wiser, walked away from this ill-fated romance. Another American who also walked away from his British girlfriend, General Dwight Eisenhower, was detailed in ABC Circle Films' *Ike: The War Years*. The Kansas-born commander's private relationship with Kay Summersby, his driver, offered some insight into wartime separation, especially for the man responsible for the Operation Overlord implementation. Here, Robert Duvall captured the mannerisms of the levelheaded general who frequently argued with Field Marshal Montgomery and, in a jocular mood, kidded his English chauffer for "seeing too many Hollywood movies."

Still other American GIs kept chasing British women. In Universal's *Yanks* the problems associated with sexual frustration exploded when thousands of American soldiers stationed in Northern England came to town looking for fun, happiness, and romance with the local women whose husbands and boyfriends were off fighting on foreign battlefields. As expected, a congenial mess sergeant (Richard Gere) quickly fell for a local beauty whose beau was in the combat zone, while his commanding officer (William Devane) courted a married woman whose husband likewise was in the service. Eventually, the sergeant and the English lass became lovers and, days before his Normandy departure, pledged everything, while the Captain, standing quietly off to the side, stared lugubriously as his British sweetheart, now reunited with her spouse, waved goodbye. He was remembering her prophetic words uttered weeks earlier, "Perhaps, I'm not a woman of the world."

In an offbeat mode, the popular horror film genre, always a staple for youthful audiences, offered many sadomasochistic productions using the war as a peripheral backdrop. General Film's *The Passage* told the macabre story of a simple Basque shepherd (Anthony Quinn) and his misadventures while guiding a fleeing family through the Pyrenees to neutral Spain while a demented Nazi psychopath (Malcolm McDowell), determined to catch these escaping refugees, followed closely. In true Caligula fashion, this repulsive German, wearing swastika-embroidered underwear, raped the daughter, chopped off and cooked a peasant's finger while strumming "chop, chop, chop, chop," and burned a gypsy alive, bragging, "I'm sending him exactly where he told me to go—Hell," before he fell victim to his own brand of cruelty. As an R-rated motion picture, the entire screenplay, imbued with one violent, nasty, deplorable scene after another, echoed Stanley Kubrick's *A Clockwork Orange*, where a deranged Malcolm McDowell portrayed another antisocial misfit, spouting blood and mayhem in futuristic London. On a lesser scale, Associated Capital's paranormal photoplay, *The Keep*, recounted the uncanny happenings in a Romanian citadel located high on a mountain pass, where *Wehrmacht* soldiers died mysteriously. Suspecting some isolated partisan activity, the Gestapo command, after an inept investigation, confronted an evil force trapped within this fortress, determined to kill anyone that prevented its escape, which prompted a professor's daughter (Alberta Watson) to exclaim, "We're dealing with a gnome! A devil!"

But *The Keep* was not the only picture to depart from a conventional mode and stray cautiously into the science fiction realm. United Artists' *The Final Countdown* gathered momentum from *The Twilight Zone* in creating the eerie story of a modern aircraft carrier—laden with sophisticated tracking equipment—on an early December 1979 patrol north of Hawaii. Inexplicably, the carrier sailed into a preternatural mist. Emerging a little shaken but unscathed from this eerie experience, the ship's leader (Kirk Douglas) realized that his modern-day flattop, the pride of the navy's fighting armada, had entered a time warp and returned to Sunday morning, December 7, 1941. After the captain explained to the crew, "I believe what we stumbled across is not man-made but a phenomenon of nature," everyone seemed confused. Now what? Should the navy launch its F-15s and destroy the approaching Japanese attack planes or simply allow history's ineluctable forces to run their course?

A copycat version of this oddball storyline, Cinema Group Ventures' *The Philadelphia Experiment*, highlighted the frolicking jaunts of two navy men who, in October 1943, somehow wound up in 1984 because of an electronic testing mishap—involving some radar and camouflage techniques—aboard their destroyer, dry-docked in Philadelphia. A wide-eyed tar (Michael Paré) seemed confused by his new surroundings and pondered, "How is this sort of thing possible?" Even so, he took the future in stride, including a childlike addiction to video games. In a similar strained photodrama, Thorn's *Holcroft Covenant* told the convoluted tale of a German boy, who was adopted by an American family during the closing weeks of World War II, lived in New York, and—as a middle-aged man (Michael Caine)—learned his father, a confidant of Adolf Hitler, left him $4 million for victims of Nazism. Now in Europe and running for his life, he discovered that a latent Fourth Reich organization planned to steal this money for their cause.

As President Roosevelt often proclaimed, any overseas combat victory first began in Pittsburgh's round-the-clock steel mills. While many factories publicized their daily outputs as morale boosters, other industrial units were strictly hush-hush institutions. Paramount's *Fat Man and Little Boy* detailed the unparalleled secrecy and intricate logistics required for the Manhattan Project, where thousands of scientists, physicists, and mathematicians gathered to plan, construct, and, subsequently, implode the first nuclear bomb. Under the leadership of J. Robert Oppenheimer (Dwight Schultz), these handpicked technicians worked assiduously, while in the background, ever mindful of security leaks, General Lester Groves (Paul Newman) glared suspiciously at the many leftists assigned to his base. The participants were often at odds with each other about politics, morality, and expediency. The hard-nosed officer hammered away at the importance of victory. "We could give this country the biggest stick in the playground, and I intend to do that." His civilian nemesis listened politely and puffed his pipe as the harangue continued, "We gotta come down out of the clouds, and get into the business of winning the war." BBC's *Oppenheimer*, another photodrama but with stronger liberal leanings, allowed Sam Waterston more philosophical latitude, permitting the scientist to ruminate, "I have become Death, the destroyer of worlds." Spelling Productions' *Day One* retold the volatile Manhattan Project story from a third perspective.

This time Brian Dennehy portrayed General Leslie Groves as a pudgy, in-your-face officer, who worked, argued, and then compromised with J. Robert Oppenheimer (David Strathairn) to construct America's first nuclear weapon. After this atomic bomb imploded on the New Mexican desert, the Army Air Corps reconfigured a B-29—one of the new high-altitude superfortresses attacking Japan—as the delivery system for this advanced weaponry. Viacom's 156-minute drama *Enola Gay: The Men, the Mission, the Atomic Bomb* praised the intricate organization that culminated when this state-of-the-art bomber became airborne on August 6, 1945, flew westward, and eventually dropped this explosive on Hiroshima. The bomber was named after the mother of the pilot, Colonel Paul Tibbets (Patrick Duffy).

Other famous war personages appeared in made-for-television productions. HBO's *Mussolini: The Decline and Fall of Il Duce* starred Bob Hoskins as the Italian leader who bellowed many orders, winked at women, and kowtowed to Adolf Hitler. Trian Productions offered a more positive interpretation with George C. Scott's performance in *Mussolini: The Untold Story*, in which the fascist leader pooh-poohed Hitler. "I don't like him; Genghis Khan in a raincoat." Stonehenge Production's *Wallenberg: A Hero* narrated the mysterious saga of the Swedish diplomat who rescued 120,000 Hungarian Jews right under Eichmann's nose and later entered the Soviet Union, never to be seen again. Richard Chamberlain portrayed the international champion. Back on U.S. soil, in Titus Productions' *F.D.R.—The Last Years*, Jason Robards depicted the American leader implementing his Doctor-win-the-war strategy. In a similar vein, BBC's *Churchill and the Generals* placed Roosevelt (Arthur Hill), Eisenhower (Richard Dysart), and Churchill (Timothy West) in a 180-minute re-creation of their ongoing discussions, arguments, and decisions.

Entertainment Partner's *Last Days of Patton* positioned George C. Scott back in his Academy Award role as the braggadocio-spouting general who died in a freak German automobile accident, while Circle Films' *Young Joe, the Forgotten Kennedy* re-created the story of this prominent family's oldest scion (Peter Strauss) and his airborne death. Globe Film's *Casablanca Express* told a convoluted story about an attempted assassination of Churchill during his North African visit. In this revisionist screenplay, the prime minister confessed to an American general that England "had a spy in Japan who was able to let us know at the end of November that three Japanese aircraft carriers were heading toward Hawaii. The most logical target was Pearl Harbor." Aquarius's *Nazi Hunter: The Beate Klarsfeld Story* recounted the turbulent experiences of a German housewife (Farrah Fawcett) who, along with her husband, organized a grassroots movement to bring Nazi war criminals before the bar. In a slightly different mode, Fawcett took another starring role as the unorthodox photographer—whose many black-and-white stills recorded the war's shaded nuances—in TNT's biographical sketch, *Margaret Bourke-White*.

Another title highlighting a wartime personage, Universal's *MacArthur*, magnified the five-star general many regarded as the war's messianic savior, the commander who pushed the Japanese back to their homeland even though numerous critics, fearful of his popularity, denounced him as a modern-day Caesar. With Gregory Peck in the leading role, the storyline began during the darkest hour of the Pacific fighting, when outnumbered and ill-supplied U.S. and Philippine troops struggled hopelessly against Japanese forces on the Bataan Peninsula. With defeat a certainty, MacArthur, now ensconced in Australia, issued his famous "I shall return" dictum and eventually organized his armed forces for the northward offensive. Always reminding his subordinates, "We are attacking," MacArthur's troops captured strategic islands while leapfrogging others. Finally, on October 20, 1944, he waded ashore at Leyte Beach and traveled inland, where in an emotionally charged scene, he reunited with the Bataan survivors. Months later, standing on the USS *Missouri*, he presided over the Japanese surrender.

Always imperious, MacArthur demanded complete authority. When ordered from Corregidor, he initially balked, threatening "to resign my commission and fight on here as a private." Later he disagreed with Roosevelt's Luzon's bypass proposal, countermanding his commander in chief, asserting, "I'm going back there next fall, even if I had to paddle a canoe." Other times, he chided indecisive officers demanding, "I want action, not complaints." Finally on Philippine soil, he pleaded with the guerrillas, "Rise and strike, in the name of your sacred dead, strike!" But with the Bataan survivors he appeared humble, apologizing to the emaciated soldiers, "Sorry I'm so late, we're long overdue."

Later, his liberal policies transformed Japan from a feudal society to a fledgling democracy by invoking land reforms and trade unions, which underscored what he told his officers: "The Japanese must be treated with courtesy and respect." But in 1950, with this conquered nation stabilized, another problem surfaced: the Korean invasion. Initially on the defensive, MacArthur's forces slowly retreated until he launched the September 15, 1950, Inchon landing, cutting his enemy's supply line. Now on the offensive, American troops moved forward. With Harry S. Truman in the White House, he promised the president a quick victory. But a few months later, Chinese forces crossed the Yalu River and attacked U.S. outposts, prompting MacArthur to exclaim, "We are now facing a new, fresh, highly trained army." Frequently at odds with Truman—who nicknamed him "His Majesty"—MacArthur issued an ultimatum to the Chinese. Tempers flared until finally the president exclaimed, "I'm going to fire that brass hat prima donna, right now." Relieved of his command, MacArthur returned to Washington, declaring, "War's very object is victory,

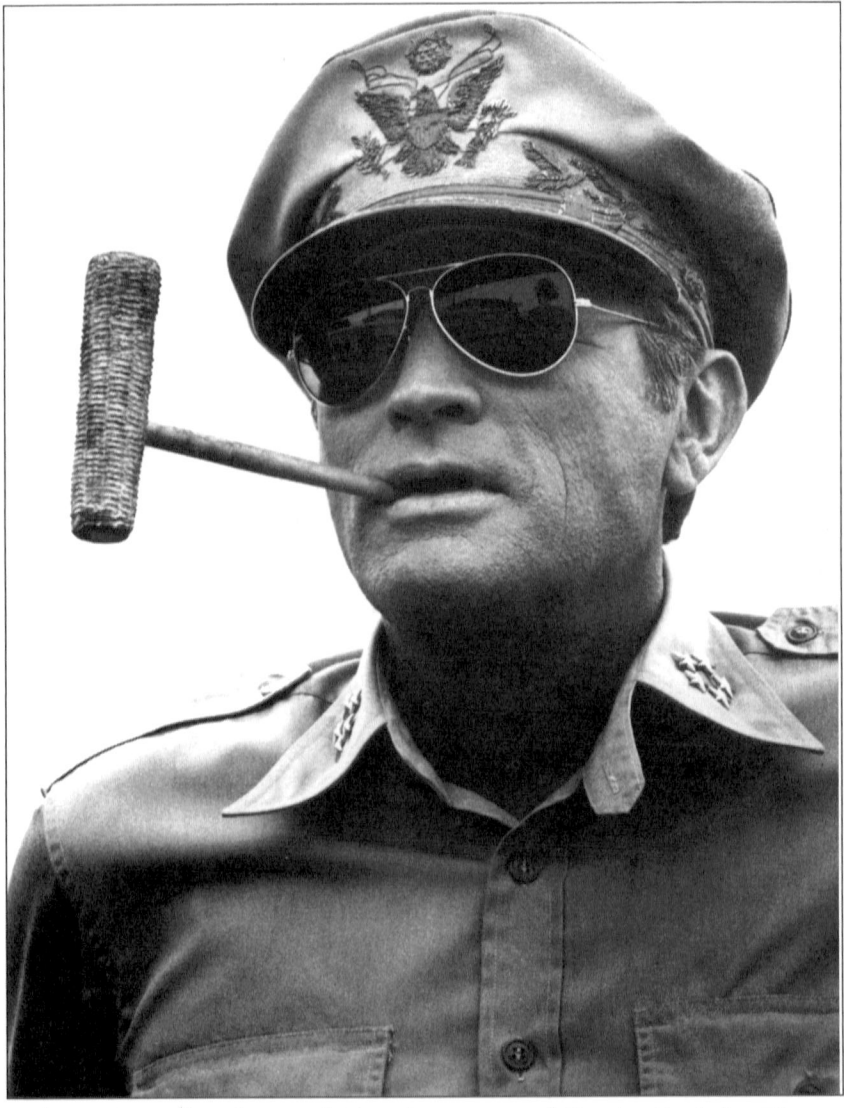

Puffing on his trademark corncob pipe, five-star general Douglas MacArthur (Gregory Peck) contemplates his next strategic move against Japanese fortifications in Joseph Sargent's photodrama MacArthur. Courtesy of Universal Pictures.

not prolonged indecision." Feted by Congress, MacArthur's famous Old Soldiers Never Die speech brought everyone to their feet in stupendous applause.

But not every screenplay ended triumphantly. Always depressing, the concentration-camp titles—the darkest side of World War II history—mirrored the horror of Hitler's Final Solution in seven made-for-television motion pictures. Time-Life's *The Wall* reenacted the April 1943 Warsaw Ghetto uprising where approximately six hundred Polish fighters held off thousands of Nazis in a fight to the finish that culminated with a German takeover. As a tough-talking resistance fighter, Tom Conti exemplified the strength of this beleaguered group that preferred death to imprisonment. Katz-Gallin's *The Diary of Anne Frank*, another version of the famous novel and play, retold the heart-wrenching story of the Amsterdam family hiding in a cramped attic, their arrest, and concentration-camp deaths. Here, Melissa Gilbert played the budding adolescent whose posthumous diary became an acclaimed international best seller. Another version of this poignant story, Telecom's *The Attic: The Hiding of Anne Frank* placed Lisa Jacobs in the leading part.

Syzygy Productions' *Playing for Time* told the surreal saga of some Auschwitz inmates, all accomplished musicians, who formed a bizarre welcoming committee for confused prisoners arriving at the death camp. With Vanessa Redgrave in the starring role, this 180-minute drama reiterated the depths of Nazi cruelty. Titus Productions' *Holocaust* traced the joys, sorrows, and life-and-death experiences of two German families caught in the lebensraum vortex. This elaborate nine-hour drama was summarized by a sadistic SS officer's (Michael Moriarty) remark, "We must keep killing them, don't you see? If we stop it's an admission of guilt!" Zenith Entertainment's *Escape from Sobibor* re-created an actual 1944 breakout from a notorious Polish death camp by six hundred Jewish prisoners who overpowered their guards and ran from the compound. Eventually, almost three hundred survived this ordeal. With Alan Arkin leading this revolt, the photodrama described the stark brutality of Hitler's Final Solution and called into question how a production company that made such a detailed Holocaust motion picture, graphically depicting torture and cruelty, could lackadaisically place the word "entertainment" in its logo. Likewise, Citadel Entertainment heralded the same misnomer in their logo when producing *Max and Helen*, another retelling of concentration-camp misery for a simple Polish couple. Yet another photodrama picture denouncing the terror of German captivity, Golan-Globus's *Hanna's War*, told the horrific story of an Israeli immigrant (Maruschka Detmer) who joined a British commando unit and returned to her native Hungary, where she was quickly captured, imprisoned, and tortured. The entire 150-minute screenplay described her Axis tormentors as savage, inhuman beasts.

In an equally horrific title depicting the Nazi war machine, International Films' *Triumph of the Spirit* narrated the true story of Greek middleweight boxing champion Salamo Arouch, who along with his entire family was shipped to Auschwitz, where he alone survived because the guards forced Jewish boxers to fight, gladiator-style, for their perverse entertainment. Starring Willem Dafoe, this poignant drama reiterated the unspeakable conditions in Hitler's extermination program. Similarly, Universal's *Sophie's Choice* told the excruciating story of an Auschwitz survivor (Meryl Streep), ordered to choose which of her two children must die in the camp. Told in erratic flashback from a postwar Brooklyn apartment, this cathartic screenplay offered graphic testimony about Nazi bestiality.

On the other side of the globe, a few motion pictures examined the sadistic nature of Japanese imprisonment. Jeni Productions' *Women of Valor* restated the misery imposed upon a group of American army nurses taken at Bataan. With Susan Sarandon in the leading role, this made-for-television screenplay—modeled after MGM's *Cry Havoc!* (1943) and Paramount's *So Proudly We Hail* (1943)—re-created the three-year struggle as beatings, rape, torture, and execution became common Japanese practices. Similarly, Yorkshire's *Silent Cries* detailed the three-year nightmare of many Australian, British, and American women captured at Singapore and sent to Sumatra. With Gena Rowlands and Annabeth Gish in principal roles, this graphic motion picture detailed the brutal treatment that caused hundreds to die from starvation and disease. Victorian Film's *A Town Like Alice* followed two lovers (Bryan Brown and Helen Morse) across three continents over a twenty-year period, including a barbaric crucifixion scene in a Malaysian camp, in this 301-minute made-for-television remake of the 1956 production. A similar drama depicting the agony of Allied soldiers in a Javanese camp, Asahi's *Merry Christmas Mr. Lawrence* explained the depravity imposed by a draconian commander (Ryuichi Sakamoto)—whose Bushido philosophy maintained that prisoners were cowards for accepting capture instead of suicide—and his interaction and possible latent homosexual desire for a British officer (David Bowie).

Another B-title elaborating the fanatical Japanese soldier obsessed by his Bushido credo, Pathfinder's *The Last Warrior* recounted the unusual circumstances of an American marine (Gary Graham) and a Japanese officer (Cary-Hiroyuki Tagawa) finding themselves stranded on a remote Pacific island in April 1945. With little chance for rescue, the Oriental soldier, hoping to die as a warrior, staged a ritualistic samurai sword-fighting contest, but the sinewy leatherneck, determined to stay alive, taunted his foe with a facetious remark, "Don't get too excited, Tojo." Then, in a gory finale, the American killed this last warrior, reaffirming that even with superior martial-arts training, the Japanese could not overpower Yankee intransigence.

Nathaniel Productions' *Pacific Inferno* offered a different perspective, depicting life in a Japanese POW camp for the Bataan survivors as a Sunday walk in the park, where navy divers received good food, pleasant housing, clean clothing, and, once in a while, a little physical romance. Here, a seaman (Jim Brown) feigned working for his captors, while in his nocturnal hours, he tiptoed out of the compound, met with some guerrillas, and then removed vast quantities of silver from Manila Bay. Eventually, the Japanese discovered his ploy, and now with his back to the wall, he chose death before capture. With numerous flashbacks to stateside cultural disparities, the photodrama took some nasty digs at contemporary racism, including a contrived scene where a navy lieutenant rationalized his behavior, "We don't bunk down with Negroes; on the ship they have their quarters, we have our quarters."

Occasionally, Hollywood toned down the horror of the Greater East Asian Co-Prosperity Sphere's occupation policies. Yanco Films' Academy Award winner, *The Last Emperor*, re-created the layered life of China's last ruler, Pu Yi. Born in 1906, he witnessed many upheavals, including the Japanese invasion, and finally in 1934 became Manchukuo's puppet head. With John Lone in the leading role, this elaborate storyline skirted historical events. In a similar vein, Warner Bros.' *Empire of the Sun* detailed the confusion experienced by a precocious eleven-year-old British boy growing up in an affluent Shanghai neighborhood when enemy forces invaded the city. Separated from his parents and interned in a civilian detention center until war's end, this free-spirited adolescent (Christian Bale) adapted to camp life, taking lessons from a Fagin-type American (John Malkovich), even though on one frivolous occasion he sang a nationalist battle hymn with some Japanese pilots.

Sometimes fictitious ideas stretched the limits of credibility. Orion Pictures' *Farewell to the King* traced the unusual odyssey of an American GI (Nick Nolte) stationed at Bataan, who spotted the Japanese approaching his perimeter, left the peninsula and, after some elaborate escapades, reached Borneo's northern coast, befriended the aborigine tribesmen, and eventually became their barefoot ruler. After three years of carefree living that included good food, pretty women, long hair, and warm breezes, a British reconnaissance patrol arrived, headed by a major (Nigel Havers) who ordered this AWOL soldier to fight some retreating Japanese forces, reminding him, "You cannot turn your back on this war." Finally, in a bloody confrontation, the GI-turned-monarch now understood the futility of battle and promised, "From this day forward, I will raise my hand against no man." With numerous nods to the Noble Savage theory, this screenplay took a few swipes at English imperialism and attitude toward people of color.

Other titles presented the global conflict in slightly different formats. Comworld's made-for-television melodrama, *The Execution*, told the unusual predicament of five San Diego women, all survivors of a Nazi concentration camp, and their involvement in the death of a local restaurant owner, a former Nazi camp doctor (Rip Torn) who, years earlier, performed gruesome experiments on young girls. Paramount's *Islands in the Stream* traced the gradual transformation of a Bimini recluse (George C. Scott) from apathetic beachcomber to hardened antifascist and his deadly confrontation with a German

U-boat while smuggling Jewish refugees to Cuba. Columbia's *A Time of Destiny* reminded audiences that the U.S. Army contained its fair share of psychotic soldiers. Here, William Hurt stalked a fellow GI, waiting for the opportune moment to kill him. Another made-for-television nine-hour saga, Universal's *Once an Eagle*, paralleled the lives of two Army officers—one (Sam Elliott) a World War I Medal of Honor winner, dedicated soldier, and straight arrow, and another (Cliff Potts) a West Point graduate, bag-of-wind conniver, and self-serving womanizer—and their many wartime experiences. A similar storyline, but twice the length, Paramount's *The Winds of War*, pushed the made-for-television concept to new dimensions with its multilayered plots, big-name stars, and varied locales. Created from Herman Wouk's best-selling novel, this eighteen-hour extravaganza traced the comings and goings of the Henry family, where the father (Robert Mitchum) became an eyewitness to military strategy, partisan politics, ill-fated romance, family conflicts, war crimes, and bumbling bureaucracy. The sequel, *War and Remembrance*, continued the saga to V-J Day even though Hitler, hiding in his bunker on April 29, 1945, declared, "I should have won this war. I did not make a single mistake."

Back on Hawaiian shores, Columbia's elaborate six-hour made-for-television remake of the 1953 classic, *From Here to Eternity*, brought back Sergeant Warden (William Devane), Karen Holmes (Natalie Wood), and Robert E. Lee Prewitt (Steve Railsback) in the multitiered storyline about sadistic NCOs, an ambitious commanding officer, a brutal stockade sergeant, a kindhearted prostitute, and, finally, the Pearl Harbor attack. In this fancy Technicolor version all the GIs wore anachronistic black neckties instead of the authorized khaki shade. Not to be outdone, Warner Bros. used the same Hawaiian locale for its spin-off version of James Jones's famous novel in their six-hour television drama *Pearl*. In this production, Angie Dickinson, Dennis Weaver, and Robert Wagner kept the soap-opera pot boiling with their many social, political, and romantic maneuverings until the early-morning Japanese aircraft rewrote history, even though most of the bombing scenes were lifted from *Tora! Tora! Tora!*

Stateside life, while far away from the hostilities, still contained its own share of problems, frustrations, and anxieties. Paramount's *Racing with the Moon* championed the high-jinks story of two California lads, anxiously waiting their eighteenth birthday to report for Marine Corps basic training. With Sean Penn and Nicolas Cage in the leading roles, the two happy-go-lucky teenagers spent their last weeks flirting with girls, imbibing some underage drinks, and fooling around with old friends. Another screenplay centering on military enlistment, Kraco Productions' *Coward of the Country* was less frivolous. Here a young southern townsman (Frederic Lehne) refused to enlist after Pearl Harbor because of a pacifist promise made to his dying father. After some unpleasant events involving his girlfriend's rape, he changed his mind, rebutted these men, and, with the help of his preacher uncle (Kenny Rogers), signed up for military duty.

On a different note, Warner Bros.' *Swing Shift* took an ambiguous look at some marital infidelity when a lonely wife (Goldie Hawn), working in an aircraft factory while her navy husband was overseas, fell for a 4-F coworker (Kurt Russell), even though the inexperienced assembler could not find a left-handed screwdriver. In an offbeat made-for-television tale, Highgate Pictures' *Summer of My German Soldier* recounted the bittersweet experiences of a Jewish teenage girl who fell for an escaped Nazi POW in a small town in Georgia. In nearby Mississippi, where a young draftee (Matthew Broderick) experienced the many vagaries of World War II military training in Universal's *Biloxi Blues*, the Brooklynite quickly realized, "It's hot. It's like Africa hot. Tarzan couldn't take this kind of hot." In a more somber mood, Columbia's *A Soldier's Story* told the unusual tale of violence, strife, and murder at a segregated training base. In CBS's *Too Young the Hero*, teenage idol Rick Schroder portrayed the real-life story of Calvin Graham, a twelve-year-old boy, who, because of his mature looks, hoodwinked navy recruiters, joined this service, and, at Guadalcanal, earned the Purple Heart. Later, after some military mix-up, he was imprisoned until everything straightened out in this made-for-television photodrama.

MGM's *Maria's Lovers* showcased the problems a returning POW (John Savage) encountered when his marriage unraveled in this sudsy, domestic melodrama. In war-torn London, Columbia's *Hope and Glory* looked at the blitz through the eyes of a nine-year-old boy (Sebastian Rice-Edwards) who imagined only fantasy and games as Luftwaffe bombs dropped near his parents' home. Village Roadshow's *Rebel* revealed more problems of the heart when a wounded American marine (Matt Dillon), recuperating in an Australian hospital, fell for a local singer, tiptoed away from a military infirmary, and moved in with the comely chanteuse. Eventually, the young leatherneck saw the light and, in a moment of reconciliation, returned to his outfit. Sometimes human emotions superseded the combat experience. TriStar Pictures' *Every Time We Say Goodbye* told the unusual situation of an idealist American flyer (Tom Hanks) who joined the RAF months before Pearl Harbor and, after some complicated adventures, wound up in a Jerusalem hospital, convalescing from a leg injury. Soon, he was romantically involved with a devout Jewish girl, but as the son of a pacifist Protestant minister, the religious differences presented numerous obstacles for a permanent relationship. In another lost-love episode, United Artists' *Captive Hearts* belabored the unlikely story of an army flyer (Chris Makepeace) who parachuted from an exploding B-25 into an isolated northern Japan region. Quickly apprehended by nearby villagers, the next few days included making friends with locals, repairing a dilapidated roof, demonstrating basic baseball rules to children, staying clear of an overage militarist, learning some falcon commands, and, finally, falling for a pretty widow, who quickly turned him into mush. Eventually, the village patriarch (Pat Morita), spotting Japanese forces nearby, trekked him to the Sea of Japan, found a small boat, and pointed to the China coast. Now, in the sudsiest of farewells, the crestfallen lovers, realizing they were "two countries, one heart," stared lugubriously at the water, fully aware, as the torch song prophesized, they may never meet again.

A few titles examined the antipodean aspect of the war. In Fauna Productions' *Attack Force Z*, some fast-moving Australian commandos, spearheaded by Captain Mel Gibson, landed on a well-guarded Japanese island, moved inland, and rescued survivors of a recent plane crash before top-secret information fell into enemy hands. With Sam Neill as the radio operator, this low-budget production reminded audiences that Anzac forces played an integral part in the victory effort. Belinon Productions' *Emma's War* examined an Australian family's difficulties revolving around a father fighting in New Guinea, a fourteen-year-old daughter's coming-of-age in a boarding school, a mother coping with separation, and a conchie (conscientious objector) trying to maintain his beliefs, especially after the Japanese bombed Sydney. Lee Remick starred in this domestic potboiler. Suatu Film's *Death of a Soldier* portrayed the negative side of the U.S. military justice system, when a mentally deranged GI was expeditiously executed for local murders. Loosely based on the Brownout Strangler incidents, this storyline portrayed MacArthur as an imperious officer, lacking remorse or forgiveness. Another screenplay depicting the five-star commander's influence, *The Last Bastion*, wove in and out of historical events and famous personages gathered in Sydney and their various roles, both defensive and offensive, against the Japanese.

Frequently, Hollywood producers opted for laughs, pratfalls, and contretemps, using the war as a convenient backdrop. In an offbeat take suggesting that the Pacific war resembled nothing more than a balmy day at the beach, Universal's remake of *Operation Petticoat* offered one gag after another when some smiling nurses came aboard a submarine operating in the Pacific theater, repeating most of the shenanigans found in the 1959 original. In this version John Austin and Richard Gilliland copycatted the Cary Grant and Tony Curtis roles in a harmless romp that included a buxom nurse blocking a narrow walkway, a smooth-as-glass ensign bird-dogging needed supplies, and, of course, an inadvertent pink paint job on the underwater vessel's hull. Another remake of an established war comedy, Fox's *To Be or Not to Be*, spoofed the Third Reich's expansion policies, mimicking Hitler when a group of Polish actors, plotting an escape from Warsaw, created a theatrical diversion and, after some fancy legerdemain, sang a few bawdy songs (including an anachronistic Pakistan reference), impersonated the führer, and finally, after a bouncy Mack Sennett car chase, flew off to freedom. With Mel Brooks and Anne Bancroft re-creating the Jack Benny and Carole Lombard 1942 roles, this 1983 screenplay rehashed much of the earlier dialogue, including Hitler's phony tantrum, "All I want is peace. Peace! Peace! A little piece of Poland, a little piece of France."

Likewise, Universal's frolic spoofing patriotism, *1941*, ran amok with its burlesque of stateside fears and widespread paranoia hours after the Pearl Harbor attack, when many West Coast residents, certain that Japanese warships were in their harbors, resorted to numerous schemes to repel these invaders. Highlighting Dan Aykroyd, Ned Betty, and Treat Williams in featured roles, this entire lark resembled the monkey business found at fraternity parties, including the madcap antics of John Belushi, who as Air Corps pilot Wild Bill Kelso flew aimlessly over the California skies proclaiming, "I've been chasing a Jap squadron for a day and a half. I lost 'em somewhere over Fresno." Another made-for-laughs title, Pimlico's *Escape to Athene*, depicted the playful adventures of some Allied POWs (Elliott Gould, David Niven, Richard Roundtree, and Sonny Bono) stashed away in a Greek island prison and their frequent fooling around with the commandant (Roger Moore). With one gag after another, including references to the greed associated with British imperialism, a quick spoof of B-Westerns, and a take on future Volkswagen sales, this film purported that the Nazi control of Greece, another dark episode of the war, resembled nothing more than a Sunday afternoon picnic.

In a similar vein, but back on home soil, Universal's made-for-television mistaken-identity gag, *Don't Push, I'll Charge When I'm Ready*, recapped the oddball adventures of an Italian POW (Enzo Cerusico) who—following one misunderstanding after another—was drafted into Uncle Sam's army. Another popcorn production, Empire's *Zone Troopers*, pushed World War II verisimilitude to its limit when a group of GIs, squirreled away in the Italian foothills from encroaching *Wehrmacht* troops, located an extraterrestrial ship and quickly struck up a friendly relationship with the funny-looking inhabitants. Soon these two groups teamed up, and within minutes, using their ray guns, routed their adversaries. With Tim Thomerson and Biff Manard in the main roles, the eighty-eight-minute put-on resembled those Saturday-afternoon cliffhangers popular during the 1930s and 1940s.

Another 1940s parody, Universal's *Dead Men Don't Wear Plaid*, rounded up numerous clips from well-known film noir classics—including *The Big*

An unnamed, friendly alien, whose flying saucer recently landed in the Italian countryside, offers his "hands" in camaraderie to American GIs in Danny Bilson's science-fictional romp Zone Troopers. *Courtesy of Empire Pictures.*

Sleep, Sorry, Wrong Number, Johnny Eager, and *Suspicion*—and incorporated these short segments into a storyline that placed a Los Angeles gumshoe (Steve Martin) one step behind a Nazi spy ring operating in his hometown, even though a field marshal's plan "to wipe out hunger, by aging cheese faster" seemed innocuous. Another spoof, Paramount's *Top Secret*, took numerous swipes at the many World War II B-quickies in an updated screenplay. Instead of swastika-wearing Nazis and banzai-spouting Japanese lurking in every frame, the 1984 villain, the East German Communists, were outfoxed by an American rock-and-roll singer (Val Kilmer). In a continuation of these parodies, an outlandish Harrison Ford played the flamboyant adventurer, erudite professor, and international roamer, Indiana Jones, in three running-wild romps, *Raiders of the Lost Ark, Indiana Jones and the Temple of Doom*, and *Indiana Jones and the Last Crusade*. In all these moving pictures, the famous archeologist butted heads with numerous Third Reich officers and their minion sheikhs, quipping, "Nazis. I hate these guys."

Once in a while, Hollywood drifted into la-la land. Vista's low-budget *The Lucifer Complex* told the aftermath of a 1986 nuclear war where deep in the South American jungle, escaped Nazi leaders, under Adolf Hitler's command, cloned numerous American officials hoping to disrupt the recovery period. With Kenneth Wynn, Robert Vaughn, Leo Gordon, and Aldo Ray in leading roles, the entire mishmash, replete with one loose end after another, drifted aimlessly, even though the führer bragged, "The Fourth Reich continues to move forward." Fox's *The Boys from Brazil* entered the same science fiction realm when an escaped Nazi doctor, Josef Mengele (Gregory Peck), now hiding in Paraguay, bred ninety-four identical Hitler clones—hoping to resurrect a new Reich—and reminded a charge, "You are the duplicate of the greatest man in history." His plans, likewise, were wrecked by Lawrence Olivier, an aged Simon Wiesenthal–type Nazi hunter.

When the 1980s came to a close, the Hollywood World War II motion picture still attracted many admirers who applauded America's fighting men leaping out of Higgins boats, running inland, and blasting their foes from their pillboxes, even though most of these viewers cheered from their living-room sofas. With their red-white-and-blue credo, frontal attacks, and hand-to-hand fighting, these screenplays highlighted major victories and recalled glorious moments from recent history. Why wouldn't they? For many young men, these cinematic adventures provided vicarious thrills about a global war that produced straightforward heroes, indisputable issues, and discernible foes.

With its ups and downs, vacillating ideologies, and skewed revisionism, these war films, in one form or another, offered tangible proof of the nation's prowess. For Hollywood this was reassuring news. But one thing seemed certain. In a few years, elaborate semicentennial celebrations would venerate this victory. Why not? Almost fifty years ago the nation's youth fought overseas, and now it was time to revere these aging veterans. And, how should the film industry join the commemoration? The answer seemed simple enough. Keep producing more spectacular motion pictures portraying U.S. forces defeating the Axis scourge. After all, as the popular song proclaimed, "Everybody loves a winner." Conversely, the lyrics continued, "But when you lose, you lose alone."

Chapter Seven

Going, Going, Gone!
Cable Television Explains the War

1990–2007

"Most people gaze neither into the past nor the future, they explore neither truth nor lies, they gaze at the television."—Czech pastor Daniel Vedra, observing his countrymen's reaction to the Communist breakdown, in Ivan Klima's 1997 novel, *The Ultimate Intimacy*

Sometime in the 1980s—an exact date is impossible to pin down—the videocassette recorder emerged as a dominant force in most American living rooms. With two competing formats (Beta and VHS), sales of this popular electronic device soared, and by decade's end over 70 percent of all households could watch their favorite motion pictures at home, either by renting titles at local stores or taping a movie from the airwaves. For many viewers this was the ideal way to enjoy a popular photodrama, even though the setup process, for the all-thumbs crowd, seemed cumbersome. Seizing on this national "problem," president George H. W. Bush—in a moment of executive levity—prophesized that by 1990 all Americans would know how to program their VCRs.

Even with its meteoric rise—by the mid 1990s many children watched VCRs in their bedrooms—this exciting technology suffered the same fate as its electronic cousins, the 78s, LPs, and 45s—when a better mousetrap appeared, the digital video disc, a compact recording that offered a sharper picture. Dubbed the DVD (since most adults associated the initials VD to mean venereal disease, the manufacturers added the superfluous letter D to steer clear of any ambiguity), sales of this equipment took off, and by 2006 the VCR, like scratch cakes, all-cotton socks, letterpress, and local bookstores, faded from the national landscape.

Hollywood, of course, moved quickly to adapt to this expanding technology. Realizing the financial impact at the box office, the moguls recognized they could sell current releases or, for greater profit, delve into their elaborate

libraries and copy motion pictures onto this format. Naturally, factory-pro-
duced movies, first on tape and later on disc, proved popular, and consumers
bought them by the handfuls. For the first time in cinema history, viewers—
instead of heading to a theater—could own (or rent) their favorite titles and
leisurely watch them. As expected, World War II dramas remained high on the
sales chart. Why wouldn't they? Ever since Pearl Harbor, these photodramas
with their red-white-and-blue endings offered tangible reminders of victory.

And what better place to show victory than France's western coastline,
where on June 6, 1944, American troops landed on Omaha Beach, ran many
yards inland, reached a tenuous seawall, and—following deadly setbacks—
destroyed the Axis bunkers, securing a wide area? Soon additional men and
matériel poured ashore and within hours, General Eisenhower announced
that, after months of logistical planning, Allied forces were on French soil.

With this historic invasion as its backdrop, DreamWorks Pictures produced
an elaborate photodrama recreating the D-Day invasion as seen through the
eyes of a small infantry squad. Directed by Steven Spielberg, *Saving Private
Ryan* expanded the boundaries of combat films with its graphic portrayal of
death, destruction, and mayhem. Probably no other Hollywood screenplay
has ever equaled the first twenty-eight minutes of this motion picture for its
realism, pathos, and horror as U.S. troops struggled forward, desperately trying to grab a foothold on Fortress Europe.

In the early hours of June 6, as hundreds of Higgins boats lumbered
through the turbulent Normandy waters toward the French coastline, one
Ranger squad stared apprehensively from their small landing craft, pondering
the next few minutes. Under the command of Captain John Miller (Tom
Hanks), these men were frightened, nauseous, and bewildered by the looming
beachfront. Suddenly, the navy driver yelled, "Thirty seconds, God be with
ya." Moments later the ramp dropped, but immediately scores of bullets entered the hull, killing and wounding the startled GIs. From their hilltop advantage, German soldiers, firing incessantly at this vulnerable landing craft,
seem indestructible. American bodies quickly filled the small boat.

"Over the side," the captain yelped, and terrified infantrymen plunged into
deep water. Some died instantly, killed by stray bullets. A few, unable to un-
tangle themselves from heavy gear, drowned, but a handful reached the surface and crawled onto the beach. Dead bodies strewed the water's edge as
American soldiers dropped rapidly from German machine-gun fire. Arms,
legs, heads, torsos, and intestines bobbled in the surf. Expiring GIs cried out
for their mothers or called upon patron saints. Some soldiers exploded from
artillery shells, others were immolated. Everywhere death and destruction assaulted the moviegoers' senses, echoing Henry V's observation, "Those who
die in battle do not die well."

Sidestepping this carnage, the squad finally regrouped, reached a small seawall, and following Captain Miller's orders, "Let's get back into the war," charged uphill, routing Axis defenders from their fortified lairs. Slowly, the tide changed as additional GIs joined the fray. Now, dead Germans lined the hillside as American forces plunged upward. Moving quickly, angry infantrymen killed anyone in their path, while their captain watched reflectively. For this small squad, this moment of triumph, a bittersweet victory, seemed tempered by the hundreds of American bodies scattered on Omaha Beach. Slowly panning across this deadly landscape, director Spielberg's camera lugubriously zoomed downward, pausing at water's edge on one isolated soldier. A name was stenciled on the fallen man's musette bag. This dead soldier was Sean Ryan.

Two days later, standing in his Washington, D.C., office, General George C. Marshall listened attentively to a report about an unusual casualty situation. Two brothers, Sean and Peter Ryan, were killed on Omaha and Utah Beaches, while a third, Daniel Ryan, died the previous week in New Guinea. For the army's chief of staff this news was exasperating because a fourth son, James Ryan, parachuted behind enemy lines on June 6, his status unknown. Recalling Abraham Lincoln's letter to a mother who lost five sons during the Civil War, the four-star general spoke bluntly, "If this boy's alive, we are going to send somebody to find him."

Back in France, Captain Miller heard his orders: select seven men, travel quickly into the Normandy countryside, locate Private James Ryan, and return him to headquarters for immediate deployment to the zone of interior. A few hours later, one GI in this small squad, miles from the safety of their front lines, grumbled openly, badmouthing the mission's logic. "You wanna explain the math of this to me? Where's the sense of risking the lives of eight of us to save one guy?" In a facetious tone, Captain Miller retorted, "Our duty as soldiers! We all have orders — we have to follow them." With this command, the Rangers trekked inland. After a few diversions — that included fighting in a village, locating the wrong James Ryan, attacking an Axis radar station, incurring two combat deaths, and destroying an SS armored truck — the Rangers finally found Private James Francis Ryan, from Iowa, holed up in an abandoned town, ready, with his platoon, to blow a strategic bridge. Quietly, Captain Miller explained his assignment. "Our orders are to bring you back." Somewhat shaken, but firm, the young paratrooper balked. "I have my orders too, Sir, they don't include me abandoning my post."

Now what? Should the straight-arrow field officer pull his rank, assert his authority, and order Ryan back, or did the GI have a point? Should they hold their position or return to the beachfront? After some soul-searching, Captain Miller issued new directives, "Disperse, you know what to do." This order needed no explanation. His troops were not leaving. For Miller, this change of heart reiterated his credo that their "objective was to win the War." German soldiers soon attacked, and, after a fierce battle, the GIs held the town. But one casualty stood out. Captain Miller—the man who once taught Ralph Waldo Emerson to high school students—had fallen on the bridge, another dead soldier miles from his Pennsylvania home. As for Private Ryan, he remained unscathed and now was heading back to his Iowa farm. For him, the war was over.

An elaborate motion picture, *Saving Private Ryan* touched every human emotion. No viewer could remain oblivious to the horrific opening scene in which untold American bodies permeated the Normandy beachfront, or a follow-up sequence back in the nation's capital, where speedy typists prepared thousand of condolence letters informing families about their sons' combat deaths, or a few scenes later when a clergyman quietly appeared in Mrs. Ryan's doorway. Clearly, the cost for the Normandy victory was immeasurable. As for the mission, the search for Private Ryan brought out the best about America. Following General Marshall's directive, no mother should bear an unreasonable burden. With soft-spoken references to the Sullivan brothers' tragedy (these five sailors, who perished on the USS *Juneau*, came from Iowa; likewise, Private Ryan was from Iowa), the senior officer's words resounded, "We are going to get him the hell out of there."

Certainly director Spielberg stretched a point here—logistically, accurate Normandy casualty information could not reach Washington the next day—but this embellishment created the storyline. With subtle elements of Fox's *The Fighting Sullivans* and *A Walk in the Sun*, this motion picture—a classic retelling of the World War II squad story—reiterated why combat men bonded, protected, and, occasionally, died in each other's arms. As for finding Private Ryan, perhaps Captain Miller had the right idea: "Ah, Ryan. I don't know anything about Ryan. I don't care. The man means nothing to me. It's just a name. You know if finding him so that he can go home—if that earns me the right to get back to my wife, then that's my mission."

Other soldiers fighting the Axis also wanted to see their friends and family. Beacon's *A Midnight Clear* recalled the adventures of six GIs from an intelligence squad, tiptoeing around the Ardennes Forest during the December 1944 Battle of the Bulge. Soon, these Americans ran into some young Germans, but instead of firing their weapons, the two sides pitched snowballs back and forth in a playful, schoolboy manner, suggesting that war—a concept created by elderly statesmen but fought by much younger people—was really a game. Basically an antiwar allegory, the photodrama downplayed all heroics but instead disparaged various officers for their callous behavior, allowing a sergeant (Ethan Hawke) to complain, "Nobody in the army ever admits that someone on our side is killed. They're either lost, like Christopher Robin, hit, as in a batter hit by a pitched ball, or they get 'it' like in hide-and-go-seek."

In sharp contrast, another portrayal of a cold December 1944 offensive, HBO's *When Trumpets Fade*, steered wide of allegory but, instead, graphically re-created the horrendous Battle of Hurtgen Forest, a confrontation in which American casualties rose every hour. With Ron Eldard in the starring role as a skeptical GI, quickly promoted to sergeant and then lieutenant, this made-for-television drama reiterated that most soldiers considered survival, not patriotism, their primary goal, echoing their leader's words, "If I can help in any way without endangering my life, I won't hesitate." A parallel storyline, with close ties to *Kelly's Heroes*, Carnaby International's *The Last Drop* recounted the misadventures of Allied soldiers, dropped behind Dutch lines during the Market Garden offensive to retrieve stolen art treasures before the Germans shipped this booty to Berlin. With Captain Billy Zane piloting the glider, "Everything," he quipped, "was on a need-to-know basis," even though two rogue Nazis were after the same plunder.

In a similar vein, Anthem Pictures' *The Fallen* focused on the October 1944 northern Italian campaign, where Axis and American troops cautiously eyed each other's movements. Loosely modeled on *The Young Lions*, this four-tier storyline reflected both sides' hopes and fears. Certainly, these ambivalent days created unprecedented problems: the ragtag German soldiers, with a handful of Italian soldiers, facing certain defeat, struggled to maintain discipline while the local partisans bickered about the merits of communism versus fascism, promising, "One day, all wars would be fought on chessboards." On the other side, the GIs—determined to stay out of harm's way—waited apprehensively, not wanting to be the last casualty.

But some Americans were less fortunate. Go Films' *Saints and Soldiers* re-created the December 1944 Malmedy Massacre where dozens of GIs—captured during the Battle of the Bulge—were machine-gunned by German soldiers near a small Belgian town. During the confusion, four infantrymen darted into the woods and for a few days dodged enemy patrols, always fearful, as one airborne sergeant warned, "They're shooting prisoners." With no weapons and little food, the foot soldiers eked out a precarious existence until a rescued British pilot, clutching a map folder, revealed he was "in possession of some crucial intelligence" and needed help. Many close calls followed this haggard group, but their luck ran out near their front lines after *Wehrmacht* forces killed three members. Following another skirmish, the two lone survivors, evading Nazi bullets, stumbled into the Allied camp, delivering the needed information. With numerous biblical, mystical, and ontological references, this ninety-minute screenplay also downplayed heroics, suggesting in an unobtrusive way that survival, a basic human instinct, was the GI's only credo.

Certain screenplays, of course, depicted the global conflict in elaborate, almost mythical proportions. DreamWorks' ten-part, made-for-television homage to a single company from the elite 101st Airborne, *Band of Brothers*, placed these men under a microscope by retelling their three-year odyssey, beginning with the unit's formation, through numerous major campaigns, until the joyous V-E Day celebration. In a 705-minute tribute, this all-volunteer group experienced every human emotion—apprehension, angst, vigilance, vengeance, euphoria, exultation, triumph, and, of course, death—testifying to the cohesive spirit that centuries earlier bonded Shakespeare's Henry V, "We few, we happy few, we happy band of brothers."

Beginning in the hot 1942 Georgia sun, a disparate group of inexperienced army men, eager for adventure and the extra allotment, worked assiduously, hoping to earn the coveted paratrooper insignia, an emblem awarded after five jumps. While this schedule pushed most GIs to their physical limits, their psychological health suffered from the frequently irrational and occasionally sadistic badgering by their commanding officer (David Schwimmer), a blowhard first lieutenant seemingly bent on proving himself. After weeks of hard training—and with some encouragement from a second lieutenant (Damian Lewis)—these newly appointed troopers bonded into the Easy Company of the 506th Regiment, realizing, as one GI exclaimed, "It don't matter where we go—once we get into combat, the only person you can trust is yourself and the fellow next to you."

Now for the war. After a cramped Atlantic crossing, Easy Company reached their English countryside base where the training intensified. Then, on the evening of June 4, the troopers geared up, ready to mount their C-47s for their invasion drop, while the company sergeant waggishly reminded his pals, "If you did not sign your GI life insurance policy, go over to Headquarters Company. Boys, don't let your families miss out on $10,000." Then the stand-down order arrived: no takeoff tonight. But the next night, all was ready. Easy Company boarded their aircraft, slid into their bucket seats, and as the carrier plane gained altitude heading for France, each man sat taut, backpedaling unknown fears.

Suddenly explosives filled the skies as German ack-ack bursts forced the troopers to hook up, stand by the door, and, as flames engulfed their aircraft, make an early jump. Now on French soil, the men of Easy Company—scattered over many miles—fought Germans, bumped into French nationals, and finally regrouped as a cohesive unit. With an operational command post delegating orders, the fast-moving squad, sensing that *Wehrmacht* forces were everywhere, stood ready to fight. Soon, they attacked an Axis weapons post and, after a fierce battle, destroyed their artillery, allowing safe access for the GIs who were storming the beaches eight miles away. With this initial victory, a stark reality emerged. Easy Company—created two years earlier with a group of green, rough-and-ready volunteers, high-spirited lads who boasted the world was their oyster—suffered its first casualties. Two men were dead and others wounded.

As an elaborate motion picture, based on Stephen Ambrose's best-selling book and utilizing fourteen directors, *Band of Brothers* downplayed flag-waving histrionics and, instead, focused on each trooper's hopes and dreams, fears and aspirations, strengths and weaknesses, in a subdued manner that allowed the group's heroism to speak for itself. For the next eleven months this unit fought at Carentan, Market Garden, and Bastogne, suffering unbearable casualties. During these encounters myriad problems and personalities emerged: one officer turned into an alcoholic while another lieutenant fell apart during enemy shelling, became mute, and was quickly relieved. A third officer became a one-man show, firing his machine gun from the hip, charging German fortifications. Enlisted men died regularly from explosives or sniper shots while ammunition, clean uniforms, and hot meals never materialized. Even the winter weather, the coldest in recent years, offered more headaches because of inadequate protective clothing. Untried replacements created added concerns because these men were either cocky or naive, unaccustomed to warfare's nuances. And sometimes, in moments of expediency, Americans shot German prisoners. Once, a U.S. captain, realizing the dangers of a nighttime patrol, fudged a morning report, claiming the nonexistent reconnaissance produced negative results.

Finally, Allied forces crossed the Rhine, and within weeks the German military collapsed, revealing unbelievable horror for Easy Company when they liberated a concentration camp, staring at the hollow-eyed, near-dead inmates. Many of these hardened paratroopers simply stared in disbelief, unable to comprehend Hitler's Final Solution, pondering the evil forces that created such despair. Even their captain looked confused: "The locals claimed that they never knew the camps existed—they say we [the Americans] are exaggerating." Days later, the men raced toward their victory prize, the führer's exclusive Bavarian hideaway, Eagle's Nest.

Why shouldn't this battle-worn group receive the lion's share? After all, one officer observed, Easy Company's goal was "to move the ball forward, one yard at a time," and ignore vulnerabilities. "We're paratroopers, we're supposed to be surrounded." But not everything worked out well. A junior officer, who landed in Normandy and suffered many close calls, waved his Dear John letter, moaning, "My wife is divorcing me. She's taking everything, taking the house, taking the kid, taking the dog." As for the notifications of combat deaths, that, too, was never pleasant, requiring proper comportment: "You tell them [the families] what you always tell them. Their sons died as heroes." And, unfortunately, that rate was high. Easy Company's attrition stood as a grim but tangible reminder of this group's achievements. As reiterated by

A paratroop officer (Neal McDonough) examines his options before ordering his squad onto a French roadway in HBO's testimony to the men of Easy Company, 506th Regiment, 101st Airborne, Band of Brothers. *Courtesy of HBO.*

a surviving member, interviewed in the late nineties for this motion picture, "I treasure my remark to a grandson who asked, Grandpa, were you a hero in the war? No, I answered, but I served in a company of heroes."

Every branch of service contained its own peril. Warner Bros. airborne saga *Memphis Belle* focused closely on the exploits of the first B-17 crew to fly the enviable twenty-fifth mission in the European theater. With Matthew Modine in the pilot's seat, this arduous flight from the bucolic English countryside to the

German port city of Bremen contained one hazard after another as Axis ack-ack blanketed the skies, and Luftwaffe fighters attacked furiously. Finally, the aircraft reached its target, and the crew—inspired by their captain's words, "If we don't drop these bombs right in the pickle barrel there are going to be a lot of innocent people killed,"—released the explosives. Following hours of white-knuckle situations, the aircraft landed safely at its home base.

The high seas presented similar risks. Castle Hill's *Proud* recounted the adventures of the first all-black destroyer crew that manned the USS *Mason* during the ship's many perilous Atlantic crossings at the height of Nazi wolf-pack attacks. Told in flashback by a surviving member (Ozzie Davis), this Eleanor Roosevelt experiment proved that black enlistees were capable and loyal mariners, men who would not flinch from duty. Reminiscing about this experience—over fifty years later—the words of a crewman said it all: "This is my land, I defended it, and the 160 Black men on the USS *Mason* defended it too!"

Over in North Africa, Allied soldiers fought tenaciously. Showtime's *Sahara* starred James Belushi as the tough-talking tank commander (Humphrey Bogart's role in the 1943 production), who with a handful of Allied soldiers prevented hundreds of haggard Nazis from obtaining needed water at an isolated desert well. Completely outnumbered, Belushi regularly taunted the Germans by suggesting his small group could drink and bathe all day long, boasting to a Nazi major that he was not "the guy with a bunch of casualties lying around for the buzzards to pick." In a different vein, Paramount's *Enemy at the Gates* examined the Stalingrad siege where Red Army and *Wehrmacht* forces collided while—off in their private war—two sharpshooters, one Russian (Jude Law), the other German (Ed Harris), trained their scopes across no-man's-land, hoping to locate their adversary. With an opening scene similar to *Saving Private Ryan*, the photodrama clearly explained how this battle became a turning point, even though an explanatory map depicted Switzerland as a recent Nazi conquest.

Wartime, of course, produced convoluted intelligence missions. Ecosse Films' *Charlotte Grey* lauded a heroic Scottish woman (Cate Blanchett), who in 1943 parachuted into France as a Resistance operative but spent much time searching for her boyfriend, a young airman (Rupert Penry-Jones). Along the way, she encountered local collaborationists, numerous infightings, and Communist sympathizers. Canal+'s *A Woman at War* recounted the harrowing adventures of a Belgian loyalist (Martha Plimpton), who became a translator for the Gestapo and sent privileged information to the underground, even though her lover (Eric Stoltz) was a traitor. Fox's *Shining Through* watched an OSS director (Michael Douglas) move unobtrusively through numerous European capitals gleaning needed war information before the Day of Infamy. After America's entry, his German-speaking secretary (Melanie Griffith)—who passed an arbitrary, ad hoc test, "to stand up, turn around, and close your eyes and tell me everything you see in the room," even though a fifty-star U.S. flag adorned the office—entered the Fatherland, and, following some comic-strip adventures, slithered into Nazi headquarters, photographed classified documents, and, with her supervisor's help, finally reached Switzerland.

Intermedia Films' *Enigma* glossed over the complex work of the Bletchley Park British code breakers, who, after much trial and error, unraveled the secrets of the German ENIGMA box, an intricate device used to relay messages between commands. Working day and night, a top-notch mathematician (Dougray Scott) finally cracked the Nazi permutations, even though "The machine has a hundred and fifty million, million, million ways of doing it, according to how you set these three rotors, and how you connect these plugs." With a new girlfriend at his side (Kate Winslet), the twosome, in a surreal subplot, stumbled upon top-secret Soviet information about the infamous Katyn Forest massacre, where Russian soldiers slaughtered most of the Polish officers corps. Loosely based on the life of famed cryptologist Alan Turing, the storyline adeptly sidestepped any mention of his homosexuality, persecution, and eventual suicide. Two other screenplays used this German machine as their fulcrum. Universal's *U-571* detailed the adventures of some U.S. sailors on a search-and-seize mission, who boarded a U-boat, overpowered the crew, and seized a code box. With Matthew McConaughey leading this American assault team, the bluejackets moved quickly to secure their prize and, for good measure, torpedoed a Nazi destroyer.

Another screenplay, Artisan Entertainment's *In Enemy Hands*, pushed credibly to the edge of space when a group of U.S. seamen—drifting helplessly in the Atlantic—were rescued by a benevolent U-boat commandant who, contrary to Hitler's take-no-prisoners policy, offered sanctuary. Then, in a surprising volte-face, the commandant requested help operating the submarine, because a runaway meningitis epidemic had crippled his crew. With basic survival at stake, this symbiotic relationship reached the straining point when, above the waves, Allied and German vessels battled. With an American victory in sight, the U.S. chief (William Macy), as a benevolent gesture, looked the other way as the Nazi officer destroyed the ENIGMA machine, rationalizing, "A promise is a promise." As a 2004 revisionist fairy tale, the entire motion picture sugarcoated every aspect of the Third Reich's brutal open-seas policy, pathetically suggesting that Nazi officers acted chivalrously in the Atlantic Theater.

The fight against Germany continued in other formats. Fine Line Features' black comedy, *Mother Night*, based on Kurt Vonnegut's novel, told the strange story of an American playwright, Howard Campbell (Nick Nolte), who married a German actress, moved to Berlin, and—dismayed by National Socialism—returned to New York. Quietly recruited by U.S. intelligence officers for espionage work, a handler politely warned him, "Your role will remain classified and Uncle Sam's official position is you're the scum of the earth." During the War, his daily anti-Semitic, anti-American radio broadcasts—employing an intricate system of pauses and coughs—contained valuable information for the Allies. After V-E Day, he slipped back into New York City, where he lived uneventfully for fifteen years until Mossad agents arrived in 1961 and, after some fancy maneuvering, spirited their prized war criminal to Israel. Now, sitting alone in a spartan cell, abandoned by everyone, he chatted amicably with Adolf Eichmann, another prisoner awaiting trial.

In a different vein, Butcher's Run Films' *The Man Who Captured Eichmann* praised the Israeli intelligence service that finally uncovered the highranking Nazi responsible for much of the Holocaust, Adolf Eichmann, who fled to Argentina in April 1945 and lived furtively for fifteen years under an assumed name. With Robert Duvall in the starring role, this made-for-television production glamorized the diligence of these agents—hardened men who patiently eyed their target, seized him off the street at an opportune moment, and, finally, returned him to Israel. Another spy screenplay, Miramax's multilayer tale of romance and intrigue, *The English Patient*, recounted the comings and goings of a Hungarian count (Ralph Fiennes), who in prewar Egypt flew over the desert, ostensibly taking photographs for a geographical society but, in reality, preparing maps for the English military. Now ensconced in a Tuscan hospital, a horribly burned combat victim unable to move, he slowly assembled segments from the past, including an adulterous relationship with a fellow-pilot's wife. Similarly, Remstar Films' *Head in the Clouds* involved the playful experiences of three friends—a Spanish Civil War nurse, a French Resistance operative, and a Nazi colonel's mistress—who frivolously experiment in some 1944 Paris ménage à trois escapades, hoping to escape from the political realities unfolding around them.

Sometimes the Italian and German forces flaunted their political differences. Universal's *Captain Corelli's Mandolin* re-created the tense mood when both armies occupied a small Greek island. Initially formal to each other, the German commandant soon locked horns with an Italian officer (Nicolas Cage) about his lackadaisical approach to military discipline and obvious interest in food, wine, music, and women. But the happy-go-lucky captain shrugged off the Nazi's complaint. "I have always found something in life worth singing about and for that I cannot apologize." However, Mussolini's departure changed everything, and now both sides battled each other. With Penélope Cruz appearing as the village beauty and, eventually, the sweetheart of the strutting, mandolin-playing captain, the storyline sugarcoated Italy's Axis Pact role, suggesting this nation was, basically, an unwilling participant. One anachronistic scene—a June 1944 radio announcement that Rome had fallen and Italy surrendered—missed its mark by almost nine months, since the Italian government capitulated in September 1943 and one month later declared war against Germany. Consequently, a good part of this screenplay was historically inaccurate.

In a lighthearted mood, Hallmark's *In Love and War* recounted the youthful adventures of the popular travel writer Eric Newby (Callum Blue) who—in 1943, as a British lieutenant—was captured by the Italians, placed in an orphanage-turned-prison, flirted with local women, and finally escaped, hiding in a nearby village with an antifascist's daughter. As a Sunday-night feature produced by a popular greeting card company, the entire screenplay depicted most Italians as totally inept fighters, solely interested in finding some vestiges of *la dolce vita.*

Life in occupied countries contained its fair share of uncertainties. In a slightly upbeat tone, Blue Wolf Productions' *Jakob the Liar* told the story of a mild-mannered shopkeeper (Robin Williams), living in an unnamed Polish ghetto amid suicide and depression, and his uncanny ability to spread phony news reports from a "secret" radio, creating a sliver of optimism for his doomed neighbors. Hollywood Pictures' *Swing Kids* recalled the problems some German students—all fans of American swing music, British fashions, and Harlem slang—endured, including their ongoing conflicts with the Hitler Youth brigades, when the Third Reich banned these decadent foreign influences. With Frank Whaley as a long-haired teenager enamored of the exuberant sounds of Benny Goodman and Count Basie, his disdain toward political issues was obvious: "No one who likes swing can become a Nazi."

The New Order disrupted everything. Stillking Film's *The Ring* rekindled the arduous struggle of a young German woman (Nastassja Kinski), who was separated from her family, imprisoned by the Nazis, released, and finally married a *Wehrmacht* officer. Then, in 1945, after the Russians entered Berlin and killed her husband, she fled to America hoping to find her family. Based on a best-selling Danielle Steele novel, this made-for-television soap opera, filmed in various locations, restated the emotional problems that nations experienced during this global upheaval. In a similar heartthrob vein, Paramount's *The Garden of Redemption* recalled the inner conflicts of an Italian priest (Anthony LaPaglia), who could mislead SS officers but could not shake off his sexual feelings for a woman in the Resistance.

Castle Hill Productions' *A Day in October* praised the quiet heroism of a Danish family's involvement with the underground movement, smuggling Jewish refugees into neutral Sweden and doing some sabotage work in a munitions plant. Amy International Artists' *That Summer of White Roses* remembered the simple lifestyle of ordinary people in a Yugoslavian riverside resort town and their ordeal when German invaders entered their lives. Hallmark's fairy tale, *Silent Night*, told a dubious 1944 Christmas Eve parable about a German mother and her son who took refuge in a family cabin near the snowy Ardennes' war front. Soon three American GIs jumped into this shelter, and moments later, three lost German soldiers arrived. Initially, the two sides behaved belligerently. One U.S. private (Romano Orzari) bad-mouthed the Axis, "I had a whole life planned until you guys invaded Poland," but eventually the *Mutter*—after some warmhearted yuletide season dialogue—convinced the combatants to halt their differences and share a Christmas dinner. Supposedly based on a true story, much of the storyline overlooked Hitler's expansionism and, instead, suggested that the war could easily be won through kindness and brotherhood.

Motion pictures about the Holocaust overwhelmed every viewer. Another depressing Auschwitz story, Lions Gate Films' *The Grey Zone*, rationalized why a few Jewish prisoners guided inmates into the gas chamber and later disposed of the ashes. With David Arquette in a leading role, this brutal screenplay pushed cinematography to its limits with unremitting scenes of torture and suffering. In somewhat better circumstances, Focus Features' *The Pianist* told the remarkable story of a Polish Jew who, with the help of some underground members and kindhearted friends, survived the war by hiding in various Warsaw locations. Based on the autobiography of Wladyslaw Szpilman, this accomplished musician (Adrien Brody) did everything to save himself, vowing, "If I'm going to die, I prefer to die in my own home." Completely surrounded with deprivation but determined to stay alive at any cost, he managed, with some unexpected good luck, to avoid capture.

Other elaborate made-for-television productions appeared on Sunday-night programming. Avnet/Kerner Productions' *Uprising* recalled the pitiful existence that thousands of Polish Jews—jammed inside Warsaw's old slum district—experienced as hunger and disease routinely claimed many lives. But in April 1943, these hapless victims, realizing that survival was impossible, armed themselves and, for the next thirty days, battled the Axis forces from street barricades, hidden tunnels, and dark cellars. Unable to continue this uprising, they were quickly overrun and subsequently annihilated. With Donald Sutherland as the Jewish Council chairman struggling with Third Reich leaders for leniency ("I try to minimize the damage"), the entire 177-minute docudrama mirrored German brutality. Foxboro Company Productions' *In the Presence of Mine Enemies* offered additional evidence regarding the Warsaw Ghetto. Here, a pacifist rabbi (Armin Mueller-Stahl) watched helplessly as ongoing deprivation and death took its toll in this imprisoned enclave. As a test of faith, he urged tolerance, while his nineteen-year-old son—full of unrealistic expectations—demanded reprisal. With many examples of Nazi cruelty, the screenplay, remaining steadfast to historical reality, retold this sad episode with dignity and clarity.

Other Sunday-night titles reminded viewers about Germany's infamous Final Solution. HBO's *Conspiracy* highlighted the 1942 Wannsee Conference, where fifteen Nazi and SS leaders gathered in a Berlin suburb to resolve what they euphemistically called the Jewish Question. Supervised by Reinhard Heydrich (Kenneth Branagh), these high-ranking officials, comfortably ensconced in a luxurious mansion, lackadaisically decreed that the Jews of Europe, regardless of their age, would be exterminated. In typical bureaucratic manner, Heydrich ordered, "From Lapland to Libya, from Vladivostok to Belfast, no Jews, not one," facetiously reminding his small audience, "Dead women don't get pregnant." Dorothy Pictures' *Anne Frank: The Whole Story* took a slightly different approach than earlier motion pictures about the Amsterdam teenager (Hannah Taylor Gordon) and her world-famous diary portraying the numerous adolescent vagaries associated with growing up—"I like watching people. I make up stories for them"—while her mother, suffering from a midlife crisis of sorts, appeared unhappy with her marriage. After months of confinement in their cramped attic and eventual deaths in the concentration camp, this gloomy drama detailed the poignancy, expectations, and fears of an ordinary family caught up in the throes of Hitler's maddening expansionist policies.

Another agonizing Holocaust story, Leucadia Film Corporation's *Alan and Naomi*, told of the simple maturation of an awkward American Jewish adolescent, Alan (Lukas Haas), living in 1944 Brooklyn, where he routinely played stickball in the crowded Williamsburg neighborhood, while his father, obsessed by the war news, listened to radio programs, studied newspaper reports, and placed colored pins on an international map. When a young, almost catatonic, French refugee, Naomi (Vanessa Zaoui), moved into an upstairs apartment, Alan's mother instructed her son to befriend this new neighbor, explaining the girl's problems stemmed from witnessing her father's brutal death at the hands of storm troopers. Unable to comprehend the girl's reticence, the fourteen-year-old Alan, eager to join his pals on the stickball field, challenged his parents' decision asking, "Why me?" But his father set him straight: "Because you're one of the lucky ones." Soon, Alan befriended the troubled Naomi and, using some ventriloquistic skills, slowly elicited from her those terrible memories of Nazi occupation until a tenuous closeness developed, culminating with an upbeat, this-too-shall-pass message.

Following the German surrender, the Allies denounced former Nazis for their role in perpetrating these atrocities. Alliance's *Nuremberg* detailed the November 1945 courtroom procedures of this international tribunal that levied one charge after another against high-ranking supporters for implementing Hitler's genocidal policies. With numerous concentration-camp newsreel inserts, this made-for-television indictment clearly documented the guilt of the Axis defendants as Chief Justice Robert Jackson (Alec Baldwin) explained point by point each man's participation in these crimes against humanity. His nemesis Reichsmarshal Hermann Göring (Brian Cox), taken aback by these accusations, proffered his own rationalization: "Everything Hitler did before the war was right. One day the German people will remember that." Finally condemned to death, Göring's suicide—he swallowed cyanide hours before his execution—remained mysterious, even though the screenplay suggested that perhaps a U.S. Army guard, out of misplaced loyalty, slipped the prisoner a poisonous ampoule.

Famous personages, always an appealing topic, received their share of made-for-television cinematic history. Gideon Productions' *World War II: When Lions Roar* re-created the November 1943 Tehran Conference when the Big Three—Franklin Delano Roosevelt (John Lithgow), Winston Churchill (Bob Hoskins), and Joseph Stalin (Michael Caine)—discussed, argued, and negotiated many issues vital to the victory effort. With much of the dialogue improvised, this 194-minute docudrama detailed an array of topics, including the upcoming Normandy invasion, Poland's demarcation, and Russia's declaration against Japan. Likewise, A&E's *Ike: Countdown to D-Day* reconstructed the months of intricate planning for Operation Overlord. Here, General Dwight Eisenhower (Tom Selleck) wrestled with thorny logistical and personnel problems, explaining to Winston Churchill, "I'm expendable, you are not," until a misty June evening when he issued the go-order, sending thousands of armed forces onto the French beaches. This biopic captured most of the general's mannerisms, idiosyncrasies, and strategies in a clear and forceful way in spite of many anachronisms: The concept of the jet stream, which began with the B-29 Japan bombings, was not understood or even named by June 1944. The acclaimed British propaganda film *Henry V* (which Ike and his staff viewed in March) was not completed until fall 1944. The Canadian maple-leaf flag insignia (prominently displayed on a Juno beach map) was not operational until 1965. And the famous walk among the airborne troops, where the supreme commander bantered and offered cigarettes, occurred on the evening of June 5, not June 6. Similarly, HBO's *The Gathering Storm* lauded Winston Churchill for his untiring leadership. This time, Albert Finney portrayed the prime minister as a pugnacious optimist, a man who asserted, "Mr. Hitler and his Nazi thugs had better look out. We're going to teach them a lesson that they'll never forget."

Other noteworthy achievements were unearthed years later. Universal's *Schindler's List* praised the real-life story of a German national—whose wartime privileges included drinking, gambling, and womanizing—and his gradual transformation from a greedy materialist to an acknowledged humanitarian, a man who risked everything to save thousands of Polish Jews scheduled for deportation and death. In his characterization of a roué turned altruist, Liam Neeson depicted Oskar Schindler as a complicated individual whose prewar ambitions included becoming a millionaire. Four years later he spent his fortune rescuing Jewish workers while defrauding the Nazis by manufacturing defective munitions, saying, "If this factory ever produces a shell that can actually be fired, I'll be very unhappy." With Ralph Fiennes and Ben Kingsley in supporting roles, the 184-minute, black-and-white, Academy Award Holocaust film paid tribute to one man's triumphs during a nightmare period. As an added acknowledgment, Ardent Productions' *Varian's War* told the quiet story of a New England idealist, Varian Fry (William Hurt)—often called the American Schindler—who unobtrusively smuggled hundreds of Jewish refugees, during the volatile pre–Pearl Harbor days, out of France, via Spain, into the United States.

On the other side of the world, Hollywood explained the Pacific fighting. Touchstone's elaborate 183-minute special-effects version of the December 7 sneak attack, *Pearl Harbor*, detailed the Japanese planning and implementation of that morning's assault, and, as a bonus, provided a goofy American love triangle. Directed by Michael Bay, this storyline traced the friendship of two Tennessee boys, Rafe McCawley (Ben Affleck) and Danny Walker (Josh Hartnett), who enlisted in the Air Corps, graduated from flight school, and were assigned to Colonel Jimmy Doolittle's (Alec Baldwin) squadron. Quickly enamored of nurse Evelyn Johnson (Kate Beckinsale), Lieutenant McCawley left for London, joined the Eagle Squadron, and fought the *Luftwaffe* during the Battle of Britain. Back in Honolulu, American admirals—studying their defensive posture against an air assault—concluded, "Pearl Harbor is too shallow for an aerial torpedo attack, we're surrounded by sub nets. All we have to worry about here is sabotage, so we bunched our planes together to make them easier to protect." Meanwhile, Japanese officers in Tokyo, examining military photographs, concluded that these clustered ships and planes made "perfect targets."

As always, the course of true love never ran smooth. From England came word that Lieutenant McCawley died in an aerial fight. Devastated, the pretty nurse fell into a depression but, a few months later, began a shaky romance with her deceased lover's best friend. After all, one onlooker quipped, "She's gotta be with someone, it might as well be you." As expected—after some moonlight coitus—this couple developed a meaningful relationship, only to learn that Lieutenant McCawley was, in fact, alive and back in Honolulu, arriving on December 6, 1941. What a predicament for the two best friends and their girlfriend.

Personifying the worst of Nazi Germany's Final Solution, a concentration-camp commandant (Ralph Fiennes) stares menacingly at the main yard, pondering the fate of hapless inmates in Steven Spielberg's epic Holocaust production, Schindler's List. *Courtesy of Universal Pictures.*

But a few hours later this problem dissipated as Japanese bombs destroyed most of the Pearl Harbor fleet. Determined to avenge this Day of Infamy, President Roosevelt ordered a Tokyo retaliatory raid. Four months later, Colonel Doolittle led this attack, and (according to Touchstone Pictures) damaged many enemy factories before veering west toward China. At the controls of two B-25s, a couple of Tennessee boyhood friends dropped their bombs, crash-landed on the mainland, fought a Japanese patrol, and later returned to Washington, D.C. Only Captain Danny Walker came home in a casket, a wartime casualty. Soon Captain Rafe McCawley and nurse Evelyn Johnson reconciled, married, and, in a typical Hollywood send-off, lived happily ever after.

Overall, *Pearl Harbor* took many liberties and employed spectacular special effects in retelling America's entry into the Second World War. Japanese aircraft zoomed through the skies, explosives shook the ground, and bombs blew apart naval vessels in such a fashion that, at times, the December 7 attack resembled a cacophonic, computerized pinball-machine game. As for the American airmen, how did they learn to fly different aircraft? Could a fighter pilot simply take over the controls of a bomber? A British Spitfire? Also, what happened to cigarettes? In the smoking-was-glamorous 1940s decade, puffers were everywhere. But in this screenplay no one smoked. Was this for real? Soldiers, sailors, and marines without their nicotine pleasure? Even President Roosevelt—whose famous cigarette holder often graced stateside newspapers—refrained. And what about that I-can-stand scene, where the chief executive rose like Lazarus from his chair without any help from his aides? Was that physically possible?

The war against Japan claimed many Americans. Fries Entertainment's *Mission of the Shark* re-created the worst World War II naval casualty. It was about the USS *Indianapolis*—a seafaring cruiser torpedoed in the Pacific Ocean—and the four-day ordeal of its crew, struggling helplessly in the water as prowling sharks killed dozens of sailors, while back in port, no record of this downing reached headquarters. Eventually rescued by dumb luck, navy commanders, in a heartless manner, moved quickly to assert blame, pointed their fingers at the captain (Stacey Keach) for various policy breaches, and convened a court-martial. Years later, however, at a 1960 shipmates' reunion, this officer received a standing ovation from the survivors, a testimony to his wartime leadership. With many close-ups depicting the savagery of the shark attacks (this entire historical episode—with all its gory details—became a prominent scene in Universal's 1975 summer blockbuster *Jaws*), it seems Kafkaesque that the film company producing this Sunday-night made-for-television drama, like many of its competitors, placed the noun "entertainment" in its trademark.

Two wartime lovers (Kate Beckinsale and Ben Affleck) struggle to maintain a modicum of normalcy against the backdrop of the December 7 sneak attack in Michael Bay's Pearl Harbor. *Courtesy of Touchstone Pictures.*

South Pacific island victories did not come easy. In MGM's *Windtalkers*, a marine sergeant (Nicolas Cage) received a difficult assignment for his unit's impending Saipan invasion. Designated a personal bodyguard for one Navaho code talker, his orders required killing a fellow jarhead—whose esoteric language formed the basis of an intricate message system—rather than allow capture by the Japanese. Fox's *The Thin Red Line* (a remake of Allied Artists' 1964 B-clunker) retold the famous James Jones novel about the army's difficult task of securing Guadalcanal. With Nick Nolte as a gung-ho infantry colonel, the elaborate screenplay provided many frontal assaults as the GIs labored to destroy the Japanese.

Other invasions offered similar risks. Many miles to the north, U.S. Marines landed on a strategic island, Iwo Jima, charged forward, and after weeks of deadly fighting, secured this sulfuric landmass. Originally the subject of the 1949 John Wayne classic, *Sands of Iwo Jima*, this victory uplifted most Americans after a photograph, depicting six Americans raising Old Glory on Mount Suribachi, appeared in daily newspapers. Taken by Joe Rosenthal, this picture made instant heroes of these five marines and one navy corpsman. In 2006, DreamWorks released its interpretation of this famous battle and its aftermath. Directed by Clint Eastwood, *Flags of Our Fathers* detailed the intricate planning, implementation, and success of the invasion, followed by the stateside problems when the three surviving flag raisers embarked on a bond-selling drive.

With Ryan Phillippe, Jesse Bradford, and Adam Beach in leading roles, *Flags of Our Fathers* traced these spirited marines' shipboard preinvasion jitters, the beachfront assault, and the many close calls from Japanese artillery until February 23, 1945, when six men raised a second, much larger American flag on the island's summit, while an Associated Press photographer snapped their picture. By evening's end, three of these Marines were dead. The survivors—after some fancy brass-hat maneuvering—were removed from combat and ordered stateside. Arriving in Washington, D.C., and acclaimed as heroes, the two leathernecks and the bluejacket balked at their accolades but eventually—after a public relations officer moaned, "The last four bond drives came up so short we just printed money"—agreed to appear at rallies. After V-J Day, the threesome took their discharges and returned home. A few years later, Ira Hayes, the Pima Indian who helped raise the Stars and Stripes on a distant island battlefield, died ignominiously in the Arizona sun, a victim of alcohol abuse and wartime guilt.

In retelling this story, director Clint Eastwood pulled out every plug with his stark depictions of beach carnage where marines died violently from explosives, fires, shrapnel, and, later, banzai charges. For the Japanese, the invasion meant American forces were defiling holy ground, since this island, geographically, was part of the mainland. Later, when the three flag raisers toured the States, different problems arose. As a Pima Indian, Ira Hayes endured numerous racial taunts and soon turned to alcohol, while his two pals had other issues. For these three men, their welcome-home-hero reception—with flashbulbs popping, firecrackers crackling, and brass-band music blaring—offered little comfort; instead, all the noise and commotion brought back deadly memories of the Iwo Jima invasion.

Clearly, this motion picture delineated the Iwo Jima fighting in unequivocal terms. On one side, eager American marines, the best of the nation's youth, moved forward to secure this strategic island. Always rough and ready, these leathernecks fought tenaciously, protected each other, and upheld the tenets of semper fidelis. As for their Japanese enemy, that was a different matter. These Japanese soldiers, imbrued with emperor-worship and a medieval death-before-dishonor mentality, mutilated American prisoners, staged numerous banzai assaults, and committed hara-kiri. The advancing marines understood their peril. Be careful at all times. The Japanese attackers wanted to kill Americans.

But a few months later, in December 2006, another motion picture, also directed by Clint Eastwood, took a different look at the Iwo Jima invasion, depicting the Japanese defenders as kind and decent people, helpless pawns in uniform, caught up in the vortex of a war created by militarists so long ago that the reasons seemed obscure, while their nemesis, thousands of offensive American marines, were determined to eradicate every Japanese they saw. Using a predominately Japanese cast, DreamWorks' *Letters from Iwo Jima* portrayed these ill-fated soldiers—waiting for the inevitable arrival of the Western barbarians—as protectors of their emperor and families. Led by a Harvard-educated general (Ken Watanabe), this officer's credo, "I am determined to serve and give my life for my country," provided inspiration for his worn-out battalion, while another shibboleth, "If our children can live safely for one more day it would be worth the one more day that we defend this island," revealed the grim truth.

For these troops, digging trenches, erecting fortifications, enlarging tunnels, and reinforcing cave entrances took their minds off the looming American invasion even though their commander's words, "Our duty is to stop the enemy right here. Do not expect to return home alive," provided little comfort. Farewell letters were written. A few reached the mainland but most never left the island. Decades later, they were unearthed in a bombed-out cave and provided worthy reading. According to the tattered letters, one soldier recalled happy hours working as a baker, another pined for his children, a third remembered his wife's softness, and an officer reminisced about cheerful horseback-riding trips. Overall, these letters limned a Norman Rockwell nation, where thoughtfulness and tenderness, not militarism and aggression, filled the air. Golly!

Swearing to uphold the Bushido creed of death before dishonor, a bemedaled Japanese officer (Ken Watanabe) salutes his beleaguered troops in Clint Eastwood's revisionist retelling of a costly U.S. Marine battle, Letters from Iwo Jima. *Courtesy of Touchstone Pictures.*

Eventually, the Marines landed, ran forward, and after weeks of fighting, captured Iwo Jima. Virtually every Japanese soldier died, most from firepower or hillside accidents. A handful were self-inflicted. A few surrendered. As for the Americans, their casualties climbed into the thousands, but one unfortunate marine, wounded near a cave, experienced kindness. Looking at the bleeding leatherneck, an English-speaking general reassured the frightened man and ordered rudimentary medical care. Hours later, however, the marine died. Staring at a dead enemy and listening to their officer read a letter from his mother, the Imperial soldiers realized this young man—over three thousand miles from his hometown—imaged themselves: peaceful, happy, and friendly. Peaceful, happy, and friendly? What kind of revisionism was Clint Eastwood peddling? Were these the same Japanese who bayoneted emaciated GIs on the Bataan Death March? Was this the military machine that routinely decapitated civilian prisoners? How about the Rape of Nanjing? Were some of these peaceful, happy, and friendly Imperial soldiers involved in that six-week orgy? How about Shanghai? How many bed-ridden patients did the Japanese slaughter? Should the moviegoer believe, as Clint Eastwood expatiated, that these troops quietly arrived, like a deus ex machina, on Iwo Jima without any prior military experience, fresh from their mainland families, to become fodder for some I-want-to-kill-you, sadistic U.S. marines?

Clearly, many World War II combat pictures contained subtle pacifist messages that echoed General MacArthur's dictum, "Only the dead have seen the end of war," and *Letters from Iwo Jima* dramatically mirrored this viewpoint. Certainly, every story has two sides, and history is always written by the winners, but it's difficult to view the Imperial Japanese army as victims. As Jerry Della Femina quipped, weren't the Japanese those wonderful folks who gave us Pearl Harbor?

As for the Japanese prisoner-of-war camps, most photodramas left nothing to the imagination in depicting the barbaric treatment imposed upon all captives. Planet Pictures' *Paradise Road* told the uplifting saga of some women from different countries and social levels who organized a vocal ensemble — in spite of their guards' resistance — to maintain a peripheral level of sanity in these untried circumstances. With scene after scene of Japanese depravity — including setting a prisoner on fire and forcing another to kneel in the afternoon sun inches away from a fatal sword — the women struggled against innumerable hardships, always mindful that, as one victim uttered, "The will to survive is strong, stronger than anything," while their Japanese tormentors grimaced menacingly. Loosely based on the aftermath of the infamous Bangka Island massacre, where Japanese soldiers, on February 16, 1942, forced twenty-one women into waist-high ocean water and then machine-gunned everyone, this Hollywood production offered quiet praise for these survivors and their three-year ordeal. A similar screenplay involving another Indonesian POW camp, NBC's *Silent Cries*, told the harrowing, three-year story of Japanese torture, starvation, rape, and beatings of helpless women, a situation so deplorable that nearly half died from their captors' treatment. Together, these two titles portrayed the Japanese soldier — some fifty years after V-J Day — in terms that few moviegoers could comprehend: uncaring, bestial, and vindictive behavior, supported by historical records.

If such blatant atrocities were routine in the female compounds, how did male prisoners of war survive Japanese captivity? Blood Oath Production's *Prisoners of the Sun* articulated the grisly story of three hundred liberated Australian soldiers from the Ambon Island compound — where Japanese guards, during a three-year period, beheaded over eight hundred prisoners and tossed the bodies into an unmarked gravesite — and the subsequent war tribunal, revealing more gruesome torture, that prosecuted the Japanese officers responsible for these atrocities. Argyll Film Partners' *To End All Wars* recounted the harsh treatment inflicted on many Scottish soldiers forced to build a railroad in the difficult Burmese underbrush. Frequently beaten and given only meager rations, the Highlanders, despised by their captors because they accepted surrender before death, gradually learned survival techniques: "Always bow before a guard, Korean or Jap. And never look 'em in the eyes when they pass you—that's pure defiance. Always look away. Rules of Bushido." Likewise, Roadshow Productions' *Return from the River Kwai* explained the depravities experienced by the Allied prisoners—who built a bridge in the Thailand jungle for their Japanese captors—and their subsequent sea voyage to their enemy's homeland. With Edward Fox and Denholm Elliott in starring roles, this screenplay depicted the sadistic, uncaring, and inhumane behavior of the Japanese soldiers.

A similar storyline, but with a strong flag-waving ending, Miramax's *The Great Raid* re-created the daring January 1945 rescue of hundreds of U.S. captives taken at Bataan three years earlier and held in the Cabanatuan camp in the Philippine jungle. U.S. Rangers trekked inland, attacked the compound, and returned the emaciated GIs to safety, validating their commander's promise: "We're going to push through our front lines right into the Japs' backyard and rescue 500 hundred American prisoners of war." With scene after scene of Japanese atrocities, including the burning alive of hapless Americans, the final moments of this red-white-and-blue extravaganza—with strong echoes of the rousing 1945 John Wayne breakthrough title *Back to Bataan*—reminded audiences, once more, about America's great World War II victories.

Sometimes the war took a back seat to lost love. Miramax's *Map of the Human Heart* traced the mushy regrets of a young Inuit from his playful Eskimo days, months in a Montreal hospital, youthful infatuation, unrequited affection, and finally, combat service in the RAF when in February 1945, on a strategic bombing run over Dresden, his aircraft exploded. Forced to bail out, his slow parachute descent into the burning city brought his life into focus, proving that true love, unlike gravity, plots its own course. With Jason Scott Lee in the leading role, the screenplay's unhappy ending reiterated the popular song's lamentation, "For all we know, we may never meet again." Another Romeo and Juliet romance, New Line's *The Notebook*, utilized the war as a backdrop, attesting that love and separation go hand in glove. Here, a young Carolinian from the wrong side of the tracks (Ryan Gosling) unsuccessfully wooed the girl of his dreams. Pearl Harbor changed everything; first enlistment, then North Africa, the Battle of the Bulge, and, finally, an army hospital. His stateside return to a lonely house retold the saddest of tales experienced by thousands of GIs.

Occasionally, a love story made a disastrous, left-hand turn, destroying everyone in its path. HBO's made-for-television *The Affair* indicted the U.S. Army for perpetuating the same old-boy, racist policies—found in southern states—on its British bases, where thousands of Americans amassed for their D-Day embarkation. Here in a small village, a soft-spoken black soldier

(Courtney B. Vance), haphazardly became involved with an introverted, married woman (Kerry Fox). When the affair became public, the confused wife, unable to handle peer pressure, cried "rape," charging the GI with this violent act. He was quickly arrested, tried, and executed. This story line blamed numerous officers for their uncaring, unconscionable attitude toward African Americans. Columbia's multitiered morality tale of adultery, Catholic guilt, jealousy, and self-doubt, *The End of the Affair*, depicted a delicate ménage à trois—a novelist, a government official, and his future wife—during the height of the London blitz. With Ralph Fiennes, Stephen Rea, and Julianne Moore in leading roles, this fleeting triangle proved once again that all was fair in love and war. A similar storyline, Fox's *For the Moment*, recounted the summer 1942 romantic entanglements among various Commonwealth airmen training in rural Manitoba and their newfound girlfriends. This time a spirited Aussie flyer (Russell Crowe) fell for a lonely married woman (Christianne Hir), even though, he mused, "The average life expectancy of a bomber pilot [in combat] is six bloody weeks." After earning his wings and embarking for England, these star-crossed lovers politely waved goodbye, realizing—for better or worse—their wartime affair combined both joy and sorrow.

The American home front, with its roller-coaster lifestyle, contained another set of problems. IRS Media's *December* examined the youthful side of unbridled patriotism, when on December 7, news of the Japanese attack resounded in the hallways at an elite, all-male, Vermont preparatory school, inciting the students into a vengeful mood. After days of debate—a mixture of solipsistic and chauvinistic arguments—a busload of seniors, with the administration's blessing, left the campus and were transported to a nearby induction center. Paramount's *A Separate Peace*—also set in a boarding school at the war's height—examined those ambiguous days where fourth-year classmates realized that graduation meant military service, bringing an end to the simplicity associated with carefree, learning days. Orion Pictures' *Radio Days* centered around a Jewish family living in Queens, spending many hours listening to war news in their modest apartment. Written and directed by Woody Allen, this droll screenplay re-created many well-known personages whose daily broadcasts molded opinions and disseminated international stories. These prompted a geography-deficient spinster aunt (Mia Farrow) to ask, "Who is Pearl Harbor?"

Fox's *For the Boys*—a peripatetic tale about two USO entertainers (James Caan and Bette Midler) who sang and danced at makeshift military sites—offered such double entendres as "Well, alone in the dark with thousands of men. There is a God after all!" to many GIs, even though one song, "Come Rain or Come Shine," was not composed until 1946. Sometimes a returning soldier learned that loneliness did not make the heart grow fonder. In another Fox production, *A Walk in the Clouds*, a decorated hero (Keanu Reeves) returned to San

Francisco, discovered his marriage in shambles, and—after some Cinderella ad-ventures—agreed to pose as the husband of a pregnant, unmarried college stu-dent (Aitana Sánchez-Gijón), hoping this ruse would placate her domineering, oenologist father. With numerous flashbacks to his South Pacific combat days, this bittersweet storyline, with fairy-tale deftness, blended good wine, young ro-mance, and wartime memories into the obligatory happy ending.

Another home-front title, Fox's *Come See the Paradise*, tackled the em-barrassing question of President Roosevelt's Executive Law 9066, the thorny legislation that authorized immediate internment of all West Coast Japanese Americans to remote, bleak camps. Based on the fearful, racist assumption that fifth columnists would aid their motherland through sabotage and dissen-sion, these U.S. citizens—the majority were women and children—endured many months of hardships and deprivation in spartan compounds. In this bar-ren landscape, a leftist labor organizer (Dennis Quaid), married to a Japanese American, struggled unsuccessfully to convince military officials that their ac-tions represented innumerable violations of law, fair play, and morality. A sim-ilar storyline, Kennedy/Marshall Company's *Snow Falling on Cedars*, reiter-ated this dark side of national history by recreating the many indignities this hapless minority underwent during their illegal internment. Warner Bros.' *American Pastime* also examined this unsavory period, only this time the GI guards played the Japanese Americans a highly charged baseball game that came down to the ninth inning with two outs. With a fifty-star flag flying over-head, the home team batting first, and a bigoted coach warning his daughter, "You're not going to see that Jap!" the entire 2007 photodrama—using a pop-ular sport as metaphor—offered many parallels to the current Iraqi War. HBO's *The Tuskegee Airmen* posited the inspiring story of the real-life African American pilots, from their early Alabama flight training to becoming a leg-endary fighting unit noted for protective air support of Allied bombers in the European theater. As tenacious aerial attackers, most of the flyers echoed a senior officer's words, "As pilots we live in the air, but we die by fire."

Overall, many made-for-television productions that used the Second World War as backdrop contained the usual Norman Rockwell pabulum needed for Sunday-evening audiences. Disney's crowd-pleaser *Chips, the War Dog* told the happy story of a hard-to-discipline family canine that was placed into the army and, with the help of a new master, became a valuable war-effort asset. With Brandon Douglas in the leading role, this photodrama offered strong ap-peal for most pet owners. A similar Pollyanna interpretation of Trillium's re-make of the Rodgers and Hammerstein classic, *South Pacific*, updated the musical wartime tale. This time Glenn Close crooned she would "wash that man right out of my hair," while a young army lieutenant, good-looking Harry Connick Jr., claimed that true love could make anyone feel "younger than springtime." Castle Rock Entertainment's *The Majestic* provided quiet praise to Bedford, Virginia, a small town that sent 134 men—the Bedford Boys—into combat, but only a handful returned. Jim Carrey sparkled as an amnesia-stricken patient who in 1951 stumbled into a tiny, Capraesque Californian hamlet, where some locals, mistaking him for a long-lost hero, explained, "All told, this town gave sixty-two of its young men to the War—more than our share; seventeen of them in Normandy alone." After some goofy Jimmy Stewart–type up-and-down adventures, everything came to light in an all-was-forgiven, brass-band ending.

Hallmark's *Decoration Day* honored a southern black tenant farmer and the problems associated with a belated Medal of Honor presentation. Here, a recluse neighbor (James Garner) stepped out of his private world to help this former GI. Quinex Entertainment's *The Incident* examined a small town's anger when a German POW at a nearby internment camp—accused of killing a popular doctor—denied this charge. Soon, a slow-talking lawyer and World War I veteran (Walter Matthau) unraveled evidence proving his client's innocence, even though the physician's widow, unable to accept her husband's medical peccadilloes, screamed, "I don't think you have the right to call yourself an American anymore!" Another title dealing with intricate legal maneuverings, Turner Pictures' *Never Forget*, told the unusual story of a concentration-camp survivor (Leonard Nimoy) and his courtroom battle with a neo-Nazi organization's claim, using discursive logic, that the Auschwitz gas chambers never existed. With Dabney Coleman portraying his attorney, the two men slowly unmasked the screwball world of Holocaust deniers, a fringe movement with a small but vociferous band of supporters. Another Hallmark Sunday-night picture, *The Little Riders*, told the quiet story of a young American girl stranded with her Dutch grandparents right after the Nazi takeover of Holland and the problems associated with the occupation, seen from a child's perspective. Sometimes a motion picture raised moral issues. A more balanced look at the Japanese home front that examined the lives of diehard Imperial officers, small children, stoic family members, and many foreigners, Greenwald Production's *Hiroshima: Out of the Ashes* detailed the traumatic seventy-two hours before and after the August 6, 1945, atomic bombing of this major seaport. Intertwining the lives of a few desperate inhabitants—an American prisoner of war, Japanese civilians, and European diplomats—and their subsequent struggle for survival amid conflagration, ruination, and radioactive fallout, the photo-drama—created for Sunday postprandial entertainment—weighted the efficacy of this first nuclear explosion against various humanistic principles.

As expected, the science fiction market—with its strong box-office appeal—offered its own interpretation of the global conflict. Trimark's *The Philadelphia Experiment II* kept the preternatural kettle boiling with the same shenanigans of the original, nine years earlier. In this sequel, a modern (1993) U.S. Air Force stealth bomber vanished into a time void, reappeared in Hitler's Germany, and subsequently dropped a nuclear bomb on Washington, D.C., enabling the Nazis to win the war. However, an American hero (Brad Johnson), whose unique DNA permitted unlimited linear travel, returned to 1943, and after some Captain Marvel adventures, changed the time sequence and thwarted the German victory, allowing "real" history to continue. With one subplot contradicting another, the whole mishmash resembled wartime *Popeye* cartoons, in which America's favorite spinach-eating sailor continuously ran the Axis forces into the ground.

Dangers lurked everywhere. Dimension Films' *Below* suggested that a U.S. submarine operating in the North Atlantic—making creepy, metal-against-metal sounds—was haunted by its former skipper's ghost, while above the waves a German ship, concerned with more practical matters, dropped explosives. With Bruce Greenwood holding a steady course, everyone's nerves snapped when an unexplained recording of Benny Goodman's "Sing, Sing, Sing" resounded throughout the hull, even though a chief petty officer concluded, "We got mechanical problems, that's all." Replete with typical *Twilight Zone* metaphysics, the entire underwater drama, with its eerie noises, occasional apparitions, and wraithlike mirrors, rattled everyone.

Science fiction travesties frequently were off the wall. King Picture's *Treasure Island* spoofed the comings and goings of two American code specialists (Lance Baker and Nick Offerman) working on a classified naval base in San Francisco Bay, deciphering Japanese messages. Basically a parody of Fox's 1956 thriller, *The Man Who Never Was*, these two men planned to drop a dead body with false documents into the Pacific near Japanese forces. Laden with soft pornography, this screenplay's many skits—Charles Atlas and his ninety-seven-pound weakling, race relations, wartime epithets, and victory celebration photographs—were overshadowed by the prurient scenes involving latent homosexuality, voyeurism, polygamy, and nymphomania.

Another screwball idea, Lions Gate's *The Empty Mirror*, rationalized Adolf Hitler's dysfunctional behavior, suggesting that the führer's problems originated in his youth. With Norman Rodway as the German leader, Camilla Soeberg as his mistress Eva Braun, and Joel Grey as Josef Goebbels, much of the screen time contained one diatribe after another as top officials blamed each other for the Third Reich's shortcomings, even though the führer denounced Joseph Stalin as "a footnote, a footnote if he is fortunate." A third photodrama, Silver Bullet's *Straight into Darkness*, depicted a group of abandoned French children—programmed by a loose-cannon caretaker (David Warner) to kill Nazis quickly and efficiently—who eventually reached safety thanks to the efforts of two U.S. Army deserters

(Scott MacDonald and Ryan Francis). Another plotline involving children, Columbia's *Hellboy*, re-created the comic-strip adventures of some Nazi weirdoes, who in spring 1945 planned to summon forth the Seven Gods of Chaos. Thwarted by U.S. soldiers and President Roosevelt's personal psychic adviser (John Hurt), this squad rescued a little red baby—equipped with horns and a tail—and subsequently raised this child to become Hellboy (Ron Perlman), mankind's greatest warrior, the sworn enemy of all evil forces.

Other supernatural storylines provided many face-covering screams for science fiction fans. Arbor Avenue Films' *Horrors of War* pushed the envelope when American troops, patrolling German forces, ran into werewolves, mutants, and zombies, unaware that Hitler's mad scientists had hatched these secret "weapons." Soon, OSS operatives, headed by Lieutenant John Schmidt, prowled the forests, discovered the sources, and finally destroyed these unusual creatures. Not to be outdone, Combat Productions' *SS Doom Troopers* fashioned additional fodder for *Frankenstein* aficionados after a U.S. intelligence squad, headed by Corin Nemic, uncovered a zany Nazi experimenter (Ben Cross) amalgamating some unexplained atomic-energy particles. He was creating a twenty-foot, hulking, megamuscled supersoldier that resembled a huge plastic action figure and was impervious to heavy gunfire, grenades, flamethrowers, tank blasts, and multiple explosions. He bragged, "An entire army of such creatures could crush the Allied advance and guarantee absolute victory for the Fatherland." Using a variety of offensive maneuvers, the GIs, after numerous setbacks, finally cornered this laboratory contraption and, with a little help from the French Resistance, destroyed the Third Reich's behemoth.

Sometimes, a Nazi monster became airborne. Concrete Productions' *Reign of the Gargoyles* provided many thrills when German soldiers uncovered some medieval pagan ruins embellished with stone gargoyles. Using the latest Third Reich incantations, these inanimate creatures were brought to life and, after some preternatural events, downed many Allied aircraft, causing a flight commander to ask, "What the hell are those things?" One bomber crew, headed by Joe Penny and Wes Ramsey, parachuted to safety, teamed up with Resistance fighters, eluded Nazi pursuers, and—using the Spear of Destiny (a weapon that once pierced Christ's side)—slew the gargoyle king, rendering all its minions helpless. With numerous scenes depicting explosions, shootouts, disintegration, and decapitations, the entire screenplay, with all its bells, whistles, and bows, resembled nothing more than a contemporary video game.

Occasionally, a screenplay floated into outer space putting an eccentric spin on world history. HBO's *Fatherland* expostulated that in 1944 the Normandy invasion failed, forcing a truce between Germany and the Allied

Powers. Twenty years later, Hitler still ruled Germany, Albert Speer created an elaborate monument to the Thousand Year Reich, Joseph Kennedy Sr. was America's president, General Eisenhower and Prime Minister Churchill died in exile, and King Edward and Queen Wallis sat on England's throne, while eighty-five-year-old Joseph Stalin, still at war with Germania (its new name) pondered his nation's next move. With numerous inconsistencies and illogical premises, this made-for-television travesty—with Rutger Hauer in a leading role—jumped from one implausible scene to another, ignoring logic, continuity, or substance, even though one Nazi general bragged, "This is the age of detente."

Certainly moviegoers witnessed many changes since the early, two-dimensional 1942 propaganda titles appeared, in which good and evil stood clearly apart. Later, colorized, wide-angled, then digital photodramas chronicled the war with expanded technology. Hollywood, of course, abandoned its antiquated back lots and filmed on locations all over the world, working in countries that offered the best tax loopholes, while at the same time distributing many foreign-made titles. At the beginning of the twenty-first century, World War II movies still appeared, albeit intermittently. But what about the audience? Was there still a market for a rousing, flag-waving go-get-'em screenplay? Would this genre survive or would the war become a spin-off, reduced to commercialized science fiction stories or comic book adventures designed for young audiences?

Chapter Eight

Sixty Years of Fighting

Why Should It End?

"What, are my deeds forgot?"—Achilles, a Greek warrior, at the gates of Troy, asking his compatriot Ulysses for clarification about his recent battlefield achievements in William Shakespeare's tragic story of unfulfilled love, *Troilus and Cressida*

"Those scraps are good deeds past, which are devoured; As fast as they are made, forgot as soon as done."—Ulysses' pragmatic reply explaining victory's ephemeral nature

"What do wars ever prove? Men, women, and children are slaughtered and a generation later, friends are enemies and enemies are friends and the whole stupid cycle starts over again."—Marlon Brando, as an anti-Nazi, German national, expatiating about wartime's chiasmatic nature in Fox's 1965 sea-voyaging saga, *Morituri*

"I loved it. I loved the war. I didn't want it to end. The idea of the war continuing on and on was really great for me."—Cult-film director Russ Meyers—whose 1965 black-and-white romp *Faster, Pussycat! Kill! Kill!* started him on the road to stardom—recalling his World War II combat experiences

When the Second World War ended in September 1945, most Americans literally jumped for joy in madcap celebrations. Why wouldn't they? The Japanese unconditional surrender meant only one thing: our boys were coming home. A few months later, when the servicemen began returning, the good times moved up a big notch. Festive parties heralded wonderful celebrations and now, the GIs—finally reunited with friends and family after years of separation—sat down and recounted wartime experiences. And what stories were told! Throughout 1945 and into 1946, one question greeted every veteran, "What did you do in the war?" Sometimes the answer was terse, in other situations, complex. Occasionally a veteran became reticent, other times, everything spilled out in a torrent of words.

But wartime jubilation eventually wore down, and by 1947, just one year later, new problems gripped the country. Unemployment fueled economic anxieties, while a former ally, the Soviet Union, repudiated its friendship with an Eastern Europe expansionist policy. On a positive note, the Marshall Plan aided Germany's recovery, while over in Japan, democratic reforms, under General MacArthur's benevolent eye, moved forward. By 1949 both Germany and Japan—two nations that once launched an unprecedented and brutal war against the United States—were now good friends with their former adversary. And not a moment too soon. On June 25, 1950, just five short years since V-J Day, the North Korean army, an acknowledged Russian puppet, attacked their southern neighbor. Within hours, U.S. troops, rifles in hand, were in a hot zone. Almost overnight, the Second World War became ancient history as a worried nation turned their eyes toward a small Southeast Asian peninsula.

Three years later the Korean conflict ended, but peace seemed as distant as the moon because two superpowers—the United States and the Soviet Union—aimed nuclear missiles at each other. Dubbed the Cold War, this unprecedented conflict shaped American life throughout the fifties and sixties as each side wondered who would launch the first explosive. In an age of jet aircrafts, low earth-orbit satellites, and computer-guided missiles, World War II armament—now squirreled away in museums—seemed, like the conflict itself, a quaint relic from the outlying past. In 1958 a realistic motion picture reflected these mainstream ideas. Directed by Edward Dmytryk, *The Young Lions* synchronized the adventures of two American draftees and a *Wehrmacht* officer. In one scene, a smooth-talking, New York City ladies' man (Dean Martin), annoyed about his upcoming induction, offered a dire prediction: "Look, I've read all the books. I know that in ten years we'll be bosom friends with the Germans and the Japanese. Then I'll be pretty annoyed that I was killed." How prescient was that?

By the early sixties, most Americans watched an impending problem festering on the other side of the world. In Southeast Asia, a jungle conflict brought U.S. troops to Vietnam, causing stateside tempers to flare about this distant entanglement. Still waving Old Glory, the World War II generation argued for a decisive victory, only to watch in dismay as college students burned flags and draft cards while taunting President Johnson with a derisive litany, "Hey, hey, LBJ! How many babies did you kill today?" Clearly, the "we're-all-in-this-together" days of twenty-five years earlier—like loose-lips-sink-ships, blackout shades, and aluminum pennies—vanished from the landscape. For all its glory and sacrifice, the Second World War, with its poignant monuments, gold-star mothers, and foreign burials became, as the popular Carole King song lamented, "so far away."

Far away? By the 1970s this global conflict seemed as remote as the Peloponnesian Wars. In 1973 a Hollywood motion picture poked fun at the nation's historical awareness. Directed by John G. Avildsen, Paramount's scathing black comedy *Save the Tiger* traced the downward spiral of a World War II veteran, Harry Stoner (Jack Lemmon), who fifteen years earlier landed in Anzio but now operated a California dress-manufacturing company teetering on bankruptcy. Frequently remembering the Italian beach invasion, he could not comprehend how "In 1944 that sand was made in blood and last year it was covered with bikinis." Soon, he ran into an offbeat, college-age hitchhiker, Myra (Laurie Heineman), and after some double-entendre generational banter (she wanted to save the tigers from extinction) the two wound up in a cozy room. Eventually undressed, she eyed his scars and innocently inquired what happened. "I got those in Italy," he mumbled. Impressed, she continued, "In a fight?" Shaking his head, he explained, "In the war." Puzzled, she asked, "In Italy?" Nodding, he confirmed, "In Italy." Looking nonplussed, the free-spirited student blurted out, "We never fought a war with Italy."

Italy? Why would the United States fight a war with such a fun-loving nation, a country with a reputation for pretty women, succulent pastas, aromatic wines, spiffy sports cars, and high-fashion clothing? By the mid-1970s—over thirty years since V-J Day—how many university-aged Americans understood the war's intricacies, its combatants, its issues, and, finally, its conclusion? How many knew that fascist-controlled Italy, under the heel of Benito Mussolini, invaded neighboring countries, deported hapless civilians to concentration camps, and as a major component of the Axis tripartite, fought against Allied forces?

If by the 1970s World War II resembled, as the love ballad suggested, "faded photographs," what about the new century? Would old deeds, as Achilles pondered, be soon forgot? At Tokyo's venerable Yasukuni Shrine, a Shinto religious site that commemorates Japan's World War II dead—including General Hideki Tojo and other convicted Class-A criminals—a new extension, the Museum of Military History, contains hundreds of mementos glorifying the nation's past. Opened in 2002, most of exhibits claim that Japan fought a war not to subjugate other countries but, instead, to gain independence from outside influences. Citing the two thousand years of freedom from invading foreigners, one display after another tones down the 1941–1945 aggression. Poignant farewell letters from kamikaze pilots highlight the virtues of sacrifice, while the 1937 Rape of Nanjing—where estimates of Chinese deaths reach three hundred thousand—is simply called the

Totally worn out from an evening with a silly coed, a former infantryman (Jack Lemmon), who was wounded during the 1944 Anzio invasion, cannot fathom the university student's marginal understanding of World War II in John G. Avildsen's black comedy, Save the Tiger. Courtesy of Paramount Pictures.

Nanjing Incident, an event euphemistically described as Japanese forces bringing stability to a troubled region. As for Pearl Harbor, a text from Emperor Hirohito rationalized the attack, expounding the military had no choice but to go forward because the United States, a belligerent Western nation, planned to force Japan into a confrontation simply as a means to end its Great Depression. Perhaps that explains a commemorative statue of India's Judge Radhabinod Pal, the only jurist who handed down a not-guilty verdict for Japan's leaders during the postwar tribunals.

Even most textbooks downplayed the war. References to the Korean occupation, including the Comfort Women, do not appear, echoing Tokyo's governor Shudo Ishihara's directive that the Nanjing Massacre never took place. At the same time, in March 2002, the Japanese appeals court ruled their government did not have to pay $7,260.00 damages to three Korean women because these sexual violations—committed by the occupying Japanese army—did not breach their nation's constitution. Earlier, in January 2000, organizers at the Osaka International Peace center called the Nanjing Massacre the biggest myth of the twentieth century. Unwilling to confront its past with anything remotely unpleasant—a Class-A war criminal was elected prime minister in 1957—the director of the Nagasaki Atomic Bomb Museum, in 1996, removed some 1937 photographs of women being jostled in Nanjing, claiming these images upset children. A chairman of a nationalist group and war veteran, Sunao Nishi, claimed categorically that Japanese troops did not kill Chinese in Manchuria, sentiments that appear in the nation's textbooks. Written by nationalist scholars, these books consistently deny historically documented atrocities committed during the war and often refer to Japanese invasions into Asian nations as "advances." Even the 2001 prime minister, Junichiro Koizumi, approved these changes. To maintain national honor, another government-endorsed textbook revision deleted all references to Japanese troops ordering the 1945 mass suicides of Okinawan villagers.

How quickly events fade. Not wanting to upset an upcoming summit applecart, on July 6, 2000, a U.S. Marine general, Earl B. Hailston, dutifully apologized to the Okinawan governor for the behavior of a nineteen-year-old serviceman in his command. The young leatherneck, who was not charged with anything, was accused of trespassing and an indecent act against a minor. In a scene echoing any number of Hollywood POW atrocity pictures—*Prisoner of the Sun* or *The Great Raid*, for example—the high-ranking officer bowed contritely and expressed his regret, while grimfaced Japanese officials stood quietly. In a similar situation in March 2001, Admiral William Fallon and the U.S. ambassador—hoping to allay some anti-American anger—bowed submissively to the homeland prime minister and apologized for a U.S. submarine accident that killed nine Japanese students in the Hawaiian waters. A few days later, the vessel's commander, Scott Waddle, also leaned forward in a gesture of submission to the parents, offering handwritten letters as a tangible token of remorse.

Music and veneration, two needed components of militarism, offered Japanese students a chance to evaluate their past. In 2004 the Tokyo Board of Education—hoping to foster ethnic pride and national identity—mandated that every school day, all students must stand, face the rising-sun flag, and sing the national anthem. During World War II, this patriotic song, "Kimigayo" (translated as "His Majesty's Reign"), was heralded by Japanese troops during their Asian invasion forays, while the prominent red-and-white flag, always displayed in public arenas, was a grim reminder to captive people everywhere of their unwanted colonial rule.

And what about Hideki Tojo, Japan's wartime prime minister who in 1948 was hanged as a Class-A criminal? Over fifty years later, his granddaughter Yuko Tojo works assiduously to transform the image of the general, who ordered the Pearl Harbor attack, from villain to national hero, a soldier who died defending his country. Her best-selling 1997 revisionist book, *My Grandfather Hideki Tojo*, extolled his patriotism, portraying him as a victim of Allied politics. The following year, a film production company used this text as the screenplay for *Puraido: Unmei no toki* (translated as *Pride: The Moment of Truth*), another slanted motion picture depicting Tojo as the nation's savior. With Masahiko Tsugawa in the starring role, this skewed photodrama became the highest-grossing Japanese movie of 1998, even though in one Tokyo suburban theater, protesters, angry at the positive portrayal of the wartime leader, slashed the screen.

Japanese revisionism lurks everywhere. In the southern town of Chiran, an elaborate kamikaze museum, opened in 1975, glorifies young pilots' sacrifices against the encroaching blue-eyed devils. The museum, which draws over half a million visitors a year, displays farewell letters and photographs that nationalists argue preserve their noble sacrifice against a barbaric enemy. This type of adulation for the approximately four thousand Special Attack Corps pilots assigned to crash their bomb-laden aircraft into Allied ships, blends nicely with current official policies to expunge Japanese atrocities from history books and reinstate patriotism into public education. At the same time, a popular 2007 motion picture, *I Go to Die for You*, written by Tokyo's governor, magnified the defensive effort as honorable and the kamikazes' role as righteous heroes who died for the common good in an idealistic crusade to free Asia from Western domination. By fall 2007, this somber motion picture, depicting the worship and enshrinement of these rightists' ideals, grossed over two billion yen in Japan. Prime Minister Yoshiro Mori's appraisal, made on May 19, 2000, was that, "Japan is a divine nation with the emperor at its core and we want the people to recognize this." Why doesn't he just yell, "Banzai?"

Across the ocean in the Mississippi Delta, a similar drama played out in the New Orleans World War II Museum. As in Chiran, each year thousands of visitors examine the many artifacts associated with America's victory effort. One of the volunteer guides, Tom Blakey—a former paratrooper who fought on D-Day and, later, across Europe—spent six years answering questions and relating his combat days to interested groups, many of which, he realized, did not know much about the war. Sometimes, the octogenarian mused, people asked, "What side were we on?" or worse, "Did we win the war?" These inquiries resounded in the lobby of an elaborate building dedicated to explaining the Second World War. A similar story, recounted by Bobbie Hamilton, detailed her childhood experiences living in Corregidor before the Japanese takeover, where playful children swam in the South China Sea right near the Malinta Tunnel. Today, the Florida resident reflected, "Very few people have heard of Corregidor and that includes many young Filipinos." Why is this? What happened? How did World War II awareness fall to the wayside? Maybe someone should ask Joe Foss.

Born in 1915 on a South Dakota farm and raised in a hunting and marksmanship environment, Joe Foss became enamored of flying—according to local folklore—when Charles Lindbergh landed at the nearby Sioux City Airport. In 1940 he earned a bachelor's degree, a civilian pilot's license, joined the Marine Corps, graduated from flight school, was commissioned a second lieutenant, and, the following year, on December 7, was the Pensacola officer of the day. On October 13, 1942, over Guadalcanal, he destroyed his first Japanese Zero. A few more kills followed until October 25, when he shot down five enemy aircraft, becoming the Marine Corps' first ace-in-a-day.

On November 7, his luck soured when his plane crashed into the Pacific waters. Initially discombobulated, he climbed aboard a raft, floated for a few hours, and was rescued by nearby locals off Malaita Island. Back in the air, his tally reached nineteen kills. On November 9, Admiral Halsey awarded him the Distinguished Flying Cross. Four more enemy aircraft dropped from the skies, but—a few days later—malaria caught up with him. Hospitalized in Australia, he returned to his unit on January 1, 1943, and on January 15 he shot down three more aircraft, bringing his total to twenty-six, equaling Eddie Rickenbacker's World War I record. All of this took place in a mere eighty days, including six weeks of convalescing. Apparently, President Roosevelt thought that was enough. Ordered stateside, on May 18 Captain Joe Foss cautiously leaned forward while the chief executive pinned the Congressional Medal on his blouse and, according to personal recollection, called the airman "young feller." A few days later, his picture appeared on the cover of *Life*. Acclaimed a national hero, he served as a training adviser for the rest of the war.

After V-J Day, more recognition followed. Initially one of the organizers of the South Dakota National Guard, he joined the House of Representatives, returned to active duty during the Korean conflict, served four years as governor of South Dakota, and from 1959 to 1966 reigned as commissioner of the American Football League. Always in the public eye and a popular speaker, retired Marine Corps general Joseph J. Foss openly greeted friends and admirers at functions, meetings, sporting events, even on the street. But years later, on January 11, 2002, at the Phoenix International Airport, everything changed abruptly. Foss became—like a character from Yevgeny Zamyatin's dystopian novel *We*—a nonperson.

After placing his jacket into the X-ray machine, the eighty-six-year-old Marine Corps ace was questioned by security personnel about a small pentagonal object inside a fancy case, whose rounded metal edges represented a potential threat to airline safety. For over forty-five minutes, Foss recalled, about eight or nine people passed around the Congressional Medal of Honor without any real understanding of what they were holding. Certainly, none of these security workers had the vaguest notion what this decoration represented, even with the inscription on the reverse side. None, of course, knew anything about Guadalcanal. For all practical purposes, that South Sea island was a planet in outer space. And World War II? What was that? Something you see in the movies? Finally, after some unpleasant back-and-forth discussion, an America West Airline representative intervened. The World War II fighter pilot—who fifty-nine years earlier went airborne for different reasons—was finally allowed on the commercial aircraft. Quietly he sat down, fastened his seat belt, and stared pensively out the window.

At least he sat quietly. Back on January 17, 1994, in Oakland, California, approximately seventy Castlemont High School students—on a special Martin Luther King Day field trip—were taken to a local theater to see Steven Spielberg's Holocaust film, *Schindler's List*. According to news accounts, most of the adolescents seemed disinterested, even bored watching this slow-moving, black-and-white picture about a subject that lacked teenage appeal. About an hour into the drama, a small but loud group laughed, joked, and cheered when a Nazi officer shot an old Jewish woman point-blank in the head. When other viewers complained, the manager halted the projection and summarily ejected every student. Someone called the local newspaper, and within hours this incident became a national front-page story.

Immediately, the board of education worked on damage control. Students apologized, and local Jewish organizations offered help in explaining the Holocaust. Even Steven Spielberg and Governor Pete Wilson showed up at an elaborate meeting in the school's auditorium. For the next few months, the controversy rebounded in school hallways. Finally, the summer vacation arrived and, like most unpleasant episodes, the events of that January afternoon faded away. Why wouldn't they? As one fourteen-year-old sophomore explained, she meant no disrespect in the theater. "World War II," she continued, "was long ago and far away and about people we never met."

At least these California teenagers did not wear a swastika to the movie house. In January 2005, twenty-year-old Prince Harry—third in line to the British crown—donned a Nazi uniform to a costume bash, hoping, one can only speculate, to impress his friends with this sartorial grand entrance. When photographs appeared in *The Sun* depicting the young prince soul-kissing a pretty partygoer, also dressed in Nazi regalia, the royal family, no stranger to scandal, issued a formal apology, claiming that young people's knowledge of World War II was limited.

British tabloids—always eager for the jugular—suggested that if this merry-making had taken place a few weeks later in the Austrian Obersalzberg Mountains, the young prince might have been spared the embarrassment. In February a luxury hotel opened on the site of Adolf Hitler's alpine German retreat. Berchtesgaden, the Third Reich's second seat of power, where the führer romped with his selected inner circle, boasts 138 rooms and twelve suites. While condemned by Jewish leaders as a place inappropriate for holiday recreation, the Bavarian State minister claimed this new five-star resort, with daily rates from 270 to 1300 euros, would give the local tourist industry a needed shot in the arm. What's next? An elaborate luxury hotel—situated majestically on Berlin's brightly lit Kurfürstendamm—named the Hotel Hitler?

Why not? As one of France's great heroes, Napoleon Bonaparte's reputation remains unblemished. Squares, streets, hotels, alcoholic beverages, clothing, logos, even a multilayered, creamy pastry use his name or image lavishly as a testimony to his many deeds. None of his admirers, of course, mentioned Napoleon's 1802 Haitian decree ordering the death of every black male over the age of twelve. How about Hitler? In the early 1960s— fifteen years after V-J Day—the hang-ten surfing crowd proclaimed the führer's coveted Iron Cross their pelagic symbol. Why shouldn't they? Doesn't this metal image enhance the appearance of any young surfer? How about the future? In two hundred years, will Hitler's cropped musta-chioed image appear on commercial products? Maybe on the label of a robust Bavarian beer? By 2200 will revisionist capitalists argue Hitler only wanted to improve his country but went about it the wrong way? Maybe someone should talk to Punit Sabhlok, an aspiring entrepreneur who, in 2006, opened an eatery in Mumbai, India, called Hitler's Cross. Taking his cue from the führer, this owner boasted that he, too, wanted to conquer the world, not militarily, but by "his food and service." What a wonderful name for a restaurant!

As for the zone of the interior, how well do most Americans remember the war some sixty years later? On May 26, 2001, Michael Bay's *Pearl Harbor* opened nationwide. To commemorate this event, a New Brunswick, New Jersey, megatheater invited members of the Pearl Harbor Survivors Association as their guests. Idling in the lobby, one of the veterans, Ernest Renda, stared incredulously as an usher, speaking with his wife Bebe, stumbled over his words. The twenty-year-old seemed confused. Wasn't *Pearl Harbor* just a movie, like *Jurassic Park* or *Field of Dreams*, he asked? Sheepishly, the young man listened to an impromptu history lesson explaining this film was not a story that some Hollywood screenwriter made up.

Maybe a few German nationals need an extemporized history lesson. In early November 2004, England's Queen Elizabeth II arrived in Berlin for a climate change conference, held informal talks with Chancellor Gerhard Schroeder, and—two nights later—attended a festive concert to raise funds for the rebuilding of Dresden's *Frauenkirche*, an elaborate, eighteenth-century cathedral destroyed by Allied bombers in February 1945. Throughout her stay, German newspaper editorials berated Her Majesty's government, the Royal and American Air Forces, and various leaders, including the late General Arthur "Bomber" Harris for the three-day aerial attack of almost sixty years ago and demanded the queen apologize for this wartime act. Undaunted (and probably confused), Queen Elizabeth, who lived through the 1940 London blitz, demurred and, after a few ceremonial functions, politely returned to London.

Apologize? Were German headlines demanding an apology from the royal family for bombing a World War II enemy target—the former Third Reich nation whose unrelenting Luftwaffe attacks destroyed city after city, including Rotterdam, during the peak of their westward offensives? What is next? Maybe the U.S. Army should apologize for liberating the concentration camps and forcing nearby adult townspeople to view their führer's final solution. Or how about the Nuremberg Trials? Maybe the Allies should apologize for prosecuting known war criminals.

As always, a fine line divides capital interests and historical realities. On Waikiki's main shopping street, Kalakaua Avenue, an elaborate twin-story hotel dominates this prime beach area. With its startling lobby, indoor waterfall, and prized oceanfront rooms, the hotel attracts many well-heeled visitors, especially Japanese nationals, who arrive in busloads, ready to enjoy the balmy Honolulu weather. For many of these tourists, this ivory-colored hotel is a honeymoon retreat where smiling couples arrive, *en famille*, for elaborate Hawaiian-style weddings and receptions.

With friendly, pleasant service as its watchword, the hotel staff offers one useful suggestion after another to comfort its guests. Fascinated by Polynesian artifacts, its island activities sheet inquires, Why not visit the famous Bishop Museum? How about an excursion to the only royal mansion on American soil? Head over to the Iolani Palace, the staff advises, to see this grand structure completed in 1882. Interested in twentieth-century history? Why not visit Pearl Harbor? Here, on December 7, 1941, the hotel's directory informs, enemy dive-bombers nearly destroyed the U.S. Pacific fleet that fateful morning.

The U.S. fleet was attacked by *enemy* dive-bombers? Where did these aircraft come from? Enemyland? On a bright, happy August 2002 afternoon, an energetic, smiling assistant manager offered a facile explanation for the hotel's language. The Pearl Harbor attack occurred nearly forty years before anyone on the staff was born, she began, and since her formative years were spent in California, the historical events were a little fuzzy. But if the Japanese actually dropped those bombs, they probably were sorry. After all, look around, she gestured. Look at all these happy people from Japan. Besides, why bring up the past? Really, she concluded, what's done is done and prudent hotel management requires simplicity. Don't you understand, her smiling faced beamed, that was long ago. Yes, it was long ago, but it certainly wasn't far away. The attack happened a few miles from the hotel. Maybe this polite representative spent the previous evening watching Columbia's 1957 desert saga *Bitter Victory*. Here a British major (Richard Burton), preparing to attack an Axis stronghold, speculated about the raid's long-term effects: "I wonder why people have short memories. Do they forget what they want to forget or don't they care?"

Maybe Hollywood can refresh past events. In the fall 2000 issue of *Voices*— a quarterly magazine published by the Pfizer Pharmaceutical Company to promulgate their blue, erectile dysfunction pill, Viagra—an unsigned article explained some seductive traits to "warm up those cool fall nights." Some suggestions included long walks, fresh flowers, stargazing, and romantic movies. Motion pictures, of course, can inspire some intimacy, and the writer singled out *From Here to Eternity* as a mood-setting title. Romance? Intimacy? Did anyone on the Pfizer staff watch this picture? Where is the romance when a sadistic stockade guard bludgeons a helpless prisoner? Will anyone feel like some intimacy after watching Japanese planes strafe Hickman Field, killing many GIs? How about the vicious treatment of an idealist bugler by some nasty sergeants? Will that instigate some lovemaking? Need more inspiration? Why not swoon over that back-alley stabbing scene where one soldier knifed another? Or, for the pièce de résistance, maybe the couple should watch *Schindler's List*. That should clinch the evening.

Certainly there were difficult experiences on the road to victory, and Hollywood—never shying away from the horror, mayhem, or destruction— would gleefully summarize the four-year conflict with a colorful noun. Photodramas such as *A Place in Hell*, *A Taste of Hell*, *Back Door to Hell*, *Between Heaven and Hell*, and *Bridge to Hell* retold many problems associated with combat. Other screenplays, *Five for Hell*, *From Hell to Victory*, *Hell Commandos*, *Hell in Normandy*, and *Hell in the Pacific* offered ongoing praise for America's champions. Likewise, *Hell Is for Heroes*, *Hell River*, *Hell Squad*, *Hell to Eternity*, *Hellboy*, and *Heroes in Hell* described numerous victories, while *Seven Women from Hell*, *Surrender—Hell*, *Ten Seconds to Hell*, *and The Walls of Hell* fought more battles. Lastly, *The Walls of Hell*, *To Hell and Back*, and *When Hell Broke Loose* demonstrated, when all was said and done, American prowess remained undaunted.

For better or worse, Hollywood remains the leading teacher of World War II, offering one version after another about America's four-year ordeal. With its ubiquitous visual appeal (even though GIs wear lipstick), high-powered amplifications, and elaborate special-effects system, their many interpretations still hold court. Can anyone doubt the influence of John Wayne, the tough American who never lost a battle? How about Clark Gable? Didn't he send those B-17s into Germany's heartland, wrecking their matériel industries? Look at Henry Fonda. Wasn't that a smart idea, attacking the Japanese at Midway? Do not forget Gregory Peck. After many setbacks he finally waded ashore, godlike, at Luzon, keeping his "I Shall Return" promise to the Philippines people. Remember to clap for Robert Taylor. He and his *Enola Gay* crew brought the war to a dramatic end. Wave the flag for James Garner and his fine-tuned Rangers. Didn't they blast those Nazis out of their mountain stronghold? Give credit to Jeff Chandler. His Red Ball Express kept the French eastward advance moving unobtrusively. Do not leave out young Audie Murphy and his daring exploits routing the Germans. What about James Cagney? His quick thinking wrecked the Japanese navy.

As for the future, where will Hollywood venture next? Can World War II screenplays remain a viable commercial interest, or is this subject, like its predecessor the Great War, dated? Will the motion-picture industry keep Old Glory, frontal beachhead assaults, commando raids, and precision daytime-bombing attacks in its production schedule, or has this subject, like the 1940s propaganda pictures, also run its course? One point is certain. Future generations will learn about this conflict from the movies they watch. No one can deny—as Marshall McLuhan told the Vietnam generation—the medium is the message. And certainly, no one can overlook Paul Fussell's prescient words, "The real war will never get into the books." Maybe a coda is needed: the real war will never reach the silver screen.

Selective Filmography of World War II Motion Pictures

1946–2007

Above and Beyond

MGM, Directed by Melvin Frank and Norman Panama,
Released 1952

A sudsy, hearts-and-flowers soap opera that details the marital problems caused by the elaborate security necessary for the crew training to drop the first atomic bomb. Good-looking Robert Taylor excels as Colonel Paul W. Tibbets Jr.—the fly-by-the-book Air Corps pilot—who demands rigid discipline for his top-secret assignment, while his wife (Eleanor Parker) cannot fathom warfare's realities. (Robert Taylor, explaining to his spouse the nature of Japanese aggression: "To lose this war to that gang we're fighting would be the most immoral thing we could do to those kids in there—and don't you ever forget it.") Eventually, the *Enola Gay* completes her mission—bringing the war to a dramatic climax—and after months of separation, the happy couple, in a corny tearjerker ending, reunite at the Washington, D.C., airport.

Act of Love

United Artists, Directed by Anatole Litvak, Released 1954

A wonderful boy-meets-girl romance in which true love takes the proverbial wrong turn and ends disastrously. Kirk Douglas radiates as a combat-experienced PFC, who in winter 1945 is assigned to Paris command headquarters. Soon, the dimpled-chin GI falls for a sweet French girl (Dany Robin), and after a whirlwind courtship the twosome agree to marry. (Douglas, explaining why he cannot stay the night: "The Army doesn't know anything about "just once"—when they say eleven o'clock, they mean eleven o'clock.") Hampered by a loudmouthed captain, Douglas is reassigned, and after a failed last-ditch effort both lovers are permanently separated. Then, in a Javert-type finale, the distraught female drowns in the Seine. As a social protest, the photodrama blasts away at those American opportunists fueling the black market and the nasty, undemocratic behavior of the officer caste system.

The Affair

Home Box Office, Directed by Paul Seed, Released 1995

A critical, no-holds-barred indictment of the U.S. Army's officer cadre system that blatantly enforces Jim Crow laws when hundreds of black GIs arrive in a British village, months before the Normandy landing. Well-mannered Courtney B. Vance sparkles as an ordinary foot soldier unaccustomed to the civility proffered by his host nation. Following a series of romanticized coincidences, he becomes the lover of a lonely married woman (Kerry Fox). Eventually discovered, the comely wife—completely discombobulated—cannot stop those events that allow a kangaroo court-martial to execute Private Vance on a trumped-up rape charge. Supposedly inspired by a "true" story, this made-for-television drama reiterates that racism and fascism permeate the commissioned ranks. (Colonel Ned Beatty, explaining why he wants an immediate execution: "We are shipping out any day. In France, the nigger boy's gun will be loaded; we estimate to lose 50,000 good men there! So, I'm not about to worry about one bad one.")

Ambush Bay

United Artists, Directed by Ron Winston, Released 1966

A slow-moving, disjointed, don't-ask-any-questions trek through the Japanese-held Philippine jungle by a wily group of U.S. Marines hoping to infiltrate an enemy camp days before General MacArthur's historic 1944 "I shall return" invasion. Here, a close-to-the-chest sergeant (Hugh O'Brien) watches helplessly as one by one his elite squad falls victim to the hostile terrain. Eventually, the resourceful noncom, along with a nineteen-year-old radio operator (James Mitchum), creates a loud diversion, sneaks into a guarded compound, and—after some fancy hand-grenade throwing—detonates a Japanese underwater mining complex, a feat that ensures the U.S. Navy safe passage for their attack vessels. Worst typecasting: former Andy Hardy all-American boy and song-and-dance man, Mickey Rooney, as a rough-and-tumble, sangfroid marine gunnery sergeant. (Sergeant Rooney, ruminating about his precarious situation: "I can't figure it out—feel like I'm in a stadium with a bunch of Jap spectators.")

An American Guerrilla in the Philippines

Twentieth Century–Fox, Directed by Fritz Lang, Released 1950

Another strong testimony to American individualism, proving once again that prowess, integrity, and determinism always lead to victory regardless of the odds. Tyrone Power moves quickly as a navy officer stranded on a Philippine island in 1942, when his command retreats to Australia. After a shaky start, this resourceful ensign—along with other isolated GIs—mobilizes villagers and, for the next three years, destroys enemy installations, harasses Japanese forces, and maintains morale, while radioing important logistical information to Allied headquarters. (Ensign Power, summarizing his work: "In short, we built an army, restored a government, sought to imbrue the people with an unconquerable faith and an inevitable victory.") Best scene: the guerrillas beam with pride as their hero, five-star General MacArthur, keeping his "I-shall-return" promise, enters their village hideout much to the acclaim of the flag-waving, native population.

The Americanization of Emily

MGM, Directed by Arthur Hiller, Released 1964

A wacky, off-the-wall, farcical, black comedy—probably the funniest World War II movie ever made—that grinds the U.S. military into the ground with its irreverent spoof of authority, leadership, and interservice rivalry. Always resourceful and quick on his feet, James Garner coruscates as a goldbricking naval aide who supplies women, booze, elaborate London hotel accommodations, and favors to numerous admirals planning the massive D-Day assault. Off to the side, his English girlfriend, Emily (Julie Andrews), slowly learns that the American method of waging war requires an oleaginous public relations staff. (Admiral Melvyn Douglas, explaining the importance of usurping any army glory: "The first dead man on Omaha Beach must be a sailor.") After a series of madcap, turnabout events—that include blatant opportunism, poor planning, unbridled alcoholism, and a canceled invasion date—the first "dead" naval man returns alive, much to the confusion of the senior officers who must scramble to reverse this unexpected contretemps.

Anzio

Columbia, Directed by Edward Dmytryk, Released 1968

An outspoken commentary pointing the finger at the U.S. Army's high command for the severe casualty rate during the January 1944 Italian campaign. Here, an accredited war correspondent living with a combat squad

(Robert Mitchum) witnesses many examples of ineptitude responsible for the decimation of an inland patrol. (Newsman Mitchum, lambasting General Arthur Kennedy: "Of 767 men there are seven survivors left to see the results of one more royal foul-up.") As a fervent Nazi officer in charge of an ill-supplied garrison, Wolfgang Preiss keeps the Allied forces bogged down on the Anzio beachhead until German reinforcements arrive. Eventually, the U.S. Army—after some leadership shuffling—initiates a dramatic breakthrough, allowing the ground pounders their first victory on the slow road to Rome.

Attack

United Artists, Directed by Robert Aldrich, Released 1956

A blatant, no-holds-barred, both-barrels salvo exposing the U.S. Army officer old-boy network where cronyism, nepotism, favoritism, and occasional incompetency flourish with impunity in a frontline outfit. Eddie Albert is outstanding as an unstable, indecisive, southern National Guard captain whose numerous blunders create many casualties during the November 1944 French hostilities. Eventually confronted by a squad lieutenant (Jack Palance), the two men square off. (Lieutenant Palance threatening his commanding officer: "Listen to me, Cooney! If you put me and my men in a wringer—if you send us out there and let us hang—I swear, I swear by all that's holy, I'll come back. I'll come back and take this grenade and shove it down your throat and pull the pin!") Basically an outspoken, leftist film, the photoplay emphasizes the futility of combat, but—in a faltering shift—its weak, Pollyannaish, red-white-and-blue ending softens the blow, reducing the screenplay's antiwar message to mere pabulum.

Attack on the Iron Coast

United Artists, Directed by Paul Wendkos, Released 1968

Another explosive damn-the-torpedoes-full-speed-ahead aquatic yarn, this one heaping dollops of praise on a fast-moving Canadian commando unit. These commandos' daring 1943 attack on a German-occupied Normandy seaport destroyed an important component of Hitler's so-called impregnable Iron Coast. Led by tough-talking Lloyd Bridges, the knife-wielding night fighters must live up to his exacting standards. (Major Bridges to staff: "Postponement is out of the question. We gotta move within six days or not at all.") With the help of a diehard naval officer (Andrew Keir), this raid, after some initial setbacks, restates the indomitable spirit of the British Empire. Best scene: Major Bridges, learning that an apprehensive sailor is only sixteen years old, gives the lad his prized cigarette lighter.

Away All Boats

Universal, Directed by Joseph Pevney, Released 1956

A quintessential 1950s Cold War–era naval adventure that highlights America's seafaring forces as indomitable sailors who methodically blast their Oriental foes out of the water. Promoted to captain of an amphibious launch vessel, hard-talking Jeff Chandler slowly hones his inexperienced tars into a first-class assault team. (Captain Chandler, laying down the law: "The singular duty of this ship is to carry a combat-loaded battalion right into the laps of the enemy.") After months of vicious fighting, the ship's luck runs out when a kamikaze, dodging hundreds of rounds over Okinawa, rams its starboard side. Unwilling to accept defeat, the fast-moving bluejackets, inspired by their officers, clear the deck, patch the hull, and literally tow their damaged vessel to safety. Using many pelagic stereotypes—including the loneliness of command, the disgruntled officer, and the innocent bumpkin—this wonderful ending reaffirms the U.S. Navy's credo that the unassailable bond between crew and ship never falters.

Band of Brothers

DreamWorks, Directed by David Frankel et al, Released 2001

An elaborate, made-for-television, straightforward account about the men of Easy Company, 506th Regiment, 101st Airborne. Beginning with their arduous Georgia basic training, they are followed through their jam-packed Atlantic crossing, nighttime D-Day drop behind German lines, difficult fight for Carentan, Market Garden, and Bastogne, poignant concentration-camp liberation, and, finally, the glorious capture of Hitler's prized Bavarian hideaway, Eagle's Nest. With a large supporting cast and utilizing eight directors, this 705-minute tribute offers strong testimony to an outfit that by war's end suffered a 150 percent casualty rate. (Lieutenant Damian Lewis, explaining his company's philosophy: "You know why they volunteered? So when things got really bad, the man in the foxhole next to them would be the best, not some draftee who's going to get them killed.") With numerous interviews of surviving members, this cinematic epic details those wartime emotions—fear, anxiety, disappointment, caution, elation, retribution, elitism, and victory—as these paratroopers move forward, mindful of the company clerk's directive, "Anyone who has not made a will, go to the supply office."

Battle Cry

Warner Bros., Directed by Raoul Walsh, Released 1955

A chest-pounding 155-minute Marine Corps hagiography—based on Leon Uris's best-selling novel—which traces the joys, camaraderie, and sorrows of some young men from their shaky San Diego boot-camp days to their eventual rendezvous with Japanese forces in the South Pacific campaign. Van Heflin stands tall as the hard-nosed father-figure commander, ordering extensive physical training for his youthful charges. (Colonel Heflin, explaining the rationale for his unremitting all-day, all-night marches: "When we go into battle again, not one of my boys will die because he's a straggler—no one's going to die because he's weak."). With James Whitmore, Tab Hunter, and Aldo Ray in supporting roles, the screenplay blends family values, the contribution of the Navaho Indian code specialists, and semper fidelis with the larger backdrop of the nation at war in a style reminiscent of the 1940s propaganda films.

Battle Force

Film Ventures International, Directed by Umberto Lenzi, Released 1977

Another low-budget, Italian-made hoopla that chronicles the glory and defeat of a small group of American, British, and German officers from a 1936 Berlin dinner through numerous battles. Finally, the combatants converge in the North African desert, where, in an elaborate tank offensive, they witness the capitulation of Rommel's Afrika Korps. Here, a seventy-one-year-old war correspondent (John Huston) watches the Nazi surrender, while back at West Point his pal, a seventy-two-year-old general (Henry Fonda), receives personal messages from the front lines. Loosely modeled on *The Young Lions*, this copycat version contains one disjointed vignette after another that caricatures both Axis and Allied soldiers. Worst German accent: *Wehrmacht* soldier (Stacy Keach) explaining lebensraum. (Lieutenant Keach to party guests: "I can guarantee, the führer has no intentions of starting a war.")

Battle of Blood Island

Bickman/Rapp Productions, Directed by Joel Rapp, Released 1960

Another grainy, B-for-bad, hackneyed sixty-four-minute earsplitter—based on a short story by Philip Roth—describing the ordeal of two GIs, who in January 1945 survive a botched Pacific island raid. Then, they spend the next few months hiding in makeshift areas, dodging Japanese patrols, and arguing ad infinitum about extraneous issues not pertinent to the war. Both Richard Devon and Ron Kennedy talk incessantly but never make a point or reach a conclusion. (Private Devon, expatiating on survival instincts: "What kind of guts does it take to stay alive?" while his pal, Private Kennedy retorts: "Do you always have to be kidding around?") Unknown to the Americans, V-J Day arrives, and in a ritualistic mood, the Japanese commit hara-kiri, allowing the soldiers two more months of prosy and tedious loquacity until a rescue party, searching for a suitable atomic bomb testing site, locates them.

Battle of Bloody Beach

Twentieth Century–Fox, Directed by Herbert Coleman, Released 1961

A bottom-of-the-barrel, 100 percent hokum, B–soap opera that follows the misgivings of an American construction worker, who roams around various Philippine islands delivering matériel to resistance groups while searching for his wife during the precarious 1942 Japanese-occupation days. Acting more like a lovesick student than a guerrilla fighter, Audie Murphy frequently stares out into space hoping to locate his missing bride, while his sidekick (Gary Crosby) suggests more vigilance. (Lieutenant Crosby, summarizing various dangers: "Last time I listened in on Tokyo Rose, they upped the reward on you to 50,000 pesos. I doubt they pay that much for General MacArthur.") Eventually, the lovers are united, but the reunion becomes strained because the wife—thinking her spouse long dead—latched onto a new beau. Finally, an oceanfront battle with Japanese forces reconciles the lovers, and in a typical ride-off-into-the-sunset ending, the twosome paddle out to a waiting U.S. submarine, leaving their conjugal problems behind on the bloody beach.

The Battle of Neretva

Republic, Directed by Valjko Brilajic, Released 1971

A typical Yugoslavian action yarn glorifying the Balkans' guerrilla warfare, with famous Hollywood stars peppered into a convoluted script, akin to the popular 1940s B-pictures. Here, Yul Brynner—a seasoned partisan thwarting the Nazis—blows up numerous bridges, while a German general (Curt Jurgens) bellows orders to his many subordinates. Eventually, the decisive battle of Neretva brings victory to the freedom fighters and death to Orson Welles, the turncoat supervising the Chetnik forces (Welles, plotting the defeat of the nationals "Let them destroy themselves.") Replete with many stock scenes—including the fight to the finish, the heroic female soldier, and the traitor in the midst—the photoplay heaps dollops of praise on Marshal Tito, the renegade Communist widely revered by his countrymen.

The Battle of the Bulge

Cinerama Productions Corporation, Directed by Ken Annakin,
Released 1965

An elaborate, overstated, and fuzzy adaptation of the Germany army's desperate
efforts to halt the Allied eastward advance in December 1944, when after weeks
of seesaw fighting, the American forces, with superior airpower, overran the
Wehrmacht in the frigid Belgian forest. Using an array of impressive stars—including Henry Fonda, Robert Ryan, Dana Andrews, Robert Shaw, and Telly
Savalas—this wide-angled, 165-minute, pseudo-travelogue ignores most historical events and, instead, provides a stylized, soap-opera account of a pivotal U.S.
victory. (Nazi tank commander Robert Shaw, explaining facetiously why his side
can win: "Germans are still the best toy makers in the world.") With one inaccu-
racy after another, including a Belgian "Alps" aerial reconnaissance and a back-
and-forth tank duel, this fiction-as-fact screenplay at time resembles a galloping
Hollywood Western, complete with a rousing, cavalry-to-the-rescue ending.

Battleground

MGM, Directed by William A. Wellman, Released 1949

A finely crafted black-and-white testimony to the men of the 101st Airborne
Division—the Screaming Eagles—who brought the *Wehrmacht* to an abrupt
halt during their protracted Battle of the Bulge. Van Johnson, John Hodiak,
and James Whitmore star as worn-out GIs, whose squad must spend Christmas week 1944 at Bastogne, dodging Nazi infiltrators during one of the War's
coldest periods. Lacking adequate supplies and cut off from their own lines,
the dogfaces maintain a shaky sense of humor (PFC Johnson and fellow GI,
kibitzing over the password: "Hello Joe, what do you know? Just got back
from a vaudeville show.") Modeled after the classical propaganda genre, the
storyline preserves the hopes, aspirations, fears, and frustrations of a small
but cohesive group of men, highlighting their eclectic backgrounds as they
fight their way out of the Belgian woodlands.

Beach Red

Theodora Productions, Directed by Cornel Wilde, Released 1967

A strong, antiwar statement—based on the novel by Peter Bowman—that
downplays heroics and, instead, focuses on the folly and egomania associated
with battle. Now a marine officer, Cornel Wilde cautiously guides his men
through the uncharted jungles of some unnamed South Pacific island, only to

witness violent death at every turn, while his psychopathic top sergeant (Rip Torn) rants and raves about everything (Sergeant Torn to Captain Wilde: "I'm a Marine! Who gives a damn about this dead Jap now? He's nothing, he's worth nothing!") Heavy-laden with numerous flashbacks depicting wholesome family life, as well as some Eisenstein-type montage, the storyline portrays both Japanese and Americans as peaceful individuals longing for their wives, children, and hearths. Eventually, large numbers of marines and Japanese perish in a gory, allegorical end-of-the-film battle, allowing Cornel Wilde another opportunity to expatiate about war's absurdity.

Beachhead

United Artists, Directed by Stuart Heisler, Released 1954

A taut, watch-your-back, steamy jungle trek involving a four-man marine reconnaissance team operating behind enemy lines to disrupt Japanese logistics hours before a major U.S. offensive at the strategic island of Bougainville. Hard-talking Frank Lovejoy, an experienced noncom, moves cautiously, guiding his small squad from one skirmish to another, while a younger leatherneck, Tony Curtis, carps about military life. (Loudmouth Curtis to his sergeant: "What did all those years in the Marine Corps do to you? Burn your nerves out?") Eventually, the devil dogs rescue a French scientist and his daughter, and—after another arduous journey—return safely to their command post. Funniest scene: Corporal Tony Curtis, crawling through the jungle with a knife in his mouth, ready to pounce upon an unsuspecting Japanese soldier hiding in the underbrush.

The Beginning or the End

MGM, Directed by Norman Taurog, Released 1947

Another B-homily that ponders atomic energy's future in the postwar period. Employing a narrative, documentary format, the photoplay traces the Manhattan Project, starting with Einstein's warning to President Roosevelt, up to the *Enola Gay*'s early morning mission over Japan. Here the flamboyant scientist, Dr. J. Robert Oppenheimer, played by Hume Cronyn, offers a conservative interpretation while Brian Donlevy—portraying General Lester Groves—keeps his military staff on their toes with his demand for expediency. (Army major, Robert Walker, working with a physicist: "Just get us that bomb and get it before Hitler and the Japs.") One scene—depicting the Los Alamos implosion—seems macabre: Oppenheimer and his staff, unaware of nuclear energy's potential, rub suntan lotion on their skin as protection against the blast from this first atomic test.

The Best Years of Our Lives

MGM, Directed by William Wyler, Released 1946

A wonderful 171-minute Academy Award epic—one of the greatest films ever made—that amalgamates the joys, sorrows, and self-realizations of three combat veterans when they return to their thriving, mid-American city months after the war has ended. Dana Andrews is outstanding as a decorated B-17 bombardier, who discovers the postwar boom has no room for the men who dropped their explosives on German targets, while Fredric March, a former sergeant back from the Pacific island fighting, begrudgingly returns to his executive banking position. (March to wife: "Last year it was kill Japs; and this year it's make money.") Harold Russell, a young sailor who lost both hands when his ship was attacked, steals the show as a shy, sensitive, Norman Rockwell–type hometown boy hoping for a modicum of normalcy. Heavy with acerbic social criticisms that blast draft-dodgers, war profiteering, unfaithful wives, America-First committees, and short memories, the film's tempo—based on the free-verse poem by MacKinlay Kantor—reiterates the various modes of opportunism that existed on the home front and calls to task the important job of helping every returning serviceman.

Betrayed

MGM, Directed by Gottfried Reinhardt, Released 1954

Another spy-versus-spy melodrama that plunges a Dutch officer (Clark Gable) into a deadly cat-and-mouse game with a Resistance traitor (Victor Mature) during the final days of the spring 1944 Holland occupation, as monocled Gestapo officers routinely unravel Allied sabotage information prior to the Market Garden offensive. Unable to ferret out the German plant, the hard-nosed Gable scrutinizes his entire staff. (Major Gable, rationalizing his skepticism: "It's my job to look for the worst in people, suspect them, mistrust them, everyone.") After some comic-book adventures—including an elaborate pseudo-double-agent infiltration into a German hospital ward to rescue an underground fighter—Gable exposes the turncoat. Funniest scene: straight-faced Lana Turner, also an Allied agent, parachutes from an American C-47, wearing a mushroom-shaped helmet that resembles mission-to-Mars headgear.

Between Heaven and Hell

Twentieth Century–Fox, Directed by Richard Fleischer, Released 1956

A strong antimilitary CinemaScope proclamation—based on the novel by Francis Gwaltney—that accuses some American officers stationed on a Pacific island in 1945, labeling them irrational, pusillanimous, and fascist. Once a combat sergeant—now busted to slick-sleeved private—Robert Wagner harbors deep resentment against the army caste system. (Private Wagner explaining his reduction in rank: "Assaulting an officer under combat conditions.") Reassigned to a dangerous forward unit, he confronts Captain Broderick Crawford, a psychopathic tyrant known simply as "Waco," who sends him off to a precarious lookout station. After a Japanese attack, the good-looking Wagner manages to warn his unit, saving the lives of many soldiers. In a typical Hollywood happy-ending format, the deranged captain falls victim to a sniper shot, and the army command, now cognizant of its personnel shortcomings, places capable, intelligent men back in command.

The Big Red One

United Artists, Directed by Samuel Fuller, Released 1980

A stand-up-and-shout tribute to the GIs of the First Infantry Division—the fighting men who wear the big, red, number one emblazoned on their left shoulder—highlighting their many combat accomplishments. Lee Marvin—a battle-hardened sergeant from the Great War—serves as a father figure to his eclectic squad, from their initial assault landing in North Africa and subsequent campaigns in Sicily, Normandy Beach, the Battle of the Bulge and, finally, to the liberation of a Czechoslovakian concentration camp. Along the way, the foot soldiers—with a diverse collection of American youthful values—share tragedy, pathos, dreams, and an occasional female with their noncom, illustrating the importance of squad unity. (GI to buddy: "You said the U.S. Army is made up of the First Division and ten main replacements.")

Bitter Victory

Columbia, Directed by Nicholas Ray, Released 1957

Another parched, black-and-white, CinemaScope, Sahara Desert adventure yarn, detailing the training, planning, and implementation of a precarious British commando raid against an isolated Libyan outpost to steal General Rommel's offensive orders. Under the command of Major Curt Jurgens, the squad reaches its target, destroys the enemy camp, takes the documents, but, after some unforeseen events, becomes stranded in an abandoned tenth-century waterhole village. Off to the side, a disillusioned colleague, Captain Richard Burton, a former archeologist, disparages the mission's usefulness. (Captain Burton's tirade: "The fine line between war and murder is distance.") After a series of mishaps—including a deadly scorpion's sting, a long, hot march, and, as always, the stereotypical sandstorm—a British rescue team reaches the beleaguered group. Acclaimed a hero, Major Jurgens, in a nod to a gentleman's sensibilities, pins his recently awarded medal on a mannequin, a gesture of war's anonymity.

Black Brigade

ABC, Directed by George McCowan, Released 1970

Another campy, pseudo-blaxploitation, seventy-minute potboiler about the feats of an all-black infantry squad picked for a dangerous assignment to seize a strategic German dam in 1944. Headed by a redneck, southern officer, Stephen Boyd, this search-and-hold mission stands on shaky ground as the Georgia-born captain, annoyed by the unit's homogeneity, offers one taunt after another. (Captain Boyd to Lieutenant Robert Hooks: "This isn't a company, it's a circus.") Eventually, seven men sneak behind enemy lines, and—after some Marx Brothers antics—reach their objective, battle the Germans, and hold the roadway, allowing thousands of American troops easy passage for their eastern offensive (Lieutenant Hooks, explaining his unit's bravery: "Every one of those men volunteered to fight—to die for his country.") With numerous speech, sartorial, hirsute, and geographical anachronisms, the made-for-television screenplay, originally titled *Carter's Army*, offers low-budget praise for African American soldiers. Worst casting: well-known comedian Richard Pryor as an inept GI unable to understand simple instructions or comprehend military time.

Born to Ride

Warner Bros., Directed by Graham Baker, Released 1991

A far-fetched, made-for-adolescents hodgepodge about the unlikely adventures of the U.S. Army's first motorcycle squadron, highlighting some of their Looney Tunes escapades against the Gestapo during the closing months of 1939. Here, John Stamos, a one-time teenage idol, portrays a smart-aleck army corporal who constantly snubs military regulations, but is allowed some impunity because of his extraordinary riding skills (base commander Slobo-dan Dimitrijevic to Stamos: "I need somebody to train my men how to ride these machines—you're the man who can do that.") Soon, the good-looking motorcyclist winds up in Franco's Spain and—with his unit—rescues an American atomic physicist from the *Schutzstaffel*. Matured and exonerated from his foolish past, Corporal Stamos receives some military kudos plus a big kiss from the colonel's daughter. Laden with implausible situations, the whole shooting match resembles the cliffhanger serials popularized during the 1940s' Saturday-afternoon matinees.

The Boys from Brazil

Twentieth Century–Fox, Directed by Franklin J. Schaffner, Released 1978

An off-the-wall, science-fictional, à la Frankenstein fish story, claiming that the führer's chromosomes are alive and well in South America. Gregory Peck portrays the infamous mad scientist, Dr. Josef Mengele, who in 1978—using unspecified body specimens—has cloned dozens of young Adolf Hitlers, who eventually will create the Fourth Reich. (Dr. Peck, explaining his screwball plan: "Ninety-three boys are exact genetic duplicates of him [Hitler], bred entirely from his cells" while another former Third Reich officer, James Mason, smiles sardonically.) Meanwhile, a doddering, world-renowned Nazi hunter, Laurence Olivier, gets wind of this plan and, after a series of cat-and-mouse travel episodes, exposes everything. Based on Ira Levin's best seller, this popular motion picture continues the fringe conspiracy theory whose advocates preach Hitler did not perish in the Berlin bunker but, instead, is roaming around various South American countries, plotting a return to power.

Breakthrough

Warner Bros., Directed by Lewis Seiler, Released 1950

A let's-go, move-up, keep-low tribute to the GIs who landed at Omaha Beach, raced to the seawall, and, eventually, routed the Nazis from their strongholds, paving the way for a dramatic Allied breakthrough miles away at Saint Lô. Dodging many bullets and explosives, Sergeant Frank Lovejoy guides his chain-smoking squad from the Normandy coast into the arduous, inland hedgerow fighting, and, finally, on the road to Paris. (Sergeant Lovejoy explaining his unit's combat experiences: "Nobody walked across Normandy, they crawled.") Along the way this small, eclectic group—that included a green lieutenant, a dog lover, a future politician, a prankster, and a teenager—bond into a cohesive unit, protecting each other. With numerous newsreel inserts (some anachronistic), much of the photodrama reiterates that the American fighting man—when pushed to his limits—fights both arduously and bravely.

Breakthrough

Maverick International, Directed by Andrew V. McLaglen, Released 1978

A West German production (using the same title as a 1950 World War II motion picture) that continues the legendary exploits of a recalcitrant *Wehrmacht* soldier, Sergeant Steiner (of *Cross of Iron* fame) and his ongoing battle against sadistic, inhuman Nazi officers who issue a fight-to-the-death decree during the July 1944 Normandy retreat. Richard Burton seems miscast as the Third Reich noncommissioned officer who nonchalantly tells an American colonel (Robert Mitchum) about an upcoming German coup, hoping his information will force a truce. (Sergeant Burton to Mitchum: "The time for laughing at Adolf Hitler is passed. In a matter of hours, we shall hear that he is dead.") After the plot fails, an American general (Rod Steiger) orders a frontal tank assault and—following some minor skirmishes—the GIs, aided by Sergeant Burton, enter a French town and secure their position. With frequent antiwar, anti-Hitler, and anti-Gestapo references, this screenplay portrays the common German soldier as a kind-hearted innocent imprisoned by a rabid military system.

The Bridge at Remagen

United Artists, Directed by John Guillermin, Released 1968

A blatant antimilitary, antiofficer, and antiwar indictment, detailing the Allied attack of a strategic Rhine installation, the Ludendorff Bridge, and the Nazi's futile March 1945 defense. E. G. Marshall radiates as a Machiavellian U.S. Army general determined to take his objectives regardless of the human cost. (Marshall to subordinates: "We're risking 100 but we may save 10,000, even 50,000! What you got to do is throw your men across!) But a battle-hardened lieutenant (George Segal) and his sergeant (Ben Gazzara) display only scorn and contempt for their senior officers, while over in the German camp a Nazi major (Robert Vaughn) and his general (Peter Van Eyck) become casualties of their superior's unique cruelty. Containing numerous examples of leadership failure, the storyline lambastes the command system found in both armies.

The Bridge on the River Kwai

Columbia, Directed by David Lean, Released 1957

A 161-minute blockbuster—winner of seven Academy Awards—that describes the ordeal of some British POW's building a Japanese railway bridge in the Malaysian jungle and the efforts of a small Allied raiding team to destroy this important military target. Basically an antiwar picture with numerous box-office stars—including William Holden, Alec Guinness, Jack Hawkins, and Sessue Hayakawa—the story line questions the efficacy of heroics, megalomania, the officer caste system, Oriental fanaticism, and death before dishonor. (Commander William Holden badmouthing his superior: "You and that Colonel Nicholson, you're two of a kind! Crazy with courage, for what? How to die like a gentleman, how to die by the rules?") One of the most controversial scenes:

Alec Guinness, a ramrod British soldier, inadvertently drops his makeshift swagger stick into the river, a faux pas unthinkable for an English officer.

A Bridge Too Far

United Artists, Directed by Richard Attenborough, Released 1977

A puffed-up, we-can-win, flag-waving, 176-minute tribute to the Allied forces and their ambitious but ill-fated attempt to seize four strategic bridges during a daring Dutch offensive—code-named Market Garden—in September 1944. Using an array of impressive motion-picture stars portraying important military luminaries, the storyline, based on the book by Cornelius Ryan, weaves in and out of various British, American, and German command posts and battle sites, expostulating how the nine-day, seesaw fighting was really a combination of unrealistic planning, logistical screwups, and ineluctable serendipity. (Dirk Bogarde, portraying General Frederick "Boy" Browning, explaining why his side will win: "We're going to fly 35,000 men 3,000 miles and drop them behind enemy lines—it will be the largest airborne operation ever mounted!) Finally, after suffering numerous losses, the Allies capitulate, leaving behind many dead and wounded soldiers. (General Dirk Bogarde, rationalizing the defeat: "Well, as you know, I always thought that we tried to go a bridge too far.")

The Caine Mutiny

Columbia, Directed by Edward Dmytryk, Released 1954

Another critical jab at military life—from the Pulitzer prize novel by Herman Wouk—that depicts the fictional 1944 account of a half-crazed ship commander aboard a U.S. Navy minesweeper in the Pacific theater and his subsequent removal by junior officers, culminating with a court-martial to decide if such actions constitute a mutiny. Humphrey Bogart's portrayal of a demented captain convinces his staff that he is unfit for duty (Lieutenant Fred MacMurray to Lieutenant Van Johnson: "Captain Queeg has every symptom of acute paranoia—just a question of time before he goes over the line.") Eventually, Bogart's trial-room comportment—rolling three steel balls incessantly in his palm—exonerates the accused, even though their defense attorney (José Ferrer), feeling he has maligned the wrong man, heaves champagne into a celebrant's face.

Captain Corelli's Mandolin

Universal, Directed by John Madden, Released 2001

Another saccharine, 1940s wartime, romantic saga that proves, once again, the heart is a lonely hunter. Happy-go-lucky Nicolas Cage portrays an Italian mandolin-playing artillery officer, whose ill-disciplined unit occupies an idyllic Greek island, Cephallonia, while a German commandant politely ignores the lackadaisical nature of his subordinates. (Captain Corelli, explaining his nation's attitude about hostilities: "We're Italian, famous for singing, eating, making love.") Soon, the opera-singing Romeo catches the eye of a local beauty (Penélope Cruz), who—after some off-again, on-again flirtations—capitulates to the strumming musician. But Mussolini's 1943 escape changes everything as Italians and Germans, now enemies, fight their private battles, culminating in a gory end-of-the-film atrocity scene that separates the lovers. Two years later, however, they are united. Funniest scene: Captain Cage, marching in formation, in a manner that resembles the typical awkwardness exhibited by clumsy recruits during their first hours of basic training.

Captain Newman, M.D.

Universal, Directed by David Miller, Released 1963

A tricky blend of pathos, tragedy, and comedy depicting the psychiatric treatment of some American servicemen convalescing at an Arizona military hospital, circa 1943, where anxious commanders order their subordinates to make on-the-spot evaluations, employ fast treatment, and quickly return patients to their overseas fighting units. Soft-spoken Gregory Peck radiates as Josiah Newman, an army medical officer whose daily encounters with red tape, shell-shocked GIs, insufficient supplies, ambitious superiors, Italian prisoners-of-war, plus a locked-up ward of psychotic patients provide a continuous flow of humor, sadness, renewal, and optimism. (Captain Newman, explaining his laid-back philosophy: "We say 'Roger' quite a bit around here—makes us feel like heroes," while off to the side, his pretty nurse (Angie Dickinson), downplaying her maternal instincts, smiles gleefully.) With Tony Curtis as the preeminent goldbricking corporal holding an endless array of midnight-requisitioned materials, the whole shebang—complete with anachronistic haircuts, uniforms, aircraft, and jargon—could easily be titled, "The Three Stooges Get Drafted."

Captive Hearts

MGM, Directed by Paul Almond, Released 1987

Another implausible, love-conquers-all fairy tale that purports an Army Air Corps pilot (Chris Makepeace), along with his gunner, bail out of a crippled B-25 over northern Japan during December 1944. Quickly captured by frightened farmers, the two officers are first imprisoned in a mountainous village, but, after some roundabout events, are released to make needed household repairs. (Lieutenant Makepeace to his sergeant: "We better start planning our way out of here.") As the locals warm up to the young flyer, the ongoing war seems far away when a pretty Japanese widow (Mari Soto) catches his eye. Now, the twosome tiptoe around, hoping their mutual affection will not upset the proverbial applecart. When Japanese troops arrive, the town patriarch (Pat Morita) acts decisively, leading the lovers to the Sea of Japan. Ensconced in a small boat heading for the Chinese mainland, the Air Corps pilot waves a tender goodbye to his newfound sweetheart, promising that someday, when the birds are singing, he will return. Most unresolved question: what was a B-25, a two-engine bomber—with a limited range—doing in northern Japan?

Carmen Jones

Twentieth Century–Fox, Directed by Otto Preminger, Released 1954

A high-powered CinemaScope musical extravaganza updating George Bizet's famous opera, *Carmen*, to a black training base in the rural South sometime during the middle of the war. Harry Belafonte stars as a clean-cut army corporal—selected for flight-training school—who only wants to marry the innocent girl of his dreams. (Belafonte to sweetheart: "There's no use in waiting till the war's over for us to get married, not when I have a twenty-four-hour pass. We can have our honeymoon tonight.") Hours before his conjugal ceremony, the naive Belafonte capitulates to the charms of the post's femme fatale (Dorothy Dandridge), and after a series of musical adventures, the twosome flee to Chicago, barely escaping the authorities. Eventually, the strain of AWOL turns the good-looking Belafonte from a straight-arrow soldier to a jealous murderer. In its own simplistic way, the storyline denounces the segregated lifestyle of the African American GIs, a situation mandated by military regulations.

Casablanca Express

Globe, Directed by Sergio Martino, Released 1989

A preposterous Italian production—modeled after the spaghetti Westerns—that purports Winston Churchill's double duped the Nazis into attacking a local train heading for Casablanca during the early days of the 1942 North African campaign, while the real prime minister rendezvoused with President Roosevelt. Here, a two-star American general, seventy-three-year-old Glenn Ford, oversees this cloak-and-dagger mission while his British colleague (Donald Pleasence)—unaware of the ruse—plans an elaborate rescue mission. (Pleasence to staff: "We can't let Hitler fly our prime minister to

Berlin—I'm sure he'd rather die!") Soon Allied forces, firing anachronistic weapons, rout the Germans in a cavalry-to-the-rescue ending while another hero (Jason Connery) rides off into the sunset with his newfound girlfriend. Lacking any synchronized dialogue, the photoplay suffers from numerous revisionist inconsistencies, including a wild claim that Winston Churchill, aware of the impending Pearl Harbor attack, did not notify the White House.

Castle Keep

Columbia, Directed by Sydney Pollack, Released 1969

A lyrical, ontological, and mystical look at war's absurdity—based on the novel by William Eastlake—employing various forms of symbolism, spiritualism, and rationalism during the precarious 1944 Battle of the Bulge. As a one-eyed army major straddling a white thoroughbred, Burt Lancaster's laconic talk seems obtuse to his seven charges seeking refuge in a baroque castle in the Belgian forest, while his host (Jean-Pierre Aumont) explains the Freudian concept of destruction endemic to both sides. (Count Aumont, expatiating on military futility: "They planned this war because there was something they hadn't yet smashed.") Eventually both Allied and Nazi forces clash in a ritualistic Götterdämmerung, and the castle's ruins offer ignominious testimony to mankind's folly. Replete with numerous juxtapositions, including Peter Falk's portrayal of a soldier-turned-baker and Patrick O'Neal's obsession as an art historian, the convoluted story line is a classical retelling of the beauty and the beast fable.

Catch-22

Paramount, Directed by Mike Nichols, Released 1970

A heavy-handed, madcap, off-the-wall, black comedy—based on Joseph Heller's runaway best-selling first novel—that fires off both barrels at the lunacy of military life, blasting away at the nepotism, opportunism, goldbricking, and megalomania found during wartime. Alan Arkin is outstanding as an Army Air Corps bombardier, stationed on an unnamed Mediterranean island, whose daily attack missions have pushed him over the edge. Pleading mental instability, the acid-tongued Arkin discovers that military regulations forbid reassigning airmen who claim psychosis. (Captain Arkin, learning the intricacies of Catch-22: "In order to be grounded, I got to be crazy and I must be crazy to keep flying. But, if I ask to be grounded that means I'm not crazy anymore and I have to keep flying.") With an all-star cast that includes Jon Voight, Richard Benjamin, Art Garfunkel, Martin Balsam, Martin Sheen, Bob Newhart, and Orson Welles, no aspect of military life escapes lampooning.

Funniest scene: the flyers bomb their own base in a surrealistic, quid pro quo deal with the Germans involving some surplus cotton.

China Doll

Romina Productions, Directed by Frank Borzage, Released 1958

An easygoing, heart-tugging story about the antics of some Air Corps Hump pilots, who in 1943 routinely traverse the danger-prone Himalaya air route, and the misadventures of their senior pilot when he innocently "buys" a young Chinese girl, a bond servant, from her obliging father for a three-month period. Unable to extract himself from this ambiguous arrangement, hard-talking Captain Victor Mature initially ignores the pretty adolescent until the moment of truth, when infatuation ends and the heart takes over. (Captain Mature's declaration: "I guess I fell in love with you right from the beginning," culminating in marriage and a baby daughter.) Months later, a Japanese aircraft kill both parents, and, after years of orphanage life and U.S. red tape, a kindly priest finally unites the teenage girl with her father's close friends in a heartwarming, happy ending.

Code Name: Emerald

MGM, Directed by Jonathan Sanger, Released 1985

Another fictionalized, B-potboiler highlighting the secrecy surrounding the Operation Overlord logistics and the Allies' determination to keep the Nazi spy machine ignorant of the landing site and date. Based on the novel by Ronald Bass, the photodrama purports that a captured twenty-one-year-old U.S. Army first lieutenant—privy to this information—eschews Gestapo interrogation until good-looking American double-agent Ed Harris can parachute into France. There, Harris seduces a comely resistance worker, and with the assistance of a benign Nazi colonel (Max Von Sydow), smooth-talks his way past the German jailers to rescue the frail-looking American. (Double-agent Ed Harris to frightened officer, Eric Stoltz: "I'm with OSS—the Nazis think I'm working for them.) Funniest scene: clean-cut Ed Harris strutting around in a meticulously tailored Gestapo uniform, bellowing reprisal threats to everyone within hearing range.

Come See the Paradise

Twentieth Century–Fox, Directed by Alan Parker, Released 1990

A strongly worded, no-holds barred, revisionist indictment of Executive Law 9066—quickly passed after the Pearl Harbor attack—that sent thousands of

West Coast Japanese American citizens to barren internment centers for the war's duration. Here, an outspoken, leftist labor organizer (Dennis Quaid), married to a Japanese American, watches helplessly as federal agents—brandishing newly printed warrants—round up his wife and in-laws, claiming these soft-spoken family members represent a threat to America's security. (Quaid to Army official: "It's unconstitutional. They had their rights taken away from them. The nisei, who were born here, are American citizens!") Laden with many examples depicting the indignities heaped upon a hapless minority, scene after scene denounces the hysteria, racism, and opportunism responsible for their illegal confinement.

Command Decision

MGM, Directed by Sam Wood, Released 1948

A microscopic examination of the Eighth Air Corps' controversial 1943 precision daylight bombing raids over Germany that destroyed many strategic targets but caused a high casualty rate for the American airmen. Clark Gable is outstanding as the ramrod general who must send out dozens of aircraft each day on such perilous but tactical missions. (Gable to General Walter Pidgeon: "It was my decision to make, Sir, and I made it.") With Van Johnson, Brian Donlevy, Charles Bickford, and John Hodiak in supporting roles, the storyline—based on the Broadway play by William Wister Haines—takes numerous digs at American politicians, past and present, who, naively, deprecate airpower but now control the purse for all appropriations. With many actual aerial scenes, the film realistically captures the fright and discomfort found in the European air war.

Commandos

Heritage Enterprises, Directed by Armando Crispino, Released 1968

Another no-one-can-stop-us, get-out-of-the-way, B-yarn about a wily team of Italian-speaking American GIs, led by a chisel-face sergeant (Lee Van Cleef), who, in October 1942, don Italian uniforms, slither into a North African oasis, stab, strangle, and shoot fascist troops, dupe some Third Reich supply officers, and kill escaping prisoners, only to learn that their operation offers no military value. (Sergeant Van Cleef, explaining his mission: "This ain't no Halloween party.") Eventually attacked by some Panzers, both Americans and Germans—after an intricate back-and-forth struggle—perish in an elaborate, gory battle that insinuates war's futility. Most cerebral scene: *Wehrmacht* and U.S. officers discuss the nuances of Goethe's *Faust*, emphasizing the eighteenth-century poet's well-known chariots of destiny passage.

The Counterfeit Traitor

Paramount, Directed by George Seaton, Released 1962

A glowing testimony to the heroic Swedish oil broker, Eric Erickson, the man who posed as a Nazi sympathizer to learn important production information that resulted in many Allied bombing missions. William Holden portrays the American-born businessman, now a naturalized Swedish citizen, and his slow transformation from ardent capitalist to deft spy. (British Intelligence officer Hugh Griffith explaining the dangerous assignment: "You'll be hated for a while, there's no doubt about that. You'll be a quisling and you'll just have to live with that.") Based on the book by Alexander Klein, the storyline details numerous close calls inside the Fatherland—including clandestine meetings with underground workers, a love affair with a German contact, plus imprisonment and flight—before he reaches Stockholm an acclaimed hero. Funniest scenes: Holden, wearing a perfectly knotted necktie while sleeping in a cellar jail or dashing from captors, while his pudgy Gestapo nemesis, oblivious to firearm safety procedures, carries a Luger in the back pocket of his trousers.

Cross of Iron

EMI Films, Directed by Sam Peckinpah, Released 1977

Another revisionist tract—from the book by Willi Heinrich—that tones down Nazi bestiality by portraying individual members of the *Wehrmacht* as decent, honorable soldiers, mere pawns in an out-of-control, maddening war machine. James Coburn is convincing as a recalcitrant sergeant who must battle both his officers and the Russians as the German army slowly retreats from the Taman Peninsula in 1943. (Coburn, expressing his rage at the command structure "I hate all officers—all the Stranskys, all the Triebigs, all the Iron Cross scavengers in the whole German army," while his superiors [James Mason and Maximillan Schell] plan his death.) Basically a caustic, violent, and riveting salvo against the Prussian caste system that allows deranged, megalomaniac German officers unlimited authority, the screenplay—employing numerous surrealist concepts—suggests that World War II was fought only on the Eastern Front, expostulating that the Red Army, not the Nazis, were the real enemy.

Darby's Rangers

Warner Bros., Directed by William Wellman, Released 1957

A fuzzy (and distorted) paean to Colonel William Darby, the founder of the army's Ranger battalions that spearheaded important 1943 victories in North Africa and Italy. Looking firm and resolved, James Garner portrays the

Arkansas-raised officer as a hell-bent fighter, who leads his tip-of-the-javelin combat soldiers into many difficult battles against Nazi forces. (Colonel Garner, explaining his military strategy: "We're kind of a mustang outfit. We use the book, but occasionally a page or two gets mislaid.") Off to the side, his loyal sergeant (Jack Warden) rationalizes most problems with succinct Yiddish phrases. When not fighting their German adversaries, the enlisted men generally seduce vulnerable woman or visit immaculate Scottish homes, while a West Point lieutenant (Edward Byrnes) sports an Elvis-style coiffure and, after ten minutes of serious thought, marries a forlorn Italian so that the bleached-blond signorina may obtain some free GI penicillin.

Day One

Aaron Spelling Productions, Directed by Joseph Sargent, Released 1989

A made-for-television docudrama that traces the development of the atom bomb beginning with Albert Einstein's historical letter to President Roosevelt and culminating with the Japanese surrender. Laden with famous names from the 1940s, the storyline proffers a quaint mixture of fact and fiction about the complex Manhattan Project. Brian Dennehy coruscates as the hard-nosed, no-nonsense, military boss General Leslie Groves, who serves as foil, friend, and tormentor to the noted physicist, J. Robert Oppenheimer, played by David Strathairn. In this version, the controversial leftist suggests a moderate position. (Strathairn to colleagues, regarding the implementation of their new weapon: "Without the bomb, they have to invade Japan—a million American casualties.") Replete with many ambiguous moral questions, the photoplay eventually fizzles down to late 1945 as Oppenheimer, dismayed by the carnage of Hiroshima and Nagasaki, ponders his uncertain future.

D-Day: The Sixth of June

Twentieth Century–Fox, Directed by Henry Koster, Released 1956

Another hearts-and-flowers soap opera that peripherally uses the Normandy invasion as the backdrop for an American junior officer's adulterous affair with an insecure, love-stricken British social worker, who still pines for her missing-in-action boyfriend. As a London-based combat veteran assigned to Operation Overlord, Captain Robert Taylor lauds the fighting man preparing for the historic assault. (Taylor, praising an errant airman: "He'll conduct himself like soldier right in the gun turret of his B-17, flying over Germany in broad daylight.") But Taylor turns to mush every time Dana Wynter mentions his wife's name. Finally, on June 6 an elite Ranger squad assaults a German stronghold and—after a series of rope-climbing adventures—the enemy capitulates. Wounded in this daring raid, Robert Taylor—now convalescing in a London hospital—relinquishes his English lover and, in a saccharine fade-out, reluctantly returns to his stateside spouse.

Deadly Mission

Film Concorde, Directed by Enzo Castellari, Released 1977

Another B-copycat version of *The Dirty Dozen* in which five American soldiers, heading for stockade imprisonment, escape their captors in the French countryside and begin a 165-mile trek to the Swiss border. Along the way they rout some German troops and, eventually, stumble into a Resistance camp. There, following more convoluted events, they agree to storm a Third Reich stronghold, gather information, board a high-security Nazi train, and steal a secret gyroscope. With Bo Svenson in charge of this volatile mishmash, much of the screenplay resembles a Road Runner cartoon—these escapees shoot, strangle, punch, kick, stab, throw, push, burn, knee, and ram many Germans until, finally, an Army colonel (Ian Bannen) grabs the important wheeled instrument, proving once more that American troops, no matter how heinous their crimes, remain loyal to the old red, white, and blue. (Bo Svenson, explaining the rationale: "I think it's about time we got started with this war.") Funniest scene: six-foot-two Bo Svenson walking with his five-foot-eight colonel in a manner resembling a Mutt and Jeff cartoon.

Death of a Soldier

Suatu Film Management, Directed by Philip Mora, Released 1986

A strong indictment against the U.S. Army's military justice system that in 1942 ordered the hanging of a mentally deranged American GI for murdering four Australian women. As expected, James Coburn radiates as the military lawyer appointed to defend the psychotic soldier. Soon, he realizes the futility of any arguments when his superiors—eager to cement the relationship with their Aussie ally—censor all his courtroom motions. (Coburn to girlfriend: "If we allow this to happen without protest, we're nothing more than judiciaries, killers, Nazis. That's what the Nazis do, isn't it?") With many scenes depicting American officers as alcoholics, degenerates, or fascists, the storyline takes numerous potshots against General MacArthur (Jon Sidney), denouncing the four-star commander as insensitive, opportunistic, and autocratic.

One unsettling scene—highlighting the whitewashing of a shooting incident between Australian and American troops—demonstrates MacArthur's dictatorial power to silence any critic.

December

I.R.S. Media, Directed by Gabe Torres, Released 1991

A psychological examination of the anger experienced by some male adolescents—residing in an exclusive Vermont preparatory school—as news of the Pearl Harbor attack blares from their radios. Soon, a clean-cut senior (Wil Wheaton) repudiates the mock heroics espoused by his roommates and, contrary to the sophomoric flag-waving atmosphere, refuses to enlist. After hours of back-and-forth arguments, the young loner produces a copy of the 1939 National Book Award title—Dalton Trumbo's *Johnny Got His Gun*—citing reasons how this novel altered his perception of patriotism. (Wheaton to friends: "This book! It made me see how crazy war is.") Eventually, with the administration's blessing, a busload of upperclassmen embark for their induction center, leaving the taciturn Wheaton to his private ruminations. Strongest scene: the headmaster burns Trumbo's book, fearful that other students will read this antiwar tract.

Decision before Dawn

Fox, Directed by Anatole Litvak, Released 1951

A well-crafted, espionage thriller—based on George Howe's novel, *Call It Treason*—that follows the thorny path some *Wehrmacht* POWs follow after agreeing to become Allied agents in their homeland, hoping such service can bring the war to a quick end and spare their townspeople total obliteration. Here, a hard-nosed American commander (Gary Merrill) wants quick results and accurate information. (Colonel Merrill, laying down the law while another officer (Richard Basehart) watches cautiously: "If we found you've betrayed us, whether you're a double agent or a plain crook, you'll wind up in front of a firing squad.") Soon, a twenty-year-old corporal (Oskar Werner) reaches his hometown and, after a series of close calls—that include meeting an old family friend, becoming friendly with a lady of the evening, falling in with a black marketeer, and, finally, posing as a medic—learns the location of troop movements. As a minor revisionist work filmed on location in Wurzberg, a bombed-out town, the screenplay suggests that not all Germans were Hitler-worshipping belligerents but, instead, decent people caught up in unfortunate circumstances.

The Desert Fox

Twentieth Century–Fox, Directed by Henry Hathaway, Released 1951

A meticulously worded, subtly distorted, revisionist whitewash that heaps dollops of praise upon one of Hitler's successful generals, Erwin Rommel, the acclaimed, hands-on officer whose North African victories earned him the sobriquet, "The Desert Fox." James Mason's precise English enunciation sounds anomalous coming from the Teutonic field marshal who—after witnessing the führer's accelerated primitivism—reluctantly joins the unsuccessful conspiratorial movement, hoping to salvage some dignity for his nation. Eventually discovered, he chooses death before dishonor (Rommel, venting his frustration: "Those hoodlums again, those thieves and crooks and murderers, those toy soldiers, those dummy generals with their books and charts and maps and posters.") With many prominent English actors in supporting roles, the photodrama often resembles a British cabinet meeting, except, this time, the participants wear swastikas and Iron Crosses instead of Savile Row morning coats.

The Desert Rats

Twentieth Century–Fox, Directed by Robert Wise, Released 1953

An all-male, hard-as-nails, flag-waving, we-can-do-it, semidocumentary tribute to the fighting men of the Ninth Australian Division. Those worn-out, down-under soldiers emerge, like desert rats, from their Libyan sand trenches to attack the *Wehrmacht* troops, disrupting Field Marshal Erwin Rommel's July 1941 Suez Canal offensive. Lt. Colonel Richard Burton bellows many orders to his noncommissioned officers, determined to keep his green charges from harm's way during the 242-day defense of Tobruk. (Colonel Burton, praising the enlisted man: "Being an infantryman is the toughest job in the Army.") Over in the German camp, James Mason portrays the field marshal as a likable bon vivant enjoying gourmet meals, bespoke uniforms, and attentive military valets. Best scene: Colonel Burton meets his old schoolmaster in the enlisted-men's ranks and—in an awkward reversal of fortunes—proffers gratitude for those formative years.

The Devil's Brigade

United Artists, Directed by Andrew McLagen, Released 1968

Another rip-roaring, go-in-headfirst commando photodrama that highlights the amalgamation of some ill-disciplined American GIs—along with a group of straight-arrow Canadian soldiers—into a well-honed fighting unit dubbed the Devil's Brigade. In this anomalous outfit, tough-talking Lt. Colonel William Holden makes no bones about his assignment, while off to the side, Major Cliff Robertson grins sardonically. (Holden to troops: " . . . I want men that are tough, love to fight, fight to win, and would rather die than quit.") Eventually, these fighters reach Italy and in a few days capture a hilltop town with dozens of German prisoners and then storm a mountain stronghold to topple a strategic Nazi observation post. Loosely based on historical facts, this screenplay—from the book by Robert H. Adleman and George Walton—offers strong testimony to this highly decorated unit and its many European victories, proving, once again, that when pushed to the limit, the Allied soldier accepts the call to colors.

The Dirty Dozen

MGM, Directed by Robert Aldrich, Released 1967

A fast-moving adventure story—based on the book by E. M. Nathanson—that takes some nasty swipes at the U.S. Army officer caste system and its harsh penal code against enlisted men. Lee Marvin sparkles as a recalcitrant combat major who must recruit, discipline, and train twelve military prisoners—misfit GIs facing execution or long prison terms—and lead them on a suicide mission behind German lines hours before the D-Day invasion. (Hard-talking Major Marvin, venting his frustration: "I didn't pick these men—the army did! Remember? And I didn't pick this assignment either!") Eventually, this oddball unit—dubbed the Dirty Dozen—parachutes into France and, after some zany comic-strip adventures, blows up a renaissance chateau, killing many high-ranking Nazi officers. Top-heavy with Hollywood stars—including Donald Sutherland, Charles Bronson, Telly Savalas, Robert Ryan, Clint Walker, and John Cassavetes—the storyline caricatures American officers as either cynical, hard-nosed, or adipose, while citing the average foot solder, regardless of his faults, as loyal, patriotic, and sacrificial.

Don't Go Near the Water

MGM, Directed by Charles Walters, Released 1957

A plush, thick-vegetation, blue-water, CinemaScope college-freshmen comedy—from William Brinkley's acclaimed novel—that suggests the 1944 South Pacific American offensive resembles the dozens of shenanigans often associated with playful fraternity life. Smooth-talking Glenn Ford radiates as a frustrated public-relations naval lieutenant working for a pettifogging commander, while off to the side, most of his colleagues concoct intricate plans to avoid combat. (Lieutenant Ford to pals: "The public relations outfit is a collection of oddballs and freaks.") Numerous subplots include blackmailing an obnoxious war correspondent, arranging a romantic tryst between an enlisted tar and a pretty nurse, building an officer's club with inexperienced maintenance people, allowing a voluptuous reporter aboard a combat destroyer, providing a school building for the native children, and, finally, in a Pygmalion nod, grooming a foul-mouth sailor into a refined speaker capable of addressing the Admiral's staff. The whole kit and caboodle downplays the carnage of this combat zone and, instead, suggests that World War II was, in reality, all fun and games.

The Eagle Has Landed

Associated General Films, Directed by John Sturges, Released 1977

A fictionalized suspense tale—from the best-selling novel by Jack Higgins—that purports in 1944 an elite Nazi commando group secretly parachuted into eastern England and, after a series of close calls, assassinated Winston Churchill. Michael Caine's Cockney accent seems strange, coming from a highly decorated Nazi who finally reaches the prime minister's countryside verandah, while his commander, one-eyed Robert Duvall—spouting aphorisms from Carl Jung's synchronicity theory—issues cryptic orders from the Fatherland. As the American officer who discovers the German plot, Captain Treat Williams finally guns down the Axis agent only to discover the "prime minister" was an impostor. Saturated with glowing references to Third Reich humanitarianism, the story line sugarcoats every aspect of Hitlerism. (Nazi colonel, Michael Caine, rationalizing his capture: "I thought the plot failed because one of my men died saving the little girl up there.")

Eight Iron Men

Columbia, Directed by Edward Dmytryk, Released 1952

Another B-story that examines the stress and frustration a small American squad endures when confined to a bombed-out French house during the war's last months, as Nazi snipers take an occasional potshot at their invaders. Here, Lee Marvin, a senior NCO in charge of the eight iron men holed up in this temporary shelter, keeps a tight rein on his charges while exasperated by the lack of tangible information. (Sergeant Marvin to Corporal Richard Kiley: "That's the trouble with this war—a lousy patrol war—crawl on your belly in the mud, stick a knife in some guy, always in the dark!") Eventually, the GIs rout their adversaries and—acclaimed as heroes—return to their rear lines. Replete with hackneyed dialogue, this B-picture contains one visual cliché after another, including the lone GI who tosses a hand grenade with deadly accuracy into a German pillbox, while offering an incantation to his baseball idol Bob Feller.

The Enemy Below

Twentieth Century–Fox, Directed by Dick Powell, Released 1957

Another deep-six, CinemaScope underwater operational narrative—based on the novel by D. A. Rayners—that pits a crafty American destroyer captain against a U-boat commander in a convoluted cat-and-mouse mission during the final days of the South Atlantic hostilities. Robert Mitchum's Yankee intransigence forces worn-out German officer Curt Jurgens to reevaluate Nazi fealty, as his submarine dives deeper to avoid American depth-charge detonations. (Commander Jurgens to aide: "I'm sick of this war—it's not a good war.") Finally the U-boat surfaces, and in an outlandish Götterdämmerung, both ships—now heavily damaged—sink ignominiously to the sea's bottom. With one pithy observation after another, the all-male storyline pooh-poohs the dangers of naval combat, suggesting that conflict is a romantic and chivalrous undertaking.

Ensign Pulver

Warner Bros., Directed by Joshua Logan, Released 1964

A lackluster, watered-down sequel to *Mister Roberts* (1955) that continues the madcap, South Pacific confrontation between a U.S. Navy cargo ship's crew and their loose-cannon commander, Burl Ives, while on the starboard side, the ship's laundry officer, Ensign Pulver (Robert Walker Jr.) keeps the pot boiling with his many sophomoric pranks. Eventually, the captain's unknown past emerges and—following some minor concessions—everyone reconciles their differences. (Robert Walker Jr. explaining Burl Ives sudden reassignment: " . . . He's saying thank you now, by leaving the ship he loves.") Most amazing feat: the makeshift medical operation where Ensign Pulver—in an astonishing six minutes—makes an incision, removes the appendix, cauterizes the stem, and, without missing a beat, sutures the patient while his medical pal, Walter Matthau, relays instructions via ship-to-shore phone.

Escape to Athene

Pimlico Films, Directed by George P. Cosmatos, Released 1979

A half-spoof, half-serious take about the Nazi occupation of an antique-laden Greek island circa 1944. This time, Roger Moore portrays a jaded German

POW commandant who keeps one step ahead of his Gestapo superiors, while Allied prisoners David Niven, Elliott Gould, Richard Roundtree, and Sonny Bono constantly upset the applecart with their recalcitrant antics. (Gould, kibitzing with his captor about his terpsichorean skills: "I can teach dancing to the men—help limber them up after all that goose-stepping.") Eventually, a serendipitous breakout frees the prisoners, destroys the Axis armament, routs the *Wehrmacht* forces, and returns the island to local control. Replete with many anachronistic weapons, language, scuba gear, and even a New York Yankees baseball cap, this part-Western, part-make-believe photodrama shuns all verisimilitude and, instead, portrays this dark page of World War II history as nothing more than a walk in the park. Funniest scene: Nazi troops, guarding a rocket station, wearing specially designed Buck Rogers uniforms.

The Extraordinary Seaman

MGM, Directed by John Frankenheimer, Released 1969

An E-for-Easy, lighthearted, oddball frolic that traces the exploits of three shipwrecked U.S. sailors who reach a Pacific island, where they discover a dilapidated vessel, HMS *Curmudgeon*. A spiffily dressed British officer, David Niven, cajoles the tars into making the ship seaworthy. Soon, these gallants take to the open waters, but the bluejackets, much to their chagrin, learn that their English host is, in fact, a ghost destined, à la Ancient Mariner, to roam the ocean until one good deed redeems him. (Commander Niven, explaining his predicament: "I have been in the Royal Navy for forty-three years; granted since my death, I have been somewhat inactive.") After a few cheery mishaps, this do-it-yourself crew destroys a Japanese vessel, allowing the wraith passage to the hereafter. Funniest scenes: Commander Niven's empty whisky glass automatically refills, allowing unlimited imbibitions.

Eye of the Needle

United Artists, Directed by Richard Marquand, Released 1981

A high-powered spy thriller—adapted from the best-selling book by Ken Follett—that traces the sub-rosa activities of a Nazi plant in war-torn London that sends coded messages about the D-Day operations to Berlin. As a rabid devotee of Hitlerism, Donald Sutherland oozes villainy in every frame, obsessed with his own megalomania. (Axis cohort to stony-faced Sutherland: "You must deliver them personally to the führer.") When his cover falls apart, the German spy eludes British officialdom, takes a twining northern escape route, and reaches a remote Scottish island inhabited by a small, caretaker family.

Attempting to make a U-boat rendezvous, the Machiavellian agent commits two murders. He is finally thwarted by a simple English woman with a hand-gun in a gory end-of-the-film death scene, allowing General Eisenhower's invasion to proceed as scheduled.

The Fallen

Anthem Pictures, Directed by Ari Taub, Released 2006

An off-centered combat tale—borrowing generously from the synchronistic format of *The Young Lions* with a nod to Chaplin's *The Cure*. The story traces the comings and goings of a U.S. quartermaster platoon, a retreating Nazi squad, a disarrayed Italian reinforcement group, and a gang of angry partisans during the October 1944 Northern Italy campaign and their eventual hillside Götterdämmerung. With numerous Freudian, Sartrean, and Jungian over-tones, the entire screenplay—using an impressive array of unknown actors—depicts the common soldier, regardless of nationality, as a frustrated, hungry, and overburdened individual, a mere pawn on a chessboard, led erratically to-ward an inglorious death by uncaring and, occasionally, inept officers. (Sergeant John McVay, explaining the ground pounder's plight: "Those in-fantry boys get killed every day of the week.") With numerous allegorical, symbolic, and ontological scenes, this 2004 screenplay, arriving almost sixty years after war's end, equates the European battlefield with Polonius's view of sixteenth-century drama: tragical-comical-historical-pastoral.

Farewell to the King

Orion Pictures, Directed by John Milius, Released 1989

An offbeat, discursive allegory that juxtaposes war's absurdity with the virtues of the Noble Savage. Nick Nolte shines as an American GI who, in 1942, deserts his Bataan post, reaches Borneo's northern coast, and—after a series of make-believe adventures—becomes king of a local headhunter tribe. Three years later, British paratroopers locate his isolated village, and soon the blue-eyed sergeant's serene world evaporates as a fleeing, ragtag Japanese army forces a deadly confrontation. With numerous antimilitary swipes, this fictional drama—based on the book by Pierre Schoendoerffer—excoriates English brutality while downplaying American heroism. (Discalced ruler Nolte, explaining his motives: "Just before the fall of Corregidor—when MacArthur skipped out—some of us figured it was time to go too.") Drollest scene: longhaired Nick Nolte's linguistic skills, articulating an esoteric native dialect to wide-mouthed, British botanist-turned-major, Nigel Havers.

Fat Man and Little Boy

Paramount, Directed by Roland Joffe, Released 1989

Another revisionist point-of-view examination of the designing, building, and implementing of the atomic bomb, emphasizing the logistical, monetary, and moral issues associated with the Manhattan Project. Paul Newman's trim waistline offers minor distraction in his tough portrayal of the outspoken, pudgy military commander, General Leslie Groves, while Dwight Schultz sparkles as the leftist physicist, J. Robert Oppenheimer. Frequently at odds with each other, the dominant General Newman finally convinces the temperamental scientist to bring an end to the Pacific war. (Newman to Schultz: "You want to sit on your hands, polish your conscience—while we might be able to end this whole thing with one shot?") Burdened with ongoing philosophical arguments, the motion picture offers strong rationalizations regarding the thorny issue of obliterating the two Japanese cities.

Fatherland

HBO Pictures, Directed by Christopher Menaul, Released 1994

A convoluted "What if?" made-for-television, fictionalized social commentary—based on the book by Robert Harris—that suggests an off-the-wall ending to World War II. In 1944 the Allied Forces—after being pushed into the sea at the abortive Normandy invasion—create a separate peace with the führer. One year later, the Americans detonate two atomic bombs on Japanese cities, forcing that nation's capitulation. Russia, now standing alone, still fights an eastern front war with Germany. By 1964 King Edward and Queen Wallis govern England, Joseph Kennedy Sr. is the U.S. president, and Hitler—still ruling Germany—remains a frail seventy-five-year-old dictator, while his nemesis, Joseph Stalin, now eighty-five, stealthily puffs his pipe. With Rutger Hauer and Miranda Richardson in starring roles, the storyline meanders from one illogical point to another as German nationals struggle to find normalcy in their troubled lives. (Nonplussed Miss Richardson, asking a naive question: "What does Final Solution mean? What happened at Auschwitz?")

The Final Countdown

United Artists, Directed by Don Taylor, Released 1980

A high-flying, science fiction kaleidoscope that shows off the U.S. Navy's modern carrier power in a manner usually found in the eerie scripts that made the popular television series, *The Twilight Zone*, a household word. Kirk Douglas stars as the captain of the USS *Nimitz*, a flattop cruising west of the Hawaiian Islands in late 1979, while Martin Sheen, a civilian observer, studies military protocol. Soon, a phantasmagoric sea storm transposes the ship back into a late-1941 time zone where the F-15s spot the Japanese armada. (Douglas to officers: "Every man on this ship knows that we have radar and visual contact with the Japanese fleet approaching Pearl Harbor on December 6, 1941.") Unable to upset the course of history, the carrier reluctantly returns to the present, allowing the sneak attack to culminate. Replete with pithy hindsight observations, this offbeat tale glamorizes every facet of life aboard an electronically operated navy fighting ship.

Fireball Forward

Twentieth Century–Fox, Directed by Marvin Chomsky, Released 1972

Another made-for-television fabrication that suggests the 1944 Normandy breakout campaign was hampered by the espionage activities of a turncoat Resistance fighter, who radios Nazi artillerists strategic Allied positions. As a former combat sergeant promoted to major general, Ben Gazzara takes command of a hard-luck outfit with a high casualty rate and, using a low-key approach, gains the respect of the enlisted men, while calling for unerring standards from his officers. (General Gazzara chiding his old pal, Colonel Eddie Albert, about military discipline: "Now you either cut the mustard or I send you back! I'd hang my brother if he screwed up a combat assignment.") Eventually, American intelligence agents eliminate the spy, and within minutes a successful frontal attack routs the Axis forces, opening the road to Paris.

Five Fingers

Twentieth Century–Fox, Directed by Joseph Mankiewicz, Released 1952

Another sub-rosa espionage thriller—based on the memoirs of a high-ranking Nazi, L. C. Moyzisch—that claims the Third Reich obtained secret information from an Albanian valet working in the British Embassy in neutral Turkey during the early months of 1944. James Mason is superb as the servant-turned-bon-vivant, whose passion for fine food, *grand cru* wines, and pretty women transforms him into a master spy photographing Allied war plans for the Axis. (Mason, explaining his deception skills: "I usually just photographed everything in sight that's stamped secret, most secret, and top secret.") Soon his luck runs out, and after taking an intricate escape route from Ankara to Istanbul, and then Rio de Janeiro, he begins a lavish lifestyle that abruptly terminates when Brazilian officials—puzzled by the thousands of British pounds being spent—discover his banknotes are nothing more than counterfeit currency, a method of payment frequently employed by the Germans.

Five for Hell

Filmstar, Directed by Gianfranco Parolini, Released 1968

Another low-budget, made-in-Italy, strictly-for-fun, B-frolic that borrowed many ideas from *The Dirty Dozen* and *Where Eagles Dare*. This one is about some oddball GIs, recruited to infiltrate an Italian villa and steal a secret Nazi plan. (General Bill Vanders, explaining the mission: "Fifty thousand of our men will fall into a death trap, unless we can find out about Plan K, proposed by the führer.") Under the leadership of a gung-ho, baseball-aficionado officer (John Garko), this diverse group—including both a safecracker and trampoline ace—finally reach their target and proceed to dupe, exasperate, somersault, shoot, stab, strangle, flip, push, and foil many Germans before extracting the needed information. While basically a frisky, picaresque story, punctuated with a snazzy musical score, the whole nine yards resembles a typical 1960s spaghetti Western in which numerous shoot-outs and elaborate pyrotechnics punctuate most scenes. Funniest casting: sinister-looking SS officer (Klaus Kinski), ranting and raving about the Third Reich's achievements. (Kinski to subordinate: "It's not for you to judge the orders of our führer.")

Flags of Our Fathers

DreamWorks, Directed by Clint Eastwood, Released 2006

A high-powered, digitally enhanced retelling of the historic Iwo Jima flag-raising photograph—snapped by Joe Rosenthal on February 23, 1945—and the bittersweet fame thrust upon three surviving members by jingoistic, oleaginous, public-relations officials intent on exploiting the elation this black-and-white picture inspired. Based on James Brady's best-selling book (his father is the sailor in the picture), the photodrama vacillates between the bloody island fighting, where U.S. casualties skyrocket (Marine officer explaining the enemy's tenacious defense: "This is Japanese soil, sacred ground—they will not leave politely") and the psychological difficulties experienced by the three men on their stateside tour, their discharge, and the eventual alcohol-related death of one leatherneck, Ira Hayes (Adam Beach), the Pima Indian who experiences heartfelt praise on the one hand, while the other receives vicious racial slurs on the nationwide bond-selling drive. Most discouraging scene: a young Marine, horsing around on a transport ship, falls into the ocean and, owing to warfare's exigencies, is left to fend for himself, while a disillusioned sailor observes, "So much for no man left behind."

Flat Top

Monogram Pictures, Directed by Lesley Selander, Released 1952

A high-flying, do-not-ignore-the-wave-off-flag, aircraft carrier, B-saga that details the training and eventual combat success of a fighter squadron during the 1944 Philippine invasion. Barking numerous orders from the ready room, Commander Sterling Hayden demands complete adherence to navy regulations, while his executive officer (Richard Carlson) suggests a relaxed approach. (Stone-faced Hayden to airmen: "Keep your noses clean, fly straight, and we're all going to get along just fine.") Produced by an original poverty-row studio—noted for cutting any conceivable corner—this attack-them-from-the-air tale often contains anachronistic newsreel or documentary footage. Typical budget-cutting insert: U.S. fighter pilots head off to dogfight advancing Japanese planes in torpedo-laden aircraft.

Flying Leathernecks

RKO, Directed by Nicholas Ray, Released 1951

Another rip-roaring, red-white-and-blue, John Wayne, blast-them-from-the-skies, action story that glorifies the volant adventures of a Marine Corps fighter squadron hard at work during the 1942 Guadalcanal campaign. Once more the commander of a close ground-support unit, Major John Wayne, with the help of Captain Robert Ryan, routs the Japanese force at every turn, demonstrating unequivocally the semper fidelis credo. (Duke Wayne to colleague: " . . . this is where we separate the men from the boys.") Replete with many documentary newsreel inserts, the photoplay depicts the heavy American losses spent for this island victory. Most risqué scene: John Wayne, home on stateside leave, kisses his wife and then—in an atypical moment—spirits her into the bedroom.

Force of Arms

Warner Bros., Directed by Michael Curtiz, Released 1951

A drawn-out hearts-and-flowers soap opera—based on a short story by Richard Tregaskis—that uses the 1943 Italian winter offensive as the backdrop for some heavy-handed romance within the officer cadre. Here, a battlefield-commissioned lieutenant (William Holden) and his dogface squad spend many days fighting the Nazis sequestered in the Roman hills. Back on leave, the good-looking Holden meets a Pollyanna Wac (Nancy Olson), and after a whirlwind courtship, the twosome marry, briefly enjoying a makeshift honeymoon. (Lieutenant Holden to Lieutenant Olson: " . . . I'm going to live forever because of you.") Returning to their units, the newlyweds' joy shatters when the husband is reported missing in action. After a protracted search, Lieutenant Olson finds her spouse convalescing in a military hospital. Reunited, the two officers—in a sudsy fade-out—swear eternal devotion.

The Frogmen

Twentieth Century–Fox, Directed by Lloyd Bacon, Released 1951

A fast-paced adventure tale glamorizing the high-risk assignments of the navy's underwater demolition teams—the frogmen—as they swim in the danger-laden waters off the Japanese homeland during the war's closing months. Leading a handpicked squad, Richard Widmark obeys all military directives punctiliously. (Commander Widmark to crew: "We're ordered to blow up the only known Jap submarine pen south of the home islands.") Chief Petty Officer Dana Andrews's approach is less authoritative or caustic. With an array of ocean action scenes, the story line highlights the elaborate training and strong camaraderie that keeps this all-volunteer outfit fine-tuned. Best scene: the frogmen's retrieval from the ocean using a small lariat, rubber lifeboat, and precision teamwork.

From Hell to Victory

Wardway, Directed by Hank Milestone, Released 1979

Another French-Italian-Spanish, dubbed-into-English production that proves once again that ineluctable, serendipitous events mold human emotions. On August 24, 1939, six close friends—two Americans, two French, one English, and one German—celebrate summer's end at a festive Paris party, vowing to make this happy occasion an annual event. But one week later, with the invasion of Poland, these plans dissolve as each person becomes involved with the ongoing global conflict. Over the years, the six lives intertwine, and in one macabre scene, the Frenchman—now a Resistance fighter—unknowingly kills his German friend, a *Wehrmacht* officer. With George Peppard and George Hamilton in starring roles, the photodrama spends much time examining lost love or missed opportunities. (American war correspondent (Sam Wanamaker) reflecting on the snows of yesterday: "It's hard to believe that kind of happiness ever existed.")

From Here to Eternity

Columbia, Directed by Fred Zinnemann, Released 1953

A strong indictment of the fascist-type mentality—that includes favoritism, bullying, torture, and death—at a U.S. Army base, a few miles from Pearl Harbor, as reported in the highly acclaimed first novel by James Jones. Burt Lancaster stars as a straight-arrow top sergeant, whose sangfroid demeanor slowly erodes when he falls for his commander's wife. (Sergeant Lancaster's view of the military hierarchy: "I hate officers—I always hated officers!") Montgomery Clift likewise shines as the lowly recluse who refuses to join a regimental boxing squad to expedite a promotion, while Private Frank Sinatra—in an Academy Award role—becomes a victim of a sadistic stockade sergeant. When the Japanese attack their outpost on December 7, all differences are quickly reconciled as the troops prepare to defend their island. Much of the photoplay depicts the negative side of army life, highlighting the abusive qualities of authority.

Gallant Bess

MGM, Directed by Andrew Marton, Released 1946

A gee-whiz, golly, Pollyannaish testimony to the nation's farmland youth, those get-up-early, hard-working lads who leave rural America and, using their homespun skills, serve in the armed forces. Marshall Thompson is wonderful as a sixteen-year-old orphan, who fudges his age, enlists in the Navy, and because of his tractor skills, joins the Seabees (Young Thompson, explaining his reasons: "You have to go, even if you have to lie to go.") Days before shipping overseas his favorite foal contracts pneumonia and quickly expires. Grief-stricken, the tar returns to his outfit and eventually lands on a Pacific island, where Japanese soldiers fight a rearguard action. Deep in the jungle he stumbles upon a wounded mare and, using common sense, nurses the horse to recovery. In a matter of days she becomes the outfit's mascot. At war's end, navy officials, pleased by this wholesome, symbiotic relationship, look the other way as feisty Gallant Bess leaps onto a cargo ship, offers the brass a few happy neighs, and joins her bluejacket admirers for the voyage home.

The Gallant Hours

United Artists, Directed by Robert Montgomery, Released 1960

A fine-tuned, quasi-documentary hagiography of Fleet Admiral William F. Halsey, the tough-talking sailor whose Kill Japs! Kill Japs!, Kill More Japs! credo, combined with some good luck, routed the Japanese invaders during the precarious 1942 Solomon Islands campaign. Former song-and-dance man James Cagney downplays the four-star officer's well-known belligerency and, conversely, portrays a soft-spoken, introspective man with a messianic plan for victory. (Bull Halsey to his command staff: "If we lose Guadalcanal, there will be nothing to stop them to go all the way down to Australia.") With fighter-pilot Dennis Weaver serving as foil, much of the storyline highlights the intricate cat-and-mouse game between Japanese general Isoroku Yamamoto and Halsey's intelligence section—and the culminating moment when the Japanese code, now broken, allows an American triumph. Using numerous religious messages, including a Roger Wagner Chorale soundtrack that constantly blares patriotic dirges, this film reiterates the righteousness of America's cause in the brutal Pacific theater.

Go for Broke!

MGM, Directed by Robert Pirosh, Released 1951

A down-to-earth testimony honoring the Japanese American GIs who formed the highly decorated 442nd Combat Team. Portraying a youthful Texas shavetail supervising a squad of nisei soldiers, Van Johnson—after a shaky start—witnesses the bravery of these tightly knit GIs as they rout the *Wehrmacht* in Italy and France. (Lieutenant Johnson, mocking a captured Nazi officer who cannot understand why Japanese men are wearing U.S. uniforms: "Didn't Hitler tell you? Japan surrendered and they're fighting on our side now!") Replete with many stock scenes, including the GI with the girl back home, the college graduate who eschews a commission, and the malcontent who eventually learns the value of teamwork, the storyline is the Wake Island saga told in reverse (this time, the Americans win). Best scene: President Truman decorates this unit at an elaborate White House ceremony.

Golden Earrings

Paramount, Directed by Mitchell Leisen, Released 1947

Another lighthearted, desultory melodrama where a vain Gestapo officer chases a British colonel during the last week of August 1939 in the Black Forest town of Freiburg. Here Ray Milland, an English undercover agent, escapes from a Nazi stronghold and, after some precarious moments, meets a sensual gypsy, Marlene Dietrich, who agrees to disguise the good-looking fugitive as a clan member. (Sultry Dietrich, applying facial make-up to Milland: "I can make a gypsy out of log of wood.") Based on the novel by Yolanda Foldes, the screenplay blatantly ignores the Third Reich's persecution of gypsies and suggests that this subculture rollicked around small Bavarian towns eking out a paltry living by palmistry, while a foreign agent—operating right under the *Schutzstaffel's* nose—unobtrusively filches a German poison gas formula and escapes to his homeland. Silliest scene: Ray Milland reading the palm of a *Wehrmacht* youth, promising the soldier good fortune and amatory adventures.

The Good German

Warner Bros., Directed by Steven Soderbergh, Released 2007

An offbeat, black-and-white, stylized, film noir homage to the 1940s spy-versus-spy melodramas produced in the same chiaroscuro, voice-over format made during that long-ago decade. Easygoing George Clooney radiates as an American journalist, who arrives in Berlin to cover the July 1945 Potsdam Conference. He is quickly enmeshed in international intrigue—black market activities, former girlfriend, and Nazi rocket scientists—while off to the side, his military driver explains the sub rosa opportunities. (Corporal Tobey Maguire to his passenger: "The war is the best thing that ever happened to me.") With scene after scene lifted from such classics as *The Third Man*, *The Blue Dahlia*, and *Murder, My Sweet*, this contemporary production lauds Hollywood's golden age, when movies were made on studio sets without special effects. Best scene: the airport ending, a wonderful copycat tribute to Humphrey Bogart and Ingrid Bergman's sudsy farewell in *Casablanca*.

The Good War

Bauer Martinez Studios, Directed by Giorgio Serafini, Released 2005

An off-the-wall allegory—supposedly based on a true story—that details the frustrations of Italian prisoners interned in Hereford, Texas, when American military officials demand the inmates sign an antifascist statement before repatriating them. Here, a seventy-two-year-old bird colonel (Roy Scheider) hobbles throughout the compound, perturbed that a combat injury has given him this stateside assignment. (Colonel Scheider, bemoaning his fate: "I've been put out to pasture.") In a strange twist of fate, as a quick-thinking Neapolitan (Luca Zingaretti) plots his escape, the camp unexpectedly closes, stranding the commander and his charge. Now in a precarious situation, the two men, with little food, put aside their differences and, for the next few agonizing days, claw at each other, dissecting war's futility. As a twenty-first century morality tale, the screenplay, ping-ponging from one solipsistic point to another, rationalizes why former allies are now enemies and former enemies are newfound allies.

The Great Escape

United Artists, Directed by John Sturges, Released 1963

Another elaborate 173-minute kaleidoscope—based on the book by Paul Brickhill—that details the planning, implementation, and eventual escape of seventy British officers from a closely guarded stalag, deep inside the Fatherland, to their freedom, capture, or death. As the only American POW in this otherwise homogeneous group, Steve McQueen sparkles with Yankee intransigence, determined to free himself from Nazi captivity. (Captain McQueen to English colleagues: "By morning, I'm going to be so far away you couldn't hear it if they were shooting at me with howitzers.") Using an all-star cast—including James Garner, Richard Attenborough, Charles Bronson, James Coburn, and Donald Pleasence—this edge-of-your-seat action yarn contains a myriad of subplots, as the captive Allies use their ingenuity to elude the Nazis. Best scene: Steve McQueen, on his motorcycle, approaching the Swiss Alps.

The Guns of Navarone

Columbia, Directed by J. Lee Thompson, Released 1961

An action-packed CinemaScope production—based on Alistair MacLean's novel—that traces the 1943 high-powered adventures of some Allied saboteurs sent onto a small Greek island, who after many close calls, destroy two massive German guns poised to attack a British rescue convoy. Appointed leader of this well-honed team, Gregory Peck, with linguistic and mountain-climbing skills plus his sangfroid, thwarts the Nazis at every turn. (Peck to colleague: "The only way to win a war is to be just as nasty as the enemy.") With Anthony Quayle, David Niven, Anthony Quinn, and Stanley Baker in supporting roles, the screenplay contains the knife-wielding marksman, the explosives expert, the traitor in the midst, the loyalty of numerous underground fighters, and the "I'll-kill-you-after-the-war" malcontent. Also included are some random antiwar scenes that—in strong, unequivocal language—lambaste the mock heroics of combat.

The Gypsy Warriors

Universal, Directed by Theo James, Released 1978

Another frivolous, made-for-television B-mumbo jumbo that suggests that World War II was an ongoing Mack Sennett two-reeler devoid of any horror or mayhem. James Whitmore Jr. and Tom Selleck portray two wisenheimer

American officers who, in June 1940, parachute into France on an espionage mission involving the ubiquitous secret Nazi chemical-weapons factory. After some Saturday-matinee heroics—coupled with a little romantic digression involving a comely gypsy (Lina Raymond)—the German production plant is rendered inoperative even though some of the military tactics resemble a Daffy Duck cartoon. (Bedazzled Captain James Whitmore Jr. to his fellow saboteur, easygoing Captain Tom Selleck: "Your West Point ring! We're on an undercover operation and you're wearing a West Point ring!) Originally titled *Deadly Wine*, this photoplay became the basis for a television series that—after eight weeks of low ratings—was yanked off the airwaves.

Halls of Montezuma

Twentieth Century–Fox, Directed by Lewis Milestone, Released 1950

A high-powered, hit-the-beaches, dig-in, go-get-'em glorification of the U.S. Marines and their many Pacific island victories. Squad lieutenant Richard Widmark steps lively leading his leathernecks from a beachhead invasion, through dangerous marshlands, and finally, to heavily fortified caves, where his men—the best of American prowess—capture enemy prisoners and, eventually, locate a strategic Japanese rocket-launching site. With Jack Palance, Robert Wagner, and Karl Malden as dyed-in-the-wool fighters, the marines, after many hardships, battle their way back to their command post much to the acclaim of Major Richard Boone. Best scene: the squad honors a fallen comrade. (Sergeant Jack Webb—paraphrasing John Donne's poetry—eulogizes a friend's sacrifice: "Now we are part of the world, the world is part of us. If any part suffers, all suffer; if any part loses freedom, all will lose it.")

Hanover Street

Columbia, Directed by Peter Hyams, Released 1979

This hearts-and-flowers melodrama proves that true love conquers all. Good-looking Harrison Ford—a B-25 American pilot stationed outside of London in 1943—stumbles into a complex romance with a married woman, bright-eyed Lesley-Ann Down. After a series of serendipitous events, the dashing airman is unknowingly paired with her husband, Christopher Plummer, to infiltrate Gestapo Headquarters in northern France. Soon the two men steal an important codebook, and their escape route—back to England—resembles one implausible B-adventure after another as Resistance fighters thwart the Nazi war machine at every turn. Now in London, the noble-minded officer quietly utters his sudsy good-bye. (Lieutenant Ford whispering his swan song to Miss Downs: "I love you enough to let you go, which is more than I've ever loved anything or anybody in my life.")

Hart's War

MGM, Directed by Gregory Hoblit, Released 2002

A unimaginative bricolage of stock scenes plucked from *Battleground*, *Stalag 17*, *Slaughterhouse-Five*, *The Great Escape*, *The Caine Mutiny*, *The Tuskegee Airmen*, *A Few Good Men*, and *To Kill a Mockingbird* that details the comings and goings of a large contingent of American GIs jammed into a German POW compound during winter 1945. Bespectacled Bruce Willis seems miscast as a full bird colonel who orchestrates a U.S. court-martial as a ruse to destroy a nearby munitions factory. Lieutenant Colin Farrell, a naive Yale graduate, works assiduously to defend his charge, a black Air Corps pilot, from the lynch-mob mentality of the makeshift trial barracks. (Lieutenant Farrell to Colonel Willis: "I'm just trying to protect my client.") Eventually, as a redemptive symbol, Colonel Willis—exhorting his honor, duty, and country doctrine—sacrifices himself in a bizarre exchange of one life for many, demonstrating once again that in war, the end justifies the means.

Heaven Knows, Mr. Allison

Twentieth Century–Fox, Directed by John Huston, Released 1957

A modern reworking of the Robinson Crusoe fable—from the novel by Charles Shaw—where a sinewy marine corporal (Robert Mitchum), adrift for days in the South Pacific, finally reaches a small island that is inhabited solely by a Roman Catholic nun (Deborah Kerr). Soon, the twosome form a polite friendship while honing their survival skills. (Mitchum to nun, explaining the improbability of a U.S. rescue: "The brass planned to bypass a lot of these islands on the way to Tokyo, at least that's the scuttlebutt.") After a series of arduous events—that include eluding Japanese patrols, recovering from illness, and sidestepping a love declaration—the twosome are saved by tough-fighting U.S. forces. With many allegorical references, the screenplay's motif—the dignity of religious institutions—restates the wholesome nature of America's participation in the global conflict.

Hell in the Pacific

Selmur Pictures, Directed by John Boorman, Released 1968

A complex parable that in an esoteric way offers insight about survival, friendship, and tolerance. As a Japanese officer marooned on a remote South

Pacific atoll during the war's closing months, Toshiro Mifune's solitary existence in such a harsh environment requires discipline. Eventually, a naval pilot (Lee Marvin) washes ashore, and the two men—initially hostile to each
other and unable to communicate verbally—concede a shaky truce. Realizing
the futility of remaining in their barren location, they construct a raft and finally reach another deserted coral island, only to perish from an explosion.
Using many theological symbols—including a crucifixion scene—this modern-day Bible story contains many religious themes. (Captain Marvin to his
Japanese companion: "How come you guys don't believe in God?")

Hell Is for Heroes

Paramount, Directed by Don Siegel, Released 1962

Another we're-all-in-this-together drama of an isolated six-man army infantry squad that must halt a *Wehrmacht* attack on the hilly Siegfried line during the perilous 1944 offensive. Here a tight-lipped, psychotic, recalcitrant
private (Steve McQueen) glowers menacingly at both American and German
forces. (Private McQueen, threatening a seventeen-year-old Polish orderly:
"You show up on the line, I'll blow your head off.") Another private (Bobby
Darin) takes a more realistic approach to combat. (Darin to replacement:
"Look, up here, this gun is your life.") Soon, the refractory McQueen—unable to accept any military regulations—starts a private war by charging uphill and destroying a strategic Nazi pillbox, only to perish at his moment of
glory. As a coda, the screenplay acknowledges that the U.S. Armed Forces
contain a fair share of deranged individuals whose violent and excessive tem-
peraments frequently undermine everyone's welfare.

Hell to Eternity

Atlantic Pictures, Directed by Phil Karlson, Released 1960

A B-grade, fictional account—supposedly based on a true incident—about an
orphaned Los Angeles boy who was raised by a Japanese American family
during the 1930s, and after Pearl Harbor enlisted as Marine Corps interpreter.
Jeffrey Hunter portrays a clean-cut leatherneck who slowly learns military
rudiments under the tutelage of his combat sergeant (David Janssen). When
their unit hits the beach at Saipan, the twosome encounter many close calls,
culminating with Private Hunter's capture of a Japanese general. (Hunter explaining to a Japanese officer that he understands his language: "I understood
that double-crossing speech! These men died without any reason.") Appalled
by the Japanese civilian casualties on this Pacific island, Private Hunter uses

his linguistic skills to rescue many nationals before they commit a ritualistic suicide. One scene—the surrender of dozens of haggard enemy soldiers to a lone marine—is a copycat version of the closing minutes of Warner Bros.' 1940 classic, *Sergeant York*.

Hellcats of the Navy

Columbia, Directed by Nathan Juran, Released 1957

Another humdrum, seafaring melodrama bemoaning the inner loneliness a naval commander endures after he sacrifices an officer's life to preserve the safety of his submarine. Here, Ronald Reagan—the skipper of an underwater Hellcat working the precarious Japanese straits—stands by his decision to lose one lieutenant rather than allow his vessel to perish. (Commander Reagan to colleagues: "Did you think I enjoy letting men drown?") Exonerated by his senior staff and encouraged by his girlfriend (Nancy Davis), the soft-spoken Reagan takes to the seas again and—in a stereotypical confrontational scene—destroys many enemy vessels, much to the acclaim of his crew and former detractors. Introduced by the famous war hero Admiral Chester W. Nimitz, this battle story glorifies every facet of Pacific theater naval operations.

The Heroes of Telemark

Columbia, Directed by Anthony Mann, Released 1965

A high-powered adventure tale glamorizing the planning and implementation of a daring British-Norwegian raid that destroyed the Nazi heavy-water plant operating on the Scandinavian peninsula. As a scientist turned saboteur, Kirk Douglas guides a handful of commandos into the German factory that is manufacturing Hitler's untried atomic weapon. (Kirk Douglas, explaining his motives to his ex-wife: "We're working for the Resistance.") With Richard Harris at his side, the raiders sneak into the plant and—with a little gravitational help from Mother Nature—obliterate this military threat. Loosely based on actual events, this historical reconstruction—reminiscent of some 1940s propaganda films—praises Norwegian intransigence toward their Axis captors.

Hiroshima: Out of the Ashes

Hallmark Home Entertainment, Directed by Koreyoshi Kurahara and Roger Spottiswoode, Released 1995

Another fiftieth-anniversary, made-for-television, let's-tell-both-sides-of-the-story, 185-minute disquisition that sifts through the moral, logistical, political, and military complexities responsible for the dropping of the first atomic bomb. Kenneth Welsh radiates as President Harry S. Truman—who along with numerous aides and advisers—must decide the most pragmatic method to end World War II. (General Lesley Groves, played by Richard Masur, demanding an immediate deployment of the weapon: "Now we got the bomb and a chance to use it. For Jesus' sake, let's use it where the Japs will feel it the most!") Using a quasi-documentary format, this in-depth screenplay depicts the numerous egos—American, English, Russian, and Japanese—responsible for the first nuclear attack.

Hitler

Warner Bros., Directed by Stuart Heisler, Released 1962

An overstated B-production that chronicles national socialism's early days, beginning with the publication of *Mein Kampf* and culminating with the Poland blitzkrieg invasion. As the domineering führer demanding blind obedience from his swastika-wearing followers, Richard Basehart suffers from an oedipal complex as he balances his emerging dictatorship with a puppy-love crush on his young niece. When the romance turns sour, the infatuated Hitler turns his amatory attentions toward Eva Braun, with a grandiose promise of a New Order. (Richard Basehart to his Nazi charges: "In that hour, I was responsible for the fate of Germany and, thereby, I became the supreme judge of the German people.") Replete with one distortion after another, the photoplay closely resembles the ad hominem format of the anti-Hitler films produced during the war.

Hitler's SS: Portrait in Evil

Metromedia Productions, Directed by Jim Goddard, Released 1985

An elaborate, 150-minute, made-for-TV analysis of the infamous *Schutzstaffel* (the SS) as viewed through the eyes of two German brothers from the early 1931 Stuggart beer-hall meetings to the Third Reich's 1945 Berlin collapse. During this unprecedented period, the older son (Bill Nighy) joins Heinrich Himmler's Gestapo, rationalizing that the reform policies will benefit the nation, while his younger brother (John Shea) prefers the Storm Troopers. Hitler's June 30, 1934, Night of the Long Knives massacre changes everything when their ideological differences openly clash. (SS Officer Nighy, venting his anger: ". . . if you have any idea what they're doing to tens of thousands of people. . . .") Eventually, the elder brother realizes his misguided loyalties and watches—with cynical resignation—the New Order's capitulation. With stellar performances from David Warner, Tony Randall, Carroll Baker, and José Ferrer, this historical storyline depicts much of the ruination caused by this dreaded organization.

Homecoming

MGM, Directed by Mervyn LeRoy, Released 1948

Another hearts-and-flowers soap opera—overflowing with oleaginous wartime-separation sentimentality—about a materialistic surgeon, who treats well-to-do patients respectfully, while ignoring backyard urban problems. In another stereotypical, he-man role, Clark Gable sparkles as a married, bon vivant doctor, who, after Pearl Harbor, joins the medical corps, completes basic training, and arrives in the European combat zone. For the next three years he lives and works with injured frontline GIs, while slowly falling for his outspoken nurse (Lana Turner). Unable to reconcile his dilemma, the smooth-talking Gable balks at any commitment until, in a typical 1940s Hollywood marriage-is-sacred, divorce-is-impossible ending, the pretty nurse dies from combat injuries, allowing her sweetheart an easy out. (Lieutenant Turner's deathbed coda to Colonel Gable: "When a soldier leaves his outfit, all debts and friendships are cancelled.") Funniest scenes: groups of doctors, gathered at various functions, smoking one cigarette after another, oblivious to any injurious health risks.

Hornet's Nest

United Artists, Directed by Phil Karlson, Released 1970

A far-fetched, high-jinks yarn describing the heroics of an American soldier who parachutes into Nazi-occupied Italy. With a motley gang of native children—plus a comely German doctor—he eludes Gestapo forces and eventually blows up a strategic dam, allowing Allied troops a counterattack. Rock Hudson—a lone GI stranded behind enemy lines—offers numerous shibboleths regarding his underground mission, while his young charges whistle esoteric warning codes. (Hudson to some Italian adolescents: "We'll kill over 10,000 Nazis by blowing up that dam.") Since the film is a joint Italian-American production, the entire plot mimics the numerous spaghetti Westerns of this period, parodying such stock scenes as the fistfight, the shootout, and the hero riding off into the sunset, only this time the handsome American leading man, lacking any equestrian support, sits in a dilapidated military truck.

Imitation General

MGM, Directed by George Marshall, Released 1958

An offbeat, fast-talking, quasi-slapstick screenplay that spotlights the afternoon antics of a combat-experienced master sergeant, who—following a series of comic misunderstandings—assumes the role of a dead, one-star army officer in the French countryside, weeks after the Normandy invasion. As always, Glenn Ford sparkles as a "general" who quickly musters some inexperienced soldiers, plans an outlandish offensive, blasts an enemy observation post, and knocks out some German tanks snared in a ditch. His wisecracking pal, Corporal Red Buttons, eggs him on and, back in the farmhouse, vivacious Taina Elg, unable to speak English, smiles approvingly. (Sergeant Ford, explaining why this ruse is necessary: "Unusual situations call for unusual solutions.") With frequent nods to Charlie Chaplin's silent one-reelers, this mistaken-identity storyline combines wartime drama with military frivolity.

In Enemy Hands

Artisan Entertainment, Directed by Tony Giglio, Released 2004

Another implausible, hot-air, three-dollar-bill fairy tale that claims a benevolent Nazi U-boat commander—acting contrary to Hitler's take-no-prisoners edict—places a group of American sailors in their cramped submarine rather than allow the bluejackets to perish on the ocean. (Nazi officer Thomas Kretschmann to Chief Petty Officer William Macy: "Do you know why I picked up your men? I'm tired of this war.") But in a few hours, meningitis strikes more than half of the German crew, and soon both sides combine their manpower for basic survival. (First Officer Kretschmann to everyone: "We are now on the same side.") Soon, the U-boat is attacked by Nazi and Allied vessels, and as a token of friendship, Chief Macy allows the German captain to destroy the valuable ENIGMA code box before an American destroyer rescues everyone. As a revisionist tract this far-fetched undersea yarn, saturated with Pollyanna dialogue, downplays the Third Reich's open-seas brutality and, instead, suggests that beneath their gold-plated swastikas, Nazi commanders are compassionate and noble individuals.

In Harm's Way

Paramount, Directed by Otto Preminger, Released 1965

A powerful, 180-minute tribute to the naval officer corps where innovative planning, strong leadership, and precision coordination obliterate a Japanese armada threatening the Pacific theater. Standing on the bridge, Rear Admiral John Wayne must lose two ships, his left leg, and his estranged son before winning a major sea battle, while his girlfriend, easygoing Patricia Neal, x-rays his fractured right arm. Based on the novel by James Bassett, the storyline amalgamates numerous plots, including Executive Officer Kirk Douglas's fall from grace and sacrificial redemption. (Kirk Douglas, shouting his jubilation over the Pearl Harbor attack: "O Rock of Ages. We got ourselves another war—a gut-busting, mother-loving navy war.") With an all-star cast that uses Henry Fonda, Burgess Meredith, Dana Andrews, and Franchot Tone in high-ranking roles, every aspect of naval life—from the mundane to the complex—seems orderly and glamorous.

In Love and War

Twentieth Century–Fox, Directed by Philip Dunne, Released 1958

Another glorified CinemaScope paean to the fighting men of the U.S. Marine Corps—based on the novel by Anton Myrer—that emphasizes the male bonding found in love and war. Jeffrey Hunter, Robert Wagner, and Bradford Dillman star as hardened gyrenes who put aside their social-class differences to fight the Japanese in a vicious 1944 Pacific island battle. Back in sunny California, their three women—from diverse backgrounds—stoically wait, each hoping her man's name will not appear in the newspaper's casualty reports. Eventually, the Marines secure their island, but one combat private cannot fathom his unit's savagery toward the enemy. (Private Dillman, shouting his disgust: "We're all butchers! Just kill and kill and kill and nobody cares why.") Best action scene: Sergeant Jeffrey Hunter blows up a Japanese tank.

The Incredible Mr. Limpet

Warner Bros., Directed by Arthur Lubin, Released 1964

A lighthearted, whimsical, just-for-fun, family-oriented romp that intersperses a conventional photodrama with animated cartoons. Timid, 4-F Don Knotts illuminates as bespectacled Mr. Limpet, an amateur ichthyologist who frequently fantasizes about piscatorial life. (Knotts, during a typical daydreaming session: "I wish I were a fish. Fish have a better life than people.") Eventually, the Flatbush bookkeeper's wish comes true and—after a series of flitting, underwater belly laughs—he teams up with a navy petty officer (Jack Weston) to pinpoint Nazi submarines operating in the North Atlantic. Acclaimed a hero after V-J Day, Mr. Limpet begins a new mission, enlisting porpoises for Cold War military assignments. Best scene: Mr. Limpet, using a little pelagic know-how, redirects German torpedoes in a 360-degree arc and smiles gleefully as the explosives detonate in their original firing tubes.

Is Paris Burning?

Paramount, Directed by René Clement, Released 1965

A detailed look at the political, social, and military events occurring in the French capital during the turbulent month of August 1944. As Allied forces prepare to liberate the City of Lights from its four years of occupation, a Nazi commandant—under strict orders from the führer—plans to demolish every building, monument, and bridge. Based on the best-selling book by Larry Collins and Dominique Lapierre, the black-and-white screenplay contains an array of impressive stars—including Kirk Douglas, Anthony Perkins, Charles Boyer, Jean-Paul Belmondo, Glenn Ford, Robert Stack, and Yves Montand—to portray famous personages, Resistance fighters, plus French, German, and American forces. Finally, the Third Reich general responsible for destroying Paris (Gert Froebe) capitulates to his humanistic values and surrenders his army. (Swedish ambassador Orson Welles praising the German's decision: "History will be grateful to you for having saved a very beautiful city.")

Judgment at Nuremberg

United Artists, Directed by Stanley Kramer, Released 1961

An in-depth examination of the controversial Allied war-crimes tribunal responsible for the onerous task of assigning guilt to dozens of high-ranking Nazis. Spencer Tracy demonstrates the best of New England jurisprudence as he spends eight months sifting through reams of ambiguous evidence, ever mindful of the political Cold War ramifications of his verdict. (Judge Tracy to colleague: "I'm a rock-ribbed Republican, who thought that Franklin Roosevelt was a great man.") Replete with intricate subplots—and a cast that includes Burt Lancaster, Judy Garland, Montgomery Clift, Richard Widmark, Marlene Dietrich, and Maximilian Schell—the *j'accuse* finger vacillates from scene to scene. Personages, laws, and loyalties are indicted for a long list of bestial crimes. Eventually, many Nazi followers must answer for their wartime activities, but their life-imprisonment sentences, considered severe by German nationals, are eventually abrogated as American statesmen—mindful of hostile Russo-American relations—seek support from their former enemy against the new Stalinism threat.

Kelly's Heroes

MGM, Directed by Brian G. Hutton, Released 1970

A heavy-handed, half-spoof account of some enterprising GIs who—after a series of Looney Tunes adventures—loot $16 million in gold bullion from a local bank behind German lines during the 1945 offensive. Clint Eastwood's deadpan smile reassures his buddies of the screwball plan's efficacy, while Top Sergeant Telly Savalas bellows numerous orders to the "heroes." Unaware of the ground pounders' impending peculation, General Carroll O'-Connor lavishly awards medals to men in his command, including a dysfunctional tank driver (Donald Sutherland). (GI Sutherland, enunciating the psychological attributes of heroism: "To a New Yorker like you, a hero is some type of weird sandwich.") Funniest scene: three GIs, satirizing the classic Hollywood Western shoot-out, lithely approach a Nazi tank, while over in his bedroom, Carroll O'Connor pins two stars onto his pajama's epaulets.

King Rat

Columbia, Directed by Bryan Forbes, Released 1965

A dreary, tiresome, pseudo-allegorical morality tale—from James Clavell's book—depicting the hardships that British, American, and Australian prisoners-of-war endure in a Japanese camp on the Malay Peninsula in 1945. George Segal scowls as Corporal King, a streetwise American soldier who manipulates both Allied officers and Japanese guards with numerous scams and black-market deals. His nemesis, British lieutenant Tom Courtenay, proffers one blowhard threat after another. (Provost Officer Courtenay to King Rat: "Like all criminals, you're greedy.") Finally liberated, the smooth-talking American, realizing his power niche is over, rationalizes his behavior. (Corporal Segal to rescue official: "There's no harm in looking after your clothes?") Most ponderous scene: Segal and his minions enjoy a mystery meal that consists of dog meat, a recipe frequently prepared in Asian culture.

Kings Go Forth

United Artists, Directed by Delmer Daves, Released 1958

Another combat-related soap opera, based on the novel by Joe David Brown, highlighting the military pursuits of a squad leader (Frank Sinatra) as he leads his army patrol into battle against German forces in the southern France theater during the June 1944 advance. In his spare time, he woos a carefree Riviera belle (Natalie Wood). (Lieutenant Sinatra philosophizing about the vagaries of war: "Some days we drink champagne, courtesy of the French, and some days we eat dirt, courtesy of the Germans.") Inevitably, a good-looking, slick-talking infantry corporal (Tony Curtis) horns in on his officer's girlfriend and, after a series of lies, innuendoes, and broken promises, wins the heart of the French lass, only to drop her like the proverbial hot potato. As retribution for his perfidy, the corporal dies in a nighttime skirmish while Frank Sinatra, now a captain and minus his right arm, returns to his lost love and the twosome, in a gooey Hollywood ending, pledge eternal devotion.

The Last Day of the War

Sagittarius Production, Directed by Juan Antonio Bardew, Released 1969

A B-for-Budget, cliché-ridden travesty about a tight American infantry squad assigned to rescue an important German scientist before a demented Gestapo officer—ignoring the formal V-E Day mandate—locates this turncoat, who is squirreled away in an Austrian hamlet. U.S. sergeant George Maharis (of *Route 66* fame) fights, stabs, and shoots many Nazi soldiers before rescuing his charge, while pulchritudinous Maria Perschy, wearing fancy high-heeled shoes during her Alpine ascent, smiles approvingly. Produced as a joint Italian, Spanish, and American venture, the storyline—borrowing heavily from the 1930s Hollywood oaters—contains one implausible situation after another. (Sergeant Maharis, explaining his secret mission, "We're looking for someone—a German scientist, civilian kraut, because the SS is looking for him, we gotta get there first.")

The Last Drop

Carnaby International, Directed by Colin Teague, Released 2005

An offbeat, part-spoof, part–Road Runner, three-tier romp about the comings and goings of a British paratroop squad, two Nazi renegades, and a loose-cannon American colonel. In September 1944 they roam around the Dutch countryside looking for Berlin-bound art treasures, while nearby, Axis and Allied forces fight the decisive Market Garden battle. As part of the English team, glider pilot Billy Zane seems confused about their mission. (British Tommy, offering a personal observation: "This ain't no cloak-and-dagger job.") When they reach a farmhouse cellar loaded with plunder, a U.S. officer (Michael Madsen) ponders his future. (German opportunist [Steve Speirs], suggesting a deal: "Surely if the spoils of wars should just happen to fall into the brave hands of such men as yourselves.") With one improbable comic-book, hodgepodge, shoot-out scene after another, much of the plot resembles a Saturday-morning cartoon. Best impersonation: Michael Madsen as Colonel J. T. Colt, a General George S. Patton wannabe.

The Last Tyrant

Group One, Directed by Carlo Lizzani, Released 1974

Another European-made docudrama outlining the final days of Benito Mussolini, the Italian dictator who created a fascist state, aligned his nation with Hitler, declared war on the Allied Forces, and, subsequently, met an ignominious death during the April 1945 uprising. As American GIs approach Milan and Nazi troops falter into the Fatherland, only glabrous Rod Steiger could mimic the egomaniacal traits of the ruler—now facing ruin—negotiating an escape to Switzerland. (*Il Duce's* aspirations: "Once the war is over, we must have our share of the glory and the reward.") An influential Roman Catholic cleric (Henry Fonda) also realizes the futility of the autocrat's reign. (Cardinal Fonda's exasperation: "This was the man who thought he was another Caesar.") Eventually, some quick-moving partisans thwart his retreat and summarily execute the leader who brought devastation to their country, even though the trains, following his edict, ran on time.

The Last Warrior

Pathfinder Pictures, Directed by Martin Wragge, Released 1989

Another B-mishmash that lifts a few scenes from *The Last Samurai*, *Hell in the Pacific*, and *Heaven Knows, Mr. Allison* to form a convoluted action yarn about a U.S. Marine sergeant (Gary Graham) stranded on a remote Pacific island with a Roman Catholic nun (Maria Holvoe) and their harrowing adventures when a sword-wielding Japanese officer (Cary-Hiroyuki Tagawa), obsessed with his Bushido philosophy, forces his American foe into an elaborate duel-to-the-death contest. After many setbacks, including an unremitting jujitsu beating, the leatherneck rallies, forges ahead, and in a gory finale kills his Oriental nemesis. (Tagawa, expatiating on defeat: "One to one, you are no match for us, except when you fight us with your machines.") With some pseudo-religious overtones, this low-cost storyline—using minimal dialogue—reaffirms the maxim that in wartime, a spiritual presence always guides the victor.

Letters from Iwo Jima

DreamWorks, Directed by Clint Eastwood, Released 2006

An overblown, simplistic, distorted, there-are-two-sides-to-every-story sugarcoating of the bloody February 1945 Iwo Jima invasion as seen through the eyes of hapless Japanese soldiers, pawns of sadistic, Emperor-worshipping officers who insist they fight until the death. (Japanese general Ken Watanabe's draconian instructions: "Not one of you is allowed to die until you have killed ten enemy soldiers.") Eventually, U.S. Marines storm this lava-encrusted island and, after fierce fighting, decimate the outnumbered defenders. With defeat a certainty, most Japanese either join suicidal banzai charges or explode grenades on their chests. As a revisionist interpretation, much of the screenplay ignores the brutal and sadistic reign of Japanese aggression and, instead, purports the common soldier's virtues—kindness, sensitivity, and nonbelligerency—come forth in poignant letters sent to their mainland families. Most contrived scene: various American officials at a plush 1929 Washington, D.C., reception first present their Oriental guest with a crafted pearl-handled revolver then, at the dinner table, taunt him about his Bushido beliefs.

The Longest Day

Twentieth Century–Fox, Directed by Ken Annakin, Andrew Marton, Gerd Oswald, and Bernhard Wicki, Released 1962

An elaborate 175-minute black-and-white blockbuster—based on the best-selling book by Cornelius Ryan—that documents the historical Normandy invasion as witnessed by Allied and Axis forces at numerous battle sites and command headquarters. Using a large contingent of famous stars—including John Wayne, Robert Mitchum, Richard Burton, Curt Jurgens, Rod Steiger, and Robert Wagner—the screenplay details the successes, good fortune, tragedy, and dumb luck that both sides experience during this longest of days. Utilizing many subplots juxtaposed against the larger issue of Allied determination to gain a foothold on Fortress Europe (tough-talking Colonel John Wayne to his taut American paratroopers: "Your assignment tonight is strategic. You can't give the enemy a break, send them to hell!"), the film offers a subtle justification for the many casualties necessary for this important victory.

MacArthur

Universal, Directed by Joseph Sargent, Released 1977

A gargantuan, I-am-in-charge, do-not-question-my-orders testimony to the five-star general whose clarion I-Shall-Return promise became an inspiring catchword throughout the Pacific theater. Hard-talking Gregory Peck depicts the many frustrations, defeats, and achievements General Douglas MacArthur experienced, including the Corregidor withdrawal, Australian regrouping, island-hopping strategies, Philippines retaking, V-J Day celebration, Japanese rehabilitation, presidential hopeful, Inchon invasion, executive dismissal, and, finally, congressional "Old Soldiers Never Die" speech. References to his low casualty rate are numerous. (MacArthur, explaining his policy: "Good commanders do not turn in heavy losses.") This hagiographical storyline reiterates MacArthur's dictum, "In war there can be no substitute for victory." Best scene: in a reflective mood, a somber General MacArthur visits the Bataan Death March survivors.

Malaya

MGM, Directed by Richard Thorpe, Released 1949

A farfetched, implausible absurdity about two American mercenaries who in 1942 surreptitiously enter this Japanese-controlled Southeast Asian country and—after a series of make-believe adventures—smuggle all the raw rubber onto the deck of a hidden U.S. Navy transport. Spencer Tracy and Jimmy Stewart portray this unlikely dyad who organize a small raiding party of modern-day buccaneers, while corpulent Sydney Greenstreet—interested in the gold bullion his fellow countrymen carry—aids in the peculation. (Stewart explaining the need for this vital raw material: "We're organized to get the rubber out without the knowledge of the Japs.") As the Japanese officer in charge of the occupation forces, Richard Loo adds another stereotypical villain role in his long career as the slimy Oriental nemesis who can bend but never break a captor's will.

The Man Who Never Was

Twentieth Century–Fox, Directed by Ronald Neame, Released 1955

An elaborate CinemaScope production that purports the 1943 Allied Sicily invasion succeeded because an intricate British intelligence operation hoodwinked the Germans into deploying their defensive forces to Greece. As a naval commander, Clifton Webb selects a cadaver, creates a detailed, bogus military identification pattern, and sends the body adrift off the Iberian Peninsula until it reaches a Spanish fishing village. Here, a Nazi agent procures his "classified" information and—after a cursory London undercover examination by Third Reich spy Stephen Boyd—the Germans accept this plan hook, line, and sinker. Supposedly based on actual events, the photoplay restates the quiet heroism of the United Kingdom. (Commander Webb to the deceased's father: "I can assure you that this is an opportunity for your son to do a great thing for England.")

The McKenzie Break

MGM, Directed by Lamont Johnson, Released 1970

Another revisionist tract depicting the numerous stratagems some bright, agile, resourceful German prisoners of war employ to escape from a British camp located in Western Scotland. Burly Brian Keith radiates as an intelligence officer assigned to prevent a rumored breakout, while his nemesis, U-boat Commander Helmut Griem, smiles sardonically at military directives. (Captain Keith, explaining his task: "I got sent up here to do a job—I'm supposed to find out what's behind that break.") After punctilious planning, including clandestine radio messages, elaborate tunnel boring, and synchronized crowd diversions, the Germans slither from their confinement. Later—following some *Mission Impossible* adventures—they reach a Nazi submarine but, in a surprising denouement, watch incredulously as their commander, just yards from freedom, surrenders unceremoniously to his English captors.

Memphis Belle

Warner Bros., Directed by Michael Caton-Jones, Released 1990

An elaborate testimony to the first crew in the Eighth Air Force to fly the coveted twenty-fifth mission, a feat allowing each man stateside duty. Youthful Matthew Modine shines as a B-17 captain who lifts his aircraft from the quiet plains of southern England to the German port of Bremen to bomb the city's industrial area on May 17, 1943. (Modine to airmen: "We were sent here to bomb a factory. If we don't do it, someone's going to have to come back and do it for us.") Constantly under attack by Luftwaffe fighters or ack-ack bursts, the bomber—damaged in its critical landing section—limps back to its home base, much to the acclaim of elated senior officers and public-relations staff. While the storyline is pure Hollywood fiction, it is, nevertheless, a paean to William Wyler's 1944 aerial documentary *The Memphis Belle*, a film that glorified this landmark crossing.

Merrill's Marauders

Warner Bros., Directed by Samuel Fuller, Released 1962

An all-male, nothing-can-stop-us, 200-mile, India-to-Burma trek by three thousand army volunteers, dubbed "marauders," to destroy Japanese strongholds in this strategic southeastern peninsula. Here, in the dense, swampy terrain, one-star General Frank Merrill (Jeff Chandler) rallies his weary men from one dangerous area to another, while his commanding officer General "Vinegar" Joe Stillwell (John Hoyt) warns everyone about the price of failure. (General Stillwell to officers: "Your job is to keep the Japanese out of India—keep them from linking up with the Germans.") Based on the book by former marauder Charlton Ogburn, this Technicolor adaptation graphically recalls the humid climate, hostile vegetation, numerous diseases, and enemy offensives these GIs endured during their three-month march, a feat responsible for expunging most Japanese forces from Burma. Strangest scenes: in numerous battle encounters, the Japanese soldiers fall to their deaths in an exaggerated, terpsichorean manner resembling dance students auditioning for ballet school.

A Midnight Clear

Beacon, Directed by Keith Gordon, Released 1992

A caustic, surrealistic, ontological look at war, death, and friendship—from the book by William Wharton—that demeans the caste system separating enlisted men from their officers. Ethan Hawke sparkles as a young, pensive sergeant who, along with five other GIs from an intelligence and reconnaissance squad, squirrel themselves in the Ardennes Forest during the Christmas 1944 German offensive. Here they come face to face with their adversaries in a symbolic snowball fight, and soon both sides realize the futility of conflict. (Sergeant Hawke, lamenting his conscription: "We want to make it clear we're not actually part of this army.") Eventually, the GIs accept the Germans' surrender offer, but in a Kafkaesque turn of events, the Americans inadvertently kill their new friends. Packed with numerous religious, allegorical, and atonement references, the photoplay labels U.S. officers as fascists, responsible for destroying the innocence of youth.

Midway

Universal Pictures, Directed by Jack Smight, Released 1976

A rousing, fly-off-the-deck, flag-waving, Sensurround extravaganza explaining the meticulous logistics, warrior determination, and old-fashioned good luck that enabled U.S. forces to defeat a large Japanese convoy at the decisive June 1942 Battle of Midway. Here, Henry Fonda portrays Admiral Chester Nimitz, the naval hero who relied on instinct to send his outnumbered ships into combat. (Admiral Fonda, stressing his perilous situation: "Our three carriers and our escorts are all that stands between the enemy fleet and the American coastline.") Off to the side, Captain Charlton Heston proffers needed advice. Basically an all-male docudrama, this 132-minute screenplay—laden with actual (and occasionally anachronistic) newsreel footage—details the heavy American pilot losses in this decisive victory. (Japanese Admiral Yamamoto [Toshiro Mifune] ruminating about lost youth: "They sacrificed themselves like samurais, these Americans.")

The Misfit Brigade

Panorama, Directed by Gordon Hessler, Released 1987

A low-budget, heavy-handed, quasi-revisionist B-spoof of American World War II screenplays, containing one mock-heroic after another. This time the easygoing, salt-of-the-earth German soldier, the traditional Hollywood villain, takes center stage as a kind-hearted, frolic-loving individual. Over on the Russian front, good-looking Bruce Davison commands a penal tank crew, composed of assorted misfits on a suicide mission to blow up a Russian train in exchange for freedom. (SS Colonel David Carradine explaining the rules: "The sacrifice of your wretched lives will bring glory to the führer."). After many Keystone Kops adventures—include leading a brothel romp, posing as Red Army fighters, and uncovering a joint German/Russian resort (complete with nude swimming)—these recalcitrants destroy the target, return to base and, as predicted, are double-crossed by General Oliver Reed. However, in a make-believe ending, U.S. fighter planes attack the base and, in a twist of fate, the misfits kill the SS officers, proving once again the righteousness of the *Wehrmacht* soldier.

Mission of the Shark

Fries Entertainment, Directed by Robert Iscove, Released 1991

A gripping, harrowing, and frightening photodrama that depicts the torpedoing of the USS *Indianapolis* on July 29, 1945 and the crew's unbearable four-day ordeal as they bobble helplessly in the South Pacific. Stacy Keach is superb as Captain Charles McVay, who can only watch in terror as marauding sharks attack his men, while back in command headquarters the cruiser's destruction has gone unnoticed. Eventually, the men are rescued, but the casualty rate became the greatest naval loss in World War II. (Captain Keach, dumbfounded by the statistics: "880 men are dead, that's a fact, a terrible fact.") As a made-for-television movie, the screenplay blasts high-ranking naval officials for their poor management and callous handling—including a kangaroo court-martial—of this terrible incident.

Mission to Death

Independent-International Pictures, Directed by Kenneth W. Richardson, Released 1966

A seventy-one-minute, B-for-bottom-of-the-barrel potboiler, produced by a cost-cutting company known for rehashing the same unknown actors, utilizing amateur photography equipment, and failing to synchronize any sound track. Jim Brewer "stars" as a tough-talking sergeant leading a platoon of U.S. soldiers to attack a Nazi radar station in Northern France during the January 1945 offensive. (Brewer, explaining his raison d'être: "I'm doing the best I can for one reason—and that's to get the job done and go home.") After destroying their first target, the GIs run into some bad luck and, in a gory, end-of-the-film shoot-out, all perish while a voice-over coda expatiates on the folly of war. Most serendipitous event: the GIs, while fighting a January war in a damp, frigid region of France, always travel in warm, sunny weather without any winter clothing.

Mister Roberts

Warner Bros., Directed by John Ford and Mervyn LeRoy, Released 1955

Another CinemaScope performance—based on the novel by Thomas Heggen—depicting a naval captain as an irrational, sadistic buffoon, who bullies his crew aboard a supply vessel on duty in the noncombatant South Pacific during the spring of 1945. As a pettifogging martinet, James Cagney is no match for his executive officer, Mr. Roberts (Henry Fonda), an easygoing ensign constantly at odds with his superior. (Fonda to Cagney: "How did you ever get command of a ship? I realize in wartime they have to scrape the bottom of the barrel, but where did they ever scrape you up?") With Jack Lemmon and William Powell in supporting roles, the storyline sustains some comical moments of pelagic life interspersed with numerous uncomplimentary remarks about the officer-privilege system, especially Captain Cagney's obsession with maintaining a palm tree on the ship's forward deck.

Morituri

Twentieth Century–Fox, Directed by Bernhard Wicki, Released 1965

A stylized, antiwar, cat-and-mouse thriller that pits an anti-Nazi national, reluctantly working as a British agent, against Gestapo officers on a German freighter delivering needed cargo to the Fatherland. Marlon Brando's Teutonic accent proffers one shibboleth after another as he surreptitiously slopes around the vessel—commanded by Captain Yul Brynner—defusing all explosives while occasionally expatiating his own brand of nihilism. (Brando to a female prisoner: "All wars are idiotic, one is not different from the other.") After a series of drawn-out events that include slinking between an Allied convoy, a rendezvous with a Japanese submarine, an abortive change-of-command plot, and, finally, detonating some dynamite to scuttle the ship, the Mozart-loving Brando, standing stoically on the damaged bridge, ponders the Roman gladiator's salute to Caesar, *morituri te salutant*—we who are about to die salute you—as he awaits rescue by the American navy.

The Mountain Road

Columbia, Directed by Daniel Mann, Released 1960

A low-grade, B-potboiler—closely akin to the 1940s sagebrush Westerns—spotlighting the heroics of an Army demolition team assigned to blow up some Chinese roadways during a strategic 1944 Allied retreat from encroaching Japanese forces. Jimmy Stewart seems miscast as an engineering major, frustrated by the anarchy that has enveloped most of the fleeing refugees. (Major Stewart to Oriental girlfriend: "I got to believe that what I'm doing means something.") Along with Sergeant Harry Morgan, the Americans escape from local bandits, destroy their objectives, and reach the safety of their command post. One scene in particular—the indiscriminate strafing of a peasant village by Major Stewart's men—shows the Caucasians as flagrant racists exhibiting strong hatred toward all Chinese. With so much Sinophobic dialogue, the storyline suggests that the Chinese, not the Japanese invaders, are the real adversaries.

Murphy's War

Paramount, Directed by Peter Yates, Released 1971

Another war-is-futile tract that pits the demonic forces of Nazism against a monomaniacal, revenge-obsessed Irish merchant seaman's rage. Peter O'-Toole's blue eyes sparkle as the lone survivor of a German U-boat attack in Caribbean waters during the first week of May 1945. Rescued by a French oil engineer (Philippe Noiret), he hastily repairs a dilapidated biplane and—armed with some homemade Molotov cocktails—makes a low-level pass, damaging the Axis ship hidden in a nearby estuary. Eventually, the submarine heads for open waters, where Seaman O'Toole—now commanding a rickety steel barge—continues the fight that culminates in a watery Götterdämmerung, destroying both friend and foe. Based on the novel by Max Catto, most scenes indict the seafaring Third Reich for their savage show-no-mercy warfare. (O'Toole venting his anger: "They shot the entire crew in the water.")

My Foolish Heart

Warner Bros., Directed by Mark Robson, Released 1949

A hearts-and-flowers soap opera—from a short story by J. D. Salinger—that traces the loneliness of a distraught coed whose army sweetheart accidentally dies in a stateside training mission, a few months after the War has started, and her subsequent rebound marriage to the wrong man. Susan Hayward glows as a caustic dipsomaniac whose school-days memories of her deceased boyfriend (Dana Andrews) only brings bitterness and unhappiness to her current husband (Kent Smith). Eventually, the stoic Miss Hayward comes to terms with the human cost of the war and agrees to an amicable divorce, allowing her best friend to walk away with her spouse. As social commentary, the storyline reiterates the nation's fears, confusion, and humor during the early months of 1942. (Character actor Robert Keith, poking fun at Private Dana Andrews' ill-fitting uniform: "Well, I must say, you are the sorriest-looking Casanova I've ever seen.")

The Naked and the Dead

RKO, Directed by Raoul Walsh, Released 1958

An elaborate adaptation of Norman Mailer's controversial novel that takes an assailing look at some of the troubled personalities in the U.S. Army leadership corps as they advance inland on a South Pacific Japanese-held island during the 1943 offensive. As a fascist-minded one-star general, Raymond Massey reiterates his Nietzschean absolutism philosophy, while his sadistic platoon sergeant, Aldo Ray, shoots Japanese prisoners to extract the gold fillings from their mouths. (General Massey to Lieutenant Cliff Robertson: "The only way you can generate the proper attitude of awe and obedience is by immense and disproportionate power.") With numerous references to unfaithful wives, the million-dollar wound, the officer/enlisted man schism, and the sexually active 4-Fs, much of the screenplay reaffirms the frustration each foot soldier endures in his jungle-fighting microcosm.

Never So Few

MGM, Directed by John Sturges, Released 1959

Another high-jinks Far Eastern adventure tale—based on the novel by Tom T. Chamales— belaboring the rough-and-tumble antics of Captain Frank Sinatra routing the Japanese during the 1944 Burma invasion campaign. With Peter Lawford, Steve McQueen, and Philip Ahn as members of a motley, behind-the-lines commando team, Old Blue Eyes—after blasting his Oriental enemies out of the jungle bush—takes a respite from combat to woo flirtatious Gina Lollobrigida. (Captain Sinatra to his shapely Italian girlfriend: "I'm going to miss you! Where I'm going, nobody smells of soap.") Eventually, the storyline takes a macabre twist when Sinatra's team crosses the Chinese border, attacks a renegade warlord's camp, and—in a highly charged scene—executes their prisoners in a manner reminiscent of the Japanese atrocities commonly found in the 1940s Hollywood propaganda films. Funniest scene: Frank Sinatra wearing a pasted-on goatee.

A Night in Casablanca

United Artists, Directed by Archie Mayo, Released 1946

An eighty-five-minute gem—featuring the wacky Marx Brothers—that parodies Michael Curtiz's 1943 Academy Award–winner *Casablanca* and, as a bonus, takes a quick swipe at Howard Hawks's 1944 war film *To Have and to Have Not*. Fast-talking Groucho Marx, now a hotel manager in postwar Casablanca, romps his way through numerous misadventures as foreign intrigue, Nazi agents, and secret treasures emerge everywhere, and Chico and Harpo create their own form of mayhem. Soon, a chief inspector bellows orders to "round up the usual suspects," while ensconced in another room, Groucho spoofs both the famous roulette game scene and the Bogart and Bergman airport farewell. (Groucho, now flying the airplane: "We have to keep going until we run out of gas.") In its own simplistic way, this photo-drama signaled the end of Hollywood propaganda pictures, allowing directors to create new themes, ideas, and motifs about the global conflict.

Night of the Fox

Dove Incorporated Production, Directed by Charles Jarrott, Released 1990

Another Yugoslavian-made adventure yarn—based on the popular novel by Jack Higgins—that employs big-name Hollywood stars in roles incompatible with their ages and acting skills. As a senior British general who orders the rescue of an American officer stranded on the Nazi-occupied island of Jersey, eighty-two-year-old John Mills reminds his subordinate, George Peppard, that the fate of the D-Day invasion rests solely on his shoulders. Soon, the pudgy American major infiltrates Gestapo headquarters, dupes numerous

German officers, and after some Saturday-afternoon cartoon adventures, rescues his man, only to learn of his commander's double-dealing. (Peppard to Mills: "Sometimes I wonder who the enemy is!") Most unrealistic scene: sixty-two-year-old George Peppard climbing down a rainspout, a feat difficult for a man forty years younger.

The Night of the Generals

Columbia, Directed by Anatole Litvak, Released 1967

Another pro-German, revisionist homily that suggests most Nazi generals were noble, high-minded, and kind individuals—interested only in assassinating Hitler—while, occasionally, one rotten officer turns up to spoil the barrel. Peter O'Toole portrays a psychopathic general whose brutal murders of local prostitutes remain unnoticed until his colleague, Colonel Omar Sharif, relentlessly investigates these mutilations. (Nazi intelligence officer Omar Sharif, explaining his obsession: "I'm interested in just one general who killed a girl and thought because he was a general he could play God in bed as well as in battle.") Eventually O'Toole's crimes are brought to justice, and his impromptu suicide serves as the coda to expiate all misdeeds. With many famous actors—including Tom Courtenay, Donald Pleasence, Philip Noiret, and Christopher Plummer—this fictional thriller whitewashes much of the horror associated with the Third Reich's occupation policies.

No Man Is an Island

Universal, Directed by John Monks Jr. and Richard Goldstone, Released 1962

A long-winded, I-will-fight-the-Japanese-from-the-hills, Pacific island action tale, loosely based on the exploits of Seaman George Tweed, a thirty-two-year-old bluejacket stranded behind enemy lines on Guam, whose three-year hit-and-miss forays frustrated the Japanese occupation forces. Good-looking Jeffrey Hunter endures many close calls as he slides in and out of different hideaways, aided by local natives. (Seaman Hunter explaining his predicament to a local Catholic priest: "You see, there were five of us. I was in charge, I'm the only one left.") Eventually, an American ship appears on the horizon, and using his Morse code skills, the quick-thinking sailor guides this destroyer out of harm's way. Acclaimed a hero and reunited with his Chamoru sweetheart, an older and wiser serviceman now understands the mystical lines of John Donne's metaphysical poem.

None but the Brave

Warner Bros., Directed by Frank Sinatra, Released 1965

A low-key, antiwar parable about some stranded Marines and abandoned Japanese soldiers on an uncharted Solomon island, circa 1943, who originally battle each other but eventually discover the futility of killing and call a truce. Now a chief navy corpsman, Frank Sinatra treats friend and foe equally. (The Voice, proffering a humanist position after amputating the leg of a Japanese soldier: "I didn't save that kid's life to see him get shot.") Meanwhile, his superior (Clint Walker), must convince his glory-hungry lieutenant the lesson of tolerance and understanding. Soon, this harmony dissipates when a U.S. rescue ship approaches—causing a resumption of hostilities—and the carnage that follows only restates the storyline's pacifist motif. Best scene: Sinatra enters the Japanese military camp to perform a lifesaving operation using only rudimentary instruments plus the omnipresent whiskey bottle.

Okinawa

Columbia, Directed by Leigh Jason, Released 1952

Another slow-moving B-potboiler describing the adventures of a five-man gunnery crew aboard a U.S. Navy destroyer during the spring 1945 Okinawa offensive, where dozens of Japanese suicide pilots—the kamikazes—aim their aircraft at American warships. The ship's captain, pudgy Pat O'Brien, fully understands the dangers of Japanese fanaticism. (O'Brien to command staff: "The most effective weapon the Japs have—kamikaze!") When Seaman Cameron Mitchell and his fellow jacktars, personifying the best of Yankee intransigence, line up the bandits in their crosshairs, most of the enemy airpower is blasted out of the sky, crashing violently into the sea. Using a generous supply of documentary footage—from both sides—the storyline details the ferocity of this final island victory.

Once before I Die

F8 Productions, Directed by John Derek, Released 1965

A high-jinx, shoot-'em-from-the-hip, equestrian yarn—akin to the Saturday-matinee B-oaters—that traces the hoofprints of some polo-playing U.S. Army cavalrymen, who galloped away from an aerial attack near their Philippine base during the early hours of December 7. Traveling west toward Manila, this spirited group, led by jodhpurs-wearing Major John Derek, statuesque Ursula Andress, and glabrous Lieutenant Richard Jaeckel, endure an array of make-believe adventures that include attacking a Japanese tank with fallen trees and burning bushes, plus a benevolent sexual experience proffered by Miss Andress to a neophyte GI so that the lad may experience coitus "once before he dies." Most prophetic scene: Major John Derek expostulates on Japanese expansionism. (Derek explaining the Greater East Asia Co-Prosperity Pact to the politically uninformed Andress: "They bombed Pearl Harbor; obviously, they're planning something big.")

Onionhead

Warner Bros., Directed by Norman Taurog, Released 1958

A low-budget comedy-melodrama that blends some Laurel and Hardy slapstick, a femme fatale's psychosis, a corrupt mess officer's duplicity, a ship's captain's morality, and a submarine attack in an eighty-four-minute screenplay that jumps from one genre to another. After joining the Coast Guard in spring 1941, a happy-go-lucky Oklahoma college student (Andy Griffith) laughs his way through basic training, receives a chief petty officer's rank, becomes a cook and, after more shenanigans, finds a Boston sweetheart. Soon, the girlfriend drops him, marries another sailor, and after her new husband sails off to Greenland, seduces the confused hayseed. Back in his kitchen, he acts decisively when he eventually discovers a theft operation that, literally, takes good food from sailors' mouths. (Chief Griffith to his staff: "As long as I'm the head cook, I'm running this galley.") Acclaimed a hero after some fancy machine-gun-firing against a U-boat, he runs into an old hometown flame and, after a quick courtship—much to the acclaim of his pals and officers—marries the pretty maiden, proving, once again, that true love comes to those who wait.

Operation Bikini

American International Pictures, Directed by Anthony Carras, Released 1963

Another cost-cutting, use-lots-of-newsreel-footage, B-for-bad, seventy-seven-minute train wreck that traces the comings and goings of a Navy demolition team assigned to destroy a U.S. submarine, lying ignominiously at the bottom of a South Pacific atoll, before Japanese forces, lurking nearby, find this vessel and retrieve important intelligence codes. Anemic-looking Tab Hunter seems apathetic about his directive while his bosun mate, Jim Backus (the voice of the popular cartoon character, Mr. Magoo), listens apprehensively. (Lieutenant Hunter, explaining the mission:

"We're here to find the sub that was sunk in the channel last month.") After a few comic-strip adventures, the unit, spearheaded by teen idol Frankie Avalon, swims many fathoms underwater, sets the charges, and, after a few close calls, demolishes the ship, much to the relief of its commanding officers. Funniest juxtaposition: Frankie Avalon's daydreaming fantasies, where, twice, he croons romantic songs to bikini-clad girlfriends, who, shaking their scantily clad bodies, offer tangible evidence of the American man's why-we-fight credo.

Operation Crossbow

MGM, Directed by Michael Anderson, Released 1965

A fabricated action tale glamorizing the sub-rosa world of some Allied agents, who in 1943 parachute into the Fatherland and—after some cat-and-mouse escapades with the Gestapo—destroy the underground factory that manufactures the V-2 rocket. Working as an American spy speaking flawless German, George Peppard sweet-talks his way out of most predicaments until starry-eyed Sophia Loren learns about the mission. Unable to trust the Italian widow, Peppard approves her execution and likewise sacrifices Tom Courteney to a Nazi firing squad. Infused with many examples of ambiguous loyalties, the storyline reiterates the aphoristic concept that all's fair in love and war. (British citizen Anthony Quayle, now aligned with the Third Reich, rationalizing his perfidy: "Before Hitler came to power we were nothing. Now, we're the greatest nation in the world—the most feared and most respected.")

Operation Pacific

Warner Bros., Directed by George Waggner, Released 1951

A straightforward, below-the-waves, blast-the-enemy adventure detailing the perilous missions that Silent Service members routinely experienced in their war against Japan. As always, John Wayne is superb as the captain of the USS *Thunder*, a submarine destroying Japanese vessels in the Pacific waters, while rescuing many downed American airmen. (Wayne, bellowing orders after torpedoing another enemy ship: "Take her down, fast and deep—rig for depth charge, rig for silent running.") With many references to the "I'm-just-an-ordinary-guy-not-a-hero" sailor, the photodrama quietly reaffirms the importance of every man's role in the combat zone and honors the many sacrifices needed for victory. (Wayne, eulogizing the *Thunder*'s chief petty officer: "Chiefs have been taking care of this man's navy for a long time.")

Operation Petticoat

Universal International, Directed by Blake Edwards, Released 1959

A pleasant, easygoing, and harmless comedy that sidesteps the horror and brutality of World War II and, instead, spoofs the global conflict as a series of wisecracking, double-entendre events. Here, suave Cary Grant radiates as the skipper of a damaged American submarine that limps out of harbor following a Japanese air attack in December 1941, while his junior officer (Tony Curtis) smooth-talks everyone for needed parts to keep the underwater vessel operational. (Commander Grant, rationalizing such behavior: "To paraphrase Mr. Churchill, never have so few stolen so much from so many.") Once on the high seas, the crew experiences an array of zany adventures that include a busty nurse blocking a narrow walkway, a voodoo blessing from a local witch doctor, two village women giving birth in the forward cabin, an askew torpedo attack that blows up a Japanese truck, and—as the pièce de résistance—the unintentional priming of the ship's outer surface that dries a bright pink.

O.S.S.

Paramount, Directed by Irving Pichel, Released 1946

An elaborate now-it-can-be-told tribute to Wild Bill Donovan's acclaimed cloak-and-dagger organization—the Office of Strategic Services—an undercover group responsible for many covert, worldwide operations that disrupted numerous Axis offensives. (Colonel Donovan to charges: "Learn how to kill—quickly, silently!") After intense stateside training, good-looking Alan Ladd moves stealthily through the Brittany back roads. There—after some smooth talking, close calls, and unexpected luck—he destroys an important Nazi railroad tunnel necessary for the Allied D-Day invasion, while his girlfriend (Geraldine Fitzgerald) maneuvers their escape. Soon, the twosome sneak across the Rhine to facilitate the U.S. Army's advance into the Fatherland where, again, they slip in and out of dangerous situations. Finally, their luck falters, and as a farewell expiation, the pretty Miss Fitzgerald sacrifices her life for a mission's success. (Tough-talking Alan Ladd, ruminating about his lost love: "I didn't even know her real name.")

Pacific Inferno

Nathaniel Productions. Directed by Rolf Bayer, Released 1979

A totally distorted and tasteless photodrama using the infamous Bataan Death March—an historical event where hundreds of emaciated American

GIs perished from Japanese savagery—as the backdrop for a preposterous underwater search-for-silver travesty. Former football running back Jim Brown, "stars" as a U.S. Navy diver, who along with other bluejackets, surrenders to the Japanese when Corregidor capitulates. Soon, these prisoners receive good food, hearty beverages, and clean housing and are put to work retrieving sunken treasure. (Imperial officer to sailors: "I bring you pleasurable food and drink. This number-one best Japan wine.") In his evening hours, Seaman Brown hooks up with some guerrillas and, after some comic-book adventures, removes the prized bullion, swims to a nearby village, and, in a gory finale, blows up a barge, kills many Japanese, and—in a nod to contemporary American racism—accepts a martyr's death. Replete with anachronistic haircuts, eyeglasses, slang, attitudes, and music, the entire production depicts POW life as nothing but a series of minor irritations.

Paratroop Command

American-International Pictures, Directed by William Witney, Released 1959

A B-for-bottom-of-the-barrel, jump-out-of-the-plane, stand-up-and-shoot yawn describing the comings and goings of some paratroopers during the 1943 Italian campaign. Here, an airborne soldier (Richard Bakalyan), unaware of an offensive ruse, accidentally kills a squad member, and soon everyone turns against him. (Corporal Bakalyan, explaining the misunderstanding: "I swear, Lieutenant, when I shot, so help me, I never knew it was the Cowboy.") Unable to shake this stigma, the downtrodden Bakalyan— hoping for redemption—zigzags across a minefield, steps on an explosive, but lives long enough to deliver a needed radio. With numerous scenes of documentary footage interspersed in the storyline, this seventy-one-minute quickie—from a production company noted for using unknown actors, watered-downed scripts, and a seven-day shooting schedule—explains the war as nothing more than a comic-book scenario.

Paratrooper

Columbia, Directed by Terence Young, Released 1953

Another unlikely airborne story glamorizing the recruitment, training, and combat assignment of some British paratroopers who distinguish themselves in a 1942 North African raid. Here, tough-guy Alan Ladd plays a former U.S. Air Corps pilot who joins the Royal Army as an enlisted man to forget some unpleasant stateside experiences. Soon, this stereotypical loner refuses any leadership assignment. (Major Leo Genn berating Private Ladd: "One fine day—whether you're wearing three stars or three stripes or nothing at all—the men are going to look to you.") Eventually, the blond-haired American, with the help of a kindly English girlfriend, realizes his folly, and in a formula film ending, accepts his wartime responsibility, much to the glee of his pals and superiors.

Patton

Twentieth Century–Fox, Directed by Franklin J. Schaffner, Released 1970

An elaborate 171-minute hagiography to the unorthodox, flamboyant, and controversial four-star general known to his men as Blood-and-Guts, the larger-than-life egocentric officer responsible for many important battlefield victories. In an Academy Award performance, George C. Scott captures the idiosyncrasies of the unconventional George S. Patton—from his Bible-quoting oratory down to his ivory-handled revolver—beginning with his 1943 North African campaign until his triumphant 1945 entry into the German capital, while his commander, General Omar Bradley (Karl Malden) spends many hours cautioning his charge about military propriety. Frequently obsessed with megalomania, the outspoken general seems hoisted by his own petard with his many diatribes. (Patton to hospital doctors, regarding admittance procedures: "Battle fatigue is a free ride—yellow bellies' ticket to the hospital. I'm not going to subsidize cowardice.")

Pearl Harbor

Touchstone Pictures, Directed by Michael Bay, Released 2001

An over-the-top, computer-enhanced, *Weekly Reader*, special-effects retelling of the December 7 attack as seen through the eyes of two Tennessee-born pals, their shared girlfriend, plus an entourage of noted 1941 personalities. These include President Roosevelt, whose famous residence, the White House, anachronistically sports central-air-conditioning ducts on the rooftop. At a Hawaiian air base, two Air Corps pilots (Ben Affleck and Josh Hartnett) chase after a pretty woman (Kate Beckinsale), while on the high seas, the Imperial Japanese fleet steams closer to their Sunday-morning target. While the love triangle reaches a discomfited stalemate, enemy air squadrons attack Pearl Harbor, destroying most of the Pacific fleet and killing thousands of civilians and servicemen. (Colonel James Doolittle, played by Alec Baldwin, assessing the damage: "You know at Pearl they hit us with a sledgehammer.") Eventually, the U.S. forces reorganize and, in a stunning coup de main, bomb

Tokyo. With numerous examples of dramatic license, much of this soap-opera-laden storyline implies that Japan attacked Pearl Harbor for the sole purpose of resolving an awkward ménage à trois.

The Pigeon That Took Rome

Paramount, Directed by Melville Shavelson, Released 1962

A lighthearted spoof that japes military bureaucracy, Prussian discipline, and Italian family life in an offbeat manner that resembles the classical farce. Here, in 1944, two Army spies—Charlton Heston and Harry Guardino—working undercover in Rome must rely on carrier pigeons to convey messages, while keeping a low profile in the Nazi-occupied city. After a series of sidestepping misadventures, that include wooing comely lasses, sweet-talking German soldiers, inadvertently eating their prized homing birds at a gala Easter dinner, and sending the wrong instructions to Allied command, the duo are acclaimed heroes as the city capitulates to the attacking Americans. Completely nonplussed by the turn of events, Captain Heston waxes philosophical. (Heston to pal: "This is no war—it's an insane asylum!") With numerous potshots at opportunistic officers, this laid-back, antiwar photodrama quips the conflict as a happy-go-lucky child's game supervised by goofy, out-of-it adults.

Play Dirty

United Artists, Directed by André Detoth, Released 1969

A cynical reappraisal of the British North African campaign where senior staff officers—perched safely behind their oversized desks—dispatch a small attack team behind enemy lines, fully aware that these Tommies will perish in the hot desert fighting. Here, the leader of this motley squad (Michael Caine) slowly realizes the sacrificial nature of his assignment as his men capitulate to the heat, terrain, and Nazi offensives. Back in headquarters, Harry Andrews—in another brash commander role—manipulates their deaths into a well-orchestrated propaganda coup, culminating with an English counterattack. Laced with strong Machiavellian overtones, the storyline depicts the worst of British forces, stressing their primordial needs. (Michael Caine, expatiating his moral code: "I want to survive here—I watch, I listen, and I say nothing.")

The Plot to Kill Hitler

Warner Bros., Directed by Lawrence Schiller, Released 1990

A pie-in-the-sky, puffed-up, made-for-television, revisionist paean to the Nazi officers, who—hoping to save their country from continued Allied bombings—

masterminded the assassination attempt of their führer. After some detailed logistics, a briefcase containing an explosive is placed next to Hitler at a July 20, 1944, staff meeting. However, the Nazi leader survives the detonation, much to the plotters' dismay. (Brad Davis as General Claus von Stauffenberg: "I set off a bomb during my conference with the führer. I saw the blast myself. No one who was in that room can still be alive.") Soon, top-ranking officers endure their own terror as Hitler—played by Mike Gwilym—orders brutal reprisals for anyone remotely associated with this plot. With numerous heroic actions, this sugarcoated photoplay suggests that most top-ranking Nazis were astute, magnanimous, and nonbelligerent nationals who could care less about lebensraum.

Proud

Castle Hill, Directed by Mary Pat Kelly, Released 2004

A heart-warming, Norman Rockwell, factual story that honors the 160 African American sailors who manned an escort destroyer, the USS *Mason*, on many dangerous North Atlantic crossings during the height of wolf-pack attacks. Ossie Davis radiates as the real-life Seaman Lorenzo Dufau, who along with his shipmates, performs laudably in an Eleanor Roosevelt experiment to determine the efficacy of black seamen. (Senior citizen Davis, explaining why African Americans fought in World War II: "The only colors that count are red, white, and blue.") During one perilous crossing, the vessel—ignoring the ocean dangers—dramatically forges ahead in high, windy, seas, providing their convoy needed support. Best scenes: a 1994 admiral's reception for these men, awarding medals—long overdue because of wartime racial policies—plus President Clinton's 2003 tribute, citing these sailors for their "Magnificent, magnificent effort!"

The Proud and the Profane

Paramount, Directed by George Seaton, Released 1956

An overblown tribute to the men of the Marine Corps—from Lucy Herndon Crockett's novel *The Magnificent Bastards*—who fought the Japanese in the South Pacific campaign and then returned to the peaceful French island of New Caledonia for training and medical care. Here a martinet battle commander (William Holden) hones his youthful charges razor sharp, disdaining any weakness or emotion. (Colonel Holden, dressing down a naive chaplain: "I want my men to be superstitious about only one thing—when they come face-to-face with a Jap in the bush, I want them to consider it very bad luck not to kill him first.") Eventually, the sangfroid colonel capitulates to the warmth of a Red Cross worker (Deborah Kerr), and following an off-again, on-again romance, the twosome are united in a saccharine end-of-the-movie fade-out. One scene in particular—Deborah Kerr placing flowers at the military cemetery—restates the high casualty rate sustained in the island-hopping warfare and, subliminally, deifies all fallen members of the Corps.

PT 109

Warner Bros., Directed by Leslie H. Martinson, Released 1962

A glamorized version of President John F. Kennedy's 1943 South Seas combat experiences—based on the book by Robert J. Donovan—that portrays the youthful naval lieutenant (j.g.) as intelligent, versatile, and resourceful. Assigned to a mosquito-boat command, good-looking Cliff Robertson quickly learns the rudiments of seamanship and, along with a fine-tuned crew, attacks a Japanese island to rescue some stranded marines. Later, an enemy ship rams their plywood hull, and following a series of close calls—including an arduous ocean swim, ducking from Japanese forces, and functioning without food or medical supplies—the sailors are rescued after Lieutenant Kennedy dispatches his famous message-inscribed coconut. (Lieutenant Kennedy, reassuring the tars: "We're getting out of here if we have to get in the water and drag this damn island back with us!")

Racing with the Moon

Paramount, Directed by Richard Benjamin, Released 1984

A wonderful, joyous, coming-of-age fulfillment that limns the hopes, aspirations, and uncertainties of two Californian youths who—in the 1942 winter—are counting the days before their Marine Corps induction. Sean Penn and Nicolas Cage portray lifelong friends eager to leave their pin-boy jobs, become leathernecks, and rout America's enemies. (Cage to Penn: "The only future we got is Germans and Japs.") As their days dwindle down, the twosome enjoy some last-minute shenanigans that include chasing after girls, drinking whiskey, and hustling some bluejackets in a pool game. Finally, the magic date arrives, and much to the acclaim of family and friends, the boys, now eighteen years old, jump on the train, confident their enlistment will bring an end to the global conflict.

The Raiders of Leyte Gulf

Hemisphere Pictures, Directed by Eddie Romero, Released 1963

A cut-to-the-bone, jerky, shoot-at-everyone, B-for-Bad soap opera that peripherally depicts the Philippines resistance movement weeks before General

MacArthur's historic "I-Shall-Return" pageantry. On a remote Malay archipelago, Lieutenant Michael Parsons leads an attack team against a Japanese stronghold to rescue an American prisoner. (Lieutenant Parsons to group, "We're still in the middle of a war.") Off to the side, his native girlfriend (Liza Moreno) whispers sweet nothings into his ear. (Liza to sweetheart: "Is it true that most Americans are afraid of lizards?) Soon, machine-gun bullets rebound, hand grenades explode, and the Japanese forces are routed, but in a sudsy fade-out, the two lovers—reconciled to any anomaly—bid a saccharine farewell, promising to unite at war's end.

The Ravagers

Hemisphere, Directed by Eddie Romero, Released 1965

Another low-light, terse-dialogue, B-quickie from a shoestring production company known for hacking out one war title after another. Unshaven John Saxon moves slowly as a U.S. Army captain leading a motley Filipino guerrilla team dodging a retreating Japanese patrol during the closing summer days of World War II. Finally, the Japanese soldiers commandeer a Roman Catholic convent but are promptly routed by the jungle fighters. (Major Saxon, explaining his offensive strategy: "If we don't lose our heads, we got a fighting chance.") Meanwhile, his subordinate (Fernando Poe Jr.), after killing many banzai-spouting soldiers, pauses to make eyes at Bronwyn FitzSimons, a disheveled American damsel in distress.

The Red Ball Express

Universal, Directed by Budd Boetticher, Released 1952

A fast-driving, no-road-too-difficult, no-trip-too-arduous tribute to the men of the Army Transportation Corps, the GIs who drove overpacked trucks hundreds of miles to supply General Patton's tanks with gasoline and ammunition during the July 1944 Normandy breakout. As always, Lieutenant Jeff Chandler takes charge of a diverse group of soldiers, quickly molds them into a tight unit, and leads them down many a hazardous thoroughfare to deliver needed matériel. (Lieutenant Chandler, explaining their mission: "The line of trucks between here and the front is almost continuous—a load of supplies will be dropping behind Patton every minute, day and night.") With Sidney Poitier as a young corporal espousing some racial harmony, the fast-moving storyline (using many grainy newsreel inserts) highlights the heroic work of the many African American GIs who served in this important outfit.

Reign of the Gargoyles

Concrete Productions, Directed by Ayton Davis, Released 2006

Another black-magic, they're-everywhere, airborne comic-strip romp detailing a mad Nazi scientist, who during the winter 1945 defensive brings to life—à la Frankenstein—hundreds of gargoyles that fill the French skies to destroy Allied bombers. (U.S. crew member, radioing his superiors: "They're slaughtering us in the air, on the ground!") Eventually, some downed airmen, led by Joe Penny and Wes Ramsey, team up with British commandos and Resistance members and, after a series of make-believe adventures, hop into a German airplane, turn a few switches, fly into a gaggle of gargoyles, and then ram a sacred spear into the "heart" of the primary monster, rendering all others ineffective. With many references to medieval sorcery, this harmless, make-believe yarn offers the same vicarious thrills found in noisy video-game arcades.

Run Silent, Run Deep

United Artists, Directed by Robert Wise, Released 1958

Another all-male, I-want-revenge, Silent Service potboiler—based on the novel by Edward L. Beach—that juxtaposes the loneliness-of-command theme against the larger issue of destroying Japanese seafaring vessels during a 1943 offensive. Clark Gable shines as an obdurate U.S. Navy submarine captain patrolling the South Pacific theater, secretly searching for the enemy ship that blasted him out of the water a year ago. When confronted by his second-in-command (Burt Lancaster) about the efficacy of a one-man show, Gable pooh-poohs his executive officer. (Gable to Lancaster: "A captain can redefine orders if he feels he has an advantage.") Eventually the Japanese vessel is spotted and—in a typical climax—sunk by some deft bowshot torpedoing. As a coda, Gable's underwater death, an expiation for disobeying military directives, deifies the men of the submarine command.

Saints and Soldiers

Go Films, Directed by Ryan Little, Released 2003

A quiet remembrance of the dozens of American prisoners murdered by German forces in the Belgian forest near the small town of Malmedy during the December 1944 Battle of the Bulge. During this infamous massacre, four GIs run into the woods, flee their captors, forage for weapons, and eventually team up with an English pilot carrying logistical information. After numerous close calls—including ducking into a cellar while Nazis frolic overhead in the living room, hiding in a farmhouse, killing a Nazi to stop a rape, freeing a simple German soldier, and finally, driving through a *Wehrmacht*'s camp wearing their enemy's uniforms, the needed information reaches the Allied command post. Young, Bible-reading Corporal Corbin Allred sparkles as the group's marksman, whose simple but competent mannerisms frequently collide with his religious convictions. (Allred to pal: "Do you believe in a life after this one?") Off to the side, his sergeant keeps a watchful eye. Best scene: each man, in a moment of fraternal bonding, reveals intimate secrets: Corporal Corbin's confession: "I never kissed my wife till the day we were married."

Sands of Iwo Jima

Republic, Directed by Allan Dwan, Released 1949

The quintessential combat film of the postwar period that—in a quiet, dignified manner—honors the Marine Corps for their many island victories. Who else but John Wayne could portray a tough, gruff squad sergeant who teaches his young charges the meaning of loyalty, teamwork, and semper fidelis? (Straight-faced Sergeant Wayne to replacements: "Before I'm through with you, you're going to move like one man and think like one man—if you don't, you'll be dead!) Soon the marines assault Iwo Jima and, along with John Apgar and Forrest Tucker, push inland to witness the historic Mount Suribachi flag rising. Here, a Japanese sniper fells John Wayne, and after a short eulogy the gyrenes—mindful of their sergeant's sacrifice—continue their attack. Using three real-life members from the Joe Rosenthal photograph in the cast, the screenplay reaffirms the high human cost of the South Pacific fighting.

Saving Private Ryan

DreamWorks, Directed by Steven Spielberg, Released 1998

An overpowering, one-of-a-kind, flag-waving accolade to the U.S. forces that landed on Omaha Beach on June 6, 1944, fought their way inland, and finally secured the beachfront. Tom Hanks sparkles as a Ranger officer who leads his squad uphill, attacks German defenders, and, finally, seizes their strongholds. A few days later, his men journey into the French countryside to locate a young paratrooper (whose three older brothers recently died in combat) and bring the private back to the command post. After many difficulties, including fighting rearguard *Wehrmacht* soldiers, discovering the "wrong" Private Ryan, and ambushing a radar station, the Rangers find their charge but, in an unanticipated turn of events, must fight against an Axis attack. (Captain Miller's appraisal: "Things have taken a turn for the surreal.") Eventually, Private Ryan reaches safety, but Captain Miller perishes defending his position. Most harrowing scene: the first twenty-eight minutes, depicting the indescribable carnage U.S. forces experienced on the Normandy coast.

The Sea Chase

Warner Bros., Directed by John Farrow, Released 1955

Another hot-air, revisionist production purporting that most German nationals were noble, austere, and kindhearted, while only the degenerates embraced Hitler's world-domination policies. Here, John Wayne, as an anti-Nazi German sea captain, slips his steamer from an Australian harbor—after the 1939 Poland invasion—determined to reach home port. After months of ocean turmoil, including the ubiquitous sea storm, a shark attack, a suicide, and pursuit by a revenge-bearing British warship, Wayne finally reaches a Norwegian fjord, where in an ambiguous ending he disappears with mysterious, bleached-blond Lana Turner. (Captain Wayne, waxing philosophically: "Immortality has nothing to do with fame.") With obvious parallels to the *Odyssey* and the *Rime of the Ancient Mariner*, this screenplay retells the "long voyage home" saga as a World War II parable, only this time, the Germans are heroes.

The Sea Wolves

Paramount, Directed by Andrew V. McLaglen, Released 1980

A far-fetched fairy tale purporting that a motley group of over-the-hill British civilians living in Calcutta formed a high-powered commando team and destroyed three Nazi warships moored in nearby Goa, a Portuguese neutral port. David Niven moves cautiously as the leader of these former cavalrymen, while two English officers—Gregory Peck and Roger Moore—supply the covert military logistics necessary to coordinate this raid. A plethora of subplots—including the mysterious femme fatale, waterfront spies, cryptic code books, secret radio room, and the ship's engine that falters before starting—add to the fast-moving action that proves, once again, the indomitable force of English prowess. (David Niven, explaining his unit's determinism: "We're a little thin on top and thick in the middle, but I guarantee you, every one of these fellows would pull his own weight.")

Sealed Cargo

RKO, Directed by Alfred L. Werker, Released 1951

Another well-deserved pat on the back for those quiet-spoken fisherman on the northeastern Canadian coast who kept a sharp eye for Axis warships. As always, Dana Andrews keeps a steady course as a Nova Scotian fishing-boat skipper who answers a distress signal from a floundering ship and tows this vessel into a nearby village harbor. Suspicious of the captain's roundabout explanation, the quick-thinking Canadian slips on board and, after some fancy footwork, discovers a secret hull containing U-boat torpedoes. Soon, the Germans return to their ship. (Nazi captain Claude Rains, revealing his rank: "I am an officer of the German Navy. You do not think I would surrender a vessel under my command to a handful of fisherman.") But they are no match for the mariners, who overcome their enemies and deftly sail it out of the harbor, await the arrival of two Axis submarines and—after some tricky maneuvering—set off an explosive, destroying both U-boats.

The Secret of Santa Vittoria

United Artists, Directed by Stanley Kramer, Released 1969

A frivolous, distorted, and oversimplified view of the 1943 Italian campaign that implies only a few nationals supported *Il Duce*'s fascist policies, while most of the Nazis strut around a village square winking at the pulchritudinous locals. Anthony Quinn sparkles as a kindhearted, bumbling peasant, who—after some convoluted escapades—becomes the mayor of an isolated hilltop village, Santa Vittoria. When the German army arrives to confiscate the town's wine harvest—over a million bottles—the denizens move quickly to hide their prized possessions. (Quinn to council members: "Without our wine, we are nothing!") Much to their surprise, the ruse works, and the gullible Germans withdraw. Based on the book by Robert Crichton, the photoplay sugarcoats Mussolini's autocracy and suggests—in a roundabout way—that most Italians, sitting in their outdoor cafes sipping vino, detest their leader's wartime policies.

The Sharkfighters

United Artists, Directed by Jerry Hopper, Released 1956

A breezy tribute to a small but important coterie of U.S. naval scientists, stationed in Cuba circa 1944, who work long hours and endure numerous frustrations to perfect a shark repellent that will protect any servicemen abandoned in the ocean. Chain-smoking, hard-talking Victor Mature, a lieutenant commander and survivor of a Pacific shark attack, heads a meticulous laboratory experimenting with numerous chemicals. After weeks of testing, they stumble upon the perfect mixture. (Mature to crew: "We got a repellent that works.") Soon, he leaps into the hostile ocean and, immersed in this solution, proves its efficacy as one shark after another diverts from its fuliginous odor. Funniest scene: Victor Mature, anxious to start work, jumps onto the research ship, heading to a known breeding area, accoutered in full navy dress uniform—jacket, tie, and shined shoes—an outfit no tar would dream of wearing for such an assignment.

Shining Through

Twentieth–Century Fox, Directed by David Seltzer, Released 1992

Another boy-saves-girl spy melodrama—based on the novel by Susan Isaacs—that spotlights the peripatetic skills of an American O.S.S. agent (Michael Douglas) as he stealthily moves between European capitals, obtaining classified information during the shaky pre–Pearl Harbor days. After war is declared, his young bilingual secretary (Melanie Griffith), eager to help the Allied cause, joins this sub-rosa group, enters the Fatherland and—following a series of Nancy Drew adventures—photographs important military information. Eventually discovered, she experiences a few close calls until the good-looking Douglas literally carries her across the Swiss border. (Colonel Douglas, pronouncing his affection: "I don't want to lose you, I want to be with you always.") Best anachronistic scene: during the 1942 winter, Colonel Douglas wears the combat infantryman's badge, a medal not yet awarded to American GIs.

Ski Troop Attack

Filmgroup, Directed by Roger Corman, Released 1960

Another sixty-three-minute, B-quickie, from a director frequently called "King of the Drive-ins," whose trademark low-budget productions contain strident music, generous newsreel inserts, and skimpy lighting. This one is about a five-man U.S. ski patrol who in December 1944 reconnoiter parts of the Ardennes, while the nearby German high command plans a surprise offensive. Straight-arrow junior officer (Michael Forest) cautiously guides his squad from one snowy ridge to another, dodging the enemy. (Lieutenant Forest's directive: "As long as this weather says socked in, the ski troops are the division's only eyes behind the lines.") Eventually, the GIs stumble upon a trestle bridge and, after some fancy maneuvering with homemade explosives, destroy this strategic overpass, stymieing the Axis attack. Best special effects scene: the popular model-railroad-train set used during the final scene, emblazoned with the manufacturer's prominent logo.

Slaughterhouse-Five

Universal, Directed by George Roy Hill, Released 1972

A wide-eyed, off-the-wall, science fiction take—based on Kurt Vonnegut's acclaimed novel—that pokes fun at armed-service protocol, prisoner-of-war-camp life, interplanetary travel, and staid opticians, while calling into question the elaborate, February 1945 Dresden carpet-bombing attack. Michael Sacks radiates as a simple, nineteen-year-old, gawky American GI, Billy Pilgrim, who is captured at the Battle of the Bulge and sent to Dresden. There, along with his pals, he squirrels inside an abandoned slaughterhouse during the Allied air raid. Eventually liberated, he returns home, marries the boss's daughter, raises children, and sells many eyeglass frames while, unknown to friends and family, he time-trips between past and future. (Sacks, explaining his history: "Dresden, I was there.") Replete with numerous absurd situations that lampoon military folly, the screenplay echoes Vonnegut's contention that modern warfare—the creation of older men—is fought by unsuspecting children, who for the most part, understand nothing about conflict.

SS Doomtrooper

Combat Productions, Directed by David Flores, Released 2006

Another space-age, comic-book adventure about a mad Nazi scientist (Ben Cross), who in winter 1945 creates a defensive weapon against advancing Allied forces—an atomized, twenty-foot Hulk look-alike supermonster, impervious to every explosive. Soon, an American commando team— headed by Captain Corin Nemec—locates this laboratory-made leviathan. (Captain Nemec's warning: "The only thing standing between the First Army and that freak of nature is us.") Following a series of wide-eyed skirmishes in a stolen tank and jeep, the team finally hotwires the monster's circuitry, causing a meltdown. With numerous tonsorial and linguistic anachronisms, including a Vietnam reference about special ops and the Stone Age, this strictly for laughs, action-figure game never takes itself seriously. Best homage scene: a frustrated GI, Private Parker Lewis, blurts out, "I can't win," a reference to Fox's popular 1990 television comedy *Parker Lewis Can't Lose*, a three-year series that starred Corin Nemec.

Stalag 17

Paramount, Directed by Billy Wilder, Released 1953

A half-spoof, half-serious look at the problems some six hundred American prisoners of war encounter in a German camp—a stalag—during the closing days of 1944 that downplays the abhorrence of Nazi brutality. William Holden depicts a close-mouthed Air Corps sergeant whose daily wheeling and dealing with his captors affords him minimal comfort, much to the annoyance of his fellow GIs, while guttural-speaking Sig Rumann plods along in another cookie-cutter "Schultz" role. Eventually, the cynical noncom redeems himself by catching a smooth-talking plant and rescuing a trapped officer from the clutches of the *Schutzstaffel*. Frequently criticized for ignoring Nazi atrocities, the storyline constantly pokes fun at Hitlerism. (GI prisoner to his buddies: "Always remember, just because the Krauts are dumb doesn't mean they're stupid.")

The Steel Claw

Ponderey Productions, Directed by George Montgomery, Released 1961

A made-on-a-shoestring, ninety-three-minute, B-adventure-yarn aggrandizing the jungle-fighting exploits of a one-handed Marine captain—wearing a homemade steel claw—as he leads a motley guerrilla band into the Philippine interior to rescue a one-star general from his Japanese tormentors. Matinee idol George Montgomery fords fast-running streams, climbs steep hills, and slithers under thick underbrush before reaching the Japanese camp, where after some more shooting-from-the-hip exploits, he realizes that the freed U.S. "general" is really an opportunist staff sergeant who wanted better treatment from his captors. (Tough-talking Montgomery to imposter: "So, you decided to play General—why didn't you drop the act when we picked you up?") Undaunted by this setback, the fast-thinking marine officer, along with his wounded girlfriend (Charito Luna), treks his charges back to the American outpost, proving once again the never-say-die spirit of a fighting man.

Straight into Darkness

Silver Bullet, Directed by Jeff Burr, Released 2005

A tasteless, repulsive, twenty-first century, pseudo-artistic travesty that highlights sexual and scatological themes in a manner usually reserved for special-effects, let-the-blood-flow horror films. Scott MacDonald and Ryan Francis "star" as two Army deserters, who, in 1945, escape from confinement, crawl through a French minefield, and finally stumble into a forlorn warehouse with a valuable art collection stashed in the cellar. There, an eccentric caretaker (David Warner) oversees a handful of physically handicapped orphans, outcast children who, under his tutelage, are now expert killers. A gory battle ensues when a *Wehrmacht* squad arrives to remove the art. (Private Francis, analyzing his situation: "They're here for the paintings.") Most of the Germans die, while Private MacDonald, in an expiatory gesture, fights to the finish, allowing his friend and the children to escape. (Private MacDonald's final words: "Quit squawking and start walking.")

Submarine Seahawk

American International Pictures, Directed by Spencer Gordon Bennet, Released 1958

Another how-low-was-my-budget underwater potboiler that rehashes pelagic themes, standard clichés, and navy jargon found in most Silent Service B-photodramas. Now, in the dangerous, Japanese-laden Pacific waters, Captain John Bentley cautiously guides the USS *Seahawk* on a reconnaissance mission to pinpoint enemy positions, while off to the side, his all-Caucasian crew grumbles about missed opportunities. Eventually, their skipper locates an elaborate Japanese reserve force, and soon American aircraft blow this hostile armada out of the water, much to the acclaim of his seagoing doubting Thomases. (Bentley to men: "We gave the Jap carrier the deep six.") With many scenes of anachronistic, documentary footage, this eighty-three-minute, black-and-white film resembles the B-propaganda quickies made during the war.

The Tanks Are Coming

Warner Bros., Directed by Lewis Seiler, Released 1951

A low-budget, "let's get moving" adulation of the Army Tank Corps GIs, the men that spearheaded the perilous July 1944 Normandy breakout. Steve Cochran stands firm as a cocky, self-centered, chip-on-the-shoulder NCO, who—despite his obnoxious behavior and frequent solecisms—intelligently maneuvers his unit out of harm's way. (Sergeant Cochran, waxing eloquently about his leadership qualities: "I ain't getting nobody killed! Ninety-eight percent of the guys in cemeteries got there because they made mistakes, which I don't do.") Frequently shunned by his squad, the loudmouth Cochran, after rescuing a corporal, quickly becomes a hero and, much to the admiration of his men, leads the first tank squadron heading for Berlin. As with most B-flag-waving productions, this photodrama contains many newsreel scenes, hoping to add a little verisimilitude to a skimpy storyline.

Task Force

Warner Bros., Directed by Delmer Daves, Released 1949

A Fourth-of-July, flag-waving testimony to the navy pilots who attacked the Japanese fleet at Midway, winning a pivotal battle and altering the war's course. Gary Cooper—a longtime pioneer for aircraft-carrier superiority—sparkles as an aviation officer whose twenty-seven-year career recalls the rudimentary flying conditions that existed just after World War I. Frustrated by the isolationist movement to denigrate naval airpower, the quiet-spoken Cooper—along with character actor Walter Brennan—eventually creates a powerful flattop fleet that forces Japan's capitulation. (Commander Cooper lambasting a cynic's criticism of floating airfields: "If the country had followed that advice, our West Coast newspapers right now would be printed in Japanese.") Using many stock newsreel insertions, this quasi-documentary format restates the navy's heroism and sacrifices in a subtle but forceful manner.

The Thin Red Line

Twentieth Century–Fox, Directed by Terrence Malick, Released 1998

A 170-minute, pseudo-epistemological, what-is-the-meaning-of-war? allegory—based on James Jones' acclaimed novel—that uses the U.S. Army's 1942 Guadalcanal follow-up invasion as a metaphor for various ontological questions inherent in contemporary society. Nick Nolte is outstanding as a rough-and-ready infantry colonel. While his top sergeant (Sean Penn) cautiously ruminates, Nolte pushes his C-for-Charlie squad into the jungle's interior to rout diehard Japanese from their pillboxes. (Colonel Nolte to subordinate: "We're going straight up that hill there.") Caught in their own heart of darkness, this small fighting unit—an eclectic mixture of spiritualism, loneliness, insecurity, and atavism—experiences numerous existentialist dilemmas before the island is secure. Most dubious casting: John Travolta, as an opportunist one-star general, prancing aboard a ship in a manner suggestive of a disco dancer, and George Clooney, as a rearguard officer, badmouthing replacements with his bag-of-wind platitudes.

36 Hours

MGM, Directed by George Seaton, Released 1964

Another spy-versus-spy thriller using the D-Day invasion as the setting for psychological intrigue. James Garner stands tall as an American intelligence officer who is first drugged, then kidnapped, and finally flown to a bogus American hospital in Germany. There, a Nazi doctor (Rod Taylor) almost convinces his "patient" that five years have elapsed since the Allies defeated Hitler, that Henry Wallace is the U.S. president, and that American forces govern Third Reich territory. Slowly Major Garner unravels their scheme and, with a little help from a concentration camp victim (Eva Marie Saint), escapes into Switzerland. (Nurse Saint, offering her assistance: "I'll do anything to help you, believe me.") As a quasi-science-fictional tale, the screenplay—in an obvious nod to 1964 Cold War politics—tones down Nazi bestiality and indirectly suggests that most Germans were kind, noble, altruistic, and anti-Hitler.

The Tides of War

Arrow Releasing, Directed by Neil Rossati, Released 1990

A low-budget, plenty-of-sunshine, comic-book debacle describing the transformation of a unsmiling Austrian naval officer from killer commando to an anti–New Order, anti-Gestapo apostate, who singularly destroys a V-2 rocket station on a remote Bahamian island during the war's closing months. After landing surreptitiously, blond-haired David Soul rationalizes his assassination of innocent British nationals as a military necessity. (Captain Soul, justifying his actions: "I lost a wife and son to an English bombing raid.") Slowly, he becomes disheartened when he witnesses the *Schutzstaffel's* cruelty to the natives building a launching site. Soon he renounces Hitlerism, becomes a fugitive, and—with the help of a missionary school teacher (Yvette Heyden)—wreaks havoc on the Nazi scheme to fire a projectile at Washington, D.C. Acclaimed a hero of sorts, his prior misdeeds are conveniently forgotten by the Allied forces when they retake the island.

A Time of Destiny

Columbia, Directed by Gregory Nava, Released 1988

An offbeat gothic thriller using the 1944–1945 Italian campaign as the backdrop to a brooding, symbolic storyline that includes family dissension, delayed love, and obsessive revenge. Here, a morose American sergeant (William Hurt) spends most of his time stalking another GI (Timothy Hutton) to avenge his father's stateside car death. Eventually brought together in a combat situation, the psychopathic Hurt—temporarily putting aside his idée fixe—proffers friendship to the unsuspecting soldier. (Hutton to new buddy, William Hurt: "It's a deal, then, O.K. You and me, we're going to live through this war.") After a series of bizarre events—including a confrontation in an Italian village—the two men separate, only to reunite a few months later at a San Diego church tower in a horrific climax. As a combat film, the theme is a constant reiteration that the U.S. forces contain a fair share of the mentally deranged.

A Time to Love and a Time to Die

Universal, Directed by Douglas Sirk, Released 1958

Another elaborate CinemaScope production purporting that most German foot soldiers, fighting on Russian soil, were kind, understanding, and victims of their superior's wanton cruelty. Here a *Wehrmacht* private (John Gavin)— on a ten-day furlough during a late-winter 1944 Soviet offensive—arrives home and learns that his parents are missing, many residents are homeless, the Allied bombing is unrelenting, and Nazi opportunism and treachery are everywhere. Then, he meets an old school friend, frightened Liselotte Pulver, and after a two-day courtship, the couple marry. (Private Gavin, on his first date: "I've nearly two years combat pay with me and only two weeks to spend it.") Back on Russian soil—one week later—the lovesick bridegroom, repulsed by war's horror, dies at the hands of some disgruntled Soviet prisoners. Adapted from Erich Maria Remarque's novel, the storyline—told from the German viewpoint—rationalizes most of the Third Reich's Eastern Front brutality.

To Hell and Back

Universal International, Directed by Jesse Hibbs, Released 1955

A quiet, unobtrusive, uplifting recollection of America's most decorated World War II hero in a manner that downplays flag waving and, instead, offers muted testimony to the fears, hopes, bonding, and frustration every foot soldier experiences. Audie Murphy portrays himself as the shy, baby-faced, laid-back, sixteen-year-old rural Texan who, following the Pearl Harbor bombing, enlists in the Army and—after extensive infantry training—embarks for the North African invasion. Soon, his regiment is reassigned, and by war's end, the soft-spoken GI fought in seven major campaigns, earned a battlefield commission, and received the coveted Medal of Honor. Best scene: the recently appointed second lieutenant, mindful of his squad's safety, leaps on a disabled tank and repels a Nazi infantry attack. (Lieutenant Murphy, ordering his men to take cover: "I'm going to stay here and see if I can get some artillery working.")

Tobruk

Universal, Directed by Arthur Hiller, Released 1966

A fast-moving, fictional, African desert yarn that highlights the combined efforts of an American officer, some British Tommies, and a tough group of Jewish commandos as they infiltrate the Nazi stronghold in Libya and subsequently blow up the Third Reich's strategic oil supply. Here, a famous hit-and-run fighter, Major Rock Hudson, encounters numerous problems—including air strafing, the stereotypical traitor-in-the-midst, and native intransigence—before reaching the port city of Tobruk. (Major Hudson, explaining his survival philosophy: "I'd never consider dying for a cause—no matter how noble!") Replete with James Bond escapades, the photoplay contains one implausible situation after another, nullifying the plot to a copycat version of the popular 1940s Saturday-afternoon cliffhangers.

Too Late the Hero

Cinerama Productions Corporation, Directed by Robert Aldrich, Released 1970

A modern-day redemption parable about a goldbricking navy officer (Cliff Robertson) who, following a series of complicated events, becomes part of a British commando raid on a New Hebrides island in spring 1942. After some bad luck, most of the squad is either captured or killed, and—along with an English corporal (Michael Caine)—Lieutenant Robertson must retreat deeper into the jungle to avoid enemy forces. (Caine, reiterating the nature of Japanese cruelty: "Treat you all right? They'll chop your bloody head off—I saw what they did in the hospital in Singapore.") Eventually, the two men reach their command post's perimeter, but only Michael Caine survives a last-ditch run to safety. With many analogies to the Vietnam conflict, the screenplay depicts war as a sadistic outlet for those mentally deranged individuals whose craving for violence requires constant gratification.

Tora! Tora! Tora!

Twentieth Century–Fox, Directed by Richard Fleischer, Toshio Masuda, and Kinji Fukasaku, Released 1970

A quasi-documentary, both-sides-of-the-story, minuscule examination of the inexplicable events leading up to the Japanese attack on Pearl Harbor, blaming numerous U.S. officers for their failure to act decisively. With an array of Hollywood male stars—including Jason Robards, Joseph Cotton, and Martin

Balsam—the 144-minute storyline weaves between Japanese and American high commands as numerous personalities scrutinize or ignore the political events responsible for December 7. (Admiral Martin Balsam, explaining why Japanese torpedo planes are ineffective in the forty-foot waters of Pearl Harbor: "A torpedo dropped from a plane will plunge to a depth of seventy-five feet or more before it levels off.") As a revisionist tract, the photoplay humanizes the Japanese officers responsible for this day of infamy, almost suggesting that FDR's embargo policy forced this Oriental nation to act so determinedly.

Torpedo Run

MGM, Directed by Joseph Pevney, Released 1958

Another fictional, high-powered, CinemaScope story about life aboard a U.S. Navy submarine in the Pacific theater, the loneliness of command, and the moral dilemma reached when innocent noncombatants perish during wartime. Here, a skipper (Glenn Ford) on a search-and-destroy mission accidentally sinks a Japanese transport vessel carrying fourteen hundred American civilians, including his wife and child. (Navy buddy [Ernest Borgnine] cautioning his friend about firing the ill-fated torpedo: "This attack is more than routine.") With stoic resignation, he gradually puts this tragedy behind him and, in a gleeful finale, blows up the Japanese aircraft carrier responsible for launching the planes against Pearl Harbor. Feeling slightly repentant for this new victory, the good-looking commander—still pondering the efficacy of his earlier misdeed—moves out to sea, ready to fight more Japanese warships.

The Train

United Artists, Directed by John Frankenheimer, Released 1965

A solid, riding-the-rails, suspense meller that proves the French Resistance's mettle once again, as these *chemin de fer* workers move quickly to prevent the Nazis from transporting stolen national artworks to Germany during their hasty August 1944 Paris retreat. Fast-moving Burt Lancaster—now a Gallic stationmaster—quietly orchestrates subtle forms of sabotage that prevent a heavily fortified train's embarkation from a small, occupied village, while his nemesis, Third Reich Colonel Paul Scofield, an obsessive, monomaniacal art collector, fumes in frustration. (Hard-talking Lancaster, explaining his mission: "To hell with London. We started this whole thing for one reason—to stop the train.") With some unexpected help from screen idol Jeanne Moreau, the Nazis cannot muster enough steam to thwart French determination to save their historical paintings from destruction or pilferage.

The Tuskegee Airmen

HBO Pictures, Directed by Robert Markowitz, Released 1995

A wonderful, made-for-television, flag-waving tribute to the African American officers of the 332nd Fighter Group, the Tuskegee airmen who flew hundreds of European missions, protecting American bombers from Luftwaffe offenses. Andre Braugher coruscates as the legendary Colonel Benjamin O. Davis, the highly decorated commander who must fight both military racism and Nazi ack-ack blasts, while back in the nation's capital, a southern senator (John Lithgow) spouts hatred and virulence against these U.S. flyers. (Colonel Braugher, defending his unit: "A fair and impartial opportunity is all we ask.") With Cuba Gooding Jr. and Laurence Fishburne in the pilot's seat, every aspect of this famous air group's history—from their early Alabama training days to their hundreds of aerial citations—receives one accolade after another.

Twelve O'Clock High

Twentieth Century–Fox, Directed by Henry King, Released 1949

An elaborate testimony to the airmen who fly the dangerous B-17 attack missions from their English countryside bases deep inside the German border. Gregory Peck stars as a group commander who slowly transforms a hard-luck bombing outfit into a precision fighting unit, while his assistant (Dean Jagger) keeps a sharp administrative eye on military regulations. Nominated for four Academy Awards, the picture—based on the book by Beirne Lay Jr. and Sy Bartlett—contains detailed aerial combat scenes, restating the high human cost involved in the air war against the Luftwaffe. As a martinet leader, who gradually loosens his grip, Gregory Peck vacillates between villain and hero. (General Peck, chewing out a subordinate for a variety of offenses: "I'm going to get your head down in the mud and trample it; I'm going to make you wish you'd never been born.")

U-571

Universal, Directed by Oliver Wood, Released 2000

A fast-paced, no-holds-barred, up-periscope seafaring thriller that pits the nautical skills of a young U.S. submarine lieutenant against the resources of the German navy during a 1942 mid-Atlantic confrontation. Motivated by national security, quick-moving Matthew McConaughey, along with a sixty-one-year-old chief petty officer (Harvey Keitel), leads a raiding party that commandeers a floundering Axis U-boat, seizing its prized ENIGMA cipher machine. Soon, the American sailors man the derelict Nazi vessel and, after a series of depth-charge adventures, surface to send a beeline bow shot at a German destroyer. (Lieutenant McConaughey exhorting a frighten seaman: "You're going to go back down in that bilge and you're going to do your job, sailor.")

Under Ten Flags

Paramount, Directed by Duilio Coletti, Released 1960

Another revisionist high-seas tale glamorizing the "true" exploits of a supposedly benign Nazi naval commander who, after shelling or torpedoing numerous Allied merchant ships—killing seamen and passengers—treats the survivors with unusual benevolence. Here, a German officer (Van Heflin) pushes credibility to its limits with his Oklahoma accent, while his staff members—wearing spiffy white uniforms and behaving like eager cruise waiters—denigrate their captain's altruism. (Heflin to Nazi crew: "As long as I am in command of this ship there will be a minimum of bloodshed, a minimum of suffering.") Eventually, the British navy destroys its seagoing enemy, and in a corny formula ending, both Nazi and English officers salute each other, oblivious to the mayhem they created.

Until They Sail

MGM, Directed by Robert Wise, Released 1957

Another heart-warming, I-will-love-you-forever, CinemaScope drama, from a short story by James Michener. This story traces the romantic ups and downs of four New Zealand sisters who—from the safety of their ocean-view cottage—watch their Kiwi men march off to war, only to be replaced by U.S. Marines training for Pacific island offensives. Here, the matriarch (Jean Simmons), along with her three siblings, witness six years of separation, heartache, bereavement, perfidy, upheaval, and, finally, V-J Day. (Miss Simmons, venting her frustration: "American supermen with more money than they ever had before in their lives, dazzling little girls who are lonely.") Eventually—after months of soul-searching—the cautious Miss Simmons, realizing that all is fair in love and war, changes her tune and admits that a well-mannered, quasi-cynical marine major (Paul Newman) is really the man of her dreams.

Up Periscope

MGM, Directed by Gordon Douglas, Released 1959

Another "all ahead full, steady as she goes, right full rudder" potboiler that aggrandizes all facets of submarine life. While not lamenting the loneliness of command, pudgy Edmond O'Brien ponders the efficacy of obtaining a Japanese codebook, located on a lightly guarded enemy island, by sneaking a frogman ashore. (Captain O'Brien to volunteer: "If we can break that code first, we're going to save a lot of ships and a lot of men.") Eventually James Garner dons a wet suit, swims unobtrusively inland, and—in a series of Captain Marvel escapades—slithers through the jungle, creates a diversion, tiptoes into a radio hut, photographs the classified information, and without blinking an eye, breaststrokes back to the submarine. Using one cliché after another—including the malcontent, the fake oil slick, and numerous depth-charge attacks—the photodrama lavishes heavy praise on the Silent Service.

Varian's War

Showtime, Directed by Lionel Chetwynd, Released 2001

A wonderful testimony to the American humanitarian Varian Fry, who during the ambiguous pre–Pearl Harbor days pulled numerous strings, affected different roles, and endured some close calls to quietly smuggle hundreds of Jewish artists, intellectuals, and scientists (including Marc Chagall, Franz Werfel, Max Ernst, Hannah Arendt, and Heinrich Mann) from Nazi-occupied France to the United States. Utilizing his best foppish mannerisms, bespectacled William Hurt spends many hours arguing his noble cause, while his assistant (Julia Ormond) spouts her free-love credo. (Hurt to colleagues: "We all know that the Nazis have a particularly cold hatred for artists and intellectuals they consider degenerate.") As a made-for-cable motion picture, the storyline—mirroring many of the ideas found in *Schindler's List*—extols the New Englander's unrelenting determination to rescue any persecuted individual.

The Victors

Columbia, Directed by Carl Foreman, Released 1963

A caustic look at the everyday life of a rifle squad, where each man experiences fear, loneliness, uncertainty, and, occasionally, elation. Sergeant Eli Wallach bellows many orders to his squad as they advance through Sicily, France, and finally Germany, watching the Axis forces slowly capitulate.

Along the way, the foot soldiers drink unlimited bottles of vintage wine, smoke one cigarette after another, and chase local women in a frivolous manner resembling a Saturday-night college fraternity blast. (Corporal George Peppard's appraisal of Sicilian females: "The place is like a barnyard.") With George Hamilton and Peter Fonda in leading roles, this screenplay—replete with subtle antiwar strains—ignores heroics and instead offers muted praise to the average GI. Most harrowing scene: a young, frightened American soldier's ordeal, when taken to an empty field, tied to a post, blessed by a chaplain, and executed for desertion.

Victory

MGM, Directed by John Huston, Released 1981

Another prisoner-of-war-escape travesty that ignores the horrific living conditions found under Nazi subjugation but, instead, suggests that military confinement resembles the shenanigans found in intercollegiate sports rivalry. Here, an American POW (Sylvester Stallone) appears too well fed and muscular, while his British pal (Michael Caine), aided by a stereotypically benign German officer (Max von Sydow), organizes a soccer match between the captives and their masters. Soon, both teams square off in a Paris stadium, and with the help of Pelé (and other international football-players-turned-actors) the Allied team snatches the prize. (POW Stallone, explaining his philosophy: "You guys do what you want, but I'm leaving. I ain't going back to prison!")

The Wackiest Ship in the Army

Columbia, Directed by Richard Murphy, Released 1960

A lighthearted comedy (with a few somber moments) depicting the misadventures of an easygoing naval lieutenant (Jack Lemmon), who—along with teen idol Ensign Ricky Nelson—is hoodwinked into taking command of a rundown sailing vessel, the USS *Echo*, and gliding this ship into the Japanese-patrolled New Guinea waters to report enemy positions during the March 1943 Battle of the Bismarck Sea offensive. (Fast-maneuvering Jack Lemmon, escaping from some Nipponese coastal attacks: "Boatswain, stand by to make sail!") With numerous subplots, the storyline occasionally parodies the exaggerated Hollywood stereotypes found in many World War II action films, including the motor that does not start, the Japanese officer who graduated from UCLA, a hold-your-breath journey through an ocean minefield, and the titular use of the noun "army," while in fact, this branch of the service is never mentioned in this ninety-nine-minute photoplay.

The Walls of Hell

Independent-International Pictures, Directed by Gerardo De Leon and Eddie Romero, Released 1964

Another eighty-eight-minute, low-grade, B-for-bottom-of-the-barrel pot-boiler from a production company noted for grinding out World War II screenplays with unknown actors, sultry actresses, and nonexistent dialogue. Once more, Fernando Poe Jr., a U.S. Army noncom, shoots, stabs, and stran-gles many Japanese soldiers in the narrow streets of the Philippine walled city, Intramuros, during the February 1945 allied offensive. (Sergeant Poe, proffering advice: "You fight your war, I'll fight mine"). His commanding of-ficer (Jock Mahoney) crawls through a narrow tunnel, dodges enemy bullets, and, after some hand-to-hand fighting, rescues his sweetheart (Cecilia Lopez) from a Japanese prison. Using a generous supply of newsreel footage, this budget photodrama depicts the Filipino guerrillas as stealthy fighters, deter-mined to rout their Oriental adversary.

The War Lover

Columbia, Directed by Philip Leacock, Released 1962

A psychological evaluation of the airmen who, in 1943, left the safety of their English bases to attack enemy targets on the European mainland. As a mono-maniacal pilot, Captain Steve McQueen derives visceral satisfaction from the risks associated with combat flying, much to the confusion of his copilot, Lieutenant Robert Wagner, and girlfriend. (McQueen to comely Shirley Anne Field, hoping his braggadocio will result in a sexual conquest: "I'm going to stay until the last bomb is dropped and maybe I'll be the one that drops it!) Eventually, his luck falters when his B-17—riddled by bullets after a German raid—cannot maintain altitude on its homeward flight. With the White Cliffs of Dover in view, Captain McQueen—the War Lover—unwilling to leave his womb-cockpit, dies in a fiery crash, symbolizing his pathological consump-tion. Based on the book by John Hersey, the storyline condemns those primeval needs—found in some military men—that crave sexual pleasure in wartime violence.

What Did You Do in the War, Daddy?

United Artists, Directed by Blake Edwards, Released 1966

An irreverent, tongue-in-cheek caricature of the 1943 Sicilian campaign that ignores the thousands of American casualties and, instead, suggests the entire invasion resembled a dizzy, college fraternity drinking party. As the junior officer assigned to seize a hilltop village, Lieutenant James Coburn agrees to a surrender bacchanalia with the Italian troops left behind. (Lieutenant Coburn to *Il Duce*'s soldiers: "Until we find Major Pott and get this surrender thing worked out, we fake a battle.") Scheming with Captain Dick Shawn, the twosome keep the charade working—while duping some unsuspecting German soldiers—and eventually, after some Bugs Bunny adventures, their commanding general (Carroll O'Connor), proud as the proverbial peacock, acclaims them heroes. Along with a handful of similar films, the photoplay purports that Italy—a member of the Axis Pact—was nothing more than a happy group of fun-seeking, wine-sipping, pasta-eating nationals, who worshipped President Roosevelt, detested Benito Mussolini, and opposed belligerency.

When Trumpets Fade

HBO, Directed by John Irvin, Released 1998

A slow-moving, horrific, all-male combat tale reiterating the sacrificial nature of the frontal assault in which inexperienced American soldiers—the greenies—die rapidly as they move forward during the 1944 autumn Hurtgen Forest offensive. Ron Eldred is outstanding as a cynical U.S. private quickly promoted to sergeant, and then to lieutenant, who must lead untried GIs into a heavily fortified area where *Wehrmacht* troops—determined to keep the Allies from breaching their Siegfried Line—fight tenaciously. (Sergeant Eldred's reaction: "I am absolutely the wrong man—request permission for a Section Eight.") With many references to uncaring commanders, unstable squad members, and survival probability odds, much of the storyline points to the futility of conflict. Most harrowing scene: after a ferocious attack, only four GIs reach the German perimeter and, finally, destroy their large guns.

Where Eagles Dare

MGM, Directed by Brian G. Hutton, Released 1968

A puffed-up, implausible adventure yarn—featuring one mock heroic after another—that subliminally spoofs the black-and-white, two-dimensional propaganda films produced during the war. Portraying a British commando sent behind German lines to an elaborate Austrian Alps hideaway, Richard Burton seems a little pudgy to parachute from an airplane, leap across moving cable cars, and climb straight up fortress walls, while his taciturn partner (Clint Eastwood) looks nonplussed by this cloak-and-dagger mission. (Major Burton, explaining Eastwood's role in a complicated spy-versus-spy showdown: "He's an assassin—a member of the American intelligence organization known as O.S.S.") Eventually, the Allied team blows up Gestapo headquarters, rescues an American general, and—during a zany escape—wreaks havoc on the German war machine in a manner suggestive of a Looney Tunes Saturday-morning cartoon.

Windtalkers

MGM, Directed by John Woo, Released 2002

A high-octane, flames-everywhere, they're-coming-at-us-from-all sides, strictly male, special-effects extravaganza honoring the U.S. Marines' Navaho code talkers, whose esoteric combat messages resulted in many island victories during the war's closing months. Thirty-eight-year-old Nicolas Cage seems miscast as an intelligence sergeant assigned to protect or, if necessary, kill the Windtalkers rather then compromise their cryptic code during the Saipan offensive. Along with another noncom (Christian Slater), the two men guard their charges assiduously. (Sergeant Slater, pondering his orders: "We're here to kill Japs, not Marines.") With recurring scenes depicting both American and Japanese bodies disintegrating, hapless men on fire, bloody stabbings, frequent mutilations, a horrific decapitation, and uncanny marksmanship, the screenplay resembles many of the antics found in the Road Runner series, where this popular, anthropomorphic comic-strip hero bounces back from every conceivable mishap.

The Wings of Eagles

MGM, Directed by John Ford, Released 1957

A well-earned pat on the back for Commander Frank "Spig" Wead, the naval pioneer who—in the 1920s and 1930s—campaigned vigorously for an independent aviation section within his own branch of service. Once more, John Wayne kicks up a storm as a blunt-talking, chain-smoking, fly-by-the-seat-of-your-pants maverick who champions the fledgling aircraft carrier. After a devastating spinal-cord injury, he leaves the service and eventually becomes a successful Hollywood screenwriter but, following Pearl Harbor, bulldozes his way back into the navy. Within months, he implements the "jeep carrier" plan, a novel way to provide immediate replacements in the combat zone. (Commander Wayne, explaining the logistics: "Now backing them up, we have these jeep carriers, loaded with planes and crew.") With many action sequences, the film demonstrates, once again, the importance of naval airpower in the Pacific theater.

Yanks

Universal, Directed by John Schlesinger, Released 1979

A poignant, happy-go-lucky look at some lifestyle changes when large contingencies of American infantrymen arrive in a small Yorkshire town to train for the upcoming 1944 European invasion. Here, the Yanks flirt with local women, offer PX items for quick favors, use military equipment for personal transportation, and occasionally trade on the back market. Soon, a good-looking mess sergeant (Richard Gere), famous for his scratch cakes, falls for a shy shopkeeper's daughter. (Gere to girlfriend: "I've never met anyone like you before.") After some on-again, off-again romance, the twosome resolve all cultural differences on the eve of his Normandy departure, proving that love crosses all boundaries. With numerous references to wartime separation, uncertain future, and payroll disparities, the storyline accurately reflects an integral part of social history. Most realistic scene: a racial fight breaks out when some southern GIs, infuriated that a black soldier danced with a white girl, attack the helpless soldier, while the townspeople, unaccustomed to such behavior, stare incredulously.

Young Joe: The Forgotten Kennedy

ABC Circle Films, Directed by Richard Heffron, Released 1977

Another made-for-television Kennedy-family saga that traces the World War II navy career of the oldest scion from stateside preflight training, through the Caribbean, submarine patrol, and, finally, to a fatal August 1944 morning when the young lieutenant—eager for aerial combat—is accidentally killed during a secret English Channel airborne mission. Peter Strauss shines as the eldest son who moves in the shadow of the patriarch's vow that someday he will become the first Irish-Catholic U.S. president. Based on the Hank Searls' biography *The Lost Prince*, the Hollywood screenplay repeats Kennedy's noncombatant frustration, while his kid brother, John, a decorated navy PT boat officer, steals much of his thunder. (Young Joe, frustrated by his limited Normandy invasion participation: "It's been a month since D-Day—I might as well drive a bus.")

The Young Lions

Twentieth Century–Fox, Directed by Edward Dmytryk, Released 1958

A superbly crafted black-and-white CinemaScope production—based on the novel by Irwin Shaw—that carefully juxtaposes the lives of two Americans, from their basic training days to their European combat with a high-minded, idealist German officer, who slowly becomes disillusioned with the horror of Nazism. Dean Martin and Montgomery Clift are outstanding as two unwilling dogfaces who eventually become hardened combat veterans after their unit liberates a concentration camp. Now a *Wehrmacht* lieutenant, blond-haired Marlon Brando cannot fathom his superiors' brutality. (Brando to commander: "I don't think it possible to remake this world from the basement of a dirty little police station.") Eventually, the three soldiers converge on a German hillside and—in a somber allegorical ending—the Nazi dies from the rifle shots of the two GIs in a manner that suggests atonement for Third Reich misdeeds.

Zone Troopers

Empire Pictures, Directed by Denny Bilson, Released 1986

An eighty-eight-minute spoof of the many B-propaganda pictures that flourished during World War II. Here, Sergeant Tim Thomerson—trapped behind German lines during the Italian Campaign—stumbles upon an alien rocket ship and, after a series of science-fictional escapades, befriends the rodent-faced extraterrestrials who man this aircraft. Soon the two sides team up and—firing both Thompson submachine guns and space ray weapons—obliterate the *Wehrmacht* forces. (Newspaperman [Biff Manard], complimenting his alien friend's marksmanship: "That's cooking, Bughead.") Loaded with anachronisms and tongue-in-cheek homage scenes, this offbeat film in many ways parodies Hollywood's cliché-ridden portrayal of the Global Conflict. (Private Timothy Van Patten, discussing the alien's homeland: "Everybody knows there's no life on Venus. He's gotta be from Mars.")

Bibliography

Adams, Michael C. C. *The Best War Ever: America and World War II*. Baltimore: Johns Hopkins University Press, 1994.

Baker, M. Joyce. *Images of Women in Film: The War Years, 1941–1945*. Ann Arbor, Mich.: UMI Research Press, 1980.

Basinger, Jeanine. *The World War II Combat Film: Anatomy of a Genre*. New York: Columbia University Press, 1986.

Beigel, Harvey. *The Fleet's In: Hollywood Presents the U.S. Navy in World War II*. Missoula, Mont.: Pictorial Histories, 1995.

Biesen, Sheri Chinen. *Blackout: World War II and the Origins of Film Noir*. Baltimore: Johns Hopkins University Press, 2006.

Birdwell, Michael E. *Celluloid Soldiers: Warner Bros. Campaign against Nazism*. New York: New York University Press, 2001.

Boggs, Carl, and Tom Pollard. *The Hollywood War Machine*. Boulder, Colo.: Paradigm, 2006.

Braverman, John. *To Hasten the Homecoming: How Americans Fought World War II through the Media*. Lanham, Md.: Scarecrow Press, 1996.

Butler, Ivan. *The War Film*. New York: Barnes, 1974.

Cameron, Kenneth. *America on Film: Hollywood and American History*. New York: Continuum, 1997.

Chambers, John Whiteclay II, and David Culbert. *World War II, Film and History*. New York: Oxford, 1996.

Chapman, Ivan. *Private Eddie Leonski: The Brownout Strangler*. Sydney: Hale, 1982.

Clarke, James. *War Films*. London: Virgin, 2006.

Cripps, Thomas. *Making Movies Black: The Hollywood Message Movie from World War II to the Civil Rights Era*. New York: Oxford, 1993.

Dick, Bernard F. *The Star-Spangled Screen: The American World War II Film*. Lexington: University Press of Kentucky, 1985.

Doherty, Thomas. *Projections of War: Hollywood, American Culture, and World War II*. New York: Columbia University Press, 1993.

Dolan, Edward F. *Hollywood Goes to War*. Twickenham, England: Hamlyn, 1985.

Donald, Ralph R. "Savages, Swine, and Buffoons: Hollywood's Selected Stereotypical Characterization of the Japanese, Germans, and Italians in Films Produced during World War II." In *Race, Gender, Media: Considering Diversity across Audiences, Content, and Producers*. Edited by Rebecca Ann Linn, 193–98. Upper Saddle River, N.J.: Pearson, 2004.

Early, Emmett. *The War Veteran in Film*. Jefferson, N.C.: McFarland, 2003.

Eberwein, Robert T. *The War Film*. New Brunswick, N.J.: Rutgers University Press, 2004.

——. *Armed Forces: Masculinity and Sexuality in the American War Film*. New Brunswick, N.J.: Rutgers University Press, 2007.

Evans, Alvin. *Brassey's Guide to War Films*. Dulles, Va.: Brassey's, 2000.

Femina, Jerry Della. *From Those Wonderful Folks Who Gave You Pearl Harbor: Front-Line Dispatches from the Advertising World*. New York: Simon, 1970.

Freitas, Gary. *War Movies: The Belle & Blade Guide to Classic War Videos*. Bandon, Ore: Reed, 2004.

Friedrich, Jörg. *The Fire*. Translated by Allison Brown. New York: Columbia University Press, 2006.

Fussell, Paul. *Wartime: Understanding and Behavior in the Second World War*. New York: Oxford University Press, 1989.

Fyne, Robert. *The Hollywood Propaganda of World War II*. Metuchen, N.J.: Scarecrow Press, 1994.

Garland, Brock. *War Movies*. New York: Facts on File, 1987.

Guttmacher, Peter. *Legendary War Movies*. New York: Friedman, 1996.

Higashi, Sumiko. "World War II Newsreels and Propaganda Film," *Cinema Journal* 37 (Spring 1998): 38–61.

Holsinger, M. Paul, and Mary Anne Schofield, eds. *Visions of War*. Bowling Green, Ohio: Bowling Green University Popular Press, 1992.

Hoopes, Ray. *When the Stars Went to War: Hollywood and World War II*. New York: Random House, 1994.

Hurd, Geoffrey. *National Fictions: World War II on Films and Television*. London: BFI, 1984.

Hyams, James. *War Films*. New York: Gallery, 1984.

Jeavons, Clyde. *A Pictorial History of War Films*. Secaucus, N.J.: Citadel, 1974.

Jones, Ken D., and A. F. McClure. *Hollywood at War: The American Motion Picture and World War II*. New York: Castle, 1973.

Kagan, Norman. *The War Film*. New York: Pyramid, 1974.

Kerr, E. Bartlett. *Flames Over Tokyo: The U.S. Army Air Forces' Incendiary Campaign against Japan, 1944–1945*. New York: Fine, 1991.

Koppes, Clayton R., and Gregory D. Black. *Hollywood Goes to War: How Politics, Profit, and Propaganda Shaped World War II Movies*. New York: Free Press, 1987.

Langman, Larry, and Ed Borg, eds. *Encyclopedia of America War Films*. New York: Garland, 1974.

Marill, Alvin H. *Movies Made for Television: 1964–2004*. Lanham, Md.: Scarecrow Press, 2005.

Maslowski, Peter. *Armed with Cameras: The American Military Photographers of World War II*. New York: Free Press, 1993.

Matelski, Marilyn J., and Nancy Lynch Street, eds. *War and Film in America: Historical and Critical Essays*. Jefferson, N.C.: McFarland, 2003.

Mayo, Mike. *VideoHound's War Movies: Classic Conflict on Film*. Detroit: Visible Ink, 1990.

McAdams, Frank. *The American War Film: History and Hollywood*. New York: Praeger, 2002.

McKrisken, Trevor, and Andrew Pepper. *American History and Contemporary Hollywood Film*. New Brunswick, N.J.: Rutgers University Press, 2005.

McLaughlin, Robert L., and Sally E. Parry. *We'll Always Have the Movies: American Cinema During World War II*. Lexington: University Press of Kentucky, 2006.

Miller, Don. *"B" Movies*. New York: Curtis, 1973.

Moeller, Susan D. *Shooting War: Photography and the American Experience of Combat*. New York: Basic Books, 1989.

Nornes, Abé Mark, and Fukushima Yukio, eds. *The Japan/America Film Wars: Propaganda Films from World War II*. Chur, Switzerland: Harwood, 1993.

O'Neill, William. *A Democracy at War: America's Fight at Home and Abroad in World War II*. New York: Free Press, 1993.

Orris, Bruce. *When Hollywood Ruled the Skies: The Aviation Film Classics of World War II*. Hawthorne, Calif.: Aero, 1984.

Paris, Michael. *From the Wright Brothers to Top Gun: Aviation, Nationalism and Popular Cinema*. New York: Manchester University Press, 1995.

Parish, James Robert. *The Great Combat Pictures: Twentieth-Century Warfare on the Screen*. Metuchen, N.J.: Scarecrow Press, 1990.

Pendo, Stephen. *Aviation in the Cinema*. Metuchen, NJ: Scarecrow Press, 1985.

Perlmutter, Tom. *War Movies*. Secaucus, N.J.: Castle, 1974.

Polan, Dana. *Power and Paranoia: History, Narrative, and the American Cinema, 1940–1950*. New York: Columbia University Press, 1986.

Quirk, Lawrence J. *Great War Films*. New York: Carol, 1994.

Ray, Robert B. *A Certain Tendency of the Hollywood Cinema, 1930–1980*. Princeton, N.J.: Princeton University Press, 1985.

Renov, Michael. *Hollywood's Wartime Woman: Representation and Ideology*. Ann Arbor, Mich.: UMI Research Press, 1988.

Roeder, George H., Jr. *The Censored War: American Visual Experience during World War II*. New Haven: Yale University Press, 1993.

Rollins, Peter, ed. *Hollywood as Historian: American Film in a Cultural Context*. Lexington: University Press of Kentucky, 1983.

Rollins, Peter, and John O'Connor. *Why We Fought: America's Wars in Film and History*. Lexington: University Press of Kentucky, 2008.

Rubin, Steven Jay. *Combat Films: American Realism 1945–1970*. Jefferson, N.C.: McFarland, 1981.

Schickel, Richard. *Good Morning, Mr. Zip, Zip, Zip: Movies, Memory, and World War II*. Chicago: Dee, 2003.

Serene, Frank. *World War II on Film: A Catalog of Select Motion Pictures in the National Archives*. Washington, D.C.: National Archives, 1994.

Shull, Michael S., and David E. Wilt. *Hollywood War Films, 1937–1945: An Exhaustive Filmography of American Feature-Length Motion Pictures Relating to World War II*. Jefferson, N.C.: McFarland, 1996.

Sklar, Robert. *Film: An International History of the Medium*. New York: Abrams, 1993.

Slocum, J. David, ed. *Hollywood and War, the Film Reader*. New York: Routledge, 2006.

Spiller, Robert J. "War in the Dark," *American Heritage*, February/March 1999, 41–51.

Strada, Michael J., and Harold R. Troper. *Friend or Foe? Russians in American Film and Foreign Policy, 1933–1991*. Lanham, Md.: Scarecrow Press, 1997.

Suid, Lawrence. *Guts and Glory: The Making of the American Military Image in Film*. Lexington: University Press of Kentucky, 2002.

———. *Sailing on the Silver Screen: Hollywood and the U.S. Navy*. Annapolis: U.S. Naval Institute Press, 1996.

Suid, Lawrence, and Dolores A. Haverstick. *Stars and Stripes on Screen: A Comprehensive Guide to Portrayals of American Military on Film*. Lanham, Md.: Scarecrow Press, 2005.

Toplin, Robert Brent, ed. *Hollywood as Mirror: Changing Views of Outsiders and Enemies in American Movies*. Westport, Conn.: Greenwood, 1996.

Uklanski, Piotr. *The Nazis*. Zurich: Scalo, 2000.

Vidal, Gore. *Screening History*. Cambridge, Mass.: Harvard University Press, 1992.

Virilio, Paul. *War and Cinema: The Logistics of Perception*. New York: Verso, 1989.

Wetta, Frank J., and Stephen J. Curley. *Celluloid Wars: A Guide to Film and the American Experience of War*. New York: Greenwood, 1992.

Woll, Allen L. *The Hollywood Musical Goes to War*. Chicago: Nelson, 1983.

Index

About the Author

Robert Fyne, an English professor at Kean University, Union, New Jersey, teaches film and literature courses. Actively involved in numerous motion-picture organizations, Dr. Fyne has published extensively in *Film & History*, *North Carolina Historical Review*, *Wind/Literary Journal*, *Christian Century*, *Journal of Popular Film and Culture*, *Literature/Film Quarterly*, *France Magazine*, *Alaska Quarterly Review*, *Historical Journal of Film, Radio, and Television*, *Social Science Journal*, *Film Library Quarterly*, *New Guard*, and *Intellect*. Other World War II essays have appeared in anthologies including *The Columbia Companion to American History*. His 1994 book, *The Hollywood Propaganda of World War II* (Scarecrow Press), examines over four hundred wartime screenplays and their contribution to the victory effort. He is currently the book review editor for *Film and History*.